Cyclopedia
of
Literary Characters II

A-Div

CYCLOPEDIA
of
LITERARY
CHARACTERS II

VOLUME ONE—A-DIV

Edited by
FRANK N. MAGILL

Salem Press
Pasadena, California   Englewood Cliffs, New Jersey

∞ The paper used in these volumes conforms to the
American National Standard for Permanence of Paper
for Printed Library Materials, Z39.48-1984.

Library of Congress Cataloging-in-Publication Data

Magill, Frank Northen, 1907-
      Cyclopedia of literary characters II / edited by
Frank N. Magill.
          p.   cm.
      Includes index.
      1. Literature—Stories, plots, etc.   2. Literature—Dic-
tionaries.   3. Characters and their characteristics in literature.   I. Title.   II. Title: Cyclopedia of literary characters two.   III. Title: Cyclopedia of literary characters 2.
      PN44.M28   1990
      809 ' .927 ' 03—dc20   90-8550
                                                              CIP
      ISBN 0-89356-517-2 (set)
      ISBN 0-89356-518-0 (volume 1)

PRINTED IN THE UNITED STATES OF AMERICA

PUBLISHER'S NOTE

In 1963, Salem Press presented its *Cyclopedia of Literary Characters*, two volumes collecting more than sixteen thousand characters from some thirteen hundred novels, plays, epics, and other classics of world literature, arranged alphabetically by title of work. The list of works from which these characters were selected was developed from the original *Masterplots* series, which provided plot summaries of the world's greatest literature. The *Cyclopedia of Literary Characters* offered readers the opportunity to become familiar with both famous and less well-known personalities from classic fiction: Major characters were presented in write-ups of one hundred to one hundred fifty words; supporting and minor characters were described in fewer words, according to their importance.

In 1986, Salem Press brought out the first in a new survey of literature, *Masterplots II*, American Fiction Series, which covered novels of twentieth century North and Latin America, never before treated in previous *Masterplots*. *Masterplots II* has since grown to twenty-two volumes addressing fictional literature and plays (as well as four volumes surveying great works of literary nonfiction). A new generation of literary characters has appeared.

Cyclopedia of Literary Characters II collects those new characters who make their appearance in the following series in *Masterplots II*: American Fiction, British and Commonwealth Fiction, World Fiction, and Drama. In addition, twenty works from the Short Stories series, generally qualifying as novellas, were chosen for character coverage. In total, 1,437 works are represented in these four volumes. *Cyclopedia of Literary Characters II* thus can be used both on its own and as a companion set to *Masterplots II*, where plot and analysis complement the character descriptions found here.

Articles are arranged alphabetically by title of work, volume 1 beginning with *Aaron's Rod*, by D. H. Lawrence, and volume 4 concluding with *Zuckerman Unbound*, by Philip Roth. Each article starts with some standard ready-reference top matter, listing author, type of work (such as novel or play), the time of action in the work under discussion, and the date of first publication (or production in the case of plays). The characters are arranged by order of importance within each article. As in the original *Cyclopedia of Literary Characters*, the central or key characters receive lengthier description; supporting and minor figures, less extensive treatment. Not every character who may have made an appearance in the works is represented here; most contributors, however, made an effort to list more characters than appeared in the listing of "Principal Characters" found in the counterpart article from the *Masterplots II* set.

Pronunciation is provided for character names that are most likely to be mispronounced (primarily foreign-language names), especially in cases where the original spelling of the name would not prompt a reasonable facsimile of correct pronunciation from the English-language speaker. Hence, the intention was not to provide pronunciation automatically for all foreign-language names (many of which, such as Heinz or Jacques, will be familiar to most readers); nor was the intention to instruct the reader in the subtleties of foreign-language pronunciation. Rather, pronunciation is offered where the editors believe that the original spelling would present an obstacle to oral discussion of these characters. A Key to Pronunciation is found in the front matter to volume 1.

Three indexes can be found at the back of volume 4, which are designed to help the user more readily access the text. First, there is a complete list of titles, including cross-references. Second, an Author Index lists titles by author; again cross-references are included. And finally, the alphabetical Character Index, listing the more than 12,000 characters herein described by last name (with accompanying cross-references where appropriate), is a valuable aid in locating the author and work or works with which a particular character is associated.

Finally, the editors wish to thank a long list of contributors, the names of whom will be found, along with their affiliations, in the front matter to the first volume. Their efforts in compiling the descriptions and complying with the project's design have made this publication possible.

CONTRIBUTING REVIEWERS

Hardin Aasand
Dickinson State University

Michael Adams
Horrmann Library, Wagner College

Patrick Adcock
Henderson State University

Amy Adelstein
Independent Scholar

Jacob H. Adler
Purdue University

Kerry Ahearn
Independent Scholar

C. D. Akerley
U. S. Naval Academy

Arthur Tilo Alt
Duke University

Daniel Altamiranda
Arizona State University

Christopher L. Anderson
University of Tulsa

Stanley Archer
Texas A&M University

Frank Ardolino
University of Hawaii at Manoa

Christopher M. Armitage
University of North Carolina at Chapel Hill

Dorothy B. Aspinwall
University of Hawaii at Manoa

Philip Auslander
Georgia Institute of Technology

Addell Austin
State University of New York College at Oneonta

Marie-Denise Boros Azzi
Rutgers, State University of New Jersey

Raymond Bach
Texas A&M University

James Baird
University of North Texas

Laura Stone Barnard
University of Wisconsin-Milwaukee

David Barratt
University of North Carolina at Asheville

Thomas F. Barry
Himeji Dokkyo University

Melissa E. Barth
Appalachian State University

Sally Bartlett
University of South Florida

Kate M. Begnal
Utah State University

Robert M. Bender
University of Missouri-Columbia

Richard P. Benton
Trinity College

Mary G. Berg
Harvard University

Jennifer E. Berkley
Independent Scholar

Robert L. Berner
University of Wisconsin-Oshkosh

Cynthia A. Bily
Siena Heights College

Harriet Blodgett
Stanford University

Harold Blythe
Eastern Kentucky University

Seth Bovey
University of New Mexico

James H. Bowden
Indiana University Southeast

Robert Bowie
Miami University

Marion Boyle
Bloomsburg University

Jerry W. Bradley
New Mexico Institute of Mining and Technology

Patrick Brady
University of Tennessee

Gerhard Brand
California State University, Los Angeles

Philip Brantingham
Loyola University of Chicago

Francis J. Bremer
Millersville University of Pennsylvania

Susan Briziarelli
Washington University

J. R. Broadus
University of North Carolina at Chapel Hill

Robert R. Brock
University of Montana

Keith H. Brower
Dickinson College

Alan Brown
Livingston University

Elizabeth Brown-Guillory
University of Houston

Carl Brucker
Arkansas Tech University

Maurice P. Brungardt
Loyola University, New Orleans

David D. Buck
University of Wisconsin-Milwaukee

Paul Budra
Simon Fraser University, Ontario, Canada

Jeffrey L. Buller
Loras College

David L. Bullock
Kansas State University

Lori Hall Burghardt
University of Tennessee

Rebecca R. Butler
Dalton College

Anne Callahan
Loyola University of Chicago

Thomas J. Campbell
Pacific Lutheran University

Edmund J. Campion
University of Tennessee

Pamela Canal
Independent Scholar

Byron D. Cannon
University of Utah

Thomas Carmichael
University of Toronto

David A. Carpenter
Eastern Illinois University

Warren J. Carson
University of South Carolina-Spartanburg

Sonya H. Cashdan
East Tennessee State University

Leonard Casper
Boston College

Jocelyn Creigh Cass
Fraser Valley College

Thomas J. Cassidy
University of Wisconsin-Steven's Point

Lila Chalpin
Massachusetts College of Art

Edgar L. Chapman
Bradley University

John Steven Childs
Polytechnic University

Dennis C. Chowenhill
Chabot College

C. L. Chua
California State University, Fresno

Patricia Clark
University of Tennessee

Karen M. Cleveland
Independent Scholar

Greta McCormick Coger
Northwest Mississippi Community College

Julian W. Connolly
University of Virginia

Bernard A. Cook
Loyola University, New Orleans

Will H. Corral
Stanford University

Virginia Crane
California State University, Los Angeles

Frederic M. Crawford
Middle Tennessee State University

Lee B. Croft
Arizona State University

CONTRIBUTING REVIEWERS

W. Gordon Cunliffe
University of Wisconsin-Madison

Noel Daigle
Independent Scholar

Donald A. Daiker
Miami University

Dale Davis
Northwest Mississippi Community College

Jane Davis
Cornell University

Jocelyn Roberts Davis
Independent Scholar

Mary Virginia Davis
California State University, Sacramento

Matthew K. Davis
Independent Scholar

Timothy C. Davis
University of South Florida

Frank Day
Clemson University

Michael P. Dean
University of Mississippi

Bill Delaney
Independent Scholar

Linda C. DeMeritt
Allegheny College

John Deredita
Independent Scholar

Don DeRose
Independent Scholar

James I. Deutsch
George Washington University

James E. Devlin
State University of New York College at Oneonta

Ikenna Dieke
Allen University

Gweneth A. Dunleavy
Augustana College

Paul F. Dvorak
Virginia Commonwealth University

Karen Dwyer
Purdue University

Bruce L. Edwards
Bowling Green State University

Clifford Edwards
Fort Hays State University

Thomas H. Falk
Michigan State University

James Feast
New York University

Gaston F. Fernandez
University of Arkansas

Jaime Ferrán
Syracuse University

Donald M. Fiene
University of Tennessee

John W. Fiero
University of Southwestern Louisiana

Daniel D. Fineman
Occidental College

Edward Fiorelli
St. John's University

David Marc Fischer
Independent Scholar

Ruth D. Fisher
Kutztown University

Louise Flavin
University of Cincinnati

Kay Kenney Fortson
Phillips University

Thomas C. Fox
Washington University

Carol Franks
Portland State University

Ronald H. Fritze
Lamar University

James Gaasch
Humboldt State University

Frank Gado
Union College

Robert L. Gale
University of Pittsburgh

Louis Gallo
Radford University

Ann D. Garbett
Averett College

Daniel H. Garrison
Northwestern University

Michael Wm. Gearhart
University of South Florida

Philip Gerard
University of North Carolina at Wilmington

Dana Gerhardt
Independent Scholar

Donna Gerstenberger
University of Washington

Jill B. Gidmark
University of Minnesota

Donald Gilman
Ball State University

Jonathan A. Glenn
Holy Cross Junior College

Jacqueline L. Gmuca
*University of South Carolina-
Coastal Carolina College*

Donald Gochberg
Michigan State University

Hazel Gold
Northwestern University

Lucy Golsan
Independent Scholar

Richard J. Golsan
Texas A&M University

Sandra Y. Govan
University of North Carolina at Charlotte

Eleanor H. Green
Ohio Northern University

Mark Haag
University of California, Los Angeles

Steven L. Hale
Morris Brown College

Jay L. Halio
University of Delaware

Natalie Harper
Simon's Rock of Bard College

E. Lynn Harris
University of Illinois at Chicago

Sandra Hanby Harris
Tidewater Community College

Melanie C. Hawthorne
Texas A&M University

Mark Allen Heberle
University of Hawaii at Manoa

Terry Heller
Coe College

Joyce E. Henry
Ursinus College

Michael Craig Hillmann
University of Texas at Austin

Eric H. Hobson
University of Tennessee

James L. Hodge
Bowdoin College

Heidi J. Holder
*University of Massachusetts
at Amherst*

William H. Holland, Jr.
Middle Tennessee State University

Michael Hollister
Portland State University

Anna R. Holloway
Fort Valley State College

John R. Holmes
Franciscan University of Steubenville

Glenn Hopp
Howard Payne University

Pierre L. Horn
Wright State University

Ruth Hsu
University of Southern California

Steven R. Huff
Oberlin College

David E. Huntley
Appalachian State University

E. D. Huntley
Appalachian State University

Geraldine L. Hutchins
East Tennessee State University

Allen E. Hye
Wright State University

CONTRIBUTING REVIEWERS

Archibald E. Irwin
Indiana University Southeast

Nalini Iyer
Purdue University

Terry Hays Jackson
East Tennessee State University

Shakuntala Jayaswal
University of New Haven

W. A. Johnsen
Michigan State University

Kathleen A. Johnson
Lake Forest College

Mary Johnson
University of South Florida

James W. Jones
Central Michigan University

B. A. Kachur
University of Missouri-St. Louis

Albert E. Kalson
Purdue University

Bettye Choate Kash
Tennessee Technological University

Richard S. Keating
U. S. Air Force Academy

Katherine Keller
University of Central Florida

Steven G. Kellman
University of Texas at San Antonio

Richard Kelly
University of Tennessee

Martin Kich
Lehigh University

Christine Kiebuzinska
*Virginia Polytechnic Institute and
   State University*

Cassandra Kircher
University of Iowa

Paul Kistel
Los Angeles Pierce College

Wm. Laird Kleine-Ahlbrandt
Purdue University

Paula Kopacz
Eastern Kentucky University

Stephanie Korney
Independent Scholar

Steven C. Kowall
Independent Scholar

Susan Kress
Skidmore College

Marlies Kronegger
Michigan State University

Lolette Kuby
Akron University

Katherine C. Kurk
Northern Kentucky University

William LaHay
Independent Scholar

Joseph Laker
Wheeling Jesuit College

James B. Lane
Indiana University Northwest

P. R. Lannert
Independent Scholar

Eugene S. Larson
Los Angeles Pierce College

Terry Lass
Columbia College, Missouri

Ellen M. Laun
Pennsylvania State University, Fayette

Bruce H. Leland
Western Illinois University

Lagretta T. Lenker
University of South Florida

Leon Lewis
Appalachian State University

Leslie W. Lewis
*Indiana University,
   Bloomington*

Terrance L. Lewis
Clarion University

T. M. Lipman
Independent Scholar

Donald E. Livingston, Jr.
Arizona State University

James L. Livingston
Northern Michigan University

Helen Lojek
Boise State University

Barbara A. Looney
University of South Florida

Janet Lorenz
Independent Scholar

Michael Loudon
Eastern Illinois University

Barbara Lounsberry
University of Northern Iowa

Philip H. Lutes
University of Montana

Reinhart Lutz
University of California, Santa Barbara

Sara McAlpin
Clarke College

Janet McCann
Texas A&M University

Janie Caves McCauley
Bob Jones University

Arthur F. McClure
Central Missouri State University

Robert McColley
University of Illinois at Urbana-Champaign

Jean McConnell
University of New Mexico

Philip McDermott
Independent Scholar

Andrew Macdonald
Loyola University, New Orleans

Gina Macdonald
Loyola University, New Orleans
Tulane University

William J. McDonald
Baylor University

Gregory McElwain
University of New Mexico

Richard D. McGhee
Kansas State University

Edythe M. McGovern
Los Angeles Valley College

John L. McLean
Morehead State University

Alan L. McLeod
Rider College

Marian B. McLeod
Trenton State College

David W. Madden
California State University, Sacramento

Coleen Maddy
University of Iowa

Helga Stipa Madland
University of Oklahoma

Philip Magnier
Independent Scholar

Martha Manheim
Siena Heights College

B. P. Mann
University of San Diego

Donna Maples
Howard Payne University

Joss Lutz Marsh
California Institute of Technology

Liz Marshall
Independent Scholar

Charles E. May
California State University, Long Beach

Laurence W. Mazzeno
U. S. Naval Academy

Patrick Meanor
State University of New York College at Oneonta

Leslie Mellichamp
Virginia Polytechnic Institute and State University

Vasa D. Mihailovich
University of North Carolina at Chapel Hill

Randall M. Miller
Saint Joseph's University

Kathleen Mills
Baldwin-Wallace College

Maureen W. Mills
Central Michigan University

Christian H. Moe
Southern Illinois University at Carbondale

Fritz Monsma
Independent Scholar

CONTRIBUTING REVIEWERS

Robert A. Morace
Daemen College

Gwendolyn Morgan
Montana State University

Robert E. Morsberger
California State Polytechnic University, Pomona

James V. Muhleman
Hawaii Loa College

John M. Muste
Ohio State University

Eunice Myers
Wichita State University

Susan V. Myers
University of New Mexico

Mary Henry Nachtsheim
College of St. Catherine

William Nelles
Northwestern State University of Louisiana

John S. Nelson
Saint Mary of the Plains College

J. W. Newcomb
Memphis State University

Terry Nienhuis
Western Carolina University

Donald R. Noble
University of Alabama

Marjorie J. Oberlander
Mercy College

Aileen O'Catherine
Independent Scholar

Kathleen O'Mara
*State University of New York College
    at Oneonta*

Robert M. Otten
Assumption College

David Patterson
Oklahoma State University

David Peck
California State University, Long Beach

Robert W. Peckham
Sacred Heart Major Seminary

William E. Pemberton
University of Wisconsin-La Crosse

Helmut F. Pfanner
University of Nebraska-Lincoln

R. Craig Philips
Michigan State University

William L. Phillips
University of Washington

Susan L. Piepke
Bridgewater College

Steven L. Piott
Clarion University

Rosaria Pipia
*Queens College of the City University
    of New York*

David W. Pitre
Episcopal School of Baton Rouge

Mary Ellen Pitts
Memphis State University

Ann L. Postlethweight
University of South Florida

Clifton W. Potter, Jr.
Lynchburg College

John F. Povey
University of California, Los Angeles

Marian Price
University of Central Florida

Victoria Price
Lamar University

Karen Priest
Lamar University

David Pringle
University of South Florida

Charles Pullen
Queen's University, Ontario, Canada

Diane Quinn
Independent Scholar

Josef Raab
University of Southern California

James H. Randall
Coe College

Tom Rash
Asheville-Buncombe Community College

John D. Raymer
Indiana University at South Bend

Jere Real
Lynchburg College

Peter J. Reed
University of Minnesota

Rosemary M. Canfield Reisman
Troy State University

Clark G. Reynolds
College of Charleston

Rodney P. Rice
U. S. Air Force Academy

Betty Richardson
Southern Illinois University at Edwardsville

Jochen Richter
Allegheny College

Jerome J. Rinkus
Pomona College

James W. Robinson, Jr.
Chaminade University

Vicki K. Robinson
State University of New York at Farmingdale

Mark William Rocha
Glassboro State College

Gisela Roethke-Makemson
Dickinson College

Peter S. Rogers
Loyola University, New Orleans

Douglas Rollins
Dawson College

Jill Rollins
Trafalgar School, Quebec, Canada

Carl Rollyson
Baruch College, City University of New York

Evelyn Romig
Howard Payne University

Paul Rosefeldt
University of New Orleans

Joseph Rosenblum
University of North Carolina at Greensboro

Natania Rosenfeld
Princeton University

Sidney Rosenfeld
Oberlin College

Stella P. Rosenfeld
Cleveland State University

Robert L. Ross
Independent Scholar

Gabrielle Rowe
McKendree College

Elizabeth A. Rubino
Northwestern State University of Louisiana

Nancy E. Rupprecht
Middle Tennessee State University

Susan Rusinko
Bloomsburg University

Dennis Ryan
University of South Florida

Chaman L. Sahni
Boise State University

John Scheckter
C. W. Post College, Long Island University

Leda Schiavo
University of Illinois at Chicago

Thomas C. Schunk
Quincy College

Jo C. Searles
Pennsylvania State University, University Park

Millicent Sharma
Independent Scholar

John C. Sherwood
University of Oregon

R. Baird Shuman
University of Illinois at Urbana-Champaign

Anne W. Sienkewicz
Independent Scholar

Caren S. Silvester
Bob Jones University

Carl Singleton
Fort Hays State University

Genevieve Slomski
Independent Scholar

Gilbert Smith
North Carolina State University

Ira Smolensky
Monmouth College

CONTRIBUTING REVIEWERS

Katherine Snipes
Eastern Washington University

Janet L. Solberg
Kalamazoo College

Marcia J. Songer
East Tennessee State University

George Soule
Carleton College

Thomas D. Spaccarelli
University of the South

Isabel B. Stanley
East Tennessee State University

Lisa S. Starks
University of South Florida

Helen Winter Stauffer
Kearney State College

Larry L. Stewart
College of Wooster

H. R. Stoneback
*State University of New York College
   at New Paltz*

Richard Stoner
Broome Community College

Ian Stuart
University of California, Santa Barbara

James Sullivan
California State University, Los Angeles

Charlene E. Suscavage
University of Southern Maine

Catherine Swanson
Oxford University

Roy Arthur Swanson
University of Wisconsin-Milwaukee

Charles Sweet
Eastern Kentucky University

Thomas J. Taylor
Independent Scholar

Terry Theodore
University of North Carolina at Wilmington

Allen Thiher
University of Missouri-Columbia

Betty Taylor Thompson
Texas Southern University

Lloyd R. Thompson
University of New Haven

Lou Thompson
New Mexico Institute of Mining and Technology

Evelyn Toft
Fort Hays State University

John P. Turner, Jr.
Humboldt State University

John Merritt Unsworth
North Carolina State University

Luiz Fernando Valente
Brown University

Russell Valentino
University of California, Los Angeles

George W. Van Devender
Hardin-Simmons University

Dennis Vannatta
University of Arkansas

Donald Vanouse
*State University of New York College
   at Oswego*

Emil Volek
Arizona State University

John C. Watson
University of Oregon

H. J. Weatherford
Georgia Southern College

James Michael Welsh
Salisbury State University

John Whalen-Bridge
University of Southern California

Susan Whaley
Independent Scholar

Cynthia Jane Whitney
University of South Florida

Barbara Wiedemann
Auburn University at Montgomery

Clarke L. Wilhelm
Denison University

Ray Willbanks
Memphis State University

Sandra Willbanks
Maharishi International University

Lori Williams
Independent Scholar

Philip F. Williams
Arizona State University

Robert J. Willis
East Stroudsburg University

John Wilson
Independent Scholar

Johnny Wink
Ouachita Baptist University

Michael Witkoski
Independent Scholar

Leigh Woods
Independent Scholar

Karin A. Wurst
Michigan State University

Jennifer L. Wyatt
Southern Illinois University at Edwardsville

Robert E. Yahnke
University of Minnesota

Vincent Yang
Pennsylvania State University, University Park

Marlene Youmans
State University of New York College at Potsdam

Michael Zeitlin
University of Toronto

Harry Zohn
Brandeis University

John Zubizarreta
Columbia College, South Carolina

LIST OF TITLES IN VOLUME 1

CYCLOPEDIA OF LITERARY CHARACTERS II

LIST OF TITLES IN VOLUME 1

KEY TO PRONUNCIATION

â	pare, stair	o͝o	book, push
ă	man, rang	o͞o	moor, move
ā	ale, fate	ou	loud, round
ä	calm, father	p	put, stop
b	bed, rub	r	red, try
ch	chin, reach	s	see, pass
d	day, bad	sh	she, push
ĕ	ten, ebb	t	to, bit
ē	equal, meat	th	thin, path
ė	fern, bird	ŧh	then, mother
f	fill, off	ŭ	up, dove
g	go, rug	ū	use, cube
h	hot, hear	û	surge, burn
ĭ	if, hit	v	vast, above
ī	ice, right	w	will, away
j	joy, hedge	y	yet, yam
k	keep, take	z	zest, amaze
l	let, ball	zh	azure, seizure
m	man, him	ə	is a vowel occurring in an unaccented
n	now, ton		syllable, as
ng	ring, English		a *in* above
ŏ	lot, box		e *in* chapel
ō	old, over		i *in* veracity
ô	order, shorn		o *in* connect
oi	boy, oil		u *in* crocus

FOREIGN SOUNDS

à	pronounced as in the French *ami*
k̲	pronounced as in the German *ich*
ll	usually pronounced like *y* in *yes* in Latin America; in Spain like the *ll* in *million*
ṅ	a nasal *n* pronounced as in the French *bon*
ñ	pronounced like the *ny* in *canyon*
œ	pronounced as in the French *feu* or the German *böse*
r̄r	pronounced as in the Spanish *barranco*
ü	pronounced as in the French *du* or the German *grün*
x	pronounced as in the German *nacht*

Cyclopedia
of
Literary Characters II

———

A-Div

AARON'S ROD

Author: D. H. Lawrence (1885-1930)
Type of work: Novel
Time of action: December 24, 1919, to November, 1920
First published: 1922

Aaron Sisson, a well-educated young man who decides not to teach but to return to the coal mine as a secretary to a miners' union. He leaves behind the oppressive responsibility of his wife and three daughters to become an orchestra flutist in London and then leaves London for Italy, following Lilly. He finds Lilly again in Florence, seeking him out to discuss a new modus vivendi.

Lottie Sisson, his beautiful wife, with whom he has a contest of wills. She half desires, half resists his attempts to return home.

Millicent Sisson, the oldest of their three daughters, who inherits the struggle of wills from her parents. At Christmas, she tries the patience of her father by testing the strength of a family tree decoration; it breaks.

Jim Bricknell, a war veteran, the son of the local mine owner. He takes up Aaron as an interesting acquaintance who represents the real working class in his superficial commitment to cultural revolution. Bricknell repeatedly proclaims his need to be loved throughout the novel.

Josephine Ford, his fiancée, an artist. She has a short affair with Sisson in London.

Rawdon Lilly, an English gentleman whose cottage Bricknell visits on the strength of his own invitation. When Lilly criticizes him too severely, Bricknell knocks him breathless. Later, Aaron arrives drunk and feverish at his Covent Garden flat, to be nursed back to health, until he, too, breaks with Lilly. Lilly knows that he is expected to save his friends by telling them some unique truth. At the end of the novel, in a long discussion, he tells Sisson that modern men and women must either love or rule.

Francis Dekker, a traveling Australian painter, whose privileged means and manner contrast with Aaron's background as they ride the train to Florence together.

Angus Guest, a traveling Welsh painter, who forms part of the English-speaking artistic set in Florence.

James Argyle, a traveling English writer, another visiting member of the Anglo community in Florence.

Manfredi, the Marchese del Torre, a colonel in the Italian army. He befriends Sisson as a fellow musician despite his awareness of the relationship that Sisson is forming with his wife.

Nan, the Marchesa del Torre, his wife. She draws Sisson into an affair by her smouldering passion, which transforms into a childlike dependency after they are lovers.

W. A. Johnsen

THE ABBESS OF CREWE
A Modern Morality Tale

Author: Muriel Spark (1918-   )
Type of work: Novel
Time of action: The early 1970's
First published: 1974

Alexandra, the recently elected Abbess of Crewe, a Roman Catholic Benedictine abbey in the English Midlands. Tall and slender, with white skin and light eyes, the forty-two-year-old abbess bears herself with a clear consciousness of her aristocratic lineage. In her quest for power, she will stop at nothing. To win the election, she bugged the abbey and the grounds, entered into a secret pact with the Jesuits to commit a burglary, and even accused her rival of being a bourgeoise instead of a lady. When she is exposed, Alexandra casts the blame on her loyal aides and is last seen en route to the pope to be exonerated. In the parallel Watergate scandal, she represents President Richard M. Nixon.

Sister Felicity, Alexandra's unsuccessful rival for the position of abbess. A tiny, red-haired woman, usually breathless and disorganized, Felicity is a crusader for change, justice, freedom, and love, demonstrating her principles in a sizzling liaison with a Jesuit named Thomas. In her headquarters, the sewing room, however, she is very tidy, and therefore, she immediately notices the theft of her thimble from her workbox. When she later finds Jesuit seminarians stealing love letters from the same box, she calls the police. After fleeing the abbey with Thomas, she exposes Alexandra and her aides. Felicity represents Senator George McGovern, as well as presidential counsel John Dean.

Sister Walburga, the prioress. A long-faced, middle-aged woman from a wealthy family, she developed her mind with a series of intellectual lovers. She has subordinated her own ambitions to those of Alexandra, however, and is her chief of staff. Realizing Alexandra's vulnerability, she insists that the abbess pretend to be ignorant of any wrongdoing in the election process. When the scandal breaks, Sister Walburga is sent to serve in an infirmary at a distant abbey. Sister Walburga represents Nixon's White House chief of staff, H. R. Haldeman.

Sister Mildred, novice mistress and Alexandra's second in command. A pretty, blue-eyed woman with an appealing heart-shaped face, she is thirty-six years old. Timid by nature, she is contented with her subordinate position. When the police are called, Sister Mildred becomes very nervous; however, she remains loyal to Alexandra and is willing to assume the blame to shield her. She is sent to the infirmary with Walburga. Mildred represents Nixon's domestic affairs adviser, John D. Ehrlichman.

Sister Winifrede, a third aide. Tall and fair, with a round face, she looks more like a British matron than a nun. Although she is stupid, she is totally loyal and, therefore, useful for menial tasks, such as preparing refreshments during planning sessions. Anticipating possible disasters, Alexandra forces Winifrede to sign a blanket confession before her final mission, when she tries to deliver hush money to the seminarians in the men's room of the British library and is arrested. Winifrede represents White House lawyer Charles W. Colson as well as John Dean.

Sister Gertrude, the abbey's foreign missionary. A Machiavellian in outlook and Germanic in accent, she communicates with Alexandra from the Congo or Tibet, where she is constantly rearranging local governments. Although she remains aloof from local abbey politics, once the scandal breaks, she points out Alexandra's errors. Gertrude represents Secretary of State Henry Kissinger.

Father Baudouin, a Jesuit priest and friend of Alexandra. A heavy, middle-aged man with gray hair, he is particularly attractive to Sister Walburga. After his role in organizing the burglary becomes known, he is sent to give American seminars in demonology.

Father Maximilian, a Jesuit priest and Father Baudouin's coconspirator. He is a fine-featured, distinguished-looking man; however, despite his obvious intelligence, he is easily persuaded to help Alexandra. Because of his part in the theft of Felicity's letters, he, too, is sent to America.

Rosemary M. Canfield Reisman

2

ABEL SÁNCHEZ

Author: Miguel de Unamuno y Jugo (1864-1936)
Type of work: Novel
Time of action: Unspecified
First published: Abel Sánchez: Una historia de pasión, 1917 (English translation, 1947)

Joaquín Monegro (hwä•kēn' mō•nĕ'grō), a physician and scientist, an accomplished orator, and a lifelong friend and secret enemy of Abel Sánchez. In this parable of contrasts and moral ambiguities, Joaquín is the dark personality, like the biblical Cain, consumed by jealousy and hatred of his closest companion. Even as a child, Joaquín believed that Abel had robbed him of everything he ever wanted, effortlessly usurping his friends and the admiration of adults. Actually, having chosen this role, Joaquín often arranged accidents that promoted his preconceptions. When he fell passionately in love with the beautiful Helena, for example, he arranged for Abel to paint her portrait, fully aware of Abel's easy success with women. When Abel and Helena became lovers, Joaquín believed that he had proved once more that Abel had betrayed him. He becomes more sly and circumspect in his zeal to outdo and even to destroy Abel. Although he is considered a cold man, Joaquín despises himself for his continual malice and actually fights off some temptations to harm Abel. When Abel and Helena are married and expect a child, he refuses to attend Helena in childbirth, lest he strangle the child at birth. He marries a tender and compassionate woman. When his wife has a baby girl, he hopes that he can gain salvation through the love of a child. He even becomes fond of Abel's son, who wants to become a doctor, not a painter like his father. Although Joaquín takes Abelin into his household as an apprentice, originally with the malicious goal of displacing Abel as parent, he grows to love the boy and becomes a good mentor, teaching him his healing arts. Yet neither the love of his patient wife nor the devotion of the young people can root out the ancient malice. When Abel becomes enthralled with his grandson, born to Abelin and Joaquín's daughter, the old jealousy arises once more. In an argument, Joaquín reaches for Abel's throat, but Abel dies of a heart attack on the spot. The wretched Joaquín dies soon after, mourning that he had killed Abel and that he had never loved anyone.

Abel Sánchez (ä•bĕl' sän'chĕz), a famous painter. Although he is devoid of malice and envy, Abel is hardly a candidate for sainthood. In fact, his character is extraordinarily flat, lacking in any depth of reflection, sorrow, or passion. He is egotistical and self-serving, though not offensively so. He sometimes disagrees with Joaquín regarding the nature of art. He paints the surface of things and insists that a man is no different on the inside from what he appears to be on the outside. That is one reason that Joaquín and even young Abelin are dissatisfied with his art, even though he is very skillful in producing surface effects. Only Abelin has suffered from his father's lack of warmth. Joaquín is probably correct that Abel does not want his son to follow in his footsteps as a painter, since that might dilute or even displace the father's fame. Though Joaquín ardently seeks truth as the highest good, Abel pursues art and beauty rather dispassionately. His marriage to Helena is thus very appropriate, though he is unfaithful to her when other beautiful women are available.

Helena Sánchez, Abel's wife. Abel met his match in Helena, a woman who seems to be all surface. She becomes enamored of Abel mostly because his portrait makes her a famous beauty. She, too, seems lacking in malice or ulterior motives. Though well aware of Joaquín's passion for her, she did not lead him on or promise him any favors. She is sometimes called a peacock or a "professional beauty." She seems to have no impact at all on her son, nor does she appear to suffer from Abel's infidelities.

3

Antonia Monegro, Joaquín's wife, personifies motherliness, tenderness, and compassion. She is drawn to Joaquín because of the sickness of his soul. A religious person, she prays for his salvation and tries to bring him back into the light through the power of unselfish love. Joaquín recognizes and seems at times to respond to her devotion. He repudiates his old infatuation with Helena, realizing the real superiority of Antonia. He welcomes the daughter she gives him as a new opportunity to learn love instead of hate. Yet even his satisfaction with his daughter is tainted with the desire to keep pace with Abel, who had sired a son. Ultimately, the long-suffering Antonia receives a final emotional wound from the remorseful Joaquín when, on his deathbed, her husband mourns that he never loved her.

Abelin Sánchez, Abel's son, idealizes Joaquín for his devotion to the science of healing. While Joaquín always preferred pure scientific research to actually helping people, he pursued the practice of medicine as more lucrative. The idealistic Abelin, who offers to organize and publish Joaquín's many recorded observations and brilliant insights about his patients, ensures that Joaquín's talent will, in fact, have a benevolent effect upon posterity. Yet it also feeds Joaquín's neurotic desire for a fame to rival Abel's.

Joaquína Monegro Sánchez, Joaquín's daughter, inherits her mother's temperament and her desire to win salvation for her tortured father. In fact, when she desires to become a nun and spend her life in prayer for that very reason, Joaquín hastily redirects her energies, begging her to marry Abelin and thus heal the rift between the two families.

Joaquiníto Sánchez, the grandchild. His name was chosen not by anyone in the Monegro family, but by Abel, the father-in-law, who becomes a regular visitor at the physician's house. The aging Abel lavishes on his grandson the affection he never accorded to his own son. The child responds to the endless drawings that Abel makes for him and soon loves Abel much more than he does his more somber grandfather. When the elder Joaquín is about to die, he has the child brought to his bedside and begs his forgiveness. The child gives it readily enough, though he understands nothing about the dying man's distress.

Katherine Snipes

ABSURD PERSON SINGULAR

Author: Alan Ayckbourn (1939-   )
Type of work: Play
Time of action: The 1970's
First produced: 1972

Sidney Hopcroft, an up-and-coming businessman who starts out running a general store but successfully expands into real estate development. In his thirties, he sports a thin mustache and, when first seen, wears a dated but well-kept suit. He is small in stature, dapper, very cheerful, and exuberant. His bustling energy, which the more urbane Brewster-Wrights find boring and gauche, suits his wife perfectly. An irrepressible handyman, he loves do-it-yourself projects and household repairs. He constantly fidgets and, when not under a sink fixing the plumbing, flits about nervously. His Christmas gift to his wife, a deluxe washing machine, is indicative of his no-nonsense, unromantic nature. Although serenely oblivious to the emotional state of others, his goodwill seems genuine and infectious. He is a spark plug, always trying to get the others to have fun, even in the most unlikely situations. Much of the play's hilarity springs from Hopcroft's inappropriate activity for the circumstances, especially in act 2, when Eva

Jackson repeatedly attempts suicide while Sidney tries to clean out her kitchen-sink trap.

Jane Hopcroft, Sidney's wife, also in her thirties. Called "Admiral" by Sidney, she has an obsessive need to clean and scrub and in her delight with such tasks seems to parody the typical wife of television commercials. She has the habit of breaking into song when busy with domestic chores, making her seem silly and inane. Like her husband, she lacks imagination and sensitivity when it comes to others. She is not as gregarious as Sidney and does not like parties or drinking, accepting her role as hostess more as a grim domestic duty than a pleasure. With dust rag in hand, she is effusive and cheerful but otherwise rather stiff and apprehensive. In the final scene, however, fortified with several drinks, she unwinds and joins in the fun with atypical abandon.

Ronald Brewster-Wright, a bank officer. A well-bred man in his forties, he is fairly imposing in appearance but not particularly distinguished. Although capable of wry observations, he is rather stuffy, deliberate, and reserved, a striking contrast to Sidney Hopcroft. Now in his second marriage, he admits that women are incomprehensible to him. Belonging to the managerial class, and thus relying on servants and tradesmen, he is totally incompetent as a handyman. He comes close to electrocuting himself when attempting to repair a light fixture in the Jacksons' flat.

Marion Brewster-Wright, Ronald's wife, somewhat younger. Cosmopolitan and sophisticated, she has a patronizing attitude toward those she considers beneath her. She is also two-faced, exuding charm and warmth when face-to-face with the Hopcrofts but making unkind comments behind their backs. On the weary and bored side, she drinks excessively, presumably to cope with life's disenchantments. Ultimately, she is incapacitated by her alcoholism, becoming an increasing embarrassment to her husband.

Geoffrey Jackson, an architect. He is a handsome man in his mid-thirties, a self-styled "sexual Flying Dutchman," who womanizes shamelessly. He has a rather arrogant self-esteem but is not the creative genius he imagines himself to be. He is humbled somewhat when the ceiling of a building he designed caves in and his professional prospects diminish. Ironically, in the building's ruins his marriage begins to be rebuilt. He finally learns to value the emotional support and loyalty his wife offers him.

Eva Jackson, Geoffrey's wife, also in her thirties. Initially, she is distraught and desperately unhappy in her marriage. She feels abandoned by her husband and uses tranquilizers to cope with her misery. Fear of madness and the numbing effect of drugs make it difficult for her to socialize or perform simple household chores, and she becomes as untidy and careless as Jane Hopcroft is neat and orderly. When Geoffrey announces that he is moving out to take up with another woman, Eva, at an emotional ebb, makes an ineffectual attempt to kill herself. Then, as if spiritually refortified by her seriocomic failure at suicide, she begins to put her life in order, and, in the last act, strengthened by the new demeanor of her husband, she reveals remarkable good sense and emotional stability.

John W. Fiero

THE ABYSS

Author: Marguerite Yourcenar (Marguerite de Crayencour, 1903-1987)
Type of work: Novel
Time of action: 1510-1569
First published: L'Œuvre au noir, 1968 (English translation, 1976)

Zeno, an alchemist, physician, and philosopher. At the beginning of the novel, Zeno is a wildly attractive twenty-year-old student of theology, tall and slim, pale and haggard, with fiery eyes. Being illegitimate, he feels the hypocrisy of social morals; furthermore, he acquires early a thirst for truth, which leads him to travel and meet all the important scientists and philosophers in his conquest of knowledge and in his search for himself. A true skeptic, this Humanist challenges established orthodoxy, since he is passionately interested in all human and scientific pursuits and experiences, often at the risk of prison or the stake. In middle age, gaunt, gray, and frugal, he hides under the alias of Sebastian Theus in his hometown of Bruges, Belgium, where he is appointed physician at a church-run hospice. As confidant to several monks, he learns of their orgies and fears for his own freedom. He decides to stay, however, for his life or death no longer matters to him. Indirectly implicated, he is arrested and tried (under his real name) for all his past activities and books and condemned to die, although he can obtain a pardon if he recants all his writings. He refuses and at fifty-eight kills himself.

Henry Maximilian Ligre (lǐ′•grə), a soldier of fortune. At sixteen, Zeno's cousin and a banker's son is tall and angular of face, with tawny hair, in love with life and poetry, as he joins France's armies to conquer the world of arms and women. Considered a brilliant soldier, he has been leading for twenty-five years the rude existence of a mercenary, often penniless, always cheerful and fearless, charming women to whom he writes sonnets and enjoying the pleasures of wine and song. He dies a captain during a sortie, the pages of his manuscript buried with him in a ditch.

Henry Justus Ligre, a merchant and banker. This corpulent and lusty Fleming loves his son Henry Maximilian and tolerates his nephew Zeno. Enjoying the pleasures of food, drink, and female company, the newly widowed and increasingly rich and influential Ligre marries a trader's daughter with whom he has a son, Philibert.

Jean-Louis de Berlaimont (bĕr•lĕ•mōñ′), the prior of a monastery. More than sixty years old, he is gentle and compassionate, refined and sophisticated, and devout and tolerant. A former courtier and diplomat, he enjoys discussing politics and theology with Zeno. During these talks, he sides with the Patriots against Spanish rule; torn between the presence of evil and God's inherent goodness, he sometimes doubts his own faith. He dies of a throat polyp after advising his friend to flee from the Inquisition.

Alberico de' Numi (nōō•mī′), a prelate. A handsome and attentive young nobleman, he seduces Hilzonda Ligre, whom he later abandons to pursue his political and clerical ambitions. Indeed, he receives the cardinal's hat at thirty, although he continues to lead a rogue's existence and is murdered after an orgy.

Hilzonda Ligre, a bourgeois woman and Henry Justus' sister. Slender and not too pretty, when young and naïve, she fell in love with Alberico, with whom she had Zeno. Ashamed of her sin, she is finally consoled by her brother's friend and business associate, whom she eventually marries and with whom she has a daughter, Martha. All three leave for Münster, renamed the City of God. There, she becomes one of the ruler's mistresses in mystical euphoria. After the imperial troops regain the city, she is beheaded.

Simon Adriansen, a merchant. He is a God-fearing older gentleman, bearded and wrinkled. In his conduct with all, he is charitable and kind as well as successful in his business and investments (he is related to the Fuggers of the famous banking house). After his death following the Münster rebellion, he is buried in a Catholic cemetery, his strong Anabaptist faith notwithstanding.

Martha Adriansen, a bourgeois woman. As a little girl, she is thin and sickly, more intellectual than her cousin Benedicta Fugger with whom she is reared after her parents die. Although a Calvinist, she lacks true fervor and, in fact, during the plague of 1549, she reveals to her half brother Zeno a cowardice of the spirit that is worse than any physical cowardice.

Benedicta Fugger (fōō·gĕr′), the daughter of Martin and Salomé (Adriansen) Fugger, a pretty girl of the same age as her cousin Martha. Martha and she are best friends and learn French, music, and drawing together; in addition, both secretly study Reformed liturgy and tenets. She dies of the plague, despite Zeno's treatment.

Bartholomew Campanus, a canon. Thirty years old, but already appearing much older, Campanus is Zeno's affectionate uncle and tutor. He is scholarly in his interest for languages and philosophy, which he teaches his pupil. At the end of the novel, he is eighty and infirm, and, while his life has been peaceful and innocent, he is desolate over Zeno's past and probable end.

Philibert Ligre, a banker. The second son of Henry Justus Ligre, he is fat and physically unassuming. Deeply interested in money and finance, he is very astute and ferocious in his business dealings. He is at first engaged to Benedicta, but when she dies he marries his cousin Martha. Becoming fabulously wealthy and powerful, Martha

and he live in ostentatious luxury and yet refuse to help Zeno (his cousin and her half brother) after Zeno's indictment.

Cyprian, a monk. He is Zeno's handsome and affable eighteen-year-old aide who, though superstitious, hardly educated, and lazy, has a certain nursing ability. He is involved in theologically inspired sex orgies with several other monks. After his arrest, under torture he confesses all and dies at the stake, along with his friends.

Idelette de Loos, a noble girl. This fifteen-year-old maiden, appropriately called the Fair One by the monks, is very beautiful, with blonde hair and blue eyes, and always well dressed. Daring, coquettish, and headstrong, she is the center of orgiastic and sexual rituals. Being an "angel," she supposedly cannot conceive, but, when she becomes pregnant, she strangles her baby. At her trial, she implicates her accomplices and, found guilty, is beheaded.

Sign Ulfsdatter (ülfs′dǎ·tər), a healer and herbalist. Referred to as the Lady of Froso, she is tall, fair, and beautiful, generous and hospitable. She is one of Zeno's few peers and the only woman he truly loves.

Pierre L. Horn

THE ACCIDENT

Author: Elie Wiesel (1928-   )
Type of work: Novel
Time of action: The 1950's
First published: Le Jour, 1961 (English translation, 1962)

Eliezer, the narrator, a journalist of Eastern European birth. After losing his entire family in the Holocaust, Eliezer has emigrated to Paris and New York. He is haunted by his past, by the guilt of having survived, and by a deeply felt responsibility to bear witness on behalf of the dead. His mind is flooded with dreams, images, symbols, and memories, especially of his grandmother, whom he loved devotedly. He finds it impossible to

live in the present: He is cynical, detached, and inexpressive. When he does speak, it is often in metaphors, philosophical assertions, and enigmas. He has been drawn to Kathleen since the moment they met, but ultimately he pities her faithfulness and her need to be deceived. Similarly, he feels disdain for Dr. Russel's inability to comprehend despair. Eliezer is weary of the suffering of life and longs to encounter death, and the

7

accident he survives is an expression of that longing.

Kathleen, a charming young woman, Eliezer's lover. Kathleen believes strongly in the omnipotence of love. From an affluent background, she is confident and decisive and not accustomed to losing battles. Yet she is blind with illusions about the goodness of the world and cannot fathom Eliezer's obsession with the past. Through their tumultuous and often cruel affair, she learns about suffering. Later, after he has left her, she is spiritually deadened by marriage to a man for whom she feels no passion.

Eliezer's grandmother, an Eastern European woman who was killed in the Holocaust. Eliezer's grandmother lives vividly in his memories and in his basic philosophy of life. She was a simple and pious elderly Jewish woman with soft white skin and an enormous black shawl. She often protected the young Eliezer from his father's temper and always treated him with compassion.

Dr. Paul Russel, the young resident who cares for Eliezer in the hospital after the accident. Russel is wise and perceptive beyond his years, and he sees in Eliezer the depth of an intense spiritual struggle. He is affable and informal at the patient's bedside but not afraid to be direct. Ultimately, his ideals and strong belief in the value of life render him unable to understand Eliezer's anguish.

Nurse, the young woman who assists in Eliezer's care. She is patient and attentive to Eliezer but commands authority when necessary. She is honest with him and responds openly to his moods and challenges. Her humor brings a much-needed lightness to his recuperation.

Sarah, a prostitute with whom Eliezer spent an evening in Paris shortly after his liberation. At the age of twelve, Sarah was forced into prostitution in a Nazi concentration camp and became the favorite toy of the German officers. She feels shame about her manner of survival and guilt in the knowledge that sometimes she even felt pleasure in such reprehensible sexual encounters. With no pretensions about her moral stature, she is fearless, even proud; yet she is unpredictable, moody, and, to Eliezer, elusive.

Gyula, a Hungarian painter and friend to Eliezer. Gyula is tall and robust in person, rebellious and mocking in spirit: in all ways a powerful and intimidating figure. He alone understands Eliezer's despair, and yet he alone, arrogant and energetic, is able to inspire the wounded man. Gyula has no patience for sentimentality and suffering: He refuses to hear Eliezer's confession but rather insists on painting a portrait that ultimately helps Eliezer see himself more clearly.

B. P. Mann

ACCIDENTAL DEATH OF AN ANARCHIST

Author: Dario Fo (1926-   )
Type of work: Play
Time of action: 1970
First produced: Morte accidentale di un anarchico, 1970 (English translation, 1979)

Maniac, a shabbily dressed man with wild hair, thin spectacles, and a goatee. The Maniac is an inventive and unpredictable subversive who has been arrested twelve times for illegal impersonations. His disguises and personae include a magistrate, Professor Marco Maria Malpiero, and—perhaps his true identity—Paulo Davidovitch Gandolpho, Prose Pimpernel of the Permanent Revolution and sports editor of *Lotta Continua*, a Jewish conspiracy newspaper. The Maniac's revolutionary fervor is grounded in a deep knowledge of fields as diverse as railroads, grammar, explosives, and psychology.

Not only is he a disciple of Sigmund Freud, but he also proudly claims to be a certified psychotic. His manner is light and cheerful, suffused with delightful mimicry and a sharply sardonic wit. His hobby is the theater, and in the police station he is at once scenarist, actor, and audience, alternately manipulating, observing, and cooperating with the police buffoons. Thus he chatters endlessly and distractingly but is equally capable of stating the truth in boldly direct terms: He is both jester and seer, a wise fool. When the discussion turns to political theory, the Maniac becomes didactic and dogmatic, a seemingly disembodied voice of communist ideology. In his subtle way, he is a moral catalyst, forcing the policemen to expose the truth about the anarchist's death and maneuvering Felleti into an inescapable moral dilemma. The Maniac himself does not offer to sacrifice his own life senselessly, but rather seems to hover above both the action and the moral questions it presents.

Francisco Giovanni Batista Giancarlo Bertozzo (bĕr·tō'tsō), Inspector of the Milan Police and its explosives and ballistics expert. Despite his simplicity and downright stupidity, Bertozzo is supercilious, arrogant, and stubborn. His devotion to the proper conduct of official business makes him an easy target of ridicule. He simply misses the subtleties of the social and political drama in which he is involved, neither knowing how to play along with pretenses nor recognizing when he is being humored or gulled.

Bellati, Superintendent of the Milan Police. Bellati is a loud and vulgar oaf with a quick and explosive temper. He is brasher and more confident than his fastidious subordinates. Though he makes an effort to maintain protocol and appearances, his sense of humor and play overcome him, and he gets caught up in the Maniac's games and diversions.

Pissani, Inspector of the Milan Police, from its political branch. Pissani is a weak, cautious, and basically unintelligent man who is baffled by irony and susceptible to the least suggestion or intimidation. Throughout the Maniac's investigation, Pissani insists unrelentingly that all the circumstances surrounding the anarchist's death were aboveboard.

Maria Felleti, a journalist from *L'Unita*, one of Milan's major mainstream newspapers. Felleti is a direct, challenging, and confrontational reporter; devoted to exposing the truth, she does not respect or defer to the official authority of the police. She is a sensible reformist who believes deeply in the existing institutions of Italian law and democracy; therefore, she does not believe that she can or should take justice into her own hands. When put to an immediate decision once the truth about the anarchist's death is known, however, she is willing to risk her life for her beliefs.

Constables, a pair of dutiful and efficient police officers. The constables are basically fearful and remain detached, by choice or ineptitude, from the investigation. On occasion, however, they inappropriately interject personal reflections and opinions.

B. P. Mann

THE ACOLYTE

Author: Thea Astley (1925-   )
Type of work: Novel
Time of action: The early 1950's to late 1960's
First published: 1972

Jack Holberg, a blind musician who becomes Australia's major composer. In his early forties by the time the novel concludes its decade of action, Holberg is a handsome, powerfully built man whose blindness seems to enhance his presence. A complex character, he is both gifted and obsessed, both kind and cruel. The novel's events and the other characters' lives revolve around his rise from an itinerant pianist in country towns to a composer of international reputation.

Paul Vesper, the "acolyte" to Holberg. In his twenties when he meets Holberg, the novel's first-person narrator subordinates his own personality to focus on the composer's story. He insists on portraying himself as a most ordinary and dull-witted man, fit only to serve the extraordinary and brilliant Holberg. Yet, through the narrative's ironic stance, Vesper emerges witty, likable, and sensitive in his own right, even as he bears the insults and humiliation of serving as an "acolyte" before the dubious altar of artistic genius.

Sadie, Holberg's aunt and former guardian. Sadie is a lively seventy-year-old woman who, in a red wig and outlandish clothes, gambles and frolics at Australia's noted resort, Surfer's Paradise. Although she is a comic character to an extent, her relation to Holberg assumes significance, for, unlike the others, she does not forgo her individuality to feed his egotism.

Jamie, Holberg's young son, actually the child of his wife's sister. A sensitive and handsome boy, he struggles to discover his identity amid the odd household, the conflicting family relationships, and his father's coldness.

Hilda, Holberg's wife. A colorless and unattractive woman in her thirties, she devotes herself entirely to Holberg and his work, even though she understands neither the man nor the art he produces. She patiently bears his cruelty and indifference, along with his frequent infidelities, and remains humble and servile, even to the point of feigning blindness at times.

Ilse, Hilda's sister and Jamie's mother. Common in appearance and personality like her sister, generally inept as well, Ilse takes a perverse delight in suffering at the hands of Holberg. Like the others, she has let her own life fall into a kind of paralysis so that Holberg's genius might flourish.

Robert L. Ross

ACQUAINTED WITH GRIEF

Author: Carlo Emilio Gadda (1893-1973)
Type of work: Novel
Time of action: 1925-1933
First published: La cognizione del dolore, 1938-1941, serial; 1963, book; 1970, expanded
　(English translation, 1969, expanded)

Gonzalo Pirobutirro de Eltino (pē•rō•boo•tē′r̄o dā el•tē′nō), a middle-aged engineer and writer. Gonzalo carries a grudge against everything and everyone, including his mother, father, and brother (the latter two are dead). He often abandons himself to bouts of anger and makes all kinds of violent accusations: He accuses the peons of thievery, the middle class of being society's disgrace, the rich of having taken advantage of the war to make money, and the military of being irresponsible warmongers. Often, Gonzalo not only insults and yells at his mother but also batters her. The last heir of the Pirobutirro family, Gonzalo is basically a misanthrope.

Señora Elisabetta Francois Pirobutirro, Gonzalo's mother. Señora Elisabetta lives in a world of illusion. She believes that the family is still wealthy, and she is more concerned with the appearance of their social status than with the emotional problems of her son Gonzalo. She is obsessed with the memory of her son who died in the war.

Doctor Higueróa (hē·gwä·rō'ä), the Pirobutirros' family physician. Doctor Higueróa is a figure who symbolizes society's point of view in its perception of Gonzalo's personality. Higueróa's thoughts act as a means of expressing society's opinion about Gonzalo's

behavior, especially the way that Gonzalo treats his mother, Señora Elisabetta.

Cavaliere Trabatta, Gonzalo's neighbor. Cavaliere Trabatta is the victim of a burglary after refusing the protection of the Nistitúo, a vigilante group. He hires mercenaries to be his guards instead, and it is they who find Señora Elisabetta after she is attacked.

Rosaria Pipia

ACROSS

Author: Peter Handke (1942-   )
Type of work: Novel
Time of action: The early 1980's
First published: Der Chinese des Schmerzes, 1983 (English translation, 1986)

Andreas Loser, a teacher of ancient languages at a high school in a suburb of Salzburg, Austria, and an amateur archaeologist who specializes in the excavation of doorways and entryways. He is in early middle age, recently separated from his wife and two children, and on a leave of absence from his teaching post. Loser is a highly introspective man in the middle of a life crisis, searching for a meaning to his existence. He is plagued by the feeling that he is merely an observer of, rather than a participant in, life. Near the beginning of the novel, he deliberately knocks down a man walking in Salzburg, and this serves to bring his situation to full awareness. He is intensely concerned with nature and the simple objects around him. Later in the novel, his desire to participate in life emerges, again in the form of a violent act. While walking at night over the Mönchberg Mountain in order to play

cards with several friends, he sees an old man who is spraypainting swastikas on the trees and rocks. He mortally wounds the man with a rock and pushes him over the side of the cliff. Loser feels that, for once in his life, he has acted decisively and experiences no remorse for his act of murder. The next day, he contemplates death and his estrangement from life. At the end of the work, he wanders around the Salzburg area and then travels to Italy to visit the bucolic landscapes portrayed by his favorite writer, the ancient Roman poet Vergil.

The old man, an unknown man, probably a neofascist. He is approximately in his late sixties. His act of defacing nature by spraypainting swastikas on the mountainside prompts the narrator's violent response.

Thomas F. Barry

ACROSS THE RIVER AND INTO THE TREES

Author: Ernest Hemingway (1899-1961)
Type of work: Novel
Time of action: Winter, 1949
First published: 1950

11

Richard Cantwell, a colonel in the U.S. Army Infantry, dying of heart failure after fighting in World War II. A battered and much-decorated fifty-one-year-old professional soldier with old steel eyes and wild boar blood, he returns to Venice, Italy, the city he loves most, to hunt ducks before he dies. In addition to a breaking heart, he has an injured leg, a crippled right hand that still cracks open, a broken nose, head wounds, and scars on his face. He defended Venice as a lieutenant in the Italian army during World War I and has many friends. Most recently, he fought in the invasion of Normandy, helped to liberate Paris, was made a brigadier general, and was later unjustly demoted to colonel. In his life, he has lost three battalions and three women. When he falls in love with Renata, a refined Venetian girl, he is able to surrender command and follow her spiritual authority, while in turn he educates her and calls her Daughter. He is a rough yet cultured man and shares with Renata excellent taste in paintings, literature, people, food, and wine. Very critical of himself, he always tries to be just to others but is inclined by nature and experience in war to be impatient, angry, and brutal. Condemning bad leadership in World War II that cost many lives, he calls himself Mister Dante. Renata brings out his saving nature and helps him purge his bitterness, fight against brutality, and die a graceful death.

Renata, a countess from an old Venetian family, in love with Richard Cantwell. Nearly nineteen, she is tall and graceful, with silky dark hair, almost olive-colored skin, a heartbreaking face, qualities of a gentle cat, and a delicate low voice that reminds Cantwell of Pablo Casals playing the cello. She is honest, brave, loyal, poetic, very intelligent, and independent; she does not care what people think of her, and her culture and spirit embody the values that Cantwell has fought for all of his life. She respects his trade as a soldier, calls him Richard the Lionhearted, and fell in love with him because of his ability to transcend pain and enjoy life fully. Throughout the novel, she bravely faces the fact that he will soon be dead and makes the best of what they have in the short time remaining to them.

The Gran Maestro, headwaiter at the Gritti Palace Hotel, an old soldier and Cantwell's best friend in Venice. Handsome from the inside out, he has a loving face; a long straight nose; kind, gay, truthful eyes; honorable white hair; ulcers; and, like the colonel, a breaking heart. The two men fought together for Italy in World War I and share traits such as realism, practicality, integrity, dedication to duty, and the rare ability to enjoy life despite suffering. In jest and hatred of all those who profit by war, they belong to a fictitious organization with only five members, called the Order of Brusadelli, named after a notorious profiteer and laughingstock. At the end of the novel, the Gran Maestro honors Renata by making her a member of the order.

Ronald Jackson, the colonel's driver, a common soldier. A sad boy from Wyoming whose brother was killed in the Pacific, he thinks the colonel is a "mean son of a bitch" who can also be very goodhearted and generous. In Venice, Cantwell unburdens him of duty and tells him to go have fun. At the end, the colonel adds to the dignity of Jackson by paraphrasing to him the last words of General Stonewall Jackson and lessens inconvenience by climbing into the backseat to die.

Michael Hollister

ADA OR ARDOR
A Family Chronicle

Author: Vladimir Nabokov (1899-1977)
Type of work: Novel

Time of action: 1850-1965
First published: 1969

Ivan (Van) Veen, the fastidious, rakish scion of an aristocratic family, matures from schoolboy to psychiatric scholar to retired traveler. Although he has many sexual partners, his life is dominated by an eighty-plus-year love affair with Ada, said to be his cousin, but in actuality his sister. Fourteen-year-old Van, who gains local fame for his unusual skill at walking on his hands, meets twelve-year-old Ada in the idyllic setting of her putative father's country estate, Ardis. There they fall in love, but Van also attracts the lifelong, obsessive love of his and Ada's half sister, Lucette. A second summer in Ardis, four years later, reaffirms Van's love for Ada, but this time the idyll is shattered by Van's discovery of Ada's unfaithfulness. Van is wounded in a duel and recovers at the nurturing hands of a family friend, Cordula de Prey, in her Manhattan apartment. Eventually Van and Ada are reunited in the apartment (now Van's), but a winter of love is interrupted by the abrupt entrance of their father, Demon, who demands that the lovers part. Van spends his adult life in the study and practice of psychiatry, with a special interest in time, space, and insanity. During a transatlantic ocean voyage, Van is surprised to learn that Lucette has contrived to become his fellow passenger. When Van, out of conscientious scruples, rebuffs her advances, she jumps overboard to her death. Van and Ada meet again, in their thirties, in Switzerland, and resume their affair, although Ada is now married. The illness of Ada's husband forces another separation, but the lovers reunite again in their fifties and spend a happy and active old age together, traveling around the world from one fabulous home to another.

Adelaida (Ada) Veen, a pale, dark-haired beauty, who is a precocious twelve year old with interests in botany and entymology when she first meets and falls in love with her "cousin" Van. As she matures, her sensuality blossoms, and she has many male lovers, as well as, eventually, a bisexual intimacy with her troubled half sister, Lucette. Van is most angered by her brief romances with Lucette's music teacher and with Cordula de Prey's cousin, Percy. After both men die, Ada spends her young adult years in a tepid career as a film actress. In between her periodic romantic reunions with Van, Ada marries and spends much of her middle age on a ranch in Arizona with her husband. Eventually, she returns to Van and spends her old age traveling with him, photographing butterflies, and helping to edit the story of their life together.

Dementiy (Demon) Veen, a fabulously wealthy, black-haired womanizer who sires both Van and Ada with his actress-mistress, Marina Durmanov, though married to Marina's mentally ill sister, Aqua; he is, however, the father-of-record of Van only, with whom he enjoys a warm relationship. The bond is badly damaged when Demon inadvertently discovers that his two children are lovers. As an older man, Demon enjoys female lovers of steadily diminishing age (ending with a difficult nymphet of ten) and finally dies in a plane crash.

Marina Durmanov Veen, a faded, red-haired stage and film actress of mediocre gifts, marries Daniel Veen but carries on a stormy love affair with his cousin Demon. As a result, Marina is the mother of Demon's daughter Ada, Dan's daughter Lucette, and Demon's son Van, though all involved pretend that Van was born instead to Marina's sister Aqua. Marina runs Dan's country estate, Ardis, and occasionally plays the role of doting mother while combining her acting career with a series of love affairs. Marina, who is looked upon with contempt by both Van and Ada, resolutely ignores the evidence that the siblings are lovers until she reaches her deathbed from cancer.

Aqua Durmanov Veen, Marina's twin sister, is married to Demon Veen and claims to be Van's mother, though Van is actually Marina's child by Demon. Aqua's life is plagued by an escalating series of episodes of mental illness, culminating with her suicide before the age of forty.

Daniel Veen, a dull, stodgy art dealer of independent means. He is married to Marina Durmanov, and he is the father of Lucette and the putative father of Ada. He visits Ardis on weekends and has very formal, limited relationships with his wife and family.

Lucinda (Lucette) Veen, a beautiful, troubled redhead, a half sister to Van and Ada. Teased as a youngster by close proximity to Van and Ada's romance, she comes to love both half siblings obsessively, enjoying sexual intimacy with Ada, but finding herself frustrated in her overtures to Van. On one occasion, all three have a brief sexual encounter in Van's bed. When Lucette's frantic, final attempt to engage Van on shipboard fails, she jumps overboard to her death.

Ida Larivière, young Ada's and Lucette's governess. She continues in this position even after achieving unexpected literary success with her plays and short stories. She is somewhat in awe of Ada, and her characteristic failure to observe keeps her from perceiving the romantic nature of Ada and Van's relationship.

Percy de Prey, one of Ada's lovers, a heavyset, hot-tempered rival of Van, and a cousin of Cordula de Prey. He is killed in military service.

Cordula de Prey, a young school friend of Ada. She remains close to Van and Ada all their lives. She nurses Van back to health after he is wounded in a duel, gives him the Manhattan apartment where he and Ada spend a memorable winter, and arranges for Lucette to procure last-minute reservations on the ill-fated ocean liner from which she plunges to her death.

Philip Rack, Lucette's music teacher and another of young Ada's lovers. A thin, self-effacing man, he eventually is poisoned by his wife and dies in the same hospital where Van is brought after being wounded in a duel.

Andrey Vinelander, a simple Russian with a ranch in Arizona. He marries Ada after Demon has surprised and separated Ada and Van. Ada remains loyal, if not faithful, to Andrey during a lengthy illness that eventually leads to his death, allowing Ada at last to return to Van.

Dorothy Vinelander, Andrey's sister, a prissy, annoying pseudointellectual, despised by both Van and Ada. In spite of her intrusiveness and inquisitiveness during a family trip to Switzerland, she fails to grasp the true nature of Van and Ada's relationship.

Laura Stone Barnard

THE ADDING MACHINE

Author: Elmer Rice (Elmer Leopold Reizenstein, 1892-1967)
Type of work: Play
Time of action: The early 1920's
First produced: 1923

Mr. Zero, a small, thin, sallow, and partially bald man in his late forties or early fifties. For twenty-five years, he has worked as a bookkeeper in a large department store, where he adds up the day's receipts after arranging sales figures in columns. For his dedicated work, he expects a raise, not having received one in seven years, but instead learns that he is to be replaced by an adding machine. His mind is preoccupied with figures, and he reveals all the prejudices of the lower middle class, though by temperament he is stolid and subdued. He is a henpecked husband, and his marriage leaves much to be desired. For diversion, he peers at a scantily clad prostitute who lives in a nearby apartment until his wife forces him to report her to the police. Following his execution for murdering the Boss, he comes to understand that he has a slave mentality and temperament, which he will never escape.

Mrs. Zero, wife of Zero for twenty-five years. She is forty-five, unkempt, shapeless, with graying hair. A chronic complainer and gossipy housewife, she amuses herself with Western and romantic films. She nags Zero constantly for his lack of ambition and possesses attitudes of petty bourgeois respectability.

Daisy Diana Dorothea Devore, a plain, middle-aged woman, Zero's assistant bookkeeper who calls out figures for him to write down. Like Zero, she wears a green eye shade and paper sleeve-protectors while working. Her affection for Zero is masked by her quarrelsome nature. She is chronically unhappy and talks of suicide, an act she carries out after Zero's execution. In the afterlife, their romance, separated from their work, achieves a brief but futile second chance.

The Boss, a middle-aged, stoutish, bald, well-dressed manager of the department store where Zero works. Dedicated to strict business principles and efficiency, he attempts to inform Zero of his termination.

Mr. One,
Mr. Two,
Mr. Three,
Mr. Four,
Mr. Five, and
Mr. Six, friends of the Zeros, about their age, and guests at an evening party in their apartment. They are dressed like Zero in every detail. They converse about the weather and denounce women's suffrage, foreign agitators, minorities, Catholics, and Jews. They form half the jury that finds Zero guilty.

Mrs. One,
Mrs. Two,
Mrs. Three,
Mrs. Four,
Mrs. Five, and
Mrs. Six, wives of the male guests of the Zeros. They are all dressed alike except that each dress is a different color. They talk of films, gossip about a recent divorce, complain about men, and explore the illnesses of their acquaintances. They form half the jury that convicts Zero.

Guide, a man in a peaked cap and blue uniform who leads curious tourists past Zero's prison cell, delivering a lecture on him as an example of a North American murderer, explaining his pending execution, and selling photograph folders portraying his criminal life to the tourists.

The Fixer, an allegorical figure with wings suggesting an angel, but one who clips his fingernails, reads comics, and smokes a pipe. Zero expects him to prevent his execution, but the Fixer declines, pointing out that Zero's life has been worthless.

Shrdlu, an apparition from the grave, shabbily dressed, wearing silver-rimmed spectacles, and smoking a cigarette. Despondent over his unmotivated murder of his mother while the minister Dr. Amarath was present at Sunday dinner, he bears a greater burden of guilt than Zero. He relives the episode and confesses his crime to Zero. He has come to accept Dr. Amarath's fatalistic pronouncement that he has a criminal nature.

Lieutenant Charles, a middle-aged man, somewhat corpulent, barefooted, dressed in red tights, and wearing a Panama hat. He conveys an air of world-weariness, pessimism, and nonchalance. An immortal, he functions in the place where souls are prepared for reincarnation and is charged with dispatching Zero back to earth, where he will operate a super-hyper-adding machine. He reveals information about Zero's previous incarnations.

Stanley Archer

15

THE AERODROME
A Love Story

Author: Rex Warner (1905-1986)
Type of work: Novel
Time of action: Shortly after the start of World War II
First published: 1941

Roy, the supposed son of the Rector and his wife. Roy (though athletic and educated at home) is a typical village inhabitant of undeveloped character. At his twenty-first birthday dinner party (a British rite of passage to adulthood), he is told that he is adopted; he responds by getting drunk. He is ambivalent about the village (representing muddling tradition) and the aerodrome (representing modern efficiency). He is both sensual and thoughtful. Though he loses and regains his desire to see the world in realistic terms, he sees that he can neither reshape nor avoid it. The story is his autobiographical narrative of the events of the year following his birthday party; the climax is his discovery that the Rector's wife is his mother and the Air Vice-Marshal his father: He sees that his self is derived in part from both of them.

The Flight-Lieutenant, an officer at the aerodrome, also twenty-one years old. He represents the link between the past and the future, tradition and modernity. He has tight, yellow curls, keen eyes, and a forward-thrusting jaw; he is considered handsome and charming. Though he is often moody, bitter, and vindictive, he is admired by Roy and is successful as a seducer; he is knowledgeable, irrepressible, a practical joker. He usually speaks with a cold voice, and he is often deeply critical of the village; he has those virtues and graces absent in Roy, though he kills both the Rector and the Air Vice-Marshal, his father, who had seduced and abandoned his mother, the Squire's sister, Florence.

The Rector, Roy's guardian and putative father. At age thirty, when a theological student, he planned the murder of a fellow student (brighter, more handsome) who had won the affections of the girl he loved and

the appointment that he wanted. Anthony, the friend, survived, left the church, and became Air Vice-Marshal. The Rector had a child, Bess, by his housekeeper, Eva, the innkeeper's wife; he is wracked by guilt and remorse, annually confessing his guilt in his prayers for forgiveness. He is now fifty-two, and his contribution is extreme, though he loves Roy and knew of his wife's pregnancy by Anthony before they were married. He has a pale face, a black beard, thin lips, and fierce, penetrating eyes, yet he is "the gentlest of men." His eternal torture, he recognizes, is the consequence of jealousy, which has brought dissimulation, deceit, and disquiet.

The Rector's Wife, a pale-faced woman with thin yellow hair and an expansive white forehead. She rarely exhibits any feeling except placidity and contentment, though on overhearing her husband's confession her look suggested both triumph and contempt. Her closest friend is the Squire's sister, Florence. Only in her confrontation with the Air Vice-Marshal, where she aims to protect Roy, does she show any strength of character.

The Air Vice-Marshal, the effaced theological student **Anthony,** who has always been marked by tremendous ambition. He is a man of great intellectual gifts and of remarkably impressive physique (though not unusually tall) and upright carriage. He is noted for his concentration, certainty, and self-control as well as for his lack of nervousness, his authoritative (and cold) voice, and his "small cordiality." He is opposed to inefficiency, waste, and stupidity, as well as to sentiment and spontaneity. His motto, "That the world may be clean," is his constant motivation, though the news of the Rector's marriage may well have been the factor that determined his character. Hatred, pride, and ambition cause him to order the death of one son (The Flight-Lieutenant) and to kill his mother; only his "accidental" death saves Roy and his mother.

The Squire, the symbol of the traditional ways of the village, who has been in declining health since his lands were confiscated to allow for the building of the aerodrome. He seems very old: His face appears small and pale, with the skin dragged back from the bones, and his deeply pitted eyes are accented by great eyebrows. Yet, he is most amiable and exudes aristocratic confidence and persuasive kindliness. He and his sister, Florence, shared mutual gratitude and devoted friendship. On his deathbed he wishes to see Roy; he says only "Your father," then "Florence," before becoming silent, and Roy infers that the Rector is not his actual father.

Florence, the Squire's sister and mother of

the Flight-Lieutenant. She is a tall, thin woman with remarkably clear gray eyes; she is interested in charities. The best friend of the Rector's wife, she was seduced and abandoned by Anthony.

Dr. Faulkner, a physician. A friend of both the Rector and Anthony, he recovered Anthony from the mountain-climbing accident and nursed him back to health; but he kept this a secret (to allow Anthony to lead a new life) and even went through a funeral for him, thus allowing the Rector to marry Anthony's pregnant girlfriend and to obtain his benefice. Dr. Faulkner is a short, fat man with an almost bald head and is the personification of the genial village doctor-mentor. His poise and authority in the confrontation between the Air Vice-Marshal and his antagonists at the end of the novel provide elucidation and credibility.

Alan L. McLeod

AFTER MANY A SUMMER DIES THE SWAN

Author: Aldous Huxley (1894-1963)
Type of work: Novel
Time of action: The late 1930's
First published: 1939

Jeremy Pordage, an Englishman hired for six months in California to catalog the Hauberk papers, twenty-seven crates of fragments of English history relating to the Hauberk family. With blue eyes, spectacles, and a bald spot on the top of his head, Pordage is a scholar and a gentleman, amazed by the vulgarity of California and of his employer, Jo Stoyte, a self-made millionaire. For Pordage, things are real only when translated into words. He is a bachelor, tied to an emotionally devouring mother. He is a civilized observer and, according to William Propter, a potential victim or murderee.

Mr. Jo Stoyte, once the local fat boy called **Jelly-Belly,** now a California millionaire who lives in a castle. His numerous business holdings include farmland with orange groves

on it and the Beverly Pantheon cemetery. He stands to make more millions buying up land in the San Felipe Valley when he gets a tip that irrigation water is coming to the valley. A small, thick-set man with a red face and a mass of snow-white hair, Stoyte is called Uncle Jo by the patients in his Home for Sick Children. He boasts that he had no education, and although he fills his castle with expensive European art works, he has a library with no books in it. At sixty years old, Stoyte has had a stroke and is terrified of death, repeating to himself like a mantra, "God is Love. There is no death." Stoyte's love for the curvaceous Ginny is a mixture of concupiscence and fatherly affection. He calls her Baby.

Mr. William Propter, a large broad-

17

shouldered man with brown hair turning gray. He is a philosopher, trying to make sense of the world. He is the author of *Short Studies in the Counter Reformation*, a book that Jeremy Pordage knows and respects. Propter talks to Jeremy and to Peter Boone about his ideas concerning reality and human behavior. A reformer, Propter puts his ideas into action, building cabins for the migrant workers working for Stoyte and using simple machines that will make him and the migrants self-sufficient. Propter knew Stoyte from his school days and befriended him then. Propter feels guilty that he might have contributed to Pete's death, though he did not.

Miss Virginia Maunciple, a twenty-two-year-old woman with auburn hair, wide-set eyes, and a small, impudent nose. Her most characteristic feature is her short upper lip, which gives her face a look of childlike innocence. Through much of the novel, as Stoyte's mistress, she lives happily in the present with no long-range desires. She is fond of Stoyte and calls him Uncle Jo. She thinks herself virtuous because since she has been with him, she has not had sex with any other man, only with two female friends. A Catholic, Ginny has had Stoyte build a shrine to the Virgin Mary on the grounds of his estate. She also has a minishrine in her bedroom with a costumed Mary doll in it. When Ginny begins a degrading affair with Dr. Obispo, she is thrown into confusion and guilt. She acts as if she has been drugged by the sexual experience. She uses her new attentiveness to Pete to make Stoyte jealous, deflecting his attention from Obispo.

Dr. Sigmund Obispo, a dark-haired, dapper man with a handsome face who put Stoyte back on his feet after Stoyte suffered a stroke. Interested in research and not in patient care, Obispo has become Stoyte's personal physician in order to get a laboratory funded. For Stoyte, Obispo is trying to discover the secret of longevity. Obispo has only contempt for religion and philosophy (and for most other human beings), and he puts his hope in science. He is a Don Juan who insults Ginny (and everyone else) with

his sarcasm, wanting her sexually but on his unromantic terms. When he gets her and when Stoyte jealously tries to kill Obispo, the doctor gets the upper hand, controlling Stoyte, Ginny, and probably the millions.

Peter Boone, Obispo's assistant in the research laboratory, an athletic young giant of a man. He is enthusiastic about liberty and justice, but he has inadequate language with which to express his feelings. He fought in the International Brigade in the Spanish Civil War in 1937, and he still feels loyalty and affection for the men with whom he fought. He is naïve, thinking that Ginny is pure and loving her. He thinks that he is unworthy of her. Idealistically, he tries to understand Propter's philosophy, and he seems willing to change his life when he is convinced. He worries whether the work that Obispo is doing in the laboratory is good. When Ginny changes from treating him like a brother to seeming to show a romantic interest, he is confused. He loses his life in the rivalry between Stoyte and Obispo, trying to comfort Ginny.

Dr. Herbert Mulge, Ph.D., D.D., the principal of Tarzana College. Contemptuous of the rich men he solicits, Mulge works tirelessly to obtain their money to expand the college. Mulge is a large, handsome man with a sonorous voice who uses pulpit eloquence to charm Stoyte into contributions. Stoyte gives the college money for a new auditorium and then for a new art school. Mulge wants to make Tarzana the living center of the new civilization in the West.

Mr. Hansen, the agent for Jo Stoyte's estates in the valley, gives worse than average treatment to the migrant workers, making the young children work all day for two or three cents an hour. He provides vermin-infested housing for the workers. Although he is a decent, kindly man in his private life, he is cruel "doing his duty" to the estates. Propter tries to make him understand the workers' needs, but Hansen does not want to know about them.

18

Charlie Habakkuk, the manager at the Beverly Pantheon. He tries to convince Stoyte to make improvements and extensions to the cemetery, especially by adding catacombs. When Stoyte refuses some of his suggestions, Habakkuk becomes angry, feeling that his ideas have made the cemetery popular while Stoyte reaps the profits. Charlie spouts cigar smoke and talks to the boss like a carpet salesman. Charlie has made the cemetery successful by injecting sex appeal into death.

The Fifth Earl of the Hauberk family, who held the title for more than half a century and was believed to die at ninety under William IV. He was the author of a notebook that Jeremy Pordage reads and catalogs. The earl collected the pornography that is part of the Hauberk Collection. Jeremy and then Dr. Obispo discover that the earl ate fish guts to prolong his life. He fathered three illegitimate children at the age of eighty-one. He faked his death and with his housekeeper Kate went underground into the subterranean passages of his house. Dr. Obispo says that slowing up the development rates of an animal is possible, but the older the anthropoid, the stupider. When the doctor finds the earl and Kate still alive under the Hauberk house, that is what he finds, two stupid anthropoids.

Kate M. Begnal

AFTER THE BANQUET

Author: Yukio Mishima (Kimitake Hiraoka, 1925-1970)
Type of work: Novel
Time of action: The late 1950's
First published: Utage no ato, 1960 (English translation, 1963)

Kazu Fukuzawa, owner of the After the Show Retreat in Setsugoan. On the high grounds in the hills near Tokyo, Kazu lives remote from civilized and noisy life. In both her garden and her restaurant, every detail is calculated to please and soothe the eye. Seeking to combine rustic simplicity with elegance and aesthetic sense, Kazu hopes that her garden conveys a sense of detachment from wordly pleasures. Her natural state is ecstatic wonder, and she exudes love as the sun gives out heat. Her energy is an eternal delight to her visitors. Her harmonious life is challenged when she marries Noguchi. While at times she identifies herself so deeply with the political views of her husband's party as to forget herself as an independent individual, she gradually becomes like an actress playing a role in a play based on the ideology of the radical party. In the end, however, she chooses not to submit to the dictates of society, politics, or even her husband. Instead, she returns to her source of spiritual solace: her garden and restaurant.

Yuken Noguchi, an intellectual of the radical party. Though the husband of the peaceful Kazu Fukuzawa, Noguchi seems to be in total disharmony with himself, with society, and with nature. He hides behind an ambiguous smile, laconic conversations, artificial attitudes, cold manners, acidulous reactions, and expressionless eyes. His stingy frugality indicates his choked emotional world, while his frigidity results from sexual desires undermined by prejudices. He is blinded by righteousness; he fails to see the essence of things. His absentmindedness in relation to everyone is in tune with the cold air and gloomy atmosphere around him, whatever the season. Noguchi is enterprising and calculating. He believes he must organize his party rationally to show a favorable balance of profits and costs. This abstract and calculating spirit proves to be only a fragment of a man. He seems to object to life rather than subject to it. His wish still to be young contradicts the aged house, outfit, and comb that he has owned for thirty years.

Totsuka, a radical pamphleteer. Wrong-headed and stubborn, he distorts the truth with brutal directness and uses irresponsible lies in a political pamphlet in order to secure forcefully the victory of his party.

Soichi Yamazaki, Noguchi's campaign manager for the radical party. He takes painstaking care in maintaining a devout and faithful friendship with both Noguchi and Kazu

Fukuzawa. He is sincere about his promise to assist Kazu at any time.

Genki Nagayama, an old conservative politician. His indulgence in lust and power, money and sex, push him to prevent an auction of Kazu's property. He is disappointed that she will not sell herself to him.

Marlies Kronegger

AFTER THE FALL

Author: Arthur Miller (1915-   )
Type of work: Play
Time of action: The 1950's
First produced: 1964

Quentin, a lawyer who agonizes over his past—the failure of his two marriages, unhappy childhood experiences, the political witch-hunts in the 1950's, and the extent to which he bears personal responsibility for what happened to his close friends and his two wives. Quentin views these past events from the perspective of the present. He has met a new woman, Holga, with whom he has fallen in love. She is European and brings with her a sense of the European past, including that of World War II, of mass destruction and the concentration camps. Quentin reacts to this grim history in terms of his own life, questioning his motives; his selfishness; his rejection of his first wife, Louise; and his inability to help his tormented second wife, Maggie. Although Quentin is not able to resolve all the conflicts within himself, with Holga's help he does come to understand better his own implication in the sufferings of others.

Holga, Quentin's fiancée who helps him come to terms with his guilt over his previous marriages. Having suffered greatly herself during the war, she has had to deal with the issues of responsibility that Quentin addresses to himself. Her calm, abiding presence throughout the play bespeaks a sensibility that has grown with experience and is able to accept the worst that Quentin can confess about his own character.

Louise, Quentin's first wife, who has been his mainstay for many years. In several flashback scenes, Quentin explores his estrangement from her. She is unable to understand Quentin's dissatisfaction with his own life and with their marriage. Her main complaint is that Quentin does not really talk to her, that he does not know how to interact with women, and that their growing separation is largely a matter of his inability to share himself with others.

Maggie, Quentin's second wife, a beautiful, sensuous woman who becomes a major recording star. When she first meets him, however, she lacks confidence and responds warmly to his encouragement and sensitivity. He makes her feel like a whole human being. At the same time, her exuberant spirit makes him, for a time, a much warmer and more giving person. Yet, as Maggie tears herself apart, a victim of self-doubt, she begins to view Quentin as a burden in her life, as someone who has used her. Although he tries to help her, he also withdraws from her more and more as she becomes hysterical and eventually commits suicide.

Felice, one of Quentin's devoted clients who appears as almost a fantasy figure. She worships Quentin and does not see the cold side of him that makes Maggie turn against him.

Mother, who dominates Quentin's family in the childhood flashback scenes. When Quentin's father loses his money in the stock market crash of 1929, she turns against him, blaming him for the family's troubles. She recurs on stage as a figure in Quentin's mind, a part of his remembrance of his difficult childhood, playing the part of the accusing woman, which reminds him of his first wife, Louise.

Lou, one of Quentin's lawyer friends whose career is ruined by his testimony before the House Committee on Un-American Activities. His radical political background has put him in a vulnerable position, especially since he admits that he lied in one of his books about life in Soviet Russia. He has asked Quentin to defend him—a task Quentin takes on with mixed feelings, worried about his reputation and concerned that his heart is no longer in defending his colleagues.

Mickey, one of Quentin's lawyer friends, who has saved Lou once before, when his academic career was threatened by charges that he had been a subversive. Mickey devastates Quentin when he admits that he is going to "name names," that is, tell the House committee about his friends who were active in radical politics.

Carl Rollyson

AFTERNOON MEN

Author: Anthony Powell (1905-   )
Type of work: Novel
Time of action: The 1920's
First published: 1931

William Atwater, the protagonist, a young museum official. He has straw-colored hair, sometimes wears tortoiseshell-rimmed spectacles, and has long, slender legs. His father is a retired civil servant, but he has twice failed to gain a Foreign Office post. He is one of the "Bright Young People" of the London Soho district, witty but bored and enervated. He secured his museum position through influence. He spends his evenings in talk, while he drifts from one situation to another.

Raymond Pringle, Atwater's friend, a painter. He is twenty-eight, has red hair, and affects a manner of dress that combines a workman's shirt with patent-leather shoes. He lives on a comfortable inheritance, with which he is rather tightfisted. He is a bad painter, but his study in Paris has given his work a certain slickness that allows him to sell an occasional painting. He has a beach cottage, which is the setting for the novel's climactic scene.

Harriet Twining, Pringle's occasional mistress. She has fair hair and dark skin and is a staple of the London party scene. She drives men quite mad, and many want to marry her immediately. Yet she tires of them, wears them out, or spends all of their money before romance can proceed to the matrimonial stage.

Susan Nunnery, a young woman desired by Atwater. He meets her at a party early in the novel. She has a quality, at least in the protagonist's perceptions, which sets her apart from the other "Bright Young People." Her large, expressive eyes are her best feature.

Lola, a model and frequent Soho partygoer. The name she bears is her own invention. She looks like an early drawing by Augustus John. She purports to read Bertrand Russell when she requires reinspiration.

Hector Barlow, another struggling artist. He is stockily built and has light eyes and black,

21

stubbly hair, which grows low down on his forehead. He wears sack-colored clothes and sucks a pipe. He was with Pringle in Paris. He has an assertive nature but is fretting over which of several girls to marry—all these alliances seem equally unlikely.

Fotheringham, an unsuccessful journalist. He is a heavily built, pink-cheeked young man, who has had a temporary job for the past five years as subeditor with a spiritualist paper. He is responsible for the advertisement pages. He dislikes spiritualists as a group, complaining of how they keep his nose to the grindstone. He longs for a new occupation and especially desires to go to America.

Undershaft, a young man who is a phantom presence in the novel. He has gone to America, thus escaping the pointless life the others are leading in London. For this action, he is variously admired, envied, and blamed.

He is rumored to be in New York, prospering as a piano player and living with a woman of indeterminate race.

Naomi Race, a patroness of the arts. No one knows her age or anything about her late husband, except that he was acquainted with Rossetti. She is like the dowager of drawing-room comedy. She has Atwater to dinner about once every two months.

George Nunnery, Susan's father. He is characterized by his daughter as a retired failure, a curious small man with a walrus mustache. He still discusses finance, but his bankruptcy, or something, has left him somewhat vacant.

Verelst, a wealthy Jew. He is dark, with bags under his eyes and a thick nose. He is almost good-looking, almost distinguished-looking. Susan goes off to America with him at the end of the novel.

Patrick Adcock

THE AGE OF WONDERS

Author: Aharon Appelfeld (1932-   )
Type of work: Novel
Time of action: 1938-1969
First published: Tor-ha-pela'ot, 1978 (English translation, 1981)

Bruno A., the Son, in 1938 a twelve-year-old schoolboy. He has to look on helplessly and semicomprehendingly as his family and their comfortable existence fall to pieces in a world of jarring anti-Semitism. Aching for love and warmth from his estranged parents, the boy's intimations of decay and doom intensify as he is shunted from provincial home to country resort and back again. In the second part of the novel, Bruno, a middle-aged man, returns to confront childhood ghosts after the breakup of his marriage in Jerusalem.

Father, an Austrian writer and literary critic. His successes bring joy neither to him nor his family. A tired, absentminded, surly man, he succumbs to bitterness and paranoia as he

is increasingly attacked for the sickly Jewish spirit of his writing. His hatred of petit bourgeois Jews and ragged *Ostjuden* (Eastern European Jews) is second only to his fear of being regarded as one of them. As anti-Semitism blocks his career and destroys his self-respect, he soothes his soul with alcohol and impossible dreams of a literary and cultural renaissance. This delusion leads him to abandon his family for a baroness in Vienna.

Mother, a tall, tight-lipped, unhappy woman. She bears her husband's physical and spiritual distance in stoic fashion and strives to preserve an atmosphere of normalcy and dignity even as Jewishness makes her family an object of derision and loathing. A woman with strong philanthropic impulses, she devotes herself frantically to charitable institutions as her personal life deteriorates. After her husband has run off to Vienna, she dutifully responds to a call from the local rabbi to join the Jews assembling in the synagogue, and that night she is imprisoned with her son and adopted daughter.

Theresa, Bruno's aunt, Mother's younger sister, and a diligent university student. Tall like her sister and marked by a clear brow that radiates her inner life, she has the air of a priestess. After a fit of depression has landed her in Saint Peter's sanatorium, she emerges for a family vacation only to be stricken by another fit of otherworldly melancholy. Her psychosis leads her to convert to Christianity with a sacrificial gesture, and soon thereafter she dies suddenly and mysteriously within the walls of Saint Peter's.

Brum, a onetime friend of Bruno's parents. He transforms himself from a thin, ascetic, cowering person into a bold and blunt character, renouncing his Judaism along the way. In the second part of the novel, he is an old, bitter anti-Semite. He receives a beating from Bruno yet never owns up to his Jewish past.

Stark, a sculptor. Born of a Jewish mother but reared at an "Aryan" military academy, he transmutes the anti-Semitism he encounters into an ever more passionate yearning for his mother's faith. Much to the horror of Father, this strong-spirited man and erstwhile champion of the family's dignity has himself circumcised and submits to the squalor of a Jewish almshouse.

Salo, Father's brother. Flamboyant and vigorous, he aims to shock his conventional family. He and his mistress are a breeding ground for scandal, all the more upsetting because Salo belongs to the merchant class that Father detests.

Danzig, Bruno's violin teacher. His attempts to root out the imperfections in his playing have made him a nervous wreck. Plagued by an inferiority complex and an uncontrollable twitching of his left shoulder, he leaves for Australia.

Louise, the nubile maid and the only vibrant and sensual element in the otherwise icy household. With her rustic innocence and high spirits, she captivates Bruno and his male relatives. Bruno later discovers that Louise, who becomes fat and devoid of charm, once prostituted herself to his uncles.

Helga, an orphan adopted by Bruno's family. She gradually loses her untamed, fearless spirit and becomes docile and domesticated.

Suzi, the illegitimate daughter of Salo and his mistress. Bruno meets her and her lesbian lover upon his return to Austria, and the turmoil and conflicts within her bastard psyche may be regarded as typical of the postwar generation.

Harry Zohn

AGENTS AND PATIENTS

Author: Anthony Powell (1905-   )
Type of work: Novel
Time of action: The 1930's
First published: 1936

Blore-Smith, a young law student. He has big brown eyes, huge ears, a shapeless face, and a speech impediment. He is recently down from Oxford, naïve, inexperienced, and in search of glamor and excitement. In London, he meets a pair of artist-intellectuals who are little better than confidence men. They exploit him mercilessly and whisk him away to absurd adventures in Paris and Berlin.

Oliver Chipchase, an art critic and amateur psychoanalyst. He has an emaciated physique and wears a severe expression. He has a history of sordid love affairs, which are the sort of love affairs he says he likes. He has a large number of eccentric acquaintances, both in London and on the Continent. He easily convinces poor Blore-Smith that the young man is in need of his psychiatric treatment.

Peter Maltravers, a friend of Chipchase and a dabbler in scriptwriting and filmmaking. He is tall and distinguished-looking, but his appearance gives no hint of intellectual aptitudes. He wishes to do a cinema verité, in which he will simply film an assemblage of intellectuals as they respond to a provocative situation. Since such a venture is commercially unpromising, he desperately needs financing that will not require repayment. This he finds in the person of Blore-Smith.

Mrs. Mendoza, the owner of a flower shop in a fashionable part of London. A tall, fair-haired, beautiful woman, she combines a tweedy appearance with a bohemian life-style. She is variously known as Mrs. M. and Mendie.

Commander Hugo Venables, a retired naval officer who is courting Mrs. Mendoza. He is about fifty, heavily built, and purple-faced. He is a rather vacant man, who finds it difficult to please his beloved.

Sarah Maltravers, Peter's wife. She is a woman of languid manner. They have a "modern" marriage, except that Peter becomes angry when she goes out with other men. Blore-Smith develops a crush on her.

Schlumbermayer, a dealer in art objects and another eccentric friend of Chipchase and Maltravers. He is a tall, bespectacled man of about forty-five, going gray and tending toward fatness. He hosts the making of Maltravers' film. There is something bogus about him, as signified by the fact that he has business cards printed in several different names.

Patrick Adcock

THE AGONY AND THE ECSTASY
A Novel of Michelangelo

Author: Irving Stone (1903-1989)
Type of work: Novel
Time of action: 1487-1564
First published: 1961

Michelangelo Buonarroti (bwō‧nä‧r̄rō′tē), a skinny, unsociable thirteen-year-old who wishes he could redraft his facial features with a crayon as the action of the novel begins. He reflects on the death of his mother when he was only six and his consequent loneliness and hunger for love. First trained as a stonecutter and then sent away to school for three years, young Michelangelo preferred drawing to the study of Latin and Greek. It is not until he becomes a student at the Medici sculpture garden at age fourteen, having spent a year at Ghirlandaio's studio, that he comes to know happiness again and forms lasting friendships. Tutored by the Plato Four, he develops a love for ancient culture and a familiarity with classical texts; at the same time, he begins working seriously in marble. After a beating permanently disfigures his face, Michelangelo never overcomes his insecurity about his own ugliness. He becomes a victim of his own drive for artistic perfection. Carving as long as twenty hours a day, he persists for months without adequate food or sleep. At one time, he sleeps in his clothes for a month; when he finally removes his boots, the skin of his feet comes off with them. Working on the ceiling frescoes for the Sistine Chapel, he becomes racked from the position in which he must

24

work and almost blind from the dripping paint. In addition to experiencing the agony of working and of being treated as a mere laborer by his patron, Pope Julius II, Michelangelo suffers the agony of producing great art only to have it destroyed. Rioting Florentines break an arm off his *David*, and the Bolognese melt down a bronze statue of Julius, which he has taken fifteen months to create, and recast it as a cannon. He is himself stoned by the rock cutters of Carrara because Pope Lèo insists that he use marble from Pietrasanta instead of theirs. Because Michelangelo feels an inner compunction to complete a significant body of works, he has no time for social niceties or a love relationship. He shares his father's pride in family, but he believes that as a mendicant artist working for long periods in self-imposed isolation, he cannot have a family of his own. Even as an elderly man, he retains the sense of the artist's responsibility to convey human emotion and the very meaning of life instilled in him long ago by the Medici circle. Although he becomes increasingly subject to multiple infirmities, he experiences little diminishing of his artistic powers. Viewing his works in his mind's eye, he feels the ecstasy of a long lifetime of work well done as his soul soars through the gaping hole that will become the dome of St. Peter's.

Lodovico di Lionardo Buonarroti Simoni, Michelangelo's father, a man tottering on the edge of social ruin who invests his hopes for reestablishing the family fortune on Michelangelo, the only one of his five sons ever to earn money. Lodovico, who went into despair after the death of his first wife, never showed any affection or understanding to Michelangelo as a child. Then, from the time of the boy's apprenticeship, he controls his earnings, over the years taking eighty percent of Michelangelo's commissions while his son lives sacrificially and eats little. Never satisfied with Michelangelo's contracts, he complains and dogs him to earn more money to buy farms for him and set his brothers up in business. When Lodovico dies on his ninetieth birthday, Michelangelo realizes his love for his father in spite of the hardships he has endured for him. He is satisfied to have been the means to the recovery of the family name.

Lorenzo de' Medici, Il Magnifico (mā′dē•chē), the untitled ruler of Michelangelo's Florence, patron of artists and intellectuals, and poet. The wealthy, powerful Lorenzo wants to liberate the human mind by fostering a renaissance in learning and the arts. After Lorenzo's untimely death at age forty-three, Michelangelo realizes that he owes all that he is to this ideal ruler-scholar whom he had known for only three years.

Contessina de' Medici, the daughter of Lorenzo de' Medici, whose youthful romance with Michelangelo is stillborn because of their social differences. After her brother Piero makes arrangements for Contessina to marry Ridolfi, she is not permitted to see Michelangelo again. They retain their feelings of affection and loyalty for many years, however, and Michelangelo attempts to intervene with Florentine authorities on her behalf during her family's eight years in exile and poverty. She is eventually restored to favor and assumes a large role in Vatican politics when her brother becomes pope. Michelangelo, greatly shaken by her sudden illness and death, maintains a lifelong relationship with her offspring.

Clarissa Saffi, a cobbler's daughter and the mistress of a Bolognese nobleman. Michelangelo is passionately attracted to her when they are both nineteen. Twelve years later, they have a brief affair, but after a few months she leaves him because he is too preoccupied with making wax models to give enough of himself to her.

Vittoria Colonna, the daughter of a powerful Italian family, the Marchesa di Pescara. She is a beautiful, regal, and kind Renaissance woman whom Michelangelo meets when he is sixty-one. They exchange his drawings and her poetry, and Michelangelo falls deeply in love with her. She is devoted to convent life and reform within the Roman Catholic church, however, and never offers him romantic love.

Tommaso de Cavalieri, an elegant and handsome Roman, Michelangelo's assistant architect for St. Peter's and his inseparable companion during his last seventeen years.

Janie Caves McCauley

ALL GOD'S CHILLUN GOT WINGS

Author: Eugene O'Neill (1888-1953)
Type of work: Play
Time of action: c. 1898-1915
First produced: 1924

Jim Harris, a black who dreams of becoming a lawyer. The play introduces him at the age of nine and follows his development over the next fifteen years. In the opening scene, he is already in love with Ella Downey, whom he later marries. Kindhearted, Jim is ashamed of his race, and his feeling of inferiority prevents him from succeeding.

Ella Downey, a white girl one year younger than Jim. As a child of eight, she admires Jim, but later she reveals a hatred of blacks. Although she realizes that Jim is morally superior to her white associates, she can never fully accept her marriage to him. As much as part of her wants Jim to succeed so that he can prove his true worth, another part of her wants him to fail and thus to confirm her belief that blacks are inferior to whites. This ambivalence drives her insane. Feeling tainted because of her interracial marriage, she refuses to associate with whites, and her bigotry drives potential black friends away.

Hattie Harris, Jim's sister, a teacher in a black school. Proud of her race, Hattie tries to accept Ella and nurse her when she becomes ill, but Ella's racism drives Hattie away. Yet Hattie, too, is not free of prejudice and is reluctant to associate with whites.

Mrs. Harris, Jim's mother. Believing in the separation of the races, she regrets Jim's marriage to a white girl. She and Hattie move from lower Manhattan to the Bronx to live exclusively among blacks.

Mickey, a white prizefighter. The same age as Ella, they are childhood friends and then lovers. Mickey abandons her after she becomes pregnant with his child.

Shorty, a white gangster and another member of the crowd that played with Jim, Joe, and Ella when they were children together. A pimp, Shorty offers to add Ella to his stable of prostitutes when she is struggling financially.

Joe, a black gangster. He cannot understand why his friend Jim is trying to become a lawyer, for he sees them both as suited only for a life on the streets. While he underestimates blacks' abilities, he recognizes that Jim wants to use money and education not, like Hattie, to prove that blacks are equal to whites but rather somehow to escape from his black heritage.

Joseph Rosenblum

ALL GREEN SHALL PERISH

Author: Eduardo Mallea (1903-1983)
Type of work: Novel
Time of action: c. 1940
First published: Todo verdor perecerá, 1941 (English translation, 1966)

Ágata Cruz (krōōs), the protagonist, a once strikingly beautiful, fair-skinned, dark-haired woman, grown pallid and harder-featured from the frustration of her barren fifteen years of married life on unproductive farms in southern Argentina. She was reared in a similarly drab setting by her widowed father, developed a need to escape, and for that purpose accepted the marriage proposal of Nicanor, whom she did not love. Life with Nicanor is even less sociable than it was with her father, stifling her inner passion. When she is thirty-five, Ágata's anguish reaches a point of crisis, and, seeking to end it all, she spends a freezing winter night outdoors and leaves doors and windows open in winter when Nicanor is inside delirious with fever. After his death from freezing, she falls into a brief affair with the lawyer Sotero. With him, Ágata is able to get out of her intense, tortured subjectivity and thereby knows fleeting happiness. When Sotero callously discards her, though, she again takes up her doomed quest for self. It leads her back to the town in which she was reared, where she ends up as a street person, roaming in closed concentration on her personal void. Ágata's suicidal tendencies are restrained by the fear that the emptiness of her earthly existence will persist after death.

Nicanor Cruz, a dry, unimaginative landowner, sunken into defeat and resentment. A failure as a farmer, Nicanor has to abandon his estate for a smaller, even less productive farm. He is passionless and uncommunicative as a husband, and his relationship with Ágata breeds only bitterness. Nicanor grows dark-skinned from contact with sun and soil, and seems as sterile as his land. His stoic, he-man attitude brings on his final illness, pneumonia, as he walks over his dead land obsessively for an entire day in a chilling rain.

Dr. Reba, Ágata's father, an inept medical practitioner. He was a reader of the Bible and a sententious reciter of its proverbs but was nevertheless an atheist. A Swiss immigrant, Dr. Reba married an Argentine woman who died at the birth of Ágata, their only child. He never remarried, and he lived a life of solitude alleviated less by his poor professional efforts than by his exercise as a tavern conversationalist. He communicated better with his tavern companions than with his daughter, who loved him despite the gulf that separated them. In later life, Dr. Reba drank heavily. He died some years before the present time of the novel.

Dr. Sotero, a worldly, opportunistic lawyer who seduces Ágata when she is a widow living in a coastal city of Bahía Blanca. Handsome, deep-voiced, good-humored, and self-assured, Sotero claims to like diffident women such as Ágata, who completely subordinates herself to him. Sotero's mysterious business dealings for a Buenos Aires entity called the Organization take him out of Bahía Blanca and give him an excuse to leave Ágata.

Ema de Volpe, a frivolous but also strong-willed woman who attaches herself to Ágata in Bahía Blanca. She is open about her own promiscuous life and does her best to wheedle intimate information out of the reticent Ágata. Conceited, perpetually overdressed, and having an exotic air about her, Ema calls herself a courtesan. She spends her evenings with Sotero, his business associate Romo, and three sisters, who are glib and slack like herself. She introduces Ágata to this group and encourages her to join them in their soirees.

Dr. Romo (r̄rō′mō), a short, heavy, sarcastic lawyer and associate of Sotero. Romo addresses everyone in an insinuating tone, and he habitually and cryptically calls Sotero "Sycophant" in front of the others. Romo visibly disdains Ágata for her docility. He is vulgar and has a taste for off-color jokes.

John Deredita

ALL MEN ARE ENEMIES

Author: Richard Aldington (1892-1962)
Type of work: Novel
Time of action: 1900-1914, 1919, and 1926-1927
First published: 1933

Antony Clarendon, a sensitive, idealistic youth. He was reared in a traditional English upper-class home, its values so secure he assumed that this contented and harmonious world would be eternal. During European travels, he falls in love with Katha, an Austrian girl, whose innocent passion satisfies his quest for beauty. All of his idyllic expectations are shattered by his experiences as an officer during the terrible battles of 1916. Overwhelmed by postwar conditions and in despair that he cannot find Katha, he becomes cynical and self-destructive. He resolves, without love, to marry Margaret, a sophisticated woman of his own class, and pretends to enjoy the social round expected of him. Her father makes him the well-paid director of the family company. Soon his whole nature rebels against this empty routine, which thwarts his spiritual principles. He separates from his wife and wanders idly, until by happy chance he again encounters Katha. In the mutuality of their renewed love, he finds final content.

Margaret, Antony's wife. She is a typical product of her class: elegant and superficial. Completely fulfilled by her role as wife and hostess, she never questions the values of her upbringing. Her unthinking acceptance of the social patterns she has inherited strikes Antony as selfish arrogance. Insensitively, she cannot comprehend why he does not relish the wealthy comfort she provides. When she cannot and will not appreciate his aesthetic yearning for simpler, less materialistic virtues, he rejects her and the world she exemplifies.

Katharina (Katha), an Austrian girl who meets Antony on a romantic Italian island, where they have a passionate youthful affair and plan a loving future that is broken off by the declaration of war. During the war and the economic dislocation of its aftermath, she suffers such poverty that she is driven to prostitution until she finds a wretched, low-paying job. Nevertheless, she retains her romantic dreams of being reunited with Antony and rediscovering their love. She personifies Antony's idealism and love of beauty and lives to share his yearning for a life free from the dictates of the snobbery of the business world.

Henry Clarendon, Antony's father. He is a dedicated amateur scientist and an atheist. His affection is limited by a cold pedantic manner and his grievance that his son is so opposed to the scientific studies in which he delights. Antony receives guidance in religion and art from his mother. Her early death leaves both men bereft.

Henry Scrope, a wealthy neighbor whose distinguished family has served England at the highest levels of government for generations. He is too independent to follow that path, preferring independent explorations in remote regions. He has a major influence on Antony, for Scrope's cavalier attitudes and extravagant ideas represent to Antony some valuable part of the human spirit that is endangered by modernity.

Stephen Crang, a gifted man with a brilliant mind. His family poverty is too extreme to allow him the education he deserves, so he accepts a subordinate teaching post. This unfairness so embitters him that he becomes viciously militant and condemns the entire capitalist system, which he blames for his deprivation. Ironically, the war gives him the opportunity to escape the constrictions imposed by class. He changes his beliefs, modifies his accent, and becomes a willing beneficiary of the system he had once rejected.

Robin Fletcher, an optimistic and idealistic young novelist who befriends Antony in Paris. Imprisoned during the war for his pacifist beliefs, he becomes a rabid Communist, who spitefully repudiates all traces of behavior that he can excoriate as "bourgeois." He changes Crang's life.

Richard Waterton, a disabled soldier. His war wound prevents him from returning to the stage or developing his skill as a sculptor, but, without despairing, he retains his generous and gentle spirit. He goes with Antony on a trip to North Africa, during which his kindly manner and quiet good sense guide Antony toward his decision to reject his marriage and his London life.

Walter Cartwright, a high-ranking civil servant who would have made an ideal husband for Margaret, because he shares her social values completely. He is handsome, somewhat pompous, openly ambitious, and utterly incapable of comprehending Antony's objections to the business world and its attendant social pretensions that satisfy him so well. He calls Antony's decision to escape "childish folly."

Julian, Margaret's young brother. Antony at first is greatly drawn to him, believing there exists in Julian a potential for a genuine appreciation of life in its most humane mode. As he grows up, Julian, to Antony's dismay, willingly accepts the standards of his peers and becomes a typical member of his class, his only priority being earning money and promotion, because these are the measures of success.

Evelyn, Antony's cousin. As an adolescent, she stays with his family, and her youthful, slim body awakes him to his first experience of gently tender sexuality. She remains as Antony's sweetest memory, until she returns to London after years in India as the wife of a senior army officer. To Antony's horror, she has taken on all the superior racist attitudes of a bigoted and self-satisfied colonial settler. Her manner appalls him and betrays the old dream, which she has long forgotten.

Babbo,
Mama, and
Filomena, the Italians who own the hotel in Aeaea where the love between Antony and Katha begins and is rediscovered. They are immensely loving, eager, and attentive toward the young couple and become, for a time, a kind of chorus as the lovers' passion develops.

John F. Povey

ALL MY SONS

Author: Arthur Miller (1915-   )
Type of work: Play
Time of action: The late 1940's
First produced: 1947

Joe Keller, a middle-aged factory owner of working-class background. He is a plain, inarticulate man with a certain peasant shrewdness. His values are simple: work and family. His purpose in life is to pass on his business to his surviving son, Chris. His moral simplicity, however, is his undoing. During World War II, he knowingly authorized the shipment of cracked cylinder heads to the army air force; the defective parts caused the deaths of twenty-one pilots. Although imprisoned and brought to trial, he avoided conviction by shifting the blame to his hapless partner, Steve Deever. Although he is accepted by his neighbors, they do not doubt his guilt, nor did his son Larry, who, ashamed of his father's actions, committed suicide three and a half years earlier during the war. Only his son, Chris, believes he is innocent. Keller is forced to face his responsibility when Larry's former girl, Ann Deever, now about to marry Chris, gives the Kellers Larry's suicide letter. Realizing that his actions caused Larry's death and that the twenty-one pilots are as much his sons as Larry (he refers to them as "all my sons" in his last speech), Keller shoots himself.

Kate Keller, the fiftyish wife of Joe Keller. She superstitiously clings to the hope that her son Larry, who disappeared during the war and is assumed to be dead, will return. This false hope complicates her surviving son's plan to marry Ann Deever. To her, accepting the marriage means that Larry will never come back; she therefore opposes the marriage and tries to get rid of Ann. Her denial of Larry's death is rooted in her knowledge of her husband's guilt. In her mind, Larry's death is linked to the pilots' deaths; denying the reality of his death is her way of denying her husband's responsibility for the deaths of the others. Her denial is shattered by Ann, who, to save her future happiness with Chris, reluctantly shows her Larry's suicide note.

Chris Keller, Keller's thirty-two-year-old, sensitive and intellectual son. He works for his father's company, which someday will be his. A World War II veteran whose combat experience has left him with a strong sense of responsibility for others, he is an idealist, though rather naïve. He loves his father, which causes him to ignore his suspicions about his father's guilt. He loves his mother, which casts a shadow over his desire to marry Ann. He is forced to choose between family responsibility and his moral idealism, which transcends family concerns. Unlike his father, he acknowledges obligations beyond the family. When confronted with his father's guilt, his moral idealism demands that he reject his father, which drives Joe to suicide.

Ann Deever, the attractive, twenty-six-year-old daughter of Joe Keller's former partner and neighbor, Steve Deever, whom she has not seen since his imprisonment. She was once Larry's girlfriend but now is in love with Chris, who invited her back to her old neighborhood so he could propose to her. Her desire to marry him over Kate's objections causes her to reveal Larry's suicide note to Kate to prove his death.

Jim Bayliss, a doctor and the Kellers' neighbor. His idealism is periodically encouraged by Chris. Like Chris, he must choose between family responsibilities and other, greater, values. He would like to do medical research but cannot support his family on the salary it would pay; although a successful doctor, he has compromised his idealism. A close friend of the Kellers and particularly of Chris, he has guessed Joe's guilt.

Sue Bayliss, Jim's wife. A practical, witty woman approaching middle age, she is threatened by Jim's stifled idealism. She too is aware of Joe's guilt and finds Chris's idealism shallow. She asks Ann to not live close to them after she marries Chris, so Chris will no longer encourage her husband's interest in medical research.

George Deever, Ann's impulsive and short-tempered brother. A lawyer, he comes to the Kellers' home after visiting his embittered father in prison, realizing that Joe Keller has destroyed his father. He tries to dissuade Ann from marrying Chris. He is almost reconciled with the Kellers, but Kate inadvertently reveals that Joe authorized the shipment of defective parts and not George's father. He again asks Ann not to marry into the family that destroyed their family; when she refuses, he leaves.

Lydia Lubey, onetime girlfriend of George Deever and the wife of Frank. She is a vibrant, beautiful woman who laughs easily. Her brief reunion with George at the Kellers shows how she too has settled for less than the ideal. She is a living reminder to George of what he lost when he went away to war; George is her reminder that she has married someone foolish and second-rate.

Frank Lubey, a foolish, insensitive, and balding haberdasher who is Lydia's husband.

30

Although only thirty-two years old, he managed to avoid military service in the war. He foolishly encourages Kate's superstition-fueled hope of Larry's return by presenting her with a horoscope "proving" that Larry did not die because the stars were "favor-able" to him the day he was reported missing. His marriage to the vivacious Lydia during the war reveals that he, like Joe Keller, profited while others died.

Lloyd R. Thompson

ALL OUR YESTERDAYS

Author: Natalia Ginzburg (1916-   )
Type of work: Novel
Time of action: The late 1930's through the end of World War II
First published: Tutti i nostri ieri, 1952 (*Dead Yesterdays,* 1956; better known as *All Our Yesterdays*)

Anna, a plump, pale girl of fourteen, the younger girl in her family. On the day her father dies, she meets Giuma, the boy across the street. Although she ostensibly prefers playing with her girlfriends, she is drawn to this social superior and begins to play with him, or rather becomes the object of his imaginative play, every day. He talks to her, tells her endless fascinating stories, and even ties her to a tree. In later years, she enjoys hearing him recite poems by Eugenio Montale and eating ice cream with him at the Paris café. They imagine themselves part of the revolution, shooting and escaping over rooftops. At the age of sixteen, Anna finds herself pregnant, but Giuma refuses to marry her because of her youth and the war. Instead he gives her one thousand lire, which he has saved to buy a boat, for an abortion. Frightened, she tells her plight to Cenzo Rena, an old family friend, who offers to keep her secret and marry her. Anna thus becomes the wife of the savior of the southern village of Borgo San Costanzo, where she gives birth to a daughter and gradually becomes sympathetic to the hard life of the peasants. She supports her husband's revolutionary activities and nurses him through a life-threatening illness. After he finally gives his life for the peasants, she, like her friends and family members, faces the future at the end of the war with courage and hope.

Cenzo Rena (chĕn'tsō rĕ'nä), a country gentleman, world traveler, and friend of Anna's father. A tall, big man with a hairy face and graying mustache, he is almost forty-eight at the time he marries Anna. A practical and generous man, he lives in an old family home high on a hill above a peasant village in southern Italy. The peasant men seek his company and advice as a revered friend and protector. He works for the improvement of their living conditions and teaches them that in a war there are no real winners. After a fugitive hiding in his cellar shoots a German, he gives himself to the Nazis and Fascists to obtain the release of ten hostages. He is shot in the village square, but he leaves to the villagers a legacy of fervor for political equality and the desire to end their cycle of poverty and misery.

Giuma (jē·ōō'mä), Anna's childhood friend and the father of her child, a boy with wolf-like teeth who is spoiled and rich. After having gone to school in Switzerland, he returns to Italy at the beginning of the war, a handsome and healthy seventeen year old. Although he despises Fascism, he will risk going to war. To everyone's surprise and his own disgrace, he fails his high school examinations and returns to school a gloomy and silent young man who reads the works of Søren Kierkegaard rather than those of Montale. Later, in Turin, he studies commercial sciences and pursues philosophy on his own. He contemplates suicide but miraculously escapes death during an air raid shortly after having apologized to Anna for making her suffer. After the war, he overcomes his guilt through psychoanalysis and marries an American physician whom he meets in Switzerland. Together they propose to bring about socialist reforms at the soap factory he has inherited from his father.

Ippolito (ēp•pō•lē′tö), Anna's brother and the loyal son of a revolutionary theorist who dies of lung cancer before the war begins. As an adolescent, he keeps a flea-ridden dog at the family's summer home and roams the countryside carrying a gun. He has a dry, smooth, thin, white face and a look of world-weariness. He does not like girls or the ordinary pleasures of youth. During his father's illness, he serves him as a slave, taking dictation, typing memoirs, reading *Faust* to him, and caring for his physical needs in the face of verbal abuse. After his father's death, he develops a close friendship with his neighbor Emanuele, the elder son of a

soap manufacturer. They become pedantic provincial intellectuals who secretly read subversive works and talk about revolution. Expecting a police raid one evening, they furtively burn a bundle of newspapers but never hear from the authorities concerning their vague ideology. When Italy enters the war on Germany's side after the fall of France, Ippolito, sitting in the public gardens, commits suicide with his father's revolver.

Giustino (jē•ōōs•tē′nō), Anna's younger brother, who ultimately fights with the Partisans in Russia.

Concettina (cōn•chĕ•tē′nä), Anna's elder sister, who has many suitors but marries a Fascist and flees Italy to protect her baby during the war.

Janie Caves McCauley

ALL THAT FALL
A Play for Radio

Author: Samuel Beckett (1906-1989)
Type of work: Play
Time of action: The 1950's
First produced: 1957

Mrs. Rooney (Maddy), a woman in her seventies, in poor health, weighing more than two hundred pounds. Mrs. Rooney's trip to meet her husband at the railway station on his birthday is a long, slow journey full of chance meetings with a variety of characters. She represents the human condition, and her dragging feet suggest the difficulty of making one's way through life. Mrs. Rooney mourns the loss of her child Minnie, and she is philosophical about the brevity of existence in her remarks about the chicken killed on the road. She tries to converse with the various people she meets but ends by estranging them, suggesting modern man's inability to communicate. Mrs. Rooney is obsessed with sex, including a "lifelong preoccupation with horses' buttocks," and many of her remarks carry sexual innuendo,

making her a symbol of sexuality. She is caring and concerned for the health and well-being of those she meets. She announces the source of the play's title in Psalm 145, which provides the text for the Sunday service: "The Lord upholdeth all that fall and raiseth up all those that be bowed down." The quotation prompts laughter in Mr. and Mrs. Rooney, showing their skepticism that they, as the "bowed down," will someday be raised up.

Mr. Rooney (Dan), the blind husband of Mrs. Rooney. Always in bad humor, Mr. Rooney is surprised by his wife's appearance at the train station on his birthday. He is preoccupied with counting, which he sees as one of the few satisfactions in life. When he and Maddy are taunted by the children on the road, he confesses an urge to kill a child, especially the boy Jerry who guides him home from the station. His job is mundane and repetitious, and he expresses a desire to end it. Chronically ill, he represents an urge toward death, unsure of how old he is and whether he will be alive on Monday.

Christy, a carter, who meets Mrs. Rooney on the road. He is walking beside a cartload of dung, which he offers to Mrs. Rooney, suggesting that the ride down the road of life may be like a ride on a dung chart. Mrs. Rooney tells Christy that she speaks only in simple words but often thinks her way of speaking is bizarre.

Mr. Tyler, a retired bill-broker. He meets Mrs. Rooney on the road and stops when he realizes his bicycle tire has gone flat, suggesting that for him, too, the journey down the road of life is difficult. Mrs. Rooney falls into a fit of mourning for her dead child, but when he attempts to console her, she interprets his consolation as sexual advances, and he rides away.

Mr. Slocum, Clerk of the Racecourse. Mrs. Rooney calls him an old admirer. He offers her a lift in his motorcar, but they are barely able to fit her in. Mr. Slocum's dry wit responds to Mrs. Rooney's suggestive remarks with literal answers. He carelessly runs over a chicken on the road, prompting Mrs. Rooney's remark on life's brevity, fore-shadowing the death of the child under the wheel of the train.

Tommy, a porter at the railway station. He helps Mrs. Rooney out of the Slocum motorcar, a maneuver that intimates parturition.

Mr. Barrell, the stationmaster, nearing retirement. He is impatient with Tommy and irritable with Mrs. Rooney, who questions him about the lateness of the train.

Miss Fitt, a lady in her thirties who professes to be very religious. She recognizes people only in church and her charity is limited, since she has to be coaxed to help Mrs. Rooney up to the platform. She describes herself as dark and "alone with her maker." She represents the inability of the religious to function in the world.

Jerry, a small boy who is hired by Mr. Rooney to lead him home from the train station. He runs after Mr. Rooney to return the ball he believes was left by him on the train. From Jerry, Mrs. Rooney learns that a child was killed on the tracks, causing the train's delay.

Female Voice, and
Dolly, a woman and her daughter at the train station. They laugh at Mrs. Rooney and Miss Fitt.

Louise Flavin

AMADEUS

Author: Peter Shaffer (1926-   )
Type of work: Play
Time of action: 1781-1823
First produced: 1979

Antonio Salieri, a court composer and later Imperial Kappellmeister to Joseph II, Emperor of Austria, who has dedicated his life and his talents to the greater honor and glory of God and has obtained fame, reputation, and the Emperor's favor. Salieri belongs to a clique of Italians who have culturally colonized the court. His composure is shaken when Mozart, an upstart Austrian prodigy from Salzburg, comes to Vienna and makes a favorable impression on the Emperor. Though he never questions Mozart's talent, Salieri becomes insanely jealous, schemes to ruin Mozart's career, and ultimately confesses to having killed Mozart before insanely attempting suicide. Salieri is an evil-minded, Satanic figure, proud, vain, and humiliated by Mozart, the main player and narrator in a parable demonstrating the sin of envy.

Wolfgang Amadeus Mozart, the genius composer, presented as a crude, vulgar, and tactless young egotist who has absolutely no modesty with regard to his talent. The victim of the drama, Mozart is innocent and naïve in the devious world of court politics, too tactless to veil his contempt for the Court Italians and Salieri's music and too naïve to recognize Salieri as his most dangerous enemy.

Constanze Weber, the daughter of Mozart's landlady in Vienna and, later, his wife. She is well-intentioned, innocent, and tolerant of her husband's behavior, but she shares his vulgarity. She drives a wedge between Mozart and his father, Leopold, who later dies in Salzburg. She secretly visits Salieri when the couple needs money to survive, taking original manuscripts, but later she is suspicious of Salieri. She loves her husband but is unable to help him at the end, when she returns from Baden to find him, dying, in the company of Salieri.

Joseph II, the Emperor of Austria, Mozart's patron, who loves music but is too dense to fully appreciate Mozart's talents. Essentially a man of mediocre intelligence and taste, he

prefers Salieri to Mozart and is therefore easily influenced by Salieri. He appoints Mozart to replace Gluck as Chamber Composer after Gluck's death, but, on Salieri's advice, at only one-tenth of Gluck's salary.

Baron Gottfried Van Swieten (fän svēt′ən), the Prefect of the Imperial Library and an ardent Freemason, who helps to support Mozart and his family after Mozart becomes a Mason, until Mozart writes *The Magic Flute* and alienates his benefactor by utilizing Masonic rituals (at Salieri's suggestion) and revealing Masonic secrets in that opera. Because of his old-fashioned musical preferences, he is known as "Lord Fugue." He pays for Mozart's pauper's funeral.

Count Johann von Strack (fôn shträk), the Royal Chamberlain, who conveys the Emperor's orders to commission Mozart to write a comic opera in German, which further alienates the Court Italians.

Count Franz Orsini-Rosenberg, the director of the Imperial Opera and part of the Italian faction, who argues against opera that is non-Italian and criticizes Mozart for employing "too many notes." He believes that "all prodigies are hateful."

The "Venticelli" (věn•tē•chēl′ē), the **"Little Winds,"** which serve as "purveyors of information, gossip, and rumor" and function as a chorus to the action.

James Michael Welsh

AMBIGUOUS ADVENTURE

Author: Cheikh Hamidou Kane (1928-   )
Type of work: Novel
Time of action: The mid-1930's to c. 1950
First published: L'Aventure ambiguë, 1961 (English translation, 1963)

Samba Diallo, a young man of the Diallobé artistocracy who is perceived by all to represent the future of his people. For this reason, the older generation of the Diallobé people struggles to influence the course of his life.

As a child, Samba evinces a profound sense of the spiritual beauty of Islam and of the Koran, whose words he repeats without understanding them. When it is decided that he will attend the French school, he becomes enamored with the Western alphabet, philosophy, and scientific method, all of which suggest that everything can be expressed, analyzed, and mastered. Undertaking university studies in philosophy in Paris, he suffers deeply over the loss of that spiritual plenitude he had known before his contact with the West. As he discusses philosophical, spiritual, and political issues with those he meets, he realizes that in the course of his "ambiguous adventure" he has internalized aspects of both cultures and is no longer completely at ease in either. Recalled to Africa by his worried father, he seems to seek out his own demise, apparently experiencing a return of faith at the moment of his death.

Thierno (tē·ĕr′nō), teacher of Islam in the Koranic school and spiritual master of the Diallobé people. The fragility and stiffness of his aging body make a vivid contrast with the ethereal joy in his soul. Thierno declines to help the Diallobé decide whether to send their children to the colonial schools. With his preferred successor, Samba, away in Paris, however, he designates Demba, a pragmatic youth of peasant stock, whose first official act is to allow the Diallobé children to attend the French school.

The Knight, Samba's father, so dubbed by a school friend of Samba (Jean Lacroix) because of his stature and noble bearing. Although working at a civil service post in the colonial administration, his contact with the West has not altered his deep faith. Indeed, he asserts that Africa's urgent mission is to restore a sense of spirituality to an impoverished Western civilization obsessed with scientific and technological progress.

The Chief of the Diallobé, secular leader of his people, brother of the Most Royal Lady, and Samba's cousin. The Chief represents a middle ground, a locus of indecisiveness in an era in which important decisions must be made. A lucid and profoundly human character, he clearly feels inadequate to play the role assigned him by his historical era.

The Most Royal Lady, Samba's aunt and the Chief's sister. Looking twenty years younger, at sixty she radiates the beauty and strength of the Diallobé aristocracy. Her principal role in the novel is to exhort her people to attend the French school. In an eloquent speech, she acknowledges that the consequences of this decision cannot be predicted; precious elements of their cultural or spiritual heritage may be lost, but the Diallobé must move forward.

The Fool, a friend of Thierno. His darting gaze, strange clothing, odd speech, and marginalized position in Diallobé society have earned for him this title. His reasons for having visited the West are unclear, but he seems to have fought in World War I and to have been permanently traumatized by his experiences. The West he describes to Thierno is a cold, hard, mechanized, dehumanized world, and he opposes any contact with it. He is grief-stricken at Thierno's death, and his efforts to force Samba to pray on the holy man's grave precipitate Samba's apparent death at the end of the novel.

Paul Lacroix (lä·krwä′), a colleague of the Knight. His principal importance is as a participant in a conversation with the Knight as the two men observe a magnificent African sunset; that sight causes them to reflect on "the end of the world." The men represent two radically different belief systems. Lacroix fears the end of the world, feeling that it could only signify human failure and would end the infinite continuation of enlightenment and scientific progress. The Knight looks forward to the end of the world as the moment when all questions and uncertainties will be resolved.

Paul Martial, a middle-aged Protestant pastor. A sympathetic and enlightened Westerner, he discusses philosophy with Samba. As a young man, he had dreamed of going to Africa as a missionary. He perceived such a mission as only a spiritual exchange between cultures, and would have refrained from the Westerner's frequent practice of combining proselytizing with "gifts" of medicine and technology.

Lucienne Martial, Paul's daughter, and a university classmate of Samba. She advocates a political (Marxist) solution to the social crisis in Africa. Samba admires her fervent commitment, observing that she has followed the road to Damascus in the opposite direction from that taken by the apostle Paul—that is, away from her Christian upbringing. Samba does not experience a similar conversion. He recognizes that for him the resolution of conflict lies in faith rather than politics.

Janet L. Solberg

AMERICA HURRAH

Author: Jean-Claude van Itallie (1935 or 1936-   )
Type of work: Play
Time of action: The mid-1960's
First produced: 1966

First Applicant (Jack Smith), an unemployed housepainter. He is proud of his profession, his union membership, his Italian heritage. He recounts an occasion when, lacking direction in his life, he mentioned to his priest that he might like to join a monastery but received no reply.

Second Applicant (Jane Smith), an unemployed floorwasher. She is of Jewish-Irish descent and has been washing floors for twenty years. She feels abandoned by her deceased husband.

Third Applicant (Richard Smith), an unemployed bank president. During his job interview, he flaunts his education, social status, and previous employment. Later, he reveals that he lost his job because of an unexplainable and uncontrollable feeling of panic that has incapacitated him.

Fourth Applicant (Mary Smith), an unemployed lady's maid. During her job interview, she brags about her family origins and the aristocratic families for whom she has worked. On the city streets, however, she becomes completely disoriented and unable to find her way.

Hal, a television ratings service employee in his late twenties or early thirties. He is cynical in outlook and enjoys tormenting George, his supervisor, with whom he feels himself to be in competition. He wants to begin a relationship with his coworker, Susan.

Susan, a television ratings service employee in her early twenties. She is engaged in an affair with her supervisor, George, who is married, but flirts with Hal. After she agrees to go to a movie with Hal, she still treats George with excessive tenderness. She is given to inexplicable fits of hysterical laughter and is in therapy.

George, a television ratings service supervisor, forty-three years old. He competes with Hal for Susan's affections, drawing attention to his greater tact and life experience, but calls off his affair with Susan after she decides to go out with Hal. He telephones his wife to tell her that he will be coming home after all, only to be greeted with incredulity. Immediately after calling off his assignation with Susan, however, he chokes on a chicken bone. When he recovers, he returns to his competitive stance with respect to Hal and tries to insinuate himself into Hal's date with Susan.

The Motel-Keeper, represented on stage by a giant *papier-mâché* puppet, spouts clichés about how "homey" the rooms of her motel are and describes in great detail the various consumer catalogues from which she has ordered its decorations.

The Man and The Woman, also represented by giant puppets, the guests staying at
the motel. They undress, use the bathroom,
make love, dance, and destroy their room to
the accompaniment of the television set and
loud rock music. After attacking the Motel-
Keeper herself and ripping her arms and
head off, they exit through the theater's
aisles.

Philip Auslander

AMERICAN BUFFALO

Author: David Mamet (1947-   )
Type of work: Play
Time of action: The 1970's
First produced: 1975

Don Dubrow, a man in his late forties, the
owner of the junkshop called Don's Resale
Shop, who unknowingly sells a rare American Buffalo nickel for what he assumes must
have been too little. He believes that by
tricking him the buyer achieves an unwar-
ranted dominance over him. Don intends to
get even by planning a robbery, one in which
he will not participate, but where he will
have the nickel restolen. This dream-fantasy
of the robbery restores to Don the sense of
power that he lost with the nickel's sale.
When the play opens, Don is berating the
dependent Bob for leaving the house he had
been sent to stake out and emphasizing his
dominance by making Bob apologize for that
action. Don's need for family is expressed by
his fatherly friendship and concern for slow-
witted Bobby, whom he tries to teach the
difference between friendship and business
but whom he betrays out of mistrust of his
own convictions and the strength of Teach's
arguments. He holds the offstage character
Fletch up to Bobby as an example of a guy
who can think on his feet, but he becomes
totally demoralized when he learns through
Teach that Fletch cheated him, a friend as
well as a business associate. Don turns violent when frustrated. His whole life seems to
exist only within his resale shop.

Walter Cole, called **Teach,** an overreactive
friend and associate of Don who is totally
unsure of his actions, although he puts up a
good front by using bold language infused
with positivism. His unsureness, however, is
echoed in his innate suspicion of others, and
he believes that everyone is motivated by
self-interest. Business in his world is necessary, and the means used to justify its execution, self-justifying. The use of deceit, physical violence, and assault are merely business
tactics, and friendship is nothing more than
a means of gain. Teach lacks the courage of
his convictions, however, and there is a great
gulf between his word and his deed. His
suspicions allow him to terrorize Bobby
physically, and even though these thoughts
turn out to be erroneous, he is never anxious
or questioning of his action. Teach utilizes
moral principles that justify his cynical outlook. His great robbery never takes place;
Teach is a bungler as well as a misogynist.
Offstage female characters illustrate his total
lack of control in his world.

Bob, a slow-witted gofer and junkie of Don,
who emphasizes the superiority Don feels.
Bob is cheated out of participation in an
abortive robbery but ironically may have
done the cheating. Bob is dependent on Don
for the cash to feed his habit. Participation
in the robbery will temporarily bring him the
cash he needs and possibly praise from Don.
Because of his habit, however, Bob must
also be committing small types of crimes,
and it could be that he committed the crime
that Teach accuses him of—getting the
American Buffalo nickel from the customer
in some foul way. Don's calls to the hospitals
in the area prove that Bob is not trusted by
Don. Throughout the play, Bob, in repeating

much of what Don tells him, uses a type of low-language slang that indicates his low in-

telligence and his inability to progress outside of Don's Resale Shop.

Marjorie J. Oberlander

AN AMERICAN DREAM

Author: Norman Mailer (1923-   )
Type of work: Novel
Time of action: 1962
First published: 1965

Stephen Richard Rojack, the narrator and protagonist, a war hero, former congressman, professor of existential psychology, televison personality, and murderer. On a late-night visit to his estranged wife, Deborah, Rojack strangles her after enduring her taunts. She challenges his manhood, and Rojack feels particularly vulnerable since he has had doubts about his character. Although he has achieved some notoriety, he has not lived up to his own heroic image of himself. Yet he weathers the police interrogation well, even though they suspect him of throwing her body out the window to make it look like suicide. Rojack's project throughout the rest of the novel is, so to speak, himself. He is determined to act as his own man, which means confronting his hostile father-in-law, Barney Kelly, and fighting for his new love, Cherry. At the end of the novel, he leaves town on a quest westward, hoping to develop a better character.

Deborah, Rojack's wife, the daughter of wealthy and powerful Barney Kelley. Although her early years with Rojak have been stimulating, she has obviously lost much respect for him and goads him into killing her at precisely the moment when he is looking for help. Deborah is beautiful, but she is cold and self-involved. She seems to have none of Rojack's vulnerabilities. She dies at the beginning of the novel, but her character and her judgments of Rojack tend to dominate his thinking about himself.

Barney Kelly, a millionaire with connections to the Mafia, who suspects Rojack of murdering his daughter. The cool and col-

lected Kelly does not reveal his emotions until the moment when Rojack—determined to prove his courage through some physical feat—decides to walk the parapet outside Kelly's apartment. As Rojack makes a turn around the building, Kelly tries to trip him. Rojack's step is steady, however, and he is able to cope with this crucial moment, which gives him enough courage to get through the traumatic night of Deborah's murder.

Ruta, Deborah's German maid, who is in the house the night Rojack strangles Deborah. On an impulse, Rojack invades Ruta's room after murdering Deborah and finds Ruta ready for his sexual advances. Rojack's taking of this woman is associated in his mind with his newfound energy. He asks Ruta not to mention this episode to the police and she complies. Only later does he suspect her of having some special connection with Barney Kelly, who may have set up Ruta to keep an eye on things in the house.

Cherry, a nightclub singer with whom Rojack has an affair. She is blonde and beautiful. She has a modest talent, but Rojack appreciates her toughness and willingness to befriend him when he first meets her at a table surrounded by gangsters. Cherry becomes Rojack's inspiration. She is the woman for whom he is willing to fight, the woman who can support him in precisely the ways Deborah was unwilling to do.

Roberts, a detective who investigates Deborah's murder. Although he is virtually certain that Rojack is a murderer, he does not have enough evidence to prove it. Instead, he tries to work on Rojack's anxieties, hoping that he will confess. At the same time, Roberts has a certain admiration for Rojack's toughness.

Shago Martin, a black man with sexual prowess who has been Cherry's lover and who becomes a television replacement for Rojack. At one point, Rojack has to fight Shago for Cherry. Although the white man and the black man share certain values—

especially their antiestablishment bias— their feelings about Cherry divide them. In a particularly brutal scene, Rojack kicks Martin down the stairs. While Rojack feels some compassion for his rival, he feels compelled to fight for this new woman and for this new sense of himself. Martin, on the other hand, behaves like a burnt-out case, trying to frighten Rojack with a knife but without the force to call him to account.

Carl Rollyson

THE AMERICAN DREAM

Author: Edward Albee (1928-   )
Type of work: Play
Time of action: The late twentieth century
First produced: 1961

Mommy, the head of the household, who dominates the play. She complains about poor service in the department store and, in general, is fixated on her role as a consumer. Mommy's main interest is to remain in control, to make life convenient for herself, which means, among other things, getting rid of outspoken and quarrelsome Grandma, who has become a nuisance. Mommy and Daddy have apparently had a child who somehow disappointed them. They hope that the visit from Mrs. Barker will help resolve things by disposing of Grandma, getting a new child, and restoring their sense of domestic bliss. Mommy does not seem to notice that she often contradicts herself. At the end of the play, she welcomes the appearance of the Young Man, who seems familiar to her, even though she cannot identify him.

Daddy, who acts in most ways as Mommy's subordinate. He is a whiner and complains about how difficult it is to get anything fixed in the apartment. His comments seem quite infantile, and he doubts himself, so that Mommy has to keep propping him up by praising his masculinity. Like Mommy, he anticipates the arrival of a new adopted child as if it were a product from the department store. Almost never thinking for himself, he is quite willing

to have Mommy or Mrs. Barker suggest the right course of action. He is so inept that Mommy often repeats herself, for she cannot be sure that he has understood her. He even has trouble finding Grandma's bedroom.

Grandma, an old and feeble but still sharp-minded woman. She knows that Mommy and Daddy are trying to get rid of her, and her sarcastic comments about their plans are astute and humorous. Grandma seems much more realistic than Mommy or Daddy and does not use their euphemisms to disguise what she says. Grandma often interrupts the dialogue between Mommy and Daddy and Mrs. Barker and interprets what they say. It is Grandma, for example, who reveals that Mommy and Daddy have made a botch of their adoption of a little boy and now want a replacement for him. It is also Grandma who dubs the Young Man who arrives as "the American dream," for he is meant to function as the fulfillment of Mommy's and Daddy's hopes and illusions about perfect family life in America. Grandma, in short, is the only character who knows how to speak her mind.

Mrs. Barker, a visitor to Mommy and Daddy's home, who announces herself to be the chairman of Mommy's women's club, which is a surprise to Mommy, who claims to have had trouble recognizing her in the artificial light. Mrs. Barker acts like one of the authorities that Mommy and Daddy have been expecting. She is more uninhibited than the other characters, taking off her dress to be more comfortable. She speaks vaguely about a number of important activities and wonders whether she has come to pick up Grandma's boxes. Eventually, Mrs. Barker learns from Grandma that she has really come to pick up Grandma.

Young Man, a handsome and athletic man, who arrives at Mommy and Daddy's apartment. He is rather dumb and without much emotion. He refers to his identical twin, who is evidently the young child that Mommy and Daddy had previously adopted. With no real motivation of his own, the Young Man seems merely to be there in order to fulfill Mommy and Daddy's desire for the perfect child.

Carl Rollyson

AMERIKA

Author: Franz Kafka (1883-1924)
Type of work: Novel
Time of action: The early twentieth century
First published: 1927 (English translation, 1938)

Karl Rossman, a fifteen- or sixteen-year-old youth who leaves his native Prague to seek his fortune in America. A sensitive, naïve adolescent who has been treated unfairly by his parents, Karl arrives in America with little money and few possessions but with a strong determination to triumph over circumstances. He is hardworking, eager to learn, willing to make sacrifices—in many ways, it would seem, the ideal immigrant. His first experiences in America, however, are nightmarish, comically so in their reversal of the immigrant's dreams. Karl sees justice travestied, is himself falsely accused and beaten, and becomes a fugitive, finding a place only among the outcast. After a hiatus in the narrative, however (perhaps several years), Karl regains hope, responding to a poster advertising jobs with the Theatre of Oklahoma (apparently a government project on a fantastic scale). In a spirit of rejoicing, Karl leaves on a rail journey across America, secure in the belief that in Oklahoma he will at last realize his dreams for himself in the New World.

Senator Edward Jacob, Karl's wealthy uncle, a proud, stuffy, self-made man, the red-faced gentleman with a thin bamboo cane whom Karl meets in the ship's office. Owner of Jacob Despatch Agency in New York, he has gained American citizenship and severed all ties to his European past. Jacob exults in saving his nephew from a life of wretchedness, doing so partly because of pity and partly because of his strong dislike for his own relatives who have set the boy adrift. He takes him in to his lavish surroundings, supporting and advising him and indulging the youth in every modern advantage. At the same time, he tyrannizes over him, expecting Karl to seek his unconditional approval in every situation. Without a word of warning, he castigates Karl for unintentionally going against his wishes. Convinced that nothing good can come from Karl's family, Jacob disappears from Karl's life just as unexpectedly as he entered it.

The Stoker, a ship employee. A huge, brawny man, he confines Karl in a tiny compartment below the decks of the ship in New York Harbor so as to have an audience for his complaints against his superior, Schubal, who, he says, bullies him. Although Karl argues for him before the captain, the Stoker loses his case, for Schubal has fifteen noisy witnesses to support him.

Grete Mitzelbach (mĭt′zĕl•bäx), the fifty-year-old manageress of the Hotel Occidental. Herself an immigrant from Vienna, she benignly takes on Karl as her protégé but finds herself powerless to defend him against the Head Waiter's charges of dereliction.

Therese Berchtold (bârk′tōlt), an eighteen-year-old Pomeranian girl who serves as Grete Mitzelbach's typist. Having warned Karl to stay away from Robinson and Delamarche, she is grief-stricken at his dismissal from the Hotel Occidental.

Brunelda, a wealthy, fat singer, the former wife of a cocoa manufacturer, who keeps Delamarche in her suburban flat with Robinson as their servant. She spends most of her time lying on a filthy couch in her red gown.

Robinson, an Irishman who attaches himself to Karl for self-gain and ultimately causes him to lose his job as lift boy. He becomes a lazy drunk who lies on the balcony at Brunelda's flat and attempts to get Karl to perform the housework so that he can care for Brunelda personally.

Delamarche (de•lä•märsh′), a Frenchman who succeeds in the New World by binding himself to Brunelda as her kept man.

Janie Caves McCauley

AMONG WOMEN ONLY

Author: Cesare Pavese (1908-1950)
Type of work: Novel
Time of action: The late 1940's
First published: Tra donne sole, 1949 (English translation, 1953)

Clelia Oitana (ō•ē•tä′nä), the narrator, a successful couturiere, who comes from Rome to Turin, Italy, to open a fashion house. Clelia, who had escaped from the Turin working-class quarter seventeen years before, returns, at age thirty-four, as an attractive, experienced woman. She had been driven by ambition to get ahead but is now aware that the life she has created is largely empty. Clelia moves among the elite young people of postwar Turin and finds them to lead frivolous, meaningless lives, escaping from boredom by slumming expeditions and by engaging in vicious gossip about one another. Clelia is not very happy with her life, but her work, at least, brings her much satisfaction. Fulfilling work is something that her friends do not have.

Rosetta Mola, the twenty-three-year-old daughter of a rich, proper Turin family. Rosetta, a serious, naïve woman, fed up with the meaningless existence of her social group and yet unable to find an alternative, attempts suicide the night Clelia returns to Turin. Clelia meets her and realizes that she is in trouble but has no answer to Rosetta's fundamental question: When life and love teaches you who you are, as Clelia has assured her it would, what do you do with what you have learned? The book closes with Rosetta's death by suicide.

Momina, a rich, well-educated, former baroness. Slightly younger than Clelia, a fresh-faced and attractive brunette, she is the center of the group of elite young Turinians, with all activities revolving around her. Momina is cynical, discontented, disgusted with life and with everyone and everything. While she can live with the emptiness of her life and dismisses it with a cynical shrug, she feeds the nihilistic void within Rosetta. Momina is dangerous, perhaps deadly, to Rosetta.

Gisella, a small shopkeeper and an old friend of Clelia. Gisella is a thin, gray woman, with a bony, resentful face, in whom Clelia sees herself if she had not escaped the working-class quarter. If Momina's group offers little to Clelia, neither does Gisella or others from Clelia's past.

Morelli, an older friend of Clelia, whom she met in Rome and who provides entrée for her into the elite circles and salons of Turin. Morelli seems to lead the same unproductive life as the other members of the Turin leisure class, but he possesses more substance. He enjoys life and points out to Clelia that she has turned work into a vice that controls her and into a criteria that she uses to judge the worth of other people. He describes to her the accomplishments of the parents of the young people that Clelia meets in Turin and shares her disgust at the aimless existence of the young, including their inability to enjoy life.

Febo, an architect, who designs Clelia's

fashion house. An attractive, young man, who possesses a talent and who works, he is a frivolous, irrepressible womanizer and playboy. Clelia sleeps with him on one occasion out of boredom and to stop him from pestering her so that he will go away.

Becuccio (bā·kōō′chyō), the foreman of the crew reconstructing Clelia's fashion house. He is a young, competent, muscular, curly haired man with an attractive smile, who appeals to Clelia. She sleeps with him out of attraction, not boredom, but recognizes, as he does, that their way of life is too different to allow any more than a passing affair. Becuccio, a Communist and skilled worker, seems to suffer none of the emptiness of his "betters."

William E. Pemberton

THE ANATOMY LESSON

Author: Philip Roth (1933-   )
Type of work: Novel
Time of action: 1973
First published: 1983

Nathan Zuckerman, the protagonist of *The Ghost Writer* and *Zuckerman Unbound,* a successful writer, author of the notorious best-selling novel *Carnovsky.* In this novel (the third of a trilogy), he is not well. For eighteen months, he has been suffering inexplicably from extreme neck and back pains that prevent him from extensive reading and even from writing, though he feels he has nothing left to write about. To make matters worse, he has turned forty. He lives alone, and to help ease his pain he not only drinks and smokes pot but also has a bevy of four girlfriends who visit him at different times and cater to his needs, including his sexual needs. Finally, in desperation, he decides to give up writing and become a doctor.

Robert (Bobby) Freytag, Nathan's college chum, now a successful anesthesiologist in Chicago, whom Nathan flies out to consult

about applying to medical school. Bobby's mother has died three weeks earlier, and at the cemetery with Bobby's aggrieved father, Nathan loses his head (he has been taking too much Percodan and drinking vodka), attacks the old man, and falls on a gravestone, fracturing his skull and sustaining other injuries.

Henry Zuckerman, Nathan's younger brother, who believes that *Carnovsky* was a terrible affront to American Jews in general and to the Zuckerman family in particular. He holds Nathan responsible for hastening the death of their father, whose dying breath sounded like a curse on his older son. A year later their adoring mother also dies, but Nathan does not arrive in time to hear her last words. Before her death, she scribbles the word "holocaust" on a scrap of paper, which Nathan carries about with him, trying to figure out what she meant.

Milton Appel, a professor and literary critic, whose severe criticism of *Carnovsky* and his other fiction Zuckerman finds it impossible to forgive. The criticism rankles still more when Appel wants Zuckerman to help defend Israeli interests by writing something "uplifting" about the country and its ideals.

Jaga, the Polish émigrée who works as a receptionist in the office of Nathan's trichologist (along with other ailments, he is suffering hair loss). At first she plays hard to get but eventually yields to Nathan's charms and becomes one of his four playmates. During their lovemaking, she utters long monologues about herself and her hopeless existence as a woman and an exile.

Gloria, wife of Nathan's accountant and another of the female comforters who visit him. She enjoys making rice pudding for him and wearing a G-string.

Jenny, a painter who lives in Vermont and tries to lure Nathan away from New York to the country, where they could live a healthy life and eat fresh vegetables.

Diana, a rich heiress and the youngest of Nathan's four lovers and comforters. A student at Finch College, she tries to help Nathan by appealing to the Protestant work ethic. She also tries to persuade him to stop hating Appel and write the essay.

Ricky, the female chauffeur who drives Nathan from the airport in Chicago to his hotel. En route, Nathan assumes the identity of Milton Appel, whom he describes as an arch-pornographer. He tries hard to entice Ricky, but he is no match against her sturdy independence and healthy mental state. Finally, after long enduring his tirades and propositions, she tells him off.

Jay L. Halio

ANDORRA

Author: Max Frisch (1911-   )
Type of work: Play
Time of action: The 1950's
First produced: 1961 (English translation, 1963)

Andri, age twenty, has been brought up in Andorra (not the small European country but a "model") in the belief that he is a Jew whom his foster father, the Teacher, rescued from persecution by the "Blacks" across the border. Since then the Andorrans have forced him into the role of an outsider and to behave like their stereotypical notion of a Jew—a rootless, greedy, lustful, heartless, oversensitive coward. Learning that he is not a Jew only exacerbates his confusion and anguish. Having been ferreted out by the totalitarian "Jew-detector," Andri is finally dragged to his doom by the invading Blacks, while his fellow Andorrans look on passively.

The Teacher (Can), a man who drinks heavily in an attempt to drown his sorrow over the stupidity, cupidity, and hypocrisy of his fellow Andorrans. As a young, idealistic gadfly and firebrand, he called his pupils' attention to the many untruths in their textbooks. Now, however, the man who cravenly disowned his son Andri has a chilling sense of doom and vainly attempts to atone for his cowardice and deception. He is the only Andorran who offers resistance to the nightmarish invaders, but eventually he feels compelled to hang himself in his schoolroom.

Barblin, the Teacher's teenage daughter. She hopelessly falls in love with Andri without realizing that their union would be incestuous. Barblin suffers the trauma of being raped by the brutish Soldier. In the end, the half-demented girl, her hair shorn, an Ophelia figure and the only Andorran who has nothing to whitewash, senselessly splashes white paint on the town's cobblestones and speaks of saving Andri's shoes for his possible return.

The Señora, a mysterious woman from across the border. She confronts her erstwhile lover, the Teacher, and accuses him of cowardice in not acknowledging their son. Suspected of being a spy for the blacks, she is killed by a stone, and Andri is falsely accused of having thrown it.

The Priest (Father Benedict), a more sensitive and insightful person than his fellow citizens, yet even he is not free from prejudice. He is the only one who really acknowledges his guilt: He enchained Andri, as it were, by fashioning for himself a fixed image of him.

The Mother, the Teacher's wife and Bar-blin's mother, vainly strives for a peaceful atmosphere in the family.

The Doctor (Ferrer), the new medical officer of Andorra, widely traveled and yet a narrow-minded, frustrated Jew-baiter.

The Carpenter (Prader), feels that Andri should not be his apprentice but become a salesman or a stockbroker. Yet he charges the Teacher an exorbitant sum for training Andri.

The Soldier (Peider), the quintessential bully, drunken braggart, chauvinist, and anti-Semite.

The Innkeeper, as hypocritical as his fellow citizens, he employs Andri as a kitchen boy.

The Journeyman (Fedri), an opportunist who is too weak to oppose his master's trickery in the carpenter's shop when the chair he has made proves inferior to Andri's.

Harry Zohn

THE ANDROMEDA STRAIN

Author: Michael Crichton (1942-   )
Type of work: Novel
Time of action: 1967
First published: 1969

Dr. Jeremy Stone, a professor of bacteriology at Berkeley, a Nobel Prize-winner, a lawyer, and a federal government consultant whose paper on the possibilities of a bacterial or viral invasion has led to his Project Wildfire, a $22 million underground containment laboratory in the Nevada desert, where the extraterrestrial enemy can be studied and countermeasures developed. Stone's papers on bacteriology and mutant reversion have led him to be compared to Albert Einstein. His insistence on a nuclear device to destroy the lab if the alien disease threatens to escape is the key to the project and to the plot. He is a thin, balding man with a prodigious memory, a sense of humor, and an overpowering impatience that leads him to interrupt speakers and to finish conversations. Four times married, this imperious man alienates colleagues but is unquestionably an intellectual power. Stone views the disaster at Piedmont as a confusing but challenging puzzle and the survivors as the central clues.

Dr. Peter Leavitt, a clinical microbiologist and epidemiologist specializing in parasitology, the chief of bacteriology at the same hospital as Hall and responsible for recruiting Hall. Leavitt's research, conducted worldwide, is famous, but ill-health made him give up research abroad. He suffers from epilepsy and is hypnotized by blinking lights, a carefully hidden vulnerability with potentially disastrous consequences when a flashing alarm renders him unconscious.

Dr. Charles Burton, a fifty-four-year-old pathologist who accompanies Stone to Piedmont and then to the Wildfire lab. Burton held a professorship at Baylor Medical and served as consultant to the NASA Manned Spaceflight Center in Houston. His specialty is the effects of bacteria on human tissues. His unruly and untidy appearance puts Stone off, but his expertise is undeniable. Burton accompanies Stone on his initial investigation of the Piedmont disaster and later is trapped in a lab with the virus released by the failure of a seal.

Dr. Mark Hall, a surgeon Stone reluctantly enlisted in the Wildfire team when another is unable to come. Known by associates as "swift, quick-tempered, and unpredictable," he operates rapidly, laughing and joking while cutting, but turning irritable when work becomes slow and difficult. He is called out of surgery to join the team and is initially not particularly welcome as a useful member (except for his knowledge of electrolytes and his unmarried status). In an intuitive leap, however, he comes to a final understanding of the terrifying disease. He describes his experiences as "horrifying" and "unfamiliar." As in H. G. Wells's *War*

of the Worlds, the alien invader finally succumbs from common earthly causes, making Hall's discovery moot, but in the meantime, as the "Odd Man" of the Wildfire instruction Manual, he is the only one who can stop the nuclear self-destruct mechanism.

Major Arthur Manchek, the Project Scoop duty officer, an engineer, who reacts to the mysterious cut-off in transmission of the satellite recovery team sent to Piedmont, Arizona, deciding to call an alert and set up flybys, scans, and laboratory studies. Manchek is a quiet heavyset man, "plagued by labile hypertension" and unable to lose the extra pounds necessary for promotion. Previously in charge of experiments in spacecraft landing methods in the Wright Patterson facility in Vandenberg, Ohio, Manchek had successfully developed three new capsule shapes that were promising. He hates administrative work and was happiest working at the wind tunnels of Wright Patterson. He notices the aged survivor on the flyby films, declares a state of emergency, and calls in the experts. Manchek disappears from the novel early, however, replaced by the Wildfire team. He reappears near the end (when he finds out about the crash of a plane that invaded Piedmont air space) and pushes for nuclear destruction of Piedmont and Wildfire.

Andrew Macdonald

ANGEL PAVEMENT

Author: J. B. Priestley (1894-1984)
Type of work: Novel
Time of action: The late 1920's, during the Great Depression
First published: 1930

James Golspie, the protagonist, is a canny, blunt, vulgar, persuasive con man who easily takes advantage of the naïve Howard Brompart Dersingham and brings financial ruin to the firm of Twigg & Dersingham, dealers in veneer and inlays for furniture makers. Returning to England after a long absence, Golspie is looking for an outlet for his inexpen-

sive wood products from the Baltic area. He is intrigued by the Angel Pavement address of Dersingham's firm, descends upon the unsuspecting group, and literally takes charge. Demanding, and getting, his commissions in advance, everything Golspie does affects the lives of those connected with the firm for good, at first, and finally evil. Medium in height, powerfully built, nearly bald, Golspie has thick bushy eyebrows and a huge drooping mustache, and he repels and attracts simultaneously.

Howard Brompart Dersingham, in his late thirties, is the owner, by inheritance, of Twigg & Dersingham, a firm slowly failing primarily because of his incompetence. He is a poor product of the English public school system; Dersingham's greed, gullibility, and ineptness make easy Golspie's destruction of the company.

Mrs. "Pongo" Dersingham, his wife, in her early thirties, the mother of two young children. She pretends to live an exciting and full social life but in fact is rather dull. She does create an optimistic outlook at the end, seeing hope in the financial disaster her husband has created.

Harold Turgis, in his early twenties, is the junior clerk in the firm. A sallow, shallow, poorly dressed, physically unattractive young man, he dreams of romance, spawned mostly through films and magazines, and fantasizes about romantic interludes with beautiful women. He meets Lena Golspie, who teases, torments, frustrates, then dismisses him. He tries, in a fit of anger, to kill her, but he is as unsuccessful at that as he is at most things. Like the others, he loses his job as the firm fails.

Lena Golspie, the young, very attractive daughter of James Golspie. She is a flirt, a spendthrift, a well-traveled and popular young lady, whose main characteristics are selfishness and a disregard of others' feelings.

Herbert Norman Smeeth, fiftyish, is the cashier and senior clerk of the firm. Apprehensive by nature and conservative by habit, he is continually concerned about his and his family's future financial status. The temporary business success brought about by Golspie only slightly modifies his attitude, a cautious approach to life and business not shared by his family or his employer.

Edie Smeeth, his wife, in her early forties, has two grown children and an obnoxious cousin, Fred Mitty, who irritates her husband. The eternal optimist, she sees a hopeful future despite the firm's failure.

George Smeeth, age twenty, their son, a mechanic. He lives a sort of relaxed life that Herbert Smeeth cannot understand.

Edna Smeeth, eighteen, their daughter. She lives for films and cannot hold a job because of her inability to resist complaining.

Lilian Matfield, in her late twenties, is the typist for the firm of Twigg & Dersingham. Aloof and cold to her fellow workers, she dominates them all, even though she is relatively new to the firm. She lives at the Burpenfield Club, a residence for working girls and women; her relationships with her fellow boarders reveals much about her thinking. Incurably romantic, a dreamer of perfection, she is at first annoyed by Golspie, then fascinated by him. She dates him but refuses to spend a weekend at the coast with him. She later agrees to go, only to be left waiting in Victoria Station as he sails for South America.

Poppy Sellers, age twenty, is hired as an assistant typist when the business expands under Golspie's direction. She shows an interest in Harold Turgis and is probably his salvation as the novel ends.

Stanley Poole, a fifteen-year-old office boy at Twigg & Dersingham who fantasizes about aviation adventures and about becoming a detective so he can "shadder" people.

Mrs. Pelumpton, Turgis' landlady, is short, broad, constantly busy, and much taken by her own sacrifices in an exasperating world. She is, however, kind to Turgis.

Mr. Pelumpton, her husband, is a garrulous, rheumatic old busybody who deals in second-hand, thirdhand, and fourthhand goods. He frequently offers Turgis advice.

Mr. Walter Pearson and
Mrs. Walter Pearson, friends and neighbors of the Dersinghams. Mr. Pearson is retired from business in Singapore.

Miss Verever, Mrs. Dersingham's mother's cousin, is a forty-five-year-old, acid-tongued professional virgin.

T. Benenden, Smeeth's tobacconist at Angel Pavement, warns Smeeth about the future. At the hospital after being hit by an automobile, he learns that his injuries are the least of his health problems. Smeeth visits him and is shocked by what he sees and hears.

Fred Mitty, Mrs. Smeeth's cousin, a loud, brash, self-proclaimed comic. His antics infuriate Herbert Smeeth and amuse almost no one.

William H. Holland, Jr.

ANGELS FALL

Author: Lanford Wilson (1937-   )
Type of work: Play
Time of action: The 1980's
First produced: 1982

Father William Doherty, a sixty-five-year-old mission priest, who controls his flock with wit, deception, and persistent hope to elevate their lives. He displays a brittle, self-effacing humor, masking a strong will that results in his major conflict with Don Tabaha. A romantic who is fond of quoting romantic verse such as from the "Highwayman," Father Doherty sees the world as transitory and man by nature as good; he has always maintained a "willing suspension of disbelief" about his life's role that makes him sympathetic with artists. These attitudes allow him to dismiss nuclear catastrophes that occur a few miles away. His great fault is his vanity in wanting Don, his surrogate son, to follow him in his mission.

Don Tabaha, a half-Indian in his mid-twenties, who was reared by his aunt, the mission's caretaker, and Father Doherty. Don is split in half by more than his racial background. While realizing his duty is to help the American Indians as their doctor, he is also aware that he could venture into the city as a research specialist. To complicate matters, Don has a love/hate relationship with Father Doherty, his father figure. All this tension has made Don surly. Yet he exhibits a natural inclination to doctor: He tries to go to the mine to treat the injured; he correctly diagnoses Niles Harris' hypoglycemia; and he warns Zappy about getting arthritis from lying on the floor. His name, Tabaha, means "by-the-river" in Navajo; it fits Don, who is at a major crossing point in his life between duty to those he loves and self-fulfillment.

Niles Harris, a fifty-six-year-old neurotic art historian and professor from Rhode Island on his way to a private sanatorium in Arizona. Niles Harris' wit is only matched by Father Doherty's, his counterpart in many respects. Borrowing from Samuel Taylor Coleridge, Harris, however, announces early in the play that he has lost his ability to continue a "willing suspension of disbelief." He also quotes Blaise Pascal in French that makes him sound almost pedantic if it were not for his own self-deprecation. While he says that the source for his despair is his lost faith in his writing and teaching, later in the play he reveals that he suffered a severe loss when his brightest student committed suicide. Niles Harris shares Father Doherty's fault of investing his vanity in a protégé. By the play's end, Niles Harris appears improved as a result of Don Tabaha's ministrations and his argument with Father Doherty

47

over Don Tabaha's decision that allows him insight into his own problems.

Vita Harris, the thirty-year-old, strikingly handsome wife of Niles Harris, and, true to her first name, a life source for Niles. She helps him to cope with his anguish in a quiet way that counteracts the abrasiveness of the other characters. Vita comments on the actions of the others but does not judge them. Rather, she shares Father Doherty's view that the world is transitory and that such problems as nuclear disasters and disposing of her dead father's many antiques are not on the same level of importance as saving Niles's sanity or rebelling against the status quo. Vita was Niles's student and now is a writer of children's books, so she understands both sides of the debate between Father Doherty and Niles Harris. At the end, Vita, a lapsed Catholic, remains to hear Mass.

Marion Clay, an attractive art gallery owner in her early forties. She is undergoing a major change in her life because of the death of her artist husband, Branch. Unlike Niles or Don, Marion handles change without the problem of betraying her calling. Always the realist, she encourages others but knows that her career is to be their caretaker. Her affair with Zappy is almost motherly. Marion Clay is as basic as her last name implies but with a dignity that Father Doherty admires. Like Vita, Marion offers support to others who need it without claim of return, because she has sure faith in herself and her calling.

Salvatore "Zappy" Zappala, a twenty-one-year-old tennis pro and Marion Clay's lover. At first, Zappy appears to be the comic relief to the play. Nervous and hypochondriac, he goes into a near faint when Don is relating the illnesses that the American Indians get. Fear of drinking the local water forces him to drink a thermos of martinis and get progressively drunk. Living up to the meaning of his first name, Salvatore, he supplies the saving revelations in the play. Because of his radio, he informs everyone on the status of the uranium mine disaster and the road's accessibility; further, he supplies a vivid example for Father Doherty's lesson on vocation by narrating his discovery of natural talent to play tennis. Zappy is Don's counterpart to the degree that he is following his calling without a quandary.

Richard Stoner

ANGLE OF REPOSE

Author: Wallace Stegner (1909-   )
Type of work: Novel
Time of action: The late 1860's to 1970
First published: 1971

Lyman Ward, a retired University of California history professor and past winner of the Bancroft Prize. Lyman, in his late fifties and suffering from a degenerative bone disease that confines him to a wheelchair, has been abandoned by his adulterous wife, Ellen Hammond Ward. To pass the time, he begins researching the personal history of his grandparents, Oliver Ward and Susan Burling Ward, who spent most of their adult lives in the American West, his academic speciality. He is extremely opinionated, and his attitudes toward the social experiments of the 1960's could not be more negative. He begins with a strong bias against his grandmother, who probably also committed adultery. Lyman is a protagonist and also the novel's narrator; during the telling of the multigenerational saga, he encounters much evidence that exposes his need for self-serving conclusions. He finds that history challenges him to be a more sympathetic and forgiving human being than the subjects of his study: He must consider allowing his estranged wife Ellen to return.

Susan Burling Ward, an Easterner and a magazine illustrator with ambitions to be an artist. Born in 1848 and reared in a small New York town, she fails to attract an aristocratic New York City husband and so marries Oliver Ward, a mining engineer, and accompanies him to California, Mexico, Colorado, Idaho, and other parts of the West. Her snobbishness and desire to return to the East prevent her from judging her husband by criteria other than those of New York City salons. After her dreams of wealth and gentility clash repeatedly with the realities of their married life, she considers leaving, and at the very least flirts with Frank Sargent, one of Oliver's assistants. After several separations, she returns to the marriage, but it has degenerated into a kind of truce, and it never improves.

Oliver Ward, an engineer and a practical visionary. Initially, he is for Lyman the bearer of all virtues, a strong, energetic man too large to tolerate the conventional social scene of the East and not sympathetic to its economics. He is a builder, not an exploiter. He has the knack for thinking "big ideas twenty years ahead of their time," such as a formula for cement or an irrigation scheme too large for private funding. His principles cost him several jobs, but his skills earn the respect of experts such as John Wesley Powell and Clarence King. His stubbornness, however, does not allow him to be a sufficiently sympathetic husband, and in Lyman's speculation, the Oliver-Susan marriage was loveless from 1890 until their deaths almost fifty years later.

Shelly Rasmussen, a young woman hired for the summer of 1970 to care for Lyman and to act as his scribe. Shelly is a young and candid California woman of the 1960's, ultraliberal, and a constant foil to Lyman. Her impertinent questions expose many of Lyman's contradictions and biases, and her politics elicit much preaching from him.

Augusta Drake, a New York City socialite and friend of Susan Ward. Augusta is Susan's ideal: Eastern, wealthy, and polished. The rather stuffy letters she sends Augusta from the West provide Lyman with much evidence for his historical narrative.

Frank Sargent, an assistant to Oliver Ward at the Idaho irrigation project. Young and handsome, Frank is for Susan a beautiful compromise between masculine energy and social grace. He kills himself after the drowning of the Wards' daughter Agnes and confirms for Oliver the suspicion of adultery.

Rodman Ward, a sociology professor and the son of Lyman and Ellen. A cocky and ironic man, Rodman finds his father hopelessly out of touch. His sociological methods, both personal and academic, define for Lyman the superficiality of the 1960's.

Ollie Ward, Lyman's father. Born in 1877, he grows up to be a bitter man, alienated by the Eastern education to which Susan sent him. He returns the favor by taking no part in the rearing of Lyman himself.

Ellen Hammond Ward, Lyman's estranged wife. Ellen, a shadowy presence, has run off with the surgeon who amputated Lyman's leg. In the end, she seeks a reconciliation and presents Lyman with what he sees as the ultimate test for his moral philosophy: Can he be a better man than his grandfather?

Kerry Ahearn

ANGLO-SAXON ATTITUDES

Author: Angus Wilson (1913-   )
Type of work: Novel
Time of action: The late 1950's
First published: 1956

Gerald Middleton, a retired Oxford professor of medieval history and author of the definitive study of Canute. Middleton, despite the respect of many of his peers, considers himself to be a personal and professional failure and lives in a state of mild depression. His conscience forces him to make a series of decisions that set him in search of truth and revitalize him as a man and as a historian. Though ultimately successful professionally, he fails to rebuild meaningful relationships with his family.

Ingeborg Middleton, Gerald's wife, whom he married when he was turned down by Dollie. Tall, of ample figure, she likes to be surrounded by gaiety. She tries to stage-manage things and people around her and demands affection from her family. Inge ignores events and other things that she finds unpleasant, including an affair between Gerald and Dollie.

Robin Middleton, the eldest son of Gerald and Inge. He is a company director of the family firm from which Gerald and the rest of the family derive much of their wealth. He is unhappy in his marriage to the social-climbing Marie-Hélène, who is a Catholic and will not consider a divorce. He is carrying on an affair with his brother John's secretary, Elvira Portway.

John Middleton, the younger son of Gerald and Inge. He is a radio celebrity and journalist with political ambitions. John is making a name for himself in conducting an exposé of the persecution of a small-market gardener by the civil service. John is homosexual and develops a relationship with Larrie Rourke, an Irishman with a criminal background. John's secretary, Elvira Portway, tries to get Gerald to bring John to his senses, but Gerald fails. Rourke, on the run from the police, goes to France, with John accompanying him. A car crash kills Larrie and causes John to lose a leg.

Dollie Stokesay, née **Armstrong,** wife of Gilbert Stokesay, an essayist and poet. Gilbert was a ruthless Nietzschean who exulted in the outbreak of World War I, in which he was killed in action. Dollie, who had rejected Gerald's suit because she found him too solemn, does have an affair with him but then drops out of his life until he looks her up as part of his investigation of the Melpham dig. The two get along well, and while a permanent relationship is out of the question there is likelihood of a continuing close friendship.

Sir Edgar Iffley, president of the Historical Society of Medievalists and a friend of Gerald Middleton. He has been urging Middleton to accept the general editorship of a new series of books on medieval history, which Middleton has been reluctant to do. Middleton's decision to accept the post is tied in with his determination to discover the truth about Melpham and represents a turning point in his life and career. Iffley supports Middleton's challenge to the authenticity of the Melpham find.

Professor Lionel Stokesay, deceased at the time of the book's action but an important figure in the earlier events which Middleton is trying to unravel. He was Regius Professor of English History at Oxford and Gerald's tutor. He was also responsible for the Melpham dig and, too eager to accept the authenticity of the pagan idol that it turns out his son planted. When he discovered the truth he concealed it to protect his son's memory.

Canon Reginald Portway, the local clergyman and antiquarian who was involved with Professor Stokesay in the Melpham dig. His granddaughter is Elvira Portway, who is John Middleton's secretary and Robin Middleton's mistress. Portway had doubts about the authenticity of the Melpham find, but had not made them public. A discovery of a conscience stricken letter which Portway had sent to Lionel Stokesay is the final proof Gerald needs that the find was a fraud.

Francis J. Bremer

ANIMAL FARM

Author: George Orwell (Eric Arthur Blair, 1903-1950)
Type of work: Novel
Time of action: The mid-twentieth century
First published: 1945

Mr. Jones, the owner of Manor Farm. After getting drunk on Midsummer's Eve, Mr. Jones fails to return in time to feed his animals. They have been thinking about rebellion anyway, and they take this opportunity to chase out Mr. Jones, Mrs. Jones, and the human farm workers. In his ineptness, he is analogous to the Czar of Russia, who was unable to hold Russia together during the stress of World War I.

Old Major, previously exhibited as Willingdon Beauty, he is the prize boar whose dream inspires the Animalist Revolution on Manor Farm. Modeled on Vladimir Lenin, Old Major is highly respected in the barnyard, a capable orator, and an uncompromising ideologue for the Animalist cause. He dies in his sleep before the rebellion can take place.

Snowball, a young boar whose chief rival is Napoleon. Snowball is modeled on Leon Trotsky and so represents brains and organizational ability rather than brute force. It is Snowball, for example, who writes the Seven Commandments on the barnyard wall, who has the idea of building the windmill, and who studies the books left behind by Mr. Jones to see what practical benefit he can extract from them. Like Trotsky, Snowball is exiled after the Revolution and is falsely made out to be the chief villain of Animal Farm.

Napoleon, a young boar who ousts Snowball and assumes complete power over the other animals. While Snowball is studying human science, Napoleon trains a litter of dogs to become his secret police force. Napoleon corresponds to Joseph Stalin, who ousted Trotsky after the death of Lenin, and who then led bloody purges against possible and imagined dissenters.

Squealer, also a young boar. Squealer is the most clever with language and is Napoleon's propagandist and chief misinformation officer. He is said to be able to turn black into white, meaning that he can persuade most animals of that which is patently false.

Boxer, a cart horse who always works hard. His two mottos are "Napoleon is always right" and "I will work harder." When he gets a split hoof, he is sent off to the glue factory, though Squealer claims he is sent to a hospital. He is good friends with Benjamin.

Clover, a maternal, hard-working cart horse. Boxer and Clover are the most faithful disciples of the pigs who run Animal Farm. They are not intelligent, and so they are easily fooled by Napoleon and Squealer. Boxer and Clover represent both the main strengths and weaknesses of the working class.

Benjamin, a cynical donkey. He alone among Animal Farm animals is not fooled by Squealer's lies. Benjamin is not exactly an intellectual but rather represents the sort of barnyard wisdom that prefers not to announce itself publicly. Benjamin, however, cries out when Boxer is taken to the glue factory.

Mollie, a young foolish mare. She cannot forget the niceties of farm life that were lost with the Revolution. She misses decorative ribbons and the occasional lump of sugar. She runs away to a farm where she is pampered.

Moses, a raven who claims the existence of Sugarcandy Mountain. He is a spy for Mr. Jones and, in his insistence on otherworldly rewards, appears to represent institutionalized religion.

Mr. Pilkington, a human enemy of Animal Farm who comes to do business with the animals.

Frederick, a farmer from Pinchfield. Although an enemy of the farm, he comes to buy leftover timber. He pays with forged currency. Frederick represents Adolf Hitler, who, despite much distrust, formed the Non-Aggression Pact with the Soviet Union and then broke it.

John Whalen-Bridge

ANNE OF THE THOUSAND DAYS

Author: Maxwell Anderson (1888-1959)
Type of work: Play
Time of action: 1526-1536
First produced: 1948

Anne Boleyn, mistress and, later, wife of King Henry VIII; she was executed in 1536. Anne is first seen in the Tower of London, awaiting death; her life with Henry is then told in flashbacks. Anne, in 1526 a not altogether innocent girl, is passionately in love with Lord Percy, Duke of Northumberland, to whom she has engaged herself, but she has attracted the attention of Henry, who separates the lovers. Embittered by his actions, she denounces the king's person and talents. Yet, her world empty with the loss of her lover, her parents applying pressure, Anne allows herself to be drawn to Henry, although she arrogantly refuses to go the way of her sister, her reputation stained and her children illegitimate. Anne demands marriage, believing that Henry cannot meet this demand because he is already married to Katharine of Aragon. When Henry seeks an annulment for that marriage, Anne is flattered by the length to which Henry will go to win her. When Henry makes her his queen, she surrenders completely, denouncing her new power and status and pleading only for Henry's love. Yet, this admission only causes Henry's love for her to wane; he increasingly turns his attention to Jane Seymour, who, like Anne earlier, is not easily won. Threatened and insecure, Anne grows more strident in her demands. Before she will try for another child with Henry, she insists on the death of Sir Thomas More and those others who will not accept Henry as the supreme religious authority in England and who deny the legitimacy of their marriage. Henry meets this final demand, but their son is born dead, and Anne thus loses her hold over Henry. He allows false charges of adultery to be brought against her, and Anne falls victim to the bloodshed that she herself, as she recognizes in the Tower, has let loose upon the land.

Henry VIII, King of England from 1509 to 1547. Henry has been attracted to all three Boleyn women: Elizabeth, later mother of Anne and Mary, and both daughters. Elizabeth remembers him as innocent and naïve; Mary recalls him as insecure, unwilling to court any woman who might reject him. By the time Henry pursues Anne, he has been corrupted by his own power, mistaking his own will for God's; he speaks of courting favor among his people but, in reality, derives pleasure from imposing his own will, whether upon his courtiers, his populace, or an unwilling woman. For Henry, the chase and capture are everything; to his courtiers, he admits that he sees no difference in this respect between deer and women. When Henry first courts Anne, this brutality is only latent within him, but her defiance and the challenges she sets him bring that brutality to the surface. Once Henry has proven capable of murdering friends such as Sir Thomas More to gain Anne, he proves equally capable of murdering Anne to gain a new love. Henry's excuses (England's need for a male heir, God's wrathful judgment on his mar-

52

riages to Katherine and Anne) are merely that, excuses that only superficially conceal the profound will to power that, in middle age, is the core of his character.

Cardinal Thomas Wolsey, lord chancellor. Wolsey compromises his religious duties to keep Henry's favor and to enrich himself at the expense of the church. He arranges Henry's liaison with Anne but is horrified at their proposed marriage. He is undermined by Thomas Cromwell, who has learned amorality from him, and fails in body and spirit when he turns his palace over to Anne.

Thomas Cromwell, adviser to Wolsey, later

to Henry. Admittedly without scruples, Cromwell gains Henry's favor by arranging the marriage with Anne but is equally willing to arrange her death, obtaining evidence against her through torture.

Sir Thomas More, statesman, author, and, later, saint. More dies rather than renounce his allegiance to Rome, confident in the faith that, in the long run, an ultimate justice governs the universe, bringing men and women the destinies they merit; his faith is validated by the fall of Wolsey and the death of Anne.

Betty Richardson

ANNIVERSARIES
From the Life of Gesine Cresspahl

Author: Uwe Johnson (1934-1984)
Type of work: Novel
Time of action: 1931-1967 and August, 1967, to August, 1968
First published: Jahrestage: Aus dem Leben von Gesine Cresspahl, 1970-1983 (English translation, 1975; *Anniversaries II,* 1987)

Gesine (gā·zēńə) **Cresspahl,** born in 1933 in the province of Mecklenburg, Germany, emigrated to New York in 1961 and has worked in a bank there since 1964. She lives in a modest apartment with her ten-year-old daughter Marie, with whom she conducts frank conversations about her own and her parents' lives, duly committed to a diary which extends from August, 1967, to August, 1968, and which mingles the present with the past. From 1939 to 1945, she underwent the normal education of a German child under the Nazis. Then, after 1945, she spent more than three years in the Russian zone of postwar Germany, where she studied diligently after the Russians arrested her father, having learned to behave cautiously. Nevertheless, she clashes painfully with a malicious bureaucracy. From Halle University, in the GDR, she flees to West Germany, where Marie is born. The child's father, Jakob, an East German railway official, is killed before they can be married, and Gesine, resolving to stay unmarried, emigrates. In New York, unhappy memories of her German past make

her an impassioned opponent of the Vietnam War and of racial prejudice. Yet, for all her enlightened views, she spares no expense in sending Marie to a Catholic private school to avoid the squalor of public education. She finds consolation in the honest, old-fashioned truthfulness of *The New York Times* (which she calls "Auntie"). The paper is full of reports of the Vietnam War and of violence in American cities (including the death of Martin Luther King). This, and New York, confirm Gesine in her dislike of violence, but she is growing attached to New York, influenced by Marie's enthusiasm. Nevertheless, she discusses her life and recent German history with a highly critical Marie. She is making good progress in her bank career, she rejects D. E.'s offers of marriage and earns the approbation of her unpleasant boss. She is learning Czech to add to her other languages with a view to working in Prague.

Marie Cresspahl, the daughter of Gesine, born July, 1957, in West Germany and brought to New York in 1961. At first, she hates the city but now would not live anywhere else and even dislikes speaking German or going to foreign restaurants. She wears a Vietnam War button in her conservative school and looks after a token black girl enrolled from a nearby slum, but finds the task onerous and takes part in a wild Halloween party to avoid having to invite the girl home. Nevertheless, enlightened principles prevail, so that she and Gesine do take the girl in for a short period. Marie's teachers are disturbed by her vehement opposition to the Vietnam War, which leads her to address an inopportune and gravely naïve question on the matter to the president of Gesine's bank. A polite child, she is highly critical of Gesine's and Germany's past.

Heinrich Cresspahl, Gesine's father, born in 1888, a cabinet-maker from Jerichow, Mecklenburg, and, for a time, the manager of a workshop in Richmond, near London. He meets his future wife, Lisbeth, on a trip to Mecklenburg and ends by agreeing to a church wedding and settling in Jerichow when Gesine is born in 1933, in a Germany celebrating Adolf Hitler's rise to power. He joins the Nazi Party although he dislikes the regime and had, while in England, helped German refugees. His behavior seems at times unorthodox: He consorts with the Jewish veterinarian and, after his wife's death in 1938, makes an extended tour of Denmark and England, where he has an illegitimate child. During the war, he spies for the British, reporting aircraft movements. He becomes mayor of Jerichow for a time during the British, then Russian occupations. He falls foul of the Russian authorities, is arrested, and returns broken in health to die in 1962. There is talk of naming a street in his honor.

Dietrich Erichson ("D.E."), born in 1928, the son of a baker in Mecklenburg, Germany, is now a professor of physics and chemistry in the United States and does secret work for the U.S. Air Force. He arrived in the United States in 1960, after defying the GDR authorities, and met Gesine in a refu-

gee camp. A skilled technician and a mediocre lecturer, he lives with his mother in a former farmhouse in New Jersey, where Gesine and Marie visit him. He no longer regards his German past as reality. He wishes to marry Gesine and is liked by Marie. He finally gives up his courtship and is killed in a plane crash in the course of duty.

Lisbeth Cresspahl, née **Papenbrock,** Gesine's mother from a well-to-do Mecklenburg family with aristocratic pretensions. She follows Heinrich to England and is anxious to please him. After the marriage, however, she finds herself unable to settle down or to discuss her difficulties. She returns to Jerichow for the birth of her child, and Heinrich eventually joins her permanently. Uneasy in her conscience, she attempts suicide by drowning and even seems willing to let Gesine drown in a barrel (her father rescues her, saying nothing). Lisbeth dies in mysterious circumstances in a fire in 1938.

Hilde Paepke, née **Papenbrock,** Lisbeth's sister. She has married a shiftless lawyer who squanders her dowry. Her three children are Gesine's favorite cousins, and Heinrich likes her. Though no friend to the Nazis, she dies with her children while fleeing from the advancing Russians in 1945.

Louise Papenbrock, Lisbeth's mother. Fanatically religious (she demands more fervor in the pastor's sermons), she rules her family, allowing her husband a regular supply of kümmel (caraway-flavored liqueur). When Lisbeth returns to Jerichow, she is ready to receive her, excluding Heinrich.

Albert Papenbrock, Lisbeth's father, a shrewd businessman with aristocratic claims he cannot sustain. He refuses to help his son Horst with his Nazi stormtroopers and unexpectedly welcomes Heinrich as a son-in-law.

Horst Papenbrock, brother to Lisbeth, born in 1900. After his brother Robert, a violent man, vanishes in 1914, he has hopes of inheriting his father's estate. He is a loyal member of the local Nazi Party and is secretly engaged to another member. According to rumor, he has had a hand in local atrocities. He tries unsuccessfully to display authority as manager of his father's granary. His father sends him to Brazil to look for his brother and to get him out of mischief. He is quieter on his return. He dies at Stalingrad.

Robert Papenbrock, brother to Lisbeth, Albert's son and heir. He leaves home abruptly but returns in 1935 to become a Gestapo official (or is he an impostor?). During the war, as a "special leader" he is responsible for atrocities in the Ukraine. He turns up in the Cresspahl house after the war, leaves when ordered, and escapes to West Germany.

Jakob Abs, Marie's father, a refugee, with his mother, in Cresspahl's house in 1945, who later becomes a railway dispatcher. After Heinrich's arrest, the mother looks after Gesine, helped by Jakob, whose strength combined with gentleness are remarkable in the postwar corruption and brutality. Returning from a visit to Gesine in Düsseldorf, he is killed, before Marie is born, under mysterious circumstances while crossing a marshaling yard in East Germany.

Mrs. Ferwalter, a stockily built Ruthenian Jewish countrywoman, born in 1922, a former inmate of Mauthausen concentration camp, now living in New York. She is the first to befriend Gesine in New York and to admire her European manners. She is unable to sleep soundly and wears, Gesine imagines, a permanently disgusted expression.

Anita Grantlik (Anita the Red), a refugee from Eastern Europe of Polish-German origins and Gesine's schoolmate. She had been raped by a Russian soldier at the age of eleven, condemned to fieldwork, and abandoned by her father, a policeman. She succeeds in becoming a Russian interpreter and in earning a new Swedish bicycle. She flees to the West and still corresponds with Gesine.

Karsch, a figure from the past of Gesine and D. E., now working for the United Nations and writing a book on the American Mafia. On a visit to New York from Milan, he is kidnapped but is rescued through Gesine's and D. E.'s efforts.

Annie Fleury, née **Killainen,** a friend to Gesine who lives in Vermont with her husband, a translator for the French. She abruptly leaves him, taking their three children to live for a time in Gesine's apartment, explaining that she has quarreled with him over the Vietnam issue.

Uwe Johnson, who makes a brief appearance addressing the Jewish American Congress in New York on postwar Germany, with Gesine in the audience. His reception is unfriendly.

W. Gordon Cunliffe

ANOTHER COUNTRY

Author: James Baldwin (1924-1987)
Type of work: Novel
Time of action: The 1950's
First published: 1962

Rufus Scott, a jazz drummer. Handsome, talented, and black, Rufus is the pivotal character in the novel, although he commits suicide at the end of the first chapter. He meets his girlfriend, Leona, a white woman from the South, while playing a gig. Their unstable relationship is torn apart by racial and other tensions between them, however, and he beats her, until his friend, Vivaldo Moore, intercedes. Rufus' ensuing depression results in his suicide: He walks out onto the George Washington Bridge and jumps.

Rufus' struggle initiates the questions the novel explores about the pain of sexual and racial identity.

Vivaldo Moore, an aspiring writer. An Italian-American, and Rufus' closest friend, Vivaldo is haunted by the thought that he could have been a closer, more sensitive friend to Rufus. He falls in love with Ida Scott, Rufus' younger sister, and she eventually moves in with him. When she begins an affair with Steve Ellis, a television producer, he tries to ignore it, but eventually takes some solace in a one-night affair with Eric Jones, a white Southern man with whom Rufus once had a brief, stormy affair. At the end of the novel, Ida and Vivaldo commit themselves emotionally to each other, but it is not clear that they can overcome the racial and emotional forces that have been tearing them apart.

Ida Scott, Rufus' very attractive younger sister and an aspiring singer. When Rufus dies, Ida promises herself never to let anyone take advantage of her emotionally the way she thinks people always treated her brother. Though she genuinely loves Vivaldo, she is determined to be successful as a singer, and she has an affair with Steve Ellis, a television producer she meets at a party hosted by Cass and Richard Silenski the same night she and Vivaldo first sleep together. Angry at herself for her behavior, and at Vivaldo for putting up with it, but also for not seeing the racial and social forces driving her and that led her brother to kill himself, she berates Vivaldo often, before finally ending her affair with Ellis and discussing her harsh feelings and actions with Vivaldo.

Clarissa Silenski, called **Cass,** a middle-class housewife. Sensitive to other people, but emotional, she begins to feel estranged from her husband, Richard Silenski, a writer who is becoming financially successful, while remaining artistically unsuccessful. In her frustration, she initiates an affair with Eric Jones, though she knows he prefers men. When her husband accuses her of having an affair with Vivaldo, she denies it, but confesses to her affair with Eric. He leaves, threatening to divorce her and take the children, Paul and Michael Silenski.

Eric Jones, an actor. A homosexual who grew up in the South, Eric is returning to New York from France, to which he had fled in the wake of his affair with Rufus. Lonely for his lover Yves, Eric agrees to an affair with Cass, assuming that it will only last until Yves arrives from France. The night Cass tells Richard about her affair with Eric, the same night Ida decides to stop seeing Steve Ellis, Eric and Vivaldo have a mutually fulfilling sexual encounter, which they both understand is only for one night.

Richard Silenski, a writer. Vivaldo's one-time English teacher, and an aspiring but not very talented writer for years, Richard finally becomes somewhat successful writing mysteries. Richard's involvement with this suspect type of success leads Cass to her affair with Eric. He leaves Cass when he learns about her affair with Eric and threatens to win custody of their sons.

Yves, Eric's French lover. A boy prostitute in his youth, Yves feels jealous of Eric when he goes back to America but hopes their lives will be able to continue together. The novel ends with Eric greeting Yves at the airport in New York, amid much doubt for both of them about what their future together holds.

Steve Ellis, a television producer. Sleazy, opportunistic, and self-justifying, he believes in Ida's talent as a singer but also wants to take advantage of her sexually, at least partly to assert his power over not only her, but also Vivaldo, who has snubbed Ellis on several occasions.

Leona, Rufus' lover. A divorcée who lost the custody of her son, she has moved up north to start a new life. Rejected and beaten by Rufus, she has a breakdown and is committed to Bellevue, until she is released in the custody of her brother, who takes her back down south.

Thomas J. Cassidy

ANOTHER LIFE

Author: Yury Trifonov (1925-1981)
Type of work: Novel
Time of action: The early 1970's
First published: Drugaya zhizn', 1975 (English translation, 1983)

Olga Vasilievna, a research biologist, recently widowed. After the early death of her husband, Sergei Afanasievich, she reconstructs by way of flashbacks their life together in an attempt to understand what went wrong and to assuage her guilt feelings about her husband's demise. In the end, she realizes that she is not to blame, that their marriage was doomed to failure through forces beyond their control, and that they both had unknowingly yearned for a life other than their own, which eventually led to misunderstandings and the tragic end. Although she has many acquaintances and female friends, gets on well with people, and is not afraid of life's complexities, she finds that she is psychologically overly dependent on other people and is therefore unable to attain happiness by living independently and by saving her husband from disappointments and untimely death.

Sergei Afanasievich, Olga's husband, a brilliant historian who dies prematurely at age forty-two without accomplishing much. Capricious and of unstable character, lacking dedication and willpower, always in trouble at the institute, he nevertheless knows how to make friends, especially among women, and ostensibly how to keep his marriage from falling apart. His main problem is a strong dependence on his mother's opinion and moods, as he feels a compulsion to explain and justify himself to her. He adores his mother and stands in awe before her for "making history" during the Revolution. Because of his subservience to his mother and his fear of disappointing her high expectations of him, he is ashamed to admit failure and to make necessary changes in his behavior. Instead of accepting Olga's help, he walks away from difficulties whenever they threaten to overwhelm him. He never finishes his dissertation, spending most of the time pursuing his theory about the unbroken thread running from generation to generation, which manifests itself in a seething, bubbling urge to dissent. While it is true that the society in which he lives saps his talents and thwarts his desire to be different, an emotional ineptitude and a compulsion to do only what pleases him dooms him to destruction as it did his ancestors.

Alexandra Prokofievna, Sergei's mother, a retired lawyer. Having chosen to live with Sergei and Olga, she wreaks havoc upon their life through her compulsive need to domineer. Once a typist in the Red Army during the civil war, she is able to dominate her son because of his weak will, while Olga escapes her clutches; yet the end result is the same—the deterioration of their marriage and the early death of Sergei. At difficult moments she always assumes an air of dignified authority, by which she tries to make herself indispensable. She shows gross insensitivity toward her son's difficulties, as well as toward her daughter-in-law, blaming her for Sergei's death.

Irinka, Sergei's and Olga's daughter. As a teenager, she is caught in the battle of wills among her mother, father, and grandmother. Having inherited many traits from her father (pliancy, instability, secretiveness, occasional thoughtlessness, and insensitivity), she is nevertheless the true victim of the family disintegration, as she is torn between the will of her father and that of her grandmother, while her mother stands by helpless. After her father's death, she finds some rapport with her mother, yet both realize that valuable time has been lost.

Galina Yevgenievna, Olga's mother. Unable to have any influence upon her daughter's life, she spends her love and energy upon her second husband, with whom she achieves a remarkable symbiosis. She lives only for his problems and illnesses and has no time for anyone else.

Georgii Maximovich, Olga's stepfather, an artist. A kind and well-educated man, he was once an avant-garde painter, but now he has sacrificed his principles for the secure and profitable life of a mediocre landscape artist. In this way, he symbolizes the irrepar-

able loss for the art of his country and the world.

Gennady (Gena) Vitalevich Klimuk, Sergei's colleague. A typical social climber and bureaucrat, he is largely responsible for Sergei's demise by making his life miserable in the institute and by refusing to show any understanding for his old friend.

Vasa D. Mihailovich

ANTIGONE

Author: Jean Anouilh (1910-1987)
Type of work: Play
Time of action: c. 600-500 B.C.
First produced: 1944 (English translation, 1946)

Antigone (ăn•tǐ′gə•nē), the daughter of Oedipus and Jocasta, engaged to marry Haemon, son of King Creon and Queen Eurydice of Thebes. After Oedipus' death, his son Eteocles ascended to the throne, but after one year he broke an agreement with his brother Polynices to share power with him. This action provoked a civil war in which both brothers were killed. Creon then became king. He ordered that the body of Polynices not be buried in order to discourage further rebellion. Antigone realized that Creon's decree violated Greek religious law, which required that a body be buried before a soul could cross the River Styx. Were she to obey Creon's arbitrary law, Antigone would violate her religious beliefs. She risks her life in order to observe a higher moral code. Creon offers to spare her life if she promises not to try again to bury Polynices. Antigone refuses, however, to compromise her moral principles. He then condemns her to death. Antigone's death provokes the suicides of both Haemon and Eurydice.

Creon, brother to Oedipus and uncle to both Antigone and Ismene, a cynical dictator who demands blind obedience to his laws from others but grants absolute powers to himself. He affirms that social order has nothing to do with moral and political freedom. He treats Antigone condescendingly and does

not want to understand Antigone's refusal to compromise her moral beliefs. Antigone correctly predicts that his abuse of power will alienate Creon from his family and his subjects. After the suicides of his son, Haemon, and his wife, Eurydice, Creon is alone, but no one feels pity for him.

The Nurse, a middle-aged woman who has cared for Antigone for many years. She wants Antigone to be happy. She relates that Antigone left home very early in the morning, but she does not imagine that it was to bury Polynices. Like all the other characters, she cannot predict that the serious but vulnerable Antigone will risk her life in order to remain faithful to her religious beliefs.

Ismène (ĭs•mē′nē), Antigone's older sister, a vain and unsympathetic character. Ismène is excessively concerned with clothing and her physical appearance. She tells Antigone that young women should be indifferent to political and moral problems. Only marriage and social success are important to Ismène. Although she claims to love her sister, Ismène, like Creon, treats her condescendingly. Ismène's superficial arguments have no effect on Antigone.

Haemon, the son of Creon and Eurydice, a young adult. He and Antigone share a profound love for each other, and they look forward to having children together. When Haemon learns that Creon has condemned Antigone to death, he confronts his father. He rejects Creon's specious assertion that maturity requires Haemon to accept unjust and amoral laws. Like Antigone, Haemon adheres to a higher moral code. Near the end of this play, both Haemon and his mother Eurydice will commit suicide offstage.

The Chorus and **the Prologue,** roles traditionally interpreted by the same actor, comment regularly on the moral and psychologi-

cal significance of the actions in this tragedy. The chorus and the prologue express ethical reactions to Antigone's self-sacrifice and to the great suffering caused by Creon's abuse of power.

The three guards, basically decent people exploited by their military and political superiors. They do not understand why Creon is so adamant against burying Polynices. The guards carry out their orders to watch over Polynices' body out of their fear of Creon.

Edmund J. Campion

THE APES OF GOD

Author: Wyndham Lewis (1882-1957)
Type of work: Novel
Time of action: Spring, 1926
First published: 1930

Horace Zagreus, born **Follett,** between sixty and sixty-four, the tall albino and favorite grandnephew of Lady Fredigonde Follett. He takes up young men as companions and "genius" and instructs them in the philosophy of Pierpoint. Famous as a practical joker, he is employed by Lord Osmund to provide entertainment at his Lenten Freak Party. In phallic costume, he gathers Daniel Boleyn, Julius Ratner, and Archie Margolin to present a magic show. After the disastrous failure of the Vanish, he leads his followers out onto Lord Osmund's lawn, carrying a large door, where he plays a flute while his followers dance. He dismisses Dan as the cause of his troubles at the party and puts Margolin in place as his newest genius.

Daniel Boleyn, a dull-witted young Irishman of nineteen drifting about London and taken up as a "genius" by Horace Zagreus, who sends him to study the "apes of god." He is self-consciously very tall, impoverished, and easily baffled. He blushes frequently and weeps easily when he thinks Horace slights him, and his nose bleeds at inopportune times. Dressed to perform as a

Yogi in Horace's magic show at Lord Osmund's party, his trousers catch fire, and he has to change into a girl's frock. He gets drunk on champagne and ruins the Vanish act. After Horace dismisses him in favor of Archie Margolin, Dan wanders through the General Strike in London until he is retrieved by Michael for Melanie Blackwell in France.

Dick Whittingdon, age thirty-six and educated at Winchester and Sandhurst, he is the six-foot, two-inch, suntanned grandnephew of Lady Fredigonde and Sir James Follett. He competes with Horace Zagreus for approval and money from the Folletts, though not liked by Lady Fredigonde. Separated from his wife, he keeps a house called Grotian Walk with ten studios for his painting. He is a famous collector of whips.

Pierpoint, a painter turned philospher, from a prominent Welsh-Irish family. He never appears in the novel except by name but is the source of many persons' ideas, especially Horace Zagreus, his contemporary in age. His analysis of relationships of society with art and artists provides the notion of Apes of God as those wealthy persons who ape art and therefore trivialize its importance.

Julius Ratner, a special kind of "ape," he is a Jewish author and publisher with an obsession to analyze psychological complexes. He married an heiress before the war and settled in Chelsea, but she ran off with a lover, and he turned to publishing. He is a source of money for Horace, and he publishes for Pierpoint. He is costumed as a "Split Man" by Horace for the magic show at Lord Osmund's party, to produce the illusion of cutting him in half. During the Vanish act, he is knocked from the stage by Blackshirt, who intensely dislikes Ratner. In consequence, he is hurt and threatens legal action, though he dances on the door to the tune of Horace's flute.

Archibald (Archie) Margolin, a small, twenty-year-old Jewish youth from the slums of London's East End. Taken on by Horace Zagreus as one of his young geniuses, he accompanies the magic show to the party of Lord Osmund, where he spends most of his time flipping matchsticks at party guests. He subsequently displaces Dan Boleyn entirely as Horace's genius.

Lady Fredigonde Follett, the ninety-six-year-old great-aunt of Horace and Dick, and the wife of Sir James, she is glad to move her head on a body otherwise rigid as plaster. She fantasizes about her collection of caps. When Sir James dies, she tells Horace he can expect money from her and offers herself, in a scene of surrealistic madness, as his bride.

Matthew Plunkett, a small, middle-aged man with an obsessive interest in shells. He was psychoanalyzed in Zurich by a Dr. Frumpfsusan, who advised him to choose his friends small and learn how to bully. He walks through Bloomsbury to a pub for his midday snack before his assignation with Betty Bligh at his flat. He is accosted by Dan Boleyn, son of his Dublin cousin. Impatiently, Matthew allows him to rest in his apartment. He returns to meet Betty, fantasizes his sexual assault, and fails because Dan lies in the bed to which he carries Betty.

Mélanie Blackwell, a wealthy painter from St. Louis of Irish immigrant parents. She married an Irish landowner and lived on his estate before he died. A thin woman, older than Dan, she lives with her dogs in London studios. She tries to lure Dan away from Horace by babying him, undressing him, and putting him to bed. After Dan is dumped by Horace at the end, she sends Michael to bring him to her in Azay-le-Promis.

The Lesbian-Ape, the artist into whose studio Dan Boleyn accidentally stumbles. Dan is made to pose in the nude until he faints from shame; he is awakened by the sound of her and her friend Borstie laughing at him.

Lionel Kein (Li), a wealthy novelist of silly books, he has an obsessive interest in Marcel Proust. Beardless, but with a military mustache, he looks like a spectacled Sigmund Freud. He has known Horace Zagreus for seventeen years since they met in Venice, but, when Horace insults him and his wife at a dinner party, he orders Horace out and never to return.

Isabel Kein, the handsome wife of Lionel, she presides over a dinner party for seventeen guests, where she openly gossips about her own guests, including Horace.

Lord Osmund Willoughby Finnian Shaw, the middle-aged son of the Marquis of Balbriggan, whom he, his brother, and his sister call Cockeye. Above six feet tall, he is fat, shaped like a pelican with a goatlike profile. Author of free verse, plays, novelettes, and novels, he is the master-ape. He blames his father as one of the old men who sent young men off to the Great War, though Osmund only spend a fortnight in the trenches. He is host of the great Lenten Freak Party at his weekend country estate, Jays Mill Manor Farm.

Lord Phoebus, Osmund's six-foot, three-inch brother, who left Harrow to become a hussar but was too ill to go to the trenches in the Great War. He is the historian of the family. At the party, he shows childhood toys to guests.

Bertram Starr-Smith (Blackshirt), Pierpoint's political secretary and business manager. A young, dark-faced, solemn Welshman, he wears the costume of a Fascist Blackshirt to Lord Osmund's party, where he rescues Dan Boleyn from the advances of an old man. He kicks an old colonel in the rear, takes Dan to the American Bar, where he gets drunk, and displays the Finnian Shaw library. Because he is editing an anthology of postwar verse, the Finnian Shaws are anxious to please him.

Bridget, Lady Fredigonde's maid, who combs the lady's hair each morning and helps choose a cap.

Sir James Follett, ancient husband of Lady Fredigonde, he dislikes his wife of more than fifty years. He spends his time lifting heavy books and looking at tigers' heads in his library. He dies of a stroke.

Francis Dallas, a forty-year-old, tanned man with a mustache and wearing white spats. Once a favorite, he accosts Horace at the edge of Hyde Park.

Zulu Blades, of mixed race and black skin, he lives below Matthew Plunkett. He entertains many women night and day, arousing jealous hatred in Plunkett.

Betty Bligh, the bow-legged, four-foot, ten-inch companion chosen by Matthew Plunkett as therapy for his inferiority complex.

Michael, a small man who blows smoke through his nose. At thirty or thirty-nine, he is a Bolshevik who does odd jobs for Mélanie Blackwell.

Willie Service, an attractive, mustached homosexual, assigned by Horace to chauffeur Dan Boleyn. An avid fan of Edgar Wallace detective stories, he views the world as crime-ridden.

Mrs. Lochore, Julius Ratner's housekeeper, who enters some of his fantasies about himself as a great writer and publisher.

Siegfried Victor, a young, Oxford-bred man above six feet in height, with a handsome Greek profile. He sucks a black pipe. He is a business associate of Julius Ratner, planning an anthology with Pickwort to be called "Verse of the Under-Thirties."

Hedgepinshot Mandeville Pickwort, a small man with blond hair who sucks a pipe and is an Oxford colleague of Siegfried Victor.

Cubbs, with an adenoidish mouth and dreamy blue eyes, he is Dick Whittingdon's servant at Grotian Walk.

Bloggie, a midget Polish lesbian with money, she is a guest of Dick Whittingdon at Grotian Walk.

Richard, a small, bald millionaire renowned as a painter of sea pictures. He is a guest at Grotian Walk, where he examines Dick's paintings and disputes with his wife whether one of the paintings has too much red in it.

Jenny, Richard's wife and guest at Grotian Walk. She puffs cigarettes and discusses colors in Dick's paintings.

Clemmie Richmond, a large-nosed friend who visits Pammie Farnham at teatime; she drips liqueur onto her dress from a chocolate candy.

Pamela Farnham (Pammie), the hostess for tea in her Kensington flat. She entertains several guests, including Dan Boleyn, whom she insults as a thing made by Horace Zagreus.

Lady "Snotty" Briggs, one of Pammie Farnham's guests, she gossips about the notoriety of Horace Zagreus as a practical joker before the war.

David Novitsky, a Judeo-Russian, bearded guest at Pammie Farnham's tea. He is very sociable and the grinning opposite of Arthur Wildsmith.

Arthur Wildsmith, a guest of Pammie Farnham, he has a gray, goatlike face with eyeglasses. Detached and aloof, he is contemptuous of Novitsky's amiability.

Jimmie, a very young man of nineteen, he is the focus of attention at Pammie Farnham's tea. He takes up for Dan Boleyn when Pammie insults him.

Hassan, a tall, dark young man in a black jacket and black trousers, with plum-black eyes and long eyelashes. He is Lionel Kein's butler, speaks a deep cockney, and exudes a troubling perfume.

Kalman, a guest at the Keins' party, he sits next to Isabel and tells stories of a hardworking middle-aged journalist with a reputation for writing about youth. Kalman is an elderly man with yellow skin, a Charlie Chaplin mustache, a large nose, and thick lips. He is taunted by Horace Zagreus into a Socratic dialogue on the meaning of "eminence."

Horty, a Midwestern, American novelist at the Keins' dinner party, he sports sidewhiskers and writes about himself.

Vernede, a guest at the Keins' dinner party, he departs early. Small, stocky, demure and childlike, he wears an old-fashioned, loose bowtie. He dislikes Kein, who once promised and then failed to set him up in a bookshop.

Lady Robinia Finnian Shaw, the wife of Lord Osmund for two years, she is a musician. Five feet tall, she has a narrow, colorless face and flaxen hair. During the party she drifts about, staring distractedly at nothing.

Eustace Mulqueen, the six-foot, three-inch cousin of Lord Osmund, he stands beside Lord Phoebus behind Osmund during the dinner that begins the Lenten Freak Party. Otherwise he contributes little.

Lady Harriet Finnian Shaw, a sister of Lord Osmund and Lord Phoebus, she writes verse. She is about forty and very fashionable. She arrives late for the party with her companion Miss Dyott, but she contributes to the stories of old Cockeye.

Kanoot, or **Knut, The Finn,** a loudmouthed guest at Lord Osmund's party, he recites passages of French poetry by Nicolas Boileau until hushed by a bored Lord Osmund. Worn out with his recitations, he falls into a deep sleep.

Sib, an old woman veiled and muffled, she sits beside Lord Osmund to supply him with gossip. Her specialty is people from the wicked 1890's, including the Wildes, Beardsleys, and Whistlers.

Mrs. Bosun, a housekeeper/nanny for Lord Osmund's family, she finds a frock for Dan to wear after his costume is destroyed by fire. She rushes with a medicine chest to administer to Lord Osmund when she hears he is wounded.

Jonathan Bell, an author, costumed for Osmund's Party as "Democracy" from a masque by John Dryden. He talks with Ratner about complexes and making love with fat women.

Richard D. McGhee

THE APPLE IN THE DARK

Author: Clarice Lispector (1925-1977)
Type of work: Novel

Time of action: The late 1950's
First published: A maçã no escuro, 1961 (English translation, 1967)

Martim, a middle-aged statistician from São Paulo. A heavyset blue-eyed man, he is in hiding because he believes that he has killed his wife in a jealous rage. He hides out for two weeks in a nearly empty hotel in central Brazil that is occupied only by a German and a servant. When he thinks they have gone to report his presence to the police, he flees overland and finds a job doing manual labor on a small farm in exchange for board and room. He spends a long time on the farm, which is owned and run by Vitória. He is involved for a while with Ermelinda, Vitória's younger cousin. Most of the action takes place in Martim's mind, as he tries to understand who he is and how he relates to his circumstances.

Vitória, a tough woman in her fifties who inherited a farm from an aunt and uncle whom she had visited in childhood. She spent her youth caring for her father, and only after his death has she been free to choose to move out to the country and run the farm herself. The farm is an isolated one, and until Martim appears, Vitória has lived with only the company of her cousin Ermelinda, Francisco the hired man, and a mulatto woman cook with a small daughter. Attracted to Martim, Vitória is impelled to explain her life to him and, in the process, come to a better understanding of herself.

Ermelinda, a young woman from Rio de Janeiro who has come to live on her cousin Vitória's farm after being widowed three years before Martim appears. Her sensuous indolence and vague spiritualism are attributed to her bedridden childhood and consequent overindulgence. Ermelinda falls in love with Martim, is sexually involved with him for a time, then falls out of love and distances herself from him again. Opposite in personality from her cousin Vitória, who works very hard on the farm and continually barks out orders to Martim and Francisco, Ermelinda drifts about eating candied almonds, sentimental and idle, believing in her vague presentiments about the future.

Mary G. Berg

THE APPRENTICESHIP OF DUDDY KRAVITZ

Author: Mordecai Richler (1931-   )
Type of work: Novel
Time of action: The late 1940's
First published: 1959

David "Duddy" Kravitz, a Montreal-born Jewish teenager and second-generation Canadian. Motherless and growing up in the shadow of his favored elder brother Lennie, dark, nervous Duddy feels closest to his *zeyda* (grandfather), Simcha Kravitz, who early in Duddy's life admonishes him, "A man without land is nobody. Remember that, Duddel." Duddy works for material success and admiration by buying land in the growing resort area of the Laurentian mountains north of Montreal. His laudable goal is to provide a farm for his *zeyda* and various philanthropic benefits for the Jewish community. Duddy's more questionable values, derived from his bleak immediate environment and developed also as a defense against the anti-Semitism he encounters in the larger French- and English-Canadian society, lead him to pursue his goals with admirable perseverance, self-sacrifice, and zeal but also with deeply ingrained ruthlessness. By age nineteen, having weathered bankruptcy and a nervous breakdown, he has struggled, ingratiated, and cheated his way into being the sole owner of about 440 arpents of prime

Laurentian land, but at the cost of the love and respect of those few who have tried to give him the admiration and emotional security he craves. Instead, he has allied himself by choice and by deed with the moral bankrupts around him.

Simcha Kravitz, Duddy's grandfather, an immigrant Polish Jew and a shoemaker. A pious and scrupulously honest though unbending man, Simcha is trusted and honored in the community. Hurt by his elder son Benjy, contemptuous of his younger son Max, Simcha tries to nurture in Duddy the principles he himself reveres. Advising his grandson that a man without land—a place where he belongs, he means—is nobody, he inadvertently plants in Duddy the insatiable desire to acquire property, whatever the moral costs.

Max Kravitz, the middle-aged father of Lennie and Duddy, a widower, taxi-driver, pimp, and big talker. His hopes and love are lavished on Lennie; his admiration, indicative of his own inability and questionable values, is reserved for the likes of the Boy Wonder. He takes little notice of lonely Duddy, whom he tolerates with casual affection at best and understands not at all. When Duddy acquires his land and gains a spurious prominence, Max only delights in this new opportunity to brag and dream.

Lennie Kravitz, Duddy's elder brother. Driven by the family's expectations, Lenny is studying to achieve the apogee of success for a poor Jewish boy as a McGill University-trained medical doctor. Longing also for acceptance among Gentiles, he agrees to perform an abortion on a Gentile socialite, bungles it, and flees. He must be saved from disgrace by Duddy, who is thus introduced to Montreal's English-speaking Gentile elite embodied in Hugh Thomas Calder.

Benjamin Kravitz, Duddy's uncle, a wealthy textile-factory owner and pseudosocialist. His childless, failed marriage to his now-alcoholic wife, Ida, has made him a bitter recluse. While he has paid for Lennie's edu-

cation, he has always perceived Duddy as grasping and deceitful; but when he is dying of cancer, he finally comes to perceive Duddy's inherent integrity. Hoping to encourage Duddy's finer qualities, Benjy wills Duddy his Outremont mansion, but his appreciation comes too late.

Yvette Durelle, in her early twenties, Duddy's French-Canadian girlfriend. Yvette alienates her Roman-Catholic, anti-Semitic family by moving in with Duddy as his secretary and lover. Because Duddy is a minor and a Jew, she buys Duddy's land in her name. Loving and patient, she endures Duddy's boorishness and lack of respect, deserting him finally when he destroys Virgil.

Virgil Roseboro, in his early twenties, an American, sweet-tempered, naïve, and epileptic. Doggedly loyal to Duddy, he allows Duddy to use him mercilessly at the expense of his precarious health and all of his money.

Jerry Dingleman, the Boy Wonder, in his late thirties and crippled by polio. Once handsome, he is now greasily florid of face, his large body dwindling to sticklike legs. A local boy, he has rocketed to flamboyant wealth and power in the American and Canadian underworlds. Now owner of a sleazy Montreal gambling joint, he uses an impressionable, ignorant Duddy to carry heroin for him across the United States-Canadian border. Having eventually earned Duddy's contempt, he tries to circumvent Duddy's land acquisition and fails.

Mr. Cohen, a wealthy, influential, middle-age scrap-metal merchant. He takes a fatherly interest in Duddy's career, giving him financial support and excusing, indeed encouraging, the ruthlessness and self-interest that eventually come to dominate Duddy's personality.

John MacPherson, a middle-age Scottish-born socialist, failed idealist, and alcoholic. A burnt-out teacher at Duddy's high school, he is victimized by the students; Duddy is probably responsible, through a prank, for the death of MacPherson's invalid wife. MacPherson's sardonic parting remark to Duddy, "You'll go far, Kravitz. You're going to go very far," dogs Duddy throughout his relentless search for success.

Jill Rollins

THE ARCHITECT AND THE EMPEROR OF ASSYRIA

Author: Fernando Arrabal (1932-   )
Type of work: Play
Time of action: The second half of the twentieth century
First produced: L'Architecte et l'Empereur d'Assyrie, 1967 (English translation, 1969)

The Emperor, the only survivor of an airplane crash on a small, deserted island. During the first act the Emperor re-creates some of the principal characters of his former, "civilized" society; he plays dictator, priest, nun, fiancée, soldier at war, doctor, and a woman giving birth. In successive roles, he frenetically mimes the ceremony, pomp, and ritual that define these characters. Then, exhausted by his own theatricality, the Emperor suffers an apparent heart attack. Shortly after this, in a long self-reflective monologue, he says he embraces the solitude of island life—a life without films, newspapers, or Coca-Cola. Addressing a scarecrow that he has placed on a throne, the Emperor speaks, in perhaps a rare moment of candor, of another life, of a job with a good salary and a wife who was happy when he finally received a raise. Painfully, before the scarecrow, he reviews his whole life and its main characters: his wife who cheated, his mother who no longer loved him, his friends who, for the most part, envied him. He talks of his dreams of becoming the Emperor of Assyria one day and of writing like Voltaire.

The Architect, the only other inhabitant of the island, the "savage" and future pupil of the Emperor. Although ignorant of the rudiments of architecture, the Architect possesses special magical powers over the forces of nature. As if a stage director, he creates light and darkness at will and is even able to command, through the magic of words, the island's animals. He nevertheless yearns to have knowledge of society's institutions and manners: What is a dictator? What is love? What is a mother? In a series of sadomasochistic games, role reversals, and acted-out sexual fantasies, the Architect is instructed by the Emperor in the ways of civilization. Not only playing the part of the valet-slave, the Architect, in a recurring gesture of cruelty, also threatens to abandon the Emperor by rowing to another island in his canoe. At one point, the Architect recounts a dream he has had to the Emperor. In his dream, he was alone on a small island and an airplane fell, creating a terrible panic. Much of the interaction between the only two characters in the play depends on re-created events—ceremonies reenacted in an erotic and cruel atmosphere of panic.

James Gaasch

THE ARMIES OF THE NIGHT
History as a Novel, the Novel as History

Author: Norman Mailer (1923-   )
Type of work: Novel
Time of action: 1967
First published: 1968

Norman Mailer, a famous American novelist, journalist, social critic, historian, and candidate for mayor of New York. Variously described in the third-person narrative as Mailer, the Novelist, or the Historian, Mailer is the major focal character, a principal witness to the historic events the novel recounts and analyzes. A literary genius who has just published a novel, *Why Are We in Vietnam?*, Mailer is a reluctant participant in public demonstrations against the war in Vietnam; he believes his own literary work is his only real answer to the war. A self-described Left Conservative, he is soon persuaded to lend his extraliterary efforts to the antiwar effort, however, and is arrested during the massive protest march to the steps of the Pentagon in October, 1967.

Robert Lowell, a much-admired rival of Mailer. He is considered the best, most talented, and most distinguished poet in America. A man of great personal attractiveness, Lowell makes speeches, reads his poetry, and marches with the protesters. Along with Mailer, Dwight Macdonald, Paul Goodman, and Ed de Grazia, Lowell is a speaker at the Ambassador Theater in Washington on the Thursday night before the Saturday march on the Pentagon.

Dwight Macdonald, a gregarious, massive, and bearded literary critic. He is a speaker at the Ambassador Theater and participant in the march. He is admired by Mailer, but their relations are touchy as Macdonald is currently at work on a review of Mailer's recent novel, *Why Are We in Vietnam?*

Paul Goodman, a speaker at the Ambassador Theater, disliked though respected by Mailer. Goodman is a social critic and essayist for *Dissent*, a socialist quarterly.

Mitchell Goodman, a former Harvard classmate of Mailer. He wrote a war novel for which Mailer wrote a blurb. A member of the antiwar group *Resist* and a principal organizer of a demonstration at the Department of Justice in support of students refusing the draft, Goodman telephones Mailer and invites him to speak at the Ambassador Theater.

David Dellinger, a principal organizer of the march, chairman of the National Mobilization to End the War in Vietnam, and editor of the anarchist-pacifist magazine *Liberation.*

Jerry Rubin, a principal organizer of the march. He is a creative, unpredictable, militant, hippie-oriented leader of the New Left and an organizer of the first mass protest of the war at the Berkeley campus of the University of California. Rubin once appeared at a House Un-American Activities Committee hearing wearing an American Revolutionary War uniform.

Ed de Grazia, a leading lawyer for the National Mobilization to End the War in Vietnam's legal defense committee and an old friend of Mailer.

William Sloane Coffin, Jr., a Chaplain at Yale. A man of great personal integrity and force, and a participant in the march.

Hirschkop, confident and powerfully built, he is the masterful chief counsel for the demonstrators. He successfully defends Mailer in a brilliant courtroom encounter with Commissioner Scaife.

Commissioner Scaife, an impressive Virginia judge who attempts to hold Mailer in jail but who is outmaneuvered by Hirschkop and thus compelled to free Mailer without bail.

Fontaine, a documentary maker who records the events of the march and interviews Mailer on camera.

Leiterman, a cameraman who assists Fontaine.

Heiss, a sound man who assists Fontaine.

Walter Teague, who is arrested during the

march and held in the same large holding cell with Mailer. A Leninist, Teague is a tireless caller for militant, antiwar activities.

Noam Chomsky, a brilliant linguist at the Massachusetts Institute of Technology. He is

arrested during the march and held in the same cell with Mailer.

Dr. Benjamin Spock, a famous pediatrician. He is a speaker at and participant in the march.

Michael Zeitlin

ARMS AND THE MAN
An Anti-Romantic Comedy

Author: George Bernard Shaw (1856-1950)
Type of work: Play
Time of action: November, 1885, to March, 1886
First produced: 1894

Catherine Petkoff, the mother of Raina and wife of Major Petkoff, of an upper-class Bulgarian family. As the play opens, she rushes into Raina's bedroom in the late evening to tell her the news that Raina's fiancé, Sergius Saranoff, led a victory in battle in the Russian-Austrian War, with the Bulgarians on the side of the Russians. Both women are thrilled, and both are very romantic in their attitudes.

Raina Petkoff, age twenty-three, she idealistically believes herself to be in love with Sergius, to whom she is engaged: what they both call "the higher love." As the play develops, a series of shocks and learning experiences, such as seeing Sergius with his arm around Louka, move her, in a typical Shavian fashion, away from idealism and toward realism.

Louka, a servant in the household, who is engaged to another servant, Nicola. She comes in to tell Catherine and Raina that the windows and shutters are to be closed and fastened, because the enemy is being chased through the town by Bulgarian soldiers. Catherine tells Raina to close them and leave them closed, and then leaves to take care of the rest of the household; Raina, however, prefers the windows open, so Louka closes them in such a way that Raina can open them and then leaves.

Captain Bluntschli, a Swiss mercenary soldier of about thirty-five years, running away after his company lost the battle to Sergius. His father owns a chain of hotels in Switzerland, and, while Bluntschli is in many ways a realist, his choosing the life of a soldier when he obviously would not have needed to is unrealistic. He startles Raina when she hears him climbing up to her balcony and coming into her room after she had blown out her candle in fright; he orders her not to expose him. She goes back and forth between treating him as an enemy and feeling sorry for him; however, when a Russian officer arrives searching for him, she hides and protects him, and eventually he falls asleep in her bed. Though shocked, Catherine and Raina finally allow him to sleep, and presumably he leaves safely the next morning.

Nicola, a servant engaged to Louka. They have a conversation at the beginning of act 2, as they do again later, and it becomes clear that they will almost surely never marry. Louka bitterly resents being a servant, while Nicola respects his role as a servant and respects the family, viewing them as a source of patronage when he saves enough money to open a shop.

Major Paul Petkoff, a commander of the Bulgarian Army and about fifty years old.

He arrives home in March, 1886, immediately after the servants' conversation.

Major Sergius Saranoff, he arrives soon after Petkoff has greeted his servants and his wife in the garden. Raina makes a dramatic entrance, and when the others leave them, Sergius and Raina express their highly romantic (and false) idea of love for each other. When Raina returns to the house, Sergius attempts to make love to Louka. Then Bluntschli arrives to return Petkoff's coat, which Raina had lent him, and, after a series of comical interludes, in which the reader learns, among other things, that Sergius' "heroism" was a stupid mistake that turned out luckily, the result is that Sergius will marry Louka and that Bluntschli (with the approval of her parents, once they learn of his wealth) will marry Raina: genuine love in both cases, not false romanticism.

Jacob H. Adler

AROUND THE WORLD IN EIGHTY DAYS

Author: Jules Verne (1828-1905)
Type of work: Novel
Time of action: October 2 through December 21, 1872
First published: Le Tour du monde en quatre-vingts jours, 1873 (English translation, 1873)

Phileas Fogg, an English gentleman living in London. A tall, well-built man, about forty years old, with light brown hair and a beard, he lives a quiet life of great regularity. Being independently wealthy, he spends most of his day at the Reform Club reading, taking his meals, and playing whist. Apparently having lived a life of travel and adventure some years earlier, he is a man of honor and integrity. Challenged by his whist partners to prove his contention that it is possible to travel around the world in eighty days, he agrees to make the trip in that amount of time and wagers twenty thousand pounds, his entire fortune. Along the way, he delays his journey to rescue the Princess Aouda from death in a suttee and later falls in love with her. Faced with numerous other delays and adversities in completing the trip, he still remains imperturbable and loyal to his traveling companions, even when apparently faced at the end with the loss of his remaining fortune.

Jean Passepartout (zhän păss•pär•tōō), a French manservant. A middle-aged man of pleasant and honest appearance with brown hair and blue eyes, he possesses a portly but muscular build. Prior to taking service with Phileas Fogg, he led a life of travel and uncertainty. As a result, the steady and methodical life-style of his new master appealed to him. Therefore, it is a great shock to him when it is announced that they will be traveling around the world out of a carpetbag. During the course of the journey, he shows himself to be brave and resourceful. His impersonation of the dead rajah makes the rescue of Aouda possible. At the same time, his actions also sometimes cause delays for his master, such as when he is arrested for violating the sanctity of a Hindu temple or is captured by the Sioux after he has saved the train. Still, through all these challenges, a relationship of mutual respect and affection develops between him and Fogg.

Fix, a detective. Small, slightly built, and nervous, he is a man of some intelligence. Coming across Phileas Fogg at Suez, he decides that Fogg matches the description of the man that recently robbed the Bank of England of fifty-five thousand pounds. He follows Fogg's party to India and then to Hong Kong, seeking to throw various obstacles in their way until arrest warrants arrive. After leaving English territory, he begins to aid the travelers in their passage to England, where he promptly and mistakenly arrests

Fogg on arrival at Liverpool causing a delay that makes it seem the wager has been lost.

Aouda (ou·ōō·də), the widow of an Indian rajah. This dark-haired, light-complected young Parsee beauty received a thorough English education that rendered her more European than Indian. After her rescue from the suttee, Phileas Fogg planned to drop her off with a relative in Hong Kong. Arriving there, it is discovered that her relative had moved to The Netherlands. As a result, she continues to accompany Fogg on his journey, and the couple fall in love. When they arrive in London and it appears that Fogg has lost his wager, Aouda proposes marriage. It is that suggestion that reveals the twenty-four-hour miscalculation and allows Fogg to win his bet by appearing at the Reform Club in the nick of time.

Sir Francis Cromarty, a British army officer. A tall, fair man of fifty, he is traveling to Benares to join his troops. After becoming acquainted with Phileas Fogg through playing whist during the train ride across India, he joins Fogg and Passepartout on the elephant ride and assists in the rescue of Aouda.

Colonel Stamp Proctor, a large red-bearded American, who almost comes to blows with Phileas Fogg during a political rally in San Francisco. Later, they meet on the train and are about to duel when the Sioux attack, and Proctor is severely wounded.

Captain Andrew Speedy, the English captain of the *Henrietta*, an irascible man of fifty with red hair and a growling voice. Phileas Fogg is forced to buy passage to Bordeaux on his vessel for an exorbitant price. Once aboard, he bribes the crew to lock up Speedy and sail to Liverpool. He later buys the *Henrietta* from Speedy and burns up its wooden superstructure for fuel.

Ronald H. Fritze

ARROW OF GOD

Author: Chinua Achebe (1930-   )
Type of work: Novel
Time of action: The 1920's
First published: 1964

Ezeulu (ĕ·zĕ·ōō′lōō), a haughty, old chief priest of Ulu in the six villages, including his own Umuachala, which comprise the federation of Umuaro. He sees himself and his god as beset by two dangers: the growing influence of a nearby Christian mission and the machinations of Ezidemili, priest of Idemili, who aspires to replace Ulu with his own god as paramount deity of Umuaro. Through pride and a misunderstanding, he angers the English district officer and is imprisoned for thirty-two days. Believing everything to be part of Ulu's design for destroying Idemili, he refuses after his release to declare the New Yam festival which allows harvesting; he thus causes incipient famine. When his favorite son dies, he goes mad.

Captain T. K. Winterbottom, a fifteen-year veteran of service in Africa, whose pride and unbending principles have kept him a district officer. His district headquarters is in Okperi, the land neighboring Umuaro and home of Ezeulu's mother. He admires Ezeulu as the only witness on either side of a land dispute between Okperi and Umuaro who spoke the truth. When Umuaro and Okperi went to war, Winterbottom intervened decisively and became known as the "Destroyer of Guns." He now intends to appoint Ezeulu paramount chief of Umuaro and summons the old priest to Okperi, which leads to perceived insult on both sides and to Ezeulu's imprisonment. Winterbottom's sudden attack of malaria leaves the matter largely in the hands of his assistant, Tony Clarke.

Nwaka, the leader of a prosperous family of Umuachala's rival village, Umunneora, one of the three citizens of Umuaro who has taken the highest possible (self-awarded) honorific title. He is the lifelong friend and cat's paw of Ezidemili and speaks openly against Ezeulu whenever he has the chance. He incites the desire for war against Okperi and later instigates criticism of Ezeulu's original reply to Winterbottom's summons.

Obika, Ezeulu's fiery, rowdy, hard-drinking favorite son. He is generally regarded as the handsomest and most accomplished young man of Umuachala. His whipping for tardiness by Wright, the public works officer in charge of building a road through the area, sets the tone of hostility in which Ezeulu later receives the summons from Winterbottom. Defying a fever brought on by the hardship of the delayed yam harvest, Obika fulfills the role of "runner" in a funeral ritual and dies.

Oduche (ō·dōō'chĕ), the son whom Ezeulu sends to the mission church/school to learn the ways of Christianity and discover the secrets of its power. He is so far converted as to trap a sacred python and put it in a trunk to suffocate.

Moses Unachukwu (ōō·nə·chōō'kwōō), a convert and the first successful missionary to his people in Umuaro, official "catechist" of the mission. His amazed outburst when Obika attempts to attack Wright for the whipping gives rise to the suspicion that he has made derogatory comments to Wright about Obika's family. His attempts to combat Good-country's inflammatory exhortations to kill the pythons fail.

John Goodcountry, a zealous convert from the Niger delta area, who advocates killing of sacred pythons by Christians. Later, he capitalizes on Ezeulu's harvest ban by offering immunity from Ulu's anger in exchange for an even greater yam tribute.

John Nwadika, a resident of Okperi, Winterbottom's servant. He guides the messenger to Ezeulu. During Ezeulu's imprisonment, he and his wife supply food, drink, and companionship.

Okeke Akukalia (ä·kōō·kä'lē·ə), the son of a "mixed marriage" between Umuaro and Okperi natives, who speaks for the ultimatum and delivers it to Okperi. Ascending insults lead him to destroy a local man's *ikenga,* a fetish which is broken only after death. He is killed, and the war begins.

Ogbuefi Akuebue (ŏg·bōō·ĕ'fē ä·kōō·ĕ· bōō'ĕ), a friend and confidant of Ezeulu. In his presence, Ezeulu unbends enough to laugh and to argue without anger; yet even he finds Ezeulu ultimately unknowable.

Edogo, Ezeulu's eldest son. He fears that Ezeulu has sent Oduche to the Christians in order to remove him from consideration as the next high priest. His fears are met with gentle contempt by Akuebue.

Ugoye and
Matefi, Ezeulu's younger and older wives, respectively. Matefi is jealous of Ugoye's favored treatment and Ugoye feels harassed by her rival's disapproving comments and actions.

James L. Hodge

ARTURO'S ISLAND

Author: Elsa Morante (1918-1985)
Type of work: Novel
Time of action: 1922-1939
First published: L'isola di Arturo, 1957 (English translation, 1959)

Arturo Gerace (gĕr·ä′chä), the narrator of the tale, who tells the story of his life up to the age of seventeen. He was born and reared on the island of Procida, in the Bay of Naples. His father, Wilhelm Gerace, was illegitimate, the product of an emigrant Italian and a German schoolteacher's affair. Arturo seeks affection from this moody and distant man, who is often away. Arturo's mother died shortly after his birth, and when his father returns one day with a new wife, Nunziata, Arturo is dismayed. The new wife is young, barely older than Arturo. At first the boy dislikes her; then he gradually falls in love with her. In the end, Arturo is disillusioned by his father, who turns out to be far from the romantic, heroic person Arturo has imagined him all these years.

Wilhelm Gerace, father of Arturo, who grew up hating women and disliking the fishing folk of Procida. He inherits a house from a blind eccentric who befriended him, and to this house Wilhelm brings his first wife. She gives birth to Arturo at the age of eighteen and dies shortly after. Wilhelm thereafter is seldom at home, leaving Arturo in the hands of various persons. His second wife, the youthful Nunziata, is partially an attempt to recapture the image of his first wife, also a young woman. With Nunziata, too, he is often away, however, and she is afraid of him. He is attracted to a convict, Stella, who is in the penitentiary on the island and brings her home, thus losing forever the loyalty of his son.

Nunziata, second wife of Wilhelm, a poor girl from the slums of Naples. She arouses resentment, then affection in Wilhelm's son, Arturo. She becomes pregnant with Wilhelm's child, but for most of her pregnancy, her husband is gone. Rather prim for her age, she looks on Arturo as a strange, emotional boy and repulses his signs of affection. When Arturo injures himself while staging a suicide attempt, she nurses him back to health, earning his devotion.

Assuntina, a widow of Procida, who becomes Arturo's mistress. She is a willing partner to his advances and sees in him a poor romantic boy, who gives her true love. She is, in a way, a surrogate for Arturo's real love, Nunziata, his stepmother. It is through making love to Assuntina that Arturo understands that his true love is for his father's second bride.

Silvestro, a youth not much older than Arturo, who is engaged by Wilhelm to watch over the boy while he, Wilhelm, is away on his many trips. He swims and plays with Arturo, and tries to shepherd him responsibly, not always succeeding. Silvestro is conscripted in the army, however, which leaves Arturo on his own. He is the person who introduces Arturo to the many beauties and recreations of Procida, helping him appreciate the uniqueness of the island.

Philip Brantingham

AS A MAN GROWS OLDER

Author: Italo Svevo (Ettore Schmitz, 1861-1928)
Type of work: Novel
Time of action: The 1890's
First published: Senilità, 1898 (English translation, 1932)

Emilio Brentani, a clerk in an insurance office. The Italian title *senilità* (senility) must refer to him but cannot be taken literally, for he is only thirty-five; metaphorically it seems not inappropriate, for his lack of energy and enterprise would better suit a

much older man. He is content to live in a shabby apartment with his pale sister and "to go cautiously through life, avoiding all its perils, but also renouncing all its pleasures." He neither pursues a literary career (he has published one novel) nor translates his liberal political opinions into action. He might seem to be pursuing life's pleasures in his affair with Angiolina Zarri, but his irresolution and capacity for self-deception bring defeat in the end. Though he is unwilling to marry, he expects fidelity from Angiolina and blinds himself to the evidence for her promiscuity. After she has deserted him and his sister Amalia has died, he yields indeed to *senilità*, looking back with "enchanted wonder" to the period of his affair and blending Angiolina and Amalia into one splendid symbol.

Angiolina Zarri (tsä′rrē), a lower-class girl of striking beauty and vibrant health. She treats Emilio with warmth and affection, but from the first her conduct is disquieting. Aside from the engagement to Volpini, there is evidence of other affairs, not only during the past but during her relationship with Emilio. Angiolina is usually adept at covering up, but sometimes the ruse is too transparent. She is perhaps self-deceived as well as deceitful, for she gets little in return for her youth and beauty and in the end elopes with an embezzler.

Amalia Brentani, Emilio's sister and housekeeper. Thin and colorless, she seems to Balli to have been born gray. Her attitude toward Emilio seems almost maternal. Her suppressed romantic longings are brought to the surface by Emilio's tales of Angiolina

and by Balli's visits; when she falls ill and becomes delirious, her love for Balli becomes obvious. When she dies, Emilio learns that she has been taking ether.

Stephano Balli, a sculptor and Emilio's friend and confidant. Though not without talent, he has had more success with women than with sculpture. He accepts Emilio because, like the women, he is easily dominated. He attempts to advise Emilio on Angiolina but ends up falling under her spell. He behaves decently with Amalia, however, and attends her during her last illness.

Margherita, Balli's mistress. She appears meek and submissive but turns out to have cuckolded Balli; in fact, she supports her family by prostitution.

Elena Chierici (kyĕrē′·chē), a widow with an unhappy past. She is a neighbor of Emilio and unselfishly volunteers to nurse Amalia in her final illness.

Volpini, a middle-aged tailor to whom Angiolina becomes engaged, perhaps to cover a possible pregnancy.

Sorniani, a shriveled little creature, a ladies' man and a malicious gossip, who gives Emilio information about Angiolina.

John C. Sherwood

AS FOR ME AND MY HOUSE

Author: Sinclair Ross (1908-   )
Type of work: Novel
Time of action: The 1930's, during the Great Depression
First published: 1941

Mrs. Bentley, wife of Philip Bentley, whose first name is never given, narrates the novel through the journal she keeps during two years of their life in Horizon. She is pale, with dark shadows under her eyes, wears no makeup, and often mentions that her clothes are shabby. She is a loyal, loving, and protective wife but also a frustrated artist, hav-

ing given up her study of the piano to follow Philip. She records her despair at Paul's growing alienation from her and from his work, her guilt at not being able to have children after giving birth to a stillborn son a year after their marriage, and her resentment of the conditions of spiritual and physical poverty in which they are forced to live. As an educated and sensitive outsider, she despises the pettiness and mean-spiritedness of many of her husband's parishioners but is careful not to offend them; she is reserved and makes few friends. Recognizing her husband's unhappiness, she takes an aggressive role in collecting his back salary from the towns where he has previously preached, saving money so that he can afford to leave the church. She also takes the lead in trying to resurrect their faltering marriage, supporting her husband's ill-fated attempt to adopt Steve Kulanich, an abandoned teenager from the wrong side of the tracks, and finally accepting Philip's illegitimate child as an adoptive son when the child's mother dies in childbirth.

Philip Bentley, a United Church minister, the illegitimate son of a waitress and a young preacher who aspired to be a painter and died before his son's birth. Philip is thirty-six; a strong, handsome man despite his tired eyes and the haggard look caused by poverty and unhappiness, he entered the Church to receive the education he could not otherwise afford, planning to repay his loans with a year or two of preaching; he now finds himself trapped financially and unable to escape to pursue a career as a painter. Solitary since childhood, Philip becomes even more withdrawn and defensive; guilty over his lack of faith and his inability to help his parishioners, or to improve his own financial situation, he is barely tactful with his congregation and repeatedly rejects his wife's attempts at intimacy. His only outlet is his drawing, often bitter, satirical portraits of the town and its people. Initially passive toward his wife's attempts to enable them to escape from Horizon, he becomes more hopeful after they decide to adopt his son.

Paul Kirby, a schoolteacher and self-described philologist. Smaller and less handsome than Philip, Paul befriends both Bentleys and is clearly infatuated by Mrs. Bentley. Although he, also, is educated and sensitive to the larger life outside Horizon, he is at peace with his surroundings and serves the Bentleys as a bridge between the

small town and the completely rural countryside from which he comes. He brings Steve into their lives and provides them with the means for a brief vacation at his brother's ranch. Paul's open admiration of Mrs. Bentley finally forces a confrontation between Philip and his wife that serves to place them on a more honest footing with each other.

Judith West, the daughter of a farm family from the hills north of town. She has returned to Horizon after taking a commercial course in the city. Failing to find work there, she now assists the town clerk in his office and also works as a servant in his home. She is striking looking, pale, with attractive eyes and a lively smile. The matrons of the congregation tolerate her because of her contribution to the choir but are otherwise suspicious of her independence. Mrs. Bentley befriends her cautiously, recognizing the potential danger of Judith's feelings for Philip. With the birth of her son and her own death, Judith provides the Bentleys with the means to begin healing their broken marriage.

Steve Kulanich, who comes to live with the Bentleys when his father and his live-in lover are forced to leave town, abandoning the twelve-year-old boy. He is quick-tempered and accustomed to fighting with the respectable boys who taunt him about his parents. His temper, which leads him to several fights with the twin sons of the influential Mrs. Finley and his persistent Catholicism, even after he is adopted by the United Church minister, disturb the congregation, and the Catholic orphanage authorities are called in and take Steve away.

Mrs. Finley, president of the Ladies Aid and "first lady" of the congregation. She represents much of what is petty and mean-spirited in Horizon. She is a thin woman, concerned with her status and power, who manages everything and increases Mrs. Bentley's feelings of inadequacy in her role as housekeeper and parson's wife.

Katherine Keller

AS THE CROW FLIES
A Lyric Play for the Air

Author: Austin Clarke (1896-1974)
Type of work: Play
Time of action: The seventh century
First produced: 1942

Father Virgilius, a middle-aged monk and guide for the younger brothers. His primary function at the monastery of Clonmacnoise is working in the scriptorum copying ancient manuscripts. As a devoted man of God, he interprets all phenomena in a specifically Christian context. He trusts in divine providence, even in the face of the gigantic storm in which they find themselves caught. He can see the operations of nature only as divine symbols and attempts to teach both Manus and Aengus that lesson.

Brother Aengus, a young brother-novice in his late teens or early twenties. More venturesome than Brother Manus, he discovers the ancient cave of a holy man, a hermit, and feels his spiritual presence very keenly. Although frightened by the stormy violence around him, he is capable of great spiritual serenity because he is open to visionary experiences. Such experiences threaten both Father Virgilius and Brother Manus. Brother Aengus' attunement to the energies of the natural and spiritual worlds makes him capable of delving into regions of the unconscious and articulating the ancient and often destructive memories found there. He, alone, knows why the eagle, at the play's conclusion, is beating herself against the rocks in agony over the loss of her eaglets.

Brother Manus, a young, naïve novice in his late teens or early twenties. He is full of fear and apprehension about everything that happens to them. Impatient and insecure, he demands that Father Virgilius explain the dangers they are undergoing in a rational way. He does not understand what is happening in either a religious or naturalistic framework. The voices that he does hear, he immediately interprets as demonic.

The Eagle of Knock, a mythic figure from ancient Irish folklore, she is propelled into action by the persistent question that her eaglets put to her—that is, has there ever been a more violent and destructive storm than the one now occurring? Her nest is also invaded by a harmless-looking ancient crow seeking rest and relief from the tempest; the crow turns out to be the evil Crow of Achill and destroys the eaglets once the Eagle of Knock ventures north to seek the answer from the wise Salmon of Assaroe.

The Eaglets, the young, helpless children of the Eagle of Knock. Their persistent question about the comparative severity of the raging tempest becomes the call to adventure of their mother, as she foolishly takes the advice of the Crow of Achill and flies to the dangerous north.

The Crow of Achill, an ancient Irish folkloric figure, the embodiment of fatality and betrayal. She begs to be sheltered by the Eagle of Knock from the raging storm and blames an injured leg for her inability to continue her journey. She claims to have been a messenger of the Hag of Dingle and to have been present at the Hag's metamorphosis into a beautiful young woman; the crow suggests that the ferocity of the storm may be caused by the Hag's latest transformation. The Crow of Achill has been the traditional betrayer and destroyer of heroes from ancient times, having betrayed Cuchillin and torn his eyelids off as he was dying. Her ability to move between human and animal life makes her the most dangerous of creatures.

The Stag of Leiterlone, a figure out of ancient Irish folklore. Like most heroes in tra-

74

ditional mythology, the Stag recites tales of his epic escapes from other Irish mythological heroes such as Bran and Flann. His entire life has consisted of being hunted by men and their dogs; his only consolation is that he ran many of them to death.

The Blackbird of Derrycairn, an old character from Celtic folklore. The Blackbird tells of how she was heard and revered by such heroes as Patric and Fionn and of how they used her song to foretell the coming of dawn and her feathers to disclose the knowledge hidden in sacred trees.

The Salmon of Assaroe, the embodiment of wisdom and knowledge in Irish folklore. Like the Crow of Achill, he, too, is both human and animal but uses his powers for good rather than evil. All immediately recognized him as the only authority who could answer the eaglets' persistent question. The Salmon derives his power and authority because he was present at the beginning of creation. He witnessed the violent evolutionary formulations of all the species. To escape the terrifying trauma of such consciousness, he descended into a primal sleep in which he can remember the formation of the animal world. He also answers the eaglets' question: The worst tempest that ever occurred was the great Flood itself, which he witnessed. Because of his privileged position in the evolutionary scale, he recognizes the reappearance of the fatal woman now under the guise of the Crow of Achill but too late to save the eaglets.

Patrick Meanor

ASHES AND DIAMONDS

Author: Jerzy Andrzejewski (1909-1983)
Type of work: Novel
Time of action: May 5 to May 8, 1945
First published: Popiót i diament, 1948 (English translation, 1962)

Stefan Szczuka (shchōō'kä), the son of a tailor, trained as an engineer. He becomes a member of the Communist Party in the period before the war and spends several years in prison for subversive activities. During the occupation, he is arrested again, this time by the Germans, and is sent to the concentration camp at Gross-Rosen. With the liberation of Poland by the Red Army, he becomes the head of the Communist Party Area Committee in the South-East. Now in his mid-forties, he is ready to help build Communism in Poland, which, he believes, must be done according to the Soviet example, although through reconciliation, not revenge and repression. His credo is that a man lives in order to shape both his own country and history. His wife Maria was killed at Ravensbruck, and he is driven to find out details of her death. When he meets someone who will give him such information, however, he realizes that this knowledge is less impor-

tant than knowing that she comforted her fellow prisoners, helping to protect them from doubts and despair. He is thus able to lay the past to rest, but this comes ironically just prior to his own death by an assassin's bullet.

Antoni Kossecki, a "stubborn, honest, and ambitious" magistrate in Ostrowiec, a moderately sized town one hundred miles south of Warsaw. He is not a man of exceptional talents but has managed to rise through hard work and perseverance. He is arrested by the Germans early in the war and sent to the concentration camp of Gross-Rosen, where, under the name of Rybicki, he becomes a camp orderly, participating in the control and beating of other prisoners. He judges this collaboration necessary in order to survive. The price, though, is a bad conscience and fear of discovery. He reconciles himself to this evil chapter in his life, however, by consciously cutting it out from the years of peace. Now, in his fifties, he believes that he may be able still to achieve peace of mind by making a positive contribution to society.

Frank Podgorski, a former law clerk of Antoni Kossecki, now the Secretary of the local committee of the Communist Party in Ostrowiec, Poland. He returns from the war, in which he fought as a member of the underground, with a strong desire to create a new social order in conformity with Marxist historical rectitude. He expects this transformation to gain the support and cooperation of the Polish people, but he has doubts. The triumph of victory seems unclear in meaning. Also, he asks himself if he is capable of making the necessary sacrifices that "the world demands." He is pessimistic that the hopes of the dead and the living will ever be fulfilled. His attitude becomes more doctrinaire after the murder of his older mentor, Szczuka. He hardens into a party operative, abandoning shades of gray for a strict Party code of right and wrong. Whereas, earlier, he could view Kossecki's weakness in the face of death with sympathy, he now turns him over to the Security Police to be tried for war crimes.

Andrew Kossecki, Antoni's twenty-one-year-old son. He served in the Polish underground while still in his teens, rising to the rank of lieutenant. His former struggle against Nazi Germany has now become one against the Communist government implemented by the Russians. His present assignment is to assassinate Party boss Szczuka, a man he does not know and has no reason for wanting dead. He questions the necessity of carrying out the mission but in the end decides to obey the orders of his superiors. Thus, the war continues.

Alexander Kossecki, the timid, seventeen-year-old younger brother of Andrew. He is involved in his own war. He is a member of a teenage gang that has vague goals of fighting Poland's enemies, whoever they might be. Alexander's diffidence and lack of resolution, typical of others in his generation, is eventually offset by a determination to start his own troop of fighters, all presumably possessing the same predilection and attraction toward violence.

Julius Szretter (shrĕt'tėr), the leader of the teenage gang of which Alexander is a member. He is tall and slender and cruel, a great bully. He kills one of the boys in his gang because he believes that the boy would betray them and is later proud that such an act helped to steel his resolve and demonstrate his worth as a leader.

Michael Chelmicki, a friend of Andrew and a coconspirator in the plot to assassinate Szczuka. The first failed attempt resulting in the death of two strangers makes him brood about the lack of justification for such violence. When he falls in love with a young woman named Christina, he wants to quit altogether, continued participation in a right-wing death squad now seeming obscene next to an ordinary relationship of life without violence. His fear at letting down Andrew, however, overcomes his reservations and prompts him to carry out the murder by himself.

Wm. Laird Kleine-Ahlbrandt

THE ASIATICS

Author: Frederic Prokosch (1908-1989)
Type of work: Novel
Time of action: The 1920's
First published: 1935

The Narrator, a nameless seeker after knowledge of the world on a pilgrimage from Beirut to Hong Kong. A twenty-two-year-old American, "strongly built" and apparently attractive, the narrator reveals little of his background, but it is clear that he is well read and open to experience. He becomes at times weary of the betrayals of his passing companions and considers a monkish withdrawal from the world, but he realizes finally that he must remain vulnerable to the world's shocks if he is to benefit from his observations of men. He makes no effort to shape his life, remaining a passive register of events. He is perhaps an innocent from the New World who deliberately seeks out the most shocking and degraded elements of the old civilizations he journeys through.

Antoine Samazeuilh (säm·a·zwē), a roguish vagabond from Rouen, France. The handsome Samazeuilh is twenty-six or twenty-seven, muscular, and blessed with curly blond hair. He is a faithless friend, accustomed to using friends of both sexes and abandoning them at a whim. He disappears while hiking through Syria with the narrator, only to turn up again improbably in Phnom-Penh before vanishing for good in Hue.

Feodor Krusnayaskov (fyō′dôr krŏō·snä·yäs′kŏf), a middle-aged Russian whom the narrator meets in Turkey. He is arrested with the narrator in Erzurum, and they spend two months together in a foul prison before escaping. He hides the narrator in his home, but the narrator flees in the night when he learns that Krusnayaskov is a dedicated Communist.

Hans de Hahn, a Dutch adventurer of dubious background. He is a fellow prisoner of the narrator in Erzurum, and they join up again in Peshawar. De Hahn, however, is traveling with a beautiful young woman, Ursule, and the hastily assembled *ménage à trois* collapses under sexual stress. The narrator later meets Ursule by accident in Saigon and travels with her and Samazeuilh to Hue, where de Hahn appears once more, only to die at the novel's end.

Mme de Chamellis, a beautiful, sophisticated Frenchwoman whom the narrator meets in Teheran, where she conducts a salon. She reappears in Rangoon and accompanies the narrator on a trip up the Irrawaddy River that results in her death.

Dr. Ainger, a French physician whom the narrator first meets at Mme de Chamellis' salon. They are separated upon the crash of the plane in which they are flying to Meshed. The narrator finds Ainger again in an outpost near Penang, where Ainger is providing medical care to the natives. He becomes one of the most interesting and psychologically complex figures in the novel, but he dies under the pressures of his grim jungle vocation.

Frank Day

THE ASPERN PAPERS

Author: Henry James (1843-1916)
Type of work: Short story
Time of action: The late nineteenth century
First published: 1888

The narrator, an unnamed, well-to-do American literary scholar. He is obsessed by a desire to learn everything possible about the life and works of the long-dead American poet Jeffrey Aspern and is willing to do almost anything to appropriate Aspern's papers. He has heard that the papers are in the possession of Juliana Bordereau, Aspern's former mistress now living reclusively in Venice. Using a false name and pretending to be a writer, the narrator rents rooms in her run-down palazzo, improves her neglected garden, and in time mentions Aspern in chats first with her niece Tita and then with Juliana, who does not mind throwing the two together. One night, Juliana, now quite sick, catches the unprincipled scholar rifling her old mahogany desk and collapses. Humiliated, he leaves Venice for several days, returns to learn that Juliana has died and is buried, and finds Tita in supposed possession of the papers, which she hints can be his, only if he becomes a member of the family. The narrator leaves in consternation, sleeps on what seems to him to be Tita's proposal of marriage, and returns half resigned to agree; Tita, however, greets him with the news that she has burned the Aspern papers.

Juliana Bordereau, an American longtime resident in Venice and the former mistress of Jeffrey Aspern back as far as 1825. She is now shrunken and puckered with age and sickness, constantly masks her once-celebrated eyes with a green eyeshade, and supposedly possesses a treasure-trove of Aspern papers. The narrator views her as sarcastic, cynical, profane, and even witchlike. She is certainly avaricious and rude, overcharging him for rent, demanding payment months in advance, and accepting his flowers ungratefully. She teases him by offering to sell him a small oval portrait of her Jeffrey for an exorbitant price and also by encouraging him to see more of her niece Tita Bordereau, whom she may want him to care for. Juliana's discovery of the narrator rifling her desk hastens her death. (Juliana Bordereau is modeled partly on Clare Clairmont, one of the long-lived mistresses of George Gordon, Lord Byron.)

Tita Bordereau, Juliana's tall, thin, pale, faded, untidy American niece (or possibly grandniece). She is middle-aged, mild, gauche, and seemingly callow. When the narrator broaches the subject of Aspern, she timidly agrees to try to help him obtain the papers. Encouraged by Juliana, the two get into his gondola to sample decorous Venetian nightlife. After Juliana dies, Tita cannot decide whether to respect the domineering old woman's privacy or to aid the narrator, the one evidently attractive man in her life. When he rebuffs her implicit proposal, however, she seems to enjoy telling him that she burned the papers "one by one." The narrator, then seeing her in a new light, concludes that she is "plain, dingy, elderly" and yet not "hard or vindictive." (In the 1908 revision, Tita is named Tina.)

Mrs. Prest, the narrator's confidante, expatriated from the United States for some fifteen years in Venice. She urges the narrator to lay siege to Juliana Bordereau by renting rooms from her and bombarding her with flowers. Mrs. Prest helps him rationalize when he feels hypocritical and duplicitous. (Mrs. Prest is modeled partly on James's socialite friend Katherine De Kay Bronson, long a resident in Venice.)

John Cumnor, a British editor and an admirer of Jeffrey Aspern's works. Cumnor does not appear in the story; however, he is a motivating force, since he encourages his friend the narrator to seek the Aspern papers by any available means.

Pochintesta, the Bordereaus' Venetian lawyer friend.

Robert L. Gale

THE ASSISTANT

Author: Bernard Malamud (1914-1986)
Type of work: Novel
Time of action: The mid-twentieth century
First published: 1957

Frank Alpine, a young Italian drifter. Tall, bearded, with eyes haunted by a profound loneliness and a deep spiritual sadness, Frank wants to escape a past full of mistakes and broken promises. Fascinated by the stories of Saint Francis he heard in the orphanage where he was reared, he continually aspires to a life of good but finds that he has never been able to keep himself on the right track. After robbing the Bobers' grocery store, his guilt is so strong he returns to the store and helps the old shopkeeper without pay; when Morris falls ill, he volunteers to work as the storekeeper's assistant and stays on even after Morris' health returns. He brings in more business and is responsible for saving the store from the brink of bankruptcy. He falls in love with their daughter Helen and cautiously woos her. His struggle between doing right and doing wrong continues throughout the novel: He steals from the Bobers, lies, rapes Helen just as she begins to warm to him; he also puts back the money he steals, saves Morris' life, and confesses to his crimes. When Morris dies, Frank puts on the grocer's apron and takes his place in the small grocery store.

Morris Bober, a sixty-year-old Russian Jewish immigrant who runs a small, failing grocery store. A heavy-set man with sloping shoulders and bushy gray hair that needs trimming, Morris is the epitome of the long-suffering Jew. He is as unlucky as he is honest; Morris believes that it is his heritage to suffer. As the novel opens, he watches one of his former customers sneaking down the street with groceries bought from somewhere else. He learns that a new delicatessen will soon be opening across from him; that night, he is attacked and robbed. Later, his generosity toward the drifter Frank is repaid by the assistant's stealing from him. His attempts to kill himself and to burn down his store for the insurance money both fail. At the end of the novel Morris dies of a heart attack.

Helen Bober, Morris' twenty-three-year-old daughter. Slender and attractive, Helen still lives at home with her parents, providing them with the necessary income from her job. An avid reader of novels, her heart is always set on some big future that she secretly despairs will never arrive. She longs for a college education, if not for herself, then at least for the man she will marry. She dreams of a man with a bright future who will fall in love and marry her, but her brief affair with Nat Pearl leaves her feeling bitter and devalued. She warms very slowly to Frank, but when she does she is betrayed.

Ida Bober, Morris' nagging wife. Fifty-one, with thick black hair, a lined face, and legs that hurt when she walks, Ida is as stingy and suspicious as Morris is generous and trusting. Her greatest fear is that her daughter will become romantically involved with a man who is not a Jew. Primarily for this reason she wants Frank to leave the store, setting various dates for his departure, but she also finds she enjoys the extra income he is bringing in.

Ward Minogue, the criminal son of the local detective. Violent and anti-Semitic, Ward engineers the crime which brings Frank to the store; it is Ward who hits Morris on the head with the gun. Later, when Helen is waiting in the park for Frank, Ward attacks her. He dies in the fire that takes Karp's store.

Nat Pearl, a Columbia University law student whose sister is Helen's best friend. Intelligent and handsome, Nat seems to hold the bright future Helen wants in a man, but Helen senses that he is unwilling to make a commitment to her, so, to his puzzlement, after a brief affair she spurns his advances.

Julius Karp, the Bobers' landlord. A highly successful liquor salesman, Karp seems to have got all the luck that Morris has never enjoyed. It is Karp's store Ward originally plans to rob, but he steals from the Bobers' instead; Karp's store burns down instead of Morris', so it is Karp who collects the insurance money.

Poilisheh, a small, sour-faced woman who buys a three-cent unseeded hard roll from the store every morning. She is unfriendly and anti-Semitic; her faithful appearance at the store signals the relentless beginning of each new day.

Dana Gerhardt

ASYA

Author: Ivan Turgenev (1818-1883)
Type of work: Novella
Time of action: The mid-nineteenth century
First published: 1858 (English translation, 1877)

N. N., a middle-aged Russian country land-owner who narrates the story of his unhappy love affair that happened many years before. Aged twenty-five, financially secure, and without responsibility, he traveled throughout Europe anxious to experience life. He found himself more fascinated by faces than by places. Though he possessed all the skills to move gracefully through society, he is nevertheless awkward around women. He has difficulty asserting his affection for them and is easily hurt by coquetry or rejection. A sensitive, self-conscious man, he seeks out natural landscapes that mirror his moods. When he meets two fellow Russians, a man his age and a younger woman, he is intrigued by their personalities and their relationship. He notes how different they are in looks and temperament, and he cannot believe that they are brother and sister as they profess to be. His friendship with the man ripens quickly, and his awkwardness around the young woman becomes infatuation. His increasing social intimacy with the brother soon collides with his increasing emotional intimacy with the sister. The moment he must choose between etiquette and passion is the climax of the story.

Gagin, former Guardsman, now a leisured gentleman after inheriting the estate of his father, who passed away four years ago. Twenty-four years old, tall, slim, and well-groomed, Gagin neither looks nor acts like (according to N. N.) the typical Russian on the Grand Tour in Europe. He spends his time showing his sister the towns and villages of the Continent and attempting to become an artist. He begins many drawings but finishes none of them; he ruefully concurs in N. N's judgment that he is a "regular Russian soul," simple, filled with noble thoughts, but without ardor and unable to

bring a great task to conclusion. Gagin shares N. N.'s delight in the countryside and, when the two become friends, confides the secret of his sister's birth. His feelings toward the girl are mixed: He loves her and cares for her, yet he feels ashamed of her origin. This latter feeling makes it impossible for him to believe that N. N. could indeed love his sister enough to marry her. Indeed, Gagin brought his sister to Europe because her existence made his life in Russian society awkward. He precipitates the flight that separates the lovers forever.

Anna Nikolayevna, called by her nickname **Asya,** an emotional young woman who falls passionately in love with N. N. Short in stature, graceful in figure, Asya is seventeen years old. Her character is mercurial, one moment prankish, the next moment melancholy. She is physically active and daring. She runs when Gagin and N. N. walk; she saunters on ledges where they fear to tread. The revelation of her parentage is the central mystery and problem of the plot. She is Gagin's half sister, born of the love match between his father and a peasant woman after the death of Gagin's mother. When the elder Gagin died, he enjoined his twenty-one-year-old son to take care of the girl. Asya proves too much of a problem for the young soldier, who neither can understand nor control her varied moods. She does not have a typical Russian soul: She possesses an inward passion that dares to strive toward completion and fulfillment.

Frau Luise, a German widow who befriends Asya. She is an elderly, wizened woman whose appearance strikes N. N. as odd, slightly malevolent. Asya visits her frequently, much to Gagin's chagrin. Asya's brother is sure that his sister's affection for the widow is only an affectation. Luise's house is Asya's refuge, however, as it is here that she escapes the leisured nondecisive pace of a gentleman's life. Here, too, N. N. and Asya have their final, tragic interview.

Robert M. Otten

AT PLAY IN THE FIELDS OF THE LORD

Author: Peter Matthiessen (1927-   )
Type of work: Novel
Time of action: The early 1960's
First published: 1965

Meriwether Lewis Moon, a Cheyenne veteran of World War II, now a soldier of fortune in quest of a significant purpose for his life equivalent to the spiritual relationship of his Indian ancestors with the natural world. An alienated rebel, driven by a combination of fierce pride and guilt about being an Indian, Moon finds himself in a fictional South American country in the Amazon jungle after wandering the world since he fled the college to which he had been sent as a representative of his people. In need of gasoline for their airplane, he and his sidekick, Wolfie, agree to bomb a village of the local unchristianized Niaruna Indians, who are hindering the progress of cutting down the forest. Moon's affinity with the Indians is kindled during a reconnaissance flight, when an Indian defiantly shoots an arrow at his plane. Shortly thereafter, forsaking the ways of civilization, he joins the Niarunas to aid them in their battle against annihilation.

Martin Quarrier, a Christian missionary from the Dakotas sent to aid in the civilizing of the Niaruna Indians. In his thirties, physically unattractive, Martin's interest in anthropology as well as religion makes him more sympathetic to the Indians than the other missionaries. After the death of his son, Martin becomes more interested in understanding and protecting the Indians than in converting them. He is a good, if clumsy, man whose religious beliefs are tempered by his experience. Finally, he too abandons the mission, and his wife, in a futile, sacrificial attempt to save the Niarunas.

Commandante Rufino Guzmán (kō·mǎn·dǎn'tä rū·fē'nō gūz·mǎn'), the prefect, the principal local government authority, head of the military police, and main property owner of the province. An intelligent but coarse person, more interested in his own well-being than that of the people he governs, a dangerous man, ruthless in his exercise of power, Guzmán is eager to bomb the Niarunas to advance his career. Holding the passports of Moon and Wolfie, he demands that they help him destroy the Indians by bombing the village from their plane. He tolerates the Protestant missionaries because as they Christianize the Indians they tame them.

Hazel Quarrier, the ungainly, unhappy wife of Martin, an uncritical believer in her religion and their purpose as evangelists. Psychologically unequipped to cope with the reality of the jungle environment, she suffers a mental breakdown after the death of their son and comes to see the jungle as the home of the Devil.

Billy Quarrier, the nine-year-old son of Martin and Hazel. He adapts quickly to his new environment. His innocence, bravery, and boyish acceptance of his new world endear him to the local people, as well as to the Indians. His death from blackwater fever triggers Martin's religious skepticism and Hazel's breakdown.

Leslie Huben, the leader of the Protestant missionaries. An athletic Christian and egotist, a coward at heart, he is able to present failure as if it were success and thereby gains much monetary support from the mission board at home. His primary interest seems to be his own fame. For this end, he is willing to sacrifice the Indians and anyone else. He offends Martin by speaking of Billy's death as a positive act of God.

Andy Huben, née **Agnes Carr,** the young attractive wife of Les. She is capable of more compassion than any of the other characters. Both Martin and Lewis Moon are attracted to her. Unfortunately, her kiss to Moon is the means of transmitting influenza to the Niarunas.

Wolfie, Moon's companion mercenary. A wandering New York Jew, he is, like Moon, a strong, good fighter, but unlike Moon he is not in control of himself. He is extremely vulgar in action and speech, and ultimately self-defeating. Wolfie attacks the village for Guzmán even as Moon is trying to protect the Indians.

Father Xantes (zăn•tĕs), the Catholic priest who precedes the Protestants in the attempt to convert the Indians to Christianity. A sophisticated, resilient man, confident with the history of the Catholic church behind him,

he knows the Protestants are doomed to failure, and he has the patience to outlast them.

Aeore (āy•ē•ôr′ē), the most heroic of the Niarunas. He is defiant and intelligent enough to see through Moon's masquerade as a god; he is a natural leader. He shoots an arrow at Moon's plane, thereby unknowingly instigating Moon's commitment to the Niarunas.

Boronai (bô•rōn′āy), the old chief of the Niarunas. He has the wisdom born of experience but is losing his ability to control his people in the face of the white man's destruction of the natural world. When he dies of influenza, Moon and Aeore compete for control.

Pindi (pēn′dē), a pretty, young Indian girl, a wife of Boronai. She is given by her husband to Moon, and she bears the child of Aeore.

Uyuyu (ū•yū′yū), or **Yoyo,** an Indian convert reared by Father Xantes as a Catholic. He went over to Huben when his materialistic prayers went unanswered. He has become an exploiter of his own people and is instrumental in the tragic conclusion of the conflict between the Indians and the whites.

William J. McDonald

AT SWIM-TWO-BIRDS

Author: Flann O'Brien (Brian O'Nolan, 1911-1966)
Type of work: Novel
Time of action: The mid-1930's
First published: 1939

The Narrator, unnamed, a none-too-diligent young university student in Dublin, who is writing a novel about another author, Dermot Trellis. The narrator tells about his carping uncle, his fellow students, his drinking and wasting of time, and reads from and comments upon his developing novel.

Dermot Trellis, a character in the novel which the narrator is writing. Trellis is him-

self writing a novel to demonstrate the consequences of immorality. Trellis is a pimply and neurotic recluse who chooses to spend most of his time in bed. In the narrator's story, the characters of Trellis' novel rebel against the roles which Trellis assigned to them, play out their own stories, and eventually attempt to kill Trellis. Trellis is saved when his servant, Teresa, enters his room, picks up some sheets of paper from the floor, and throws those pages which sustain the existence of the rebel characters into the fire.

John Furriskey, an original character concocted by Dermot Trellis. Furriskey, a well-built, dark, and clean-shaven man of medium height, is intended by the author to be the embodiment of immorality and rakishness, but he rebels. He marries the servant, Peggy, whom Trellis intended that he dishonor. Peggy has discovered that Trellis' control over his characters is suspended when he sleeps. Furriskey conspires with the other characters first to drug Trellis so that they can live independently of him while he sleeps and finally to torture and kill Trellis.

Orlick Trellis, the illegitimate son of Trellis and Sheila Lamont, one of Trellis' characters. Sheila was to have been a girl of virtue and refinement, whose honor is destroyed by Furriskey. Trellis, however, is so taken with the beauty and refinement of his literary creation, Sheila, that he assaults her. Their offspring, Orlick, came into the world full grown. Sharing his father's writing talent, as well as pimples, Orlick, who comes under the influence of the evil Pooka, is recruited by the other rebel characters to write a novel in which Dermot Trellis is grossly abused and then, as a preliminary to his execution, placed on trial before all the characters.

The Pooka Fergus MacPhellimey, an Irish devil conjured up by Trellis as a character in his novel. The Pooka, like Trellis' other characters, has a will of his own. By besting the Good Fairy in a game of cards, the club-footed Pooka wins the right to influence Orlick Trellis, whose inherited talent for writing is turned against Dermot Trellis. In Orlick's story, the Pooka serves as the prosecutor as Dermot's trial.

Finn MacCool, a legendary hero of Irish folklore who is "hired" by Dermot Trellis for use as an elderly character in his novel. He was intended by Trellis to be an elderly father outraged at the violation of his daughter, Peggy, by the villain Furriskey. The rebellious character Finn MacCool, however, forces himself upon Peggy.

King Sweeny, the subject of a tale told by Finn MacCool. King Sweeny of Dal Araidhe assaults a saintly cleric by the name of Ronan, who then invokes a curse upon him. Sweeny is transformed into a bird man, fated to fly from roost to roost around Ireland, eating wild crest and acorns. In MacCool's tale, Sweeny composes an epic lay describing his physical and mental anguish.

Paul Shanahan and
Antony Lamont, minor characters borrowed by Trellis for his novel. Shanahan is an older man who appeared in many of the writer William Tracy's romantic Westerns. Lamont is Sheila's brother, who was to demand satisfaction from Furriskey after he had taken advantage of her. Shanahan and Lamont do not play the roles assigned to them but become instead principal conspirators against Trellis. They relish his physical torments and are simultaneously judges, jurors, and accusers of Trellis in the story written by Orlick.

Slug Willard and
Shorty Andrews, two tough cowboys borrowed from the Westerns of William Tracy by Dermot Trellis as minor characters in his novel. They also serve as accusers and judges in Orlick's story.

The Good Fairy, a character drawn from Irish folklore by Dermot Trellis for his novel. The Good Fairy, an invisible pocket-sized creature, is intended by Dermot Trellis to contrast with the evil of the Pooka, but, escaping the control of Trellis, the Good Fairy gives up the right to influence the newborn Orlick to the Pooka, who had beaten the penniless fairy at poker.

Peggy, a domestic servant, created by Trellis as one of his characters. Trellis intended for Furriskey to take advantage of her and betray her. In fact, Furriskey behaves honorably toward her, and they marry.

Jem Casey, a workingman's bard, who joins the other characters for the trial of Trellis.

Brinsley, the narrator's friend and fellow student. Brinsley is the narrator's drinking partner and the audience and critic for his developing manuscript.

Uncle, unnamed, the narrator's penurious and rather small-minded, but well-intentioned uncle, with whom he lives in Dublin. Uncle is fat, with a red complexion and coarse and irregular features. A third-class clerk at Guinness and a commonplace man, he is deeply concerned over his unstudious nephew's apparent slothfulness. He is appropriately pleased when his nephew passes his final examination with honor, and presents him with a used watch.

Bernard A. Cook

AUGUST 1914

Author: Aleksandr Solzhenitsyn (1918-   )
Type of work: Novel
Time of action: August, 1914
First published: Avgust chetyrnadtsatogo, 1971; revised, 1983 (English translation, 1972)

Alexander Vasilich Samsonov, a fifty-five-year-old general of cavalry. After a number of years of steady, but generally uneventful, service with the cossack regiments, he is called, only three weeks before the outbreak of war, to command the Russian Second Army on the Polish-German front. This responsibility makes him uneasy, since he has not seen serious operational duty for at least seven years. Samsonov attempts to fulfill his tasks with a maximum of military professionalism, choosing subordinates on the basis of military records, not connections. He is convinced that, as the crisis of war deepens, the nation's cause will take precedence over personal interests and effective command will result. Discomfiture comes quickly, however, when Samsonov realizes that powers higher up are not really aware of the situation near the front. His dealings with supreme commander Zhilinsky are plagued by erroneous or contradictory orders and a personal relationship not between military colleagues, but between a "bullying cattle drover" and a too-often powerless but ultimately responsible subordinate. Samsonov is continuously pursued by the fear that his greatest error as a general might be the result not of an action taken, but of a failure to act when necessities, not orders, demand. This frustration mounts as miscalculation af-ter miscalculation by the Russian High Command leads to the loss of thousands of Second Army soldiers. Unable to bear the weight of responsibility for disastrous military moves he had been obliged to implement, Samsonov commits suicide, giving the High Command an excuse to condemn him for "excessively independent" operations, running counter to orders.

Georgii Mikhalych Vorotyntsev, a General Staff colonel who, following duty in the Russo-Japanese war, had seemed content with gradual professional advancement and the security of marriage. Now, embroiled in the events of August, 1914, he is particularly conscious of the responsibility of commanding miserable peasants. Their reward if they survive war, he imagines, is simply staying alive. Vorotyntsev is perplexed over his position in life, not knowing what reward might possibly be his if he survives the coming events. Throughout his life, Vorotyntsev has believed that one should do his best to assist his country, but that belief turns to despair time and again because of the harmful effects of incompetence, especially in positions of authority. This depressing result is his experience again following the first disaster of the war, when advantage was turned to defeat as a result of ineffective command structures. Yet here, and in a number of other highly pressured situations during the August, 1914, campaign, Vorotyntsev shows resiliency and an ability to call upon reserves of physical and psychological strength to salvage whatever is possible in the face of extremely adverse conditions.

Arsenii (Senka) Blagodaryov, a strong, rough-hewn, twenty-five-year-old peasant soldier. Although Senka is somewhat clumsy because of his size, he possesses a sharp intellect. Perhaps because of this asset, he gains an appointment as Colonel Vorotyntsev's orderly. In this post, he shows a remarkable ability to see the consequences of others' decisions in advance, which, coupled with his willingness to accept dangerous assignments, gains for him compliments from his commanding officer. Seen from Senka's somewhat naïve perspective, the task of fighting is a grim but necessary reality, which he hopes can be concluded at least by October 1, the traditional date of village feasts. This simplistic view does not distract from his dedication to Vorotyntsev's and the army's service; such service is simply unconnected with any higher principles of glory or patriotism.

Sasha Lenartovich, a twenty-four-year-old platoon commander who believes that Russia and the world will someday be transformed as a result of a great event. Earlier, he viewed the abortive 1905 Revolution in Russia as a call to his student generation to join the oppressed classes' struggle to break the chains of czarist tyranny. Thus, when he is drafted in August, 1914, Sasha is driven by an overwhelming despair that he should not be on the front but serve the real cause of revolution elsewhere. The ignorant troops of his platoon appear to be completely unaware, not only of class struggle but also of their own fate as pawns "driven forcibly to fight against another and equally unfortunate mass of men." He considers various routes of escape from the senselessness of his situation: court martial and expulsion from the army as a political agitator, or even surrender to the enemy. While attempting to desert his regiment, Sasha ironically falls into the entourage of Colonel Vorotyntsev, who, no longer able to marshall an effective fighting force, is reduced to attempting to break through the German lines to seek safety for a heterogeneous body of loyal survivors.

Isaakii (Sanya) Lazhenitsyn, the most intellectual of the characters. Isaakii is one of only two students from the steppe village of Sablya. He clings to the ideal of maintaining ties with traditional village values while cultivating new ideas as a student. The novelty of his ideas, especially on necessary social change in Russia, earns for him the nickname of *"Narodnik"* (stargazer). In fact, he is so inspired by the example of Leo Tolstoy that he travels to the latter's estate, meets with the great writer, and professes his loyalty as an intellectual disciple. In spite of this high idealism, when the war breaks out and Russia is attacked, Sanya feels that he has a responsibility to come to the assistance of his country. With a fellow student and covolunteer on the way through Moscow to join the army, Sanya encounters an enigmatic itinerant scholar (Varsonofiev). Their discussions wrestle with the shortcomings of *narodnik* idealism. When Sanya is asked to consider the contention that "above all, each one of us is called upon to perfect the development of his own soul," he remains perplexed, not understanding what larger laws or principles ultimately govern history. Self-proclaimed philosopher Varsonofiev's conclusion that response to the trumpet of war is a necessity, not for history, but merely for the maintenance of "self-respect" further clouds the mind of this youth torn between idealism and practical politics.

Zakhar Tomchak, owner of a prosperous northern Caucasus estate near Rostov, plus extensive lands in the Kuban purchased from titled aristocrats in St. Petersburg. Descendant of a family of migrants who originally came to the Ukraine as hired laborers, Tomchak, with his "craggy features" and "gargoyle-like" nose, still reflects his rough origins. When he goes into the city of Rostov wearing a formal suit, he strikes a somewhat comical figure. This rusticity does not keep Tomchak from using his native intelligence to further the productive goals of his agricultural domain. Many of his ideas, like the most up-to-date machinery he purchases, come from abroad or are borrowed from the German colonists whose labors have produced visibly superior results in Russia. Tomchak views Russia's declaration of war against Germany to be a great mistake. Out of fear that mass conscription will harm the effective running of his estates, he uses his influence to secure military exemptions for his son Roman, and all foremen, laborers, and cossacks in his service.

Irina (Orya) Tomchak, Roman's wife. Irina is a tall erect woman, with an elaborate coiffure. Although she is accustomed to urban standards of elegance, she avoids displays of finery in the presence of her father-in-law. By ingratiating herself with the stern Tomchak patriarch, Irina escapes the continual reprimands that plague other members of the family. Her favored position is also reflected in the fact that Tomchak relies on her reading of the *Novoe Vremya* newspaper, to the exclusion of all other sources, to learn news of Russia and the world. Irina spends long hours, both days and nights, lost in dreams that, through their romantic content, help her remove herself psychologically from the rough conditions and unpleasant associations that surround her.

Roman Tomchak, Zakhar's son. Roman tends to reflect the idleness of privilege. His main concern for the future is to secure the best possible conditions of inheritance. In the meantime, he concentrates on filling the role of a future estate owner, paying particular attention to his elegance. Roman is no friend of the declining Russian monarchy, nor does he subscribe to orthodox conceptions of religion. For propriety's sake, however, he keeps outward appearances of Christian faith and patriotism. This hypocrisy serves to distort even more the purchased privilege of military exemption arranged for him by his father.

Xenia Tomchak, the youngest of the Tomchak children. With the questionable exception of her brother Roman (who is seventeen years older), Xenia is the only member of the family to profess progressive political views. She reads widely from different Western European literatures and is tempted to abandon a standard university education to pursue a career in ballet, irrespective of the effect this switch could have on her status as an heir to the Tomchak estate. Through the special efforts of her father, Xenia enters a private provincial high school known for its "left-wing liberalism" and befriends the head mistress' family. It is Xenia's intervention that saves the daughter of the head mistress from ostracism as a result of an awkward marriage situation. Xenia herself chafes under her father's insistent pressures to marry her off. Even though her educational experiences promise to provide an opening for her into Muscovite society, she comes to realize that she has most in common with her adopted family, which has espoused liberalism out of conviction, not convention.

Byron D. Cannon

AUNT DAN AND LEMON

Author: Wallace Shawn (1943-   )
Type of work: Play
Time of action: The 1950's to the 1980's
First produced: 1985

Leonora (Lemon), Susie and Jack's daughter. A sickly young woman living alone in London, Leonora, or Lemon as she was called by Aunt Dan, sits in her apartment and subsists on bread and fruit and vegetable juices. Lately, her time is spent sleeping, masturbating, and reading books about the Nazi death camps. During her childhood, Lemon would lie in bed and listen to the stories told by Aunt Dan. Lemon later explains that when she was eighteen, she felt physically attracted to Aunt Dan, but because Aunt Dan was sick at the time, she did not make the advance. Lemon's defense of the Nazis and their cruelty appears to have been influenced by Aunt Dan's beliefs that governments will survive only through the use of violence.

Danielle (Aunt Dan), an American academic living in England, a friend of Jack and Susie's. As a young woman, Danielle became friends with Susie and later introduced her to Jack. She is nicknamed Aunt Dan by the eleven-year-old Lemon. At night, she would sit and tell Lemon stories about the great man Henry Kissinger. According to Aunt Dan, the former American secretary of state carried the problems of an entire nation on his shoulders. She defends every decision that Kissinger made during the Vietnam War, for she understands that governments must use force if they are to survive. Aunt Dan also has an affair with the prostitute Mindy after she kills a man for sexual thrills.

Jack, Lemon's father, an American who came to England to study at Oxford. After marrying Susie, Jack went to work in an auto parts manufacturing company. Never wanting to admit that he is wrong in his actions, Jack, now the owner of his own auto parts business, feels compelled to defend his own work against that done by intellectuals in the universities, perhaps as a way of assuring

himself that leaving Oxford after marrying Susie was the right thing to do. Cold and impersonal in his feelings, Jack also argues that Susie and her anxieties are the causes of Lemon's eating disorder.

Susie, Lemon's mother, an English girl. Loving and kind, Susie is also an emotionally sensitive young woman. She becomes distraught about young Lemon's eating disorder. He anxieties worsen when Jack tells her that her worrying is the cause of the problem. Susie opposes Aunt Dan's defense of Henry Kissinger and his decision-making involvement concerning the Vietnam War as well as Aunt Dan's ideas that nations must exert violent force so that others do not have to. Susie tells Aunt Dan that, although she does not know Kissinger, she feels certain that there are some people who cannot curb their violent natures, their lust for blood. Susie's opposition to Aunt Dan ultimately causes a falling out between them.

Mindy Gatti, a London prostitute. Blonde and attractive, Mindy is an amoral and violent woman. Mainly for thrills, she strangles and kills Raimondo, a foreign drug dealer, after engaging in oral sex with him. After she kills him, Mindy wraps the body in a plastic sack and hides it in the trunk of a car. Later, she tells Aunt Dan about the murder, and the two make love, for Aunt Dan finds herself emotionally and sexually attracted to Mindy while listening to the story. Mindy's act of murder exemplifies Aunt Dan's idea that violence is necessary in order to survive. The two begin an affair that lasts only a week. Aunt Dan breaks off the affair before her feelings for Mindy sour.

Dale Davis

AUNT JULIA AND THE SCRIPTWRITER

Author: Mario Vargas Llosa (1936-   )
Type of work: Novel
Time of action: The 1950's
First published: La tía Julia y el escribidor, 1977 (English translation, 1982)

Mario, the narrator-protagonist, a confident college student who is underemployed as a radio news writer. He is waiting for the chance to devote himself completely to a literary life, preferably in Paris. Other than being a novelistic character, hardly anything distinguishes Mario—indiscriminately and purposely called by the author's nicknames as a young man—from the real Mario Vargas Llosa. Mario/Varguitas/Marito serializes comically and romantically his courtship of Julia, an aunt by his uncle's marriage, and his apprenticeship as a writer under the guidance of Pedro Camacho, a scriptwriter for radio soap operas. Mario's "autobiography" is an exercise in indiscretion at the literary and empirical level, even though his depiction of himself as an intelligent, tall, dark, and handsome extrovert is rendered truthful by the other characters. Mario sees marriage alternately as a challenge or as an adventure, all of which can be turned into literature, specifically short stories. As the narrator of the final chapter, he summarized in one page how he reunites with Julia to share a life that would last eight years.

Aunt Julia, fourteen years older than Mario, a divorced Bolivian who cannot bear children. Physically attractive, she dazzles the young Mario with what he perceives to be healthy cunning and spontaneity. Despite the close family ties that would prevent their ever getting together, it is Julia who is decisive and ultimately responsible for their union. She is warm, brave, and has a wonderful sense of humor, which is what really allows her to continue, despite her awareness that their relationship will not last. Her divorce from a marriage that lasted three more years than she expected is told strictly from Mario's point of view.

Pedro Camacho, like Julia, a Bolivian working in Peru, brought in by the radio station in which Varguitas works single-handedly to organize and produce the soap operas they broadcast. Introverted and rather mechanical, he thinks only in catastrophic terms. His stories rely on extensive melodramas that are so repetitive and lacking in imagination that at times he loses characters or switches them from one program to another, without knowing he is doing it. In the final analysis, he is his own excessive creation. The readers really know little about the true Pedro but can intuit a certain madness. Marito, echoing the real Vargas Llosa, attributes his own ability to organize a narrative's totality to Camacho's type of truly professional, even if perverse, influence.

Will H. Corral

THE AUNT'S STORY

Author: Patrick White (1912-   )
Type of work: Novel
Time of action: c. 1900-1940
First published: 1948

Theodora Goodman, a spinster in her forties. Theodora has devoted much of her adult life to caring for her difficult, antagonistic mother. Once old Mrs. Goodman dies, however, Theodora decides to travel: She journeys first to pre-World War II Europe and then to America. Before leaving, she recounts the story of her youth to her young niece, and soul mate, Lou Parrott. Theodora was decidedly unfeminine as a girl, all bones and angles. She would say startling things and preferred going hunting with her beloved father to practicing the piano. Although clever and perceptive, Theodora has few friends; men in particular are repulsed by her. Except for occasional illuminating encounters with fellow individualists such as Moraïtis, Theodora has led a quiet life with her domineering mother. Following her tour through the Old World, Theodora lingers at the Hôtel du Midi, where her own fragile identity and grip on reality start to unravel as she comes into contact with other eccentric guests. For one (a Russian general), she takes on the role of his deceased sister Ludmilla. Theodora becomes increasingly confused, and as her sense of self begins to disintegrate, the other characters come to seem merely projections of her fervid imagination. Tensions mount in the hotel and it self-combusts; Theodora escapes and resurfaces in the New World. She rides a train across the United States, alights in the middle of nowhere, and gradually divests herself of all of her wordly possessions. It is only once she encounters Holstius that the healing process begins: He speaks to Theodora's higher self, helping her to gather the pieces of her fractured spirit. Like the characters in the hotel, Holstius seems not to exist except in Theodora's imagination. Eventually, she is taken away to an asylum by concerned, well-meaning people.

Frank Parrott, Theodora's brother-in-law. Although Frank is beefy and inarticulate, he and Theodora were good friends at one time.

Fanny Parrott, Theodora's younger sister. Married to Frank and mother to Lou, Fanny is entirely vapid and materialistic.

Lou Parrott, Theodora's only niece. Young Lou is clever and sensitive like her aunt; they see things the same way, and the one thing Theodora prizes above all is her relationship with her niece.

Mr. George Goodman, father to Theodora and Fanny, husband to Julia Goodman. George is a well-meaning, kind, and educated man who is naïve when it comes to financial matters. He sells off his estate bit by bit in order to satisfy his wife's desire to travel to exotic places. He understands and loves Theodora and encourages her individualism.

Mrs. Julia Goodman, mother of Theodora and Fanny. Julia prefers her plump, rosy daughter Fanny to her plain, difficult, older girl. A vain and selfish woman, Mrs. Goodman dominates her eldest daughter throughout their lives.

Moraïtis (mō•rī•ī•tǐs), a visiting Greek cellist. A small, dark, sad man, he also sees beyond the superficial and conventional in life; he and Theodora recognize each other at once as kindred spirits. Although unmusical herself, Theodora attends one of Moraïtis' recitals and emerges profoundly moved by his music.

Huntly Clarkson, a dilettante friend of Theodora. Huntly is a social somebody, a refined, well-to-do bachelor who collects art for its value and people for their idiosyncrasies. Although frequently repulsed by shabby, abrupt Theodora, Huntly cultivates her as a friend because she has a knack for cutting through social hypocrisy.

General Alyosha Sergei Sokolnikov,
Mrs. Elsie Rapallo, and
Katina Pavlou, respectively, a retired Russian military man, a wealthy American, and a young girl, all fellow guests at the Hôtel du Midi. There is some doubt that these characters are who they say they are: Throughout their stay in the hotel, each antagonizes and argues with the others, hurling accusations about others' identities. Theodora becomes the General's confidante, but she also plays friend to Mrs. Rapallo and aunt to Katina. These characters appear only in the second section of the novel. They say and do remarkable things throughout, but their speech and actions (like Theodora's) become increasingly disjointed and bizarre.

Holstius, a treelike man with whom Theodora communes in the third section of the novel. They encounter each other in an abandoned shack in the middle of nowhere in the United States. Theodora, having shed all traces of her former identity, looks to Holstius to help her reconcile and reunite the disparate halves of being such as joy and sorrow, illusion and reality, life and death. He advises her simply to accept the whole and to love elementary things such as chairs and tables. Despite Theodora's perception of Holstius as real, his presence goes unde-tected by others, who in turn apprehend Theodora for seeing him.

Susan Whaley

AURA

Author: Carlos Fuentes (1928-   )
Type of work: Novel
Time of action: The early 1960's
First published: 1962 (English translation, 1965)

Felipe Montero, a young historian and part-time private school teacher. Bored with his present job of teaching "useless facts" to "sleepy pupils," he desires a change from his daily routine, and he is drawn to an advertisement that seems addressed personally to him. Restless and curious, he is particularly susceptible to the strange events and relationships that he encounters when he accepts the job of translating the memoirs of Señora Llorente's dead husband. Felipe leaves the known outer world and enters Consuelo's dark, moldy home; in this mysterious, gothic setting he meets Aura, the ancient woman's niece. Gradually, he is drawn into a series of bewildering, grotesque occurrences that suggest the fantastic bond between the two women. His growing desire for Aura is consummated when he makes love to her and swears, "Nothing can separate us." Eventually, Felipe realizes that this "sterile conception" engenders another self, his own double, the embodiment of Consuelo's late husband General Llorente; through his sexual union with young Aura and his promise of undying love, Felipe completes his role in Consuelo's morbid scheme to perpetuate her youth and passionate marriage to the General. Felipe is too bewitched to protest; as he caresses Aura, he knows she is only the image of the withered, exhausted Consuelo, but he embraces her in shadowed moonlight and accepts his dark destiny.

Señora Consuelo Llorente (yō·rĕn'tĕ), Aura's strange, eccentric aunt, who Felipe figures is about 109 years old. Obsessed with prolonging her youth and unwilling to relinquish the past, Consuelo dabbles in the occult, keeping odd medicines in her decrepit house, growing exotic herbs and plants in a dank garden, and performing obscure rituals and bizarre communion feasts before dim candles and a tortured black Christ. She married General Llorente at age fifteen and was widowed thirty-four years later in 1901, but she has remained ageless through her illusory double, Aura, waiting for the fated reappearance of her beloved groom.

Aura (ou'rä), Consuelo's young niece. Pale, beautiful, with loose black hair and astonishing green eyes, Aura seduces Felipe, luring him into the old widow's plot to re-create her dead husband and preserve their love forever by mating Felipe with the young girl. Aura is lovely, provocative, and spectral; Felipe sees her only in shadows; he senses her more than he actually feels her, although she inflames his desire for her and he does possess her. In loving her, Felipe loses himself, for Aura is merely Consuelo's imagined self, a materialization of the old woman's past; Aura's role is to open herself sexually and "like an altar" to Felipe until he is spent and drained of his own will, his animus submerged in the dark anima figure, whose "fleshless lips" he kisses at the end.

John Zubizarreta

AUTO-DA-FÉ

Author: Elias Canetti (1905-   )
Type of work: Novel
Time of action: Probably the 1930's
First published: Die Blendung, 1935 (English translation, 1946; also as *The Tower of Babel,*
    1947)

Dr. Peter Kien (kēn), a world-renowned sinologist. Kien is a forty-year-old recluse who wants to live only for his scholarly work in his private library of twenty-five thousand books. His life is totally regulated, and his library is cared for by his housekeeper Therese, whom he decides to marry in order to assure the continuance of this good care. The marriage, however, changes this misogynist's life into a nightmarish existence. In searching for his bankbook and will, Therese makes Kien's life so unbearable that he is forced to leave his home and library. Kien is rescued by Benedikt Pfaff, who in turn imprisons and brutalizes Kien in Pfaff's cellar apartment. Eventually, Kien's brother George comes from Paris to rescue him. George reestablishes the original order of Peter's life by removing Therese and Benedikt from his home and restoring his library. Believing that everyone is satisfied, George returns to Paris. At this point, however, Peter Kien has a complete breakdown. Fantasizing that all (including his books) are plotting against him, Peter sets fire to his library and hurls himself onto the flaming pyre.

Therese Krumbholz (krōōm'hōlts), his housekeeper, a fifty-six-year-old spinster who is seeking material wealth and security for her old age. Mistakingly believing that Peter Kien has considerable wealth (which he does not), she sets out to obtain his bankbook and to become his sole heir after they are married. Her vicious greed and her merciless babbling of unbearable clichés and platitudes drive Kien from his home. Therese also has an absurd view of her physical and sexual charm, although she is really a repulsive hag. This obsession, for example, leads her to misunderstand the flattery of a furniture salesman (referred to as "that superior young man") for amorous advances, to be followed by an encounter in the showroom of the store, where she removes her skirt and tries to embrace him with her fat and ugly body, much to the amusement of the crowd of shoppers. While Kien's insanity leads him to bookishness, Therese's mania makes her pursue her greed and sexual frustrations. When George Kien tries to help his brother reestablish his life, he provides Therese with a small dairy-produce shop on the outskirts of the city on the condition that she never return to Peter Kien's home.

Fischerle (fĭsh'ĕr-lə), also known as **Siegfried Fischer** (zēg'frēd fĭsh'ĕr), a hunchbacked dwarf whose mania drives him to imagine that he can become the world's chess champion. He exploits Peter Kien's psychosis, first, by being his assistant while "unpacking" his imaginary books from his head, and then, by organizing a group of four friends who "sell" books to Kien at the municipal pawn shop (the Theresianum), while Fischerle makes off with most of Kien's money.

Benedikt Pfaff (pfäf), a retired policeman and caretaker of the apartment house where Kien lives. He lives in a cellar apartment, from where he exploits and brutalizes everyone who enters or leaves the house. After Therese has driven Peter Kien out of his home and library, Pfaff becomes her lover. Together they set out to sell the library to the municipal pawn shop. Pfaff rescues Kien from the police, who think he has murdered Therese, only to incarcerate him in a dungeonlike room of his cellar apartment, where Kien is then subjected to physical harassment and brutality while Pfaff is enjoying life upstairs with Therese. After Peter Kien's brother arrives, Pfaff is set up in business near Therese in another part of town.

George Kien, Peter Kien's younger brother, a psychiatrist and director of an asylum for the insane in Paris. Although George may be the only sane character, he too is portrayed as suffering a touch of madness in his unorthodox methods of treating his patients. It is quite obvious that his analysis of his brother's mental condition is completely incorrect, as it quickly leads to Peter Kien's demise.

Thomas H. Falk

THE AUTOBIOGRAPHY OF AN EX-COLOURED MAN

Author: James Weldon Johnson (1871-1938)
Type of work: Novel
Time of action: Between the Civil War and World War I
First published: 1912

The Anonymous Narrator, a musician and composer. The son of a black woman and a rich white father, the narrator moves from Georgia to Connecticut at an early age. He is extremely light-skinned, and the truth of his race is kept from him; indeed, his discovery that he is black is a traumatic one. Having been reared by his mother, he develops into an extremely sensitive adult. He is well read and has good manners and considerable culture. He is, however, also naïve and somewhat cowardly. The latter trait is most clearly seen when, upon being an eyewitness to the lynching and burning of another black man in the rural South, the narrator elects to pass for white from that point on. Even after he becomes moderately successful and comfortable, he sometimes regrets his decision to leave the black race but is much too afraid to live as a black man based on the lynching experience.

The Mother, a seamstress. A former servant who has a child by her white master, he in turn arranges for her and the child to move to Connecticut. She is well read and possesses considerable knowledge of black life and history, which she passes on to her son. Indeed, she is the major force in his life. She dies shortly after his graduation from high school.

Shiny, a boyhood friend of the Narrator. So called because of his extremely dark complexion, Shiny is the smartest person in the class and delivers the valedictory address on Toussaint-Louverture. This speech kindles in the Narrator a love and appreciation for black history and culture. Shiny works his way through the University of Massachusetts at Amherst and goes on to become a professor at Fisk University. A chance meeting between Shiny and the Narrator in New York leads the Narrator to disclose his race to his white girlfriend.

Red, a boyhood friend of the Narrator. So called because of his red hair and freckles, Red is not disposed to become a scholar; indeed, the Narrator helps him through school, and they become fast friends after Red comforts him following his discovery of his blackness. After high school graduation, Red's ambition is to work in a bank.

The Millionaire, the Narrator's benefactor. The Millionaire encounters the Narrator while frequenting a club where the Narrator plays ragtime. He hires him to perform at his private parties and later takes him to Europe. When the Narrator elects to return to the United States, the Millionaire provides generously for his expenses.

The Cuban Exile, a cigar factory worker. He befriends the Narrator upon his arrival in Jacksonville. The Narrator rooms with the Cuban and his wife, and the Cuban helps him get a job at the cigar factory. He also schools the Narrator on the Cuban revolution, which broadens the Narrator's awareness of the plight of people of color throughout the world.

Warren J. Carson

THE AUTOBIOGRAPHY OF MISS JANE PITTMAN

Author: Ernest J. Gaines (1933-   )
Type of work: Novel
Time of action: The early 1860's to the early 1960's
First published: 1971

Miss Jane Pittman, a former slave and life-long agricultural laborer and domestic. Small but wiry, perhaps 110 years old at the time of the narrative, Miss Jane is, with her oral autobiography, a living repository of the American black experience in the Deep South. An inspiration to her community, Jane has survived a long life of neglect, abuse, and oppression through a combination of endurance, tenacity, and necessary forbearance. She weathers the brutality and dehumanizing effects of institutionalized racism and the grief of personal loss with a wisdom and vitality that affects even her white social superiors. The autobiography she narrates so reflects her personality and attitude that she shapes the novel with an eyewitness' sense of historical immediacy. At the end of the novel, in a culmination of her century-long life, she asserts her independence and freedom by staring down a white plantation owner as she leaves for town to lend her support to a civil rights protest.

Ned Douglass, Miss Jane's adoptive son, Spanish-American War veteran, schoolmaster, and community leader. In his late thirties at the time of his murder, Ned is tall, powerfully muscled, with intense eyes and a natural orator's persuasive ability. As a small child Ned is unofficially adopted by Jane—herself barely more than a child—after his mother and infant sister are brutally murdered by nightriders shortly after the Emancipation. Calling Jane "Mama," Ned is the child Jane can never have biologically; his departure to the North at seventeen or eighteen devastates her. He is assassinated because of his independent thinking and his campaigning for the minimal civil rights of black citizens.

Joe Pittman, Jane's common-law husband, a widower with two daughters, an expert breaker of wild horses. Joe accepts Jane's inability to bear children with compassion, earning her supreme compliment, "He was a real man, Joe Pittman was." His expertise as a horse tamer leads him to seek employment on a ranch in western Louisiana, where he becomes locally renowned for his courage and ability. His talent as "chief breaker," in fact, earns for him the poignant title "Chief Pittman." Joe is killed trying to tame a huge black stallion. The seven or eight years Jane and Joe spend together are the most carefree and peaceful of Jane's life.

Jimmy Aaron, a young civil rights worker, born on the Samson plantation, shot dead by white racists in the nearby town of Bayonne. Tall and thin, with "eyes very very serious," Jimmy is from birth considered a Moses-savior figure in the black community. He is constantly identified as "the One" upon whom black hopes rest for a leader. Jimmy's intelligence and articulateness lead him not to the pulpit—as universally hoped among the black community—nor to the teacher's lectern, but into civil rights action after the example of Dr. Martin Luther King, Jr. After successfully motivating black citizens to attend a protest in Bayonne en masse, Jimmy dies a martyr's death.

Jules Raynard, an elderly white man, godfather to Tee Bob Samson and "like a second father" to Robert Samson, Sr. Jules, a big man with white hair and a red face, apparently an asthmatic, intervenes in the crisis triggered by Tee Bob's suicide. A man of intelligence and compassion, Jules speaks truths with Jane about the insidious effects of institutional racism—outworn but not yet repudiated—on modern young people. Jane respects Jules more than any other white person.

Albert Cluveau, a Cajun ne'er-do-well and paid assassin, murderer of Ned Douglass. Pock-faced, bowlegged, with patchy, unkempt white hair and watery blue eyes, Cluveau admits dispassionately to Jane to killing numerous people, black and white. Oddly attracted to Jane, Cluveau seeks her company, runs errands for her, sips coffee and fishes with her. Yet he shows neither hesitation nor remorse about cold-bloodedly shooting Ned Douglass, knowing that Jane loves Ned as her son. Believing afterward that Jane has put a curse upon him, Cluveau dies terrified, in a delusion of being attacked by demons.

Robert Samson, Sr., the owner of Samson plantation, father of Tee Bob, defender of Old South values and attitudes. Robert is a tall, thin man with brown hair and gray eyes. Like his natural son, Timmy Henderson, Robert is high-spirited and loves practical jokes. For all his energy and sardonic humor, however, Robert remains finally an entrenched member of the racist status quo. He is not personally vicious, but he lacks any sympathy for black civil rights.

"Tee Bob," Robert Samson, Jr., Robert's legal heir and only child, who commits suicide after falling deeply in love with the mulatto schoolteacher on his father's plantation. Childlike in appearance (though a college student), with a soft red mouth, large, sorrowful eyes, and fair, smooth skin and a beardless face, Tee Bob loves Mary Agnes LeFabre with a love that transcends racial boundaries and social mores. His love rebuked by the adults, black and white, as well as by his closest friend, Tee Bob takes his own life. Jane is saddened by Tee Bob's death and is touched by the tragic circumstances of his impossible love for Mary Agnes.

Mary Agnes LeFabre, the mulatto ("Creole") teacher on the Samson plantation, and the object of Tee Bob's love. Beautiful, of medium height, fair-skinned, with long black hair, Mary Agnes resembles the Italian-Sicilian descendants living in the Bayonne area. Mary Agnes perceives Tee Bob's basic decency and enjoys his boyish attention from a respectful distance, but she rejects Tee Bob's confession of love for her with a painful but truthful, "We can't have nothing together, Robert." She is forced to leave the state in anonymity after Tee Bob's suicide.

Timmy Henderson, Robert Samson, Sr.'s natural child by a black woman, Verda Henderson. Tall and thin, with reddish-brown hair and brown eyes, Timmy even has his father's hook nose. Beyond the striking physical resemblance, Timmy has his father's personality. His confusing identity and confused social status lead Timmy into a violent confrontation with a jealous white overseer. For Timmy's own safety, Robert sends his natural son away from Samson. Timmy's character and story powerfully convey the destructive effects of the South's institutionalized racism.

Miss Amma Dean Samson, Robert Sr.'s wife, Tee Bob's mother, the mistress of Samson plantation. Mrs. Samson comes across as the domestic heart of the Samson enterprise, worrying over the supervision of the black staff and keeping a nervous watch over Tee Bob. Although she knows of Timmy Henderson, she is resigned to his existence and allows him to be Tee Bob's playmate and companion. She is devastated by Tee Bob's suicide, even though Jane has tried to warn her of his love for Mary Agnes.

The Narrator, a black history teacher who travels to the Samson plantation to interview Miss Jane in 1962. Although more a presence than a developed character, the narrator provides the frame story for Jane's dramatic autobiography. The narrator also establishes the importance of Jane's life and story as the oral history of all black Americans in the South.

David W. Pitre

THE AUTUMN OF THE PATRIARCH

Author: Gabriel García Márquez (1928-   )
Type of work: Novel
Time of action: The late nineteenth and early twentieth centuries
First published: El otoño del patriarca, 1975 (English translation, 1975)

The patriarch, also called **the general, the "All Pure," the "Magnificent,"** and so on, an unnamed Latin American dictator who is somewhere between the ages of 107 and 232. At one point, he writes a note to himself reading "my name is Zacarías" (sä•kä•rē′äs), but because this event occurs after his senility has progressed, the note, like many other events in the novel, is suspect. Superstitious, paranoid, and ruthless, illiterate but peasant-shrewd, he rules from a palace that has been converted into a marketplace. It is overrun with soldiers, prostitutes, cows, and lepers seeking miraculous cures from the patriarch; the state of his palace is that of his nation, and the decrepitude of both palace and nation results from and mirrors the patriarch's deteriorating mental state. The general, old beyond memory, has the huge flat feet of an elephant, a herniated testicle that whistles at night, and no lines on his smooth hands (which renders him immune to prophecy). In a sense, he is the only character in the novel, since all other characters are rendered in relation to him and the novel fluctuates between third-person reports of his actions, first-person statements made to the patriarch, and first-person interior monologue of the general's responses to characters and events. He is the history of his nation, and, as he becomes increasingly senile, he even remembers the arrival of Europeans in the New World; these memories are never convincingly proven or refuted. The novel begins with and repeatedly returns to the discovery of his body, mutilated beyond recognition by vultures in the presidential palace.

Manuela Sánchez, beauty queen of the poor whose supernatural beauty astounds the nation. The patriarch dances a waltz with her out of ceremonial obligation, then gradually becomes obsessed with her (to the extent that he has reveille played at three in the morning and changes the nation's clocks to distract him from his nocturnal fascination with her). The patriarch courts her in the traditional manner, coming to her house with presents, but he rebuilds entire neighborhoods to elevate her slum origins. She disappears during a total eclipse of the sun, and the general's agents are unable to locate her anywhere on earth, although rumors abound.

Benedición Alvarado (bĕ•nĕ•dē•syōn′ äl•vä•rä′dō), the patriarch's mother by an unknown father, a former prostitute who paints common birds in order to sell them as exotic songbirds. During most of her son's reign, she lives frugally in a suburban house in the capital city, coming to the palace to clean up after and criticize her son. She serves to keep him in touch with his peasant roots, deflating much of the pomp and ceremony that grows about the general's person. He nurses her during her fatal illness, washing her pustulent sores with various quack remedies. After her death, her son has her embalmed and sends her corpse on a tour of the provinces; rumors of her miraculous preservation lead to his insistence on her sainthood. This demand results in his expulsion of the Catholic church from the nation, the expropriation of Church property, and the institution of Benedición Alvarado as a "civil saint." She persists in his increasingly senile memory as the last person other than himself he remembers.

Leticia Mercedes María Nazareno (lĕ•tē′ syä mĕr•sĕ′dĕs mä•rē′ä nä•sä•rĕ′nō), the patriarch's wife, a former nun. A stocky girl, she is noticed, in a crowd of nuns, by the patriarch during the exodus of the Church from the nation. His notice of her is enough to persuade his agents to kidnap her and ship her back, stripped, to his bedchamber. He keeps her there for two years before they consummate their affair, after which she becomes the power behind his throne. With much difficulty (and many embarrassments, owing to his lack of decorum in repeating his lessons), she teaches the patriarch to read. As a result of her influence, the cult of his mother is overthrown in favor of a reinstitution of the Catholic church; yet flowers wilt, vegetables rot, and meat festers at her touch. During the Catholic marriage ceremony that will legitimate the heir she carries, she gives birth at the altar just as the archbishop asks for the bride's response. As time passes, she becomes gradually less and less spiritual; as she yields to the material benefits of being the patriarch's concubine, her passion is spent in shopping at the expense of the government's credit (a ritual that is controlled by the actions of the presidential guard, who occupy the bazaar before she can arrive). Her extravagance in shopping threatens to bankrupt the already-insolvent government. In a plot laid by a cabal of the ruling junta, she is torn to pieces in the marketplace, along with the patriarch's son and heir, by dogs trained to attack her outfit and the heir's uniform. A purge ensues.

Patricio Aragonés (pä•trē′syō ä•rä•gō• něs′), the general's perfect double, who is arrested in the provinces for impersonating the leader and purveying spurious miracle cures. He loyally serves the general as a stand-in (after having his feet flattened with a mallet), but his naturally lighthearted and outgoing personality gradually merges with and transforms into the taciturn and brutal nature of the general. His services hasten the growth of the general's reputation for ubiquity, a major part of the general's mystique that will eventually confound any attempts to make sense of the nation's history. When Aragonés is fatally poisoned (relatively early in the patriarch's reign), he castigates the general in a deathbed speech; the general uses the confusion following the fake state funeral to launch another of his political purges. Aragonés' death presages and becomes confused with that of the patriarch, further muddling efforts by the general's countrymen to make sense of events.

General Rodrigo de Aguilar (rō•drē′gō dě ä•gē•lär′), an artilleryman and academy graduate, the general's right-hand man (often called "my comrade of a lifetime") who serves as minister of defense, director of state security, and commander of the presidential guard. His loyalty and friendship to the patriarch make him a stable reference point in the swirl of conspiracy and cabal that surrounds the government; he has even been granted the privilege of beating the patriarch at dominoes after losing his right arm to a would-be assassin's bomb. During a period of political unrest, he is late for a palace dinner held in honor of the high command; his arrival is to signal the final revolt against the dictator. After the officers fret for a while, General Rodrigo de Aguilar is brought in on a silver tray, cooked and stuffed; the general doles out equal portions to each officer present.

José Ignacio Saenz de la Barra (hō•sě′ ēg•nä′syo sī′ěns dě lä bä′rrä), **"Nacho,"** a sadistic torturer. Described as a "dazzling and haughty man" and an impeccable dresser who always travels with a huge Doberman on a leash, he emerges late in the general's rule to bring the patriarch's realm into the twentieth century of systematic (rather than arbitrary) torture and totalitarian government. To fill the bags full of human heads he insists on bringing the general, he butchers the patriarch's adversaries, friends, and those who are neutral, seemingly impartially, as he assumes full control of the new secret police that will, in time, come to dominate the government. A representative of the old aristocratic classes, de la Barra's rise is the final movement in the process that has brought the patriarch's revolution full circle: Any reforms or changes brought by the revoltion have been gradually effaced by time and events. Nacho himself is killed in a popular uprising, instigated by the patriarch to forestall a military coup; the torturer's body is mutilated and strung up in a public square.

Emanuel, the patriarch's infant son. At birth, he is appointed a major general "with jurisdiction and command"; he shows an uncanny aptitude for politics, ceremony, and diplomacy that belies his years. He is killed with his mother by dogs trained to attack his uniform.

David Pringle

AVALOVARA

Author: Osman Lins (1924-1978)
Type of work: Novel
Time of action: 200 B.C., 1908-1940, and 1938-1970
First published: 1973 (English translation, 1980)

Abel, a writer from Northeastern Brazil, where he was born in 1935. A student in Paris at twenty-seven, then a cashier at the Brazilian Fiscal Commission in Recife, where he has been since 1962. He makes love with three women at different times in his life. He is married but separated from a woman who kills herself. He is murdered by Hayano.

Anneliese Roos (Rose), his German lover in Paris, where she has been since 1951, though she has work as a receptionist in Amsterdam. She leaves Abel for her husband, in a Lausanne sanatorium.

Cecília, his androgynous, Brazilian lover in Recife, works for hospital social services. Her brothers, one a policeman, beat her and Abel. Pregnant by Abel, she dies in an accident.

O, his twenty-three or thirty-two-year-old lover in São Paulo. Reared by her grandparents, she married Hayano when she was still in school and attempted suicide on her wedding night. Her lovemaking with Abel is rendered in strong physical detail, during which she recalls her previous life of first love, husband, grandparents, and feeling for the bird Avalovara. She is killed with Abel by her husband, who finds them in sexual embrace.

The Fat Woman, Abel's mother, who had been a prostitute since fifteen in 1929. She was married to The Treasurer at nineteen, but refused to give up sleeping with other men; she has mothered many children by different men.

Raul Nogueira de Albuquerque e Castro (ăl•bōō•kərk′ ē kăsh′trōō), **The Treasurer,** married to The Fat Woman. He helped care for her children while working for a bank. He is killed by a truck, and it is unknown whether it was suicide or an accident.

Publius Ubonius, a Pompeiian merchant in 200 B.C. He offers Loreius freedom if he invents a phrase that can be read left to right and backward.

Loreius, a slave of Publius Ubonius, discovers the mysterious phrase that unites the novel. He kills himself after his phrase is stolen.

Tyche, Pompeiian courtesan who steals the mystical phrase from Loreius and sells it to Ubonius.

Julius Heckethorn, a German clockmaker, mathematician, harpsichordist, and expert on Mozart, born in 1908. His father was British, his mother German. He was shot as a traitor in 1939 by Germans in Holland. He makes the clock, which he began constructing in 1933, found in the room where O and Abel make love. It was brought to Brazil from Europe by the wife of the Brazilian ambassador after the war.

Heidi Lampl, marries Julius Heckethorn in 1930.

97

Olavo Hayano, the husband of ☿, whom he met when they were both children. According to ☿, he is a "yolyp," or sterile freak of nature. A Brazilian soldier, he commands a detachment during the funeral for Natividade and murders his wife and Abel.

Natividade, black maid in Hayano household. A childless virgin when she dies at seventy-five, it is her funeral procession that winds through the streets of São Paulo during the novel.

Hermelinda and **Hermenilda,** old women of Recife. Though not twins, they do look alike; they sew surrounded by cats and introduce Cecília to Abel.

Richard D. McGhee

AWAKE AND SING!

Author: Clifford Odets (1906-1963)
Type of work: Play
Time of action: The early 1930's
First produced: 1935

Bessie Berger, a working-class Jewish-American housewife, struggling to hold her family together during the Great Depression of the 1930's. An Earth Mother type, Bessie values the appearance of respectability above all else. Her greatest fear is that she and her family might be put out of their home and thrown into the street as an old lady near them has been. Bessie is domineering and self-righteous. She does not think deeply. Her life is centered on her family, three generations of which live in a cramped apartment in the Bronx.

Myron Berger, Bessie's husband, a follower rather than a leader. Myron is a broken man, totally controlled by Bessie, who is much stronger than he. He once studied law at night school but did not complete his studies. He tries innocently to overcome the hardships of the Depression by buying chances on the Irish Sweepstakes or by betting a few dollars on a horse, convinced that the government would not let such enterprises be crooked, thereby convincing himself that he stands some chance of winning, which is his only tangible hope for the future.

Ralph Berger, Myron and Bessie's idealistic son, who scrapes by on the sixteen dollars a week he earns only by living at home and contributing much-needed dollars to the family coffers. He has a girlfriend, Blanche, but cannot entertain any realistic idea of marrying her because they cannot afford to marry. Bessie's moral posture, the appearance of respectability at any price, appalls Ralph, a decent person who has never had an even break. When he was a child, there was never money to have his teeth fixed or to buy him a pair of roller skates he wanted. Now that he is on his own and is earning money, little has changed. He still barely survives economically; he still cannot live his own life.

Hennie Berger, Myron and Bessie's daughter has a streak of independence in her, although she is slowly being crushed by the same economic forces and insecurities that threaten the rest of the family. When the family's boarder, Moe Axelrod, gets Hennie pregnant, Bessie, to preserve the appearance of respectability, forces Hennie into a marriage with the unsuspecting immigrant Sam Feinschreiber, whom Hennie does not love. She finally abandons her family and compromises her child's future by running away with Moe, thereby asserting her independence but also demonstrating her self-centered willfulness.

Jacob, Bessie's father, lives with the family. He and Ralph share a philosophical kinship.

Jacob quotes the sayings of Karl Marx, using Marx to support his contention that families such as this one should not exist. Jacob and Bessie are at opposite poles: Jacob the almost total idealist, Bessie ever the pragmatist. Jacob finally commits suicide by plunging off the roof of the Berger's apartment building, having written his small insurance policy over to Ralph so that Ralph can have a new beginning.

Uncle Morty, Bessie's affluent, cigar-smoking, womanizing brother and Jacob's son. He comes to the Bergers' so that his father can cut his hair. He represents the practical businessman who has ceased to be a person. He is, rather, what the people he does business with require him to be. He is loud, rich, and totally insensitive, a character corrupted by the very capitalistic system that has made him affluent. He refers to Jacob as a nut.

Moe Axelrod, the Berger's sexually tempting boarder, a lady's man who has lost one leg in the war and now lives on a decent disability pension. Moe is no more sensitive than Uncle Morty. He may not be rich, but he has the security of his pension, which is important in the bleak days of the Depression. Having impregnated Hennie and refused to marry her, he then proceeds to destroy the marriage her mother arranged for her by virtually forcing her to leave her husband and baby to run off with him to an uncertain—and likely not very enduring—future.

Sam Feinschreiber, a lonely immigrant with whom Myron works. Myron brings Sam home to dinner to meet Hennie, who has no interest in him. Sam, however, is the vehicle through which Bessie can preserve her family's respectability when Hennie turns up pregnant.

Schlosser, superintendent of the building in which the Berger's live, informs the family of Jacob's suicide. Schlosser is German. His wife ran away with another man twenty years earlier, leaving Schlosser to rear their daughter, as Hennie is about to do. The daughter did not turn out well, and Schlosser has lived a life of desperation and frustration for two decades.

R. Baird Shuman

BABEL-17

Author: Samuel R. Delany (1942-   )
Type of work: Novel
Time of action: The distant future
First published: 1966

Rydra Wong, the most famous poet in five galaxies and, although still only twenty-six years old, already considered the voice of her age. In addition to writing poetry, Rydra is a skilled cryptographer, a linguist, and an interstellar captain. These fields of accomplishment, as diverse as they may seem, are all aided by Rydra's total verbal recall. While always having had this talent to some degree, she developed it rapidly after a severe illness in her youth. Rydra is also telepathic and frequently knows what people will say before they say it. Her own assessment of this skill, however, is that she is merely "reading" the expressions of others with great precision. By the time that she was twelve, Rydra had already learned seven earth languages and five extraterrestrial tongues. In the intervening years, Rydra has studied many other forms of communication, including six languages used by the Invaders. She is considered very beautiful and has high cheekbones, copper-colored pupils, and oriental features. Her hair is long and frequently cascades over her shoulders. Five years earlier, Rydra was part of a triple, a form of marriage among three people. One of these partners has since died and another, suffering from an incurable illness, has been placed in suspended animation.

Dr. Markus T'Mwarba (Mocky), a psychologist and teacher. When Rydra was twelve, she was sent to T'Mwarba for treatment in psychotherapy and neurotherapy. Since that time, they have become close friends. T'Mwarba holds a black belt in Aikido and is the one person in whom Rydra places complete trust.

Danil D. Appleby, a customs official who helps Rydra assemble the crew of the *Rimbaud*. With his crew-cut red hair and wire-rimmed glasses, Appleby is, at first, the very image of the punctilious bureaucrat. After meeting Rydra, however, he develops a new sense of confidence and humor, coming to enjoy wrestling matches and ultimately even undergoing cosmetisurgery to have a mechanical dragon implanted in his shoulder as a decoration.

General Forester, the officer who is supervising the decipherment of Babel-17. Forester is a large man in his fifties; he is authoritarian and has a brisk and efficient manner. He falls in love with Rydra almost immediately upon meeting her.

Mollya Twa, Navigator-One, a member of the twenty-one-person crew of Rydra's spaceship, the *Rimbaud*. An attractive woman from Pan Africa, Mollya had committed suicide seven years earlier, when her two co-navigators were killed. Rydra, in need of a Navigator-One, has Mollya restored to life for the mission. Mollya has short, graphite-colored hair. Initially, she speaks only Kiswahili, but she learns English quickly.

Calli, Navigator-Two, another crew member of the *Rimbaud*. Calli seems rough and threatening upon first acquaintance, but he is actually competent and good-hearted. His face is heavily pockmarked, and he has mechanical lights implanted all over his chest, shoulders, arms, and legs. His stellarimeter is grafted directly onto his palm.

Ron, Navigator-Three. A small, thin man of about nineteen, Ron was the youngest member of an earlier triple, which had also included Calli. As a result, he is the one who grieves most deeply over the loss of their former Navigator-One, Cathy. Towheaded and sapphire-eyed, Ron has muscles that are sharply defined. His only cosmetisurgery is a rose that emerges from his shoulder.

Brass, pilot of the *Rimbaud*. Brass is very muscular with brass claws, yellow plush paws, golden eyes, and a mane. While walking, he prefers to move about on all fours. Cosmetisurgically implanted fangs have left Brass unable to pronounce the sound of the letter *p*. He is chosen as pilot for the *Rimbaud* after Rydra watches him wrestle, a skill that illustrates the reflexes of potential pilots.

The Slug, a fat man whose eyes, hair, and thin beard are all black. The Slug moves slowly but thinks quickly and performs a number of supervisory functions on the *Rimbaud*, including that of ship's medic.

Jebel, the pirate captain of the spaceship *Jebel Tarik* ("Jebel's mountain"). Jebel commands a "shadow ship," which hides in the Specelli Snap. He lives by hijacking the ships of the Invaders and, when necessary, those of the Alliance as well. Jebel is craggy faced and wears outmoded clothing, including a plastic garment that automatically contours to his body like armor. He drapes a deep-piled black cloak over one shoulder and wears high-laced sandals. Jebel's cosmetisurgery includes false silver hair and metallic eyebrows. One thick silver ring hangs from a distended earlobe.

The Butcher, one of the most important crew members on the *Jebel Tarik*. The Butcher is a mysterious figure who has no knowledge of his own past and does not understand the terms (or concepts of) "I" and "you." He is muscular and round-shouldered and wears only a breechcloth. Cocks' spurs, used as brass knuckles, have been grafted onto his wrists and heels. His hair is amber but has been closely shaved.

The Butcher is branded with the convicts' mark from the penal caves of Titin. The mis-sion to decipher Babel-17 eventually becomes a mission to determine the Butcher's identity.

Jeffrey L. Buller

BADENHEIM 1939

Author: Aharon Appelfeld (1932-   )
Type of work: Novel
Time of action: 1939
First published: Badenheim, 'ir nofesh, 1975 (English translation, 1980)

Dr. Pappenheim, hotel "impresario" and director of the summer festival of perform-ing arts at the Badenheim resort. Encourag-ing and accommodating, he works very hard at providing the hotel guests with the best of entertainment. His attitude is quite positive, and, when the Jews face deportation to Po-land, he looks forward to a new and exciting life in a new land, feeling that no real life remains in Badenheim.

Trude, the pharmacist's wife. She is a sickly woman who worries constantly that her son-in-law Leopold beats her daughter Helena. Haunted by a hidden fear, she fades into hallucinations about ferocious wolves. Her hallucinations are replaced by childhood memories of Poland, and she believes all will be well when she, her husband, and her daughter reach Poland.

Martin, the pharmacist. He is a sorrowful man who constantly looks after his sick wife, to the point of ultimately absorbing her sickness. He is forever promising her that all will be well, despite his own anxieties.

Leon Samitzky, a Polish musician who has wonderful memories of his childhood in Po-land. He longs to return to his homeland and stirs feelings of melancholy and nostalgia in Dr. Pappenheim with his stories of his child-hood. A heavy drinker who is always in debt, he looks forward to deportation to Poland.

Professor Fussholdt, a vacationer at the re sort and a famous historian. Hostile to ev-erything Jewish, he denounces such figures as Theodor Herzl and Martin Buber. His en-tire stay in Badenheim is spent reviewing the proofs for his latest book.

Mitzi Fussholdt, the very young wife of Professor Fussholdt. A vain and unfaithful woman, she is interested only in clothes and cosmetics, and understands nothing of her husband's work. She is saddened at finding no friends or lovers in Badenheim and de-velops nightmares as a result of her fear of deportation.

Frau Zauberbilt, an escapee from a nearby sanatorium. A divorced woman, she is happy and gay, until she falls ill and begins to cling to her belief in an afterlife.

Dr. Schutz, a vacationer and mathematician who lives off his mother's money. He is boy-ish and loved by all, and chases after a young schoolgirl.

A schoolgirl, the delicate, frail girlfriend of Dr. Schutz. She wants him to take her away from Badenheim and becomes pregnant with his child. Once she is pregnant, she rarely speaks to her lover, but she has no fears and no regrets.

Karl, a divorced vacationer who terrorizes people and has a fascination for the fish in the hotel aquarium. Forever thinking about his sons in a military academy, he takes up with a married woman and invites her to go to Poland with him.

Lotte, Karl's girlfriend, who is married to

an agent for a large business firm. She is filled with sorrow and feels her life is over.

Two poetry readers, identical twins, tall and thin with a monkish look. They carry a dark secret, eat nothing, and go into seclusion. They have a passion for Rainer Maria Rilke.

Princess Milbaum, patroness of the twins. Tall and elegant, she feels there is a conspiracy against her because people avoid her. She soon shuts herself into her room, where she writes letters complaining of how the *Ostjuden* (Eastern European Jews) have spoiled Badenheim. In the end, she is a body without a soul.

Nahum Slotzker, the *yanuka*, or boy singer, from Poland. Frightened and spoiled, he grows fat at the resort and loses his voice, as well as his innocence.

Salo, a traveling salesman who grew up in Poland and looks forward to going back. Ca-

pricious and given to drink, he delights in living off his expense account.

Gertie and
Sally, prostitutes age forty and forty-two, respectively. Inseparable friends, they are kind and generous. They take care of the *yanuka*.

Peter, the pastry shop owner. Hostile and indignant, he refuses to let Sally and Gertie in his shop. He hates Dr. Pappenheim and most of the hotel guests.

Professor Mandelbaum, a master violinist who is sent to Badenheim because he is a Jew. He forces his trio to practice constantly as they await deportation.

An old rabbi, sick and confined to a wheelchair. He is forever asking questions in a mixture of Yiddish and Hebrew, and his eyes are filled with an ancient grief.

Dr. Langmann, an angry man who denies his Jewishness and dislikes Jews.

David Patterson

BAGA

Author: Robert Pinget (1919-   )
Type of work: Novel
Time of action: Unspecified
First published: 1958 (English translation, 1967)

Architruc, the narrator. He is king of Fantoine and Agapa. He describes himself as fat, with varicose veins, a flat head, pimples, sandy-colored hair, a nose like a potato, and cauliflower ears. When Architruc is fifteen, his father is killed in a revolt, and his mother assumes the regency until the youth comes of age. He mopes about the palace, delighting only in a garden that he plants with lily-of-the-valley and crowfoot. He falls in love with Baga, who is also the lover of Architruc's mother; as soon as Architruc becomes king, he names Baga his prime minister. At first Architruc travels about his kingdom to dispense justice, but eventually he grows

bored with this practice and, like his father, cloisters himself within the palace. For him, each day is identical: He arises at noon, performs a few simple exercises, and examines his collections of pebbles, shells, leaves, eyeglasses, and watches. Then his barber arrives to shave him. Afterward, Architruc waters his plant, Ducky, and sponges its leaves. Dressed in white, the king next appears at lunch, his chief delight, where he always eats beef, an omelette, and cheese before he retires to his room once more. War with Novocardia disrupts this pattern. Following his victory, he retires for a century to a hut in the forest. When he returns to the palace, a visit from Queen Conegrund again upsets his routine. While overseeing the construction of a castle in the valley of Rouget, he wanders off to join a small convent and becomes a woman for a time.

Baga, Architruc's prime minister. Baga appears subservient, bringing Architruc his morning tea and chamber pot, carrying the king's umbrella, planning the royal menu, helping the monarch dress. Yet Baga also conducts foreign and economic policy without consulting Architruc, converting his country into the world's leading exporter of rat pelts and building up an arsenal for eventual war with neighboring Novocardia.

Corniflet, the royal barber and part-time molecatcher. About thirty, he has red hair and blue eyes.

Piston and
Vielle, the royal musicians. The cornetist once had long hair, but now he and the hurdy-gurdy player are both bald. One formerly had worked as overseer in a print shop, the other as a milkboy, but Architruc's father trained them to their present occupation. Though they are sixty, they look eighty. They live in the forest in a one-room house that was formerly a hunting lodge. Each day the king sends a car to bring them to the palace to play the banquet overture.

Sister Louise, a godly woman who lives on prayer and vegetables. For a time, Architruc shares her house.

Mary, a pretty young woman who joins the convent of Architruc and Sister Louise. She and Architruc sleep together until he recovers his masculinity.

Queen Conegrund, ruler of Doualia. Fat and red-faced, she wears a red wig and a diamond crown. A voracious eater and lover, she tries to bed Architruc, but she accepts a black dishwasher in his stead. Her visit to Architruc strains the treasury, but her purchase of the dishwasher for a thousand rupees helps replenish the coffers.

Rara, an orphan adopted by Architruc to become his heir. Between ten and twenty years old, Rara is pale, blue-eyed, tall, and frail. He is a voracious reader.

King Gnar, a cave dweller who receives the letters that Architruc writes while living in the forest. Gnar may be the real power behind the throne: When Gnar tosses a dirty sock in the direction of Architruc's palace, the king at once decides to open a sock shop. Gnar has a serpent for an adviser.

Mougre, Baga's predecessor as prime minister.

Joseph Rosenblum

THE BALCONY

Author: Jean Genet (1910-1986)
Type of work: Play
Time of action: The 1930's
First published: Le Balcon, 1956 (English translation, 1957)

Irma (The Queen), the proprietress of the Grand Balcony, a brothel specializing in role-playing games. Approximately forty years old, she wears severe clothing and jewelry that reflect her bent for business matters and the riches they bring. Predisposed to calling her wealthy customers "visitors" instead of "clients," she fears a workers' revolt that would threaten her establishment. Although she appears to have some genuine affection for one of her employees, Carmen, as well as for the chief of police, George, her good standing with them seems largely predicated on their usefulness to her. In scene 8 she becomes The Queen, wearing an ermine cloak and, on her brow, a diadem.

The Chief of Police (George), a cigar smoker who wears a heavy fur-lined coat and hat. He wishes that "The Chief of Police" would become one of the figures portrayed at the Grand Balcony. A politically ambitious freemason, he dreams of being enshrined in a tomb by the subjects of an empire he aspires to command. In scene 8 he becomes **The Hero;** later in the play, he seems to have achieved his goals. It is also revealed that he wears a toupee.

The Bishop and
The Judge, clients at the Grand Balcony who first appear in versions of their customary garb, wearing garish make-up, twenty-inch-high tragedian's cothurni, and other accoutrements that make them seem unusually large. Later in the play, they appear to have actually assumed their roles in Irma's regime.

The General, another client, a retiring-looking gentlemen who is first shown being dressed in a complete general's uniform by The Girl, an employee of the Grand Balcony. He, too, appears to assume his role in Irma's government.

Carmen, an employee favored by Irma who is in charge of bookeeping at the Grand Balcony. Possibly the daughter of a cavalry colonel, she talks of bringing toys and perfumes to her own daughter, who lives at a nursery in the country. Proud of her skills, she is particularly attracted to playing female saints and other religious heroines. She uses her familiarity with clients and other employees to spy for Irma.

Chantal, a former employee who has left the Grand Balcony to join her lover, Roger. Her acting ability is coveted by the revolutionaries, who desire a fiery woman who will inspire their followers. She leaves Rog-er's side to join them, only to be assassinated in a plot devised by The Bishop.

Roger, Chantal's lover who admires her spirit but also wishes to control her. After her death he becomes the first client at the Grand Balcony to play the role of Chief of Police. Interrupting the fantasy by asking Carmen if she knew Chantal, he then appears to castrate himself.

The Executioner (Arthur), an employee, a physically intimidating figure who helps enact The Judge's fantasy. At heart a retiring soul who clings to the security of his job and his sycophantic relationship with Irma, he is shot in the head at the end of scene 5.

The Envoy, wears an embassy uniform styled as a tunic, and speaks enigmatically of The Queen in his first appearance in scene 7. Unaffected by the revolt, he advises Irma on matters of state once she assumes the role of The Queen.

The Man, a nervous and sloppily dressed client who stands before three mirrors as he awaits the whip and louse-infested wig that comprise his costume props. His reflections are played by three actors. As **The Beggar** he cries "Long Live the Queen" in scene 8; as **The Slave** he partakes in Roger's fantasy at the Grand Balcony.

The Woman (Rosine, The Penitent)
The Thief, and
The Girl, young female employees who interact with The Bishop, The Judge, and The General and The Man, respectively.

Three Men with Machine-Guns, rebels who lead Chantal away from Roger in scene 6.

Three Photographers, earnest young men dressed in black leather jackets and blue jeans who take profile shots of The Bishop, The General, and The Judge in act 7.

David Marc Fischer

THE BALD SOPRANO

Author: Eugène Ionesco (1912-   )
Type of work: Play
Time of action: The late 1940's or early 1950's
First produced: La Cantatrice chauve, 1950 (English translation, 1956)

Mr. Smith, an utterly boring, illogical husband living in the suburbs of London. He discusses inconsequential trivia with his wife and with their guests, another couple, and, subsequently, the Fire Chief. He is lacking in genuine communication with his wife. They do not listen to each other. His absence of rational arguments and his numerous fallacies are especially satirized. These include sweeping generalization, ignoring the question, circular reasoning, faulty argument by analogy, non sequitur, oversimplification, and faulty assumptions. Frequent contradictory statements are made. When he refers to all the members of a large, extended family as having the name Bobby Watson, both men and women, the author thus satirizes lack of individuality and the blurring of sex lines. Also, he refers to someone as a "living corpse," reflecting the author's view that those in the play are, indeed, living corpses.

Mrs. Smith, a middle-class housewife married to Mr. Smith. She opens the play by discussing the three helpings she and her husband each had at dinner, gluttony thus being satirized. She misuses words. Her topics of conversation are utterly trivial. She turns the conversation quickly to death. She, as her husband, abounds in illogical arguments. For example, when the doorbell rings three times, she sees no one there and insists that the doorbell rings because there is never anyone there. She criticizes men as effeminate, only to have Mr. Smith counter that women are doing masculine things, such as drinking whiskey.

Mary, the maid at the Smiths' home. She enters, stating the obvious, that she is their maid, as if they did not know. Having been given permission by Mrs. Smith to go out for the afternoon, she, on returning, finds the Smiths' dinner guests at the door, waiting

for Mary to return home as they did not dare enter by themselves. When the Smiths leave to change into dinner clothes, she invites the Martins in. She uses faulty logic to "prove" that Mr. and Mrs. Martin are not who they are. When the Fire Chief arrives later, she embraces him, glad to see him again at last. She insists on reading to the guests her poem, "The Fire," which is woefully repetitious and atrocious verse, a satire of amateur poets.

Mr. Donald Martin, a middle-class friend of the Smiths, husband to Mrs. Martin. While they wait in the living room for the Smiths to enter, Mr. Martin does not know where he has met Mrs. Martin, as if they are strangers. They make so little impression on each other that they cannot even remember being together. They finally deduce that they sleep in the same bed, thus the author satirizes marriage as lacking real unity. Mr. Martin's conversation when the Smiths appear is preposterously banal.

Mrs. Elizabeth Martin, a middle-class woman married to Mr. Martin, both being rather embarrassed and timid. She reports seeing a man on the street bend down to tie his shoelaces, a hardly believable sight, the ordinary seeming to her extraordinary. Her class prejudice against Mary is also satire.

The Fire Chief, who has come on official business to ascertain if there is a fire in the house since he has orders to extinguish all fires in the city. He complains that his business is poor now since there are few fires, and hence his profits on output are very meager, an attack on commercialism in public service. The Fire Chief points out that he does not have the right to extinguish clergymen's fires. This ties in with Mrs. Smith's comment that a fireman is also a confessor.

That is, she sees him in a religious light, in that fire involves warmth, which is related to life and also to love, which religion aims to foster. Thus, the Fire Chief is like a priest and hears confessions. Mrs. Smith inverts the relationship, however, seeing the Fire Chief as the confessor. Mrs. Smith had earlier misused the word "apotheosis," which refers to exaltation to the rank of a god. The author's irony indicates that these people are degraded instead. When Mary enters, she embraces the Fire Chief. He observes that she had extinguished his first fires, implying, perhaps, a previous hot relationship. The Fire Chief refers to a bald soprano, from which term the play takes its title, and which implies a lack of something customary and desirable, namely, hair. "Soprano" refers to a mode of communication in the higher range, but by implication ironically satirizes these people as low in their level of communication. After the departure of the Fire Chief, the play builds to a lengthy crescendo of hostility and nonsense. Then, with the lights going off and then on, the play begins again, but with the Martins this time saying exactly the same lines that the Smiths used earlier.

E. Lynn Harris

THE BALKAN TRILOGY

Author: Olivia Manning (1915-1980)
Type of work: Novel
Time of action: 1939-1941
First published: 1981: *The Great Fortune*, 1960; *The Spoilt City*, 1962; *Friends and Heroes*, 1965

Harriet Pringle, the twenty-two-year-old wife of Guy Pringle. She is thin and dark with an oval face. She has been married to her husband for less than a week and has known him only three weeks when she accompanies him to his job in Bucharest, Romania. The child of divorced parents, neither of whom wanted her, she has been reared by an aunt who regarded her as a nuisance; she looks to Guy for security, but she finds security neither in him nor in a Romania threatened by Nazi invasion. Harriet is increasingly resentful of Guy's simple, almost religious, faith in Marxism, by his boyish enthusiasm for various educational and theatrical projects, and by his tendency to bring eccentrics home for her to house. Her interests are metaphysical and personal; his are rational and impersonal. Fleeing Bucharest for Athens with Guy, Harriet finds a job in the British Information Office. She meets and is attracted to Charles Warden, but she cannot break faith with Guy nor commit herself to Warden. As Athens, too, readies for invasion, Harriet realizes that her marriage has survived both its periods of illusion and disillusion. She and Guy are still together when they flee Athens for Egypt.

Guy Pringle, in charge of the English department at Bucharest when his professor is made head of British propaganda in the Balkans. A large, nearsighted, twenty-three-year-old bear of a man with a mild face, Guy is a committed Marxist, hostile to religion and convinced that Russia alone can save Europe. He is subject to many enthusiasms that he insists on indulging; fond of having his own way, he does not want to be limited or defined by anyone, and he expects Harriet to understand when he diffuses his energies, not on marriage, but on crowds of strangers. Harriet believes that he uses his projects to avoid accepting reality and to ensure that he is the center of attention. As Bucharest falls, Guy produces the story of the fall of Troy (William Shakespeare's *Troilus and Cressida*), reveling in the spotlight as the political situation darkens. He doggedly prepares for a new school term up until the time that they must leave Bucharest. In Athens, betrayed by mediocrities he has befriended in Bucharest, he must struggle to find work. He begins a new project, a revue to entertain troops, and spends his spare time in a Marxist café. Prodded by Ben Phipps, he intervenes when Harriet is attracted to Warden, but he is not sympathic to her discontent, although he is hurt when she reveals doubts about their marriage.

Prince Yakimov (Yaki), a former society playboy, now impoverished. Son of an Irish mother and White Russian father, Yaki is tall, thin, with a face like a camel's. He has light green eyes and a long, delicate nose. A gourmet, a gourmand, and a heavy drinker, Yaki is resentful at the tricks fate has played on him. He has lived with the seemingly wealthy Dollie Clay-Callard, only to find that, at her death, she was in debt and left him nothing. Then he receives an income from his mother, but it ceases with her death. Increasingly ragged, Yaki is forced to beg for the luxuries he craves. Harriet is at first resentful when Guy brings him home to live in their spare room, but Guy is turning Yaki into an actor, training him for the role of Pandarus in his Shakespearean production. Yaki is quite successful, but the success does not bring him the food and drink he had anticipated, and, after the production, Guy loses interest in him. Resentful, Yaki betrays the presence in Guy's flat of a suspicious map and a Jewish escapee. Fleeing to Athens, Yaki takes a job delivering English news sheets on a bicycle. When Guy stages a revue there for the troops, Yaki is again successful, this time, in a blonde wig and false eyelashes, as Maria in *Maria Marten.* On the eve of the Nazi invasion, Yaki is fired from his job. Before he can escape Athens, he is shot by police for lighting a cigarette in a blackout.

Second Lieutenant Charles Warden, in Greece on mysterious British military assignments. Born to wealth and possessing the appearance of a handsome schoolboy, Warden studied classics until the war interrupted. Harriet perceives him as a romantic, even sacrificial, figure marked for death, but does not perceive the depth of his feeling for her until he is leaving the city. She has encouraged his friendship but has been unable to commit herself to a love affair. When Harriet and Guy leave Athens for Egypt, Warden is left behind with the retreating army.

Alan Frewen, British Information Officer in Athens. A heavy, square-built, middle-aged man, Frewen is withdrawn and silent; his one constant companion is his dog, Diocletian. Although a loner, Frewen efficiently helps those in need, hiring Yaki, Harriet, and two pathetic English sisters. A lover of Greece, he refuses to leave in the face of the German invasion; he plans to hide out on the Greek islands.

Inchcate, an aging professor of English in Bucharest, later British Information Officer there. Once contemptuous of officialdom, he becomes a self-important official, denying danger in the face of all evidence and occupying himself in reading Henry James and Marcel Proust. Refusing to give up his office or his summer school because a prestigious British academician has been scheduled to visit for a lecture, he remains oblivious to reality until his office is vandalized and he himself is seriously injured while reading Jane Austen. He collapses when reality then becomes impossible to ignore.

Sasha Drucker, the sheltered son, in his twenties, of the powerful banker Emanual Drucker. Sasha has been Guy's student. He is tall, thin, and narrow shouldered, with the manner of a nervous animal. Protected and indulged, he finds his world shattered when his father is arrested, imprisoned, brutalized, and put on trial. He himself is sent to the army, where he witnesses the brutal anti-Semitic murder of a friend. He runs away and finds refuge with Harriet and Guy. When they are out, the apartment is raided and Sasha and a servant vanish. Harriet mourns. When Harriet accidentally meets him in Athens, she learns that his family purchased his freedom. By then, his innocence is lost. Harriet cannot convince him that he was betrayed by Yaki, not by the Pringles themselves; Sasha refuses any longer to trust anyone outside his own Jewish faith.

Clarence Lawson, on cultural assignments from the British Council. Brutalized by his father and his schoolmasters, Clarence has the cringing manner of someone who expects to be hurt and even wants to be. He is attracted to strong women, such as Harriet, who will inevitably reject him. When he leaves Bucharest, he takes with him Sophie Oresanu, who marries him, and, upon receiving her British passport, leaves him for a series of wealthier men.

Sophie Oresanu, a law student. Pretty, part Jewish, dark, with an excellent figure, Sophie is clearly interested in Guy and hostile when Guy brings Harriet to Bucharest. She even threatens suicide to gain Guy's attention. Harriet is resentful, but Guy points out that, as a part-Jewish orphan with no dowry and too much freedom to suit Romanian conven-

tion, Sophie must capture a husband any way she can.

Ben Phipps, a free-lance journalist who has published with the Left Book Club. Short and thick-boned with black bristly hair, Phipps wears thick glasses that conceal hard black eyes. In Athens, he becomes Guy's friend, but Harriet senses that he dislikes all women and is a natural enemy of married life. Phipps wants Guy's attention; he wants Harriet to remain in the background. Nevertheless, his need to control people and events causes him to point Guy toward Harriet's growing fascination with Warden. Phipps believes in worldwide, fantasic political plots. Harriet disbelieves in them, but, nevertheless, it is Phipps's sense for plotting and his need to control events that lead to a way for English citizens to leave Athens ahead of the Nazi invasion.

Betty Richardson

THE BALLAD OF PECKHAM RYE

Author: Muriel Spark (1918-   )
Type of work: Novel
Time of action: The late 1950's
First published: 1960

Dougal Douglas, a new employee of the English textile firm Meadows, Meade & Grindley. A twenty-three-year-old Scot with a deformed shoulder, a captivating smile, and a complete disregard of convention, Douglas is hired in the vaguely defined position of "Arts man" by virtue of his M.A. from the University of Edinburgh. Later, under another name, he takes a similar position with a rival firm. Because he is able to play any role which occurs to him, Douglas can adjust himself to almost all of the characters he meets, and as a result, he elicits their secrets, draws them into his whimsical plans, and complicates their lives. Finally he leaves for Africa, a later stint in a monastery, and, eventually, a career as a writer.

Humphrey Place, a refrigeration engineer who lives in the same rooming house as

Dougal. Handsome but weak-willed, Humphrey is fascinated with Dougal and takes his opinions as gospel. Under Dougal's influence, Humphrey rejects his fiancée in mid-ceremony. Two months later, however, when Dougal is no longer present, he marries her.

Trevor Lomas, an electrician and a gang leader. Tall, strong, and quarrelsome, he is jealous of Dougal, who has attracted Trevor's girl. Convinced that Dougal is either the leader of a rival gang or a police agent, Trevor and his thugs threaten and attack Dougal's friends. During his escape, Dougal is ambushed by Trevor but disarms and defeats him.

Dixie Morse, Humphrey's fiancée, a typist at Meadows Meade. A tall, attractive, dark-eyed, black-haired girl of seventeen, Dixie ruins the engagement period by her insistence on making and saving every penny she can, so that she can have a perfect wedding and a fully furnished home. Devastated by Humphrey's rejection, she nevertheless recovers enough to marry him later, when Dougal's influence has dissipated.

Leslie Crewe, Dixie's half brother. Although only thirteen, he is a member of Trevor Lomas' gang. When Dougal refuses to pay him blackmail to keep quiet about the two jobs, Leslie becomes his bitter enemy.

Merle Coverdale, the head of the typing pool at Meadows Meade. At thirty-seven, she has tired of her long-term relationship with her married employer but finds that she cannot extricate herself. Because of her friendship with Dougal, she is murdered by her lover.

Vincent R. Druce, the managing director of Meadows Meade. Trapped in his miserable marriage to a well-off wife, he has set up a permanent relationship with Merle Coverdale. After he hears the rumors that Dougal is a police agent, he is so nervous about business misdeeds that he plans to flee the country. Before he can make his plans, however, he snaps mentally, accuses his mistress of informing on him, stabs her to death with a corkscrew, and is later arrested.

Maria Cheeseman, a retired actress and singer. Into her autobiography, which Dougal is writing, he incorporates bits of the stories told him by the residents of Peckham Rye, as if they were part of her experience.

Jinny Ferguson, Dougal's girlfriend and fellow student at the University of Edinburgh. After he deserts her when she is ill, she breaks off their relationship and marries someone else. Dougal's tears over Jinny's rejection bring him the sympathy of his female fellow workers.

Richard Willis, the managing director of a competing textile firm. A Scot, he sees Dougal as a possible ally, hires him for a vague research job, and makes plans to place him on the firm's board of directors.

Rosemary M. Canfield Reisman

THE BALLAD OF THE SAD CAFÉ

Author: Carson McCullers (1917-1967)
Type of work: Novella
Time of action: The 1930's
First published: 1943

Miss Amelia Evans, the owner of the sad café, a tall, powerful, independent woman, with crossed eyes. A solitary child reared by her widowed father, she inherits the largest store in the tiny town and becomes the richest woman for miles around. With uncommon industry, as a shrewd businesswoman, a self-educated doctor, a determined litigant, a carpenter, meat packer, and moonshiner, she turns things to profit. Yet, she is ill at ease with most people in town, and they take keen interest in her scandalous relations with Marvin Macy and Cousin Lymon. Shortly after her father's death, she had married Marvin, only to storm out of the bedroom on their wedding night. Within ten days, she had run him off her premises and acquired title to all of his property. Years later, she falls in love with a diminutive hunchback who appears out of nowhere claiming to be a distant cousin. Mellowed by this new love, her heart warms to the community as she gradually converts the store to a café. Her café brings the townspeople a new pride, for there they can forget the cheapness of their lives and let her liquor reveal the secrets of their souls obscured by drudgery and petty routine. Amelia's newfound happiness is ruined, however, when Marvin comes back from prison. She is mortified by Lymon's fondness for him. Her usual resolve dissolves in emotional confusion. She makes no move to curb Lymon, even when he invites Marvin to move in with them. She tries to poison Marvin once, but the plates get switched and her revenge is foiled. After losing a fight to Marvin and Lymon, Amelia turns in on herself. She raises the price of everything in the café to one dollar. Business falls off. The place is boarded up, and passers-by only occasionally see her grief-ridden face gazing out of the shuttered window.

Cousin Lymon Willis, the hunchback stranger beloved of Amelia. Standing only about four feet tall on his crooked legs, he shows up one day claiming kin with Amelia. Frail, moody, and prone to crying fits, he nevertheless possesses an uncanny ability to relate to strangers. Thus, he penetrates her loneliness and engages the townspeople's emotions, helping to make the café a success. When Marvin comes back from prison, Lymon evinces a weird affinity for the man, following him around in public, tugging at his pants' leg, and wiggling his ears to attract Marvin's attention, though he is violently rebuffed. Lymon precipitates a crisis by bringing Marvin into Amelia's living quarters. Later, with a flying tackle, he saves Marvin from being beaten in a fair fight with

Amelia, and the two men run off together after wrecking the café. Beloved of Amelia and lover of Marvin, Lymon demonstrates McCullers' idea that the quality of human love depends on the lover's ardor rather than the characteristics of the beloved.

Marvin Macy, Amelia's husband, the handsomest man in the region. An abused and abandoned child, he grows up wild, wicked, bold, fearless, and cruel, seducing young girls for laughs, fighting, stealing, and probably killing. His character undergoes a brief reversal during his courtship of Amelia, but he fails to bed her on the wedding night, and the marriage lasts only ten days. She winds up with all of his property, including ten acres of land and a gold watch. After spending years in prison for robbing three gas stations, he comes back to town. There befriended by his former wife's hunchback companion, he draws dangerously closer to her by visiting the café, taking meals with her, and eventually rooming with Lymon in her upstairs living quarters. His love-hate relationship with Amelia culminates in a bareknuckled fight between them in the café, which he would have lost, except for Lymon, who intervenes before she can strangle him. After stealing the gold watch and wrecking the café, the two men leave town together.

John L. McLean

BANANA BOTTOM

Author: Claude McKay (1889-1948)
Type of work: Novel
Time of action: The early 1900's
First published: 1933

Tabitha (Bita) Plant, a Jamaican village girl adopted and educated by the Craigs, who are British missionaries. At age twelve, she had had her first sexual experience, to which she was a willing partner, but propriety required that it be represented as rape; accordingly, when adopted, she is sent to Europe for seven years to be transformed into a dark-skinned Briton of Calvinist outlook, a proper model for the local villagers. She rejects hypocrisy, enjoys sensuality, identifies with the folk and their institutions and beliefs, and adopts a philosophy and life-style that is an amalgam of Caribbean and Continental cultures, of colonial and metropolitan ways. She is the quintessential woman of the West Indies: physical, intellectual, attuned to island life.

Malcolm Craig, a Calvinist minister of the mission church in Jubilee, whose grandfather had founded the mission. Well-built, frank, hearty, and a God-praising soul, he had grown up in the village and loved the countryside; however, his religion was unforgiving, confining, and joyless. His true motive in adopting and educating Bita was to demonstrate his theory that natives could be transformed into civilized individuals and weaned from the joys of the flesh.

Priscilla Craig, one of only two ordained clergywomen in the colony. She is a middle-aged, small woman full of high-class anxiety, a feminist related to British suffragettes, and one whose face flushes with beatific light whenever she sings in church. Her own son, an adult, is a crippled idiot, and she is unable to agree to her husband's wish to adopt a boy as a possible successor; she nevertheless agrees to adopt Bita, whom she wishes to rear as "an exhibit." Like her husband, she denigrates affection and intimacy. She is generous in her expenditure of resources for Bita's education, but she is niggardly in her expenditure of love.

Crazy Bow Adair, the descendant of a Scots settler who had bought the vast mountain estate of Banana Bottom and married one of the blackest slaves whom he liberated. Precocious, intellectual, and the color of a ripe banana, he was schooled for a white-collar job; he was competent as a musician, able to play bamboo flute, guitar, banjo, and fiddle, even the school piano. He and Bita romped in the riverbank grasses, and, though he was twenty-five, he was considered harmlessly light-headed. Bita succumbed to his music, caressed him, and with passion induced her own seduction. Educated, musical, older, and physical, he represented those things that Bita admired in life.

Hopping Dick, a fine-strutting dandy. On her return from Europe, Bita meets him at a local market: She is impressed by his undisguised and acknowledged physicality, by his dancing and romancing. He is a follower of the primitives' god Obeah and is anti-intellectual, yet he attracts Bita for a time, for he represents that aspect of her that the Craigs have attempted to expunge. His backing out of their engagement, conversion to Christianity, and forsaking of his unrestrained folkways leaves Bita disillusioned and frustrated.

Herald Newton Day, a theological student. The elder son of Deacon Day, he was being groomed to succeed the Craigs in the Free Church at Jubilee. Local belief was that the Craigs intended that he should marry Bita. Mrs. Craig describes him as a worthy young man, but he is essentially proud, affected, sanctimonious, and lacking in any racial identification and self-esteem. He is an absolute hypocrite: His joy in preaching is in hearing his own voice; his sermon on the sufficiency of God's love is negated by his defiling himself with a nanny goat. He is yet another example of the failure to transform human nature; he is not the herald of the new town or the new day that his name suggests.

Squire Gensir, a freethinking British settler of aristocratic mien and background who is a serious student of Jamaican culture and an advocate of black self-esteem. He is an opponent of the Craigs and their philosophy; he is instrumental in having Bita accompany him to a "tea meeting," at which she dances with skill and enthusiasm, recognizing her affinity with the folk of Jamaica. According to one local preacher, Gensir was decadent because he collected folklore; however, Gensir stood firm against discrimination in accommodations, he was given to simple dress, and he loved the island and its common people. His high intellect, however, precluded him from being wholly submerged in the austere simplicity of village life. He was essentially "a lonely man living a lonely life," but he was the catalyst for Bita's transformation and ultimate self-fulfillment.

Jubban, the elderly drayman of Jordan Plant, Bita's father. He is thoughtful, hardworking, and an emotional, responsive, yet responsible lover and husband. He is serious, strong, proud of his race and of his own accomplishments as a worker; he is sure, firm, kindly, and characterized by splendid

qualities. He is the true complement of Bita and the foundation of her contentment.

Marian B. McLeod

BANG THE DRUM SLOWLY

Author: Mark Harris (1922-   )
Type of work: Novel
Time of action: The early 1950's
First published: 1956

Henry "Author" Wiggen, the narrator, who is the star left-handed pitcher of the New York Mammoths and author of an earlier novel, *The Southpaw.* He chronicles the final months in the life of his friend, the Mammoths' third-string catcher, Bruce Pearson. Henry is Bruce's constant companion; he holds out for a contract that stipulates that Bruce can only be traded or released if Henry receives the same treatment; he protects Bruce from the hooker Katie; and he tries to keep their teammates from making Bruce the butt of their jokes and tricks, keeping Bruce's condition a secret from everyone except Henry's wife and two teammates. While doing all these things, he pitches the Mammoths to the pennant and a World Series championship.

Bruce Pearson, a journeyman catcher told by the doctors at the Mayo Clinic that he has Hodgkin's disease and only a few months to live. Bruce is stupid and slow, but under the threat of death he begins to appreciate life more, taking each day as it comes. He even plays better, helping the Mammoths in their difficult drive for a pennant and becoming more of a student of the game. The divided team comes back together for the pennant race when Bruce's condition becomes generally known and the knowledge breaks down the animosities that have grown up during the season. Bruce catches the pennant-clinching game and collapses on the field at the end. He returns from the hospital for the start of the World Series, and then his father takes him home. He dies, back home in

Georgia, shortly after the end of the World Series.

Holly Webster Wiggen, Henry Wiggen's wife, who gives birth to a daughter late in the season. She does Henry's taxes, handles his finances, and supports him in his efforts to help Bruce and keep Bruce's insurance money out of Katie's hands.

"Dutch" Schnell, manager of the Mammoths. His team does not perform up to its capabilities, causing him great frustration, which he tries to take out on Henry. He knows that something is wrong but cannot figure it out, even after hiring a private detective to find out what secret Henry and Bruce share. He is tough, threatening to release Bruce or trade him for a better catcher, but when he eventually finds out about Bruce's illness he keeps him in the lineup.

Katie, an expensive prostitute. Bruce has been in love with her, but she has fended him off until she figures out that he is dying and that he has a large insurance policy. She will marry him if she is made the beneficiary, but Henry prevents this.

"Goose" Williams, an aging catcher who at first rides Bruce unmercifully. He is the first player Henry tells about Bruce's illness, and thereafter he is protective of Bruce.

Joe Jaros, coach with the Mammoths and Henry's partner in a kind of con game called Tegwar, in which the rules change all the time. He rejects Henry because of the latter's insistence on letting Bruce play the game, which Bruce does not understand.

"Red" Traphagen, retired catcher and Henry's mentor, now a college professor. He returns to the team as a coach and counselor during the final weeks of the season.

"Piney" Woods, rookie catcher for the Mammoths, sent back to the minors but recalled near the end of the season. He plays the guitar and sings the dirge "Streets of Laredo," which contains the words of the book's title.

John M. Muste

BANJO
A Story Without a Plot

Author: Claude McKay (1889-1948)
Type of work: Novel
Time of action: The early 1920's
First published: 1929

Lincoln Agrippa Daily (Banjo), a black vagabond from the South who has skipped the ship that brought him to Marseilles. He is a wastrel, womanizer, dreamer, and loafer whose improvidence leads him to depend on instinctive actions and chance encounters to survive. He is essentially trusting and basically generous; however, he is philosophical when he is tricked out of his banjo, which he values above all. He is seldom sober, though wine affords him decreasing pleasure; his charismatic personality allows him to become leader of the small band that he organizes from the polyglot beachboys of the port. He deprecates blacks who attempt to "pass"; he stresses racial pride, being influenced much by Ray, with whom he decides to continue his vagabondage in Europe rather than return to the West Indies as a crewman on a tramp steamer. His pervasive melancholy is muted by Latnah, who cares for him after a hospitalization; in fact, she is the instrument of his metamorphosis. He is the cohesive element of his group.

Ray, a would-be writer and an educated West Indian beachboy. A drifter who has absconded from his family responsibilities to follow his own interests and whims, he regards happiness as the highest good and difference as the greatest charm of life. Moderate in his views (except for being rather strident in his antiwhite sentiments), he is dependable in-

sofar as his immediate colleagues are concerned. He rediscovers his African roots and is proud of belonging to a race that has been "weighed and tested." Finding life in the Ditch (the Marseilles black slums) palling, he opts for an itinerant working life.

Latnah, an Earth Mother-type of lover and prostitute who offers succor to Banjo and his colleagues. She was born in Aden of a Sudanese or Abyssinian mother and an unknown father; she is "not young and far from old," and has enviable physical attributes, though she is small. Her complexion is olive-toned, she runs like a gazelle, and she is as graceful as a serpent. She is caring, energetic, and sensual, and when she swims nude in the ocean, her beauty excites her companions, for she is lovely, limber, and sinewy. She regards herself as superior to the other women denizens of the Ditch, for her difference from them is obvious. Her compassion for her companions is generous, and Ray and Banjo find it difficult to leave her for their new life as migrant workers.

Bugsy, a small, wiry, aggressive boy, dull-black in complexion. He was given his nickname because his companions thought him "bughouse," and he was delighted with his new name. He is sardonic, he dislikes French food (especially wine and horsemeat), and he is the soberest of the group. Ray describes

113

him as "the toughest black boy I ever knew," but Banjo criticizes him for being "the meanest monkey-chaser I evah seen" (in other words, vehemently antiwhite).

Taloufa, a Nigerian who has been in Wales and the United States and is a supporter of Marcus Garvey's Back-to-Africa movement. He has been educated out of his native ways by Christian missionaries, yet he is opposed to "coon stuff." He represents the blacks who have been cut off from African village life but not made part of Western urban life. Like the others, he is broke but not broken.

Buchanan Malt Avis (Malty), the best drummer on the waterfront. He is an ebullient, indefatigable West Indian who led the beachboy band before the arrival of Banjo. He received his name from the trade names on boxes of goods found in the kitchen where his mother worked. He started life as a boy on Caribbean fishing boats; then he sailed as a "boy" to New Orleans, became a full-time seaman, and had never returned home. Skilled on the guitar, ukelele, and mandolin, and possessed of a "shining, black, big-boned, plump, jolly face," he is a close friend of Ray and Latnah and accompanies them on their grape-picking excursion. Like McKay, he is the versatile, irrepressible companion of both men and women.

Goosey, a "yaller nigger" from South Car-olina who has lived in New Jersey and obtained a high school diploma. An aggressive person, he has had contretemps with his ship's officers and has been paid off in Marseilles with his friend Talpufa, the guitar player. Goosey, a flute player, is thoughtful and a pseudophilosopher on race relations, Ray thinks him an "accident-made nigger" and a bonehead given to sophomoric musings. Goosey is naïve: He is tricked out of his money almost immediately after his landing. A child of the Cotton Belt, he is no cosmopolite. Advocating the piano, harp, and violin rather than the banjo (which he sees as a symbol of bondage), he adheres to the uplift philosophy of the Harlem Renaissance intellectuals. He is mainly a foil to the sophistication of the longtime black beachboys of the Ditch.

Ginger, a long-term Ditch inhabitant, a former seaman and former convict. He is chestnut colored and has drab brown curly hair. He has lost his seaman's papers and stolen another's; he has become proficient in French. He always advises taking the line of least resistance, and he has ponderous opinions on all topics. When the others consider leaving the Ditch, Ginger prefers to stay and take his chances. He has succumbed to the familiar and is not cut out for the vagabond life.

Alan L. McLeod

BAREFOOT IN THE HEAD
A European Fantasia

Author: Brian W. Aldiss (1925-   )
Type of work: Novel
Time of action: The near future
First published: 1969

Colin Charteris, the main character, a Serbian, who after the psychedelic wars does resettlement work for the Italian government. Seeking stability he drives north to Metz, where he has a vision of the multiple paths of human life. His visionary powers lead him to England, where he becomes a popular messiah figure. Later, he preaches his brand of multilogic through England and then arrives in Ostend. On the way to Brussels, he switches cars with Banjo Burton, who crashes into a truck. Since he survives, all think that he has risen from the dead. When the movement gets dictatorial, he resigns and wanders eastward with Angeline.

Angelina, a young waitress who works at the hotel in Metz. She refuses to sleep with Charteris and is not heard from again.

Phil Brasher, a young psychedelic who survives an airplane crash and believes himself to be a savior. He resents Charteris' coming, and in a fight Charteris pushes him in front of a car.

Angeline, Brasher's wife. After his death, she becomes Charteris' mistress and his most loyal follower. She bears his child and is the only one faithful to the end.

Banjo Burton, a hitchhiker whom Charteris picks up in Great Britain. He is a member of a rock group and introduces Charteris to Phil Brasher.

Army Burton, Banjo's brother, also a musician, who enthusiastically encourages Charteris to become the leader of the whole world.

Robbins, a young musician and disciple of Brasher, who turns to Charteris after Brasher's death.

Ruby Dymond, another musician who is in love with Angeline and writes songs for her, but never becomes her lover.

Greta, a groupie who is distraught by Brasher's death.

Featherstone-Haugh, another musician.

Cass, a disciple of Charteris who wants him

to become a world leader. When Laundrei comes along, he teams up with him, abandoning Charteris.

Ranceville, a prop man for Boreas. He is so moved by the accident that kills Banjo that he wants to be in the car, otherwise populated by manikins, during the filming of the crash.

Elsbeth, a young Jewish girl who temporarily becomes Charteris' mistress.

Jan Koningrijk (yän kŏn·ĭn·krēk), the chief of the rescue squad for the Belgian freeway system. He is called to the accident that kills Banjo Burton in Charteris' car, leading the people to believe that Charteris has risen from the dead.

Marta Koningrijk, the young schizophrenic wife of Jan, who becomes Charteris' mistress after the accident.

Nicholas Boreas, a Belgian film director, middle-aged and fat, who partakes of questionable sexual activities. He wants to make a film on the life of Charteris. He is seen recreating the accident scene.

Kommandant Laundrei, a local military chief, middle-aged and pompous, always dressed in a splendid uniform with many medals. He arrests Charteris for loitering and then tries to get Charteris to help him become the leader of Germany by teaching him self-control, but Charteris refuses.

Hirst Wechsel (hėrst vĕk′zəl), an aide to Kommandant Laundrei; he introduces Charteris to him. Later he seems to turn into a bird.

Robert W. Peckham

BAREFOOT IN THE PARK

Author: Neil Simon (1927-   )
Type of work: Play
Time of action: Several days in February in the early 1960's
First produced: 1963

Corie Bratter, a newlywed married only six days. She is young, pretty, and full of enthusiasm for the future. Impulsive and fun-loving, she considers herself a Do-er, not a Watcher. Her impetuosity is not shared, at first, by her mother or husband, and they are aghast when she cheers the crazy antics of Victor, a neighbor. Corie eventually learns to appreciate dependability and quiet strength.

Paul Bratter, Corie's husband, a twenty-six-year-old attorney in his first job. Both his dress and outlook are very conservative. Extremely proper and dignified, he always knows the right thing to say. He is level-headed and practical and keeps his emotions in check, perhaps too much so. Nevertheless, after Corie accuses him of being a fuddy duddy, he shows her that he, too, is capable of walking barefoot in the park.

Ethel Banks, Corie's mother. She is in her late forties, and, while still pretty, she has fallen out of step with the fashions. She lives alone in West Orange, New Jersey. Consciously or unconsciously, she has adopted a rather narrow image of herself as someone with a sensitive stomach, a bad back, and no need for romance. It takes a wild evening out with Victor for Ethel to rediscover her carefree and spontaneous self.

Victor Velasco, the Bratters' upstairs neighbor. Fifty-eight years old, he is a very colorful character. Although capable of looking positively natty in a double-breasted pin-striped suit, he has also been known to wear Japanese kimonos and berets. He is vain, flamboyant, and quite without shame when it comes to letting someone else pick up the tab. Married three times, he is a terrific flirt. He is also a gourmet cook; Paul refers to him as the "Hungarian Duncan Hines." Yet there may be signs that Victor is beginning to slow down. After an exhilarating evening of his own creation, he suffers a broken toe and an upset stomach.

Harry Pepper, a telephone repairman. He witnesses, to his mortification, a fight between Corie and Paul.

Liz Marshall

THE BARK TREE

Author: Raymond Queneau (1903-1976)
Type of work: Novel
Time of action: The early twentieth century, probably the 1920's
First published: Le Chiendent, 1933 (English translation, 1968)

The narrator, or **"I,"** a shadowy figure who often seems to be following the other characters, though he never reveals more than that about himself.

Étienne Marcel, a Parisian bank employee. Étienne is at first a "one-dimensional character," but after being observed by Pierre Le Grand, he acquires three dimensions and begins to question things. He is a typical Parisian who works in the center of the city and returns every day by train to his house in the suburbs. He is married, has a son, and eats a disgusting meal every day in a cafeteria. This routine is broken after Pierre sees him nearly run over in front of a train station.

Étienne then stops at a suburb, Blagny, where, in a café, he meets the other characters and becomes embroiled in the question of the treasure behind Old Taupe's door. Étienne becomes a near-philosopher as he awakens to questions about the world, such as the presence of two rubber ducks swimming in a shop window, especially with the help of Pierre. At the novel's end he is drafted into the army when the French and Etruscans declare war on one another, leaving his wife to disappear and his son in the hands of the evil Bébé Toutout.

Pierre Le Grand, an observer and thinker. He is an enigmatic character who, upon being asked if he is a novelist, declares that he is a character. He is the only character conscious of Étienne's transformations and may appear under other names in the novel, such as Pierre Troc. He is something of a philosophical midwife to Étienne in helping him to learn to think and is also involved in the comic misunderstanding when people begin to believe that Old Taupe has a fortune hidden behind his door.

Madame Sidonie Cloche (klōsh), a midwife and an abortionist. She is another observer, taking special pleasure in seeing people run over. She is instrumental in fostering the belief that Old Taupe has a fortune and gets the young servant girl Ernestine to marry him for it. A meddling old woman who is vaguely criminal, she shows up at the end of the novel during the French-Etruscan War as Queen of the Etruscans, or Mrs. Olini (in French, Missize Aulini, recalling Mussolini), and is unhappy about being written about in a novel.

Dominique Belhôtel, a café proprietor. Brother of Madame Cloche, he owns the café in which Étienne stops one day for French fries. Another rather dubious figure, he achieves his ambition when he buys a brothel in order to have enough money for his son Clovis to become an engineer when he grows up.

Saturnin Belhôtel, brother of Madame Cloche, a concierge. He has ambitions of being a writer and confides in Narcense, who lives in his hotel.

Old Taupe (tōp), a bum. Taupe is clearly with no means of support except selling junk and lives by a railroad track where he has placed a door, behind which the others believe he has a fortune after Étienne and Pierre visit him. He marries the young servant girl Ernestine in an epic wedding feast at the café.

Narcense, a musician and would-be writer. Narcense is unemployed and spends most of his time pursuing women in the street. Alberte, Étienne's wife, attracts him to their suburb, where he spends time trying to meet her.

Bébé Toutout (tōo·tōo'), a parasitic dwarf. He imposes himself on the Marcel household and comes to live there. Another figure associated with evil, the dwarf helps set up a brothel in the house after Étienne leaves for the war.

Théo, Étienne's son. A typical adolescent in some respects, he prefers looking at obscene photographs to reading philosophy and is mainly interested in sex. He befriends Bébé Toutout and tries to thwart Narcense.

Alberte, Étienne's wife. She is very attractive and has men pursuing her constantly, especially Narcense.

Madame Pigeonnier (pē·zhēōn·yā'), a neighbor of Étienne. She is attractive and interested in Theo.

Jupiter, a dog. This poor pet has the misfortune of leaping in on a coffin during a funeral and is hanged.

Allen Thiher

BARNABO OF THE MOUNTAINS

Author: Dino Buzzati (Dino Buzzati Traverso, 1906-1972)
Type of work: Novella
Time of action: The early twentieth century
First published: Bàrnabo delle montagne, 1933 (English translation, 1984)

Barnabo, a young forester and the only one of his guard not called by a last name. Although proud and somewhat quick-tempered, Barnabo is also sensitive and considerate, as demonstrated by his pretense of allowing another forester (Pietro Molo) to win a fight rather than be humiliated. Later, he stops to help a wounded crow, not having the heart to kill it, unlike his comrades who kill and pluck crows to be cooked for dinner. Barnabo is disgraced and his career ruined when cowardice overcomes him and he is unable to help his fellow foresters in a battle with the brigands. His only solace in exile is his special relationship with the crow that he had rescued right before the battle. When Barnabo does have a chance to redeem himself many years later, he finds himself once again unable to kill, though for a different reason: It is not cowardice but compassion that makes Barnabo allow the brigands to escape forever.

Giovanni Berton, another young forester and Barnabo's friend. The son of a carpenter, Berton is fascinated by the mountains and can spend hours merely watching them. It is he who sees the smoke of the brigands in the mountains and persuades Barnabo to join him in an expedition in search of the bandits. Berton covers up for Barnabo when Barnabo is accused of cowardice, by saying that Barnabo was not near the scene of the battle. Many years later, he urges Barnabo to return to San Nicola from exile and resume his life there, though not as a forester.

Antonio Del Colle, the commander of the foresters when the novel begins. He is a short, elderly man who is still sprightly enough to carry heavy loads and hike through the mountains, and his eyes are still keen enough that, when he shoots his rifle, he does not miss a target at a hundred meters. He is murdered by the brigands, and his body is buried on the same mountain where another forester, Darrìo, died. It is Del Colle's death that sparks the foresters' obsession with capturing the brigands; Del Colle is succeeded as commander by Giovanni Marden.

Angelo Montani, another forester. A suspicious and dour man, Montani neither likes nor trusts Barnabo. Montani is very efficient and regimented, and he does not talk much. Sometime after Barnabo leaves in disgrace, Montani has a run-in with a bandit who, astonishingly, knows Montani's name. Obsessed with this mysterious stranger, Montani returns several times to the mountains to try and either capture or kill the bandits but never succeeds.

T. M. Lipman

BAROMETER RISING

Author: Hugh MacLennan (1907-   )
Type of work: Novel
Time of action: Eight days in early December, 1917
First published: 1941

Neil Macrae, twenty-eight, the orphaned nephew of Geoffrey Wain and unknowing father of his cousin Penelope Wain's daughter Jean. At the French Front, Geoffrey Wain, commander of Neil's regiment, had been preparing to court-martial his nephew for failing to carry out an impossible order when shelling had occurred. Wounded and temporarily amnesiac, Neil was mistakenly identi-fied as a British private. Using his false identity, Neil has returned to Halifax to clear his own name. Still in poor health, Neil's strength of character is not at first discernible; nevertheless, this sometimes-impulsive son of Jamsie Wain, rebellious daughter of the British loyalist Wain family, and John Macrae, a respected Cape Breton craftsman, embodies the best of a new breed of Canadians forged out of World War I and freed of colonialist dependence on England. An M.I.T.-trained engineer who excels in the new field of submarine design, an impatient Neil now knows exactly what he seeks. During the eight days that include the horrendous, historic Halifax explosion, this modern Odysseus is freed of Geoffrey Wain, reunited with his Penelope, and aided by his true friends in clearing his name. He finds a focus for his restless energy in the monumental rescue work following the explosion. The novel's conclusion finds the uncompromising Neil facing a bright future.

Penelope Wain, twenty-nine, Geoffrey Wain's daughter, a woman of strong character and great ability with a deceptively fragile appearance. A reserved woman, Penny suffers quietly the loss of Neil and her false relationship with her daughter Jean, adopted for propriety's sake by her uncle and aunt Fraser. Penny sustains herself with her successful career as a talented ship designer; she also provides her young brother Roddie with the love and guidance the motherless boy needs. Almost ready, like the mythical Penelope, to succumb to a persistent suitor, Penny's patience and hope are rewarded when Neil returns and they find their love undiminished.

Colonel Geoffrey Wain, a tall, broad-shouldered, impressive-looking man in his middle fifties, his military appearance enhanced by his close-cut silver hair and black mustache. Temporarily relieved of his command at the French Front, Wain is reluctantly home in the city and country he contemptuously regards as a colonial backwater, though he enjoys his family's traditional social superiority. Hereditary head of the booming Wain shipyards, Wain exudes authority but has actually led a life of few challenges. He is obsessed with hatred for Neil, especially when he hears that Neil is alive in Halifax, thus threatening to dash Wain's hope of resuming a military command. Wain passes some time in a desultory affair with his petite, ambitious, vulgar young secretary Evelyn Phillips; in the explosion, Wain dies at Evelyn's apartment, his tawdry death belying his lifetime of presumed superiority.

Doctor Angus Murray, in his late forties, a widower, medical officer in Geoffrey Wain's battalion in France, currently home on leave recovering from shrapnel wounds. Tired and disreputable looking, Murray fights loneliness and and impending despair with frequent bouts of drinking. He is a sensitive, self-aware man, with deeply felt ideas about Canada and its future. Galvanized by the explosion, he sets up a hospital in the Wain house and completes his rehabilitation, physical and mental, with ceaseless surgical work. Deeply in love with Penny, he gracefully relinquishes her to Neil and indeed champions Neil, seeing to the practical details of his vindication, yielding to Neil as the New Canadian.

"Big" Alec Mackenzie, in his mid-forties, a craggy Nova Scotian Highlander, married and father of three, missing his Cape Breton life but now making a better living in wartime Halifax. A corporal in Wain's battalion in France, Mackenzie was privy to the Wain-Neil fiasco; unaware that his job at the Wain shipyards is a bribe for his silence, Mackenzie is the best wharf foreman Wain ever had, bringing to his job the diligence and integrity with which he approaches life. An inarticulate man, born to carry out orders, Mackenzie always gives his best. In the explosion, he supports with brute strength beams from his wrecked home, saving his wife but dooming himself when a spike pierces his lung. Rescued by Neil and Murray, Alec survives just long enough to give Murray the vital testimony needed to clear Neil's name.

Jill Rollins

THE BARON IN THE TREES

Author: Italo Calvino (1923-1985)
Type of work: Novel

Time of action: The late eighteenth century
First published: Il barone rampante, 1957 (English translation, 1959)

Cosimo Piovasco di Rondò (pyō•văs'kō dē rŏn•dō'), twelve years old at the narrative's outset, the eldest son in the Piovasco family and successor as baron of the Ombrosa estate. Cosimo is energetic and determined, an idealist who insists on acting on his principles. The central figure in the story, he sets the main action going when he refuses to eat a meal of snails prepared by his sister, and, sent from the table, he climbs into a holm oak on his family's estate and vows never to descend from the trees. Cosimo eventually develops instincts and senses different from other humans, as a result of living in the wild and having to be ever watchful and alert. This vigilance becomes "his natural state, as if his eyes had to embrace a horizon wide enough to understand all." Despite his arboreal life, he becomes studious and well read in the philosophy of the Enlightenment; as a reader as well as a tree dweller, he acquires, virtually and literally, a bird's-eye view of his era.

Biaggio Piovasco di Rondò (byä'jyō), eight years old at the outset of the action, the brother of Cosimo, who narrates the tales of Cosimo's extraordinary life. Though regarded by Cosimo at first as weak, because of his failure to resist their father more strongly, Biaggio is a close friend and confidant to Cosimo. Biaggio takes his brother food and supplies when needed and keeps Cosimo informed of what is going on that Cosimo cannot observe. Throughout the narrative, Biaggio maintains an attitude of wonder and awe at his brother's exploits.

Violante (Viola) Ondariva (ōn•dä•rē'vä), neighbor to the Piovasco family and member of the rival Ondariva family, which has claim to some of the same lands as the Piovasci. Approximately Cosimo's age, Viola is attractive, blonde, capricious, and independent. She meets Cosimo shortly after he has entered the trees, when she is swinging in her garden and he greets her from a tree. She attracts Cosimo immediately with her teasing coyness and her being a member of the family his father has declared a sworn enemy. Known to a youthful gang of fruit thieves as Sinforosa, she occasionally assists them from her white horse by alerting them to where ripe fruit is and sending them an alarm when danger is near. At every chance, Cosimo attempts to impress her, and, according to Biaggio, it is partly to demonstrate to her his strong will that Cosimo continues for his whole life in the trees. Later, after being widowed, Viola becomes Cosimo's lover.

Arminio Piovasco di Rondò, the Baron of Ombrosa, father of Cosimo, Biaggio, and Battista. A dreamer aspiring unrealistically to higher nobility, Arminio dresses, in powdered wig and formal French court attire, in the outdated style of Louis XIV. His response to the turbulence of his age is that of a reactionary, attempting to regain a lapsed dukedom. His otherwise harmless pretensions disgust Cosimo, whose first impulse to live in the trees is an act of rebellion against his father's authority. Arminio's principal reaction to his eldest son's rebellion is to become too embarrassed to go out or to face his friends among the nobility.

Corradino di Rondò, formerly **Konradine von Kurtewitz,** also called **the Generalessa,** wife of Arminio and mother of Cosimo, Biaggio, and Battista. She is called the Generalessa by her children because of her martial bearing and her preoccupation with military matters, which she learned from her father, a general who had commanded the Empress Maria Theresa's troops and took his daughter with him from camp to camp. The Generalessa is domineering and strict, but protective of her children. Like her husband, she is so absentminded in rearing her children that her sons grow up left to their own devices, enjoying much freedom. With Cosimo, she is solicitous and caring, and one of the first to accept Cosimo's decision to live in the trees.

Battista di Rondò, sister of Cosimo and Biaggio. Battista's countenance is compared by Biaggio to a rodent's, with her staring eyes, narrow teeth, yellowish skin, and starched hair. She became confined to her home, dressed as a nun, after she had attacked the young son of a noble family visiting her father. Battista's main interest as a youth is cooking bizarre, revolting dishes, including rats' livers, pigs' tails, and porcupines. She is the cook of the infamous meal of snails that her brother Cosimo refuses to eat. Battista eventually marries the young Count of Estomac, thus ensconcing herself in the self-aggrandizing aristocratic life that Cosimo has devoted himself to protesting.

Dennis C. Chowenhill

THE BARRACKS

Author: John McGahern (1935-   )
Type of work: Novel
Time of action: Post-World War II
First published: 1963

Elizabeth Reegan, forty, a former nurse, now married to a sergeant in the Irish police force and stepmother to his three children. After a nursing career in London during World War II and a passionate love affair which does not work out, Elizabeth returns to the west of Ireland and marries against her family's advice. The novel covers the year during which she suspects, confirms, and fails to live through the cancer which has invaded her body. The real issue, however, is not Elizabeth's physical cancer, but the cancer of her growing conviction that life is essentially without meaning. Her confrontation with death merely confirms and emphasizes her conviction that the human condition is inherently one of isolation. Though she continues to rejoice in natural beauty and human kindness, she is sustained only by the endless routine of repetitive tasks which make up her life—repetitions echoed by the police rounds her husband makes and by the seasonal rounds. The barracks within which the Reegans make their home, then, is a microcosm of the world, for both barracks and world would fall into chaos without the cycles of duty and year to impose a hint of order.

Sergeant Reegan, fifty, Elizabeth's husband. A member of the freedom forces which achieved Irish independence in 1921, Reegan has been rewarded with a position in the newly formed police force. After thirty years as a sergeant, however, he tastes the increasing bitterness of his position. Independence has made no real change in Ireland, but it has changed his life. Without it, he would either have stayed on the farm, which he loved, or emigrated to the United States. Constantly at odds with his superintendent, he dreams and plans for the day when he can buy a farm and work only for himself. He is moody and occasionally irascible, but he is also kind to Elizabeth, generous, and even sensitive. He does not begrudge the expense of her illness, though it puts off achievement of his dream. Yet he is aware that he does not really know his wife (who never calls him by his first name, or by any name for that matter) and that they will end their days caring for each other but still essentially alone.

Michael Halliday, about thirty-five, the London doctor with whom Elizabeth has an affair. Michael introduces Elizabeth (who is deeply in love with him) to an unfamiliar world of books, concerts, fancy restaurants, and ideas. Eventually, however, he confesses that he no longer loves her and that all along he has been using her to stave off his growing sense of the meaninglessness of life and his growing tendency toward suicide. He still wants her to marry him, but Elizabeth refuses. It is his cynicism which affects and infects her the most, and increasingly during the course of the novel she finds herself echoing ideas he has formulated for her years before. She ends by wondering whether Reegan has not been to her what she was to Halliday, a device to postpone the suicide which is the ultimate result of such cynicism.

Superintendent John James Quirke, roughly fifty, Reegan's supervisor. A small-minded authoritarian, he spends a good bit of his time sneaking around and spying on the guards to be sure they are fulfilling the exact letter of their responsibilities (which they frequently are not). He is a capricious, often vicious man whose lack of reason in the use of authority echoes the apparent lack of reason in whatever authority governs the world.

Teresa Casey, the childess wife of Ned Casey. A bit at loose ends without the routine responsibilities which sustain Elizabeth, she delightedly takes over care of the children when Elizabeth falls ill. They give her life structure, meaning, focus—and so her experience echoes Elizabeth's and Michael's, for only routine and activity can ward off despair.

Willie,
Una, and
Sheila, ages twelve, eleven, and nine. Reegan's children by his first wife. They like Elizabeth, and she likes them. They are good to her, and she cares for them. Yet there is no close emotional bond or genuine understanding, and indications that they can do without her threaten her sense of purpose and coherence.

Helen Lojek

THE BASIC TRAINING OF PAVLO HUMMEL

Author: David Rabe (1940-   )
Type of work: Play
Time of action: 1965-1967
First produced: 1971

Pavlo Hummel, an army private and medic during the Vietnam conflict. Pavlo has red hair and green eyes, is five feet ten inches tall, and weighs 152 pounds. Estranged from his family, Pavlo has had his name legally changed from Michael to spite the father whose identity he has never known. He worries about whether or not to hug his mother when he returns home. Although he grew up in New York City, Pavlo is inexperienced and innocent; his street-smart persona is an act, and the other men see through it easily. Neurotically obsessed with the impression others have of him, Pavlo lies about his sexual exploits and his experiences in crime. He claims to have stolen twenty-three cars and to have had an uncle who was executed at San Quentin prison for killing four people. He never suspects or realizes that the other men know he is lying and that they are

laughing at him. Pavlo thinks that he can win friends by being a good soldier, so he resorts to flattering sergeants and volunteering for difficult tasks. When he realizes that no number of push-ups will win the friendship and respect he craves, Pavlo swallows one hundred aspirin, but he is saved by the squad leader, Pierce. Pavlo is determined to prove himself in the infantry, but he is assigned to be a medic. He follows his orders to the letter but is ashamed of his job and repeatedly asks to be transferred to the battlefield. At one point Pavlo talks Sergeant Brisbey out of committing suicide, but his efforts lack sincerity. Parham is wounded by Viet Cong and cries out for Pavlo's help while Pavlo is asking for transfer. Pavlo carries Parham's body to safety but more out of a desire to impress others with his bravery than out of any concern for Parham. Finally,

Pavlo is assigned to the fighting. Pavlo is wounded three times and earns the Purple Heart before he wants out, but ironically his request is refused. Pavlo is finally killed in a senseless incident arising from a fight over a prostitute. A grenade rolls into the room, and Pavlo scoops it up and is holding it when it explodes. He takes several days to die. Despite the changes in Pavlo Hummel as he becomes harder and more cynical, the young man never gains any real insight.

Ardell, Pavlo's fantasized soldier. A black man in sunglasses and a strange uniform with black ribbons and medals, Ardell enters and exits throughout the play to advise Pavlo. Ardell's is the experienced and prophetic voice, as he teaches Pavlo about the army and war. Ardell says that Pavlo is black inside, hiding such intense pain that the young man cannot even see himself clearly.

Sergeant Tower, the drill sergeant. A tough black man, Tower singles out Pavlo and makes him do punitive push-ups on the first day of basic training. Throughout the play, Tower gives instructions on combat and first aid. He tells the soldiers what to do when they are lost.

Kress, one of the men in Pavlo's unit. Large and muscular, Kress does not understand much. He flunks the proficiency test and has to repeat basic training. Kress is always complaining about being cold, even in the furnace room. Kress despises Pavlo.

Yen (ĭng), a Vietnamese prostitute. Dressed in purple silk pajamas, Yen is the first woman with whom Pavlo has sex; he visits her regularly.

Pierce, squad leader. Pierce does not participate in the harassment of Pavlo, but he understands why the other men dislike him. Pierce's main concern is his responsibility as leader. He is afraid of how violent incidents will reflect on him, tarnishing his military record.

Sergeant Wall, a friend of Sergeant Brisbey. After being beaten in a fight with Pavlo over Yen, Wall throws a grenade in the room.

Sergeant Brisbey, one of Pavlo's patients. Brisbey stepped on a mine and has lost his testicles, both legs, and one arm. He is very bitter and wants to kill himself.

Mickey, Pavlo's half brother. Tougher than Pavlo, Mickey does not care what others think. He is a womanizer and heavy drinker and is disrespectful of their mother.

Mrs. Hummel, Pavlo's mother. A small, dark-haired, plump, fashionably dressed woman, Mrs. Hummel appears distracted when Pavlo returns home. She recounts a story of a mother who learns that her son was killed in Vietnam.

Lou Thompson

THE BASS SAXOPHONE

Author: Josef Škvorecký (1924-   )
Type of work: Novella
Time of action: The 1940's
First published: Bassaxofon, 1967 (English translation, 1977)

The narrator, a male jazz musician in Kostelec, a small town in Nazi-occupied Czechoslovakia. An eighteen-year-old Czech dandy and jazz saxophonist is swept into a band concert for the Nazi occupation forces by his fascination with a beautiful rare bass saxophone. Wearing a false mustache to escape recognition by other Czechs, he dons the green, purple, and orange costume of Lothar Kinze's German orchestra in order to play the bass saxophone. His personal passion for music battles his fear of political reprisals.

Interrupted and unmasked, he flees the hotel concert hall, but the secret experience remains for him an emblem of his youth and the mysteries of life.

Horst Hermann Kühl, a Nazi official in Kostelec. Kühl once confiscated one of the narrator's jazz records when it was accidentally broadcast in the cinema. Although the narrator suffered no SS prosecution for his offense, he continues to suffer from fear of Kühl and his power. Kühl attends the concert by Kinze's orchestra.

Lothar Kinze, the leader of and violin player for a small German orchestra traveling by bus through occupied territories. A seedy refugee from circus performances, Kinze recruits the narrator to replace his ill saxophonist.

The man on the gilded bed, the regular bass saxophone player in Lothar Kinze's orchestra. Interrupting the narrator's performance, he takes the stage in a stirring performance that elicits the ire of Kühl and burns itself into the memory of the narrator, a moment of pain that shakes complacency.

Virginia Crane

THE BATHHOUSE
A Drama in Six Acts with a Circus and Fireworks

Author: Vladimir Mayakovsky (1893-1930)
Type of work: Play
Time of action: The late 1920's
First published: Banya, 1930 (English translation, 1963)

Chudakov, a Soviet inventor. He is a visionary, desirous of building a time machine that will enable people to extend moments of joy and contract periods of sorrow. Single-minded, serious, hardworking, and without government support, he succeeds in making contact with the future. At the end of the play, his invention carries him and many others a hundred years into the future.

The Phosphorescent Woman, an emissary from the year 2030, contacted by Chudakov's invention. She comes from the time when Communism has triumphed worldwide. Articulate and authoritative, she intends to bring into the perfect state those twentieth century citizens most responsible for building it. Her Communism is humanitarian rather than ideological, commonsensical rather than doctrinaire.

Pobedonosikov, Chief of the Federal Bureau of Coordination. He is a Soviet bureaucrat in love with power. Though he speaks the jargon of an egalitarian people's revolution, he delights in acquiring privileges and pulling rank. He maintains authority by reminding everyone of his (self-inflated) role in the 1917 Revolution. When the Phosphorescent Woman arrives to carry the best Communists into the future, he tries to control the operation but instead is left behind.

Velosipedkin, an official from the Young Communist League. A worker dedicated to socialism, he is practical-minded, aggressive, and savvy. At first skeptical of Chudakov's invention, he later becomes its strongest advocate. He battles bureaucrats in the attempt to get government support and, after the arrival of the Phosphorescent Woman, helps choose the best Communists for transportation to the future.

Optimistenko, secretary to Pobedonosikov. The quintessential bureaucrat, he shields his boss from the petitions of ordinary citizens. He is dedicated to following procedures rather than to achieving results. For each petitioner in the long queue, he has a different excuse why his boss cannot help today. While worrying if the time machine has food service, he is left behind.

Polya, Pobedonosikov's wife. Tired of her husband's marital arrogance and extramarital affairs, she is a secret supporter of the time machine. Ironically, she secures money from an embezzler in Pobedonosikov's office to finance a key phase of Chudakov's experiment. She persuades the Phosphorescent Woman that she belongs in the future when married couples will be more honest and more affectionate with each other.

Isaac Belvedonsky, a painter and photographer. He lacks artistic ability and artistic integrity. He sells his work to Pobedonosikov by catering to the bureau chief's ego and acquisitiveness. He specializes in bourgeois objects with a revolutionary twist, for example, a Louis Quatorze sofa decorated with hammer-and-sickle fabric.

Pont Kich, a British visitor in Russia to admire Soviet achievements. He speaks a kind of fractured Russian, mixing English vocabulary and Russian syntax. He indiscriminately praises what he sees. He uncritically accepts what his bureaucratic guides tell him: that the Soviets have already achieved the Communist ideal.

Madame Mezalyansova, an interpreter who escorts Pont Kich. She is Pobedonosikov's mistress and flaunts her status in front of Polya.

The Director of the Play, who becomes a character for one scene. Close to exasperation, he reasons with the actors who perform the bureaucrats when they threaten to abandon their parts. The actors complain that they portray ignoble, unworthy social types. Desperate to save the play, he convinces them to continue the performance by introducing an uplifting, ideological pantomime into the play.

Robert M. Otten

THE BATTLE OF PHARSALUS

Author: Claude Simon (1913-   )
Type of work: novel
Time of action: 1968
First published: La Bataille de Pharsale, 1969 (English translation, 1971)

O., narrator and principal character in a series of events that are not told chronologically but are instead presented as the free play of his memory, which acts as a kind of "mobile," circling and changing position around a few fixed points: the four or five most important events of his life. O.'s profession is never stated, but he is a classical scholar of sorts, and he is fascinated by the Battle of Pharsalus, which he read about as a schoolboy and the exact location of which, as an adult, he has tried to find in the north of Greece. His translations of Caesar, however, are awkward and his interest in Roman history limited to this battle and to Caesar's profile on the coins and bills of the countries he visits on a train trip through Europe. O. is not a writer, but he is interested in the multiple meanings of words, and lists of Latin words, with their French meanings, are scattered throughout the narrative. The visual possibilities of letters fascinate him—the *A* in "PANTALON" becomes a pair of pants in an advertisement for a clothing store. O. is not an artist, although he is writing an essay on a painting in a German museum and greatly admires battle paintings by Nicolas Poussin, Piero Della Francesca, and Paolo Uccello. Only briefly is O. seen in an office, which is probably in the old home on the family estate in southern France. He counts out small piles of money in it, just as Uncle Charles used to do, to pay the dirty, shadowy men waiting outside in the dark hallway. This place is where he still lives, with a wife whom he does not love and two children whom he does.

Odette, O.'s lover, an artist's model, with dark eyes and a cloud of black hair, her child's face made-up like a "poisonous flower," sometimes lying among cushions and surrounded by porcelain and vases of flowers, sometimes wearing a Japanese kimono after posing for the painter, Van Velden. Sometimes, she is with O., wearing a cheap street dress and chipped fingernail polish. Her promiscuity is well known and drives O. to behavior of which he is later ashamed.

Uncle Charles, a relative whom O. remembers as being in the office, which smells of old wine and tobacco, seated at his desk, holding a half-smoked cigar in his bony hand, wearing on his nose eyeglasses that reflected the light. He is correcting, often ridiculing, the young O.'s translation of Caesar's account of the battle of Pharsalus.

O.'s grandmother, a matriarchal figure in her old-fashioned clothes of serge or dark silk, with a high collar and small tucks across the bodice, a cameo at her throat. There is majesty and importance to her position and her age, and, to the young boy, she represents death.

Lucy Golsan

BEACHMASTERS

Author: Thea Astley (1925-   )
Type of work: Novel
Time of action: The early 1980's
First published: 1985

Tommy Narota, the leader of a rebellion on a tiny South Pacific Island. Son of a native woman and a British planter, Narota, at age fifty or so, is a gentle and naïve sort, not at all a typical revolutionary. Yet his firmly held belief in the native people's right to govern themselves on their own island inspires them to revolt, albeit unsuccessfully, against the European powers that have so long dominated them.

Gavi Salway, a teenage boy, who learns at the rebellion's start that he is a half-caste, even though he had been reared believing that he was the child of British planters. Possessing a keen sensitivity and awareness, Gavi sets out to grasp the significance of this discovery, and during the short-lived rebellion he makes his passage into manhood.

District Agent Cordingley, the island's major British official. In appearance, speech, and actions, the middle-aged Cordingley is a near caricature of British colonial adminis-

trators. Typically, he responds to the rebellion in a bumbling, cowardly manner.

Bonser, a crude, bigoted, and exploitative Australian expatriate, who works as a mechanic on the island. The rebellion to him simply provides a way to make money through gun smuggling.

Père Leyroud, an aging Roman Catholic priest who has spent forty years on the island. The rebellion serves to heighten his sense of failure and his disillusionment with the religion he preaches.

Salway, a British planter and Gavi's grandfather, who has been an island resident for fifty years. Wise and gentle, he sees the rebellion as a sign of a passing era and the end of deception concerning Gavi's true parentage.

Woodful, the school's middle-aged headmaster, who displays more understanding of the natives than most of his fellow Anglo-

Saxons on the island. Woodful realizes that the rebellion has undone all of his years of well-intended struggle, and he accepts that truth.

Chloe of the Dancing Bears, an aging prostitute of British descent. A minor character, Chloe stands out as a representative of several such decadent colonial types portrayed briefly in the novel; having long used the island as a retreat from shattered lives that they cannot face, they ignore the revolution as well.

Letty Trumble, the middle-aged wife of a minor British official. Prudish, pretentious, racialist, and sexually frustrated, Trumble represents a typical kind of woman that colonialism produced.

Belle Cordingley, the American wife of District Agent Cordingley. She is a brassy blonde, whose responses and actions border on the comic as she expresses bitterness and disappointment over her husband's past failures and his pathetic behavior during the rebellion.

Robert L. Ross

THE BEAUTIFUL AND DAMNED

Author: F. Scott Fitzgerald (1896-1940)
Type of work: Novel
Time of action: 1913-1921
First published: 1922

Anthony Patch, a playboy and dilettante. Most of the novel is narrated from the point of view of this good-looking, intelligent, and fundamentally decent man and concerns his moral deterioration between the ages of twenty-five and thirty-three. He stands to inherit the lion's share of his grandfather's estate, worth in the neighborhood of $75 million. This inheritance has a debilitating effect on Anthony because it stifles any motive to do anything for himself, although he continues to entertain notions of writing about history. His parents died when he was a child, along with his paternal grandmother, who was rearing him in their stead. These tragedies left him with a chronic paranoid anxiety and help to explain why he is passive, immature, and lacking the aggressiveness to carve out a career for himself. With nothing serious to occupy his mind, he takes to drinking and becomes a hopeless alcoholic.

Gloria Gilbert Patch, Anthony's wife, three years his junior. Just as Anthony has never had to develop any strength of character because of his grandfather's riches, Gloria has never had to develop any strength of character because of her remarkable beauty. She is spoiled, selfish, and narcissistic. She feels that her beauty conveys a certain nobility upon her, so that she does not have to do anything but merely has to be. Gloria is the worst possible wife for Anthony because she is just as feckless and incompetent as he. She is Fitzgerald's model of a flapper: She is one of the first socialites to bob her hair and wear daring fashions. When her beauty begins to fade with age and dissipation, she is a lost soul.

Adam Patch, a millionaire and philanthropist, Anthony's grandfather. In his prime Patch was a ruthless businessman, but in his old age, with death staring him in the face, he suddenly develops a conscience and begins trying to reform the world. He advocates hard work and sobriety—virtues that his grandson completely lacks. When Anthony learns upon the old man's death that he has been disinherited for his wild conduct, he and Gloria are thrown into desperate straits. Anthony continues squandering the meager capital he inherited from his mother and becomes involved in a seemingly endless lawsuit to overturn his grandfather's will.

Richard Caramel, Gloria's cousin and Anthony's best friend, a successful novelist. Pudgy and unattractive but talented and warm-hearted, Caramel graduated from Harvard with his head full of ideals about "service to humanity." His first novel was a sincere work of art; then he gradually becomes corrupted by literary fame and the need to keep making money. His later works are potboilers—the sad thing being that he does not even recognize them as such.

Maury Noble, another of Anthony's friends from Harvard days. This handsome, brilliant young man might have made important contributions to some branch of human thought. Yet, he can find no meaning in a mechanistic universe; he goes into business and becomes hardened and cynical while growing more and more prosperous. He is another illustration of Fitzgerald's thesis that the

blind forces of nature have countless ways of corroding innocence and beauty.

Joseph Bloeckman, a Jewish motion picture producer. He is in love with Gloria but loses her to Anthony, who appears to have more to offer in terms of wealth and social prestige. Bloeckman serves as a foil to Anthony: Through his brains and ambition he acquires money, power, and even the upperclass polish that he initially lacked. His success in spite of disadvantages highlights Anthony's weakness of character.

Dorothy Raycroft, Anthony's mistress during World War I. Anthony is sent to training camp in South Carolina, where he meets this pretty, unsophisticated country girl of nineteen. After the war ends, she follows him to New York and causes him to have a nervous breakdown by demanding his love when he is in the final stages of his character disintegration and has nothing left to give anyone.

Bill Delaney

BEAUTY AND SADNESS

Author: Yasunari Kawabata (1899-1972)
Type of work: Novel
Time of action: 1961
First published: Utsukushisa to kanashimi to, 1961-1963, serial; 1965, book (English translation, 1975)

Toshio Oki, a fifty-four-year-old novelist. He is a sentimental man, in the ascetic and reserved manner of the Japanese aesthetic. When Oki was thirty and newly married, he had an affair with a fifteen-year-old girl. This affair he later fictionalized, and the resulting book has become his best, most acclaimed, and most enduring novel. He sets the present-time action of the novel going with an impulsive action: He arranges to meet his former mistress and to listen with her to the tolling of temple bells at midnight on New Year's Eve. Instead of resulting in the hoped-for insight and perspective, the meeting brings more involvement; Oki finds himself starting a romance, parallel to his

first affair, with his former mistress's young protégée, meeting the same dilemmas and making the same flawed choices.

Otoko Ueno, a traditional Japanese painter, who at the age of fifteen was Oki's mistress. A reflective woman, she spends much of her time reminiscing, musing about her life and the poignant, never-to-be-spoken feelings that became the subjects of her paintings. Although she has a firmly established career and a new lover, her affair with Oki, their love, the stillborn baby they conceived, and her eventual mental breakdown and hospitalization are still the foremost events in her life. Otoko wonders whether she should lay the hold that the affair has over her to the power of art, rather than to an enduring grand passion. Oki's novel, although idealized, has kept their affair alive in the memory of the public. Otoko herself has forged an attachment to her lost baby by working on an idealized portrait, a picture of a child she never saw. Although she had been Oki's saucy young lover, the main mark of her character is reflection. She is largely passive as her unreserved young companion undertakes to complete the story of Oki and Otoko's affair.

Keiko Sakami, Otoko's student, companion, and lover. She is young, full of passionate energy, and without reserve, even ruthless, in her actions. She is beautiful (she reminds many of the young Otoko), and although she asserts that she hates men, she has no reservations about using her powers of seduction against them. To Otoko's horror, she announces her plan to revenge Otoko on Oki and his family. It may be that the revenge is directed as much against Otoko as for her benefit. Against Oki himself, although she does cause him some trouble with his wife, she does nothing that she might not have done had she merely wanted to be his lover. Later, however, she seduces his shy son, Taichiro. Knowing that he cannot swim, she entices him into a motorboat. She survives an apparent accident, he dies by drowning.

Fumiko, Oki's wife. Formerly an office typ-

ist, she is now established in the life and sentiments of an Oriental wife and mother. Newly married, and in her early childbearing years when Oki started his affair, she reacted sometimes with jealous rage and sometimes with displays of tragedy. In one of the latter, she had endangered the health of her baby, the young Taichiro. When she read Oki's novel about the affair, she suffered a miscarriage. Still later, she had become reconciled to the affair, saying even that she should have given Oki his freedom. In the present time of the novel, Fumiko's rage and tragic pathos have muted, and she and Oki have made a kind of peace over the affair. It is neither forgotten nor an open rift between them.

Taichiro, Oki's son, a university professor specializing in traditional Japanese Literature. Shy and scholarly, and still living with his parents, he has not, despite his advanced position, become fully his own man. He is a committed antiquarian, knowledgeable and enthusiastic about Japanese history and literature, subjects he is afraid may die from inattention. He is taken aback by Keiko's ignorance of her own heritage. Nevertheless, he is easy prey for her seduction. In her company, he makes progress toward adulthood. As she leads him to take steps away from his family, however, she is only accomplishing her plan of revenge and arranging his seemingly accidental death.

Fritz Monsma

THE BEAUTYFUL ONES ARE NOT YET BORN

Author: Ayi Kwei Armah (1939-   )
Type of work: Novel
Time of action: The 1960's
First published: 1968

The Man, deliberately given the generality of anonymity, a clerk who works for the nationalized railway system in Ghana, West Africa. He and his wife, Oyo, and their children live in comparative poverty because of the Man's unflinching determination not to accept bribes but to live on his inadequate

salary in a society that finds such behavior incomprehensible. In spite of the temptations that come to him from every side, the constant nagging of his bitter wife, and his own awareness of the hardships his abstinence imposes upon his children, he continues to maintain his unalterable moral stance. His determination is in some measure justified when a coup destroys the regime and the corrupt are arrested, but as he begins to rejoice in the vigorous national purge of corruption, he witnesses the same old crookedness immediately reactivated. The Man represents, to an exaggerated degree, an idealized portrait of a truly noble man in a degraded society.

Oyo, the Man's wife. She has no sympathy with her husband's honesty and all but despises him for it. Indifferent to the principles involved, she can only see how well others are managing as a result of their acquiescence to wrongdoing. She has a deep envy of the successful and yearns for the luxuries that other women enjoy. Only at the end does she commend her husband when she sees the painful consequences that come when the criminals are arrested.

Koomson, a government minister who epitomizes the grossly corrupt African politician of the postindependence years. He has come up the hard way, starting out as a tough dockworker. He is gross and vulgar but can convincingly assume a cheerful, hearty public manner that appeals to voters. He distributes bribes freely, indulging his family with all the most visibly ostentatious material things—invariably from Europe, for in this country only the expensive foreign imports are evidence of success; local products are for the failures. Koomson swindles the Man's mother in a tax-evasion dodge to buy a boat, which he uses for his escape from the police when the new regime orders his arrest. At the end, he is a frightened and defeated fugitive, using his last bank notes to bribe his way to safety.

Estella, Koomson's wife, an egregious snob who embodies the pretensions of the nouveau riche. Ironically, her behavior is patterned after the arrogance of the white colonials from whom her country has been liberated politically but not yet culturally. When her husband escapes into exile, the new administration does not prosecute her, and she survives to live on in Ghana in reduced circumstances.

The Teacher, another generalized figure, the Man's teacher, guide, counselor, and guru. The Teacher supplies him with the intellectual rationalization for his search for moral order in a delinquent and disintegrating society, and reinforces his personal determination with philosophic precedent. The Teacher plays no active part in the events of the novel, but his long conversations and debates with the Man allow the author to air his angry response to the overwhelming corruption that festers within his country.

John F. Povey

BECKET
Or, The Honor of God

Author: Jean Anouilh (1910-1987)
Type of work: Play
Time of action: The twelfth century, 1154-1189
First produced: 1959

Henry II, the high-strung Norman King of England, who defines his power in terms of his relationship with his friend, adviser, and eventual adversary Thomas Becket. Henry's demeanor as well as his age changes as he goes from young optimistic monarch to disillusioned sovereign. Initially, he believes that all he has to do to accomplish something is to give the order and have it obeyed. This simplistic attitude changes as he discovers that vested interests are formidable bulwarks. Furthermore, people develop different priorities as circumstances change. Their attitudes in life alter as their roles in life differ. Henry becomes more withdrawn and isolated; he feels deserted by everybody and realizes that he must learn to be alone. In his desperation, he cries out for others to save him, thus preparing the way for the play's ultimate tragedy.

Thomas à Becket, a Saxon of common birth whose love of luxury and desire to elevate himself from his despised origins leads him into a friendship with King Henry, with whom he helps pass the time drinking and wenching. Henry believes that Becket is his man and appoints him Chancellor of England and then Archbishop of Canterbury. In doing so, however, he precipitates Becket's transformation from a servant of the crown to a servant of God, putting him on a collision course with his authority. Becket regains his honor and atones for having cheated his way into the ranks of the conquerors of his people through his martyrdom.

Gilbert Folliot, Bishop of London, "a thin-lipped, venomous man" who is led more by his antipathies than by his principles. Thus, loyalty to the Church proves less durable than his hatred of Becket. Yet, he is not without courage, although predisposed to believing that the interests of church and state are one, making it easy for him to become an agent for the condemnation of Becket.

Gwendolen, Becket's young Welsh mistress, acquired by him as a spoil of war, but who grows to love him. She becomes a symbol of Becket's devotion to Henry when Henry demands she be delivered to his bed as a favor. Gwendolen goes without protest, but when Henry tries to embrace her she commits suicide.

The Four English Barons, Henry calls them his "four idiots" and his "faithful hounds." Indeed, their unswerving loyalty to the crown gives him reassurance of his own worth. These men are so willing to please that they respond to the royal will even without a direct order. They, therefore, symbolize the triumph of the ethical state that has no higher goal than loyalty to itself, and

they serve it even should their path lead to murder.

The Archbishop of Canterbury, Becket's elderly predecessor, an old-time server who tries to reach an accommodation with the state by appealing to reason. When that fails, he is not above using his office to get his way. Yet, he knows that he is too old for a confrontation with the king over the issue of taxation of the Church, and he urges circumspection, hoping that Becket will, in time, prove an ally.

Louis, King of France, "a burly man with intelligent eyes," who shows that the nature of his position is to make things as difficult for England as possible. Thus, he is not averse to becoming involved in the struggles between the English Catholic church and the state. He grants Becket his royal protection, at least until the political climate might change. Louis knows that there is no principle in politics, save inconsistency.

The Pope, a thin, fidgety small man with a problem: He needs money but believes that if he takes it from the King of England, he cannot give support to Becket, who is fighting for the rights of the Church. He wants to survive in a world of high intrigue and will apparently make any kind of deal as long as he can hold on to a good reputation.

Cardinal Zambelli, the swarthy and somewhat grubby adviser to the pontiff, who tells the pope that he should play a double game: relieve Becket of his functions as Primate and then immediately reappoint him, thus scoring points against both him and the King of England. In this world of high papal politics, epitomized by this cardinal and pope, everything is a game played by constantly changing rules.

The Queen Mother, the quintessential "I-told-you-so" figure. She believes that if her son Henry had only listened to her, he would not be in the mess he is in now.

The Young Queen, Henry's wife. She is a

constant object of his abuse. She is naturally disturbed that her husband preferred debauchery with his friend Becket to attending to his duties as a father and husband. In her bitterness, she becomes a nag.

Henry and **Richard,** Henry's young sons. He treats them with great contempt, as his family generally becomes the object of his scorn and ire.

Wm. Laird Kleine-Ahlbrandt

THE BEDBUG
An Extravaganza in Nine Scenes

Author: Vladimir Mayakovsky (1893-1930)
Type of work: Play
Time of action: 1929
First produced: Klop, 1929 (English translation, 1931)

Ivan Prisypkin, alias **Pierre Skripkin,** a former worker and Communist Party member. A man with philistine values and tastes, intent on improving his social status, Prisypkin pretentiously adopts the French name Pierre and abandons his working-class girlfriend, Zoya, to marry Elzevira, a member of the petit bourgeoisie. Amidst the drunken revelry of his wedding celebration, the house burns down. All the bodies of the wedding party are recovered except Prisypkin's. Fifty years later, when Prisypkin's frozen body is discovered in an ice-filled cellar, he is unfrozen. The boisterous, vulgar Prisypkin, who curses, drinks, sings, and plays the guitar, finds himself out of place in a sterile, rationally planned, regimented futuristic society. Placed in a cage in a zoo when other citizens are infected by his contagious behavior and begin to imitate him, he is put on display along with the bedbug resurrected with him as a specimen and relic of the bourgeois past. In the final scene of the play Prisypkin, alone and dismayed, suddenly turns to the audience and joyfully recognizes the spectators as fellow human beings who share his weaknesses and vices.

Zoya Berezkina, a working girl. A simple, modest, unpretentious young woman in love with Prisypkin, Zoya is driven to despair when she is jilted by Prisypkin and shoots herself. Resilient, she survives the suicide attempt and reappears fifty years later as a professor's assistant, who witnesses the resurrection of Prisypkin. Confronted again with Prisypkin, she realizes her folly in having attempted suicide over such a vulgarian.

Elzevira Davidovna Renaissance, a manicurist and cashier of a beauty parlor. Prisypkin's fiancée, Elzevira is an attractive young woman who fusses over Prisypkin and lavishes him with kisses and endearing nicknames. During the drunken revelry at her wedding, she is pushed onto the stove, her veil catches fire, and she perishes in the blaze.

Rosalia Pavlovna Renaissance, a hairdresser. Elzevira's mother, Rosalia, is an enterprising, energetic woman eager to have her daughter marry Prisypkin to obtain the privileges that come with Prisypkin's labor union membership. Protective of her interests, she curses and threatens Zoya when Zoya claims Prisypkin as her own.

Oleg Bayan, an eccentric house-owner. A clever, witty man and amateur poet, he comments ironically on Prisypkin's behavior, pointing out his shortcomings. He acts as Prisypkin's companion and mentor, attempting to educate Prisypkin and to raise him to a higher cultural level. Slightly intoxicated, he delivers the main toast at Prisypkin's wedding.

The Zoo Director, orders that Prisypkin be used as a source of nourishment for the bedbug and has them both placed in a glass case to be exhibited to the public. He pompously delivers the major address at the ceremonies unveiling the resurrected Prisypkin and the bedbug, denouncing both as parasites.

A Professor, an elderly scholar, knowledgeable about the past, who supervises the unfreezing of Prisypkin and explains Prisypkin's anachronistic speech and behavior to the doctors who assist him.

The Master of Ceremonies, the man who coordinates activities at the celebration to present the resurrected Prisypkin to the public.

The Chairman of the City Council, the man who warns citizens about the cultural danger of Prisypkin's anachronistic behavior.

A Speaker, the President of the Institute for Human Resurrection. He polls the country and records the vote to resurrect Prisypkin.

David Osipovich Renaissance, a hairdresser, Elzevira's father, who plays a minimal role in the play, appearing only at Elzevira's wedding.

Jerome J. Rinkus

BEETLECREEK

Author: William Demby (1922- -)
Type of work: Novel
Time of action: The American Depression era
First published: 1950

Johnny Johnson, a black teenager. Johnny has come to Beetlecreek, West Virginia, from Pittsburgh to live with his uncle, David Diggs. His mother is severely ill and has been placed in the county home and cannot care for him. Johnny has arrived too late in the year to enter school, so he lounges around his aunt and uncle's house until school is dismissed; then he associates with the Wilson gang, the Nightriders, a group of four other black youths his age. When the story opens, a white hermit, Bill Trapp, chases the gang from his property because they are stealing apples. Johnny is trapped in the tree, but the man invites him down and into the house for cider. Johnny becomes friends with the old man, and they pass many interesting times together. Later, as part of his initiation into the Nightriders, and as part of their retaliation against Trapp for a crime that he did not commit, Johnny burns the old man's house to the ground.

Bill Trapp, a white recluse. Having grown up as an adopted child, along with his sister, Hilda, Trapp has always been melancholy and withdrawn. In order to attain the kind of respectable life that his sister always wanted for him, he works a variety of jobs: in a blacksmith shop, a garage, and as a handyman for a traveling carnival, the Harry Simcoe Continental Show. After tiring from the rigors of the traveling show, Bill Trapp purchases the May farm on the outskirts of Beetlecreek. Here he keeps to himself, venturing into town only to buy supplies and drinking heavily to ease the pain of loneliness. Trapp comes to life again after becoming friends with Johnny Johnson and his uncle, David Diggs. Trapp gives a cartload of pumpkins to the two Tolley sisters for the fall carnival, and he gives a party to which he invites the little black and white girls in order to encourage friendship between the races. At this party, one white girl, who was not invited, tears a picture from one of Trapp's anatomy books and fabricates a story that portrays him as a child molester. This rumor turns both the black and white communities against him. Bill Trapp collapses at the sight of his burning house.

David Diggs, a sign painter. A tall, slender man, at thirty-two years of age, he is frustrated, having dropped out of college to marry a young woman whom he had gotten pregnant while on a visit to Beetlecreek in pursuit of Edith Johnson. He has no drive, no ambition, and no job, except for occasional work painting signs. When he goes to rescue his nephew from Bill Trapp, he finds the old man to be an interesting and genuinely likeable person, and befriends him. When Edith Johnson returns to Beetlecreek to attend her adopted mother's funeral, David is renewed. At her invitation, he leaves Beetlecreek for Detroit with Edith Johnson on the night of the fire and the fall carnival.

Mary Phillips Diggs, a maid, David's wife. Mary has become a pious woman since her child was born dead. She wraps herself in her job as maid for the Pinkertons, a prominent white family, and in her church activities, principally, the Women's Missionary Guild, of which she aspires to be president. Although a passionate young girl when she first meets David, she has become unkempt, uninteresting, and also unattractive. She does have a successful night selling gingerbread at the fall carnival, completely unaware that her husband has left town with another woman, or that his nephew has set fire to Bill Trapp's house.

Edith Johnson, a city girl. A former resident of Beetlecreek and a college classmate of David Diggs, Edith returns to Beetlecreek to attend the funeral of her adopted mother, whom she hated. At twenty-seven, she is attractive, well-dressed, and schooled in the ways of the city. The people of Beetlecreek assume that she is a prostitute; for them, Edith Johnson has nothing but the deepest contempt. After settling her mother's affairs, she returns to Detroit along with David Diggs, whom she has encouraged to leave Beetlecreek.

The Leader, a Beetlecreek teenager. He is the callous, insensitive leader of a youth gang called the Nightriders. The gang meets in a secret hideaway to smoke, tell dirty jokes, look at pornography, and masturbate, all of which Johnny Johnson finds disgusting. Yet when the Leader offers to make him a member, he jumps at the chance. The Leader issues the condition for membership on the night of Johnny's initiation: Johnny must burn Bill Trapp's house as an act of reprisal for Trapp's alleged molestation of the Tolley girls.

Pokey, a white girl who was not invited to Bill Trapp's party. She tears a picture from one of his anatomy books and fabricates the story that Trapp molested the girls at the party.

Telrico, a café owner. As an Italian, Telrico tries to stay out of the comings and goings of Beetlecreek because he is keenly aware that he is an outsider. His cafe serves as a meeting place for the men of the town: David Diggs brings Bill Trapp to Telrico's for a drink on the night he first meets him; Edith Johnson and David also meet regularly at Telrico's.

Sarah Tolley and
Mary Ellen Tolley, two young Beetlecreek sisters. They ask Bill Trapp for pumpkins for the fall carnival. Later, they are invited to Trapp's party where the alleged molestation is to have occurred. The girls know that Trapp is innocent but are not allowed by their mother to tell the truth.

Mr. Tolley, a barber. The father of Sarah and Mary Ellen, his barbershop is the gathering place for the town and the center for discussion for all the important business in Beetlecreek.

Warren J. Carson

A BEGGAR IN JERUSALEM

Author: Elie Wiesel (1928-   )
Type of work: Novel
Time of action: 1967
First published: Le Mendiant de Jérusalem, 1968 (English translation, 1970)

David ben Sarah (his surname means "son of Sarah"), a wanderer and first-person narrator of the novel. A survivor of the Holocaust, the forty-year-old David is rebellious and skeptical of any value in a world that has lost its innocence. He is filled with memories of his childhood and spends much of his time exchanging tales and testimonies with a group of beggars in Jerusalem. At the outbreak of the Six Day War, he joins a tank unit commanded by an old friend and there meets Katriel. Soon after their meeting, he makes a pact with Katriel that if one of them should survive the war, then he will bear witness for the other. David's tale, then, is a process of bearing witness for Katriel, a man whom he envies for his compulsion to magnify humanity in an inhuman world.

Katriel, a teacher who goes back into the army to fight in the Six Day War at the insistence of his father, a blind rabbi from Safed. Tall, slim, and quiet, Katriel knows how to tell tales and how to listen to them. He loves life and the mystery of life, despite the death of his child Sasha; he is distinguished by his power to affirm the dearness of life, and in this lies his importance to David. At the time of the war, he has been married for twenty years. The one thing that most disturbs him during the war is that he has had to kill others. When the war is over, he is missing in action, leaving David to tell his story.

Malka, Katriel's wife, a strong and beautiful woman. She met Katriel when both of them were serving in the army in their youth. An orphan and a widow, she seeks out David so that he may tell her about her husband's last days. When the beggars see her, they take her for a divine apparition. To David, she represents every woman he has ever loved, and she stirs in him a hunger for love and forgiveness. She, too, is very much attracted to him.

Lieutenant Colonel Gad, head of David's tank unit and a friend from David's years in postwar Europe. As young men, he and David had long conversations about life and its meaning. He is a career soldier, who refuses to believe in defeat, no matter how mad the belief in victory might be. Aggressive and courageous, he leads his men to the Western Wall only to be killed shortly thereafter.

Gdalia, a Yeminite Jew in David's tank unit who serves as a mediator between Katriel and the other soldiers. Talkative and jovial, he is schooled in philosophy and likes to interpret Katriel's tales.

Dan the Prince, a beggar who is constantly writing reports to politicians and journalists. Once a historian in Europe, he claims to be the emissary of a mysterious king. His friends know him to be dignified, melancholy, intelligent, and compassionate; yet they regard him at various times as a psychotic, a rogue, and an embezzler.

Velvel, a beggar and a dwarf with only one eye. He is a gambler who knows how to rejoice and how to mock authority, even— or especially—the authority of reason.

Anshel, a street hustler who sells postcards in the Old City of Jerusalem. Having served in three wars, he is ridden with guilt feelings.

Yakov the Timid, a beggar and former schoolteacher who plays war games with children, teaching them not to be afraid. He is known as a peacemaker.

David Patterson

BEGGAR ON HORSEBACK

Author: Marc Connelly (1890-1980) with George S. Kaufman (1889-1961)
Type of work: Play
Time of action: The 1920's
First produced: 1924

Neil McRae, a pianist and composer. At about age thirty, he seems to be a fellow without prospects because his impracticality borders on the irresponsible. He is, however, personable and engaging, and his apparent indifference to material well-being springs more from his artistic creed than sloth or carelessness. Wholly dedicated to his music, he lives an independent, quasi-Bohemian life that is much too quixotic to suit the Cady clan. Although not in love with Gladys, Neil proposes to her when his need to be "subsidized" is pressed by Dr. Rice and Cynthia Mason, who tells him that she, Cynthia, is moving away. In his sleeping-pill induced dream, Neil envisions a nightmarish future with Gladys and his in-laws. He wakes up a wiser man, in love with Cynthia, the proper person, determined to reject all that the Cadys represent, including the prostitution of his art.

Dr. Albert Rice, a long-standing friend to Neil and of the same age. He is humorous and amiable and considerably more practical than Neil. He has a genuine concern for his friend's health, material welfare, and artistic future. In addition to providing the pills that put Neil to sleep, he enlists Cynthia's help in convincing Neil to propose to Gladys. As do the other characters, he appears in other guises in Neil's dream, first as the minister who marries Neil and Gladys, then as a reporter at Neil's trial.

Cynthia Mason, Neil's neighbor, also a musician, about twenty-five years old. Initially, she seems too motherly toward Neil, taking him to task for his wasteful behavior and forgetfulness. Her concern, however, springs from love and great respect for Neil's talent. More practical than Neil, at first she is willing to suppress her own desires to advance his career, but then, fortuitously, has second

thoughts. In the dream vignettes, it becomes clear that she is much better suited to Neil than is Gladys.

Gladys Cady, Neil's only piano student, presumably of Cynthia's age. She is on the spoiled and flighty side, determined to keep life amusing and fun, which, thanks to her father's wealth and her shallowness, is very possible. Her tastes are entirely wrong for Neil, but it is only in his nightmarish dream, in which they are married, that he comes to realize it. It is fortunate for both of them that Gladys encounters an old flame and wants to squirm out of the engagement.

Mr. Cady, a no-nonsense businessman and patriarch of the Cady family. Bossy and brusque, he is a cultural philistine who believes art, like any commodity, is good only if it can be sold at a profit. He is dedicated to two things: making money and playing golf. In Neil's dream, he is caricatured first as a crude and blustering but extremely rich manufacturer of "widgets," then as the hanging judge at Neil's murder trial.

Mrs. Cady, Mr. Cady's wife, mother to Homer and Gladys. She is a rather air-headed woman caught up in small-town speculations and gossip. Like her daughter, she is shallow and silly, traits that become exaggerated in her depiction in Neil's dream. Her pampering of Homer helps explain his unpleasant nature.

Homer Cady, son to Mr. and Mrs. Cady and brother to Gladys. He is a surly and suspicious young man who is no more refined than his father. Although he claims to be delicate, he is a recalcitrant and loutish hypochondriac who takes issue with anything said. His appalling lack of taste is reflected by his garish yellow tie, which, in

136

Neil's dream, grows larger and larger. Increasingly Neil's nemesis, in the dream trial he becomes the prosecuting attorney.

Jerry, an obliging young porter in Neil McRae's apartment house. Affable and polite,

he appears as a jack-of-all-roles in Neil's dream, assuming identities ranging from elevator boy to ticket taker at the murder trial to executioner.

John W. Fiero

THE BELL JAR

Author: Sylvia Plath (1932-1963)
Type of work: Novel
Time of action: 1953
First published: 1963

Esther Greenwood, a bright college student who apires to be a writer. At nineteen, brown-eyed and brown-haired, Esther feels somewhat out of place in the world of high fashion and money that she is introduced to as a result of winning a fashion magazine contest. Yet even though she gets to her prestigious college on a scholarship, Esther is not one to sit in the corner feeling insecure; instead, she meets the world with a lively touch of sarcasm that colors her description of New York City, her friends, and herself. After her month in the city, however, her sense of daring becomes coupled with a feeling of disappointment over life. She attempts suicide and has a nervous breakdown, which is followed by recuperation in a series of hospitals and sanatoriums.

Buddy Willard, a medical student whom Esther has dated. He is an only child, and his parents encourage his relationship with Esther. Buddy has a fairly realistic view of life. Although he has prided himself on his health, as a first-year medical student he contracts tuberculosis and must spend time in a sanatorium. When Esther visits him, he proposes to her, but by this time she has lost interest. Later, he visits her in the sanatorium, but by now for him, too, there is nothing but curiosity about their relationship and a lurking fear that he may have contributed to her emotional condition.

Mrs. Greenwood, Esther Greenwood's wid-

owed mother. She tries to let Esther alone and not pressure her too much. Since the death of Esther's father ten years earlier, she has reared Esther alone and supported the two of them by teaching business courses at a city college in Boston.

Doreen, another winner in the same competition that Esther won. Doreen comes from a finishing-type school in the South. She is a striking young woman, with white hair and deep blue eyes. She is much more sophisticated and daring than Esther, who is quite taken with her. Doreen does not feel any need to follow the schedule set out for the girls or to worry about doing the work assignments. She takes Esther to places where, alone, she would never have thought to go; her behavior and outlook suggest to Esther a new and different approach to the world.

Jay Cee, the famous editor at *Ladies' Day* whom Esther was assigned to work under during her special one-month internship. She tries to help Esther learn the work and consider her future and her opportunities, but at this point in her life, Esther has another agenda.

Philomena Guinea, a novelist and alumna of the college that Esther attends. She provided the scholarship that made it possible for Esther to attend the private women's college in Massachusetts. She continues to assist Esther after her breakdown by financing a move from a public mental institution to a more exclusive, and more expensive, private one.

Doctor Nolan, a female psychiatrist who treats Esther at the hospital where she is recuperating. She administers shock treatments, but they are not so grueling to Esther as the shock treatments administered by Doctor Gordon earlier.

Joan Gilling, an acquaintance of Esther. She becomes more important in Esther's life when they find themselves at the same mental institution and have a gentle rivalry regarding privileges, freedom, and ultimately release.

Paula Kopacz

BELLEFLEUR

Author: Joyce Carol Oates (1938-   )
Type of work: Novel
Time of action: Five years in the 1930's, and 1806-1826
First published: 1980

Leah Bellefleur, daughter of Della Pym who marries her first cousin Gideon. A dominating figure in the family who is believed to have the power to control events, Leah is beautiful, energetic, and passionate. Her youthful sexual hunger develops into an obsession with winning the release of convicted mass-murderer Jean-Pierre Bellefleur II and reuniting the 3-million-acre Bellefleur empire.

Gideon Bellefleur, son of Noel Bellefleur who marries his first cousin Leah. Gideon is strikingly handsome, emotionally reserved, and physically reckless. Although he is a gambler and womanizer, Gideon is often the stable personality that holds the Bellefleur family together. After the death of his friend Nicholas Fuhr and his alienation from Leah, Gideon becomes increasingly distant. In the end, he is the one who destroys the family by crashing a bomb-laden airplane into the mansion.

Jedediah Bellefleur, Leah and Gideon's great-great-grandfather, a hermit who seeks God on Mount Blanc but discovers only madness, hallucinations, and murder. After years in seclusion, he learns that his brother Louis has been murdered, and he returns to marry Louis' widow, Germaine, and continue the Bellefleur line.

Germaine Bellefleur, Leah and Gideon's daughter, who seems to possess magical powers. A precocious and withdrawn child who suffers through the gradual dissolution of her parents' marriage. Germaine is saved from the destruction of her family, which occurs on her fourth birthday, when her father reneges on his promise to take her on a birthday ride in his airplane.

Raphael Lucien Bellefleur, Leah and Gideon's great-grandfather, who builds the Bellefleur mansion. Frustrated in his efforts to win political power, Raphael leaves a bizarre will that demands that his remains be skinned and made into a cavalry drum.

Felix (Lamentations of Jeremiah) Bellefleur, Leah and Gideon's grandfather, who is shamed when his grandiose plan to raise silver fox concludes disastrously, losing most of the fortune that Raphael had accumulated. Felix, who was renamed Lamentations of Jeremiah by his father, drowns in a great storm while desperately trying to save his remaining horses.

Jean-Pierre Bellefleur II, Leah and Gideon's uncle who is sentenced to life in prison for murder. After Leah wins his release, Jean-Pierre murders again.

Noel Bellefleur, Gideon's father. Noel is an outwardly ordinary man who secretly keeps a small jeweled vial of cyanide on his person.

Della Pym, daughter of Felix who marries an ambitious young bank clerk named Stanton Pym. Pym dies in a tobogganing race on which several of the Bellefleur men are wagering. Della never forgives the family for the senseless death of her husband.

Hiram Bellefleur, Leah and Gideon's uncle who is plagued by sleepwalking. He survives numerous close calls during his nighttime rambles, including a wartime walk that takes him through the enemy lines. In the end, he dies from an infected cat scratch.

Ewan Bellefleur, Gideon's brother. Ewan, less physically attractive than Gideon, is nevertheless similarly reckless. He becomes the bullying county sheriff, leading a violent and corrupt life until he is gunned down in his mistress' bed. After his remarkable recovery from his numerous gunshot wounds, Ewan repents his former sinful life and leaves the Bellefleurs to join a religious order.

Samuel Bellefleur, Leah and Gideon's great-uncle, who vanishes in the Bellefleur mansion's Turquoise Room when he is abducted by spirits that come to him out of a large mirror. The family nails shut the room after Samuel's disappearance.

Vernon Bellefleur, son of Hiram and the family poet. An iconoclastic coward, Vernon rebels against the Bellefleur power and status, persisting in reading his proletarian poetry in country taverns and mills. He is finally bound and thrown into a river by some drunken workmen; however, there is some mysterious evidence that he may have survived the murder attempt.

Bromwell Bellefleur, son of Gideon and Leah. Painfully intellectual, Bromwell is sent off to a private school that he cannot stand. He runs away and gains admittance to a distant research institution, where he produces a mammoth volume on the existence of antimatter.

Jean-Pierre Bellefleur, the American founder of the Bellefleur family who was banished from France by Louis XV because of his radical ideas. Jean-Pierre managed to purchase nearly 3 million acres of wilderness, which became the basis for the Bellefleur fortune.

Raphael Lucien Bellefleur II, son of Ewan who is nearly drowned in Mink Pond by a local farm boy. Raphael continues to have a symbiotic relationship with the pond throughout his life and disappears mysteriously when the pond finally dries up.

Nicholas Fuhr, Gideon's best friend, who dies in a horse racing accident that seems to be brought on by Leah's mysterious powers.

Garnet Hecht, one of Gideon's mistresses who bears his child. Conceived on the night of Germaine's birth, the illegitimate infant is stolen by a giant predatory bird. After failing in a suicide attempt, Garnet marries an English lord.

The Varrells, a family of low-born, poorly educated people with whom the Bellefleurs carry on a lengthy and bloody feud.

Carl Brucker

A BEND IN THE RIVER

Author: V. S. Naipaul (1932-   )
Type of work: Novel
Time of action: The late 1960's to the mid-1970's
First published: 1979

Salim, the narrator. Born and reared on the east coast of Africa, Salim does not feel himself to be a true African because his ancestors were Hindus of Northwestern India. From an early age, Salim detached himself from his familiar community and now feels insecure and uncertain about his future in postcolonial Africa. Although nominally a Muslim, he lacks the religious sense of his family. When Nazruddin, a Europeanized Muslim and family friend, offers to sell him his shop in an unidentified country in central Africa, Salim accepts and drives there to take over the business. Racked by recently won independence, military coups, and civil war, the town is not at all like the place that Nazruddin's enthusiastic descriptions had led Salim to expect. Gradually, the town comes back to life, business improves, and Salim becomes acquainted with a few of the non-African townspeople. Disorder returns to the town, however, and Salim again decides to break with his community. He travels to England to see Nazruddin's daughter, to whom he has been informally engaged for many years, but, by mutual agreement, they end the engagement. Salim returns to the town, but, in his absence, the town has become radicalized, and Salim's shop has been taken over by a state trustee. Salim is betrayed and arrested for illegally possessing ivory, but he escapes. At the end of the novel, Salim leaves the town by steamer, presumably for Europe, moving down the river in darkness, away from the last scene of battle.

Ferdinand, a boy of fifteen or sixteen when he first comes from his isolated village, entrusted to Salim by his mother Zabeth, one of Salim's principal traders, who is also a sorceress. Ferdinand is ignorant and proud, diligent and eventually successful, becoming an official of the government, but disillusioned and despairing. One of the "new Africans," he knows that he, too, is doomed by the turmoil and treachery of his countrymen.

He helps Salim escape after Salim is betrayed by his assistant, Metty, and jailed for illegally possessing ivory.

Metty, the half-African boy who had been a slave in Salim's family compound and who comes to live and work with him. Their relationship is uneasy and ambivalent. During the course of the novel, Metty grows up, fathers a family secretly, and betrays Salim, who has protected and cared for him.

Father Huismans, a Belgian priest who teaches at the *lycée* that Ferdinand attends as a boy. An ardent lover of African art and culture, Father Huismans is senselessly killed by enraged bushmen during one of his collecting trips.

Raymond, a scholarly, reclusive European who is also an expert on Africa, in its political and historical aspects. He serves as an adviser to the president until the insurrection. Salim meets him at a party, but the two do not really become friends. Raymond is abandoned by the president and disappointed in his hopes but does not leave the town.

Yvette, Raymond's glamorous young wife, with whom Salim has a passionate affair. When she insults him by comparing him to Raymond, Salim beats her in uncontrolled fury, and the affair ends as she returns to her husband.

Mahesh and
Shoba, an elderly Indian couple who become Salim's closest friends. Deserted by their family, they live and act as if they were still at home in India. During the boom, they establish a Bigburger Shop, which brings them out of their self-imposed seclusion; the shop is a novelty in the town and very successful. When Salim leaves, he cannot bring himself to say good-bye to them.

Natalie Harper

BEND SINISTER

Author: Vladimir Nabokov (1899-1977)
Type of work: Novel
Time of action: The first half of the twentieth century
First published: 1947

Adam Krug (krōōg or, Russian, krōōk), aged forty, a world-famous philosopher living in a small Eastern European country where the language is a blend of Germanic and Slavic roots. A portly, arrogant man, Krug is contemptuous of lesser brains. Not interested in politics, he assumes, rather naïvely, that he has nothing to fear from the Ekwilists, who have taken over his country and instituted a police state. In a benumbed state of mind because of the recent death of his wife, he vacillates, postponing his departure abroad. His colleagues at the university and friends are arrested one after another. Krug finally attempts to flee, but it is too late.

Olga Krug, Adam's wife, aged thirty-seven. She dies at a hospital in the first chapter of the book.

David Krug, their son, aged eight. He is a bright, engaging child whom Krug loves inordinately. The Ekwilists eventually realize that Krug can be forced to support their oppressive policies if they take David as hostage. They seize him but then bungle everything and allow him to be murdered by a group of deranged persons participating in an experiment in group psychology.

Paduk, nicknamed (by Krug) **The Toad,** Krug's former schoolmate who becomes leader of the Ekwilist Party and later dictator of the country. A bully as a boy, the fat, powerful Krug used to torment the unpopular Paduk by tripping him and then sitting on his head. Paduk is apparently homosexual and in love with Adam Krug. His political philosophy emphasizes the virtues of collectivity and a total equality that will reduce everyone to the lowest common denominator. His Party of the Average Man is based on a somewhat distorted version of Fradrik Skotoma's works.

Ember, Krug's friend and fellow scholar. He has translated Shakespeare into his native language. Along with many others among Krug's acquaintances, he is arrested by the Ekwilists.

Azureus, a university president who submits immediately to the demands of the new police state and tries to influence all the professors to do the same.

Dr. Alexander, the Assistant Lecturer in Biodynamics. He doubles as an informer and secret police functionary for the Ekwilists.

Professors Edmond Beuret (French literature),
Gleeman (medieval poetry),
Yanovsky (Slavic scansion),
Hedron (mathematics),
Rufel (political science), and
Orlik (zoology), all eventually arrested, some murdered.

Fradrik Skotoma, a political philosopher who was famous in the sixties of the previous century. He is still alive. His philosophy advocates redistribution of human consciousness so as to make all persons absolutely equal in brains, talent, and the like. His quixotic "Ekwilism," impossible to realize in any practical sense, is transformed by Paduk's police state into a political doctrine attempting to enforce spiritual uniformity.

Mr. Etermon and
Mrs. Etermon (Everyman), mindless cartoon characters roughly resembling Blondie and Dagwood Bumstead of the American comic strip *Blondie*. Paduk makes them the symbol of his Ekwilism and models his own dress and behavior for a time on that of Mr. Etermon.

Hustav and
Linda Bachofen, secret police officers who arrest Ember.

Mac, a beefy thug who arrives, together with Linda Bachofen, to arrest Krug.

Mariette Bachofen, the younger sister of Linda Bachofen. She is a police spy who is sent to work as a maid for Krug and, probably, to seduce him.

Doctor Amalia von Wytwyl, the eldest of the three Bachofen sisters, who is in charge of the experiment in communal psychology that leads to the murder of David Krug. Nabokov uses characters such as her to suggest that the methods of Freudian psychology are compatible with forced collectivism and police-state brutality.

Phokus, a student, apparently the leader of the conspiracy against the Ekwilists.

Peter Quist, the owner of an antique shop, who offers to help smuggle Krug and David abroad. He is an *agent provocateur.*

Crystalsen and
Schamm, government officials in the Paduk bureaucracy. Schamm had been another tormented schoolmate of Krug.

The narrator, as is usual in a Nabokov novel, a problematic character resembling Nabokov himself but probably a front figure for Nabokov. He frequently blends with Adam Krug, in that certain passages may refer to Krug, to the narrator, or to both. Toward the end of the book, the narrator slides down a beam of light and relieves the tormented Krug of his sanity. The final passages describe the narrator getting up from his manuscript, stretching himself, and observing the hawk moth that keeps hammering against the screen of his window.

Robert Bowie

BENEFACTORS

Author: Michael Frayn (1933-   )
Type of work: Play
Time of action: The 1970's and 1980's
First produced: 1984

David Kitzinger, an architect and father of three. David is a dreamer and a schemer, a man of vision who gets caught up in ideas and concepts, especially his own. He loves architecture for the thrill of creating concrete reality from scratch and the challenge of overcoming practical obstacles. He conceives a plan to build high-rise public housing on a tract of slum land on Basuto Road in southeast London, but the scheme grows and expands until it proves overwhelmingly unpopular. Accepting the defeat of his plan breaks his spirit. David is very concerned with helping others, but his concern is seldom responsive to their particular tangible needs. His mathematical mind is reflected in his moral attitudes: To him, independence—the integrity of things or people—is a supreme virtue. Yet his desire to be fair and objective, to respect everyone's rights and desires and never to take sides, results in a kind of moral blindness. His purported magnanimity is often only a silver-coated form of arrogance and egoism, most clearly evident in the patronizing attitude and pity he exhibits toward Colin and Sheila.

Jane Kitzinger, David's wife. Jane is a former anthropologist who has been helping with David's architectural practice and eventually becomes a caseworker with a housing trust in southwest London. Jane is a realist, a woman who retains a healthy perspective on life and accepts things exactly as they are. She plays devil's advocate to her husband's schemes when necessary, but she is generally an extremely supportive wife and assistant. Intelligent, organized, and industrious, Jane is capable and often takes on more than her share of problems and responsibilities, and never begrudgingly. She truly enjoys accommodating others, generously and diplomatically, and works hard to make things run smoothly for everyone in her life. When pushed, however, she can become fiercely possessive and territorial; having a strong sense of herself, she will fight for her own needs. She begins with an ironic awareness of economic injustice and, as a result of her involvement in both Basuto Road and the Molyneuxs' domestic life, ultimately arrives at a truer sense of social mission.

Colin Molyneux, David's friend and neighbor and a father of two. Colin, a former classical scholar, works on a women's magazine and is editing an encyclopedia of sexual terminology. Eventually, he leaves his job and his home to become a squatter in Basuto Road and organizes its poor inhabitants against the skyscraper scheme, which he considers a vulgar expression of David's maleness. Colin is a dark personality, a man full of anger and hatred, who adopts a sardonic attitude and cold reserve toward everything he encounters. He is intelligent and perceptive to the point of prescience, and he enjoys commenting on what is happening as it happens, creating a jarring social self-consciousness. His actions are often without motivation: He likes to mock others and to provoke arguments, and he considers kindness and sentiment to be crimes. He never shows tender-

ness, and, when his jaded veneer drops and he really becomes angry, he is absolutely ruthless. Having married Sheila out of pity and paternity, Colin is now bored and frustrated with her, as he is with the complete mediocrity his life has assumed. In breaking away over the Basuto Road scheme, he discovers a refreshing simplicity of mind and the positive energy to fight fervently for a modest cause.

Sheila Molyneux, Colin's wife and Jane's friend. Sheila is a quiet, simple, innocent soul virtually lacking in ego and confidence. She is a housewife who looks after her children, Matt and Lizzie, rather awkwardly and tentatively; later, she takes a job at the Kitzingers' house as David's secretary and assistant. Self-assured people like David and Jane terrify her, and she envies their clarity of purpose and apparent happiness. Her simplicity allows her to find a rich and spontaneous joy in simple experiences and poetic ideas, and she truly admires and delights in David's creative vision without fully understanding it. Sheila aspires to be a person who helps others, but she is hopelessly dependent on those around her for her emotional and practical needs. Intent on pleasing Colin, she is more often thwarted and baffled by him. She feels guilty for holding him back and terrified that he will leave her. Once she takes the children and leaves him, she expresses the deepest hatred for him, and her accumulated rage at last explodes in a horrible act of blind and sudden violence.

B. P. Mann

BERLIN ALEXANDERPLATZ
The Story of Franz Biberkopf

Author: Alfred Döblin (1878-1957)
Type of work: Novel
Time of action: Autumn, 1927, to spring, 1929
First published: Berlin Alexanderplatz: Die Geschichte vom Franz Biberkopf, 1929
    (*Alexanderplatz, Berlin*, 1931; best known as *Berlin Alexanderplatz*)

Franz Biberkopf (be′bər‑kōpf), an unskilled laborer and convicted criminal. Approximately thirty years old and of stocky build, Biberkopf has been a cement worker, furniture mover, tie-pin hawker, newspaper vendor, notions peddler, burglar, fence, pimp, and assistant doorkeeper. After his release from Tegel prison, where he spent four years for the involuntary killing of Ida, his fiancée, Biberkopf is at a loss as to what to do with his life and suffers from a sense of disorientation. He resolves to begin a new life as an honorable man, but he finds that after four years in prison his real punishment is yet to come. Ida, whom he killed in a fit of jealous rage, had a sister Minna who is married to Karl, a locksmith. Franz is drawn to the place of his crime and he visits Minna and, on an impulse, rapes her. As a criminal convicted of a violent crime, Biberkopf receives official notice of his imminent expulsion from Berlin. The prison welfare association, however, intervenes, and he is allowed to remain in the city. He manages to stay on the path of blamelessness and earn his livelihood peddling notions, though he spends his evenings in the bars around Alexander Square in the city's center, slum and high crime area, where he soon becomes involved in racketeering.

Mieze (mēts'ə), whose real name is **Emilie Parsunke,** also called **Sonia,** an attractive prostitute under twenty years of age. Eva introduces her to Franz Biberkopf, and she becomes his third mistress after his release from Tegel prison. Mieze has a gentleman friend of means, and Biberkopf becomes her pimp. Mieze and Eva are friends and, in order to make Biberkopf happy, she suggests to Eva that Eva bear him a child, because of Eva's continued feelings for Franz. Eventually, Eva has a miscarriage. Biberkopf and Mieze are in love, and, after her murder by Reinhold, Biberkopf loses his inhibitions concerning him and seeks to avenge her murder.

Eva, whose real name is **Emilie,** a prostitute and lover of Herbert Wischow, her pimp. Eva was in love with Biberkopf before his imprisonment and still is after his release. She and Herbert were instrumental in sending Biberkopf to a private hospital outside the city (in Magdeburg) and in seeing

to it that no awkward questions about the crushed arm would be asked. Eva and Herbert pay for Biberkopf's recovery in their apartment, and Eva nurses him back to health. She sets him up as Mieze's pimp. Eva is expecting a child by Franz but has a miscarriage. When Franz is sought by the police, she hides him in her uptown apartment in the borough of Wilmersdorf.

Reinhold, a member of Herr Pums's gang of burglars, a man in his thirties. Seemingly sickly (he is hollow-cheeked and has a "yellow face"), he stutters and wears a shabby army coat. Because of Reinhold's friendliness toward Biberkopf and Biberkopf's fascination with Reinhold's views on politics and life, he succeeds in involving Franz in his affairs with women. Franz shares his girlfriends of whom he has tired in exchange for certain gifts. Thus, Biberkopf lives with Fränze and Cilly. Because Biberkopf was protesting his innocence and was not a willing member of the gang, he is pushed by Reinhold from a moving car, with Reinhold, therefore, responsible for crippling Biberkopf, who loses his right arm. Reinhold betrays Biberkopf a second time when he falsely accuses him of having helped him murder Mieze. Reinhold is tried, convicted, and, because of mitigating circumstances, sentenced to only ten years in prison.

Herbert Wischow (vēsh'ŏf), a pimp and petty thief. He and Franz Biberkopf were friends before the imprisonment of the latter. Herbert and Eva help Franz get the operation and recuperate. Eventually, Wischow is arrested and sentenced to two years in prison for a number of property crimes.

Karl Matter, a tinsmith and member of Pums's gang. He has a falling out with Pums over profits and is befriended by Mieze. He is implicated in her murder because he and Reinhold had taken her on an excursion to Freienwalde. Eventually, he and "wheelwright" commit their own burglaries and thus become independent. Karl informs on Reinhold once he establishes that he will not be prosecuted for his role in Mieze's murder.

Karl and the "wheelwright" are caught and sent to prison.

Polish Lina (Lina Przyballa), Biberkopf's first girlfriend after his release from prison. She hailed from Czernowitz and her father Stanislaus was a farmer. She had two miscarriages.

Otto Lüders, Lina's uncle. He peddles shoelaces and rapes and robs a young widow whom Biberkopf had befriended.

Gottlieb Meck, a member of the cattle dealers association, Biberkopf's friend. He tries to get Biberkopf a job.

Herr Pums, leader of the burglary gang that Biberkopf joins. He and Biberkopf meet in one of the gang's and Biberkopf's favorite bars.

Cilly, Biberkopf's second girlfriend after Tegel and one of Reinhold's former mistresses. She returns to Reinhold when she is pressured by him to abandon Biberkopf.

Willy, an ex-convict and a pickpocket. He meets Biberkopf in a bar and takes him to political meetings. Willy is described as young and "cocky."

Arthur Tilo Alt

BETRAYAL

Author: Harold Pinter (1930-   )
Type of work: Play
Time of action: Winter, 1968, to spring, 1977
First produced: 1978

Emma, Robert's wife. Thirty-eight years old at the beginning of the play, which moves backward in time, Emma is dissatisfied in her marriage and ready to separate from her husband. Her marriage has failed because of an affair she had with her husband's friend Jerry, a writer. Emma apparently has also been intimate with another writer, Roger Casey. Emma is angry because she believes that Robert has been unfaithful to her, yet she ascribes little importance to the fact that she has betrayed both Robert and Jerry. This obliviousness to the consequences of her own actions is a main facet of her character.

Jerry, a forty-year-old (in 1977) writer. Jerry is inherently a romantic, and it is this impulse that leads him to betray Robert, his best friend. Jerry's affair with Robert's wife, Emma, also betrays his own wife, Judith. Jerry instigated the affair with Emma while a party was in progress at Robert's house in 1968 by making a drunken pass at her. Jerry is the more romantic of the two men and the more naïve. He does not realize that Robert has discovered the affair at least as early as 1973. Jerry only comes to understand the situation four years later, which is when the play begins.

Robert, the cuckolded husband of Emma, also forty years old in 1977. He is a publisher, in fact he is the publisher of both Emma's lovers, Jerry and Roger. He is a realist and something of a detective; he seems to be the play's most clever character. He discovers Emma's infidelity while on holiday with her in Venice in 1973, when he finds a letter Jerry has written to her. From that point on, he has had the upper hand in the play. He baits Jerry with insinuations that the unsuspecting Jerry is incapable of understanding. Jerry only discovers in 1977 that Robert has been observing him for years with this knowledge of betrayal.

James Michael Welsh

BETRAYED BY RITA HAYWORTH

Author: Manuel Puig (1932-   )
Type of work: Novel
Time of action: 1933-1948
First published: La traición de Rita Hayworth, 1968 (English translation, 1971)

José Casals (Toto), the main character. The novel follows him from infancy in the small provincial town of Vallejos, Argentina, to age fifteen at George Washington High School, a boarding school in Merlo, a suburb of Buenos Aires. Bright and inquisitive but self-centered and spoiled, he grows up being first in school and having his own way. He matures into adolescence and is exposed to an ever-widening world in which he is not always the center of attention, although intellectually he has a competitive advantage over others. Hungry for knowledge, experience, and power, he continually seeks the company of older students and adults who possess these attributes. Confused about his own sexuality and the more intimate details of sex, his own sexual predilections are still to be determined. As a child, he fantasizes about the romantic images of the world that come to him principally through Hollywood films, novels, and the influence of his doting mother. As he grows up, he is forced away from her protective feminine world and has to face a harsher, nastier reality. There, too, he wants to be first. He manipulates people in his search for power and prestige, which to him are the signs of success in this larger world. What is in doubt is how his search will be resolved. Will he prefer males or females? Will he be abusive and exploitative in his use of the power that will probably be his?

Mita, Toto's mother. A college graduate, she marries Berto, a man with less education who reminds her of an Argentine film star with whom she had danced. First she works in the hospital then the pharmacy, but, when the family is finally financially secure, Berto forces her to resign and devote herself to family. She consents and has a second child, who dies still unnamed. A third infant, rarely mentioned, is also born. She rears her husband's nephew Héctor, dresses down, uses little makeup, gains weight, and accepts the matronly role assigned by her husband. She fantasizes and escapes her small-town existence through novels, films, and her son Toto.

Berto, Toto's father. A proud Spaniard who struggles through a difficult childhood in Spain that brings the early death of his mother and the tyranny of his brother. When he is pulled out of school to work in his brother's factory, he is deprived of an education. Then, when his brother sells the factory, he is forced to emigrate to Argentina. There, haunted by his earlier misfortunes, he steels himself in the ways necessary to become successful. He marries above himself yet refuses to accept help from his wife's family in La Plata. He keeps his family in Vallejos and, through great effort and sacrifice, gradually becomes a successful businessman. He makes sure his family has more than enough. He even takes his brother's son, Héctor, and rears him, although not with the attention he lavishes on Toto. He avoids the womanizing and roguish tendencies of his brother. He opts for business and familial rectitude as the appropriate strategy for success.

Héctor (ĕk'tōr), Toto's cousin. He lives with Toto's family until age twelve, when he is sent away to a boarding school near Buenos Aires. Except for a vocational school, Vallejos has nothing beyond the sixth grade, and Héctor's Aunt Mita is afraid he will be nothing more than a mechanic if he does not go away to school. Héctor returns to Vallejos during school breaks and summer vacation. He is moved by the thrill of girls and soccer. Handsome, he seduces three bookish but good-looking girls—the young schoolteacher Mari, Pug-nose, and Corky—in one summer. His dreams of the future are to leave the boarding school and return to Vallejos to play in the local soccer matches, become a great sports star, and seduce the girls. Many of the older female students interact with Toto because they are attracted to his cousin Héctor.

Paquita (pä•kē′tä), a lower-class schoolmate of Toto in Vallejos who is three years older. Her father is an impoverished Spanish immigrant from Galicia who is a tailor. She dreams of her sexual encounters with Raúl Garcia but is tormented by guilt and her fear of mortal sin. At the end of the novel, her wedding is being planned.

Esther (ĕs•tĕr′), a student from a humble Buenos Aires suburb. She wins a scholarship to George Washington High School. There she is a classmate of Toto. She is enamored of Héctor and eagerly awaits an encounter

arranged by Toto. Toto has designs on her, however, and has only used Héctor as bait. When she protests his change of plans and tries to maneuver him out of the picture, Toto snubs her by referring to her lower-class origins. She sees that she is not accepted socially and begins to see the logic of the class-consciousness and worker solidarity of the people from her own background who are committed to the Peronista labor movement.

Cobito (kō•bē′tō), a schoolmate of Toto. He is vulgar, crude, and mean. He resents school, study, and the prospects of returning to his hometown of Paraná and working behind the counter of the family store run by his brother. Jealous of the intelligence, wealth, and success of Toto, he twice tries to sodomize him.

Maurice P. Brungardt

BEYOND THE BEDROOM WALL
A Family Album

Author: Larry Woiwode (1941-   )
Type of work: Novel
Time of action: 1935 to the mid-1960's
First published: 1975

Otto Neumiller, the patriarch of a German, Catholic family. He emigrates to North Dakota in 1881 when twenty-four years old, marries Mary Reisling, and fathers Lucy, Augustina, and Charles. Energetic and civic-minded, he farms, donates to the church, and serves on the county commission, school, and grain elevator boards until the 1927 Crash, when, concerned for the welfare of others, he loses all but his original homestead in a failed attempt to keep the elevator operating. His rise in life and subsequent decline are recalled by his son, who travels to Mahomet in 1935 to bury him on his homestead as he requested.

Charles John Christopher Neumiller, a carpenter, farmer, and school janitor, born in

1891 to Otto and Mary. He is dedicated, solemn and taciturn, generous, community-oriented, and a conscientious Catholic. With his wife, Marie, he fathers Martin, Elaine, Vince, Fred, Jay, Emil, Rose Marie, Tom, and Davy. A controlled man, he tenderly, but in a businesslike manner, prepares his father for burial in a homemade coffin. Yet, he feels chastened by the openly expressed affection written in a birthday letter from his oldest son to his deceased father, and he wonders why he seldom thinks of the past. He admits that he can best express emotion in song, and his children remember his deep bass voice and wish for a pipe organ in their church. When he sells the North Dakota farm in 1938 and moves Marie and the younger children, his attachment to his farm animals prevents him from watching the sale. He has to be busy, frequently consults his watch, and with sons Fred and Tom, operates a contracting company in Illinois. His grandson Jerome recalls that he always seemed prepared for any situation that arose. Together with his father, he represents the root and potential of a family from which later generations draw strength, but from which they also drift.

Marie Neumiller, the wife of Charles and described by her grandson Jerome as "such a bulwark of authority it seemed she was carrying within her a part of the country of Germany and a great deal of the Catholic church." Proud that her family produced a cardinal and a scholar of ecclesiastical law, she cannot tolerate the drunken behavior of Ed Jones, whose daughter her son Martin marries.

Augustina Neumiller, a sister of Charles, born in 1888. Out of fear, she never marries; is high-strung, terrified of strangers, and subject to spells; and is tirelessly devoted to her father. Following his death, she remains on the North Dakota farm with hired man Clarence Popp.

Martin Neumiller, teacher, principal, life insurance salesman, plumber, and handyman, born in 1913 to Charles and Marie. In the late 1930's, he marries a non-Catholic, Alpha Jones, with whom he has five children: Jerome, Charles, Timothy, Marie, and Susan. He shares his father's work ethic but is more introspective, enjoys telling stories of his past, and hopes to write a book about his life. As evidence of his sensitivity, he loves to talk with people, cries over books, and is easily affected by radio dramas. He practices his faith more loosely than do his parents, and without compunction he promotes life insurance by using a picture of the holy family. Alpha's questions about faith he ignores, preferring instead simply to believe. Though he is talented, diligent, and possesses the sensibilities of a poet, his life is more disappointing than successful. To earn more money he gives up his principalship and eventually follows his parents to Illinois, where finan-

cial considerations force him to move his family into his parents' basement, then into an old garage, which he converts into a home between jobs as a plasterer. The move contributes to his wife's death, at which time he contemplates suicide, but his resolve to keep his family together ultimately sustains him. Eventually he remarries and moves to Eglington, Illinois, to work as a guidance counselor. His own life experiences call into question his ability to guide, for though he keeps his children together, they grow up haphazardly, and four of them suffer terribly the loss of their mother. Emblematic of Martin's inability to fully manage his life is his struggle to make sense of it by writing about it; to the very end, he feels overwhelmed by all the material that he wants to include.

Alpha Jones, the wife of Martin, born in 1916. Big-boned and slightly overweight, she labors on her father's farm like a hired hand. Her life as a schoolteacher and years dating Martin are chronicled in a diary. Because she dies giving birth at age thirty-four, her brief diary and children's recollections of her are the primary means of establishing her character. Deeply troubled by the suicide death of her talented brother, she names her first son after him. Father Krull, the priest, describes her as "passionate," but her sensuality is neither fully understood nor appreciated by her husband. She converts to Catholicism only after several years of instruction, when she decides that its rituals tie her to a more ordered past. Her questions about faith and religious practice explore one of the novel's themes.

Ed Jones, an alcoholic farmer and father of Alpha, born in 1871. Napoleonic in stature and demeanor, he speaks crudely and roughly but actually regrets his inability to relate well to Alpha. With his wife Electra, he fathers Elling, Conrad, Alpha, Jerome, Bernice, Kristine, and Lionell. Threatened by his wife's poise, beauty, and height, he reacts churlishly. As a former baseball catcher, dancing instructor, and Shakespearean actor who still wears his worn, hand-tailored suits and shirts, he seems ill-suited to farm. For financial reasons, he sends his two oldest sons to labor for relatives and his two youngest daughters to live with maiden aunts. As he ages, his physical ailments render him almost totally dependent upon his wife. His crude humor and jokes contrast with the seriousness of the Neumiller family.

Electra Jones, the wife of Ed and mother of Alpha. Tall and attractive with long hair, she is frail annd plagued by psychosomatic illnesses. Though she is righteous and moral, she tolerates her husband's vulgarity and possesses some blatant prejudices about life and people.

Jerome Jones, a brother of Alpha, born in 1921. Unattractive, skinny, and reclusive, he is an avid reader and extremely precocious. His interest in flowers and animals leads him, without success, to form a wildlife club. Following his graduation and valedictory speech, he commits suicide by drowning himself at a class picnic. His sensitivity links him to nephews he never meets, Alpha's sons, Charles and Timothy.

Jerome Neumiller, a doctor and the oldest son of Alpha and Martin. More confident and self-secure than his siblings, Jerome's interest in psychology leads him to perform a battery of tests on his brother Charles. Upon the death of his grandfather, his analysis of his family helps to establish the nature of several characters within the novel. No longer practicing a faith, he represents his generation's distance from the strong Catholic doctrine that directed their great-grandfather, Otto, and grandfather, Charles.

Charles Neumiller, an actor and second son of Martin and Alpha. He marries Katherine and has a daughter. As a child he seeks his mother's approval and is traumatized by her death. A dream about trying to reach her and communicate with her provides one source for the novel's title. His uncle Lionell, with whom he spends summers, relates to him only by criticizing him, and Lionell forces Charles to masturbate him. This relationship produces in Charles an unpredictable behav-

ior and savage energy that confuses and worries his father and siblings. Jerome determines that Charles is a borderline psychotic. When older and living in New York, Charles reacts with surprise when his father admires his voice and approves of his work doing television voice-overs. Typical of the missed communications in his life is his touching letter to his grandmother, Electra Jones, which arrives after her death.

Timothy Neumiller (Tim), poet, teacher, and third son of Martin and Alpha. He marries Cheri and has three children. When his mother dies, he loses his serene nature and retreats into his own world of concocted languages and voice imitations, and he calls himself Tinvalin, a name which only his wife will use. His life becomes more stable when he lives temporarily with his mother's relatives. As an adult, his recollections of the Neumiller family keep him awake at night. Yet paradoxically, he freely accepts his family's description of him as being apathetic, self-indulgent, and neglectful. This contrast between his own thoughts about family members and their perception of him is indicative of his generation's condition. Tim's generation is united by shared experiences, but its members do not feel the solidarity of a generation earlier, when the Neumiller business flourished and Martin moved to live closer to his parents.

Marie Neumiller, the fourth child and oldest daughter of Martin and Alpha. She never marries. Though a handsome child who hums and sings, Marie is heavy, and her spendthrift ways and disorganized room anger her father. Sensitive and quiet, she likes candles, cries over soap operas, carefully decorates the house for Christmas, and majors in Special Education. When too young to be embarrassed, both she and Susan permit themselves to be fondled by their sexually curious brothers.

Susan Neumiller, the fifth child and youngest daughter of Martin and Alpha. She quits college to marry and works as a bookkeeper for a physician. She provides a first-person description of her stepmother, Laura. While her father dates Laura, Susan resentfully stays home and grades his school papers. She admits that the family piano is unattractive, but she feels threatened by Laura's desire to abandon it and move to Chicago. Considered by her brothers and sisters to be bright and carefree, Susan actually represents that element within the family that seeks to preserve common ties. Having little to no recollection of her mother, she claims that she has heard enough to see her mother however she pleases.

Laura, Martin's second wife, a devout Catholic, former music teacher, executive secretary and private bookkeeper. When she marries Martin, she and her daughter, Ginny, move into the Pettibone, Illinois, house. An organized and careful planner, she never overcomes the discomfort that she feels in Martin's home, and thus she urges him to move. Her death from breast cancer brings the family together and closes the novel, just as Otto Neumiller's death opens it.

Father Schimmelpfennig, a Catholic priest in North Dakota. He hosts weekly card parties where players drink beer and place bets. He ministers to the Neumiller family and travels to Illinois to deliver Alpha's eulogy. Sensing the instability in young Charles's life, he takes Charles and Lionell Jones on a fishing trip during a summer when Charles stays with his uncle. His periodic appearances function as a reminder of the family's geographic and religious origins in North Dakota and the Catholic church, origins which, for a time, bind them together.

Barbara A. Looney

THE BIG KNIFE

Author: Clifford Odets (1906-1963)
Type of work: Play
Time of action: The late 1940's
First produced: 1949

Charlie Castle, a film star of considerable renown. He is rich, ruggedly handsome, virile, charming, frequently cynical, and dependably candid in dealing with people. Charlie's studio is pressuring him to renew his contract, which he does not want to sign, although it is for fourteen years at four million dollars a year. One skeleton lurks in Charlie's closet: Once when he was driving drunk, he had an accident in which someone was killed. He permitted Buddy Bliss to take the rap for him and to go to jail for vehicular manslaughter. The studio uses this information in its attempt to blackmail Charlie into signing his new, extended contract. Instead, he commits suicide.

Marion Castle, Charlie's wife. Disenchanted with the falseness of life in Hollywood, she is living apart from her husband and vows that she will return to him only if he refuses to commit himself to the long-term contract his studio is trying to inveigle him into signing. Marion is a totally honest person. She has discovered that honesty is a liability in the society in which she has been forced to travel as a star's wife, but this quality is too ingrained in her nature for her to change now.

Patty Benedict, a Hollywood gossip columnist whose loyalty is strictly to herself. She is a powerful woman who rules by intimidation and communicates by innuendo. She knows Charlie's dark secret and uses this knowledge in her attempts to manipulate him. She is as deceitful as Marion is honest. The two have a strained relationship, generally civil but little more, when they are forced into each other's company.

Buddy Bliss, Charlie's agent. He is humorless, loyal, stubborn, and not very bright. He goes to jail after Charlie's accident, willingly covering for Charlie by taking his punishment to spare the film idol the embarrassment and public humiliation he would have been subjected to had the truth surfaced. Buddy is an innocent; he is dazzled by Charlie's success and by his prowess with people. He tries to save him from all unpleasantness or from doing anything that might tarnish his manufactured image. Buddy is the sort of person who was born to be exploited.

Marcus Hoff, the pudgy, self-assured head of the studio to which Charlie is under contract. The middle-aged Hoff is bright, able, and manipulative. He dresses the part of someone who runs a studio, attired in suave, expensive, tailor-made suits of subdued colors. He frequently puffs on choice Havana cigars. He is imperious, capable of observing all the amenities but then of turning full circle and destroying anyone who gets in his way.

Coy Smiley, Hoff's lean toady who does Hoff's bidding deftly and unquestioningly. He is competent and calculating, cynical, calm, and unfailingly courteous. His Irish lineage is evident in his face and demeanor. He essentially is detached and alone. One would be unlikely ever to consider him a friend.

Nat Danziger, a man in his sixties, the agent acting as middleman between the studio and Charlie. Nat is basically good, kind, and fatherly, although the system within which he lives is corrupt. He is sentimental and religious in the broadest sense. Although he is competent in his business dealings, he seems a misfit among the jackals of the film industry.

Connie Bliss, Buddy's wife, a lissome blonde on whom clothes look superb. She has about her a hardness, mitigated slightly by her desire to please. She has a good mind.

Hank Teagle, a fifty-year-old friend of Charlie. He limps slightly and is unpretentious, quiet, and mature. He has an undeviating devotion to Charlie.

Dixie Evans, a woman who escaped her poor Boston family and her department store job four years ago to work in Hollywood. Despite her overindulgence in liquor, she puts up a good front of brightness and competence.

Ralph, the Castles' black butler, through whom one comes to see glimmerings of the real Charlie Castle.

Dr. Frary, the Castles' next-door neighbor and friend.

R. Baird Shuman

THE BIG SLEEP

Author: Raymond Chandler (1888-1959)
Type of work: Novel
Time of action: The 1930's, after the end of Prohibition
First published: 1939

Philip Marlowe, a private detective. Tall, dark, and rugged, with a poker face and a quick wit, he is attractive to women but wary of them and of all entanglements. Though cynical and hard-boiled, a heavy drinker capable of violence, Marlowe is idealistic, even puritanical. Contemptuous of money, he is an honest loner in a corrupt world. Hired to deal with a blackmail threat, Marlowe is embroiled in a more deadly game by Sternwood's two spoiled daughters, whose advances he spurns. Independent to the point of insubordination, he refuses to stop investigating the case, even when Sternwood pays him off.

General Guy de Brisay Sternwood, an oil millionaire. Crippled and cadaverous, he subsists on little more than heat. A survivor, he is a man with no moral code but respects the independence that he admires in Marlowe and his son-in-law, Regan. At the beginning of the novel, he hires the detective to protect his younger daughter but turns out to be just as interested in finding the missing Regan.

Vivian Sternwood Regan, the general's older daughter. Tall and rangy with black wiry hair and black eyes, she looks like trouble to Marlowe but turns out to have her sister and father's interests at heart. Spoiled and bored, she spends much of her time at Mars's casino gambling away her allowance. Her attempts to manipulate Marlowe and throw him off the track instead point him in the right direction.

Carmen Sternwood, the younger daughter. Coy but cruel, she is an unsettling blonde with drugged, expressionless, slate-gray eyes and an alluring body which she likes to expose. Expecting men to respond to her charms, she can be deadly when they do not. Her unexpected appearances throughout the novel complicate the plot, leading finally to her exposure as Regan's killer.

Terence Regan (Rusty), Vivian's missing husband. A tough former bootlegger and IRA officer who returned Sternwood's respect, his mysterious disappearance disturbs the General.

Eddie Mars, a gambler and gangster, owner of the Cypress Club. A gray, sporty man with official connections, he is followed everywhere by his henchman but is not quite as tough as he thinks. Suspected of killing Regan, he is mainly interested in keeping his wife (and the truth) hidden in order to blackmail Vivian.

Mona Mars, Eddie's wife. Blue-eyed, with a platinum wig and a silver voice, this former singer threw over Rusty for Eddie. As the novel begins, she has supposedly run off with Regan, but Marlowe tracks her down, giving her the chance to save him from Canino's clutches.

Norris, the Sternwood butler. Old and gravely polite, with acid-blue eyes, he is secretive and extremely protective in his role as the General's factotum and go-between with Marlowe.

Owen Taylor, the Sternwood chauffeur. Dark and boyish, he is in love with Carmen and kills Geiger, taking the glass negative to protect her before ending up along with the car on the ocean floor.

Arthur Gwynn Geiger, a pornographer and blackmailer. A soft man with a fat face and a Charlie Chan mustache, his bookstore is only a front and his attempt at blackmailing the General precipitates the book's action. He is shot while taking a photograph of the drugged and naked Carmen.

Agnes Lozelle, Geiger's secretary and Brody's girlfriend. A sexy green-eyed blonde, she always ends up with the half-smart guys, like Brody and Jones. She leaves town with the $200 that Marlowe pays to learn where Mrs. Mars is.

Joe Brody, a blackmailer and Agnes' boyfriend. He takes over Geiger's stock of pornography and tries to blackmail Vivian with the photograph of Carmen.

Carol Lundgren, Geiger's homosexual lover. This dark, handsome young punk kills Brody in the mistaken belief that he is Geiger's murderer.

Harry Jones, a small-time hood. A small man with brilliant eyes, he is not as tough as he pretends when he approaches Marlowe to sell information on Mrs. Mars's whereabouts, but he later has the courage to protect Agnes at the cost of his own life.

Lash Canino, Mars's hired killer and Mona's guard. A short, heavy-set man, always dressed in brown, he is a ruthless killer who poisons Jones and is shot by Marlowe.

Bernie Ohls, the District Attorney's chief investigator. Marlowe's friend and official connection, he takes him along to see Taylor's body, a favor reciprocated whenever Marlowe has anything to give the police.

Captain Al Gregory, chief of the Missing

Persons Bureau. This burly, slow-moving man maintains friendly relations with Mars but, claiming to be as honest as he can be in a corrupt system, provides Marlowe with background information on Rusty.

Philip McDermott

BILLIARDS AT HALF-PAST NINE

Author: Heinrich Böll (1917-1985)
Type of work: Novel
Time of action: September 6, 1958
First published: Billard um halbzehn, 1959 (English translation, 1961)

Robert Fähmel, or **Faehmel,** a forty-three-year-old architect, demolitions expert, and widower. He is a distinguished-looking gentleman with a red scar on the bridge of his nose. His days are spent according to a strict routine that stresses an almost total withdrawal from public life. Even his business associates and former army buddies do not, as a rule, see him. His secretary Leonore only sees him for an hour every business day. Robert Fähmel inherited his father's architectural firm. On the day of the novel's plot, Robert reminisces about his life. His father had built the abbey of St. Anton and he, Robert, had demolished it in the closing days of the war. He had done so on a military pretext. His real reason, however, was revenge. The monks and their abbot had partaken of "the sacrament of the buffalo," that is, they had supported the Nazis. Robert has managed to keep his culpability a secret; not even his son, Joseph, who rebuilt the monastery, knows; only his father suspects. Robert, as a young man, had resisted Nazism, and he was persecuted for it, even as a schoolboy. He and another of his classmates had to seek refuge in Amsterdam. Robert's mother, who was acquainted with the administrative head of the province, intervened and secured his amnesty in exchange for the promise that her son never again meddle in politics. Robert spent the war years as a demolitions expert in the army. He rose to the rank of captain. Since his return to his hometown, he has hewed closely to a rigid and intensely private

routine. Every day at half-past nine, he plays billiards in the Prince Heinrich Hotel. Only Hugo, the bellboy, is allowed in the room. It is to him that he tells his life's story. In the end, he adopts Hugo as his son and signs over to him his land holdings. He adopts him in lieu of a son that his wife, Edith, might have borne him if she had not been killed in an air raid. Robert seeks to come to terms with his own past and with that of his country, and he seeks to avoid or to punish all those whom he knows to be tarnished by their Nazi past. Thus he has given strict instructions to Leonore not to allow anyone near him excepting his family and Alfred Schrella, his childhood friend.

Heinrich Fähmel, an eighty-year-old architect, privy councillor, and Robert's father. He is slim and robust, the son of a peasant. He is the founder of a well-known and respected architectural firm. At the age of thirty, he won the competition for best design of a monastery. This propelled him into the forefront of architects in town and made him a well-to-do man. He cultivates the public image of an unusual man and artist by adhering to a rigid daily routine that includes a special breakfast at the Cafe Kroner. He marries Johanna Kilb, the daughter of the attorney who supervised the competition. He served as a captain with the army engineers in World War I. He won two iron crosses, which he later discards as a token of his antiwar and anti-imperialist sentiments. He

had lost one of his sons to the Nazis, because he permitted him to admire military
power, and he wishes to avoid that in the
future for the sake of his grandchildren.
Heinrich and Johanna had seven children, of
whom Robert is the sole survivor. Heinrich
tells his life's story to Leonore, whom he has
hired for the day to tidy up his office. His
eightieth birthday is about to be celebrated in
the Cafe Kroner when he learns of his wife's
arrival at the Prince Heinrich Hotel. The
party at the cafe is cancelled and takes place
in his office instead.

Johanna Fähmel, a seventy-year-old patient
in a mental hospital and Heinrich's wife. She
is a resolute and principled woman, although
felt to be obsessive at times. In her unswerving opposition to power and privilege, to lies
and terror, she refuses any advantage that
might accrue to her because of her husband's
prominence. Thus she gives away bread, but-
ter, and honey from the abbey and forces her
family to subsist on their official food rations
alone. Her losses during the war, Otto's allegiance to the Nazis and his death at the
front, and Robert's persecution have taken
their toll. She has a nervous breakdown.
Once committed to a mental hospital, she
finds it convenient to feign continued illness,
allowing her to oppose the regime with im-
punity. On her husband's eightieth birthday,
she resolves to kill the leader of the "blue-
tunics," a neo-Nazi group led by a former
Nazi and persecutor of her son, Ben Wackes.
She contrives to steal a pistol from the hospital gardener. Instead of Wackes, however,
she shoots a minister of the government at
the hotel. The man is wounded, but he survives.

Alfred Schrella, a childhood friend of Robert and his brother-in-law. Alfred and Robert
were in Amsterdam together as refugees
from Nazi persecution. Schrella, however,
continues in exile until September 6, 1958.
He has returned to his hometown after
twenty-two years abroad in Holland and
Britain. He is now stateless. He tells Robert
that he will not stay, because he cannot live
in a country that does not "tend its lambs
and breeds wolves" instead.

Joseph Fähmel, Robert's twenty-seven-year-
old son, an architect. Although he is only a
young and reluctant architect, he has been
given the task of rebuilding the abbey of St.
Anton. Even at the dedication ceremony he
is ignorant of his father's role in its last-
minute destruction. He is married to Marianne, a victim of her parents' Nazism. She
was reared by foster parents after the war.
Henrich Fähmel likes her and looks upon her
as a worthy successor to Johanna, one who
will assure the continuity of the family.
Joseph, just as his father and grandfather before him, does not seek wealth and power
and hence is undecided about continuing in
the family tradition of serving the region as a
prominent architect.

Arthur Tilo Alt

BILLY PHELAN'S GREATEST GAME

Author: William Kennedy (1928-   )
Type of work: Novel
Time of action: 1938
First published: 1978

William (Billy) Phelan, a young gambler
and bookmaker. Billy Phelan is a pool hustler and a familiar figure among Albany's
shadowy nighttime crowd. A gambler with a
gift for sizing up his opponents, he earns his
living on the fringes of society but in the
center of a netherworld in which he moves
comfortably and securely. He is also a
bookie operating with the permission of the
powerful McCall family. When the McCalls
ask him to perform a service for them that
would violate his personal code of ethics,

however, Billy must decide where his allegiance lies.

Martin Daugherty, a newspaper columnist and Billy's friend. Martin has spent his life in Albany, growing up next door to Billy's father. A journalist in the Damon Runyon tradition, he is at ease with mobsters, gamblers, and prostitutes, and is given to accurate visions and premonitions. He is also the son of a successful playwright, and he struggles throughout the book with his conflicting feelings toward his father. Martin plays a central role in Billy's story, placing a bet with him that leaves Phelan sorely in need of money and chronicling the events surrounding Billy's confrontation with the McCalls.

Francis Phelan, Billy's father, an alcoholic drifter. Francis Phelan abandoned his family when Billy was nine and his reappearance in Albany after years of aimless drifting forms one of the book's important subplots. Billy has grown up without his father's guidance, and his meeting with Francis provides him with an opportunity to measure himself against the man whose absence has shaped the course of his life. What he finds is an alcoholic vagrant, battered and ill from his life on the road and little more than a shell of the man Billy remembers.

Morrie Berman, an acquaintance of Billy's. Morrie is a shady figure on the fringes of Albany's criminal underworld: a former pimp, a gambler, and a grave disappointment to his family of tailors and political radicals. He is suspected by the McCall family of having a part in the kidnapping of Charlie McCall, and Billy is asked to spy on him by the McCalls. Billy's conflict over where his loyalties lie makes Morrie a crucial factor in his story.

Charlie McCall, son of the city's most powerful family. Charlie is a likable young man grown soft from a life of indulgence. It is his kidnapping that sets the story in motion.

Bindy McCall, Charlie's father. Bindy runs all the gambling in Albany, and his influence over who is allowed access to the town's clubs or is permitted to act as a bookie is absolute.

Patsy McCall, Bindy's brother and Charlie's uncle. Along with his brother Matt, Patsy McCall is the most powerful man in the city, a ruthless behind-the-scenes manipulator who controls Albany's political life. To free his nephew, he will use all of his considerable influence.

Melissa Spencer, an actress and Martin's former lover. As a young woman, Melissa had also been the lover of Martin's father and the inspiration for his best-known play, in which she is now appearing in Albany. A beautiful, sensual woman, she has been an odd link between Martin and his father.

Edward Daugherty, a playwright and Martin's father. Although he appears only near the end of the book, Edward Daugherty's presence is felt throughout segments focusing on his son. Now senile and in a nursing home, he was once a man capable of turning the scandal that drove his wife mad into a successful play.

Emory Jones, the editor of Martin Daugherty's paper, the *Times-Union*. When Charlie McCall is kidnapped, it falls to him to persuade the rest of the press to delay printing the story until the McCalls okay its publication.

Janet Lorenz

BILOXI BLUES

Author: Neil Simon (1927-   )
Type of work: Play

Time of action: 1943
First produced: 1984

Eugene Morris Jerome, an army recruit from Brooklyn, New York. Eugene is a young Jewish man who aspires to be a writer. He records his deepest thoughts and impressions fervently in his journal, often leaving himself more an observer than a participant in human interactions. He does have principles—respect, compassion, open-mindedness—but is hesitant to act on them. He always sees the lighter side of life, and he enlists his quick and acerbic wit to ease him through difficult situations. Having lived a sheltered life, Eugene is eager and determined to lose his virginity and fall in love, though, at least at the beginning of the play, he does not quite know the difference.

Arnold Epstein, an army recruit from Queens, New York. Epstein is a stubborn Jewish intellectual, who has very strong principles and absolutely refuses to compromise them. He has a nervous stomach and resents being in basic training, and he cannot understand why rigorous discipline and blind obedience are considered superior to respect and compassion in the shaping of soldiers. He immediately identifies Toomey as his enemy and squares off for a fierce battle. To Epstein, life is serious business, a continuous moral quandary. He is clever and sardonic, but rarely light-spirited. He can distance himself only far enough to recognize the irony of social and political injustice, and, when humiliated, even when beaten on his own terms, he accepts defeat stoically.

Joseph Wykowski, a recruit from Bridge-port, Connecticut. Of Polish descent, Wy-kowski is a physical being with a stomach of steel and an irrepressible sex drive. Wy-kowski accepts the rigors of army discipline without question: To him it is a game that, like any game, he can win. He is decidedly unintellectual and occasionally anti-Semitic, and has no patience for moral ruminations. He is the self-proclaimed leader of the platoon, and his simple strength and basic clearsightedness validate his arrogance.

Roy Selridge, a recruit from Schenectady, New York. Selridge is a young man with an engaging, though often overbearing, sense of humor. He falls in behind Wykowski as a coarse masculine voice in the group but ultimately lacks the courage to speak out or stand alone. Yet though his bravado is often hollow, his spirit is always generous and optimistic.

Donald Carney, a recruit from Montclair, New Jersey. Carney loves to sing—he sings in his sleep—and dreams of becoming a recording star. He is basically honest and good-natured but thoughtful to a fault: He has a hard time making decisions. He is faithful to his fiancée in Albany but views the prospect of marriage with serious trepidation.

James Hennesey, another recruit. He is a timid young man, relatively innocent and humorless. He misses his family but seems to be adapting well enough to army life, until he is discovered in a homosexual liaison with another soldier.

Merwyn J. Toomey, army sergeant overseeing the platoon's basic training. Toomey is a hardboiled Southern military man, who knows how to deal with trickery and back talk. He pits the recruits against one another to subjugate them to army discipline. He accepts the special challenge that Epstein directs at him and determines to win the battle of wills. He has a steel plate in his head, a souvenir from the North African campaign, that accounts for his wholehearted commitment to the rigorous treatment of his soldiers, for his sublimated sense of sadness and doom, and, ultimately, for his premature retirement from active duty.

Rowena, a Biloxi prostitute. Rowena is direct and realistic: She is a happily married woman, whose business is satisfying the sexual needs of young soldiers and peddling perfume and lingerie for them to send home to their girlfriends.

Daisy Hannigan, a local Catholic school-girl. Daisy is friendly and pretty, yet innocent and dutiful. The daughter of a journalist from Chicago, she likes books and is enchanted with Eugene's literary aspirations.

B. P. Mann

THE BIRDS FALL DOWN

Author: Rebecca West (Cicily Isabel Fairfield, 1892-1983)
Type of work: Novel
Time of action: The early twentieth century
First published: 1966

Laura Rowan, an eighteen-year-old girl who is half English and half Russian. A beautiful, intelligent, quiet girl, Laura is a perceptive observer of the people around her and responsible beyond her years. When she accompanies her grandfather on the train and hears Chubinov's declaration that Kamensky is a traitor, her imagination runs wild with scenes of Kamensky killing her because she knows the truth. These imaginings, it is later revealed, are warranted. At the novel's end, she decides to leave London and live with her mother in Russia.

Count Nikolai Nikolaievitch Diakonov, a former minister in the czar's government, living in exile in Paris for reasons of which he is unaware. A tall, broad, elderly man, he is stubborn and cantankerous despite his failing health. His death, halfway through the novel, is caused, in part, by Chubinov's revelation that Kamensky is a traitor and spy.

Countess Sofia Andreievna Diakonova, his wife. Once beautiful, the small, slight countess is now ugly and weak, partly because of her age and partly because of a serious illness (which is presumably cancer). In an attempt to hide her radium treatments from her husband, Sofia persuades him to take a trip to the coast to visit relatives.

Tania Rowan, Laura's mother, the count's daughter, who lives in London. Unusually good looking, Tania is tormented throughout the novel because her marriage is failing. Although distracted, she is nevertheless a car-ing mother to her daughter and a devoted daughter to her aging parents. At the novel's end, she decides not only to leave her husband but also to return to Russia, thus abandoning her sons and life in London.

Edward Rowan, Laura's father, a young member of the English parliament. Handsome and somewhat celebrated for his position in the British government, Edward seems interested only in Susie Stainton, his wife's one time protegée, with whom he is presumably having an affair. Although he comes to France when Laura summons him by telegram, he is distracted and cold toward his family.

Vassili Iulevitch Chubinov, the son of a minor Russian aristocrat who knew Nikolai when they were both living in Russia. A middle-aged, middle-sized, unkept man, Chubinov has dedicated his life to revolutionary activities. After tailing Laura and her grandfather onto the train, he confronts them and speaks at length about his past associations with Nikolai. Finally he reveals that Kamensky is a spy—an allegation that the Count tries to deny, but that greatly upsets him. At the end of the novel, Chubinov shoots Kamensky in the street because he believes that Kamensky intends to kill Laura.

Alexander Gregorievitch Kamensky, also known as **Gorin, Kaspar,** and **Sasha,** the Count's secretary and confidant. A small Russian man in his early forties, Kamensky is a superb confidence artist. For years, he has worked for Nikolai Diakonov, endearing himself to both the count and his wife, when, if Chubinov's story is correct, Kamensky is actually spying against them. He is murdered by Chubinov.

Cassandra Kircher

THE BIRTHDAY KING

Author: Gabriel Fielding (Alan Gabriel Barnsley, 1916-1986)
Type of work: Novel
Time of action: August, 1939, and November, 1941, to July, 1945
First published: 1962

Ruprecht Waitzmann (vīts'män), the second son of a wealthy widow (Frau Waitzmann) who owns Waitzmann Industries, a conglomerate that operates pulp and textile mills. He is an ambitious, wordly young man, who is hindered from taking over the business by his religious elder brother Alfried. To further his ambitions, he cultivates the friendship of the noble Baron von Hoffbach's wife, a promiscuous, gossipy woman. Her machinations in favor of Ruprecht lead to the imprisonment and torture of Ruprecht's brother, much to the shame of all concerned.

Alfried Waitzmann, the eldest son of the aforementioned widow, is torn between his love of the German aristocracy and his religious calling. An unsuccessful affair with a German woman wanting to be a nun in the United States does not solve his dilemma. He refuses his vocation to the priesthood, and he is finally imprisoned in the concentration camp and tortured. When the torture fails to break him, he is made a medical aide in the camp, in which position he reports to the American commander after the war.

Frau Wilhelmina Waitzmann, the aging, nearly blind widow and mother of Ruprecht and Alfried. She runs Waitzmann Industries during the war, waiting for her favorite son, Alfried, to decide whether he wants to take her place. Her role is a passive one in regard to the story, a waiting and hoping that her family will come out of the war intact.

Baron Nicholas von Hoffbach (fôn hôf' bax), a wealthy German nobleman in his fifties, who operates as go-between for Waitzmann Industries and the Nazi government. He continually upholds the ideal of the old German aristocracy in the face of what he considers Nazi barbarism. When he finds that his wife's indiscretion has led to the imprisonment of his friend Alfried, he refuses to cooperate any longer and takes part in a plot to assassinate Adolf Hitler.

Carin von Hoffbach, the baron's promiscuous French-Prussian wife, who cultivates younger men. Her affair with Ruprecht leads her to insinuate accusations against his brother Alfried to a local Schützstaffeln (SS) man, ending in Alfried's imprisonment and torture. She vainly tries to prevent her husband from getting involved with the assassination plot.

Leo von Hoffbach, the son of the baron and Carin, he seems interested only in his family's forest holdings, spending his entire life in the woods hunting; he briefly falls in love with the young Alexandra, but she turns down his proposal.

Eva de Luce, the mother of Carin von Hoffbach. She is a senile elderly woman who appears in only one scene, showing the same petulant sensuality as her daughter, titillated by the "advances" of Hubertus Grunewald and Ruprecht Waitzmann.

Onkle Fritz, a cousin of Ruprecht and Alfried Waitzmann. He is a member of the board of directors of Waitzmann Industries and a good friend to Frau Waitzmann. His role in the story is that of the wise and helpful confidant.

Alexandra von Boehling (fôn bœ' lĭnk), a noble young lady from a noble German family living in Italy, visiting with the von Hoffbachs as a way to make her way toward a good marriage. She is drawn toward both Leo von Hoffbach and Ruprecht Waitzmann, neither of whom she seems to love. Her innocent passivity is a foil to the ambition of Ruprecht and to the cruel barbarism of the Nazis.

Felix Grunewald (grōōn'ə·vält), a middle-aged member of the SS, who is in charge of a concentration camp. He prides himself on his rational and cultured approach to his prisoners. He is attracted to Alfried Waitzmann when the latter is imprisoned with him

and eventually has him, as a trustee, do work around the commandant's house. When the Russians enter the city, he commits suicide in obedience to the Führer.

Gudrun Grunewald, a neurotic and withdrawn woman. She believes that her husband is not treating her properly. When Alfried arrives, she comes out of her cell, devoted to the Nazi cause. She commits suicide with her husband.

Hubertus Grunewald, the son of Gudrun and Felix. He is even more caught up in the Nazi mystique, writing a diary of his Nazi feelings, which he thinks will be published later as an epic of the *Götterdammerung*. Yet he chooses life over suicide when the time comes.

Robert W. Peckham

THE BIRTHDAY PARTY

Author: Harold Pinter (1930-   )
Type of work: Play
Time of action: The 1950's
First produced: 1958

Stanley Webber, a boarder at a seedy seaside home. In his late thirties and unkempt, he indulges in fantasies about exotic cities in which he had performed as a concert pianist. In Kafkaesque fashion, he speaks of a career that was ended by persons he refers to as "them." Filling his landlady's need of a lodger and son, he is comfortably ensconced as a member of the household until his position is threatened by the arrival of two strange, surrealistic guests, Goldberg and McCann. He even suggests that the two have come to cart Meg, his landlady, away in a wheelbarrow. In the climactic scene, his birthday party, Stanley beats the drum Meg has given him as a present, the tempo savagely increasing as he marches around the room. During a game of blindman's buff, the lights go out. When the lights come on, he, glasses broken, is standing over Lulu, who lies spread-eagled on a table. The next morn-

ing he appears—in striped trousers, black jacket, white collar, bowler hat—and is carted away by Goldberg and McCann to a mysterious healer, "Monty," for treatment.

Meg Boles, wife of Petey, with whom she operates a rundown boarding house. A mothering person in her mid-sixties who dislikes going out, she devotes her time to Petey's meals and comfort, and, more significantly, to their boarder, Stanley, upon whom she dotes as a surrogate son. The surrogacy, however, takes on an Oedipal cast. Although Stanley protests to the contrary, Meg insists that it is his birthday, whereupon Goldberg suggests that a birthday party be held. At the end, seemingly unaware of Stanley's departure, she is enjoying reminiscing about being "the belle of the ball."

Nat Goldberg, a menacing new guest in his

159

late fifties and a "smooth operator" who takes charge of things, including his accomplice, McCann, with whom he quarrels at one point. In cryptic questions about their pasts, their beliefs, and the forces that shaped their lives, Goldberg attacks first Lulu, then Stanley, and takes on the configuration of a surrealistic-allegorical figure symbolizing the destructive impersonality of the modern world and its guilt-producing threat to the sensitive individual.

Dermot McCann, a man of thirty, serves Goldberg in the nefarious activities in which they conspire. He makes an indelible impression with his neat, precise tearing of a sheet of newspaper, column by column. McCann, Irish-Catholic, and Goldberg, Jewish, suggest the Judaic-Christian influence that has shaped the modern Western world.

Petey Boles, a man in his sixties, husband

of Meg, and deck-chair attendant. A compliant husband, he functions in the story primarily to exchange breakfast banalities with Meg or with Stanley, their boarder. His blandness puts into sharp focus the strange behavior of Meg and Stanley and the menacing threats of McCann and Goldberg. He returns from work one day to announce the arrival of their two new guests. At the end, he returns to his routines as husband and deck-chair attendant as though nothing unusual has happened.

Lulu, a woman in her twenties. She appears mysteriously with a package. Flirting with both Stanley and Goldberg, she departs the next morning after being interrogated accusingly by Goldberg and savagely ordered by the puritanical "unfrocked" McCann to confess.

Susan Rusinko

THE BLACK HERMIT

Author: Ngugi wa Thiong'o (James Ngugi, 1938-   )
Type of work: Play
Time of action: The 1960's
First produced: 1962

Remi, a youth of the Maura tribe sent to the city to attend the university and return to his village as a political and social leader for his people in the government of a newly independent country. As a student activist, he has convinced his small tribe to support the Africanist party that now governs, but he has stayed on in the city as a clerk in an oil company. Before his departure from home, his father and the Elders of the village prevailed upon him to marry the widow of his brother, recently killed in an accident. Because he has secretely loved her, and believes that she could not have loved him and married his brother, he goes through with the ceremony but flees the reality of the marriage by staying on in the city and becoming the lover of a white South African student, Jane. When he returns home with a friend

from another tribe, he decries racism and tribalism, and spurns his wife.

Nyobi, devout Christian convert, mother of Remi, confidante and supporter of his wife, Thoni. Her concern for Thoni and longing to see Remi prompt her to bless the mission of the Elders, undertaken in the name of the old religion. Repenting, she adjures the pastor of the Christian church to go on the same mission.

Thoni, legal wife of Remi. She has loved him from the first but has no socially acceptable way of telling him until she leaves him a note before committing suicide.

The Leader of the Elders, spokesman for the religious conservatives, who believe that

Christianity has been taking the best men of the tribe. Remi's father was only brought back to his ancestor's religion by imminent death, when he appealed to the Elders for help in convincing Remi to do the traditional thing and marry his brother's widow. He and the other Elders chafe at local administrators not of their tribe. They want Remi to return and do his duty as their educated citizen by forming a political party.

The Pastor, a strict interpreter of morals according to the Christian view. He sees Nyobi's task as completing Thoni's conversion, and Remi's continued absence as a defection from the church to the devil's work of the Africanist Party. Only Nyobi's flattering pleas convince him to go to the city himself. When Remi agrees to return, the pastor feels sure that Christ has won a victory.

Jane, a white South African student at the university. She has been Remi's lover and companion in a year of frenetic partygoing. She learns of his marriage shortly before he returns home.

Omange (ō•män′jə), Remi's friend and fellow activist. He is much more skeptical of the new government than Remi seems to be, and he fears the repressive possibilities of tribal politics. When he hears Remi's story of his thwarted love for Thoni, he urges Remi to go home.

The Elders, who accompany their leader to the city to convince Remi to return.

The woman, who meets Thoni leaving the village. She fears what Thoni intends, but cannot persuade her to stay.

First neighbor, who announces Remi's arrival. This neighbor emphasizes the freedom and political advantage to be gained from his return.

Second neighbor, who reports on Remi's speech. The effect was that of a stinging rebuke to the Elders.

James L. Hodge

BLACK MISCHIEF

Author: Evelyn Waugh (1903-1966)
Type of work: Novel
Time of action: The early 1930's
First published: 1932

Seth, newly crowned Emperor of Azania. He is a twenty-four-year-old Oxonian and the grandson of Amurath, first emperor of this polyglot East African country. He has a naïve faith in the future and in progress, and he is determined to modernize the country at all costs. Yet his progressive impulses are constantly at war with his tribal background and superstitious nature. He has acquired enough information at Oxford to prove Alexander Pope's famous maxim that a little learning is a dangerous thing. His efforts are largely ineffectual. He gives boots to his barefoot army, and the soldiers eat them. He shows films on birth control all across the country, but they evoke only sympathy from

the audiences for the poor, unfortunate man on the screen who has so few sons.

Basil Seal, an adventurer and one of the "Bright Young People." He is handsome, charming, opportunistic, and unscrupulous. He once had Seth to lunch at Oxford. This tenuous association has lured him to Azania, where he finds himself High Commissioner and Comptroller General of the Ministry of Modernization.

Sir Samson Courteney, the British Minister to Azania. He is eccentric, inattentive, and comparatively unsuccessful in diplomatic life. The interminable assassinations, coups, and wars that characterize Azanian political life never touch him. He regards the slightest request from any of His Majesty's subjects in Azania as a gross personal imposition.

Prudence Courteney, Sir Samson's daughter and Basil's mistress. She is a silly girl who has but two enthusiasms: sex and the *Panorama of Life*, a written collection of her callow observations. She is fated for an exotic demise, as the main course at a Wanda cannibal feast.

General Connolly, a mercenary in Seth's service. He has wide experience in the internecine wars of Africa. He is an enigmatic man with a mysterious past.

Krikor Youkoumian, Basil's financial secretary in the Ministry of Modernization. This shrewd, unprincipled, indefatigable Ar-

menian entrepreneur is perfectly fitted for the political and economic life of Azania. While those around him are periodically assassinated or put to flight, he survives each change of regime and turns a nice profit besides.

William Bland, a junior member of the British legation. His surname is an apt representation of his personality. His tepid romance with Prudence is quickly terminated by Basil's charisma.

Dame Mildred Porch, a formidable Englishwoman who much prefers animals to people. Along with her friend Miss Sarah Tin, she is visiting Azania on behalf of the League of Dumb Chums. Upon discovering a family living with their goats in an abandoned motor truck, she observes that this arrangement cannot be healthy for the goats.

Patrick Adcock

THE BLACK PRINCE

Author: Iris Murdoch (1919-   )
Type of work: Novel
Time of action: The 1960's
First published: 1973

Bradley Pearson, a writer and the narrator of the novel. Bradley, middle-aged and solitary, has retired from his job as an inspector of taxes to devote himself to his writing, at which he works painstakingly. His life radically changes when he suddenly realizes that he passionately loves Julian Baffin, whom he idealizes. This love transforms his sterile existence, finally allowing him to write his great book, which he completes while unjustly (probably) imprisoned for the murder of Arnold Baffin.

Julian Baffin, a young woman of twenty. The daughter of Bradley's friends Arnold and Rachel Baffin, Julian has asked Bradley to give her informal tutorials on great books, for she wants to be a writer. It is during her

Hamlet tutorial that Bradley realizes that he loves her; later, she tells him that she has admired him since she was a child. She idealizes and romanticizes Bradley, but ultimately their relationship seems to have had little impact on her.

Arnold Baffin, a prolific writer. Bradley encouraged his early efforts and helped to find him a publisher for his first novel; they have been friends ever since. Bradley is often drawn into Arnold and Rachel's domestic quarrels. Arnold is outraged when he learns of Bradley's love for Julian. Bradley is convicted for Arnold's murder; suggestions of professional jealousy help convince the jury of his motive.

Rachel Baffin, Arnold's wife. A dissatisfied, unfulfilled woman, Rachel attempts to seduce Bradley. She confuses Bradley because her confidences to him often contradict what she has told him previously. She draws Julian away from Bradley by making the attempt at seduction seem Bradley's and not her own. She seems ready to believe that Bradley killed Arnold although it is apparently she who hit him with the poker.

Francis Marloe, Bradley's ne'er-do-well former brother-in-law. A doctor who has been dropped from the lists for impropriety in prescribing drugs, Francis arrives at Bradley's flat hoping that Bradley will be able to persuade Christian to give him money. Bradley asks Francis to take care of Priscilla while he is away with Julian. Francis is a drunkard, and Priscilla then commits suicide while in his care. Francis later sets himself up as a psychologist, and, in his epilogue, he claims that Bradley was a latent homosexual in love with Francis.

Christian Evandale, Bradley's former wife and sister of Francis. After their marriage failed, she married a wealthy American and has recently returned from Illinois a widow. A showy, friendly woman, she helps care for Priscilla, flirts with Arnold, and proposes

that she and Bradley remarry (which, in her epilogue, she denies doing).

Priscilla Saxe, Bradley's younger sister. Desperately unhappy and hysterical, she shows up on Bradley's doorstep after leaving her husband. She tries to commit suicide with her sleeping pills and is successful on her second attempt. Bradley does not leave his tryst with Julian upon her death; when Julian discovers that, she finds it horrifying.

Roger Saxe, Priscilla's husband. Bradley has never liked him and indicts him as cruel and unfeeling when he goes to pick up Priscilla's things. He has been having an affair for years; now that Priscilla has left him, he wants to marry his girlfriend.

Marigold, Roger's pregnant girlfriend. She feels sorry for Priscilla and persuades Roger to give Priscilla some of the pretty things Priscilla is so obsessive about.

P. Loxias, the editor of the book. He becomes Bradley's friend and teacher in prison and encourages Bradley to write the book. He solicits the comments from Christian, Rachel, Julian, and Francis that form the epilogue of the novel.

Karen M. Cleveland

BLACK ROBE

Author: Brian Moore (1921-   )
Type of work: Novel
Time of action: 1635
First published: 1985

Father Paul Laforgue, a Jesuit priest and missionary to the Huron Indians. A slight, pale, thin-bearded intellectual, born and educated in France, he dreams of the glory of martyrdom in the wilderness. Fired by religious fervor, he learns the Algonkian and Huron languages and prepares meticulously for work among "the Savages." Confronted with the realities of life among the Indians, he accepts his own misery and physical suf-

fering with courage; he is forgiving of the sins of others but is haunted by guilt at his own human weaknesses. Initially secure in the correctness of his culture and religion, he comes to respect many of the Indians' ways and to question his religious certitudes. A man of conscience, he refuses to acquiesce in the religious sophistry of Father Jerome and baptize the Indians before they understand and accept the faith. Because his own faith is not absolute, he comes to see himself as unworthy of martyrdom. In the midst of his crisis of faith and unsure of God's will, he dedicates himself to working on in hope and out of compassion for the Indians as fellow human beings.

Daniel Davost, accompanies Father Laforgue on his journey to Ihonatiria. Not yet twenty, he has been in New France for one year after having promised to serve God for two years in a distant land. Intelligent and adaptable with a talent for languages, he is thought of highly by the priests. He wants to go with Laforgue not out of religious devotion, as he claims, but to continue the sexual relationship he has secretly begun with the Algonkin girl Annuka. Suffering feelings of guilt and convinced of his own damnation, he is critical of doctrinaire Christianity and is gradually drawn to the Indian way of life. He deserts Laforgue to follow Annuka and asks to marry the girl, declaring the Indians his people. He returns with Chomina and his family to help Laforgue, but all are captured by the Iroquois. After their escape, Laforgue agrees to marry Daniel and Annuka. When the couple finally join the priest at Ihonatiria, Daniel is dressed and painted like the Algonkin he wishes to become.

Annuka, a beautiful Algonkin girl in love with Daniel Davost. Formerly promiscuous, she promises to be faithful to Daniel and wants to marry him, despite her father's objections. After her father's death, she goes with Daniel to live among the Hurons at Ihonatiria.

Chomina, an Algonkin elder and Annuka's

father. He acts as a moral conscience for his people and fears that they are becoming greedy and materialistic like the French. Keeping the promise he made to help Laforgue on his journey, he is captured by the Iroquois, who kill his wife and son, torture him and his daughter, and inflict wounds that later prove fatal; he acts with bravery and explains rather than condemns the brutality of his enemies. The principal spokesman for the Indian beliefs and attitudes toward life, he engages Laforgue in philosophic debate, rejecting baptism and the Christian belief in a better life after death.

Father Fernand Jerome, one of the Jesuit founders of the mission at Ihonatiria and the man Laforgue is sent to help. At age forty-four, he has suffered a series of strokes and has difficulty moving his tall bulky frame. He has a heavy gray beard and a pale, half-paralyzed face with one eye enlarged and discolored. His assistant, Father Duval, has been murdered by the Indians, and Jerome is drifting in and out of consciousness when Laforgue arrives. With a final burst of what Laforgue sees as a misplaced religious zeal, Jerome uses the Indians' superstitions and fears to convince them that they should be baptized. Before he can reap his "harvest of souls," however, he is murdered by a terrified Indian who blames the Blackrobes for the fever that is decimating the Hurons.

Neehatin, a powerful and duplicitous Algonkin leader who secretly consults his wife on decisions and stubbornly pursues an explanation for his dreams.

Douglas Rollins

BLACK THUNDER

Author: Arna Bontemps (1902-1973)
Type of work: Novel
Time of action: The 1800's
First published: 1936

Gabriel Prosser, a slave, and the leader of the slave rebellion. He is the coachman on the Prosser plantation, located near Richmond,

Virginia. He is twenty-four years old and the tallest of three uncommonly tall brothers who is considered by the other slaves to be a "man of destiny" because of the reputation he acquired after defeating Ditcher, a black slave driver, in a fight. After the death of the slave, Bundy, he changes from a silent dreamy person to one who speaks with quiet dignity and excitement about his revolutionary plans. His rebellion fails because of the treachery of two fellow slaves, and the slaves are impeded by a devastating storm. Gabriel escapes capture for some time but is finally captured and brought to Richmond for trial, where he refuses to give any signficant information about the conspiracy before his execution.

Ben, one of the traitors of the slave rebellion, a house slave, and the old gray-headed servant to the elderly slave master, Mossely Sheppard. Ben does not share the other slaves' love and desire for freedom, and he is distrusted by the other slaves, who do not share their plans for the rebellion with him. At the end of the novel, he is the target of the wrath of the remaining slaves on the plantation after the execution of Gabriel and the conspirators.

Pharaoh, a slave and the second traitor of the slave rebellion. He wishes to lead a fighting line during the rebellion, but because Gabriel does not trust Pharaoh, Gabriel will not permit this. Pharaoh's anger and resentment turn him into a traitor. After Gabriel's execution, he turns into a madman. Upon learning of Gabriel's defeat, other slaves wear Pharaoh down by throwing knives at him at every opportunity. At the end of the novel, he climbs a tree and begins barking like a dog.

Juba, a young slave woman who is in love with Gabriel and who is the only woman participant in the slave rebellion. She is described as a tempestuous brown wench who on the night of the revolt rides the colt Araby as a signal for the conspirators. She is a strong and defiant personality and never cries out, even though she is beaten unmercifully by her slave master for her part in the revolt. She is later sold on the auction block.

Bundy, an elderly, rum-drinking slave who

is killed at the beginning of the novel when his master, Thomas Prosser, allows his horse to trample him because Prosser considers Bundy to be useless. Bundy's murder serves as a catalyst for Gabriel's revolutionary plans.

Melody, a free, apricot-colored mulattress with enameled black hair and barbarous hoops in her ears. She is a friend of the Frenchman and the black conspirators and leaves town after the revolt fails. She aids Gabriel in his flight.

Mingo, a black freeman whose distinctive characteristic is his ability to read. He is a saddle maker and a friend to the slaves because his wife and children are still slaves. He reads to the slaves from the Bible and thereby gives the conspirators inspiration and courage.

Alexander Biddenhurst, a Frenchman who is eager and hopeful about race relations. He is a friend of the mulatto Melody, but he is forced to flee Richmond after the slave rebellion because the whites think that he is one of the authors of Gabriel's plans as well as a fellow conspirator.

M. Creuzot, a Frenchman who is a printer of religious pamphlets. He believes that the prospects for the unity of poor whites and blacks are negative. He is forced to flee for his life after the slave revolt because the whites believe that he has conspired with the revolting slaves.

Thomas Prosser, Gabriel's master and a cruel and inhumane slave owner who tramples the old slave, Bundy, with his horse.

Mossely Sheppard, an elderly, rich, feeble old white man who is Ben's master. Ben reveals the plans of the rebellion to him.

Ditcher,
General John Scott, and
Criddle, slave participants in Gabriel's revolt.

Betty Taylor Thompson

THE BLACKER THE BERRY
A Novel of Negro Life

Author: Wallace Thurman (1902-1934)
Type of work: Novel
Time of action: The 1920's
First published: 1929

Emma Lou Morgan, the extremely color conscious, and therefore self-conscious, protagonist. Because of her very dark skin, young Emma Lou has been repeatedly ostracized and victimized by her fair-skinned family in Idaho, her white high school classmates, fellow students at the university she attends, and the people she meets when she flees from Southern California to Harlem. Naïve, intellectually pretentious, and an elitist, Emma Lou has internalized self-hatred; she worships light skin and, ironically, is herself biased against the other dark-skinned people, generally finding them ugly and unattractive or too poor and unsophisticated for her. Having left college to work in New York, Emma Lou finds her color prevents her from obtaining "congenial" jobs or suitable championship. She works first as a maid for a white actress, learning how whites think blacks act and live in Harlem. Toward the end of the novel, she completes a teacher training program and begins to teach. Because of both the color bias of others and her own excessive color consciousness, however, she remains largely isolated and alienated from the Harlem community.

Alva, Emma Lou's racially mixed Harlem lover. A charming, though heavy drinking ladies' man considered attractive largely because of his "high yellow," or parchment, complexion and his sophisticated manners, Alva cynically uses Emma Lou for both sexual gratification and as a means of financial support. He perceives her loneliness and turns it to his advantage by courting her and introducing her to Harlem nightlife despite the laughter of his friends, who mock his attentions to so dark a woman. Eventually, he tires of her heightened color sensitivity and tells her frankly about her own prejudices. Toward the end of the novel, although

his charms are considerably dissipated by alcohol and fast living, Alva is still able to manipulate Emma Lou.

Braxton, Alva's roommate and a would-be hustler, gambler, and youthful ladies' man as well. Braxton thinks of himself as a slightly duskier version of the white matinee idol Rudolph Valentino. Proud, vain, and physically attractive. Braxton never has money because he will not work yet cannot successfully make his living off his looks, his women, or his skills at gambling and hustling. He never says anything kind to Emma Lou and has no regard for dark-skinned Negro women.

Arline Strange, a white actress playing the part of a mulatto in the theater. She employs Emma Lou as her maid and attendant. She and her brother are the first people to introduce Emma Lou to Harlem's more celebrated nightclubs.

Geraldine, Alva's light-skined girlfriend whom he marries after she moves in with him, declaring that she is pregant with his child.

Maria Lightfood, Emma Lou's maternal grandmother in Boise, Idaho. Both class and color conscious, Mrs. Lightfood contributes to the social isolation Emma Lou endured as a child.

Jane Lightfood Morgan, Emma Lou's mother whose one act of bravery was marrying a man with ebony skin. Insensitive and ashamed of her daughter because of her dark complexion, she offers Emma Lou very little emotional support

Joe Lightfood, Emma Lou's uncle and the

166

only relative who does not belittle her color. He persuades Emma Lou to attend the University of Southern California thinking she could find "a larger and more intelligent social circle" where the color bias would be less intense.

Jasmine Griffith, a West Indian immigrant renting a room in the same Harlem boarding house as Emma Lou. She functions as a foil to show the mutual suspicion and distrust American blacks and West Indian immigrants once shared.

Gwendolyn Johnson, Emma Lou's one friend in Harlem. Educated, helpful, and sensitive to the effects of intraracial prejudice, Gwendolyn attempts to help Emma Lou by introducing her to the proper and respectable Harlem circles and by repeatedly deprecating light-skined Negroes, despite her own light complexion.

Tony Crews,
Cora Thurston,
Paul,
Truman, and
Aaron, all young artists and intellectuals representing the "New Negro" intelligentsia of the Harlem Renaissance era. Tony Crews is modeled upon Langston Hughes; other characters are thinly veiled portraits of authentic members of the Harlem literati.

Clere Sloane, former actress who employs Emma Lou as her personal maid, almost companion, when Arline Strange decides to go to Europe without her maid.

Campbell Kitchen, husband of Clere and a celebrated writer and intellectual. A white liberal with a sincere interest in exploiting Harlem and the Negro vogue of the times, Campbell encourages Emma Lou to read and to go back to school for her teaching certification.

Sandra Y. Govan

THE BLACKS
A Clown Show

Author: Jean Genet (1910-1986)
Type of work: Play
Time of action: The 1950's
First published: Les Nègres: Clownerie, 1958 (English translation, 1960)

Archibald Absalon Wellington, a black actor in the role of master of ceremonies in a play about the rape and murder of a white woman. He is a man who demands strict obedience to the script as he directs his troupe's performance for five white members of the royal court, who are seated on an upper stage. Archibald's purpose is to present his black actors in the light of the white court's expectations. Since the whites assume the blacks are liars and thieves, he instructs his actors to play those caricatures. He charges them to manufacture hate and to delete any word or gesture that might suggest love or humanity. At the close of the performance, he thanks his actors and congratulates them on portraying the stereotypes the whites expected.

Dieudonné Village (dēœ•dō•nā′ vē•läzh′), a black actor who plays the part of rapist and murderer. He is the only male character to express love, and it is directed toward Vertu, the black whore. His desire to obey Archibald, though, compels him to temper his love with words of despite. He leaves Vertu behind to reenact the slaughter of a white woman and seduces another actor, the black male Diouf, who is dressed as the female victim. He then rapes and strangles her. Although hunted down by the court, he assassinates them one by one. He returns to Vertu with words of love.

Mademoiselle Étiennette-Vertu-Rose-Secrète Diop (ä•tē•ĕn•nĕt′ vĕr•tü′ rōz sə•krĕ′ dē•ōp′), a black actress and prostitute. She is a woman of reason and balance and believes that there are bad blacks as well as good ones. She is the only female character to express a love interest, which is directed toward Village. Vertu does not participate in the murder of the white girl.

Samba Graham Diouf (dē·ōōf′), an old black actor who is the voice of order and reason. He seeks moderation and urges the blacks to be conciliatory. He pleads compromise, which falls on deaf ears. When ordered by Félicité to play the part of the slain white girl, Diouf dons a dress, a blond wig, and a white girl's mask. Immediately prior to his rape, Diouf is aided by Village in giving symbolic birth to five puppets representing the five members of the court. Diouf is then seduced by Village, taken behind a screen, raped, and strangled. He next appears—still as a white girl—on the upper stage, a symbol of the white man's territory. From there he gives an account to the Negroes of what it is like to be in the white man's land.

Madame Félicité Gueuse-Pardon (gœz pâr·dōn′), an imposing sixty-year-old black actress often perched on a throne. She displays strength, courage, and wisdom. It is she who orders Diouf to assume the role of the murdered white girl, while she portrays the girl's mother. When confronted with the white queen on her own turf, she executes an eloquent battle of words that she easily wins. In this discourse, she expresses her vision of an all-black world.

Madame Augusta Neige (nězh), a hostile, defiant black actress. She is moody, rebellious, and hatefully jealous of white women. She advocates rape and murder but condemns Village, whom she claims felt love for the woman he strangled. She seethes with white hatred, even boasting that she will drink the blood of whites. To her, all blacks are good, all whites bad. In the reenactment of the murder, she plays the white girl's sister.

Mademoiselle Adélaïde Bobo (à·dā·lä·īd′ bō·bō′), a black actress. She is a calculating, cold-blooded woman, who adheres to the script the court wants to see performed. She preaches that the ideas of blacks must spring from hatred. In the murder of the white girl she plays the victim's neighbor.

Edgar-Hélas Ville de Saint-Nazaire (vēy də săǹ·nä·zār′), a black actor who, like Diouf, makes an attempt at reason. He appears at intervals during the play to inform the black actors of events taking place outside the theater. There are hints of an antiwhite revolution and Newport News is assigned the duty of assisting in the offstage murder of a black traitor.

The Queen,
The Governor,
The Missionary,
The Judge, and
The Valet, all members of the court who are viewing the performance from the upper stage. They are all frauds playing the role of whites but are actually blacks wearing white masks. They are bigoted figureheads with little power, scanty intelligence, and no passions. As vapid creatures who are not open to the truth, they demand drama from the blacks that fit neatly with their presupposed, stereotypical ideas. They assume that blacks are inhuman rapist-murderers, which is the only way they will tolerate them portrayed. In horror, they watch as the blacks rape and strangle a white girl. The heinous crime validates what they already knew to be true, and they go to Africa (the stage below) to avenge the girl's death. Although they give lip service to justice by claiming not to indict all of Africa for one man's crime, they immediately turn around and claim that any black can be killed to pay the price for the crime. One black is as good—or bad—as another. One by one, the members of the court remove their white masks, and one by one they are assassinated by the blacks.

Steven C. Kowall

BLITHE SPIRIT
An Improbable Farce in Three Acts

Author: Noël Coward (1899-1973)
Type of work: Play
Time of action: The 1930's
First produced: 1941

Charles Condomine, a novelist, in his forties. Charles is bright, sophisticated, articulate, and debonair but somewhat at the mercy of his wives (past and present). His interest in spiritualism as a subject for a novel leads Charles to ask Madame Arcati to dinner and a séance. He, of course, is completely skeptical, but becomes a believer when the ghost of his first wife appears— and stays. From then on, poor Charles is a shuttlecock between the women battling for his affections: Ruth, his living wife, and Elvira, his dead one. If the truth were known, Charles prefers Elvira.

Ruth Condomine, Charles's second wife. Like her husband, Ruth is witty and sophisticated, quite the society matron. Ruth is a bit stuffy, however, a little predictable. She is convinced that Charles has lost his mind when Elvira appears, since she at first can neither see nor hear her. Throughout much of the play, Ruth is the concerned wife, trying to restore Charles to normalcy.

Elvira, ghost of Charles Condomine's first wife. Elvira is gray from head to toe, and only Charles can see or hear her. In life, Elvira was spirited, outgoing, wild, and care-free. In death, she is no different, she has cocktails with Genghis Khan. She does love Charles, if somewhat casually, and is quite jealous of Ruth. Her attempts to monopolize the attention and conversation of Charles after she reappears form the central tension of the play.

Madame Arcati, the local spiritualist and medium. Elderly but spry, Madame Arcati bicycles into the play wearing slightly outlandish clothes and talking to an eight-year-old contact on the other side. As everyone soon finds out, however, Madame Arcati is no fraud. She is truly in contact with the other world and has inadvertantly been the "medium" through which Elvira is called back to this one. The problem is, Madame Arcati cannot figure out how to return Elvira to the other side.

Edith, the maid. Edith plays a tiny part in the bulk of the play, but turns out to be a central character indeed. For it is Edith, not Charles, who has the extrasensory powers that called Elvira back from the dead. And only Edith can make Elvira return.

Evelyn Romig

THE BLOOD KNOT

Author: Athol Fugard (1932-   )
Type of work: Play
Time of action: The early 1960's
First produced: 1961

Morris Pietersen, a "Colored" (mixed race) male of unspecified age who lives with his brother, Zachariah. One of Morris' most important characteristics is the fact that, in contrast to Zachariah, he has light skin— skin light enough so that he has been able to pass for white. As a result, Morris seems to feel guilty toward his dark-skinned brother, needing to prove to himself and Zachariah that they do indeed have a "blood knot" and

169

that they are, in fact, tied as brothers in a valued, however troubled, relationship. An essential aspect of Morris' personality is that he seems driven to become closer than he has been to Zachariah. This desire is shown, in part, by Morris' taking a servile position to his brother. For example, ironically, it is the brother with near-white skin who assumes the domestic chores in the house, such as cooking and preparing Zachariah's foot baths, among other things. Furthermore, another important characteristic is Morris' dream that the two of them will someday move to a deserted land to escape other negative aspects of society. Thus, a main part of his outlook on existence is improving his relationship with his brother. Yet, Morris' desire to be close to Zachariah is sometimes undercut by his absorption in South Africa's racialism. A central part of the plot, for example, is Morris' exhibiting a latent dislike of blacks, as is shown when the two brothers play a game in which Morris pretends to be white, while Zachariah acts as a subservient black man. Morris' inner feelings are shown by the fact that, while he is at first unable to act the role of a white man, he soon is so carried away by the role-playing that he wishes to be abusive to Zachariah, wanting to poke him with an umbrella. Morris, therefore, expresses the plot's intention to show both his inner conflict as well as showing the tension that lurks below the surface of the two brothers' relationship.

Zachariah Pietersen, a mixed-race male of unspecified age. In contrast to Morris, who does the domestic work at home, Zachariah works at a park—ironically, keeping blacks from entering. One of his most important characteristics is his dark skin. Unlike Morris, Zachariah has always had to live a life subjected to the laws pertaining to "Coloreds"; he, unlike Morris, is unable to "pass" for white. It is not surprising, therefore, that he is the more reality-bound of the brothers, having little interest in Morris' illusion of a new life in a deserted land. Moreover, his realistic nature is emphasized even as he and his brother play games of imagination; for example, he tells Morris how to "act white" as the brothers are pretending that Morris is a white man and that Zachariah is a black in a submissive role. Another important element is that Zachariah is conflicted in his feelings toward his brother. He recalls bitterly that their mother favored the light-skinned Morris, for example. Zachariah also feels that Morris, who at time seems to push his illusions and opinions on him, is a burdensome brother. Resentment and jealously, therefore, lurk beneath Zachariah's feelings toward his brother.

Jane Davis

THE BLOOD OF THE LAMB

Author: Peter De Vries (1910-   )
Type of work: Novel
Time of action: The 1920's to the 1950's
First published: 1962

Don Wanderhope, the son of pietistic Dutch immigrants in south Chicago. As a youth, he works for his father, who has a garbage-collection business, and attends the University of Chicago. As his name suggests, he can neither believe nor disbelieve in divine providence. Times of hopefulness and happiness in his life are invariably followed by suffering and loss. He decides finally on reason, courage, and grace—but insists that the grace is solely humanity's to give, that there is no God to make all things right in the end.

Ben Wanderhope, Don's father, an intelligent but ill-educated immigrant businessman. He wavers between a variety of Dutch Calvinism that allows grace only to the elect and no belief at all. His faith is rekindled when he thinks that he is drowning in a garbage pit and again when profession of belief will lead to reduced fees for Don's treatment at a church-run sanatorium. Finally, he becomes so depressed that he has to be institutionalized for the remainder of his life.

Louie Wanderhope, Don's older brother and hero, who dies while a medical student at the University of Chicago. Always a scoffer, on his deathbed he assures those in attendance that he has "no doubts" whatsoever as to what is to follow. His smile at Don lets his brother know exactly what he means by his statement, though the others are pleasantly misled.

Greta Wigbaldy, a girl from the same milieu as Don, later his wife. Following their marriage, which takes place after his return from treatment for tuberculosis, her personality becomes increasingly disordered. Already the mother of a given-up-for-adoption child, this by a married man, she is unfaithful to Don, drinks too much, and eventually kills herself, leaving to Don her daughter by him.

Carol Wanderhope, Don and Greta's beautiful and precocious daughter. Don's love for his daughter is intensified when he learns that she has leukemia. It is only after her death that he discovers—via a tape recording which she left behind—that she knew for some time what was coming.

Rena Baker, a decent Calvinist girl whom Don meets and loves at the tuberculosis sanatorium in the Rockies. Her piety seems as genuine as her love for Don. Two days after the near consummation of that love, she has to undergo an operation and dies.

James H. Bowden

A BLOODSMOOR ROMANCE

Author: Joyce Carol Oates (1938-   )
Type of work: Novel
Time of action: 1879-1900
First published: 1982

John Quincy Zinn, a gentleman inventor. Fifty-two in 1879, John Zinn is tall, wide-shouldered, and handsome despite the dagger-shaped birthmark on his left temple. The son of a dishonest pedlar whom, as a child, he saw tarred, feathered, and burnt, Zinn was adopted by a farm family, became a radical schoolmaster influenced by transcendentalism, and finally, lionized by Philadelphia society, married into the wealthy Kiddemaster family, which supports his experimental laboratory and large family. Convinced of the inevitability of progress, Zinn believes that inventions will bring the perfectibility of mankind, and, at his death, is engaged, under government patronage, in devising weapons of destruction, including the basis of nuclear weaponry. Despite the radicalism of his early years, he regards Deirdre, Constance Philippa, and Samantha as dead when they run away to live their own lives in violation of the conventions of the Kiddemaster class.

Prudence Kiddemaster Zinn, John's wife. In 1879, stout, stern, matronly, and conventional, she once was the highly independent headmistress of a girls' school. Renouncing her independence to pursue Zinn, her spirit is broken by a series of pregnancies, sometimes difficult labors, miscarriages, and occasional deaths. In old age, however, she leaves Zinn to return to militant feminist causes.

Deirdre Louisa Bonner Zinn, an adopted Zinn daughter. Sixteen when, in 1879, she is abducted in a mysterious black balloon, Deirdre is dark-haired, pale, and small; she has a marked widow's peak and piercing silvery-gray eyes. Unhappy in her adopted home, she is disliked by the Zinn sisters, and spiritual manifestations have plagued her since childhood. After her abduction, she reappears as Deirdre of the Shadows, a distinguished and successful trance medium. When she is investigated by the Society of Psychical Research, her spirits drive three men to their deaths, thus convincing even the most skeptical of the powers that control her. She suffers a breakdown in 1895 and retires. When she returns to Bloodsmoor because of Edwina Kiddemaster's will, she is revealed to be Edwina's daughter by a secret early marriage, and she is named heir to the vast Kiddemaster wealth, which she shares with her adopted family.

Constance Philippa Zinn, later **Philippe Fox,** the oldest Zinn daughter. Twenty-two in 1879, she is tall, striking, and satiric. Because her family desires socially impressive marriages, she becomes engaged to a twice-widowed, sinister German baron, but, on her wedding night, she flees the hotel, leaving her husband unknowingly to consummate the marriage with a dressmaker's dummy. Going west, she becomes a gambler, journalist, and lawman, among many other things. She undergoes a sex change. When she returns to Bloodsmoor because of Edwina's will, she is the masculine Philippe Fox, who then elopes with a childhood friend now imprisoned by her vicious husband, and again disappears.

Malvinia Zinn, the daughter who is the family beauty. Age twenty in 1879, Malvinia is tall, blue-eyed, and vain, with rich, dark hair. Courted by a man of wealth, she runs off with an actor and launches a successful stage career, to her family's horror. After a life of dissipation, marred by the hereditary Zinn Mark of the Beast, she repents, becomes a teacher, and marries a man whose life she had harmed in her childhood.

Octavia Zinn, placid and plump, she is the Christian and conventional Zinn daughter. Twenty-one in 1879, she is a born lady; she has a warm smile, plump cheeks, and brown eyes. She marries a tyrannical and narrow retired Lutheran minister, Lucius Rumford, whose exotic sexual practices she, in her innocence, regards as normal. (These practices cause his death.) She bears three children; two die young, one perhaps killed by another, but she later finds a happy second marriage with Sean McInnes, successful investor, attorney, and U.S. Congressman, whom she had once adored when he was merely the son of their Irish coachman.

Samantha Zinn, the daughter who serves as John's laboratory assistant. Small and immature, red-haired and freckled, Samantha frightens off suitors with her intelligence. Pressured by her mother to marry a decadent aristocrat, she runs off with Nahum Hareton, her father's other assistant, a man of dubious background. (As a small boy, he had disappeared from a time machine John Zinn had manufactured when a schoolmaster.) She herself is an inventor, focusing on time-saving devices for housewives such as disposable diapers.

Edwina Kiddemaster, Prudence's aunt, author of more than seventy etiquette books. Enormously wealthy, she is conservative in her writing but less so in her private life. Her will stipulates that the Zinn daughers must be reunited at Bloodsmoor, where Deirdre is revealed to be her daughter by a disastrous marriage.

Sarah Whitton Kiddemaster, Prudence's mother. Conventionally female, an autopsy reveals that, at her death, she has virtually no internal organs. She has sewn an antimacassar 1,358 yards long.

Betty Richardson

BLOODY POETRY

Author: Howard Brenton (1942-   )
Type of work: Play

Time of action: 1816-1822
First produced: 1984

Percy Bysshe Shelley, an English Romantic poet. Thin, sallow, sensitive, and neurotic, Bysshe, who passes through his mid- and late twenties in the course of the play, champions the cause of workers, though he is the son of an aristocrat. He is a teetotaler and fights for the rights of women, yet he abandons his first wife, Harriet, to prostitution and takes Mary Godwin as his lover. Though he marries Mary after Harriet's suicide, he is never faithful. He sleeps with Claire and, later, a boatman's daughter. Bysshe advocates free love but confesses that he does not feel free. His careless actions cause the death of his first wife and of his daughter Clara. In the end, Bysshe drowns in a boating accident.

George, the Lord Byron, a Scottish Romantic poet. Byron is a talented, flamboyant, and rich profligate in his late twenties and early thirties. He is a priapic bisexual who sleeps with all manner of boys, virginal girls, and married women. He suffers from alcoholism and syphillis. Byron domineers over the other characters in the play, especially the hapless Dr. Polidori. He impregnates Claire then rejects her. He takes their daughter Allegra away from Claire and places the child in a convent, where she dies. While Byron causes pain in the life of anyone who cares for him, he is nevertheless energetic, charming, and devastatingly attractive.

Mary Shelley, Bysshe's second wife. Mary, who is also a writer, is nineteen when the play begins and only twenty-five when she is widowed. She is the voice of reason in the play, handling all the practical details of life while Bysshe follows his dreams. She has a son, William, by him and later a daughter, Clara, who dies on a journey to follow Bysshe to Venice. Mary proposes marriage to the reluctant Bysshe after she learns of his first wife's death, even though she knows that he has been sleeping with the pregnant Claire, who is expecting Byron's child. Mary's practical nature causes her to worry about her family's tenuous financial situation.

Claire Clairemont, Mary's half-sister and Byron's lover. Only eighteen years old when the play begins, Claire is obsessed by her unrequited love for Byron, and she unsuccessfully tries to get him to marry her by bearing his child. Claire, Mary, and Bysshe share a passionate triangular relationship, though it is Mary who weds Bysshe and bears his children.

Dr. William Polidori, Byron's biographer. Puritanical, jealous, vain, highly strung, and obsessed, Polidori follows Byron and Bysshe all over Europe, alternately fascinated and repulsed by their antics.

Harriet Westbrook, Bysshe's first wife and, later, a ghost. Twenty-one, sad, and beautiful, Harriet drowns herself two years after Bysshe abandons her with two children to a life of prostitution. She quotes one of his love poems to her as she throws herself into the Serpentine River. Later, she haunts the stage near Bysshe and comments ironically on his actions.

Pamela Canal

THE BLUE BIRD
A Fairy Play in Six Acts

Author: Maurice Maeterlinck (1862-1949)
Type of work: Play
Time of action: The early twentieth century
First produced: L'Oiseau bleu, 1908 (English translation, 1909)

Tyltyl (tēl·tēl), a woodcutter's son. Dressed in a light-blue jacket, scarlet knickerbockers, and white knee-length socks, he is innocent and naïve. At the beginning, which takes place during Christmas, he notices the abundance of gifts and cakes enjoyed by his rich neighbors. Accepting his situation without rancor and jealousy, he participates vicariously in their pleasures. The Fairy Bérylune appears at night and asks him to seek the Blue Bird needed to cure her ill daughter. Adventurous and courageous, he finds the Fairy interesting and stimulating, and he answers her questions on her grotesque appearance forthrightly and accurately. His good nature prompts him to seek the Bird, and the Fairy arms him with a magic diamond that enables him to defeat possible adversaries. Along with his sister Mytyl, his dog, and his cat, and everyday commodities that are personified (for example, Bread, Sugar, Fire, Water, Milk), he undertakes a journey leading to four successive realms. Though he becomes afraid during his encounter with the Oak and the other personified elements seeking revenge for past human wrongs, he finds the strength and courage to endure pain and to keep his promise to the Fairy. He encourages Mytyl to share the dangers and difficulties of the quest. At the end, he returns to the security of his home. Realistic, he acknowledges his failure to capture the Bird; however, he generously relinquishes his own blue bird to Madame Berlingot, who, in turn, gives it to her daughter. Cured, the neighbor's daughter finds momentary happiness. Yet just as the Blue Bird eludes capture, Tyltyl's bird escapes. Resigned to the situation, Tyltyl recognizes the continual need to seek the Bird. By pursuing the quest of happiness, he is prepared again to undertake a voyage to a deeper understanding of life.

Mytyl (mē·tēl), Tyltyl's sister. Appearing in a Red Riding Hood costume, she resembles her brother in innocence and purity. She loves her family, expressing joy in being reunited with her deceased grandparents, brothers, and sisters. In undertaking the journey to capture the Blue Bird, however, she lacks Tyltyl's resolve and fortitude. During her encounter with Night, she gives in to anxieties, crying and complaining as Tyltyl is about to open the door to the Forest. In contending with nature's elements, she emits horrifying screams, and unlike her brother, appears more human than heroic. The search for the Bird reflects a growth of self-understanding and wisdom: She distinguishes the differences of character between the dog and cat and, like her brother, discovers the secrets of life, the significance of duty and sacrifice, and the elusive and transitory nature of happiness.

Bérylune (bā·rē·lün), a fairy who appears at the end as **Madame Berlingot** (bər·liṅg·ō), the woodcutter's neighbor. Initially, she enters crippled and grotesque, walking with a cane and appearing with a conjoining nose and chin. She asks Tyltyl and Mytyl to capture the Blue Bird needed for the recovery of her daughter, and, giving them a magic diamond, she provides them with a supernatural force to assure their safety. In order to persuade them to undertake the quest, she uses the enchanted jewel to undergo a self-transformation from a hag to a beautiful princess and, then, to instill life into the furniture and other inanimate objects. At the conclusion, she reappears as the neighbor, accompanied by her beautiful young daughter, who is lame. Tyltyl's bird brings about a miraculous cure, which, in turn, induces gratitude from Madame Berlingot.

Tylo (tē·lō), a bulldog personified during the journey. Instinctively, it opposes the character of Tylette, the cat. Consistently loyal to the children, it fights valiantly during the battle with the elements and often shows excessive affection to its masters.

Tylette (tē·lĕt), the cat. Constantly wary of Tylo, the dog, it is hypocritical and independent. It attempts to dissuade the children from carrying out their promise of capturing the Blue Bird, and it informs Night of the children's intention. At the same time, it pretends to help them to locate the Bird. Unlike Tylo, it does not defend them in the battle

174

against the elements, and, as a character contrary to the dog, it seeks to confine and denigrate its natural adversary.

Light, the Fairy's assistant, who guides the children on a journey to insight into life's secrets and the meaning of happiness.

Donald Gilman

BLUE BOY

Author: Jean Giono (1895-1970)
Type of work: Novel
Time of action: c. 1900-1914
First published: Jean le bleu, 1932 (English translation, 1946)

Jean (the Blue Boy), a boy of about seven, when the story opens, who grows to maturity by the end of the book, when he joins the French army in 1914. Jean lives with his mother and father in the Provençal hills at the Italian border. He is the narrator of this fictionalized autobiography, in which he recounts incidents in his life and those around him from a boy's point of view, observing grief, sickness, death, and cruelty, as well as joy and delight. An impressionable, imaginative, solitary child, he spends hours watching people from the windows of his parents' apartment, looking into the windows and doors of the neighbors' apartments, and down into the sheep pen that forms the "courtyard" of the apartment building. Much of his time is also spent in his mother's laundry on the ground floor and in the cobbler's shop of his father on the third floor. Carefully dressed, with a starched white collar and a sky-blue silk tie, he attends the convent school of the Sisters of the Presentation. Much later, when he has become a young man, he gets a job at a bank, where he must wear blue livery, feeling divided into two parts, the one that carries out orders and performs menial tasks, and the inner one, whom he calls "Blue Boy," and who has been taught how to escape into the world of poetry, music, and compassion for the sufferings of others.

Père Jean, the Blue Boy's father, a cobbler and a healer, the real hero of the book. The boy sees many people come to his father's workroom seeking help with problems of all kinds, physical and spiritual. The cobbler welcomes them all without question or judgment and does what he can to relieve their sufferings and enable them to continue their lives with renewed strength and courage. The father keeps cages filled with songbirds. After a long period of yearning and saving, he buys a small plot of land for a garden, where, as he grows old and ill, he sits under the trees he planted and feeds the rabbits. It is here and in the workroom that Jean and his father have their last conversations. The old man speaks his thoughts about living in order to heal and to comfort through extinguishing wounds and composing poetry. If he learns these things, the father says, his son will become a man.

The shepard Massot and
His wife, with whom Jean is sent by his father to live for a year so that the boy can regain his health after a long illness. Jean plays with their shy little girl, Anne, and he spends the summer with "the dark man" who has also been sent by Père Jean to be healed. The two tend the sheep, talk, and immerse themselves in the *Iliad*. Thus, both the boy and the man are healed.

Décidément and
Madame-la-Reine, a violinist and a flutist, respectively. The two brothers share an apartment in the house where Jean lives. Jean's father sends his young son to listen to the musicians, recognizing that for the boy the pleasure of hearing the music is greater than the act of performing it. The two musicians are

175

among the most memorable of the myriad characters who people the book. The death of Décidément occurs shortly after Jean returns from his year at Corbières with the Massots.

Natalie Harper

THE BLUE MOUNTAINS OF CHINA

Author: Rudy Wiebe (1934-   )
Type of work: Novel
Time of action: 1919-1970
First published: 1970

Jakob Friesen IV, a guilt-ridden exile who abandons his son to escape persecution. A brooding, cynical man, Friesen never recovers from his high-handed betrayal of his son (whom he abandoned in Russia), even living among the Mennonite community with which he emigrates. As a hard-hearted immigrant to Western Canada, he spends his life contemplating the paradoxes of the Christian faith and the tenacity it takes to persevere in the middle of suffering and brutality. As one losing his faith in man and God, Friesen poignantly counsels the younger John Reimer toward the end of the novel, tempering with his introspective realism the wild-eyed, radical idealism of the naïve missionary.

Frieda Friesen, a cousin of Jakob, who with the children of other Mennonite immigrants, attempts to make a new life in Western Canada, far away from her parents' native Russia. Her own character is revealed solely through the memoirs that help give the novel its thematic structure. Her journal entries burn with a faith that acts as a calming influence on her family and others caught in spiritual turmoil. Her quiet peace in the face of the temptation to be assimilated by a new, wordly culture in the West rests upon her boundless perseverance and her unshakable faith in God. Her character exemplifies the core of Mennonite faith, particularly their determination to be faithful unto death.

David Epp, a heroic, second-generation Mennonite missionary. Epp's spirit is informed by the lofty faith of Frieda Friesen. A warm, unselfish believer, Epp trades his own life in martyrdom at the Chinese border for the lives of those whom he is helping to emigrate from Russia. Fiercely independent, Epp believes in the impossible; his pioneering, indomitable faith leads him to principle and eternal destiny above earthly comfort and safety. Epp thus becomes a model of missionary fervor to those who emigrate to the West.

Samuel Reimer, an average churchgoer and wheat farmer who suddenly believes he is called by God to be a prophet. After confrontations with the local pastor and his immediate family—who deny God speaks today—Reimer emerges as a tragicomic figure who defies the more prudent of his family members who are incredulous at his announced mission to preach peace to war-torn Vietnam. Wounded by their rejection, Samuel dies of a broken heart.

John Reimer, Samuel's brother, a missionary who travels across Canada with a cross on his back. Youthful, naïve, and idealistic, Reimer returns from a missionary training stint in Paraguay intent on taking the gospel to the secular Canadian culture, with the visual symbol of the cross on his back. His confrontation with the hardened Jakob Friesen IV forms the climax of the novel.

Emily Reimer, Samuel's wife, whose concern for the material prosperity of the household accelerates Samuel's insistence on his own austere prophetic career.

176

Jakob Friesen V, the only son of Jakob IV. He is abandoned by his father in Russia before he is exiled.

Erna Epp, David Epp's wife and, later, widow.

Bruce L. Edwards

THE BLUE ROOM

Author: Georges Simenon (1903-1989)
Type of work: Novel
Time of action: The mid-twentieth century
First published: La Chambre bleue, 1964 (English translation, 1964)

Antonio (Tony) Falcone, a thirty-three-year-old man arrested and tried for poisoning his wife, Gisèle. As three officials question him, he reveals the relevant facts of his life. He is proud to have established his own business selling and repairing agricultural equipment. A devoted family man, he appreciates his wife's homemaking, takes his daughter to church on Sundays, visits his aged father regularly, and vacations with his family at the seaside. Yet, Tony also takes advantage of sexual opportunities. To him and the women involved, these encounters are isolated incidents that entail no obligations. He maintains this attitude during his passionate affair with Andrée Despierre, who, however, is determined to marry Tony, even though he wants to end their relationship. Andrée murders her husband and his wife, and both she and Tony are sent to prison for life.

Andrée Formier Despierre (fôr·myä′ dəs·pē·yĕr′), daughter of a local hero, Dr. Formier. She lives with her mother in the Château in Saint Justin. They are proud provincial bourgeoises who have fallen on hard times; it is obvious that she marries Nicholas Despierre for money. Andrée is a tall attractive woman, with dark hair that contrasts with her white, translucent complexion. Revealing her sexual aggressiveness, she initiates an affair with Tony Falcone. During their eight meetings at the Hôtel des Voyageurs in the blue room, she expresses intense sexuality and possessiveness. She wants Tony to leave his wife and marry her. After Tony makes it clear that their affair has ended, she sends notes reminding him of their relationship. Driven by passion, she poisons Nicholas and Tony's wife, Gisèle. While she is arrested for the first murder, Tony is arrested for his wife's death. At his trial, she brazenly states that his passion for her is as strong as hers is for him, and that he intended to get rid of Gisèle in order to marry her. She is triumphant when the jury sentences both of them to life imprisonment, for she interprets the sentence as their means of remaining together forever.

Madame Despierre, the most respected and wealthiest citizen of Saint Justin. A mean-spirited woman who always dresses in gray, she spends most of her time working in a grocery store, one of her many properties. She grudgingly retires, however, when Andrée, her son Nicholas' wife, comes to work at the store. She reveals the depths of her malicious nature during Tony Falcone's trial for the murder of his wife. Although he is innocent of poisoning her, Madame Despierre tells the court that only Tony had the opportunity to put strychnine into the jar of plum jam. She lies because she wants both the guilty Andrée and the innocent Tony to be punished for her son's death.

Gisèle Falcone, Tony's wife, a small, quiet, and shy woman. After she marries Tony in Poitiers and moves with him to his village of Saint Justin, she contentedly keeps house and helps with his accounts and bookkeeping. Tony appreciates her devotion and at times feels a profound tenderness toward her that he cannot express. Although the villagers do not know her well, they recognize her kindness and are incensed when they find out that she has been murdered.

Françoise, a sturdy peasant woman about thirty years old who has worked in cafés and hotels from the age of fifteen. While employed at Vincente Falcone's Hôtel des Voya-geurs, she reveals her bold and adventurous character by challenging Tony to have intercourse with her. Afterward, their relationship reverts to what it had been originally. This incident typifies the sort of sexual relationships Tony has with many other women and contrasts with his liaison with Andrée.

Frank Ardolino

BLUEBEARD

Author: Max Frisch (1911-   )
Type of work: Novel
Time of action: The late twentieth century
First published: Blaubart, 1982 (English translation, 1983)

Felix Theodor Schaad (shät), a Zurich physician. Schaad is a fifty-four-year-old internist who is accused of brutally murdering his sixth wife, Rosalinde Zogg, by suffocating her and strangling her with his tie. The novel begins three weeks after Schaad has been acquitted of the crime and consists of his reliving the hearing. At the time of the murder, he is remarried to his seventh wife, Jutta. The question whether Schaad is pathologically jealous and capable of violence toward women is continually raised by the prosecuting attorney, but answers are inconclusive. Schaad's philanthropy and public service are pointed out. The doctor emerges as a complex and tormented individual who is perplexed by male-female relationships, particularly in their modern incarnation. After the acquittal, Schaad returns to his medical practice but is unsuccessful in resuming his former life. He tries drink, travel, and billiards, and finally returns to the town where he was born, confesses to the murder, and drives his car into a tree. He recovers from the accident and is told that his confession is false because the murderer, a Greek student named Nikos Grammaticos, has been found and taken into custody.

Rosalinde Zogg (tsōk), Schaad's sixth wife. After her divorce from Schaad, Rosalinde is supporting herself as a call girl, receiving visitors in her elegant and tastefully fur-nished apartment. Books scattered about the apartment suggest that she may be intellectually inclined. Schaad believes her to lack self-confidence, because she did not fulfill the expectations her father, a major, had for her. She was raped by an air force captain, and her first marriage occurred when she was nineteen.

The Prosecuting Attorney, no description of the personality or references to character traits of the prosecuting attorney are discernible. The prosecuting attorney is mentally revived by Schaad as the interrogator of witnesses and himself during his trial for the murder of Rosalinde.

Herr Pfeifer (pfī'fər), a friend of Schaad and a witness. Herr Pfeifer states that he once heard Schaad say he could strangle Rosalinde. Schaad helped Pfeifer complete his studies, supporting him with the sum of twenty-five thousand dollars.

The Son, a witness. The son explains that he believes his father to be egocentric but that he is not a murderer.

Lilian Schaad, formerly **Habersack,** a nursery school teacher. Lilian is the mother of Schaad's son. She testifies that Schaad kept notebooks, often resorting to writing down his thoughts after a marital squabble. She and all other former wives deny that Schaad was ever violent toward them.

Gisela Schaad, formerly **Stamm,** a medical assistant and one of Schaad's wives. Gisela testifies that she and Schaad were closer before their marriage, while Schaad was still married to someone else, than afterward.

Corinne Schaad, formerly **Vogel,** one of Schaad's wives. Corinne complains that Schaad kept her from sleeping with his incessant intellectual lecturing.

Andrea Schaad, formerly **Padrutt,** one of Schaad's wives. She states that Schaad is affectionate but possessive, a trait which led to their divorce. While married to Schaad, Andrea conducted an affair with a married man.

Major Zogg, Rosalinde's father and witness. Zog testifies that Schaad and Rosalinde wished to remain friends after the divorce.

Herr Zogg, Rosalinde's brother. Zogg often saw Rosalinde with eyes red from weeping.

Herr Rossi, a witness. Schaad saved Rossi, who intended to commit suicide, because he listened to him in a kind and patient manner.

Herr Schwander (shvänd'ər), Rosalinde's former husband and a witness. Schwander was a friend of Schaad's and still married to Rosalinde when she and Schaad were having an affair.

Helene Mathilde Jetzer (yätz'ər), formerly **Knuchel,** the first wife of Schaad and a witness. Helene appears to be a mature woman who believes the cause of her divorce from Schaad to be mutual disappointment in the marriage. She is the only one of Schaad's former wives to whom he responds with a gesture indicating good will.

Herr Neuenburger (noi'ən·bûrg·ər), a friend of Schaad and a witness. Neuenburger, who has known Schaad for at least thirty years, makes derogatory remarks about his friend's, and all physicians', intellectual capacities. He enjoys drinking wine with Schaad.

Jutta Schaad (yōō'tə), Schaad's seventh and present wife and a witness. Jutta is a thirty-six-year-old film editor who does not live with her husband, because she had promised herself never again to live with a man. Their marriage ends after Schaad's acquittal, when she announces that she intends to leave him for the cameraman with whom she has been working in Kenya.

Helga Stipa Madland

BLUES FOR MISTER CHARLIE

Author: James Baldwin (1924-1987)
Type of work: Play
Time of action: The 1960's
First produced: 1964

Meridian Henry, a minister in a small Southern town. A civil rights activist, he had urged his fellow blacks to adopt a nonviolent posture in response to threats and violence committed against them by whites resisting changes in the status quo. He had placed his faith in God and a liberal white friend to influence others and effect social change in due time. The racially motivated death of his son causes Meridian to reevaluate his non-aggressive strategy for civil rights. He begins to question God's allowance of the suffering of African Americans and has doubts concerning his white friend's willingness to eliminate the privileged position of whites.

Richard Henry, Meridian's murdered son. Seen in flashback sequences, he is a musician whose attempt to find fame in New York ended bitterly with his incarceration for heroin addiction. In his twenties, he returned to his hometown still resentful of his father's inaction concerning the suspicious death of Richard's mother. To whites, Richard is abrasive, threatening, and too boastful of his sexual prowess, especially in regard to white women. To blacks, he represents a proud, bold young man who refuses to suffer quietly the indignities experienced by African Americans in a racist society.

Lyle Britten, a store owner suspected of murdering Richard. He is a lower-class, uneducated white man who speaks crudely. A family man, he has aspirations of expanding his business to be able to provide better the means to care for and educate his infant son. Though he admires his white wife and is proud to be a racist, he prefers sex with black women. Lyle feels threatened by the unwillingness of Richard to acquiesce to the town's racial social order.

Josephine Gladys Britten (Jo), Lyle's wife. Better educated than her husband, she married Lyle out of love and a desire not to end life as a spinster. She suspects her husband of infidelity and knows that even before Richard's murder Lyle had killed a black man (the husband of his mistress). Still, she staunchly defends her husband's virtue and lies about the events leading up to Richard's murder.

Parnell James, the editor of an unpopular town newspaper. Reared in a wealthy household, he is an iconoclastic middle-aged white man. He labels himself as a liberal but enjoys his privileged racial status. He cannot reconcile his private feelings about the exotic nature of blacks with his public statements claiming no difference between the races. Caught between his friendship with Meridian and Lyle, Parnell claims he wants the conviction of Richard's murderer. He appears unwilling to divulge evidence, however, which would cast doubt on Lyle's innocence in the crime.

Juanita, a college student and civil rights activist. A black woman of strong convictions, she aspires to be a lawyer and use the judicial system as a means to achieve racial equality. Highly attractive, she is desired by Meridian and Parnell but chooses to become Richard's lover.

Joel Davis (Papa D.), a black owner of a juke joint. Though considered an Uncle Tom by blacks, his disclosure that Lyle was the last to see Richard alive forces the authorities to arrest the white man for suspicion of murder.

Lorenzo,
Pete,
Ken, and
Arthur, black college students and civil rights activists. They distrust the judicial system and have little hope for the conviction of Richard's murderer.

Hazel,
Lillian,
Susan,
Ralph,
Ellis,
Reverend Phelps, and
George, friends of Lyle; bigoted and narrowminded white townspeople. They are adamantly opposed to social change, especially that which promotes racial equality.

Addell Austin

THE BLUEST EYE

Author: Toni Morrison (1931-   )
Type of work: Novel
Time of action: 1940-1941
First published: 1970

Claudia MacTeer, the nine-year-old black girl who possesses the most consistent narrative voice in a novel resonant with several different narrative voices, all used to reveal the personal histories of significant characters. Claudia tells the story of Pecola Breedlove as both child narrator, present at critical moments in Pecola's life, and as reflective adult looking back at particular events and signs. Psychologically and emotionally healthy, sturdy, loyal, and compassionate, Claudia and her sister function as dramatic counterparts to Pecola Breedlove. Both girls befriend Pecola and both are apparently the only characters who can feel sorrow or pity for her.

Pecola Breedlove, the novel's tragic unassuming protagonist and ultimate victim. At age eleven, Pecola, her family, and virtually everyone she meets, except the MacTeers, is convinced of her alleged "ugliness." Her lack of self-esteem is generated by the destructive idea that no one values a black child and also by the neglect and contempt heaped upon her by others. A pathetic figure, abused by her parents, denied by other adults, and the target of vicious attacks from other children, Pecola believes that acquiring blue eyes will lessen her loneliness and cause others to see her in an entirely new and more appreciative light. At the novel's close, she has been raped by her father, driven into madness, and into a quest for "the bluest eyes."

Pauline (Polly) Breedlove, Pecola's mother, a maid and frustrated artist who prefers keeping order in the homes of the whites she works for than attempting to do so in her own home. A complex character suffering from both a physical and an emotional disability, Pauline is still a young woman, in her early thirties, when Morrison initially introduces her. She works hard and attends church regularly, yet just as regularly initiates arguments that typically degenerate into fights with her husband, Cholly. Seldom deliberately physically abusive, Pauline is nevertheless an emotionally abusive parent who can neither show love nor demonstrate affection or concern for her own children or her

husband. The only people she nurtures are the whites who employ her. Convinced of her own ugliness by images from the movies, Pauline has internalized this belief, acts it out daily, and has transferred it to her family.

Cholly Breedlove, Pecola's father and the father of the child she bears. Although he has committed incest, Cholly is not a one-dimensional villain. A strong young man despite the trauma of his childhood and youth, Cholly brought his young wife north in an effort to better their lives. Even in Ohio, however, he finds himself frustrated, "burned-out" and embittered by the demands of marriage and the social conditions facing black men. He turns to drinking and fighting with Pauline to escape the limitations surrounding him. He can neither be the dependable romantic hero Pauline wants nor the full economic provider his family needs. His first sin is that he causes his family to be placed "outdoors"; his worst sin is the drunken, but "tender" rape of his daughter.

Frieda MacTeer, Claudia's ten-year-old sister and the more knowledgeable, more mature, and more sophisticated sibling. Frieda knows what menstruation is and is able to explain to Pecola and Claudia that this change in a girl's body permits her to have a baby, as long as the girl has "somebody to love" her. A woman-child, Frieda is the quintessential elder sister who makes most of the decisions about actions and activities she and Claudia undertake. She is also more judicious, knowing when to fight for the protection of another child and what to do when her own rights are about to be violated. Both Frieda and Claudia remain supportive and loyal to Pecola despite her misfortunes.

Micah Elihue Whitcomb (Soaphead Church), a misanthropic odd old man who, despite his antipathy toward humankind, ironically works in professions designed to assist people. Soaphead, so called because of the texture of his hair, emigrated from the West Indies. He collects things and he has a tortured family history that includes a brief marriage. Despite perverse sexual leanings (he is a pedophile), Soaphead was a former Anglican priest; currently, he makes his living as a psychic reader or spiritual adviser and healer. In this capacity, it is Soaphead Church who, for a fee, grants Pecola's wish for blue eyes and subsequently writes a letter to God indicating why he took this action.

Maureen Peel, a newcomer in the town who creates havoc at school. Well-to-do and considered pretty because of her fair skin and long hair, Maureen upsets relationships between children and has a largely negative psychological impact. She is far more acceptable to most adults, to the teachers, and to other students at school than the dark-skinned Pecola. She causes conflicting emotions in the MacTeer sisters, who are jealous of her preferred status, yet who want to be her friend.

Sandra Y. Govan

THE BOARDING-HOUSE

Author: William Trevor (William Trevor Cox, 1928-   )
Type of work: Novel
Time of action: August, 1964
First published: 1965

William Wagner Bird, a boardinghouse owner. He dies in the first chapter and leaves his boardinghouse to two difficult boarders, Nurse Clock and Studdy. His diary provides background on the history of the residents. Nothing in the behavior of the new co-owners or the chaos they create provides a clue about why they were chosen.

E. A. Clock, a visiting nurse, resident, and co-inheritor of the house. Bilked by a charm school when she was young, she is brusque, efficient, and intrusive. Her major focus is in alleviating the pain of the elderly. To that end, she decides unilaterally to turn the house into a nursing home, ordering "undesirables" to locate elsewhere. She is the central intelligence of the novel, being the only one who realizes the nefarious nature of Studdy.

Studdy, alias **Moran,** a petty crook, blackmailer, resident, and coinheritor of the house. He preys on women: an invalid from whom he bilks money; a woman who brings the "meals on wheels"; Mrs. le Tor, whom he sees in a tea shop; and Miss Clerricot, a timid secretary. He writes anonymous letters to terrorize victims, not necessarily for money but for the enjoyment of power over people. He dislikes Nurse Clock so much that he wears a pin in his lapel with which to prick her.

Miss Clerricot, a middle-aged secretary and resident of the house. She innocently goes with her employer, Mr. Sellwood, on a business trip to Leeds. When she discovers he has other ideas, she leaves. Nevertheless, she is tormented by Studdy's saying that her employer's wife is looking for her.

Rose Cave, a middle-aged resident. She is haunted by her dead mother. A gentle soul, Rose cries out often in her sleep. She is flattered that Nurse Clock wants to keep her on as an employee when the house is converted to a nursing home.

Major Eele, a middle-aged resident. His reminiscences about a brief disastrous marriage supply humor. His fantasies about women and Mrs. le Tor in particular are based on his one recreation—viewing pornography in films and magazines.

Thomas Orpen Venables, a forty-nine-year-old resident and office worker. He lives his life in fear of vengeance from the parents of a young woman whom he had gotten pregnant but would not marry. As a result, he suffers severe stomach pains and appears to be dying.

Tome Obd, a Nigerian and a failed law student. For twelve years he has been bringing flowers and love letters to the closed door of Miss Tonks. When she finally confronts him and spells out her rejection of him, he sets fire to the boardinghouse and commits suicide.

Mr. Scribbin, a resident who is a railroad fancier. His only enjoyment is playing phonograph records of trains. Nurse Clock evicts him because of the noise. Someone

(Studdy?) breaks three of his records. For the first time, he stands up to people.

Mrs. Slape, the cook. She is dedicated to her work.

Gallelty, the cook's helper, a Manx girl. One day she had asked Mr. Bird for directions and ended up living in the house, helping the cook.

Mrs. le Tor, a prospective resident. She has a humorous date with Major Eele and is blackmailed by Studdy.

Lila Chalpin

BOESMAN AND LENA

Author: Athol Fugard (1932-   )
Type of work: Play
Time of action: The late 1960's
First produced: 1969

Boesman, a "colored" (mixed-race) South African in his fifties. He and his wife, Lena, wander along the mudflats of a South African river after being driven away from their home by white authorities as part of a slum clearance. The major characteristic of Boesman's personality is how he reacts to this situation. Boesman accepts his and Lena's bleak life with a hardened demeanor. That this dispossession is the latest in a series of such incidents in Boesman's and Lena's lives helps to explain Boesman's cynical personality. His manner is exemplified by his refusal to stop and ponder why he and Lena—or, in fact, South Africa's nonwhites—suffer such a grim fate as his and Lena's represents. Indeed, Boesman believes that asking such questions of existence is futile. He feels it is sufficient to know only the surface of life, merely to endure what life deals him and Lena, and not to question or complain. For these reasons, Boesman is in conflict with Lena, which makes up the major tension of the play.

Boesman's rationale for his feelings that he and Lena must concentrate solely on the

present and not probe into the reasons for the hardships of their existence is that life is solely the present and that the past—or how he and Lena got to the present—is irrelevant. These beliefs are central to Boesman's and the play's development. Indeed, the height of both the play's and Boesman's development comes when he reveals why he holds the beliefs he does about his and Lena's condition. He reveals that a main component of his personality is his disillusionment with the powerless life he has led, believing that his and Lena's lives themselves—and not merely their situation—are futile and meaningless. Thus, the plot of the play hinges on Boesman's reactions to and interpretation of his and Lena's plight and how the two of them clash on these issues.

Lena, Boesman's wife, a mixed-race woman in her fifties. In comparison to Boesman, a major aspect of her personality is her compulsion to ask why their situation is as bleak as it is. One of the major aspects of Lena's outlook on life is her belief in questioning: She clearly believes that in order for life to be worth living, one must examine it. Lena, for example, unlike Boesman, wants to delve into the past, to retrace their steps so she can know how the two of them arrived at their present situation. In addition, another main component of Lena's personality, unlike Boesman's, is that Lena regrets their lack of companionship, both in terms of their relationship with each other and with the outside world. Both in her outlook on their lives and in her desire for human companionship, Lena exacerbates the conflict between herself and Boesman.

Old African, a man of an unspecified age but who is, according to Fugard, the quintessence of old age and decay. He meets Boesman and Lena on the mudflats. His presence is important in showing the futility of Lena's desire for communication with others (he speaks only Xhosa, which Lena does not understand) and in making clear the frustrating nature of humanity's desire to overcome loneliness, for he also wishes to communicate with Lena about his exhaustion, the fact that he is lost, and his own impending death. In addition, the appearance of Old African heightens the conflict between Boesman and Lena. To Lena, the man is a possible link to humanity; to Boesman, he is merely an anonymous and intrusive old black man. The Old African, therefore, serves two purposes: to show Lena's need for human companionship and to develop the tension and contrast between Boesman and Lena.

Jane Davis

BOGMAIL
A Novel with Murder

Author: Patrick McGinley (1937-   )
Type of work: Novel
Time of action: The 1970's
First published: 1978

Tim Roarty, proprietor of a pub in the County Donegal village of Glenkeel. Tall, bearded, and bald, he emits an air of pessimism, considering himself a man of action condemned to an idle existence. A former seminarian, he has been impotent since he was twenty-eight. His wife died seventeen years earlier after giving birth to a daughter, Cecily, to whom Roarty is devoted despite his not being her natural father. When barman Eamonn Eales turns his attentions to Cecily, Roarty sends the girl to London, kills his employee, and buries him in a bog, deeming this murder a triumph of intelligence. His smugness is shattered when he finds himself the victim of a blackmailer who he decides is Kenneth Potter, whom he also attempts to murder. After Roarty accidentally shoots Rory Rua, the dying man reveals he is the blackmailer.

Kenneth Potter, an Englishman living in County Donegal while working for a mining firm. The introspective Potter has become increasingly lonely since turning forty and losing his ardor for his Irish wife, who remains in Dublin. He finds himself revitalized by Irish village life and his affair with Nora Hession. Attempting to become part of the community, he leads the opposition to Canon Loftus' replacement of the wooden altar in the village chapel with a limestone one only to have the priest convince the villagers that Potter's company is exploiting them. Fired from his job, he returns to London.

Nora Hession, housekeeper for the local priest. Intelligent and sensitive, she has been forlorn since being mistreated by a lover seven years earlier. She is transformed by her love for Potter and, when she becomes pregnant, agrees to go away with him until she discovers that he is married.

Canon Loftus, the priest of Glenkeel. A morose man, he blames the miseries of the world on women. He spends most of the week working on his farm with little time for his parishioners. He has had built a new chapel that the villagers think ugly but that conveys for him the austerity of true spirituality.

McGing, the village police sergeant. Headstrong, obstinate, with an inflated sense of his intelligence, he has waited all his life for a mystery only he can solve. Faced with the murder of Eales, he thinks of himself as Sherlock Holmes locked in a battle of wits with a wiley Moriarity, but he always draws the wrong conclusions, deciding the murderer is Rory Rua after it is too late to arrest him.

Gimp Gillespie, a reporter for the *Donegal Dispatch*. He collects news by sitting and drinking in Roarty's pub. Potter's closest companion in Glenkeel, he betrays his friend by changing sides in the conflict with Canon Loftus and by writing an article for a Dublin newspaper attacking the motives of Potter's firm.

Cor Mogaill Maloney, the village eccentric. A young Marxist, he is thought of as an intellectual, since he carries copies of the *Irish Times* and a history of Ireland in his knapsack. His odd behavior includes looking up the exhaust pipes of automobiles, but he is the only one to stand by Potter against the priest.

Rory Rua, Potter's landlord, a lobster fisherman. After Roarty ignores his first blackmail note, he cuts a foot off Eales's corpse and sends it to McGing. He uses his blackmail proceeds to purchase a run-down farm that Roarty has been trying to buy for years.

Eamonn Eales, Roarty's barman and victim. Secretive, sharp-tongued, and overconfident, this vagabond ladies' man from Kerry travels with two predatory black cats. Roarty regards him as the personification of evil.

Crubog, a poor elderly pensioner, owner of the farm Roarty covets. After insisting he will never sell, he enrages the publican when he gives in to Rory Rua.

Michael Adams

THE BONE PEOPLE

Author: Keri Hulme (1947-   )
Type of work: Novel
Time of action: The 1970's
First published: 1984

Kerewin Holmes, the protagonist, a painter. A large-boned woman in her thirties who likes to adorn herself with rings, she lives alone in a tower-house that she has built for herself. In her desire to avoid human contact, she has cut herself off even from her own family. She is kind to Simon, however, when he appears in her Tower and later comes to love both him and Joe, his foster father. Through her involvement with them, she learns her own need for others. At the end of the novel, she marries Joe and establishes a real home for Simon.

Joseph (Joe) Kakaukawa Gillayley, a part-Maori factory worker. A dark-skinned, broad-shouldered man in his thirties, he has a deep, musical voice and an appealing smile. Since the death of his wife Hana, Joe has indulged in alcohol and in brutality, regularly beating his foster son, even though he loves the boy. In the process of the novel, Joe exorcises his demons and commits himself to the Maori tradition, as well as to making a new family with Kerewin and Simon.

Simon P. Gillayley, a child of unknown parentage who was washed ashore from a shipwreck and adopted by Joe and his wife some three years before the time of the novel. A small, thin, sharp-featured boy of about six with a shock of blond hair, Simon cannot speak and communicates by gestures and by writing. His missing teeth and body scars are evidence of the beatings he has endured. An affectionate child, he is, however, a compulsive thief, and he is given to fits of violence and vandalism. Despite Joe's brutality, Simon loves him deeply; after the earthquake, he runs away from a foster home to find Joe. In Kerewin, for the first time he finds a real mother.

James Piripi (Piri) Tainui, Joseph's cousin. A Maori, he is a thin, slight man with large, gentle brown eyes. It is he who picks up Simon from Kerewin's Tower when the boy first appears there. Along with his parents, he is deeply concerned about Joe's abuse of Simon, but he hopes that the problem can be resolved within the family.

Marama Tainui, the mother of Piri. A kind, elderly woman, she has deep maternal feelings for both Joe and Simon. Aware that Joe is beating Simon, she takes the child whenever she can, and she continues to urge Joe to let Simon live with her and her husband, Wherahiko. To Kerewin, Simon confides that he does not want to go to Marama because she cuddles him and weeps about his father, a reminder to Simon of the brutality that he wishes to keep secret. In the celebration that ends the book, Marama is seen surrounded by all of her grandchildren, who can sleep safely beside her. Thus, she represents the ideal of the close Maori family, an ideal that will be attained by Kerewin and Joe in their new relationship.

Tiakinga Meto Mira, an elderly man who considers himself the keeper of the Maori faith. A brittle, shriveled man of seventynine, he has lived for sixty years in an isolated place by the sea, guarding the stone and the rotting canoe that mark the home of the old gods. Having inherited his charge from his grandmother, he has been waiting for his successor. When he rescues and nurses Joe after his suicide attempt, Mira realizes that Joe is that successor and passes his charge to him. Mira also tells of his encounter with Simon's father, a heroin addict, who died there. Relieved of his responsibility for the sacred place, Mira dies and is buried by Joe.

Rosemary M. Canfield Reisman

BONECRACK

Author: Dick Francis (1920-   )
Type of work: Novel
Time of action: The late 1960's
First published: 1971

Neil Griffon, financial consultant temporarily acting as head of Rowley Lodge stables. At age thirty-four, he is attractive and extremely intelligent, and has a highly developed business sense that has allowed him to make a small fortune of his own. He is called upon to look after Rowley Lodge stables, where he grew up, after his father is in an automobile accident. That puts him in direct confrontation with Enso Rivera, who is obsessed with the idea of having his son Alessandro ride the favorite, Archangle, in the Derby. Despite threats from Enso, including attacks on three horses and having his own collarbone brutally smashed, he manages to avoid giving in to this unreasonable demand. Ultimately, he proves himself a success at managing the stable, and he weans Alessandro away from the insane influence of his father at great personal risk.

Alessandro Rivera, apprentice jockey. He

is young, arrogant, and completely self-centered. He decides almost as a whim that he wants to ride the favorite horse, Archangle, in the Derby, despite the fact that his only experience has been riding in a few amateur races in Europe. By using threats, his father has him taken as an apprentice at the stable where Archangle is trained. He offends everyone at the stable. It is only after his father's thugs destroy two horses that he begins to see that his own actions are unacceptable. Realizing that Alessandro really wants to be a jockey, Neil Griffon is able slowly to teach him to be more human and, in doing so, turns his affections from his insane father. As a result of this shift in affection, the father takes action against Griffon that causes the death of another promising horse, his own henchmen and himself, and ultimately leaves Alessandro free to become the outstanding jockey he wants to be.

Enso Rivera, international fence. He is aging, fat, and, as a result of syphillis, driven by an insane megalomania. Despite being extremely wealthy, he does not spend money when a threat will work as well. He believes all he has to do is threaten Neil Griffon and his untrained son will be allowed to ride the favorite horse in the Derby. He is obsessed with the idea of giving his son anything that he wants no matter what the cost to others.

As a result of his obsession, he accidentally sets his own thugs to murder his son while Alessandro is exercising the race horses, thinking it is another jockey. He prevents the murder by killing his own men, and in the fight with them, he is himself killed.

Neville Griffon, owner of Rowley Lodge stables. At the time of the action, he is hospitalized with a broken leg after an automobile accident. At sixty-seven, he is as cold to his son as he always has been and is convinced that Neil knows nothing about running a stable and will destroy his business. He resents it when Neil makes a success of the racing season, but father and son finally come to an uneasy truce on the subject. He dies suddenly of a pulmonary embolus without ever leaving the hospital.

Etty Craig, head stable hand at Rowley Lodge. A woman of forty-three, she is the only female head stable hand at Newmarket, and she has held the position for six years. She values horses above humans, yet it is by using her knowledge and instinct for racing that Neil is able to make a success of the business. At first, she reports everything privately to Neville Griffon, but finally she realizes that Neil knows what he is doing and gives him her full support.

C. D. Akerley

THE BOOK OF BEBB

Author: Frederick Buechner (1926-   )
Type of work: Novel
Time of action: The early 1970's
First published: 1979: *Lion Country*, 1971; *Open Heart*, 1972; *Love Feast*, 1974; *Treasure Hunt*, 1977

Antonio Parr, Bebb's son-in-law. Antonio, the narrator of the tetralogy published as *The Book of Bebb*, is a free-lance writer, high school English teacher, and track coach who wants to write an article exposing the questionable activities of the evangelist Leo Bebb; instead, his life becomes inextricably intertwined with that of Bebb. Antonio is

thirty-four years old when the novel begins, has an Italian mother, and is said to have sympathetic El Greco eyes which attract people and lead them to confide in him. He and his twin sister Miriam were twelve years old when their parents died. On his visit to the Manse in Armadillo, Florida, where Bebb and his family live, Antonio meets Bebb's apparently adopted daughter, Sharon, whom he later marries. Antonio and Sharon move into his Manhattan apartment but later settle in Sutton, Connecticut, where, temporarily, their house becomes a refuge for dislocated family members including, for a while, Leo Bebb himself. Antonio seems to be obsessed with Bebb but never entirely understands him. Possibly because Bebb represents something that is essentially foreign to the educated, eastern Antonio, Bebb fascinates and intrigues him. Basically tolerant and even-tempered, Antonio makes peace with himself and the troublesome Southern family into which he married.

Leo Bebb, an evangelist. Bebb, in his fifties, is a bald, fleshy man who wears a tight, black raincoat and a narrow-brimmed hat. His Church of Holy Love, Inc., of Armadillo, Florida, ordains any male who answers Bebb's ad. Bebb and his assistant, Brownie, also operate the Gospel Faith College, which furnishes advanced theological degrees to applicants who complete its requirements, namely, reading and outlining a number of paperbacks. When Bebb is forced to leave his church in Armadillo because of lewd behavior during the ordination of Herman Redpath, the wealthy Redpath builds for him another church on his ranch in Texas where Bebb holds Sunday services for the Native Americans. After Redpath's death, Bebb no longer is content at the ranch, and he and his wife move in with their daughter and son-in-law. Redpath has left Bebb $100,000, and Bebb eventually starts a church, Open Heart, in Connecticut, which fails to attract a sufficient number of worshipers and mysteriously burns down. On a trip to Europe undertaken by Bebb, Antonio, and Sharon after Lucille's disappearance and subsequent suicide, Bebb meets the wealthy and eccentric Gertrude Conover, with whom he travels around the world and lives in Princeton, New Jersey. A sumptuous Thanksgiving dinner at her luxurious mansion is the site for the beginning of Love Feast, an eating, drinking, and preaching event intended to attract college students. Haunted by the insurance company, which has investigated the burning of

his previous church, and the Princeton police, who are enforcing the campus decision to prevent Bebb from preaching there, Bebb leaves Princeton and goes into hiding. His final gesture is to steal an airplane and, along with Clarence Golden, to buzz the campus, blanketing it with "Love is a Feast" leaflets containing a photograph of Bebb. An accident occurs in which Bebb and Clarence appear to have been killed, but the wreckage is so complete that no sign of their remains can be found. The possibility that Bebb and Clarence purposely staged the accident in order to escape the authorities but bailed out is considered by Antonio, Sharon, and Gertrude Conover. Indeed, they discover a tape with Bebb's voice and drive to the place of his birth in South Carolina where, however, they do not find Bebb but his twin brother Babe. Along with the narrator, the reader discovers that Leo Bebb is a complex character with an unusual zest for life. Although he exploits a system in which fraudulent religious ordination is so easily obtained, this former Bible salesman is not without positive qualities and certainly not without charm. As Gertrude Conover puts it, he was always good company.

Sharon Bebb, the Bebbs' adopted daughter. Sharon is young, willowy, and seductive; she has a sullen, untrustworthy, and self-indulgent face; and her language is ungrammatical and sprinkled with invective. She has a sense of humor, and her wry commentary is a successful counterpart to Antonio Parr's more seriously self-conscious attitudes. Upon being transplanted to the East, the southern young woman suffers a loss of identity and feverishly takes up speed-reading, guitar playing, and yoga so she, too, can be accomplished at something. She has a brief and senseless affair with her husband's teenage nephew Tony, and it remains unclear whether her second child, a girl, was fathered by Tony or Antonio. During the trip to South Carolina, Sharon discovers that Leo Bebb is her biological father and that her mother is the wife of Bebb's twin brother Babe. Sharon, who loves and seems to understand Bebb better than anyone else, takes this discovery in stride.

Lucille Yancey Bebb, Bebb's wife. Lucille, who has brown hair and hazel eyes, is in her mid-fifties. In a drunken stupor brought on by her husband's lengthy and frequent absences during his Bible-selling days, she inadvertently killed her baby and accepted the adoption of Sharon as a substitute. Her days at the Manse in Armadillo are spent sitting in front of the television set wearing dark glasses and drinking Tropicanas. A lonely woman, she claims that Brownie is her only friend. Lucille disappears from Antonio's and Sharon's house and commits suicide in Texas.

Laverne Brown, Bebb's assistant. Brownie, like Bebb, is in his mid-fifties and is convinced that several years ago Bebb raised him from the dead, a feat which has earned the evangelist Brownie's unflinching admiration and gratitude. Brownie prefers colorful clothing, bright sports shirts and shorts that give him a clean look but not a sporty one. Wearing rimless glasses and acting as dean of Gospel Faith College, he takes his duties there and his calling as a representative of Jesus as seriously as his devotion to Bebb. Brownie stays in Texas to carry on the activities of Bebb's church there.

Gertrude Conover, a wealthy and eccentric lady. Gertrude is seventy-five years old when Leo Bebb meets her on a trip to Europe. A professed theosophist, the blue-haired lady unleashes her colorful imagination in fantastic tales of prior existences: She claims to have known Leo Bebb in several previous lives and welcomes him as a soul mate in this one. She is only too happy to have his lively company and not only participates in but instigates several zany episodes that take place. The imperturbable Gertrude Conover is past eighty when she suggests the drive to South Carolina to search for Bebb, suggesting that, if indeed dead, he may have been reborn. She briefly takes a fat and bald baby for the reincarnated Bebb but gives up the idea when there are no definite signs confirming her belief.

Babe Bebb, Leo Bebb's twin brother. Babe

does not share his brother's rhetorical talent nor his charm and seems to be jealous of him. The fact that Leo fathered a child with Babe's wife, while he is unable to impregnate her, has spoiled his life.

Bertha Bebb, Babe Bebb's wife. Having lost her hair as the result of an experiment conducted by Babe, the large and chain-smoking Bertha wears a gray wig. As a young girl she had difficulty choosing between Leo and Babe, and finally married Babe because the Bible-selling Leo was gone too often. Bertha is Sharon's biological mother.

Miriam Blaine, Antonio Parr's twin sister. Miriam's illness, which has confined her to a hospital, is one of the reasons for the narrator's move to New York. She seems to have lost the will to live and eventually dies of cancer. Her apparently unhappy life and painful death greatly trouble the narrator.

Charlie Blaine, Miriam's husband. Charlie is a hypochondriac who spends most of his time sleeping. Unable to care for his two sons after Miriam's death in spite of the fact that he has another woman live with him, he lets his brother-in-law take the boys into his house.

Chris Blaine, Miriam and Charlie's son. Chris is a bookish and poetically inclined young man who takes care of Antonio's and Sharon's young son Bill, while Sharon is taking her various lessons.

Tony Blaine, Miriam and Charlie's son. Tony is primarily interested in athletics. He and Sharon have a brief affair, a fact he confesses to his uncle. Later he marries Laura Fleischmann.

Ellie Pierce, Antonio Parr's girlfriend. Ellie was the narrator's girlfriend before his marriage to Sharon Bebb. Cultured and well educated, she is Sharon's antitype. Ellie does volunteer work at the United Nations and is primarily interested in supporting various social and political causes.

Clarence Golden, a friend of Leo Bebb's.

Clarence was Leo Bebb's cell mate when the latter spent five years in jail for an unrevealed offense. After the Open Heart Church has burned down, it becomes known that Clarence had been jailed for arson. He helps Bebb arrange his escape from Princeton and leads Sharon and Antonio to the hideout where Bebb is staying before the airplane stunt occurs.

Herman Redpath, a wealthy American Indian and Bebb's benefactor. After Bebb ordains him, Redpath becomes the evangelist's major financial supporter.

Nancy Oglethorpe, a free-lance secretary. A single woman in her thirties, Nancy moves to Princeton because of its cultural advantages. She goes astray when her secretarial activities take her to the rooms of graduate students but is saved through Love Feast and becomes one of Leo Bebb's most ardent followers.

Laura Fleischman, a high-school student. Laura, who takes an English class from Antonio Parr, repeatedly appears in his thoughts, particularly when marital difficulties arise. She and Antonio have a very brief affair, and later Laura joins the family as Tony's wife.

Harold Callaway, Gertrude Conover's gardener. Harold, who has been in the employ of Gertrude and her late husband for many years, drives her, Sharon, and Antonio to South Carolina, where racial prejudice is evident in his treatment by Babe Bebb.

Helga Stipa Madland

THE BOOK OF LAUGHTER AND FORGETTING

Author: Milan Kundera (1929-   )
Type of work: Novel
Time of action: 1968 through the 1970's
First published: Le Livre du rire et de l'oubli, 1979 (English translation, 1980)

The Narrator, Milan Kundera, who comments freely about the act of writing, about his own life, about his characters—some of whom are based on real people and some of whom are frankly imaginary—and about the history and fate of his native country, Czechoslovakia.

Mirek, a well-known intellectual and television personality, actively involved in the Prague Spring reforms, a campaign of openness, relative freedom, and rich cultural activity initiated in response to long years of Communist oppression in Czechoslovakia. With the invasion in 1968 of Russian tanks and 500,000 Russian troops, the Prague Spring was crushed. Some half a million supporters of the Prague Spring—Mirek among them—were pushed out of their jobs or arrested, while some 120,000 Czechs left the country as exiles. As the novel opens, Mirek is attempting to recover his youthful love letters, which he wrote to Zdena, who is now as always a fervent supporter of Communist rule and the Russian State. Returning from his unsuccessful attempt to recover the letters, Mirek is arrested in his apartment, and he, his son, and many of his friends are put on trial and imprisoned for antistate activities.

Zdena, twenty-five years previously, a lover of Mirek. An ugly woman, Zdena has never forgiven Mirek for leaving her and has transformed her unrequited love into an unwavering political loyalty to the state and the Central Committee of the Communist Party.

Karel, married to Marketa, has long lived by the slogan, "As far from Mother as possible." Now that his father has died and his mother is old and alone, however, he feels pangs of guilt and so invites her for a week's visit. Dissatisfied with the sexual restrictions attendant upon monogamy, Karel develops a sexual relationship with Eva and convinces her to befriend his wife, Marketa. As the story opens, Marketa has invited Eva for a visit, which coincides with that of Mother, who overstays her welcome.

Marketa, Karel's devoted but jealous wife. She has invited Eva, whom she believes she has met first and introduced to her husband, to spend the day with her and Karel. A *ménage-à-trois* ensues.

Mother, an old woman who has trouble keeping her memories straight. Asked to stay only until Saturday, she pretends to have misunderstood and stays until Monday, and thus is present for Eva's visit and for some strange goings-on.

Eva, a tall, slender, and sexually adventurous young woman, interested only in friendship and sensuality.

Madame Raphael, a teacher of a summer-school course for foreigners in a small town on the Riviera. She has asked her students to present an analysis of Eugène Ionesco's play *Rhinocéros*.

Gabrielle and
Michelle, American students in Madame Raphael's class. For comic effect, they dress up as rhinoceroses, wearing cardboard cones on their noses as they present their analysis.

R., a shy, delicate, and intelligent editor of an illustrated Prague weekly for young people. She has asked Milan Kundera, who has lost the privilege of working after the Russian occupation, to write an astrology column under a pseudonym. Interrogated by the secret police and compelled to reveal Kundera's identity, she warns him, and he leaves the country.

Tamina, a thirty-three-year-old widow, and a waitress in a small café in a small Western European town. A Czech exile, she tries to recover memories of her dead husband, who was fired from his job after the Russian inva-

sion. Denounced and slandered after leaving the country, Tamina's husband dies. Unable to return to Czechoslovakia, Tamina tries unsuccessfully to have her cruel mother-in-law in Prague send her old love letters and notebooks.

Hugo, a café regular, a young writer with bad breath who has published only one article. He tries repeatedly but unsuccessfully to impress Tamina, whose mind seems always to be elsewhere.

The student, a young, romantic, and sexually frustrated young poet and student of poetry who conceives a passion for a butcher's wife. Inviting her to spend the night in his Prague attic apartment, the student learns that he in turn has been invited the same night to the Writers' Club, where the country's best poets will meet. Faced with this painful dilemma, he tries to work out a compromise.

Krystyna, a woman in her thirties, a butcher's wife who has occasional extramarital encounters with a mechanic. Swept off her feet by the charmingly shy student, Krystyna agrees to meet him in Prague.

Voltaire,
Goethe,
Lermontov,
Yesenin,
Petrarch,
Boccaccio, and
Verlaine, the names Kundera ironically gives to the famous poets who argue about women and poetry as they get drunk at the Writers' Club in Prague.

Raphael, an angel who guides Tamina to a boat that takes her to a children's island.

Edwige, the frankly sexual, feminist lover of Jan.

Jan, a forty-five-year-old man who is leaving the country. Before he goes, he wishes to explore the borders of sexuality, for he finds sexuality without borders to cross exhausting.

Passer, a tenacious lover of life and of mankind, he is terminally ill but is a table-pounding optimist to the end.

Barbara, a middle-aged woman who presides impatiently at the orgies she throws at her home for twenty or so invited guests.

Michael Zeitlin

THE BOOK OF LIGHTS

Author: Chaim Potok (1929-   )
Type of work: Novel
Time of action: 1950-1957
First published: 1981

Gershon Loran, the protagonist, a Jewish chaplain in Korea and a student of Cabala (Jewish mysticism). A shy and melancholy man, unkempt and poorly groomed before his metamorphosis in Korea, he is given to having visions and other mystical experiences. Gershon also has a brilliant mind, a fact clear to nearly everyone but himself. His life seems random to him, made up mostly of unlucky chances, and he faces it numbly and without enthusiasm, never really knowing what he wants to do. Keter and Malkuson both want Gershon as a disciple; Keter wins him because Malkuson's Talmud and Bible hold little mystery for Gershon, and Keter sees life as mostly mysterious, mostly posing unpleasant and unanswerable questions. Gershon's unexpected common sense and his willingness to face and accept the dark side of life make him a good chaplain in Korea and a good friend to Arthur Leiden, though Gershon typically does not recognize his own goodness. His successes never remove from him the sense he has throughout the story that he is always waiting.

Arthur Leiden, Gershon's roommate at the Riverside Hebrew Institute and fellow chaplain in Korea, a suave and handsome Bostonian. Arthur's life is dominated by an obsession with his father's role (and, by extension, the role of the Jewish people) in the development of the atomic bomb. His sense of guilt and his wish to atone for it drive him to Korea, whence he can visit Japan: Kyōto, which his mother (an art historian) was in-

strumental in saving from bombing, and Hiroshima, which his father (a physicist) was instrumental in destroying. Formerly a gifted physics student at Harvard, Arthur has turned to religion out of fear; he sees it as safer than science and as less likely to destroy the world. Emotionally very unstable throughout the novel, Arthur dies in a plane crash while trying to return to Japan. A letter from Arthur received by his parents after his death reveals that he has learned acceptance and new hope from his association with Gershon.

Jakob Keter, a visiting professor of Cabala at the Riverside Hebrew Institute and Gershon's mentor. At fifty-five, Keter is tall, trim, and bald, with a long face, bright eyes, and a humorless teaching style; his typical dress is a dark suit and a red bow tie. Having contemplated a career in mathematics or physics when a young man, Keter has given himself instead to the scientific study of Cabala, because he believes it to be the soul of Judaism, "the demonic that leads to life, rather than the demonic that leads to death."

Nathan Malkuson, a great scholar and Gershon's Talmud professor at the Riverside Hebrew Institute. In his fifties, Malkuson is of medium height, with cold eyes and a disdainful smile. Malkuson considers Cabala foolishness and wants Gershon to become a Talmudist because Talmud, the law, is the mind of Judaism, its rational meaning. After Arthur's death and Gershon's return to New York, Malkuson is Gershon's spiritual adviser.

Karen Levin, Gershon's girlfriend. Karen, who has no illusions about her looks, has single-mindedly devoted her life to academic pursuits. She earns a Ph.D. in philosophy from Columbia and teaches at Barnard and the University of Chicago. She would like to marry Gershon but is prevented by his uncertainty about his own life.

Roger Tat, Gershon's first assistant in Korea. Roger's passions are music and his girl back home. Although urged by Gabriel Rosen to find a Jewish assistant, Gershon keeps Roger, a Mormon, and finds him intelligent, efficient, and forethoughtful. Like John Meron, Roger is a significant non-Jew in Gershon's life, helping him avoid the closed-mindedness he so hates in Gabriel Rosen.

John Meron, Gershon's Roman Catholic roommate at the engineering battalion. An electrical engineer, John finds in Gershon a good friend and travels with him to Japan.

Gabriel Rosen, a Jewish medic, Gershon's assistant after Roger leaves Korea. To Gershon, Gabriel represents "road map" religion, "the smug superiority of those certain of salvation." Gershon dislikes Gabriel and what he represents.

Toshie, a young Japanese woman, a geisha, black-haired and beautiful, whom Gershon meets and befriends in a Tokyo club. Toshie acts as translator for Gershon and Arthur on their tour of Japan, which culminates in Hiroshima. In spite of Gershon's carefully platonic arrangements with Toshie, she is upset by a situation wherein she cannot physically repay his kindness to her. Arthur asks Toshie's forgiveness for his family's role in developing the atomic bomb.

Jonathan A. Glenn

BORDERLINE

Author: Janette Turner Hospital (1942-   )
Type of work: Novel
Time of action: The 1980's
First published: 1985

Felicity, an art historian and curator of a private gallery in Boston. Strikingly beautiful with cornsilk hair and slightly uneven eyes, the thirty-three-year-old Felicity has been a magnet for danger and confusion all of her life. She longs for her dead father, avoids committed relationships, and collects newspaper clippings that confirm her suspicion that reality and unreality are never far apart. She is not easily surprised. When she and Gus stumble upon Dolores Marquez, a Salvadoran refugee, hidden in a carcass of beef, they instinctively help her get across the border. This act brings Felicity into the center of an international intrigue, as mysterious figures on both sides try to locate the refugee. As she tries to cope with being stalked, having her apartment ransacked and her car disabled, and answering conflicting pleas for help, Felicity thinks through her own past and tries to find sense in it all. Because she has always been imaginative and introspective, no one takes her story seriously until she disappears.

Augustine (Gus) Kelly, a traveling insurance salesman from Ontario. A middle-aged Catholic with thinning hair and four daughters, Gus drinks too much, talks too much when he is drunk, and is habitually unfaithful to his wife. After he and Felicity smuggle Dolores Marquez over the border, Gus's guilt over his unfaithfulness, his lack of success in business, and his failure to rescue Dolores takes over, and he has drunken visions merging imagery of his wife, Dolores, the Virgin Mary, and various saints. Gus's wife mistakes frantic telephone calls from

Felicity for calls from a mistress and leaves him. Attempting to contact Felicity, Gus calls Jean-Marc and tells him what he knows of Dolores. To rescue Dolores and save his marriage, Gus rents a room in Montreal, where he drinks constantly and eventually finds Dolores again. Trying to take her to safety, he is killed, leaving a large insurance policy for his family.

Jean-Marc Seymour, the narrator, son of Felicity's former lover. Jean-Marc has hated his father since he was ten, and yearned for Felicity in a way that none of them understands. He and Felicity have confided in each other, relied on each other, and it is to him she turns when danger nears. The twenty-five-year-old homosexual piano tuner casts doubt over the story even as he tells it: He admits that he cannot remember the sequence of events; he tells himself different versions of what may have happened; he raises the possibility that he has imagined the entire thing. Trying to piece together the bits and pieces that he can remember (for he never really believed Felicity's story) a year after Felicity has disappeared, he also works through his relationship with his father.

Dolores Marquez, a Salvadoran refugee, known also as **La Salvadora, La Desconocida,** and **La Magdalena.** She has the face of Perugino's fifteenth century painting, the *Magdalena*, with high cheekbones, long dark hair, and dark brown eyes. Widow of a Salvadoran guerilla, she is suspected by both the guerillas and the government of being a spy. She has suffered the murder of her husband and the death of a child born while she was fleeing her homeland. Dolores is either a victim of oppression whose strongest loyalties are to her mother and two surviving children, or a violent player in a deadly struggle—or both.

Cynthia A. Bily

BORN IN CAPTIVITY

Author: John Wain (1925-   )
Type of work: Novel
Time of action: The late 1940's
First published: 1953, in Great Britain, as *Hurry on Down* (U.S. edition, 1954)

Charles Lumley, a job-seeker. A young man in his twenties whose appearance is as unimpressive as his university degree, Lumley has no money and no idea what to do with his life. Highly imaginative, he often defends himself by making up outlandish tales. At other times, when pressed, he abandons his usual apologetic manner and gentlemanly self-effacement to become verbally abusive or physically violent. In his attempt to avoid living up to his parents' expectations, he takes jobs as a window-washer, a driver, a hospital orderly, a bouncer, and a chauffeur before finally becoming a radio gag writer and, despite his best intentions, a financial success.

George Hutchins, a university fellow. In his early twenties, he has a heavy build and a ruddy complexion. Hardworking, humorless, and ambitious, he is ashamed of his working-class parents. To distance himself from his background, he has imitated his professors, acquiring an upper-class accent, a pipe, and the affectation of modesty. His encounters with Lumley always prove disastrous. When he appears at the Braceweight estate as a tutor, he causes an accident that costs Lumley his job as chauffeur and later, angry because of some harmless prank telegrams, frames Lumley for theft.

Veronica "Roderick" or **"Flanders,"** Lumley's beloved. A small brunette in her twenties, she pretends to be the niece of her lover, a wealthy businessman. Because of his love for her and his need for money, Charles gets into drug smuggling. Later, even though

Veronica has returned to her keeper, Charles's memory of her keeps him from proceeding with his wedding plans. When he becomes prosperous, Veronica comes back into his life.

Edwin Froulish, a would-be novelist. Another university acquaintance of Charles, he is plump, untidy, and nervous. Convinced of his genius, he lives on the allowance of his slatternly girlfriend. For a time, Charles lives with them. After Edwin has succeeded as a radio gag writer, he finds Charles a job with his team.

Ern Ollershaw, Charles's partner in a window-cleaning business. A stocky, middle-aged man with missing teeth and a broad Lancashire accent, Ern makes up for his lack of elegance with his loyal and generous nature. He wins Charles's heart by beating up a bully who has attacked him, and later, while he is being led away by the police for involvement in a car theft ring, he makes sure that Charles gets his proper share of the window-cleaning profits.

Bunder, the head of a drug smuggling gang.

A tall, awkward young man with prominent white teeth and a mustache, he dresses expensively. After the police raid his operation, he takes Charles on a high-speed chase. When Charles pulls at the hand brake, Bunder pushes him out of the car, and, as a result, Charles is badly injured and must be hospitalized for some time.

Mr. Braceweight, a rich chocolate manufacturer. In late middle age, he is pale and thin, with a colorless personality. Hospitalized for a tonsillectomy, he meets Charles, who has taken a job as an orderly, and hires him as a chauffeur. Because he is so kind, Charles is extremely unhappy when Mr. Braceweight loses faith in him as a result of George Hutchins' vicious frame.

Walter Braceweight, the son of Mr. Braceweight. Sixteen years old, he is a mechanical genius. It is the vehicle he has invented that crashes into the Daimler. By protecting Walter, Charles loses his job as chauffeur but is therefore free to be employed as a gag writer and to become wealthy.

Rosemary M. Canfield Reisman

BOSNIAN CHRONICLE

Author: Ivo Andrić (1892-1975)
Type of work: Novel
Time of action: 1806-1814
First published: Travnička hronika, 1945 (English translation, *Bosnian Story,* 1958; better known as *Bosnian Chronicle*)

Jean Baptiste-Etienne Daville, a French consul in Travnik. As a representative of French power and civilization, Daville has the difficult task of upholding a semblance of civility in a remote Balkan town ruled by the Ottoman empire. Caught in a constant silent struggle between the other two powers, Turkey and Austro-Hungary, he accomplishes the task adroitly but not without a price to his personal life. He writes an epic poem about Alexander the Great and adores his mentor and idol, Napoleon Bonaparte. Perhaps because of the stifling environment,

but more likely because he is not exceptionally clever and gifted, he fails to develop his intellect fully and to embrace new ideas sweeping Europe. His faith in human values, however, which he saw symbolized in Napoleon, helps him to survive the fall of his idol and keep a decor of civility even when it seems out of place. After his tour of duty, he leaves Travnik battered but not defeated, saddened but not bitter, content with a job well done.

Josef von Mitterer, an Austrian consul in

195

Travnik. Daville's counterpart, von Mitterer is made of a different fiber. Capable and efficient, with an unerring sense of purpose, polite but unemotional, he accomplishes his task unwaveringly. Even though he realizes that Daville represents the Western values similar to his own, von Mitterer seems to enjoy sparring with his French partner, only as a professional, to be sure. Lacking the inner life and mental agility of his French partner and conditioned by his military upbringing and diplomatic vocation, he necessarily sacrifices human qualities to his sense of duty and expediency. Unlike Daville, however, he does it firmly convinced of doing the only thing he is called for.

Mehmed-Pasha, the first of the Turkish viziers. A former slave from Georgia who climbed his way to a high position in the Turkish hierarchy thanks to his natural abilities, Mehmed-Pasha never forgets the power that he serves and represents, yet he always shows a friendly face and a smile, which hide his real thoughts and feelings. When Mehmed-Pasha is replaced after an internal struggle at the Turkish court, Daville feels a personal loss of a polite partner with whom he could talk and do business.

Ibrahim-Pasha, Mehmed-Pasha's replacement as a vizier, the exact opposite of his predecessor. Beset by various illnesses, "a walking ruin," morose and ill-willed most of the time, surrounded by a similarly dispositioned group of assistants (the local people call them "a museum of monsters"), Ibrahim-Pasha is much more difficult to work with, although under this unpleasant veneer Daville discovers a very unhappy man with whom he can still work.

Ali-Pasha, the third Turkish vizier, who turns out to be the worst of the three. Upon taking over, he proceeds to execute all the undesirable elements, such as thieves, gamblers, idlers, and political prisoners. Once his rule of iron hand is established, however, he becomes polite and even seemingly friendly with the two Western consuls. At the same time, neither he nor the other viziers ever forget that the power that they serve cannot hold foreign territories without the rule of iron fist.

Madame Daville, the French consul's wife. Small and frail in appearance, she is a dedicated wife and a determined helper in her husband's difficult task. Her practicality and strong religious beliefs make it easier for her to overcome various misfortunes, such as the loss of a child for lack of medical help. Her gentle nature of simple yet true nobility serves as a beacon of devotion and reason in the midst of a primitive and often hostile environment. She is the most redeeming character in the entire novel.

Amédée Chaumette des Fossés, Daville's assistant. Des Fossés represents a new breed of French diplomats. Much more flexible and open to changes, practical and expedient, he is better suited for the rough-and-tumble world of power-politics.

Cesar d'Avenat (Davna), the vizier's doctor and interpreter. An adventurer and connoisseur of people, Davna is the most colorful, even if less important, character in the novel, befitting its milieu. Born in Italy of French parentage, he travels to many places and serves many masters, and Travnik, with the plethora of races and international intrigue, becomes a perfect stage for him.

Vasa D. Mihailovich

BOTCHAN

Author: Sōseki Natsume (Kinnosuke Natsume, 1867-1916)
Type of work: Novel
Time of action: 1894-1895
First published: 1906 (English translation, 1918)

Botchan, a very impulsive, unsophisticated young man from Tokyo. Sometime after the death of his parents, he accepts a job as a mathematics teacher in a junior high school in a small town on the island of Shikoku. His innocence is repeatedly threatened by the school's rambunctious students, devious and fractious teachers, and cravenly weak administration. His personality and values conflict with those of the small town, and he lasts less than a year at the school. Botchan gets into one scrap after another but leaves with his honor and innocence intact after giving Red Shirt and Clown a well-deserved physical drubbing with the help of his friend, Porcupine.

Kiyo, longtime servant of Botchan's family, who dotes on her young master and wants to keep house for him. She advises Botchan, sends him money, and serves as his mother figure and standard of value.

Badger, the principal of the school. He studiously assumes an air of superiority and encourages Botchan to become a model teacher and mentor. He cannot live up to the ideal he requires of others, however, and is easily manipulated by Red Shirt.

Red Shirt, the school's head teacher, a two-faced man who lies and connives to ruin other teachers and force them out of the school. He engineers Koga's transfer to another school to steal Miss Toyama's love, makes Botchan believe that Porcupine has stirred up the students against him, and involves both Porcupine and Botchan in a stu-dent riot to bring about their resignations from the school.

Yoshikawa, nicknamed **Clown** by Botchan, a drawing teacher who slavishly flatters the educational establishment, Badger, and Red Shirt. He connives with Red Shirt to manipulate Botchan to join their faction.

Hotta, called **Porcupine,** the senior mathematics teacher and Botchan's immediate superior. A physically strong, gruff man with a sense of honor, he befriends Botchan on his arrival but becomes his temporary enemy as a result of the lies of Red Shirt and Clown. His behavior at a faculty meeting gains for him Botchan's respect, as does testimony about him from Mrs. Hagino.

Koga, a mild-mannered English teacher nicknamed **Hubbard Squash** by Botchan because he is pale and fat. Once betrothed to Miss Toyama (the Madonna), he is tricked into allowing himself to be transferred to another, distant, even more isolated school by Red Shirt, who is courting Miss Toyama.

Ikagin, Botchan's first landlord, an antique art dealer who constantly, but unsuccessfully, tries to sell bogus artworks to Botchan and Porcupine.

Mrs. Hagino, Botchan's refined, aristocratic landlady, recommended by Mr. Koga. A local gossip, she informs Botchan of Koga's broken engagement to Miss Toyama and that he is unhappy about being transferred.

Joseph Laker

THE BOYS IN THE BAND

Author: Mart Crowley (1935-   )
Type of work: Play
Time of action: The 1960's
First produced: 1968

Michael, a guilt-ridden, thirty-year-old homosexual whose sole purpose in life is to avoid his feelings. When unable to cope on a daily basis, he escapes into characterizations of past female screen stars. If reality becomes more threatening, he jets off around the world, spending extravagant sums of money he does not have. Until recently, alcohol had been another escape. After selling one unproduced screenplay, he has given up writing and, since he does not have any other source of income, he spends most of his time avoiding creditors. Michael backslides to the bottle when the all-male birthday party he is throwing for his friend Harold is crashed by Alan, his former Georgetown University roommate who is straight and not aware of Michael's homosexuality. Michael grows increasingly hostile to the point of inventing an insidious emotional game bent on hurting and demoralizing his guests.

Donald, a responsible, hardworking gay man who scrubs floors for a living. At age twenty-eight, he views his life as a failure and is committed to therapy. He is an intelligent man and an avid reader. At the birthday party, it is revealed that he has had a one-night stand at a bathhouse with Hank's lover Larry.

Hank, a math teacher in superb athletic condition. Thirty-two-year-old Hank has left his wife and children for a relationship with Larry. Deeply in love, he is frustrated by Larry's unwillingness to be faithful. This tension prompts continuous barbs between the two. Hank becomes the only gay man with whom the straight Alan can relate.

Larry, a commercial artist and Hank's twenty-nine-year-old lover. He has a strong sexual appetite and, even though he confesses during Michael's game to loving Hank more than anyone else, he still cannot promise to be monogamous in their relationship. Although he becomes jealous of the attention that Alan is giving to Hank, he continues to flirt with Donald.

Emory, an effeminate, campy interior decorator. The small, frail thirty-three year old is a somewhat pathetic character. Shunned by mainstream society, he has found a friend in another minority—Bernard, the black man whom he incessantly derides.

Bernard, a library employee in the circulation department. Although he has experienced prejudice by being black as well as gay, he feels more fortunate than the flagrantly effeminate Emory. That is why he allows Emory—and only Emory—to belittle him at times. Yet, as proud as Bernard is, Michael manages to humiliate him during his game. He coaxes Bernard into phoning a white man—a man Bernard has loved since the time he and his mother had worked for the boy's family.

Harold, an unattractive, gay, Jewish man. Harold is thirty-two and it is his birthday being celebrated. With an obsession about his lack of good looks, poor complexion, and fleeting youth, Harold arrives at the party late and intoxicated. He receives a beautiful but moronic male hustler as a gift from Emory.

Alan, a thirty-year-old lawyer with a wife and two daughters. Although Alan is Michael's former roommate from Georgetown University, he is unaware of Michael's homosexuality. When he arrives at the party uninvited, he finds he is the only heterosexual present. Someone as effete as Emory is repulsive to him, and Alan physically attacks him. During the game in which he is compelled to participate, Michael tries to extract a homosexual confession. Instead, Alan calls his wife and pledges his love to her.

Cowboy, a muscular, good-looking, and vacuous twenty-two-year-old hustler. He is Emory's twenty-dollar birthday present to Harold.

Steven C. Kowall

BREAD GIVERS

Author: Anzia Yezierska (1885-1970)
Type of work: Novel

Time of action: The early twentieth century
First published: 1925

Sara Smolinski, youngest of four daughters of Reb Smolinski and his wife. As early as age ten, Sara is intelligent enough to understand the unhappiness and frustration imposed upon her Jewish immigrant family by the poverty and squalor of their Hester Street tenement and the zealous domination of her Old World father. Sara also sees the failure of her sisters to free themselves from the domestic tyranny of their father. With a strong will and sense of purpose, she rebels against the old values and follows her "Americanized" way to personal and social freedom. Her aspirations impel her to leave home and to live on her own wages as a laborer in a laundry. She becomes educated and begins her career as a teacher.

Reb Smolinski, Father, Polish-born despotic zealot and Hebrew scholar who stubbornly applies the literal meaning of the principles of the Torah to life in America. In obvious conflict with the New World values, Reb's religious views make him a selfish tyrant. He insists, as the Torah commands, that his daughters work to support him in his studies. Every penny that they make must be turned over to him; every action that they perform must be geared to his own comfort and needs as a holy man of God. He himself is impractical, unable to survive on his own, totally dependent on his wife.

Mrs. Smolinski, Mother, Reb's wife. She sees the disparity between Reb's ideals and the demands of the new life, but she supports her husband as a dutiful wife. She respects him for his principles, but she is clearheaded about the need for survival and often scolds Reb for his foolishness. Strong and practical (she rents out part of the apartment for income), she is nevertheless sensitive to her daughters' wants, especially to Sara's attempt to succeed.

Bessie Smolinski, the oldest daughter, the first to bear the burdens of "giving bread" (financial support) to the family. If she had any aspirations, she has buried them in the selfless performance of her duty. At her father's behest, she marries Zalmon the fish peddler, a widower with a large family, to whom Bessie becomes a second mother and a drudge.

Masha Smolinski, Sara's beautiful sister. At first, Masha's love of finery and an "American" life-style keeps her above the squalor of immigrant life, but ultimately she, like Bessie, accedes to Reb's arrangements and marries a dull, loveless parvenu in the garment business. Though Masha initially "escapes" from the Hester Street tenement, she is no more liberated in mind and spirit than Bessie is in body.

Fania Smolinski, the last sister, delicate and childlike. Her life is ruined when she, like all but Sara, marries a man chosen by her father. The husband turns out to be a gambler, and Fania lives on the verge of starvation.

Hugo Seelig, the principal of Sara's school. A quiet, educated man whose parents came from a neighboring village in Poland, he falls in love with Sara, in whom he sees a kindred spirit. He does not believe Reb's accusations of Sara's familial disloyalty but gains the old man's respect and approval by becoming Reb's pupil and learning Hebrew. At novel's end, Hugo and Sara become engaged.

Edward Fiorelli

BREAK OF NOON

Author: Paul Claudel (1868-1955)
Type of work: Play

Time of action: The 1900's
First published: Partage de Midi, 1905 (English translation, 1960)

Ysé, a wife and mother. Thirty years old, beautiful, and the mother of two children, Ysé is a bundle of contradictions: She is a pragmatist and a dreamer; she is strong and weak; she is free and yet easily controlled. Lonely, fickle, passionate, guilty, and driven, she struggles to find her place in the world and yet remains always aware of the unsuitable nature of each choice she makes.

Mesa, the Commissioner of Customs in China. In his thirties, Mesa is not particularly handsome, of medium height, and rather undistinguished physically. A successful government officer, he is plagued by his awareness of the superficiality of his success. He has attempted to renounce the world to seek spiritual fulfillment but felt rejected by God. A virgin and a loner, he is an unhappy person who has a highly philosophical perspective on life. His meeting with Ysé seems an act of destiny, and the attraction between the two of them is the motivating action for the play.

Amalric, a businessman. Perhaps forty years old, Amalric has no distinguishing physical qualities. He is a realist among a group of dreamers. Though in love with Ysé, he is not controlled by the passion of love. He seeks a means to make money to live comfortably, and he is not controlled by strict ethical or moral codes. In act 3, he is living with Ysé, even though she is legally married to de Ciz and has a child by Mesa.

De Ciz, an adventurer and entrepreneur. Married to Ysé, he is young and adventurous, though without a great sense of personal strength. Although he is intelligent and clever, he is easily manipulated by both Ysé and Mesa because of his need for risk, riches, and success.

John C. Watson

THE BRIDAL CANOPY

Author: Shmuel Yosef Agnon (Shmuel Yosef Czaczkes, 1888-1970)
Type of work: Novel
Time of action: The mid-nineteenth century
First published: Hakhnasat kala, 1931 (English translation, 1937)

Reb Yudel Nathanson, a Hasid (member of a Jewish mystical sect) who has devoted his life to the study of Torah (Jewish sacred literature). An ascetic who has no concern with earthly goods, he wears rags, sleeps on a floor mat, rises early to begin the long day's study and prayer, and eats only to keep body and soul together. At the beginning of the novel, he leaves his town of Brod (Poland) to wander far and wide among Jewish villages to seek a bridegroom for his eldest daughter. Naïve as a child, he is exposed by his journey for the first time to a vast array of people, each with his own story to tell, and he is involved in continuous adventures and misadventures. He finds a moral and a purpose in all things, and all that he sees and hears draws from him an endless stream of commentary and gloss from Hebrew holy books. All problems he lays in the lap of the Almighty, including his total ineptitude in fulfilling the goal of his travels. Through a series of coincidences and fortunate accidents, he arranges his daughter's marriage to the son of a very wealthy man, and he happily returns to his life's work of prayer and study.

Nuta, the drayman, who takes Yudel on his search. Fat and robust, he is as secular as Yudel is religious. As he and his wife are constantly quarreling, he is eager to accompany Yudel for as long as possible and finds no greater happiness than to fill his belly with fine food and drink and to listen to the stories of those they meet on their travels. He is not above an occasional minor theft or deception, but after meeting an old man who is a saint he gradually becomes transformed, establishes a good relationship with his wife, gives up the occupation of drayman, and is appointed inspector of weights and measures.

Frummet, Yudel's long-suffering wife and mother of his three daughters. She and the daughters earn their meager livelihood by plucking feathers to use for pillow stuffing. When her husband disregards her insistence that he must arrange for the daughters' marriages before they are too old, she appeals to the holy Rabbi of Apta, who orders Yudel to fulfill the commandment of the bridal canopy. Near the end of the novel, Frummet discovers the hidden treasure which enables her daughter to match the twelve thousand gold pieces offered by the groom's family as their half of the dowry.

The Old Man, a holy man, one of the Thirty-Six Hidden Saints for whose sake the Almighty preserves mankind. He humbly digs clay for Jewish women to spread on the floors of their homes, and they pay him handsomely in wine, food, and candles. He and his aged wife live in the forest in a booth constructed of the materials of forest and field. His intervention in the decree which prohibits the marriage of minor men allows Yudel's daughter to wed her youthful groom.

Reb Ephraim (ĕ•frä′ĕm), the hospitable, one of scores of people Reb Yudel encounters in his travels. His former poverty leads him to excess in food and drink following his marriage to a wealthy woman. He soon forswears his gluttony and adopts a most spartan diet, interspersed with prolonged fasts. Eventually, he eats only when he can share the bounty of his table with a guest. All travelers and beggars, Yudel among them, are immediately taken to his house and are occasions for rejoicing, for without them Reb Ephraim might have starved.

Reb Vovi Shor, the father of the groom, a wealthy man, practical, efficient, and decisive in word and action.

Reb Yudel Nathanson, a wealthy man from Brod for whom Yudel the Hasid is mistaken.

Lolette Kuby

A BRIEF LIFE

Author: Juan Carlos Onetti (1909-   )
Type of work: Novel
Time of action: The late 1940's
First published: La vida breve, 1950 (English translation, 1976)

Juan María Brausen, the protagonist, who is suffering an existential crisis at the time that both his vacuous job as a Buenos Aires adman and his marriage are dissolving. Outwardly conventional, cautious, and repressed, he considers his life to be a form of death. Inwardly, though, he lives an artist's fantasy life. To save himself from the outer void, he takes on two new identities: an impersonation that he assumes so as to enter the life of the prostitute who lives in the apartment adjacent to his own, and his fictional surrogate, the protagonist of a film scenario that he is alternately writing and imagining over the course of the novel. All three levels of his identity merge ambiguously at the end of his story, when, fleeing with the young man who has independently carried out the murder of Arce's prostitute, Brausen ends up in the imaginary town of Santa María, the setting of the scenario.

Juan María Arce (är′sĕ), the name under which Brausen moves in with Queca, the

201

prostitute, who is unaware that he lives next door as Brausen. He virtually becomes a kept man. A channel for Brausen's repressed violent instincts, he develops a sadistic relationship with Queca and plans to kill her, essentially as a gratuitous act but also because she taunts him as a perpetual cuckold. When Ernesto murders her for his own reasons on the same night that Arce planned to do the job, Arce adopts a protective, paternal attitude toward the younger man, recognizing that Ernesto is in effect a more active part of himself, of the already divided Arce-Brausen.

Dr. Díaz Grey (dē'äs grāē), Brausen's fictional alter ego, a slim provincial physician with thinning blond hair. Díaz Grey, like Brausen, is middle-aged and repressed. He is a bachelor, but is awakened to love by the appearance of Elena Sala in his life. He faithfully accompanies Elena on her quest for a young man whom she wishes to save from desperation. Quite corruptible, Díaz Grey supplies Elena with regular injections of morphine and after her death accompanies her husband to Buenos Aires to procure drugs for illicit trade, without questioning the wisdom of such an endeavor. At the end of the novel, he is newly devoted to a woman, the young violinist, and on the verge of being apprehended by the police with Lagos. Díaz Grey is thus last seen in Buenos Aires, having left behind his fictional habitat, Santa María, and effectively changed places with his creator, Brausen.

Gertrudis (hĕr·trōō'dēs), Brausen's wife, originally from Montevideo, Uruguay, as he is. She has grown corpulent in her maturity, and has had a mastectomy just previous to the action of the novel. She is saddened by both her mutilation and the loss of love between her and her husband. Brausen is put off by her new physical state but also by the routine of marriage that Gertrudis represents. She leaves Brausen and goes to live with her mother in a Buenos Aires suburb. He derives his more seductive fictional character Elena Sala from Gertrudis.

Raquel (r̄rä·kĕl'), Gertrudis' younger sister, twenty years old, still living in Montevideo. Slender, reddish-haired, green-eyed, she gives rise to a nostalgic fascination for youth in Brausen, who seduces her on a trip he takes to her city, although she has recently married. Later, naïvely wishing to make a clean break with Brausen, she visits him in Buenos Aires, but he treats her harshly and orders her out of his apartment. Raquel is visibly pregnant by the time of her visit, one of several signs that her youth is behind her.

Enriqueta "Queca" Marti (ĕn·rē·kĕ'tä kĕ' kä mär·tē'), the diminutive prostitute who lives and works in the apartment next door to Brausen's. Queca's vulgar, chatty vitality paradoxically attracts Brausen-Arce, as do the irreality and inauthenticity of their relationship. She is as insincere as he is, constantly telling him lies about herself. Her only moments of truth and intelligence with him are when she is describing her obsession with "them," invisible spirits who torment her when she is alone. As time goes on, Arce routinely beats Queca, and she verbally abuses him and seems to intuit his desire to kill her.

Ernesto, a tall, bony, dark-haired, impulsive young man, one of Queca's lovers. He finds Brausen-Arce with her in her apartment one night, beats him up, and throws him out the door. Eventually Ernesto kills Queca, and after the murder, Brausen-Arce takes charge of the disoriented young man and attempts to help him escape via Santa María.

Elena Sala, the tall, blonde, married woman with a lewd smile who one day shows up in Díaz Grey's office to get morphine, and who continues to receive it from the doctor, along with his discreet attentions and his devotion. She controls their curious relationship with her self-possessed manner and quiet determination, right up until the night that she gives herself to him sexually and then dies of a drug overdose. Elena's search for young Oscar may be motivated by love in addition to altruism.

Horacio Lagos (ō•rä'syō lä'gōs), Elena's aging husband, a short, pudgy man, formal and tedious in speech and manner, but intelligent, and mysterious in his actions. Setting himself up as a cuckold, he indulges Elena's interest in the young Oscar Owen in Buenos Aires, and then effectively gives her over to Díaz Grey in Santa María when she embarks on her search for Owen in the Argentine provinces. After her death, Lagos organizes the final drug deal as, in his cryptic words, a revenge and an homage. Díaz Grey initially despises Lagos, but in Buenos Aires he sympathizes with him, even though there is evidence that, since no real escape plan has been made, Lagos' revenge is aimed at his companions and himself.

Oscar Owen, known as the Englishman, a tall, elegant, pipe-smoking young man with a thin face and a cocky look who introduced the Lagoses to drugs and acted as Elena's escort in Buenos Aires. Lagos considers him a gigolo, perhaps somewhat effeminate, and insists to Díaz Grey that Owen did not have a sexual relationship with Elena. Owen participates indifferently as driver in the drug deal toward the end of the novel.

Annie Glaeson, a talented teenaged violinist whom Díaz Grey meets during the search for Owen and whom Lagos convinces to accompany him, Díaz Grey, and Owen to Buenos Aires for the drug operation. Her motivation for the trip is not specified, but Díaz Grey transfers his affection from the deceased Elena to the young violinist, and at the end of the novel the two of them walk off slowly and happily into the sunrise of the day when they are all likely to be apprehended.

Julio Stein (hōō'lyō stīn), Brausen's bantering, alcoholic colleague at the Macleod advertising agency, who prides himself on taking life less seriously than Brausen. Stein suggests that Brausen write a commercially viable film scenario, which Brausen never delivers to him but uses as a projection for his own identity crisis. Stein also warns Brausen that Macleod is about to fire him.

Miriam, also called **Mami** (mé'ryäm, mä'mē), a sentimental, fifty-year-old French prostitute and madam, still beautiful, with whom Stein has been involved since he was twenty and she was thirty-five. Mami is nostalgic for Paris; she sings chansons and pores over the street map of the French capital. One of her songs gives the novel its title: "La vie est brève."

Macleod, the ruddy-faced, sixty-year-old North American owner of the advertising agency where Brausen and Stein work. Almost a caricature of the Yankee businessman, Macleod is religiously devoted to his profession, and when he is dismissing Brausen, he recommends that in the future his erstwhile employee forget about himself and give himself completely over to business.

John Deredita

A BRIGHTER SUN

Author: Samuel Selvon (1923-   )
Type of work: Novel
Time of action: New Year's Day, 1939, to late 1945
First published: 1952

Tiger, a Trinidadian peasant of East Indian descent. Curious, ambitious, diligent, and determined to become a man, he moves, after an arranged marriage at age sixteen, from a traditional community on a sugar estate to a multiracial village near Port of Spain. Contemplating life's mysteries and dreaming of what education might have afforded him, he sometimes resents the burden of his young family but resolves to understand and control more of his life. Turning from most of the old ways and prejudices toward the ideal of a more integrated society, he learns to read and consciously changes and improves his use of language to prepare for the inevitable changes and opportunities he envisions. He develops a love for his pastoral surroundings but, seeking advancement and contact with a bigger world, obtains employment with the American military constructing a highway. He is fearful of becoming like Sookdeo, but, tense and culturally confused, he drunkenly beats his pregnant wife, causing her to lose their hoped-for male child. Penance paid, in his early twenties he is mature and responsible, a nascent community leader with an uncertain but optimistic view of his and his nation's future.

Urmilla, Tiger's wife. Long-haired and frail with sad black eyes, she is married at sixteen and soon pregnant with a female child. Although she is friendly with her Creole (black) neighbor Rita and would like to laugh and talk with Tiger and share his worries, she is a traditional Hindu wife, passive, obedient, hardworking, and anxious to please.

Joe Martin, a laborer and Tiger's Creole neighbor. Born to a prostitute in a Port of Spain slum and reared by his great-aunt, Ma Lambie, he suffered physical abuse, hatred, and hunger until, at sixteen, he finally beat her in return. Big, strong, and without ambition, he works for the Americans and gives his money to Rita, who tries to moderate his tough, slovenly behavior in a suburban setting. Content in his illiteracy and limited knowledge, he is initially against mixing with his Indian neighbors but, as a result of Rita's influence and his own essential good nature, gradually becomes their friend.

Rita Martin, Joe's common-law wife. Generous, decent, strong-willed, and combative, she lifts Joe and herself above their slum origins and, unable to have children, rears her nephew Henry as her own. Rita ignores racial differences to befriend Urmilla, serving as her midwife and acting as the principal agent in the Indian couple's assimilation.

Ma Lambie, Joe's brutal great-aunt. A large,

frowning, ugly black woman with huge breasts, she is a barren former prostitute who seeks comfort in her old age from Joe, a child abandoned at birth, whom she routinely terrorizes and beats. When Joe hits her, she becomes a cringing and obsequious old woman fervently singing for salvation at roadside prayer meetings. After it becomes clear that she will get nothing from Joe, she turns her hostility and sharp tongue on Rita.

Boysie, an East Indian farmer and friend of Tiger. Familiar with both the country and the city, he is an influence on Tiger and introduces him to the cosmopolitan life of Port of Spain and a broader horizon. An advocate of racial mixing and bored by the village ways, he enjoys shocking traditional Indians by showing off his Creole girlfriend. He saves money to leave for England or America after the war.

Sookdeo, an old East Indian farmer who teaches Tiger to read. Misshapen by work, small, and dark with a gray beard and straggly hair, he is the village drunk and trickster, but his comic antics hide feelings of fear and desolation at growing old and never having a son.

Tall Boy, a Chinese shopkeeper with many children. Popular, fair, clever, and generous, he gives his customers credit and has integrated well into the community, adopting local manners and habits. Hardworking, ambitious, and frugal, he sends money to relatives in China.

Larry and
Chief, two white American servicemen with whom Tiger works. Good-humored, enthusiastic, and naïvely secure in the superiority of their own values, they enjoy the superficial introduction to the exotic foods and customs of poor East Indians that Tiger and Urmilla provide. Ignorant of the dislocation their visit has already caused and relaxed by too much rum, they unwittingly encourage the further breaking of taboos; the result is Tiger's drunken beating of Urmilla.

Douglas Rollins

BRIGHTON BEACH MEMOIRS

Author: Neil Simon (1927-   )
Type of work: Play
Time of action: Autumn, 1937
First produced: 1982

Eugene Morris Jerome, a fifteen-year-old Jewish boy in Brooklyn, New York. Eugene is an enthusiastic, energetic, and persistent boy with a passion for baseball, especially his hometown Dodgers. Newly aware of girls, he is impatient for sexual knowledge and lusts after his cousin Nora. He is young enough to take life and his family and all their problems lightly and clever enough to be very humorous in the process. Nevertheless, he gets blamed for everything and must continually cover his tracks. Behind his innocent cleverness is the sharp and insightful mind of an aspiring writer, and storytelling and entertaining are already basic elements of Eugene's highly expressive manner.

Kate Jerome, Eugene's mother. Kate is an optimistic yet realistic forty-year-old woman. Her belief in God and providence and her determination to find the good in all the bad things that happen are balanced with a xenophobic distrust of anything or anyone not immediately familiar. Her generous and nurturing nature can become overprotective; her capacity to worry and dominate sometimes overwhelms the members of her family. Kate works hard to keep them all going but harbors deep anger and resentment for the sacrifices she must make and the trials she must endure.

Blanche Morton, Kate's widowed younger sister. Blanche is a mournful woman who suffers from asthma and headaches and is gradually losing her eyesight from overwork at her sewing machine. She does her best to rear her daughters but feels woefully inadequate and looks to Kate and Jack for help. Her dependence on them—having housed her family under their roof for three years— feeds her feelings of guilt and powerlessness. Not interested in remarriage, she is content to wallow in self-pity over her undeserved

tragedy until a fight with Kate inspires her to accept some responsibility for her life.

Nora Morton, Blanche's pretty sixteen-year-old daughter. Nora dreams of being a Broadway dancer and is hungry for independence. She misses her father dearly and has come to resent both Blanche's inability to make parental decisions and the excessive attention paid to Laurie's fragile condition. Headstrong and enthusiastic, Nora says what is on her mind.

Laurie Morton, Blanche's thirteen-year-old daughter. Laurie has a heart flutter that makes the family members treat her like an invalid, and she has learned to indulge in their attention and exploit their concern. She studies hard and has no interest in boys yet. Precocious and contrary, she delights in correcting people and meddling tactlessly in their discussions and problems.

Stanley Jerome, Eugene's older brother. Stanley is a sincere and serious young man with a strong belief in principles and a sense of underdog morality. Despite his honesty and good faith, he somehow manages to get himself into trouble, alienating his boss and gambling away an entire paycheck. At eighteen, he is seasoned and wise about teenage lust and proves a good adviser to Eugene. For all his wayward tendencies, Stanley is in awe of his father and generally acts out of selfless devotion to his family's welfare.

Jacob Jerome (Jack), Eugene's father. Between a day job cutting raincoats and a night job selling party favors, Jack is horribly overworked, and his labors have made him older than his forty-two years. Yet at the end of an exhausting day, he is the authority figure to whom all the family members look for guidance, and he manages to deal patiently and sensitively with their various dilemmas. He has both strong ideals and a business-man's sense of compromise; rather than give orders, he offers advice.

B. P. Mann

BRIGHTON ROCK

Author: Graham Greene (1904-   )
Type of work: Novel
Time of action: The 1930's
First published: 1938

Pinkie Brown (The Boy), a frail, seventeen-year-old gang leader. Pinkie's Catholic background makes him haunted by a growing sense of his eternal damnation; still, he wildly hopes that even "between the stirrup and the ground" there is a chance for repentance and salvation. Initially, he sets out with his gang to kill Fred Hale, the man who betrayed Pinkie's mentor to a rival gangster. A sixteen-year-old waitress named Rose sees Spicer, one of Pinkie's men, shortly before Hale's murder and, to have her conceal what she knows of the crime, Pinkie pretends an attraction to her even though he is disgusted by thoughts of sex or physical closeness with Rose or anyone. When he learns from Rose that a woman is inquiring into Hale's death, he acts to solidify his position: He kills Spicer, who was thinking about going to the police, and he arranges a marriage with Rose so that she cannot be forced to testify against him. Increasingly desperate, he takes Rose into the country and tries to talk her into shooting herself by pretending to agree to a suicide pact. Suddenly a fellow gang member arrives with a policeman, and Rose throws away the gun. Pinkie assumes that he has been betrayed. He smashes a bottle of vitriol, his face steaming as the acid blows on him, and throws himself over a cliff to his death.

Fred Hale (Kolley Kibber), the man who betrayed Pinkie's mentor, Kite, to a rival gang leader, Colleoni. Hale has a deep inner humility but an intense pride in his profession. His job at the moment is to pose as a newspaper's Kolley Kibber, a character who leaves cards along a route printed in the newspaper and who pays out cash prizes to people who find the cards and recognize him. Hale is certain that he will be killed during a holiday at Brighton by Pinkie's gang out to revenge Kite's death, but he proudly continues his work nevertheless. As he feared, he is attacked by the gang while he waits for a companion and dies of a heart attack.

Spicer, one of Pinkie's gang. Spicer has twenty-five years' experience in the gangs, having begun before Pinkie was even born. He is easily made nervous and opposes Hale's death from the start. He limps because of a corn on his left foot and has pustules around his mouth, another sign of his nervousness. His job is not to kill Hale, but to take Hale's Kolley Kibber cards and leave them along the route to suggest that Hale continued his assigned work. In planting a card at a restaurant, Spicer is spotted by Rose, a new waitress, who later recalls that Spicer's appearance did not match the photograph of Hale printed in the newspaper. Spicer's restlessness makes him expendable, and Pinkie later kills him.

Ida Arnold (Lily), becomes the amateur detective who probes into the murder of Fred Hale. Ida, a fortyish, coarse, lover of life, is first seen singing in the public bar, where she meets Hale. Unlike Pinkie, Ida has no sense that there is more to life than the here and now. She operates entirely on a temporal and societal plane with a better understanding of right and wrong than of good and evil. Because Hale seemed likable—she was his companion at the time of his death—and because a certain mystery surrounds his death, she investigates to see that justice is served.

Rose, a sixteen-year-old waitress. Rose shares Pinkie's fear of eternal damnation, and she offers him an unselfish, redemptive love. She is also aware that their civil marriage constitutes mortal sin. Her love for Pinkie eventually reaches the point where Ida Arnold cannot reason with her and make Rose see that Pinkie intends to kill her. She is perfectly willing to be damned, so long as she can share her fate with Pinkie. She hesitates in killing herself out of a normal fear of death when Pinkie gives her the gun for their suicide pact. This delay allows others to arrive; Rose is spared, and Pinkie falls to his death from a cliff. At the end of the novel, her final illusion about Pinkie is about to be shattered as she walks home to play for the first time a phonograph record he made for her, on which he has spoken not of his love, as she thinks, but of his hatred.

Glenn Hopp

THE BROWNING VERSION

Author: Terence Rattigan (1911-1977)
Type of work: Play
Time of action: The 1940's
First produced: 1948

Andrew Crocker-Harris, a schoolmaster in an English public school. A failure in both his teaching of the classics and in his marriage, "the Crock," as he is dubbed by his pupils, is retiring for health reasons, one year short of qualifying for a pension. He assumes that since there is precedent, he will be granted a pension. With a reputation for giving students grades that are neither more nor less than they deserve, he seems an anachronism in a time when younger masters curry favor with students. Emotionally repressed, he gives no outward sign of his knowledge of his wife's infidelities, the latest involving Frank Hunter, a popular and younger master. On this, his penultimate day at the private school, he experiences for the first time in many years an emotional release which he describes as the twitchings of a corpse. His pupil, Taplow; his colleague, Hunter; and his replacement, Gilbert serve as catalysts for this release. Confronting his personal and professional failure openly, he breaks down his traditional English "stiff upper lip" and makes hard choices: to leave Millie, to take a position at a crammers' school, and, indeed, to follow rather than precede a popular master in speaking at term-end exercises. In these choices, he has begun to rejoin the human community and gain a self-respect that enables him to face his future with a new dignity. The most famous of Rattigan's many successful failures and patterned after a Mr. Coke-Norris from Rattigan's own schoolboy experience, Crocker-Harris is one of England's best-loved dramatic characters.

Millie Crocker-Harris, the unfaithful wife of Andrew. Bitter about his professional failure and their marital failure, she has been involved in a desultory affair with Frank Hunter. She expresses her contempt for her husband in a grippingly climactic moment when, in the presence of Hunter, she taunts Andrew with the fact that she had witnessed Taplow's mimicking him (Andrew). She reacts even more cruelly to Andrew's emotional display when he receives a gift from Taplow—a secondhand copy of Robert Browning's version of Agamemnon. She describes the gift as a few bob's worth of appeasement for a grade.

John Taplow, a plain, "moon-faced boy of about sixteen with glasses." Entering the

Crocker-Harris flat for a final Greek tutorial, he is soon joined by Hunter, who has arrived for his final farewell to Andrew. The two have an easy, informal exchange, during which Taplow mimics "the Crock." Despite Andrew's reputation for teaching Agamemnon as an exercise in translation, rather than as an exciting story about a woman who murders her husband, Taplow confesses to a sympathy for Andrew. His sympathy is expressed in his inscription in his gift, a quotation from a speech of Agamemnon to Clytemnestra: "God from afar looks graciously upon a gentle master."

Frank Hunter, a ruggedly built younger man with the confident bearing of a popular schoolmaster. Intending for some time to bring his relationship with Millie to an end, he now does so out of anger over Millie's devastating cruelty to Andrew. In an offer of friendship which he convinces the reluctant schoolmaster to accept, Hunter promises to visit Andrew when he (Andrew) is settled in his new position.

Dr. Frobisher, a stereotypical headmaster who conveys to Andrew the rejection of the latter's application for a pension and who only makes matters worse when he attempts to assuage the impact of his disappointing news by suggesting that Andrew precede rather than follow the more popular master as speaker at the end-of-term ceremonies. The latter would be embarrassingly anti-climactic; Andrew refuses.

Peter Gilbert, the young replacement for Andrew. During his visit to look over the Crocker-Harris' flat, into which he and his wife will move, he inadvertently lets slip the headmaster's description of Andrew as the Heinrich Himmler of the lower fifth. Apologizing for the unintentional tactlessness of his comment, Gilbert, like Taplow and Hunter, serves as a catalyst for Andrew's confrontation with his failure to communicate with the young boys. The two men reach an understanding and a human community of which Andrew was in much need.

Mrs. Gilbert, the young wife of Peter. In a marriage only two months old, she seems superficial and immersed in petty concerns, so that Peter reacts harshly to her inaccurate account of what he describes as their sordid encounter, their first meeting. Their marriage seems destined for a fate not unlike that of the Crocker-Harrises.

Susan Rusinko

BRUNO'S DREAM

Author: Iris Murdoch (1919-)
Type of work: Novel
Time of action: The mid-1960's
First published: 1969

Bruno Greensleave, a terminally ill old man. Bruno's illness has disfigured him so that he looks somewhat like the arachnids he studies; his head seems bulbous and enlarged, but his limbs are wasted and thin. Aware that he is dying, Bruno wishes to make amends for the missteps he has made along the way. He wants to reunite with his estranged son, Miles, and regrets that he did not go to his dying wife when she called for him.

Miles Greensleave, Bruno's son. He has been estranged from Bruno since his first marriage to an Indian woman, Parvati. He works as a minor civil servant but considers his vocation to be poetry. He married Diana several years after Parvati's death and lives a quiet, contemplative life. He realizes that he loves Lisa, Diana's sister, who lives with them. He idealizes Lisa, and the loss of her enables him again to write poetry.

Danby Odell, Bruno's son-in-law. He has managed Bruno's printing business since his marriage to Gwen, Bruno's daughter, who has now been dead many years. Danby idolized Gwen, to whom he always felt slightly inferior. Danby takes care of Bruno, who lives in Danby's house. Women find Danby charming, and he has been having an affair with Adelaide for some time before he flirts with Diana and then falls in love with Lisa.

Diana Greensleave, Miles's second wife. She first saw Miles in the market and fantasized that she could assuage his pain. Upon their marriage, she creates for Miles a safe haven and does ease his anguish. She accepts her second place in Miles's heart, Parvati being his great love. She returns Danby's flirtation and is greatly hurt when both Miles and Danby fall in love with Lisa. She tends and loves Bruno at the end of his life. By the end of the novel, she becomes a kind of divine figure, bearing others' pain and watching over them benevolently.

Lisa Watkin, Diana's sister. Lisa had a varied career before coming to live with Miles and Diana. After receiving a first-class degree at the University of Oxford, she taught in Yorkshire and joined the Communist Party. Later, she converted to Catholicism and joined the Order of Poor Clares. After leaving the order, she went to Paris and came down with tuberculosis. She teaches school in the East End of London. Lisa has always been considered the emotionally fragile sister, an image belied by her career. She returns Miles's love but refuses to have an affair with him. To shatter Miles's idealization of her, she has a happy, hedonistic affair with Danby.

Adelaide de Crecy, Danby's housekeeper and mistress. She greatly loves Danby and at first would have agreed to an affair even had he not promised to support her. She is devastated when Danby falls in love with Lisa, and eventually she marries her cousin, Will Boase, amid floods of tears.

Will Boase, Adelaide's cousin. Will is a temperamental, out-of-work actor who is given to violent passions. He loves Adelaide but tries to use her position in Danby's household to gain money. He eventually becomes a great actor.

Nigel Boase, Adelaide's cousin and Will's twin. He works as a nurse to Bruno and is very tender with him. He believes himself godlike and spies on others to gain knowledge about them. He informs Will of Danby's affair with Adelaide and tells Diana that she will watch over others benevolently.

Karen M. Cleveland

BUCHANAN DYING

Author: John Updike (1932-   )
Type of work: Play
Time of action: The 1860's, the Civil War era
First published: 1974

James Buchanan, the fifteenth president of the United States (1857-1861). This three-act closet drama opens in 1868 with Buchanan, a big man in his late seventies, lying on his deathbed at his estate in Pennsylvania. Because of age and decrepitude, he is in an abnormal mental condition. Most of the people who were important in his life appear in his bedchamber as hallucinations. Among the forty-odd characters who make cameo appearances in this biographical pageant are such famous historical figures as Andrew Jackson, Stephen Douglas, James Polk, Jefferson Davis, and Abraham Lincoln. There are also less illustrious people, including relatives and personal friends. Most of those who confront Buchanan accuse him of one fault or another, depending upon their individual perspectives and relationships with the former chief executive. Among the many accusations are that he was a cold, selfish, scheming pettifogger who betrayed his country by conspiring with the proslavery faction on the eve of the Civil War and was mainly responsible for that tragic conflict. From Buchanan's explanations of his various actions during his long period of public service, it becomes apparent that he was an exceptionally hard-working, conscientious, and circumspect if not brilliant man who was just as concerned as his successor, Abraham Lincoln, with preserving the Union. Buchanan dies a lonely, friendless, disappointed old man but a much more sympathetic figure than generally portrayed in the history books.

Harriet Lane Johnston, Buchanan's niece, First Lady during Buchanan's term of presidency. She appears at different ages throughout the play: at first as a vivacious blonde teenager, later as a mature woman, and finally as a stately matron. Buchanan was the only bachelor ever to become a U.S. president, and he chose his intelligent, spirited niece to act as his first lady during his term of office. She was an accomplished hostess and became extremely popular in Washing-

ton circles as well as with the American public. In the play, she serves mainly as an interlocutor to Buchanan in order to bring out biographical material in a conversational format.

Anne Coleman, Buchanan's fiancée. This slender, hypersensitive, aristocratic brunette died at the age of twenty-three. Her death was attributed to "hysteria" resulting from her breaking off her engagement to Buchanan in a fit of irrational jealousy. There were many rumors, however, that she had committed suicide. Her tragic death was the single most important event in Buchanan's life. He told many people that his unrequited love for Anne explained his never having married. Her portrait hangs above the fireplace mantel in the old man's bedchamber. Hostile contemporaries believed he was simply too cold, self-centered, and cerebral a person to engage in matrimony. In the play, he is accused of having been more interested in his fiancée's family fortune than in her person. She appears in his hallucinations to discuss these and other matters of a nonpolitical nature in order to round out the portrait of Buchanan as a human being as well as a politician.

Bill Delaney

BULLET PARK

Author: John Cheever (1912-1982)
Type of work: Novel
Time of action: The 1960's
First published: 1969

Eliot Nailles, a middle-aged chemist turned advertising man whose current project is the promotion of a mouthwash called Spang. He lives in the "village" of Bullet Park, a suburb of New York City, where he works. He loves his wife and son in a desperate and finally futile way, wishing to impart to them a sense of the blessedness of autumn leaves and thunder but not quite knowing how to do so. Baffled by the affluence of Bullet Park, the "modern conveniences" of television, the

liquor, and, finally, drugs, he succeeds in saving Tony Nailles, his son, from Paul Hammer's murderous machinations and in bringing about an apparent return to normalcy on the part of his family. In the book's final paragraph, however, he is drugged and blankly "happy."

Paul Hammer, a middle-aged man who is independently wealthy and who moves with his wife, Marietta Hammer, to Bullet Park and becomes a neighbor of the Nailles family. He appears initially to be eccentric and proves finally to be psychotic. He has traveled through the world in search of images that will lay to rest a constant malaise which he refers to as his *cafard* and *bête noire*. The most prominent of these images is a yellow room, and Hammer eventually occupies such a room somewhere outside the city, but he has it tarnished by his "bewitching" wife, who paints it, after Hammer has lost faith in its ennobling powers. Arrived in Bullet Park, Hammer determines to authenticate himself by some bizarre act. He decides to immolate Tony Nailles on the altar of Christ Church in Bullet Park. Thwarted in this attempt by a chainsaw-wielding Eliot Nailles, Hammer is sent to a mental institution.

Nellie Nailles, the middle-aged wife of Eliot Nailles. She is loved by her husband, principally on the basis of her radiant thighs. She appears initially to be the stabilizing influence in the family but becomes dislocated after going into the city and attending an avant-garde play featuring a nude scene. Nellie returns to Bullet Park and strives to regain her composure but realizes that her composure is possibly contemptible, depending, as it does, upon "shutting doors." Despite her good heart, she is as impotent as her husband is in the matter of helping her troubled son.

Tony Nailles, a high school football player and the son of Eliot and Nellie Nailles. He is addicted to television and later, after his father has flung the television from the house, develops a mysterious ailment that renders him unwilling to leave his bed. Tony is the only character in the novel who appears to be headed in hopeful directions after his cure by Swami Rutuola, but he drops out of the book after being healed and returns only at the end as the would-be sacrificial victim of Paul Hammer.

Swami Rutuola, a black of unspecified age and a self-proclaimed healer. He is the head of the Temple of Light, which is located in the slums of Bullet Park. Commissioned by Nellie Nailles to try to help her son, he does so by teaching Tony to chant what he calls "place cheers" (sentences that invoke healing images of places) and such words as "valor" and "love." The Swami appears to be utterly sincere in his ministrations, and they work. He refuses pay for his services.

Gretchen Shurz Oxencroft, the mother of Paul Hammer. A gray-haired, fiercely blue-eyed eccentric, she lives in Kitzbühel and is afflicted by a sense of the overwhelming mystery of life and by a determination that only an act as radical as a crucifixion will wake the world to life's mystery. She tells her son these things, perhaps influencing his attempt at homicide.

Mildred Hoe, a high school French teacher and a spinster. Miss Hoe constantly fears that she will be brutally raped and murdered. In a conference with Tony Nailles about his poor performance in French, she is told by Tony that he could kill her if he wished. She screams for help, says that she has been threatened, and presses charges. After several harrowing hours in the police station, Tony is released into his father's custody.

Marietta Hammer, the middle-aged, beautiful, blonde wife of Paul Hammer. She refers to her husband as a "henpecked doormat" and prophesies that he will never find what he is looking for but will, rather, always be lonely.

Mrs. Emma Hubbard, a thirty-year-old war widow. She meets Tony Nailles at a bookstore, and they subsequently spend a night together. The next day Mrs. Hubbard and Tony have a rather uneasy lunch with Tony's parents, after which Tony promises his father, in Mrs. Hubbard's absence, never to do anything so unseemly again.

Johnny Wink

BURGER'S DAUGHTER

Author: Nadine Gordimer (1923-   )
Type of work: Novel
Time of action: 1962-1977
First published: 1979

Rosemarie Burger (Rosa), the daughter of white South African Communists, now seeking her own identity. Rosa is a complex, serious young woman who was reared in a household dedicated to the struggle against apartheid. Both her parents were imprisoned at various times throughout her childhood, and their deaths have now left her emotionally at sea, uncertain whether her identity as "Lionel Burger's daughter" is one she wants—or is able—to live up to. The book's story is that of her slow journey toward self-knowledge and self-acceptance.

Lionel Burger, Rosa's father, a committed Communist activist. Lionel Burger is a hero of the antiapartheid struggle, a well-known figure in whose home blacks and whites are equally welcome. His final imprisonment ruins his health, and he dies in jail. A kind and intelligent man, he leaves a legacy of idealism that is both stifling and overwhelming for his daughter.

Cathy Jansen Burger, Rosa's mother and Lionel's second wife, also a committed activist. Cathy Jansen was a young union organizer when she met and married Lionel Burger. The couple had two children, Rosa and a son, Tony, who drowned as a boy. Like her husband, Cathy's life is dedicated to the fight against apartheid and she, too, is imprisoned several times before her death after a long illness.

Colette Swan Burger Bagnelli (Katya), Lionel Burger's first wife, a former dancer. Katya leaves South Africa and the Communist Party after her divorce from Lionel and is a plump older woman living comfortably in the South of France when Rosa meets her. Warm and sunny by nature, she represents for Rosa the possibilities beyond her life in South Africa.

Conrad, a young student who becomes Rosa's lover. A dreamer with an unstructured life-style, Conrad provides Rosa with a refuge, after her father's death, from her responsibilities as Lionel Burger's daughter. Their conversations force her to reexamine and analyze her childhood.

Bernard Chabalier, a married teacher, Rosa's lover in France. Rosa meets Bernard while she is staying with Katya and falls deeply in love. Although he is married and a father, the two make plans to continue their relationship in Paris, until Rosa decides that she must return to her own country.

Zwelinzima Vulindlela (Baasie), a young African boy taken in by the Burgers when Rosa was a child. Although the two were reared for a time as brother and sister, Baasie is an angry and bitter young man who rejects what Rosa has become when the two meet years later in England.

Marisa Kgosana, the wife of an imprisoned black leader. A proud and beautiful woman, Marisa has been a longtime friend of the Burgers.

Fats Mxenge, Marisa's cousin, a boxing promoter. Fats opposes a total boycott of white society, hoping to arrange fights for his black boxers with white opponents.

Richard Terblanche and
Ivy Terblanche, friends of the Burgers, also dedicated Communists and antiapartheid activists.

Clare Terblanche, Dick and Ivy's daughter. A plain, awkward girl, she has taken the path of commitment avoided by Rosa.

Flora Donaldson, a wealthy white liberal.

Generous in her financial support of the anti-apartheid cause and a close friend of the Burgers, she herself is not on the front lines of the struggle.

Brandt Vermeulen, an influential Afrikaner and apartheid supporter. He helps Rosa obtain a passport for her trip aboard.

Janet Lorenz

BURIED CHILD

Author: Sam Shepard (Samuel Shepard Rogers, 1943-   )
Type of work: Play
Time of action: The 1970's
First produced: 1978

Dodge, in his seventies, very thin and sickly looking, with a chronic cough. He spends most of the play lying on the couch and eventually on the floor, as he gradually weakens throughout the play and dies at play's end, after willing the house and property to his grandson Vince. Dodge has apparently drowned an illegitimate, and perhaps incestuous, child of Halie and then buried him in the backyard, providing the play's title and the source of the family curse, which may or may not be expiated by his own death and the admission of guilt he has made during the play.

Halie, his wife, about sixty-five years old, with pure white hair. At the beginning of the play, she comes down from her room upstairs veiled and dressed entirely in black, as if in mourning. She speaks primarily in monologues, seeming not to notice her family. In the last act, returning after spending the night away with Father Dewis, she has changed, perhaps symbolically, to a bright yellow dress, with her arms full of yellow roses. She is slightly drunk and giddy, more communicative than in the first act, though at the end of the play she returns to her room offstage upstairs.

Tilden, their eldest son, in his late forties. He dresses plainly and has a burned-out expression. Apparently, he has suffered some psychological trauma, only vaguely alluded to, but probably the result of either a trip to New Mexico (and thus perhaps related to his

son Vince, who is on his way out there and apparently comes from there) or else his suggested incestuous relationship with Halie (and thus related to the buried child, his other son). During the play, Tilden's primary action is twice to bring in armloads of vegetables from the backyard, which prepares for the climactic scene at the end of the play when he carries the freshly exhumed body of the buried child into the house.

Bradley, their next eldest son, an amputee. He is a big man with muscular arms and shoulders, developed from using crutches. His left leg is wooden, having been amputated above the knee, and he walks with an exaggerated, almost mechanical limp, accompanied by a squeaking sound of leather and metal from the harness and hinges of the false leg. At the end of the first act, he cuts off the hair of the sleeping Dodge, weakening him further, and eventually replaces him on the couch, but by the end of the play his leg has been taken away by Shelly, weakening him in turn, and he is replaced on the couch by Vince.

Vince, Tilden's son, about twenty-two, a musician. He is visiting his family after six years' absence. At first, he is rejected by the family, but by play's end has come to fit into their bizarre patterns of behavior and has inherited the family house (though perhaps not the family curse), symbolically replacing Dodge as the patriarch and taking over his position on the couch.

Shelly, Vince's girlfriend, nineteen and beautiful. Unlike Vince, she at first seems to fit into the family and to be accepted by them. By the end of the play, having elicited the story of the buried child from Dodge and become a witness to Vince's altered behavior, she rejects the role she has been forced into and leaves.

Father Dewis, a Protestant minister, a distinguished looking gray-haired man in his sixties, evidently having an affair with Halie.

William Nelles

BURMESE DAYS

Author: George Orwell (Eric Arthur Blair, 1903-1950)
Type of work: Novel
Time of action: 1926
First published: 1934

John Flory, a timber merchant stationed in the village of Kyauktada in Upper Burma. Now about thirty-five and with a face stained by a prominent birthmark, Flory seems destined to a lonely bachelorhood in the insular company of the few other British subjects of the area. Like them, he spends much of his time living the life of the "pukka sahib," the loyal representative of British values and European styles of living. Like them he spends much of his spare time drinking and gossiping at the British Club. Flory is sensitive and observant, however, and, unlike most of his bigoted countrymen in Upper Burma, he has a genuine respect for oriental culture. He counts the Indian Doctor Veraswami as one of his closest friends and even proposes him for membership in the British Club. When Elizabeth Lackersteen arrives at the village seeking a husband, Flory hopes that he has found a soul mate. Her rejection of him ultimately precipitates his suicide.

Elizabeth Lackersteen, the orphan of a bankrupt drunkard, who has come to Burma to find a suitable husband. At twenty-two she is pretty and stylish but superficial and self-absorbed. At first her eagerness to find a mate makes her receptive to Flory's attentions, but she always distrusts his interest in native culture, and Lieutenant Verrall's interest in her, coupled with rumors of Flory's Burmese mistress, make her quickly drop him. Heeding her aunt's warnings about the fates of obstinate women who refuse to accept able offers of marriage while in the East, Elizabeth marries Mr. Macgregor when Verrall decamps.

U Po Kyin, Subdivisional Magistrate of Kyauktada. A grossly fat man of fifty-six, he has made a career of corruption as a parasite of the British. A lifelong lover of politics and power, during the novel's action his main attention is given to anonymous attacks of Dr. Veraswami and to the secret backing of a native rebellion in Thongwa Village, actions he takes in order to secure himself an invitation to join the British Club as its first native member. He expects to make himself look a hero by putting down the rebellion and by discrediting his only serious rival.

Doctor Veraswami, an Indian physician, the only doctor in Kyauktada. He also superintends the jail. A small, plump black man, Veraswami treasures Flory's friendship and maintains a high regard for Europeans in the face of their repeated insults to his race. As a physician who treats Europeans, he is the most likely candidate for native membership in the British Club and thus has become the object of U Po Kyin's slanderous anonymous letters. When Flory's death deprives him of his only European friend and defender, the main source of his status, his ruin has been accomplished as he has foreseen all along.

The Honourable Lieutenant Verrall, a polo player and Military Policeman. Burdened by his debts, Verrall has moved to the Indian Army from a British Cavalry unit because it is cheaper and less demanding of his time, which he prefers to spend on polo. He despises all things oriental and insults everyone who does not share his regard for physical fitness. His evening rides with Elizabeth become a sort of courtship which is nonetheless scuttled when he leaves Kyauktada to escape his debtors.

Ma Hla May, Flory's beautiful Burmese mistress. In her early twenties, she enjoys her life as a European's mistress and the clothes and gifts it involves, even though she has little fondness for Flory. When Flory discharges her to protect his tenuous relationship with Elizabeth, her pride is hurt, and U Po Kyin easily persuades her to try to blackmail Flory.

Mr. Macgregor, the British Deputy Commissioner to Kyauktada and the model of the pukka sahib. Bulky, humorless, middle aged, but good hearted, Macgregor's devotion to exercise and proper behavior makes him stand in sharp contrast to Flory. After Flory's death, Macgregor marries Elizabeth and becomes more humanized.

Ann D. Garbett

THE BURN

Author: Vassily Aksyonov (1932-   )
Type of work: Novel
Time of action: 1970-1973, with flashbacks to 1949, 1951, 1953, 1956, 1961, and 1968
First published: Ozhog, 1980 (English translation, 1984)

Pantelei Apollinarievich Pantelei, also called **Pantik, Academician, Pantelyusha,** and **Pant,** a writer. Forty years old in 1972-1973, he wins at the racetrack, flies to Yalta, and ends up in a sobering-up station. Arrested in Moscow, he shares a dream in jail with the other heroes (Kunitser, Sabler, Khvastishchev, and Malkolmov); their identities merge with one another and with Tolya's.

Aristarkh Apollinarievich Kunitser, also called **Kun** and **Arik,** a forty-year-old physicist and space scientist. He takes Nina Lygher-Cheptsova, his lover, to political meetings at Argentov's.

Samson Apollinarievich Sabler (Samsik), a forty-year-old jazz saxophonist in a Moscow nightclub. He faints during rehearsal and discovers he has emphysema.

Radius Apollinarievich Khvastishchev (khvá'stĭ•shchəf), a forty-year-old sculptor. He invites a cloakroom attendant to pose, then learns the attendant is Lygher.

Gennady Apollinarievich Malkolmov (Genka), a forty-year-old physician who, in 1961, met Masha at a United Nations hospital in Katanga. Summoned to care for the injured Cheptsov, he allows him to die.

Tolya von Steinbock (Tolya Bokov, Anatoly Apollinarievich Bokov), seventeen in 1949, in Magadan, Eastern Siberia, where Tolya lives with his mother and loves Lyudmila Guly. He witnesses his mother's second arrest and Cheptsov's torture of Sanya.

Alisa, married to Fokusov, a seventeen-year-old Magadan camp inmate in 1949. She is a sexually promiscuous Moscow beauty with reddish-blonde hair in the 1970's. When Pantelei confronts her, she chooses her husband's wealth. Blazer says she is in the KGB.

Sanya Gurchenko (Father Alexander), a Catholic camp inmate and carpenter who escapes to the West in 1951. He introduced Tolya to the underground world of "Crimea." As Father Alexander, he encounters Panatelei/Khvastishchev in Rome in 1965-1966.

Patrick Thunderjet, an Anglo-American friend of the heroes. He met Malkolmov and Masha in Katanga in 1961. He spends an evening with Khvastishchev, Toma, and Klara. He and Academician win at a Moscow racetrack and fly to Yalta, where he drunkenly requests political asylum. In 1972-1973, he is at the University of Sussex, England.

Stepan Cheptsov, a retired KGB officer who arrested Tolya's mother and Sanya Gurchenko twenty years earlier. Retired to Moscow, he holds menial jobs to support Paulina and his stepdaughter Nina, whom he rapes. He gets drunk and beats his head bloody before he is taken to the hospital.

Nina Lygher-Cheptsova, Lygher's daughter. In Magadan during the Stalinist era, she is adopted by Cheptsov in Moscow where she lives with him and her mother in 1972-1973. Kunitser's lover, she types for counterrevolutionaries.

Alik Neyarky, a big former ice hockey player. He joins Academician and Patrick Thunderjet at the racetrack and on the flight to Yalta.

Tatyana Nathanovna von Steinbock, Tolya's mother. Arrested in 1937 as a counterrevolutionary, she served ten years in Magadan before being allowed some freedom as housekeeper in an orphanage. In 1949, she is arrested again, by Cheptsov.

Apollinary Ustinovich Bokov, Tolya's father, found in a dream, in his native village of Fanino.

Martin (Philip Yegorovich), a German Catholic political prisoner in Magadan. He lived with Tolya's mother and practiced homeopathic medicine.

Boris Yevdokimovich Lygher, a second cloakroom attendant at the National Hotel in Moscow, where Khvastishchev meets him. His name derives from *la guerre* (French for "war"), making his patriotism suspect.

Paulina Ignatievna, Lygher's wife and Nina's mother. She had been prominent in Magadan society during the Stalinist era. In 1972-1973, she is the mad wife of Cheptsov in Moscow.

Lyudmila Guly, the daughter of a colonel of security forces in Magadan. She scorns Tolya.

Sergeyevich Mukhachov-Bagrationsky (Blazer), a friend to Pantelei, whom he wants to write screenplays for Western consumption. An honorary member of the Moscow police, he has immunity from arrest.

Vadim Serebyanikov, an alcoholic, former friend of Pantelei. Once first violin in an orchestra of "new voices," he is now a solid Party member.

Academician Fokusov, Alisa's husband. He is middle-aged and a famous tractor designer.

Jan Strudelmacher, a blonde, athletic, joking mercenary. In an attack on the United Nations hospital in Katanga in 1961, he tries to rape Masha.

Mademoiselle Marianne Coulagot (Mashka, Masha), a Russian Frenchwoman and Swiss citizen, the beautiful ex-mistress to Kunitser/Sabler/Malkolmov/Khvastishchev/Pantelei, she meets him (them) while riding the streets of Moscow with Patrick Thunderjet. She first met him/them (as Malkolmov) in the United Nations hospital in 1961 in Katanga, where she was a Christian Sister of Mercy.

Silvester, who composes music for Sabler's jazz group and helps Sabler to plan a concert in 1973. With his long hair and mustache, he looks like a Western intellectual, though he once had a 1950's-style crew cut.

Zheka Buzdykin (Fatface), a musician who plays jazz with Sabler. Sabler dislikes him on account of the Czechoslovakia uprising in 1968.

Marina Vladi, a woman who was in the

audience when Sabler played at Leningrad in 1956. She inspires him to musical invention.

Arina Belyakova, Sabler's young lover in Leningrad, where she studied medicine in 1956. In 1973, she treats him for emphysema.

Klara Khakimova, a rich Asian girl from Uzbek and student at Moscow University. She was with Sabler in the Blue Bird in 1970.

Tamora Filchenko (Toma), a KGB agent who meets Academician as Khvastishchev at the National Hotel.

Tinatina Shevardina, a female student of Malkolmov. She meets him for a party and a drive through Moscow.

L. P. Fruitozov (Agent Silicate), who investigates the incident at the Moscow Hotel National.

Silly Zoika, a plump, dark small woman who provides sexual pleasures for Academician, Patrick, and Neyarky at a party in Afanasy's new apartment.

Afanasy Seven-For-Eight, Silly Zoika's fiancé, a songwriter without talent.

Petyusha, a young Party official on the plane to Yalta.

Fyodorich, an older companion of Petyusha's. He looks like Cheptsov.

Natalya, who is lured to Yalta by hopes of a film career but is raped instead. She meets Academician, who gives her money to throw along the beach.

Vitaly Yegorovich Chuikov, the director of the Party sanatorium and commander of children's war games at Yalta. He is a retired major-general who carouses with Patrick, Neyarky, and Academician.

Boris, a Magadan guard who, with Cheptsov, tortures Sanya Gurchenko.

Sergeant Ryumin, who is in charge of prisoners, including Academician and friends, in the Yalta courtroom. He wants more severe punishments.

Aunt Varya, a political prisoner. She is a friend of Tolya's mother in Magadan.

Igor Yevstigneyevich Serebro (yĕv·stĭg·nyĕ′yĕ·vĭch), a sculptor and friend of Khvastishchev's. Interviewed on BBC in 1973 after his defection, he admits he was a KGB agent.

Major Paly, who accompanied Cheptsov to arrest Tolya's mother the second time in Magadan.

Zilberantsev, a medical colleague of Malkolmov's. He knows about the serum, Lymph D.

Nikodim Vasilievich Argentov, a fellow scientist of Kunitser's. In his rooms, a meeting is held for a new political party in Moscow in 1973.

Makkar, a twenty-year-old guitarist for Sabler's new group in 1973.

Grisha Koltun, an army major and Nina's new husband. He had participated in the invasion of Czechoslovakia in 1968.

Richard D. McGhee

BURNING WATER

Author: George Bowering (1935-   )
Type of work: Novel
Time of action: The early 1790's and the late 1960's
First published: 1980

George Vancouver, the commander of the British warship *Discovery*. A short, thickset man resembling a bulldog in appearance and temperament, Vancouver is willful, impatient, and unyielding. He is a strict and capable captain and an almost fanatically precise surveyor who does not believe in the existence of a Northwest Passage. A homosexual, he feels great affection for Admiral Quadra as both a father figure and a lover. Toward the end of the *Discovery's* voyage he suffers severely from tuberculosis and from the emotional trauma of Quadra's death. He hates Menzies because in him he sees a mirror of his own flaws. He prefers warfare to trade and would rather be fighting the French than expediting commerce in the New World.

Archibald Menzies, botanist and surgeon, a civilian passenger on Vancouver's ship collecting plants for the Royal Society. When the ship's doctor falls ill and returns to England, Menzies takes over his responsibilities. Witty, argumentative, and intelligent, he is Vancouver's only intellectual equal on board the *Discovery*, which perhaps accounts for the tension between them. Almost despite himself, Menzies cannot seem to refrain from antagonizing and provoking the short-tempered Vancouver. Menzies takes a scientist's interest in the lands they visit and in the customs of the native people, things for which Vancouver has little patience. When a negligent sailor allows Menzies' painstakingly collected plant specimens to be destroyed during a storm, Menzies, infuriated by the commander's indifference, murders Vancouver.

Don Juan Francisco de la Bodega y Quadra, a Peruvian-born nobleman. Quadra is the naval commander of Spanish-held Nootka. Sophisticated, urbane, and a lavish, luxury-loving host, Quadra is also Vancouver's teacher and homosexual lover.

Lt. Peter Puget, a blunt, rude officer on the *Discovery*, notable for his fierce dislike of and contempt for the natives he encounters.

Joseph Banks, a member of the Royal Society. He is reponsible for placing Menzies on Vancouver's voyage; consequently, he is despised by Vancouver.

John Meares, an unscrupulous trader. He provides the Indians with rum and firearms, which is contrary to British policy. He serves as an emblem of the crass commercialism that motivates much of the exploration of the New World and that Vancouver hates.

First Indian, a young man who fancies himself an artist and visionary. He is eager to be considered a full man of the tribe. Impulsive and imaginative, he initially believes Vancouver's men are a vision, or gods who have sailed from the sun on a giant bird.

Second Indian, older and more practical than the first. He likes to tease and deflate the callow and boastful first Indian. He believes the Europeans are ordinary men. The dialogue between the two Indians serves as an objective if not entirely comprehending commentary on the actions of the Europeans.

First Lieutenant Zachary Mudge, a pragmatic and affable sailor on Vancouver's ship. Clever and forthright, he is one of the few men on the ship who can talk back to Vancouver.

Captain James Cook, commander on Vancouver's early voyages, including one to the Sandwich Isles. Vancouver sees Cook as another father figure. Cook is ultimately killed and eaten by Sandwich Islanders.

The Author, referred to as "he," who narrates the portions of the novel taking place at the time of its writing. He travels from his home in Vancouver, British Columbia, to Trieste, Venice, Guatemala, and South America in an attempt to understand his characters better by familiarizing himself with the places in which they lived. Introspective and solitary, he feels a strong though not uncritical affinity with his protagonist.

Catherine Swanson

BURR

Author: Gore Vidal (1925-   )
Type of work: Novel
Time of action: 1833-1840; and Burr's memoirs, covering 1776-1807
First published: 1973

Aaron Burr, (1756-1836), a Revolutionary War officer, U.S. Senator, investor, vice president of the United States (1801-1805) under Thomas Jefferson, killer of Alexander Hamilton in a duel (1804), acquitted of treason charges of trying to separate the Western States from the Union (1807). The Burr of the plot is seventy-seven, marrying a rich widow who spends the next four years, his last four, suing him; enjoying life in spite of two strokes and continuing financial disasters; and mildly enjoying his reputation as "the hellish Aaron Burr [who] meant single-handedly to disband the United States." Colonel Burr, as he is now called, is "an eighteenth-century man," inspired by the words of Voltaire and the deeds of Napoleon I (who after the trial refused offers of his service), who could still "grin like a randy boy of fourteen." Burr studiously aided and indulged his young protégé, Schuyler, giving no hint of paternity and skillfully avoiding the furious politicking to deny the election of 1836 to Van Buren by associating him with Burr. The Burr of the memoirs is a "Themistocles." His strategy for taking Quebec was correct and ignored and so on through the Revolution and the establishment of the Republic. Even his view of ambivalence on the Constitution was closer to Supreme Court decisions and amendments than Jefferson's position. Burr in the memoirs was never wrong. He could have been elected president in 1800 but chose honor over deals. Of the duel with Hamilton, Burr said, "the principal difference: At the crucial moment his hand shook and mine never does." Burr died without regret "that history, as usual, has got it all wrong."

Eliza Bowen Jumel Burr, Burr's second wife. He called her "Madame." Wealthy, litigious, hoarding treasures and memoirs of a past both sordid and elegant—she claimed intimacy with Napoleon I—she was worthy to be the second Mrs. Burr.

Theodosia Burr Alston, Burr's daughter, named for her mother. A plump, dark girl, she was lost at sea. Madame said that she was the only person whom Burr truly loved. Intelligent and well educated, she corresponded with Jeremy Bentham, whose Principle of Utility is discussed in the novel. She represents a noble side of Burr's character and was, he told Charlie, the cause of the duel.

Charles (Charlie) Schuyler, the narrator of the novel, twenty-five in 1833, Burr's law student and a writer for the *Evening Post*. There, under the pen name "Old Patroon," he achieves local fame. With blue eyes and yellow hair, he is, he wrote, "the caricature of a Dutch lout." He is paid to find proof that Burr is the real father of Van Buren and to write an anonymous pamphlet that will cause Van Buren to lose the election. Burr gives Charlie his memoirs and recollections and, in his way, his love. In 1840, as U.S. Consul in Naples, Charlie learns that Burr was his father and is happy.

Helen Jewett, Schuyler's mistress. He wanted to marry her; she refused, miscarried their son, and returned to Mrs. Townsend's, where she was murdered. She was the sad note in Charlie's life—perhaps everyone has to have a Helen to love but who does not want to be loved.

Mrs. Rosanna Townsend, formerly "one of the gayest," who had known Burr, Hamilton, Eliza, and "everybody." She ran the famous establishment at 41 Thomas Street where Charlie met Helen, read philosophical and religious works such as *Pilgrims*

Progress, and tried to educate Charlie in "real life."

William Legett, Schuyler's editor at the New York *Evening Post*. Age thirty-two, he seemed older as a result of the yellow fever contracted while he was in the navy. He was courtmartialed for dueling. Out to destroy Mr. Biddle's bank, promote free trade, abolish slavery, and help workers' unions, he was helpful to Charlie and Charlie was tolerant of his radicalism.

William Cullen Bryant, editor of the *Evening Post*, in his forties with carved lips and full face whiskers. His New England manner disguised whatever pleasure he found as "America's First Poet."

William de la Touche Clancy, who edited the magazine *America*. An unreconstructed Tory, he found "even the Whigs radical, the Adams family vulgar, and Daniel Webster a *Sans-culotte*." He represents the diversity of the New York press.

Thomas Skidmore, an egalitarian machinist, who made the embarrassing point "until we give each man his due, there is no society but a tyranny of the rich." Many sought their "due" in the West, as Burr foresaw.

Martin Van Buren, (1782-1862), eighth president of the United States (1837-1841). Burr called him "Matty Van." Charlie saw a physical and psychological resemblance to Burr. Taciturn to a fault, Van Buren was a key player with Jackson in the stand against the "Virginia Junto" and the South led by Henry Clay. His election is the focus of the novel.

Andrew Jackson, (1767-1845), U.S. General, seventh president of the United States (1829-1837), he had supported Burr in his Western adventure in 1806, dining him royally at the Hermitage in Nashville; Charlie was later to describe a White House feast that Jackson hosted. In the novel, the question is whether Jackson would live until Van Buren's election.

George Washington, (1732-1799), first president of the United States (1789-1797). In his memoirs, Burr found his commanding officer during the American Revolution inept in war, but unsurpassed in courting junior officers and Congress—a headquarters general who made an appropriate "god" for the new Republic.

Thomas Jefferson, (1743-1826), Secretary of State under Washington, third president of the United States, Burr referred to him as "my sovereign." Burr and Hamilton both called him "Massa Tom." He, not Hamilton, is the villain of the memoirs. Tall and red-headed, he was, Burr wrote, "the ugliest man I have ever seen," an opportunist who slandered as a monarchist anyone who stood in his way. Of brilliant mind, he was more imperialistic than Burr (or Napoleon, whose empire slipped away) and ordered Burr tried for treason in order to retain complete command of the country. He and Burr argued about the Constitution, Jefferson insisting on its perfection, Burr ambivalent.

Alexander Hamilton, (1757-1804), Washington's aide and the first Secretary of the Treasury. As young officers, Hamilton and Burr recognized each other as equals in ambition. Burr regretted killing him because his fortunes were in decline and only death could have made him famous.

James Wilkinson, Commanding General in Western Territories. In 1805 he was fat, soft, vain, over-uniformed, and in Spanish pay. He urged Burr to lead the West in war against Spain, and then, to save his skin, he became the chief witness against Burr.

John Marshall, (1755-1835), Chief Justice of the United States (1801-1835), presided over Burr's treason trial. Always suspicious of his cousin Tom, Marshall prevented Jefferson from using the trial to weaken the judiciary.

James Madison, (1751-1836), fourth President of the United States (1809-1817). "The only true Republican among us," Burr wrote,

"Second fiddle to Jefferson, he played better music."

Washington Irving, (1783-1859), a famous American writer, described as elderly in 1833 though only fifty, stout, shy, pro-Dutch, pro Van Buren. He was sure that Van Buren could not be Burr's son. He disliked James Fenimore Cooper (1789-1851).

Mathew L. Davis, an ancient Burrite, editor, biographer of Burr, Tammany Sachem, split with Van Buren over the bank.

Frederic M. Crawford

BUS STOP

Author: William Inge (1913-1973)
Type of work: Play
Time of action: The 1940's
First produced: 1955

Cherie, an attractive chanteuse, slightly past her prime, who has been singing in a Kansas City nightclub but is now traveling West, allegedly for a film test at a Hollywood studio. She is hotly pursued by Bo Decker, who, having heard her rendition of "That Old Black Magic" at the nightclub where she entertained, was so completely captivated by her that he ended up losing his virginity to her. Now he insists that she must marry him, presumably to make him an honest man. Unsentimental about her fleeting affair with Bo, Cherie does not want to go off to live on Bo's farm in Montana, although, as she considers her options, the prospect of marrying Bo seems possibly to be a reasonable out for her.

Bo Decker, a young, extremely innocent cowboy whose infatuation with Cherie consumes him. He will not leave her alone and is completely dismayed when she does not want to marry him. More financially secure than most of the men Cherie has met, and certainly not unattractive, Bo is really a good catch, but it takes Cherie a while to realize that. Cherie enlists the sheriff's help to keep Bo from pursuing her, but finally she accedes to going to Montana with him.

Virgil Blessing, Bo's surrogate father and traveling companion. Virgil is a lonely man, who has devoted himself to rearing Bo, whose parents are dead. Now that Cherie has come into Bo's life, however, Virgil gives his blessing to their forthcoming union and bows out as they leave together on the bus for Bo's ranch in Montana. Virgil represents pure love, and he ends up—quite literally—being left out in the cold when the bus pulls out.

Dr. Gerald Lyman, an egocentric former professor, given to drinking too much, who now spends most of his time on buses traveling aimlessly from one place to another. As the play develops, it becomes clear that his problem is nympholepsy. He tries to arrange an assignation in Topeka with the teenage Elma Duckworth but finally, in a rare moment of conscience, calls it off and, perhaps for the first time in a long while, does the right thing. Although the audience is never told explicitly that Lyman is in trouble with the law, his concern about getting over the state line as fast as possible suggests that he is running away from something.

Grace, a middle-aged waitress who works long hours at the café where the bus stops on its route from Kansas City West. Grace is good-hearted and unattached. During the play, she sneaks off with Carl, the bus driver, for half an hour, taking him to her apartment above the café. As the play ends, Virgil has no place to go and the town is completely closed up, but Grace has had her satisfaction for the night, so she does not invite the for-

221

lorn Virgil to share her bed, although to do so would have been to provide a reasonable solution for both of them.

Elma Duckworth, a high school student who loves literature and who romanticizes life. Innocent and nubile, Elma is Grace's helper in the café. When Grace goes off with the bus driver, Elma takes over, going from customer to customer and eliciting information from all the passengers on the bus, serving the function of a one-person chorus. She and Dr. Lyman do a scene from *Romeo and Juliet*, and she is about to be drawn into Dr. Lyman's web, but his conscience apparently forestalls their meeting in Topeka.

Carl, the bus driver, who, realizing that the blizzard raging outside will make it impossible for him to keep his schedule, seeks comfort in Grace's bed.

Will Masters, the sheriff, a tall, hefty man with a stubble of beard and a scar on his forehead. Cherie turns to him for protection when Bo's pursuit bewilders her. It is he who first tells Grace that the bus that is about to arrive will not be able to make it to Topeka because the road is blocked by drifting snow. His role is essentially that of a conciliator between Bo and Cherie.

R. Baird Shuman

BUTLEY

Author: Simon Gray (1936-   )
Type of work: Play
Time of action: The 1970's
First produced: 1971

Ben Butley, lecturer in English literature at London University. A childish, irresponsible, disorganized cynic who smokes constantly and drinks heavily, Ben is always quoting Beatrix Potter and T. S. Eliot and ridiculing others with his abrasive wit. Separated from his wife, Anne, he lives with his office mate, Joey Keyston, with whom he also lived before his marriage. Ben tells students that he cannot see them because of his administrative burden, but he declines to speak with his department chairman because he claims to be too busy with tutorials. After a visit by Anne, who reveals that she is going to marry someone else, he also learns that Joey is leaving him. Frustrated at losing both wife and friend, Ben taunts Joey's lover, Reg Nuttall, into striking him.

Joseph Keyston (Joey), Ben's colleague and roommate who began his relationship with Ben as his student. He is Ben's opposite: neat, organized, ambitious, timid. Joey, who is working on an edition of Robert Herrick's poetry, is concerned that Ben's

recklessness will interfere with his promotion in the English department, but he is too frightened of his friend to tell Ben that he is moving in with Reg. Despite himself, he gets caught up in Ben's cynical games, inventing a stereotyped Yorkshire working-class background for Reg. Joey accuses his mentor of attempting to make a mess of his life just as Ben has done for Anne, charging him with spreading futility.

Reg Nuttall, a London publisher. He invites Ben's ridicule by being knowledgeable about food, proud of his time in the National Service, enthusiastic about the Leeds football club, and sensitive about his homosexuality. In addition to stealing Joey away, Reg infuriates Ben by agreeing to publish a novel by the latter's rival, Tom Weatherley.

Edna Shaft, an English literature professor in her late forties. She is upset that Ben has encouraged a student, Gardner, to complain to the head of the department about her dull teaching. She irritates Ben by inducing Joey to move into an office near hers and by finally completing the book on Lord Byron she has been working on for twenty years.

Anne Butley, Ben's estranged wife and mother of their daughter, Marina. Jealous and contemptuous of Joey, she comes to Ben's office to ask for a divorce and to reveal that she plans to marry Tom, whom Ben considers the most boring man in London.

Carol Heasman, a student. She forces Ben to listen to the essay she has written about William Shakespeare's *The Winter's Tale* and is humiliated by his sarcastic response.

Gardner, a slovenly student in a feathered hat and sandals. He wants to study Eliot under Ben but is rejected as being uninteresting.

Michael Adams

BY LOVE POSSESSED

Author: James Gould Cozzens (1903-1978)
Type of work: Novel
Time of action: A September in the 1950's
First published: 1957

Arthur Winner, Jr., a lawyer whose actions and consciousness over forty-nine hours in mid-September make up the content of the novel. He has lived his fifty-four years in Brocton, a small county seat town near the Delaware Valley; he is highly respected in his profession, his church, and his community for his wisdom, capable advice, and willingness to serve. He has been married twice, first at twenty-five to Hope Tuttle, dead in childbirth eight years earlier. Of their children, Warren is dead from a foolish training accident in World War II; Lawrence is a tax lawyer in Washington; and Ann is a teenager at home under the tutelage of Clarissa, his second wife for four years. He has modeled his life on his deceased father, the "Man of Reason," yet his life is tempered by love of family, friends, and Brocton's institutions. In his legal work and personal relationships, he contends with the circumstance into which his clients have been placed by their inability to control (their "possession" by) passions and emotions. At the end of the novel, he struggles with the degree of his responsibility for an adulterous affair with Marjorie Penrose, for Helen Detweiler's suicide, and for consequences of his discovery of Noah Tuttle's illegal acts. Though weary, he resolves that he will continue to pit reason and strength against the tangles of passion, and to be content with inevitable compromises with certainty.

Noah Tuttle, dean of the local law profession. He is eighty-two, grumpy, and failing in health and memory, with strong resistance to the moral standards of the present generation. A distinguished scholar of estate and trust management and for forty years partner of Arthur Winner, Sr., he is now senior partner of the firm of Tuttle, Winner, and Penrose. Since he has been trusted and respected for his administration of many local trusts, it is shocking when it is revealed at the end of the novel that he has commingled money from many trusts with his own account, in personal, well-intentioned, but illegal attempts to protect from financial disaster those who had trusted him.

Julius Penrose, the third partner in the law firm. Since joining the firm thirteen years earlier, he has become Arthur's closest friend; although he is thought hard and cynical by many, Arthur finds their long legal and philosophical discussions very congenial. His paralysis from polio ten years earlier has increased his bitterness about the course of his life. Arthur admires Penrose's courage and sensitivity when he finally reveals that he has kept secret his knowledge of Noah's embezzlements and Arthur's affair with Marjorie, his wife. He convinces Arthur to join him in concealing Noah's misappropriation of funds and in attempting gradually, with luck and skill, to maintain control of the unsavory tangles.

Marjorie Penrose, the wife of Julius Penrose. Possessed by wild emotions, nymphomania, and alcoholism, her seduction of Arthur soon after Hope Winner's death has led to a guilty fear of death and a conversion to Roman Catholicism to structure her penitence.

Mrs. Pratt, a college friend of Marjorie. After twenty years, she has returned to assist in Marjorie's conversion. Her religious beliefs and vicarious interest in the sexual activities of others are distasteful to Arthur, who must suffer the revelation in a long interview that she knows of his affair with Marjorie.

Helen Detweiler, secretary to the law firm. After the accidental death of their parents, she has devoted herself to rearing her younger brother and to serving Noah and Arthur. Now twenty-nine, she is fearful of unpleasantness and uncertainty; when her brother Ralph demonstrates his incapacity to deal with his life, she commits suicide by poison.

Ralph Detweiler, Helen's brother. At eighteen, he is weak, immature, and spoiled by his sister. He has impregnated one girl, Joan Moore, and is accused of raping another, Veronica Kovacs. Although Arthur manages his defense and arranges bail, Ralph steals money from one of Helen's boarders and flees.

Clarissa Winner, Arthur's second wife. Formerly the beautiful, athletic director of a summer camp for Brocton girls and now in her mid-thirties, she has taken over the role of mentor for Ann Winner and reintroduced supportive love in Arthur's life.

Ann Winner, Arthur's daughter. Now fifteen, her growing sexual and social maturity frequently enters her father's consciousness.

Dr. Whitmore Trowbridge, the new rector of Christ Church. He seeks counsel from Arthur, a vestryman, on many matters, including removing the control of the Orcutt trust (which supports the church) from Noah to a Diocesan Investment Trust.

William L. Phillips

THE CAINE MUTINY

Author: Herman Wouk (1915-   )
Type of work: Novel
Time of action: 1943-1945
First published: 1951

Lieutenant Commander Philip Francis Queeg, the captain of the U.S.S. *Caine.* A neurotic officer of mediocre ability, he is not typical of his fellow Naval Academy graduates. He comes to the *Caine* from a somewhat murky background and seems determined, at least initially, to correct whatever has happened in the past to make him a below-average officer. Within a few weeks, however, he shows himself to be an incompetent martinet incapable of seeing the big picture. As a result, he evokes in his officers and men reactions ranging from pity to rage and, finally, to sincere concern for the safety of the ship. During a typhoon, this concern will lead to his relief and subsequent disgrace.

Lieutenant Stephen Maryk, an executive officer of the U.S.S. *Caine* during the mutiny. A naval reservist, he is an officer of excellent potential, typical of the young men asked to hold the line early in World War II. Solid and dependable, Maryk is torn between the requirement of loyalty to a skipper who seems mentally ill and what he perceives is best for the ship. When his sea sense tells him the *Caine* is doomed during a terrible storm, he relieves Captain Queeg of command and saves the ship. Indicted for mutiny, he is acquitted in a dramatic trial but, as is sometimes the way in the service, his career is ruined, and he disappears from the scene.

Lieutenant Thomas Keefer, an aspiring novelist and the communications officer of the U.S.S. *Caine*. Self-satisfied, witty, and urbane, Keefer is the first to suggest that Captain Queeg may be paranoid. Keefer is a petty intellectual who looks down on all career military men and relishes any opportunity to embarrass them. More than any officer in *Caine's* wardroom, he is responsible for the mutiny. Ironically, Keefer becomes commanding officer of the *Caine* after the court-martial and, ultimately, proves that he is a physical as well as a moral coward.

Ensign Willis Seward Keith, a Princeton graduate and volunteer officer. As a young man he has rarely been challenged, but there is in his character a core of hardness that will emerge under the adversity of combat and a neurotic skipper. He initially falls under the spell of Thomas Keefer, but through hard work and natural ability he overcomes the mistakes of inexperience and develops into a competent officer. He will eventually become a party to mutiny, a hero, and the final commanding officer of the U.S.S. *Caine*.

Lieutenant Barney Greenwald, a fighter pilot and lawyer. Greenwald, a brilliant attorney in civilian life, plays a small put pivotal role as defense counsel for the mutineers at their court-martial. He quickly realizes that Keefer is the real culprit in the affair and wants to expose him but is reluctant to use him as a witness. Instead he destroys Queeg, a task he performs with no enjoyment. His flair and skill during the court-martial results in the acquittal of Maryk.

May Wynn, a nightclub entertainer. An uneducated but bright young woman, May provides the romantic interest in a story primarily about men at war. Her alternately hot and cold relationship with Keith is skillfully woven into the novel, but she has no impact on the events of the mutiny or on Keith's service thereafter.

Noel Daigle

CALIBAN'S FILIBUSTER

Author: Paul West (1930-   )
Type of work: Novel
Time of action: c. the 1960's
First published: 1971

Cal, a frustrated novelist working as a hack writer. He has contracted to script a television movie entitled "Geisha from Venus," due to begin production in Japan. At an all-time personal low, he undergoes a tortuous psychological exercise in which he creates a nonstop drama in his head utilizing his traveling companions as actors in a bizarre trio of scenarios. His "filibuster" is an attempt to repress the actual events of his flight from California to Japan and to vent his growing despair over the direction in which his career is moving. He periodically threatens to quit his job but never carries through on the impulse.

Sammy Zuess, a film producer and Cal's employer. He is self-indulgent, overweight, arrogant, and an acquirer of great material wealth. He speaks in a strange accent and appears in Cal's filibuster as a merciless God-like figure.

Murray McAndrew, an actor starring in Zuess's film. Although doomed to hopeless mediocrity, he is vain and self-centered. He appears in various roles in Cal's musings.

P.D. Malchios,
Mephos,
Tophel,
Kopfhalstam,
Mc Call,
Doctor Greenfell,
Kop,
Kol,
Sadako,
Yakamoto, and
Kamiko, productions of Cal's imagination who are introduced and disappear with little explanation or description. These minor characters serve to facilitate the psychological ramblings of a frustrated man, which substitute in the novel for any traditional sense of plot.

Michael Wm. Gearhart

CALIGULA

Author: Albert Camus (1913-1960)
Type of work: Play
Time of action: A.D. 37-41
First published: 1944, in *"Le Malentendu" suivi de "Caligula"* (English translation, 1948)

Caligula, the youthful Emperor of Rome. Caligula responds to the death of his sister Drusilla by launching a reign of terror against the Roman patricians (or nobles). This oppression has no political end and lacks any clear pattern. Indeed, Caligula's goal is to demonstrate the meaninglessness or absurdity of life and therefore the impossibility of human happiness. As such, Caligula strikes at random, at times punishing the innocent and sparing the guilty. He aims merely to humiliate and outrage the patricians. Finally, after three years of mounting atrocities against them, the patricians rise up and Caligula is assassinated.

Cherea, a philosopher and writer. Cherea is criticized by Caligula for being a man of letters and, as such, promoting the fiction that life is meaningful. Cherea sees the radical implications of Caligula's campaign from the start and organizes the insurrection that ultimately leads to Caligula's death. Caligula learns of Cherea's conspiracy but allows him to live.

Scipio, a poet and close friend to Caligula. Scipio's father is put to death by Caligula, but the poet's bond with the emperor is so powerful that even this act cannot fully alien-

ate him. Scipio's artistic sensitivity puts him in touch with Caligula's suffering soul, and Caligula, in turn, names Scipio the victor in a poetry competition. Refusing throughout the play to conspire against Caligula, Scipio, in an abrupt reversal, is among Caligula's assassins in the final scene.

Helicon, Caligula's chief assistant. Neither a sycophant nor a conniver, Helicon remains loyal to Caligula. It is he, for example, who first alerts Caligula that there is a conspiracy afoot. Yet Helicon is curiously detached from the events of the play. He is well aware of Caligula's private anguish but does not share it. For Helicon, questions regarding the meaning of life are too airy to be taken seriously. Eminently practical, Helicon maintains a studied obliviousness to the ambiguities of human existence that have driven Caligula to his radical course of action.

Caesonia, Caligula's mistress. Caesonia is unswerving in her loyalty to Caligula, assisting him in his often theatrical machinations and attempting to assuage his personal agonies with love. Unlike Helicon, who understands the futility of Caligula's quest and remains detached from it one way or another, Caesonia seems to believe that her passion for Caligula can ease his pain and perhaps moderate his course. Incorrect in her assumption, Caesonia is strangled by Caligula just before the play ends.

The Old Patrician, one of the patricians terrorized by Caligula. The old patrician is conspicuously timid and cowardly. He also seeks to betray his coconspirators in return for Caligula's favor, a deal Caligula refuses. The old patrician is Caligula's polar opposite, clinging to life with such desperation as to be an even less attractive figure than Caligula, who wantonly destroys life whenever he has the urge.

Mucius, a victim of Caligula's campaign of outrage and humiliation against the patricians. Mucius is forced to listen as Caligula makes love to his (Mucius') wife in the next room. Though clearly angered, he offers no resistance. This passivity is typical of the patricians throughout most of the play.

Ira Smolensky

THE CALL

Author: John Hersey (1914-   )
Type of work: Novel
Time of action: 1878-1981
First published: 1985

David Treadup, a courageous, vital, and self-sacrificing man who devotes his life to Christian and humanitarian missions in the shifting, violent world of China during the first half of the twentieth century. Given to binges of vandalism in his youth, David pursues classical learning to escape the hard life of his parents' farm. Following his religious conversion in 1903, his mind and body thrive. A handsome, large young man, he finds an outlet for his leadership skills and personal magnetism in the campus YMCA. At the age of twenty-seven, he embarks for China with a burning desire to evangelize that land through Gospel preaching. Soon disillusioned with the methods of old-fashioned missions, Treadup looks for another door into the Chinese mind. With his overpowering body and charisma, Treadup mesmerizes millions during his lectures on the gyroscope, airplane, and wireless, convincing them that the Unseen is real and propelling them toward the modernization of China. He perseveres even during a bout with dysentery, delivering his lectures from a horizontal position onstage. During the early years of communist revolution in China, Treadup develops a hatred of violence. Suffering through years of diabolical Japanese occupation, Treadup experiences uncertainty, loneliness for his wife, deprivation, and a frustrating halt to his work. Confined to a prison camp, a defeated, exhausted, and totally broken man, he ceases his prayers and loses touch with God. At last he comes to believe that there is no God. His unexpected release by the Japanese brings great sorrow to Treadup, for he must leave the work of a lifetime. When Treadup returns to China in a war rehabilitation position, he is arrested by the People's Liberation Army. As their prisoner, he experiences total deprivation. Accused of being an agent of American capitalism, he undergoes the ultimate humiliation: the voices of the Chinese people convict him in an open-air trial. Shortly after his expulsion from the People's Republic of China, he dies in Thornhill, New York, at the age of seventy-two.

Emily Kean Treadup, an attractive, serene woman who brings love and balance into David Treadup's life. During periods of potential fretfulness as his wife, Emily becomes hyperactive in community works, founding the Anti-Footbinding League in Tientsin and working against child labor, opium dens, prostitution, and the horrible

227

working conditions for women in factories. Throughout her life, she grieves for the loss of her baby, Nancy. Usually, she is submissive; yet, she is self-confident as she rears her three sons on the mission field. Emily is a beautiful woman who remains sensual through her middle years, but, when she finally returns to the United States alone during the Japanese occupation of China, she becomes frail and ancient-looking. She dies shortly after David's return to New York, seemingly as a consequence of being relieved of her duties at Thornhill Free Library.

Johnny Wu, an ambitious, American-educated young Chinese who, with David Treadup's help, develops a program for Chinese literacy. He estranges Treadup by retaining only nationals in the organization after it is off the ground, but the missionary admires his ebullience throughout all China's woes.

Lin Fu Chen, a Westernized Chinese intellectual, Treadup's most influential friend during his early years in China. He opens Peikai University for the teaching of science, economics, and liberal arts.

James B. Todd, the handsome blond evangelist who directs YMCA's foreign missions from his elegant office in New York City. Motivated by self-love and overconfidence, he is skeptical, at times even antagonistic, toward Treadup's philosophy and programs. He manages, however, to manipulate the missionary, who holds his power and charisma in awe.

Roscoe Hersey, a missions volunteer who relieves the young Treadup in Tientsin for language study. Later, he becomes General Secretary of YMCA. He is devoted to his work and the Chinese and is serious, gentle, and tactful. After working in flood relief, he becomes ill with encephalitis and returns to the United States.

Phineas Cunningham, an irrepressible British physician who becomes Treadup's only English friend in a whole lifetime. A brilliant man of letters and student of culture and religion, he is an agnostic who chips away at Treadup's Christianity during their work together improvising medical care in Tientsin and Japanese prison camps.

Janie Caves McCauley

CANCER WARD

Author: Aleksandr Solzhenitsyn (1918-   )
Type of work: Novel
Time of action: 1955-1956
First published: Rakovy korpus, 1968 (English translation, 1968)

Oleg Filimonovich Kostoglotov, a land surveyor. A loner, unmarried and without relatives, fiercely independent, and rebellious by nature, the thirty-four-year-old Kostoglotov is a former army sergeant and inmate from a Stalinist labor camp, arrested for making politically disparaging remarks about Joseph Stalin. Exiled to the remote central Asian town of Ush-Terek, he has been sent to a hospital in another unnamed central Asian city for treatment of stomach cancer. Skeptical of all authority, Kostoglotov clashes with his political opponent, the Stalinist bu-

reaucrat and fellow cancer patient, Rusanov, who defends thought control and police-state methods. In medical matters, he confronts Dr. Lyudmila Dontsova and insists on his right to know the exact details of his illness. When he discovers that the hormone injections he is being given may save his life but will result in the loss of his sexual capacity, he persuades Zoya, a nurse with whom he is sexually involved, to discontinue the treatments. Later, on the insistence of Dr. Vera Gangart, with whom he develops a close personal friendship, he resumes the treatment, his cancer is temporarily cured, and he is released from the hospital. Torn between his attraction for Zoya and Vera, he ultimately ends his relationship with both women, thanking Zoya for their sexual intimacy which he will always remember and explaining to Vera that their relationship would be incomplete without the hope of sexual fulfillment. Amid rumors of a forthcoming amnesty for political exiles, Kostoglotov returns to Ush-Terek to live a life of simplicity similar to his fellow political exiles, Nikolay and Yelena Kadmin.

Pavel Nikolayevich Rusanov, a prominent Communist Party bureaucrat. An arrogant, forty-five-year-old careerist and status seeker, Rusanov expects special privileges in the hospital as a result of his party affiliation. He is an authoritarian official who has risen through the bureaucratic ranks by denouncing his coworkers and cooperating with the secret police. His stay in the cancer ward is marked by his numerous confrontations and arguments with the democratic Kostoglotov, whom he despises. Apprehensive about the future because of the uncertainty of his medical recovery and the political changes occasioned by the liberalization brought about in Soviet society following the death of Stalin, he nevertheless clings to Stalinist principles. Responsible for the denunciation of innocent citizens during the purge years of 1937-1938, he dreads the reintegration of victims of the purges into Soviet society. Although confronted with death and the ultimate question of the meaning of life, Rusanov learns nothing from his stay in the cancer ward and leaves the ward physically cured but psychologically unchanged.

Dr. Vera Kornilyevna Gangart, a radiotherapist. A small, shapely woman in her early thirties, shy, naturally kind, idealistic, and seemingly more innocent than a twenty year old. Having fallen in love with a schoolboy in her youth, she has remained faithful to his memory after he was killed during World War II. Determined to continue her life, she became a doctor and pledged herself to heal the afflicted. Inspired by the ded-

ication of her mentor, Dr. Dontsova, she has been working as a resident doctor for eight years. When she meets Kostoglotov, she is personally attracted by his strength of character but finds herself in conflict with his insistence on questioning medical authority. A woman of deep inward convictions, she believes explicitly in the established methods of medical treatment. Dedicated to saving lives, she urges Kostoglotov to continue his hormone treatments, even though they will result in the loss of his sexual capacity. Attracted by Kostoglotov's strength of character, she contemplates developing a relationship with him, but he refuses to sacrifice her personal happiness to his sexual inadequacy.

Dr. Lyudmila Afanasyevna Dontsova, the head of the radiotherapy department. A hardworking, conscientious, dedicated doctor, nearly fifty years old, Dontsova is referred to affectionately by her younger resident doctors as "Mama." A professional woman, mother, and housewife burdened with both professional and domestic duties, she is frequently weary from overwork but tirelessly pursues her goal of alleviating pain and curing patients. She comes into conflict with the rebellious Kostoglotov when she insists on the doctor's right to make decisions concerning a patient's treatment based on the doctor's specialized knowledge without consulting the patient. Ultimately she convinces Kostoglotov to acquiesce in undergoing hormone treatments, believing that any impairment in a patient's physical condition, including loss of sexual capacity, is justified in order to save a patient's life. Ironically, Dontsova herself is stricken with abdominal cancer. Stunned by this unexpected event, she seeks the medical advice of her mentor, Dr. Oreshchenkov, who together with Dr. Gangart realizes the seriousness of her condition and recommends that she go to Moscow for further tests.

Zoya, a nurse. An attractive twenty-three-year-old woman reared in a broken home, Zoya has become independent and self-reliant, working part-time in the hospital to support herself while studying at a medical institute. Cheerful and fun-loving, she enjoys life and has had numerous affairs but is seeking a serious, stable relationship and is consequently attracted by Kostoglotov's perseverance and strength. Sharing his independent spirit, Zoya agrees to Kostoglotov's request for medical information about cancer and provides him with a medical book. When she becomes sexually involved with Kostoglotov, she also agrees to his request to discontinue his hormone injections, since they will result in his sexual impotency. As their sexual attraction for each other wanes, Zoya resumes the hormone injections out of fear of losing her job when Dr. Gangart discovers that Kostoglotov has not been receiving the hormone therapy.

Dyomka, a lathe operator. An idealistic sixteen-year-old student whose father was killed in World War II and whose stepfather deserted his sexually promiscuous mother. Dyomka harbors bitter feelings toward his mother for her promiscuity and for abandoning him. He is befriended by Kostoglotov, who encourages him after his leg is amputated to learn to use a crutch. Resilient and confident about the future, he resolves to return to work.

Sharaf Sibgatov, a young Tartar slowly dying from cancer of the sacrum, a gentle, polite man who endures his suffering meekly and is grateful for the medical attention he receives. He arouses the pity of Dr. Dontsova, who redoubles her efforts to save him but is ultimately unsuccessful.

Alexey Fillipovich Shulubin, a librarian. An old, idealistic Bolshevik, defeated and despondent, tired of living and guilt-ridden for his complicity in the Stalin purges, Shulubin has lost his self-respect but still believes in socialist ideals. He supports Kostoglotov in Kostoglotov's numerous arguments with the unrepentant Rusanov.

Vadim Zatsyrko, a geologist. Handsome, talented, dedicated to self-sacrifice and hard work, the twenty-six-year-old Vadim passionately desires to make an important geolog-

ical discovery before he dies of terminal cancer. A Communist Party member, he is contemptuous of his intellectual inferiors and supports Rusanov in Rusanov's ideological arguments with Kostoglotov.

Yefrem Podduyev, a worker. A hardy, middle-aged man under fifty, crude, vulgar, and promiscuous, Yefrem is conscience-stricken after reading Leo Tolstoy's moral tales. Engaged by the precept that human beings should live by Christian love, he is denounced by Rusanov and Vadim for spreading alien religious ideology, but he is vigorously defended by Kostoglotov.

Dr. Dormidont Tikhonovich Oreshchenkov, a general practitioner. A warm, compassionate, seventy-five-year-old family doctor, Oreshchenkov cherishes his private medical practice. He shows kindness and sympathy to his former student, Dr. Dontsova, when she learns that she has cancer and encourages her to go to Moscow for further tests.

Avieta Pavlovna Rusanova, a journalist. Young, intelligent, talented, and energetic, Rusanov's eldest daughter, Avieta, seeks to follow her father's example and make connections to advance her career. She supports Rusanov in his ideological disputes and defends his role in the purges.

Lev Leonidovich, the head surgeon. Nearly forty years old, Lev is a conscientious, dedicated doctor, popular with his patients for his cheerfulness and optimism, inspiring respect for his common sense with Kostoglotov and his confidence in Dyomka, who chooses him to amputate his leg.

Asya, a schoolgirl. An attractive seventeen-year-old girl, lively and energetic, sexually active since the ninth grade, Asya believes that one must live for romantic love. In despair when she learns she must have a mastectomy, she turns to Dyomka for consolation.

Prokofy Semyonovich, a tractor driver. A strong, young Ukrainian suffering from a tumor of the heart, Prokofy is optimistic about his recovery and eager to return to work. When he shows his release papers to Kostoglotov, Kostoglotov, out of compassion, refuses to translate the Latin phrase indicating that Prokofy's tumor is inoperable and incurable.

Elizaveta Anatolyevna, an orderly in the radiology department. Not yet fifty years old but premarturely aged, Elizaveta is a former political exile, intelligent and educated, who serves tirelessly and uncomplainingly as a scrubwoman. Agonizing over her memories of the purges, she is urged by Kostoglotov to tell her eight-year-old son the truth about the labor camps.

Rodichev, an engineer. A former friend of Rusanov falsely accused by Rusanov of belonging to a counterrevolutionary organization, Rodichev has spent eighteen years in a labor camp. His release from the camp causes Rusanov great anxiety.

Kapitolina Matveyevna Rusanova, Rusanov's wife. A fashionably dressed, energetic, intelligent woman, married to Rusanov for twenty-five years, Kapitolina is a faithful wife and true friend to her husband. Like her husband, she has grown accustomed to privilege and status.

Yura Rusanov, a lawyer. Rusanov's eldest son, Yura is a disappointment to his father for his failure to assert his rank and cultivate the proper acquaintances. Unlike his father, Yura is humane, compassionate, and interested in justice.

Maxim Petrovich Chaly, a black marketeer and speculator. A lively, jovial man whose offer to obtain good automobile tires through the black market for Rusanov's new car is accepted by Rusanov when Rusanov is released from the hospital.

Nikolay Ivanovich Kadmin, an obstetrician. He is a lively, sixty-year-old doctor and political exile who lives a simple, unassuming life in Ush-Terek and corresponds with Kostoglotov.

Yelena Alexandrovna Kadmina, Nikolay Kadmin's wife. She is a warm, compassionate, fifty-year-old political exile in poor health, who shares her husband's friendship with Kostoglotov and joy in living a simple life.

Auntie Styofa, a grandmother, a humble, warm, compassionate Christian who consoles Dyomka and attempts to reconcile him to his fate.

Lavrenty Pavlovich Rusanov, Rusanov's second son. An average student, talented in sports, named by his parents in honor of Lavrenty Beria (bâ′rē•ə), the head of Stalin's secret police. Egged on by his father, he maliciously attempts to run down Kostoglotov with his father's automobile when Kostoglotov is released from the hospital.

Maika Rusanova, Rusanov's youngest daughter. An average pupil unable to achieve good grades on her own, Maika was placed on the honor roll because her teacher knew Maika's parents.

Jerome J. Rinkus

CANNERY ROW

Author: John Steinbeck (1902-1968)
Type of work: Novel
Time of action: c. 1940
First published: 1945

Doc, owner and operator of Western Biological Laboratory, who was graduated from the University of Chicago. Doc is small, strong, and wiry and loves science, beer, women, classical music, books, and prints. He is a thoroughly civilized man and the acknowledged, but unofficial, "mayor" of Cannery Row in Monterey. He is a fountain of wisdom, philosophy, and sometimes medical and psychiatric advice. Doc has a pointed brown beard and is described as half-Christ, half satyr. Doc has a fear of getting his head wet. He is beloved by all but is nevertheless a lonely and remote man.

Mack and the Boys, a group of unemployed men, drinkers, sometimes called winos (but not in this book). They are open, honest, and generous in their way, kind and understanding, and sometimes extremely compassionate. They have no greed, meanness, egotism, or self-interest. Much of their charm rests in the eye of the beholder.

Mack, the leader of the Boys who live in the Palace Flophouse. Once married, Mack is very intelligent and without conventional ambition. To the others, he is mentor, sage, and sometimes exploiter. He leads the frog hunting expedition and plans Doc's party. It is said that Mack could have been the president of the United States if he had so wanted. Mack loves food, drink, contentment, and, sometimes, women and fighting.

Dora Flood, proprietor of The Bear Flag Restaurant, which is really a decent, clean, honest, old-fashioned sporting house. Dora is probably in her late sixties and, the narrator says, is respected by the intelligent, learned, and kind and hated by spinsters and prudish women whose husbands respect the home but do not like it in their community. She is a great big woman, with orange hair and a big heart. During the Depression, she paid for groceries for many poor families; she is a large donator to local worthy causes. During the influenza epidemic, she put her cook to work making soup and her girls to work delivering it.

Hazel, one of the Boys, twenty-six years old and dark-haired, not too bright but without viciousness or guile. He occasionally helps Doc with the collecting of marine life and is good at it. Hazel, who has had four years of regular school and four years in reform school, was named for his great aunt by his exhausted and confused mother, who had had seven children in eight years.

Eddie, one of the Boys, the understudy bartender at La Ida, from which he brings home jugs full of dregs from all the drink glasses.

Gay, one of the Boys, married to a woman who sometimes beats him while he is asleep. Gay is an excellent auto mechanic but drinks too much and is often in jail.

Lee Chong, Chinese grocery store owner and owner of the Palace Flophouse. He stands behind the cigar counter, in front of the whiskey shelves, wearing half-glasses and extending credit judiciously. Lee Chong is shrewd but kind and can be generous and sentimental. He is a wise man, sometimes abused but always tolerant.

Henri, the painter, who is not French and whose name is not really Henri. He sometimes paints with chicken feathers, sometimes with nutshells. He loves all things French and all modernisms. He is swarthy and morose. Henri has been married twice and has had many, many other women, but they always leave him because he lives in an unfinished boat, up on blocks and with no plumbing.

Alfred, pimp/bouncer at The Bear Flag. He is accepted by the Boys. His talent is for keeping order without actually hurting anyone.

"The Captain," owner of the frog pond raided by Mack and the Boys. The Captain, whose wife is in politics, is clearly henpecked, but she is away.

Frankie, a mentally retarded and physically

uncoordinated eleven-year-old. Filthy, with dark hair, Frankie loves Doc absolutely but sadly is unable to function in society.

Wilbur, the pimp/bouncer who worked for Dora. He wanted to be one of the Boys but was never accepted by them.

Sam Malloy and
Mrs. Malloy, who live happily in a boiler in a vacant lot until Mrs. Malloy gets the urge to decorate with window curtains. Seeing an opportunity to go into business, they rent small pipes to single men.

Mary Talbot, a woman with red hair, golden skin, and green eyes. She is a loving, kind woman of infinite optimism.

Tom Talbot, Mary's husband, an as-yet-unsuccessful writer. Mary cheers him up.

Old Chinaman, a mysterious figure who walks, for years, into the ocean at dusk with a wicker basket. He emerges at dawn. Some think that he has powers; some think that he is God, others, death.

Donald R. Noble

A CANTICLE FOR LEIBOWITZ

Author: Walter M. Miller, Jr. (1923-   )
Type of work: Novel
Time of action: c. A.D. 2500, 3174, and 3781
First published: 1959

Brother Francis Gerard, a young, fresh-faced novice of the Albertian order of Leibowitz. Brother Francis discovers a fallout shelter containing relics of the Blessed Leibowitz (who, apparently, was a scientist in pre-nuclear holocaust America). Francis' discovery causes a stir in the abbey, especially since rumors allege that the pilgrim he saw prior to his discovery was Leibowitz himself.

Pilgrim, or **Benjamin Eleazar bar Joshua,** or **Lazarus,** an old man who may be the **Wandering Jew.** His figure appears in each of the three sections of the book, though he is not overtly identified as the same man each time. As the pilgrim, he marks a stone for Brother Francis that leads to his discovery of the fallout shelter. As Benjamin Eleazar, he discusses with Dom Paulo the rise of a secular state and waits for a messiah. As Lazarus, he is assigned the role of the man whom Christ raised from the dead and smiles wryly at Abbot Zerchi's hope that a nuclear holocaust will not happen again.

Dom Arkos, the abbot of the Leibowitz Ab-

bey in the first section of the book. Arkos attempts to quash the rumors surrounding the man whom Francis met in the desert and turns the examination of the fallout shelter and its contents over to another order. Toward the end of Arkos' tenure, Leibowitz is declared a saint.

Brother Fingo, a sport with an unusual pattern of melanin distribution. Fingo carves a wooden statue of Leibowitz, which, over the years, vaguely reminds Brother Francis, Dom Paulo, and Dom Zerchi of someone they cannot identify. The implication is that the statue reminds them of the Wandering Jew.

Dom Paulo, the abbot of the Leibowitz Abbey in the second section of the novel. He presides over the abbey during a period in which the secular and religious worlds are beginning to diverge. He refuses to send to the secular capital the ancient manuscripts (the Memorabilia) that the abbey holds, but he allows the secular scholar Thon Taddeo to examine them in situ.

Thon Taddeo Pfardentrott, a brilliant secular scholar. An illegitimate son of the ruling

233

family, he was reared in a Benedictine abbey, which provided him with an excellent education. He nevertheless argues the superiority of secular scholarship and scoffs at religion, saying that science should not be constrained by ethical or religious concerns. Thon Taddeo's abstract work on the nature of electricity leads Brother Kornhoer to construct an electric light.

Brother Kornhoer, a monk at the abbey who constructs a dynamo to generate power for an electric light.

Brother Armbruster, the librarian at the abbey who sees Brother Kornhoer's work as heretical.

Marcus Apollo, a papal nuncio to the court of Hannegan, the ruler of Texarkana. Apollo tries to warn Dom Paulo about Thon Taddeo's secular loyalties. He is later executed for treason because of his support of New Rome over the political government.

The Poet, a guest at the abbey. He has one removable eye, which he claims enables him to see more clearly. The brothers call it "the Poet's conscience." After the Poet, while playing the fool, accuses Thon Taddeo of avoiding the responsibility that should accompany scientific advances to prevent their misuse, he tells Thon Taddeo, who has picked up the glass eye, that he has need of it.

Dom Jethrah Zerchi, the abbot in the novel's third section. He must confront the certainty of another nuclear holocaust. He tries to defend the faith in a world gone mad and must argue against euthanasia despite its seeming kindness. The shock wave of a nuclear bomb hits the abbey as he hears the confession of Mrs. Grales, and, as he lies trapped in the rubble, he receives the Eucharist from Rachel.

Mrs. Grales/Rachel, a two-headed woman. Mrs. Grales is confessing her sins when the shock wave of a nuclear bomb hits the abbey. The effects of the bomb apparently kill Mrs. Grales while raising to life Rachel, her previously dormant other head. Rachel seems to Abbot Zerchi an incarnation of innocence, perhaps another Mary, mother of Christ.

Brother Joshua, a former astronaut. He leads a group to colonize another planet, escaping the effects of the holocaust. They take with them the Memorabilia on microfilm.

Dr. Cors, a Green Star worker. He argues with Dom Zerchi about euthanasia, which the doctor has recommended to a young woman and her baby.

Karen M. Cleveland

CAPRICORNIA

Author: Xavier Herbert (1901-1984)
Type of work: Novel
Time of action: The 1880's to the 1930's
First published: 1938

Oscar Shillingsworth, a civil servant and later, cattle rancher. He is a tall, erect, neat man who in his maturity wears a huge mustache. Determined to get on in life, he works assiduously for the government, marries well, and leases a large cattle station in Australia's rough-and-ready Northern Territory (called "Capricornia" in the novel). At the

beginning, he is somewhat prim and self-interested, but his wife runs off, and various other problems of life make him a more generous, concerned man in the long run. In his thirties at the beginning, he dies in early old age.

Mark Shillingsworth, Oscar's younger

brother, who comes to Capricornia with him to work as a government clerk. He is twenty-two and less ambitious than Oscar to please the society of middle-class clerks and shopkeepers; almost immediately, he falls in with a happy group of gamblers and drunkards. Tall and handsome, attractive to women, and prone to alcoholic excess, he soon falls out of work and society, has a child with an aboriginal girl, and kills a Chinese merchant in a brawl over money. He disappears and is believed to be dead for much of the novel but turns up as a middle-aged man, still prone to get into trouble but often rather innocently so.

Norman Shillingsworth, Mark's illegitimate son, named **Mark Anthony Shillingsworth** but known in his childhood, while living as a half-caste, as **"Nawnim,"** an aboriginal version of "No Name," which is gradually anglicized as "Norman." His mother dies soon after he is born, and Mark Shillingsworth never takes responsibility for him. Yellow-skinned, black-eyed, and handsome, he lives from hand-to-mouth until Oscar Shillingsworth takes him into his family and rears him as a white child. He is educated as a draughtsman but has natural gifts as a mechanic and ambitions to work on the railroad. He becomes a genial, attractive young man, but he is clearly of mixed blood, which he is told is part Javanese—less socially offensive than being part aboriginal. Much of his difficulty in life comes from his ignorance of his past and the reluctance of Australian society to accept him as a full member of a white family.

Heather Poundamore, Oscar Shillingsworth's sister-in-law. A pretty young woman, she falls in love with Mark and has a stormy relationship with him because of his drinking and his relations with native women. She takes a job as a barmaid to keep an eye on Mark and after his disappearance remains faithful to his memory. She is a kind, sensible woman, careful with money and a good businesswoman, which is fortunate since she will be a great help to both Mark and Norman when they get into trouble with the law.

Charles Ket, a young laborer from the west coast of Australia. He originally passes himself off under the name of Harold Carlton and is getting on in Capricornia white society until it is revealed that he is of mixed white, Oriental, and aboriginal blood. His narrow black eyes and hair betray his Chinese connection, and his swarthy skin give away his aboriginal lineage. He is a bitter, vicious man and a dangerous enemy, not disinclined to do physical harm up to and including murder. He is to become a great hater of the Shillingsworth family since he had some ambition to marry Oscar's daughter.

Frank McLash, a big, low-browed twenty-year-old, shaped like a kewpie doll, with an egg-shaped head. From his early years prone to trouble with the law, he serves time in a reformatory while in his teens. He is torn between being a thief and a railway engineer, but the latter job is torn from his grasp over and over again, sometimes by bad luck and sometimes by his own stupidity. He serves in World War I and survives it, but after that it is one disaster after another, particularly when he teams up with Charles Ket in a short life of crime.

Pansy McLash, Frank McLash's long-suffering, widowed mother. She keeps a kind of hotel, the Siding House. Although she has a strong love for liquor, she has an even stronger love for her feckless son, and she has sacrificed financially and otherwise for him all his life. She can be a good friend but is an enthusiastic enemy.

Tocky, a half-caste who becomes involved with Norman and, in her way, loves him. Beautiful, full-lipped, with long, enticing eyelashes, she brings out the worst in men. She is lively and charming and has survived a life of physical misery by her wits. She rarely does what she is told, and when she does—by Norman—it ends in disaster for her and their child.

Charles Pullen

235

CAPTAIN BLACKMAN

Author: John A. Williams (1925-   )
Type of work: Novel
Time of action: c. 1971, with dream sequences ranging from 1775 to 2001
First published: 1972

Abraham Blackman, a powerful black man, about forty years old, a career soldier who is highly sensitive to the exploitation of black soldiers throughout America's history. He teaches a seminar on black military history to the men in his command (C Company) in Vietnam, a command predominantly composed of blacks, Puerto Ricans, and crackers, the detritus of the white world; he is very effective in uniting the allegiances of his men, particularly the black men, who do not seem fully aware of the injustices visited upon them during their tours of duty. While leading a patrol, an activity unusual for one of such high rank, Blackman draws enemy fire to protect the men in his squad and is severely wounded. He enters a dream state and relives a part of each conflict in which the United States has taken part, beginning with the Revolutionary War. Blackman gradually works his way up in rank through his imaginary experiences, beginning as a raw foot soldier in 1775 and finally appearing as a lieutenant in World War II; at the time he is wounded, he is in reality a captain but is promoted to major while he recuperates. Many of his current associates appear in these illusions with him, playing roles which correspond to their actual characters in his life. He also encounters historical figures and locations which probably played an important part in his history lessons, men and places such as Peter Salem, Prince Estabrook, John Pitcairn (Revolutionary War), Andrew Jackson (War of 1812), Nurse Helen Gibson (Civil War), Brit Johnson, Forsythe, and Philip Henry Sheridan (Cavalry action in the Western United States), President Theodore Roosevelt, Brigadier General Garlinton, Brownsville (Cuba), John Joseph Pershing, Ferdinand Foch, the Argonne (World War I), Brigade Commander Copic, Captain Springhall, Oliver Law, Albacete, Aragon (Spanish Civil War), Louis-Antoine de Bouganville, Tombolo (World War II). Although Blackman is not aware of his displacement in time during these illusionary activities, he is highly cognizant of the inequities visited on the black soldiers by the whites and of their methods of maintaining control. This vision leads him to devise a comprehensive plan for a black coalition to conquer the white-dominated nation, and in the dream at the close of the novel, the scope of his ideas apparently takes the complacent whites totally by surprise and is easily successful.

Mimosa Rogers, a member of the U.S. Foreign Service, probably in her late twenties, Blackman's girlfriend. His female counterpart, she is tall, very attractive, highly intelligent, and devoted to helping Blackman achieve his goals, which she shares. After he is wounded, she is fiercely protective of Blackman. She appears in many of the historical time frames during Blackman's dream; nearly every encounter is marked by an intense sexual experience.

Ishmael Whittman, Blackman's principal antagonist, a blond, blue-eyed representative of the inferior white who holds a superior position only by virtue of race. He encounters Blackman several times during their real military careers, outranking him despite the fact that Blackman is the better soldier. Both men are aware of this situation; Whittman is extremely pleased to hear of Blackman's serious wounds and hopefully awaits news of his death. Whittman appears in most of the dream sequences always as an officer of superior rank to Blackman, though an ineffective leader, and his fear of the black man who is more intelligent, braver, and of stronger character is expressed through a desire to eradicate, or failing that, to subjugate that which he fears, a fear symbolized by the collective white vision of the marauding black penis. Although in the final dream segment Whittman has attained the rank of general, Blackman, through his superior intelligence and ability, is able to defeat Whittman and everything for which he stands.

Robert Doctorow, a white member of Blackman's command. Sensitive to bigotry through his Jewish heritage, Doctorow joins the black military history seminars, in spite of opposition from the black grunts, at least for long enough to prove that he will not be intimidated by them. An aspiring writer, he keeps a notebook of his experiences as preparation for the book he intends to write and is committed to influencing social change, a desire exemplified by his role of idealistic volunteer in the Spanish Civil War sequence of Blackman's dream. He is slightly injured in the rocket attack which kills Harrison and Belmont.

Luther Woodcock, a soldier in Blackman's command, white in appearance (except for his enormous Afro) but black by heritage. He is an example of the new black attitude which emerged in the late 1960's and early 1970's; rather than trying to blend into the white world, Woodcock flaunts his black roots proudly. A medic, Woodcock administers first aid to Blackman when he is wounded. He appears in the World War I sequence as one of the few black officers and friend to Blackman, and in the final dream he is instrumental in the defeat of the whites. He is wounded slightly in the rocket attack on the base.

David Harrison (Little David), a black

sergeant in Blackman's Vietnam squad. He is a small man physically, but he is of imposing character and refuses to bend to the idea of white supremacy; this pride leads to his death at the hands of white soldiers in the U.S. Cavalry segment of Blackman's dream. He appears as a dependable close friend in the U.S. Cavalry and Civil War sequences. Harrison is killed in a rocket attack after Blackman's patrol returns to their base on the hostile perimeter and Blackman is placed in a helicopter for transport to a hospital.

Belmont, the black radioman in Blackman's company. His grandfather was a much-decorated flying ace in World War I, highly respected in France, but reduced to lackey's status upon his return to the United States because of his color. Paul Belmont, the grandfather, is mentioned in the World War I dream. Belmont is also killed in the rocket attack on the base.

Johnny Griot, a black soldier of C Company who appears in the War of 1812 sequence with Blackman. He inspires Blackman to repel a group of drunken whites who try to abuse the sleeping black soldiers in this segment of the dream.

Antoine (Black Antoine), another black soldier in C Company who appears in the War of 1812 sequence. As a result of their actions in this conflict, the black soldiers are granted a section of land, although the government refused to grant freedom (to those who might survive the practice of placing black soldiers on the front lines) to entice the slaves to fight.

Mary Johnson

THE CAPTAIN WITH THE WHISKERS

Author: Benedict Kiely (1919-   )
Type of work: Novel
Time of action: The late 1940's to the early 1950's
First published: 1960

Owen Rodgers, the narrator, in his mid- and late twenties, a former medical student

who eventually becomes a successful hotel manager. An incurable romantic leaning toward alcoholism, he is obsessed with the fall of the house of the Chesney family and haunted by memories of its patriarch, Captain Conway Chesney. He becomes the chaste lover of Maeve Chesney, who represents to him, ironically, the idealized queen of his dreams, while he becomes the actual and fatal lover of the other Chesney daughter, Greta. He ends up marrying his first love, Lucy, who, after bearing him three children, dies. He spends his remaining days in Dublin ruefully singing songs in seedy pubs.

Captain Conway Chesney, the head of the Chesney family and patriarchal commandant of Bingen House, a hero of the Boer War, and Owen Rodgers' mentor. In spite of his death early in the story, his commanding presence remains and persistently manifests itself in the corrosive crippling of his children emotionally and spiritually. He is a small man, virulently anti-clerical, and willfully vindictive, not only to his children but also to the entire area. His greatest sin is changing the name of his estate from its original Irish name of Magheracolton, to its British name, Bingen House, thus severing the natives from their cultural and linguistic heritage.

Maeve Chesney, one of the captain's two daughters, lively, beautiful, and sexually desirable. She becomes Owen Rodgers' idealized beloved but in reality is promiscuous, fun loving, and rather shallow. Owen runs into her again late in the novel in Dublin with her teenage son, after she has lost much of her allure and most of her memories.

Doctor Grierson, a sophisticated parish priest of the area, with a doctorate from Louvain, an alcoholic. He tends to his priestly duties conscientiously but suffers under the heavy hand of his ecclesiastical superiors, who have exiled him for his intelligence and compassion. He spends most of his time drinking heavily, recovering, and advising young Owen Rodgers. He considers the Captain to be irredeemably wicked and possesses little hope for humanity.

Lucy, Owen Rodgers' first girlfriend. She is in her twenties, plumply attractive but rather unimaginative and ordinary. Owen leaves her to pursue both Chesney women only to return to marry her and take her to Dublin, where she bears him three children and then dies in middle age.

John Rodgers, Owen's cultivated and highly intelligent father. He is fully conscious of the evil effects of the Captain's influence, not only on the Chesney family but also on the entire area. A loving preserver of Irish books and music, he hates the Captain principally because he has destroyed the cultural coherence of the local area by replacing the Irish names with English ones. He is also Dr. Grierson's closest confidant and most sympathetic listener.

Greta Chesney, hardworking, practical, and quietly attractive. She tries unsuccessfully to escape the life-denying effects of her father and commits suicide following a disastrous affair with Owen Rodgers.

Alfred Chesney, nicknamed **Slobber,** the Captain's oldest son, brutalized by his father for associating with members of the lower classes. Alcoholic, ugly, and desperate for love, he is arrested for the rape of a minor and sent to prison for a year.

Edmund Chesney, the Captain's second son, soft, corpulent, and loquacious. He manages to escape to England temporarily but returns home after his father's death, blaming the Captain for his older brother's sexual misconduct.

Francis Chesney, the Captain's third son, pimply faced and sallow. He manages to escape to study for the priesthood, although he is almost disqualified by his sister's illegitimate child and Greta's suicide. After returning from studies at Louvain, he becomes increasingly alcoholic and disillusioned and grasps scrupulously to the rituals and rules of the Church.

Patrick Meanor

CASSANDRA
A Novel and Four Essays

Author: Christa Wolf (1929-   )
Type of work: Novel
Time of action: c. 1200 B.C. in the novel
First published: Voraussetzungen einer Erzählung: "Kassandra" and Kassandra, 1983,
    2 volumes (English translation, 1984)

Cassandra, the story's narrator, a princess of Troy in Anatolia, a seer, and a priestess of the god Apollo. Captured by Mycenaean Greeks under King Agamemnon, Cassandra meditates about her life in the now-ruined citadel of Troy as well as about the terrible future her captors face. Cassandra proudly recalls having been King Priam of Troy's beloved favorite. Painfully, however, she also recalls how he cast her in prison because she dared prophesy Troy's imminent doom.

Priam, the proud king of Troy, who chose not to heed the counsel of seers prophesying Troy's downfall, the chief of whom being his own daughter Cassandra. Noble, wise in many ways, yet stubborn and unyielding, Priam hoped to stave off fate. With his overthrow, he becomes one more Trojan leader in a sorry succession to endure defeat in war.

Hecuba, the wife of King Priam. Along with Cassandra and others in the inner court of Troy, Hecuba hated Troy's arrogance while, at the same time, wished for its success in battle against the Greeks. The bearer of many children, including Cassandra, Hector, Paris, and Troilus, she saves her youngest son from the wrath of the Mycenaeans by sending him abroad to Thrace, where he is subsequently murdered by the Thracian king. Wise to the world's cruel and capricious ways because of the many tragedies she has endured, Hecuba is a thoroughgoing skeptic.

Aeneus (ă•nē'ŭs), a Trojan warrior and lover of Cassandra who, after having taught her about love, vanishes. Cassandra, still dazzled by the intensity of their brief tryst, sees his disappearance as one more legacy of the war between Troy and the Greeks. Aeneus is em-

blematic of the young heroes who died for a lost cause.

Hector, son of Priam and Hecuba. He is a large, rather sluggish young man of few words, admired by his sister Cassandra for engaging in warfare though it goes against his torpid nature to do so. Hector's misfortune is to be chased down and killed by the vengeful Greek warrior, Achilles.

Anchises (ăn•chī'zēs), a Trojan shepherd. From his legendary union with Aphrodite came a son, Aeneus.

Agamemnon, the great, powerful king of the Greek city-state Argos and leader of the Mycenaean forces in the Trojan War. Cruel, resourceful, and cunning, Agamemnon, cuckolded by Paris—who abducted his wife, Helen, to Troy—takes his revenge eupon the city, razing it and killing or enslaving all its inhabitants. Among these captives is Cassandra who, at the novel's outset, is to be killed behind Mycenae's Lion Gate.

Achilles (ă•kĭl'lēz), the most famed of the Greek warriors who sacked Troy. Achilles, proud to the point of being haughty, self-directed, and moody in the extreme, is hated intensely by Cassandra. She particularly detests his brutal nature.

Panthous (păn'thŏos), a priest in Apollo's service and Cassandra's overseer in her role as priestess. Cassandra envisons Panthous as an envious and evil-minded man given to craftiness and outright treachery. Nevertheless, she admires some of his actions, such as putting an end to human sacrifices in Troy.

John D. Raymer

THE CASTLE OF CROSSED DESTINIES

Author: Italo Calvino (1923-1985)
Type of work: Novel
Time of action: The mythic past
First published: Il castello dei destini incrociati, 1969; revised, 1973 (English translation, 1977)

The first narrator, a traveler (perhaps a knight) who comes upon the castle in the woods and joins the guests who recount their tales through the medium of tarot cards. Weary from many recent trials and combats, the narrator feels unstable and confused in his perceptions, which contributes, as the story unfolds, to his uncertainty about reading the various stories accurately. The uncertainty of reconstructing stories from emblematic representations, a dominant theme of the book, originates in this state of mind of the narrator.

The Alchemist, who selects the King of Cups tarot card to represent himself. He is identified with Faust, and the tale of the bargain with the devil for the secret formula of gold begins with the alchemist's reading of the Ace of Cups and the Popess cards, which conclude the tale of a knight who narrates before him. The alchemist interacts with the others around the table also in challenging them with his elliptical and allusive style in representing his story. The many symbolic possibilities of the cards he employs and the rich complexity of the Faust legend make his audience restless and impatient for clear exposition.

Roland, the mythical knight of Charlemagne legend, who identifies himself with the King of Swords card. Roland is referred to as gigantic, moving his leaden arms and ironlike fingers slowly and cumbersomely. Domineering and threatening, he hoards the most beautiful of the tarot cards for the colorful tale of his going mad in pursuit of Angelica. As he recounts his tale, Roland undergoes a visible transformation. Ending with the card of the Hanged Man, he takes on a serene, radiant expression, from which

the narrator infers an acceptance of reason over the paladin's former unrestricted passion that led to his defeat.

Astolpho, the English knight who in Ludovico Ariosto's *Orlando Furioso* recovers the wits of Roland. The first narrator, longing for further testimony of Roland's adventures, finds this small, humorous, childlike youth among the guests and hands him the Knight of Clubs card. The youth tosses it in the air, and when it alights on the table begins the tale of Charlemagne sending Astolpho to the moon to find Roland's reason. His tale, however, maintains the theme of defeat that links the tales of the other guests. The youth ends his tale cryptically, with suggestions of failure and foreboding. Rather than discovering harmony of sense and meanings on the moon, he reports that the moon is a desert, an empty horizon where all poems and discourse begin and end.

The second narrator, who finds himself, like the first narrator, at a banquet with other travelers who are struck mute and communicating their adventures with a tarot deck. The second narrator, like his fellow banqueters, is white haired from the sudden fear of finding himself in the mysterious forest. This narrator sees himself mirrored in three cards: the Knight of Swords, the Hermit, and the Juggler. He describes himself as a writer whose impetuosity and anxiety are akin to those of a warrior. He reads his fate as a writer also in the images of famous paintings of Saint Jerome and Saint George. The first, the hermit and saint, represents his solitude and devotion to finding order in chaos; the second, the dragon slayer, depicts his struggle with confronting inner and outer demons. The narrator, thus, sees himself as representing the other travelers and all who attempt to recount and interpret the elusive meanings of their lives.

The Queen of Clubs, a woman who identifies herself by beginning with the tarot card of this name. A gigantic maiden of powerful arms and hands, she impels the narrative forward by controlling the cards when others are grabbing wildly, threatening to take control and disarrange the cards. The maiden jostles her fellow travelers and wrests the cards from them until the guests are subdued into watching her unfold her own tale of her birthing twins by a prince and controlling his father.

Dennis C. Chowenhill

CASTLE TO CASTLE, NORTH, and RIGADOON

Author: Louis-Ferdinand Céline (Louis-Ferdinand Destouchès, 1894-1961)
Type of work: Novel
Time of action: July, 1944, to March, 1945
First published: D' un château l' autre, 1957 (*Castle to Castle*, 1968); *Nord*, 1960 (*North*, 1972); *Rigodon*, 1969 (*Rigadoon*, 1974)

Ferdinand Céline (sā•lēn'), a doctor and novelist. Ferdinand is the name Céline uses for himself in narrating these quasi-fictional memoirs of his sojourn and flight through Germany at the end of World War II. In these novels, Ferdinand is a doctor who has returned to Meudon, near Paris, after the war and recalls his adventures when he fled France after the Nazi defeat became imminent. Fearing execution as a collaborator—and guilty of notorious anti-Semitism—Ferdinand threw in his lot with the Germans, though his ultimate goal was to get to the money he had sent earlier to Denmark. In *Castle to Castle*, Ferdinand is billeted with French refugees in a castle in the German city of Sigmaringen, where he shows himself to be quite adept at survival in a time of total crisis. He cynically consorts with the officials of the French collaboration government of Vichy, who still try to delude themselves with thoughts that Germany might still win the war in 1944. In the second published novel, *North*, Ferdinand tells of his earlier flight from France before arriving at Sigmaringen. Céline is sent by the German authorities to a village near Berlin, called here Zornhof, where he observes the antics of German aristocrats on the eve of defeat. In *Rigadoon*, the doctor-narrator tells of his travels under bomber-filled skies after he leaves Zornhof first to go north toward the Danish border, then to the south of Germany and Sigmaringen; after which he then returns, after the experience of *Castle to Castle*, to the north, where under bombardment he finally can flee to the Denmark that he hopes will offer him asylum. Throughout these novels, Ferdinand is the supposedly lucid observer who sees the often-insane pretensions of the characters—fictional and historical—with whom he consorts. He is also an angry narrator who believes that the present era, that of the France of the late 1950's and early 1960's, is condemned to decadence, and he takes great delight in predicting that the white race will eventually disappear as the yellow and black peoples of the globe breed with them.

Lili, Céline's wife. Lili accompanies Céline through the entire trip. She is a silent character, who, much like their cat, shows great resilience in surviving their ordeal.

Bébert (bā•bĕr'), Céline's cat.

Le Vigan (vē•gäṅ'), also called **La Vigue** (vēg), a French cinema actor who had been condemned by the Resistance as a collaborator. He accompanies Céline and Lili during the first part of their travels in Germany and also reappears from the dead in the opening section of *Castle to Castle* when the

241

narrator has a hallucination about seeing Charon, the ferryman who conveys the souls of the dead across the river Styx. As the novels progress, he takes on a character of his own, especially when he seems to become demented, acting out roles from his films or claiming to be a murderer.

Achille Brottin (brō•tăn′), Céline's publisher. This is a fictitious name for the publisher Gaston Gallimard, about whom Céline says rather unpleasant things.

Norbert Loukoum (lōō•kōōm′), an editor. This is a fictitious name for Jean Paulhan, an editor and writer working for Gallimard, whom Céline mocks.

Marshall Petain (pə•tăn), head of the Vichy government. Petain was a hero in World War I and in his old age was called upon to lead the government of France that collaborated with the Nazis after the French defeat in 1940. He was interned at Sigmaringen.

Jean Bichelonne (bē•shə•lŭn′), minister of industry in the Vichy government. He is one of many historical personages who fled France and were interned by Adolf Hitler in the castle at Sigmaringen, immediately before the Allied victory.

Ferdinand de Brion (brē•ŏn′), a journalist and Nazi collaborator also interned at Sigmaringen.

Abel Bonnard (bō•nárd′), a writer and member of the French academy also interned at Sigmaringen.

Restif (rĕs•tĕf′), a member of the French militia. Céline is very impressed by the talents of this paid assassin and collaborator who can apparently slit a throat with ease.

Doctor Harras, a high functionary in Hitler's Reich. As a collaborator with Céline, he helps him by sending him and his group to live in a village in the north of Germany, Zorhof, then to the south to Sigmaringen.

His motivation for helping Céline is not clear. In his verbose ranting he often seems to offer a double for Céline's point of view.

Rittmeister von Leiden (fôn lī′dən), an aristocrat in northern Germany. This aging Prussian is a masochist, emblematic of the insane who populate Céline's Nazi Germany. He sets out alone on horseback to stop the Russians and is beaten by prostitutes who roam the northern plains.

Marie-Thérèse, Rittmeister's sister, a paranoid who plots against her family.

Inge (or **Isis**) **von Leiden,** daughter-in-law of Rittmeister von Leiden. She wants poison from Céline so that she can get rid of her husband, a legless cripple.

Otto von Simmer (fôn zĭm′ər), the *Landrat*, or district president. This nobleman is apparently a homosexual and is murdered at *North's* end.

Kretzer (krĕt′zər), a medical functionary for the Reich. As a doctor Céline must deal with this hostile character.

Frau Kretzer, wife of Kretzer. She has lost two sons in the war and is mentally ill. She and Inge set fire to the manor in *North*.

Roger Nimier (nē•myä′), a novelist and adviser to Gallimard. He was one of the first to support Céline and defend his works after World War II.

Robert Poulet (pōō•lä′), a writer and critic. He is another early champion of Céline, though Céline succeeds in alienating him with his new racism.

Erbert Haupt (houpt), a doctor. He makes Céline and his companions get off the train at Rostock when they first attempt to go into Denmark. A follower of Friedrich Nietzsche and apparently a racist, he believes in the doctrine of natural selection.

Captain Hoffman, a member of German

general staff. He helps Céline on his way from Rostock back to Ulm.

Captain Siegfried, a fireman. Encountered in Ulm, this fireman has seen too much destruction and only wants to drink.

Odile Pomaré (pô•mä•rā′), a French teacher.

On the way to Hamburg, she is fleeing the Russians with forty-two children.

Felipe, an Italian worker. This brickmaker accompanies Céline north on the final leg of his journey when Céline is hit on the head by a flying brick.

Allen Thiher

THE CAT

Author: Colette (Sidonie-Gabrielle Colette, 1873-1954)
Type of work: Novel
Time of action: The early 1930's
First published: La Chatte, 1933 (English translation, 1936)

Alain Amparat (äm•pər•ä′), the only son and heir to Amparat et Fils (Amparat and Sons), an old and respected Parisian silk manufacturing firm, which employs him as its figurehead director. Alain carries himself with the arrogant, slightly bored self-assurance that often accompanies both "old money" and natural good looks. He is twenty-four, tall, handsome, and very fair, with good teeth, long cheeks, a slightly equine nose, natural waves in his over-thick golden hair, and clear, grayish-green eyes framed by lush dark lashes. He considers himself to be condescending to marry Camille, whom he characterizes pejoratively as a "typical modern girl." His commitment is shallow and perfunctory. He fully accepts and loves only his mother and Saha, his cat, the one thing in his life that he has chosen for himself. Soon after Alain's wedding, he begins to feel restless, lose weight, and resent his wife's corresponding heartiness. Because Camille outstrips Alain both sexually and in her ability to live life, he turns from her to Saha, whom he can dominate and who expects no more from him than love and sensuality. Only with Saha, Alain realizes, can he truly be himself. He begins to dread the day when Camille will move into his family home and is relieved when her attempted murder of Saha gives him an excuse to end the marriage and escape back to his childhood paradise with his beloved cat.

Camille Malmert (mä•mâr′), Alain's bride, he nineteen-year-old daughter of a newly rich manufacturer of washing machines. Her family has more money but less social status than the Amparats. She is slim, healthy, dark, and attractive, with good teeth, white skin, small breasts, a resonant voice, stubby fingers, and large, almost black eyes surrounded by bluish-looking whites. She seems to Alain to be slightly commonplace because of her lack of modesty, her determination to speak her mind, and her love of jazz, slang, fast cars, and nightclubs. After Alain brings Saha to live with them, Camille views her as a rival, especially after Alain begins sleeping on the divan with the cat on his chest. She is both mystified by and jealous of Alain's ability to empathize and communicate with Saha and irritated by his inability to understand and respect her. As her jealousy grows in direct proportion to her husband's increasing indifference toward her, Camille forces a resolution to this strange love triangle by acting rashly. Her unsuccessful attempt to murder Saha by pushing her off their ninth-floor balcony gives Alain the excuse that he is looking for to leave Camille and return to his family home. The end of her marriage does not break Camille's spirit. At the end of *The Cat*, she leaves Alain, busily making plans for her life and future without him.

Saha, a three-year-old purebred Russian

Blue cat, which Alain had purchased as a five-month-old kitten at a cat show. She is proud and suspicious, with deep-set golden eyes, big cheeks, a small body, a perfect face, and moonstone-colored fur. For Alain, she represents the nobility of all cats because of her natural dignity, innocence, modesty, and disinterestedness, as well as her ability to accept the inevitable, bear pain in silence, and love both freedom and order. He believes that such cats have affinities only with the finest type of human beings—those who can understand and communicate with them. Saha loves Alain: She instinctively dislikes and distrusts Camille. After Alain and Camille marry, Saha is left beind at the Amparat family home, where she refuses to eat. Her health deteriorates so greatly that Alain brings her to live with him and Camille. Here she eats, but only enough to keep alive. After Camille's attempt to murder her, Saha and Alain return to his maternal home, where she once again begins to play, hunt, eat normally, and gain weight.

Mme Amparat, Alain's widowed mother, an aging upper-middle-class society matron. She considers Camille her social inferior, judging her to be "not quite our type."

Émile, the Amparats' elderly, taciturn, family butler, who has oyster-colored eyes and prominent whiskers. He reflects the Amparats' condescending attitude toward Camille.

Mme Buque (būk), Alain and Camille's housekeeper and cook. She is a large, fat, red-cheeked woman who cooks food well and serves it badly.

M. Veuillet (vüē•yā′), Alain's father's oldest partner. He does most of the decision-making at the Amparat silk firm.

Adele, another elderly family servant who exhibits a patronizing attitude toward Camille.

Nancy E. Rupprecht

THE CATCHER IN THE RYE

Author: J. D. Salinger (1919-   )
Type of work: Novel
Time of action: Saturday to Monday in December, the late 1940's
First published: 1951

Holden Caulfield, a tall seventeen-year-old, with prematurely graying hair. In a California sanatorium where he is undergoing treatment for a physical and mental collapse, he narrates the very subjective account of his almost two-day sojourn in New York City shortly before his breakdown. Just before the last Christmas break, he had fled Pencey, an exclusive boys' preparatory school in Pennsylvania from which he had been expelled. Alienated, lonely, and sad, afraid to go home until the date his parents expected him, Holden roamed New York City seeking comfort and understanding from past friends and acquaintances, from strangers, and, stealthily, from his adored little sister, Phoebe. Still mourning his younger brother

Allie's death from leukemia three years earlier, Holden nurses a morbid sensitivity behind a façade of adolescent loudmouthed belligerence, bravado, and apathy that has cost him friends and family approval and caused this third expulsion from a school. Longing for emotional support, Holden perversely trusts almost no one. He views his world, not incorrectly, as being full of "phonies"; often, he fantasizes about a solitary life as a self-sufficient deaf-mute. Holden longs for an idyllic world epitomized for him in the words of Robert Burns's "Coming Through the Rye." He wishes himself the "catcher," protector of children's innocence, in a kind of sunlit never-never land where life's ugly adult realities—and even death—

are kept at bay. He wryly admits, though, that such a world cannot exist. His temporary retreat is this collapse from which he is now recovering by warily recounting his experiences and feelings to a shadowy listener, probably a psychiatrist.

Sally Hayes, Holden's longtime friend in New York City, a little older than he and certainly more worldly. A pretty, vain, wealthy, and self-absorbed social climber, she disappoints Holden's hopes of a comforting and yielding companion when they meet for a Sunday date in downtown New York City. When she naturally rejects Holden's wild scheme for a romantic trip to northern New England, he publicly insults her, and she flounces out of Rockefeller Plaza alone. Holden appreciates her physical charms but ultimately rejects her as shallow and smug.

Phoebe Josephine Caulfield, Holden's wiry, red-haired, and bright ten-year-old sister. Regarding Phoebe as a living copy of all that he loved in Allie, Holden creeps home Sunday night to seek out her loyal companionship and her understanding. He is comforted by Phoebe's jauntiness and vitality; he yearns to protect her from the ugliness he perceives in the world around them. A last coherent memory he has before his breakdown is of a rush of happiness as he watches Phoebe serenely riding the Central Park carousel, a tangible link with much that was joyous in his own childhood.

D. B., Holden's older brother, a successful Hollywood scriptwriter. Holden views D. B.'s life and career as "phoney" and wishes he would return to "pure" artistry as the short fiction writer he had been.

Jane Gallagher, a friend Holden's age from his summers in Maine. Holden and Jane enjoyed an unintimidating, platonic, late-childhood relationship in which each derived comfort from the other, especially when their separate private griefs intruded. At Pencey, when Holden discovers that his roommate, the "sexy bastard" Ward Stradlater, has a blind date with Jane, he is distraught, jealous and repelled by the thought of Jane at the mercy of handsome, conceited Stradlater. His concern precipitates his physical and verbal attack on Stradlater and his flight from Pencey later that Saturday night, marking the start of his odyssey.

Mr. Antolini, a youngish man now married to a wealthy older woman and once Holden's English teacher at another preparatory school. Holden had respected Mr. Antolini as a teacher and valued him as a compassionate, trustworthy confidant, especially after seeing Antolini's selfless response to a violent student death. In New York City, Holden seeks out Antolini for solace and shelter after he must flee discovery by his parents at home. He finds Antolini welcoming, ready with measured advice, but drinking steadily. Only disquieted when he settles to sleep on the Antolinis' couch, the self-absorbed Holden seems not to perceive the restless cynicism that pervades Antolini's response to his problems and perhaps explains the ever-present highball. Holden flees in panic when he awakes to find Antolini patting his head, a gesture Holden interprets as "perverty" though he later regrets his precipitous flight when he remembers Antolini's previous kindnesses. This betrayal of trust contributes further to Holden's overwhelming sense of depression and alienation. It is perhaps Antolini above the several other flawed people Holden meets who most embodies the moral emptiness and irrelevance of Holden's world.

Jill Rollins

CATHLEEN NI HOULIHAN

Author: William Butler Yeats (1865-1939)
Type of work: Play
Time of action: 1798
First produced: 1902

Cathleen ni Houlihan, "The Poor Old Woman," who symbolizes impoverished Ireland, seeking independence from British rule. A stranger, she has come to the countryside of Killala to enlist the help of the Irish in regaining her four stolen fields. She entrances Michael Gillane to leave his home and join her cause. His sacrifices and those of others transform her old age into youth. She steps from the Gillanes' door a young queen.

Michael Gillane, a young man about to be married the day after meeting Cathleen ni Houlihan. His life is full of promise: He is engaged to a pretty girl whose parents have given a dowry of one hundred pounds. He rejects domestic bliss, however, to fight for Ireland. In joining the French forces against the British, he risks his life, knowing that death will bring eternal fame.

Peter Gillane, Michael's father, a farmer who is much interested in the dowry brought by his future daughter-in-law. Her amount will make possible the buying of livestock for 10 acres of their land. When he begrudgingly offers Cathleen ni Houlihan a shilling,

he is amazed by her refusal, for money dominates his life.

Bridget Gillane, Peter's wife, who is angered by her husband's remark that she brought no dowry with her. A hardworking, practical woman, she wants the best for her two sons. With Michael about to be married, she begins to plan Patrick's future as a priest. Full of hospitality, Bridget directs Michael to open their door to Cathleen and bids her husband to offer the old woman money.

Patrick Gillane, the Gillanes' twelve-year-old son. He functions to announce the events of the outside world: the approach of the old woman to their neighbors' home, the cheering that greets Cathleen ni Houlihan, the landing of the French at Killala, and their being joined by the Irish. It is Patrick who proclaims the transformation of Cathleen ni Houlihan.

Delia Cahel, the young girl Michael is to marry. She loses the struggle for Michael's affections and their life together; their love is overshadowed by his devotion to Ireland.

Jacqueline L. Gmuca

CAT'S CRADLE

Author: Kurt Vonnegut, Jr. (1922-   )
Type of work: Novel
Time of action: The early 1960's
First published: 1963

John, surname unknown, the narrator. A Cornell-educated journalist, John spends the course of the book interviewing the friends and children of Dr. Felix Hoenikker for a book about the day the atom bomb was dropped. John is always perfectly gracious and objective in his interviews, even when his subjects are hostile and impute ulterior motives to his writing. His research takes him to the island nation of San Lorenzo, where he unintentionally becomes president

and witnesses the unleashing of *ice-nine*, which freezes the world.

Dr. Felix Hoenikker, a Nobel Prize-winning atomic scientist and creator of *ice-nine*. He is already dead as the book opens, but much of his later life is uncovered by the narrator. Fascinated by the puzzles of nature, Hoenikker has very little interest in people. He had no interest in the human implications of the atom bomb he helped create, nor in

246

the potential human harm his invention of *ice-nine* may cause; the novel ends with Hoenikker's invention freezing, and thus destroying, the entire earth.

Newt Hoenikker, a midget, the youngest child of Dr. Hoenikker. Newt is a cynical young man whose one-week marriage to a Ukranian midget named Zinka was apparently a ruse designed to obtain the secret of *ice-nine* for the Soviet Union. An incident from his childhood explains the name of the novel: On the day the atom bomb was dropped on Japan, Dr. Hoenikker dangled a string in the form of a "cat's cradle" in front of six-year-old Newt, causing the boy to cry.

Angela Hoenikker, later **Mrs. Harrison C. Conners,** Newt and Franklin's sister, the eldest of Dr. Hoenikker's children. Tall and homely, Angela dropped out of high school in her sophomore year to take care of her father and brothers when her mother died. Her only diversion was playing the clarinet. When her father died, she lost much of her purpose, until Harrison C. Conners, a handsome researcher in her father's lab, met and married her shortly after. She paints a storybook picture of her marriage, although Newt asserts that her husband is unfaithful. Franklin implies that Conners married her only to get the secret of *ice-nine* for the U.S. government.

Franklin Hoenikker, the middle child of Dr. Hoenikker and Major General and Minister of Science and Progress in the Caribbean republic of San Lorenzo. An immature-looking twenty-six-year-old, Frank came to San Lorenzo after escaping the Federal Bureau of Investigation, which sought him for smuggling cars to Cuba. As an adolescent, Frank was ignored by classmates, who called him "Secret Agent X-9" because he kept to himself. His time alone was spent building models, though near the end of the book he reveals that he had not always been alone: He had had an affair with his boss's wife.

"Papa" Monzano, the dictatorial president of San Lorenzo. A native of the island republic, Monzano is the handpicked successor of Corporal Earl McCabe, an American who began the current regime on San Lorenzo in the 1920's. Like McCabe, he pretended opposition to Bokonon. Tiring of a system based on lies, Monzano, now in his late seventies, brought Frank Hoenikker to San Lorenzo as a way of turning to science. Learning from Frank the secret of *ice-nine*, Monzano commits suicide by swallowing it, thereby freezing himself and, by contact with him, all the water on earth.

Lionel Boyd Johnson, Bokonon, a philosopher and opponent of Monzano. Born on the island of Tobago in 1891, Johnson washed up on the shores of San Lorenzo in 1922, along with U.S. Army Corporal Earl McCabe. McCabe became the island's ruler and, discovering that he could not relieve its poverty, sought to make its people happy with harmless lies. Johnson ("Bokonon" in the native dialect) created a new religion, which McCabe pretended to suppress, playing the evil dictator while Bokonon became the good holy man in the jungle. His religion, Bokononism, is based on the principle that all religions are *foma* (harmless lies), including Bokononism.

John R. Holmes

THE CAUCASIAN CHALK CIRCLE

Author: Bertolt Brecht (1898-1956)
Type of work: Play
Time of action: c. A.D. 900; Prologue, 1945
First produced: Der kaukasische Kreidekreis, 1948 (English translation, 1948)

Grusha, a young, attractive, unmarried, helpful kitchen maid in the family of the governor of a Caucasian city. The governor, returning from Easter mass, is killed in a political uprising. His wife, concerned about fleeing with her elegant dresses, forgets her baby, and the kindhearted Grusha cares for him. Fleeing for safety to her brother's distant home in the mountains, she protects the child. Grusha's sister-in-law, concerned about an unmarried girl with a baby, has Grusha married to a supposedly dying man who revives immediately after the wedding. Grusha, however, is still loyal to her Easter morning betrothal to the soldier Simon. When the child is brought back for the governor's wife by soldiers, Grusha pleads in court for the child. The governor's wife needs the son for access to the family estates, but Grusha loves him and is best for him. She wins him, is given a divorce, and her love for Simon is also rewarded.

Azdak (äz·däk′), a village scrivener, suddenly elevated, during a time of political chaos, into the role of judge for two years. He is a drunken rascal given to stealing chickens and rabbits. During the political war, he befriended a beggar, sheltering him from the police, only to learn later that it was the Grand Duke. Azdak, upset at being a traitor to his own class, wants to be tried in court but instead is made judge. His rulings, using a feigned stupidity, reflect sympathy for the poor and weak. When he seems sympathetic to the governor's wife, Grusha berates him, touching off his guilt for betraying his own class. When the birth mother pulls the child from the chalk circle and Grusha refrains out of love so as not to maim him, Azdak grants her the child.

Simon Shashava, a soldier and a guard at the palace. He has watched Grusha from behind a bush as she went to the river to do the wash, putting her bare legs in the water. Simon, ordered to accompany the governor's wife into exile, first wins Grusha's promise of marriage, expecting to return in a few weeks. He follows her to her husband's home in the mountains and then to court, willing to accept the child and marry Grusha.

Georgi Abashwili, a governor for the Grand Duke, rather lackadaisical about his responsibilities and in recognizing realities. When the palace is captured after Easter mass, he is killed.

Natella Abashwili, the governor's wife, a whining, superficial, self-centered woman concerned more about her dresses than about her child or the danger of the situation. It is clear that she is seeking the child mainly to get control of his large estates.

Michael Abashwili, their child. He is well-behaved and cooperative on the difficult twenty-two-day journey with Grusha. He reciprocates Grusha's love.

Arsen Kazbeki, a fat two-faced prince who shows deference to the governor and then engineers the palace revolt and kills the governor.

E. Lynn Harris

CAUGHT

Author: Henry Green (Henry Vincent Yorke, 1905-1973)
Type of work: Novel
Time of action: 1939-1940
First published: 1943

Richard Roe, a widower in his mid-thirties who has volunteered for duty in London's Auxiliary Fire Service. Badly hurt by the death of his wife, Roe, a product of an affluent, cultured home, learns what life holds in store for members of the working class when he signs on as a fireman and lives among them. Roe, in his detached way, loves his son, Christopher, but their relationship grows distant after Roe's sister Dy takes over his duty as parent. Ironically, one of the things that happens to Christopher in his absence is that the boy is abducted for a short time by the sister of his superior officer, Albert Pye.

Albert Pye, sub-officer of the London Auxiliary Fire Service station and Roe's superior officer. Pye, a rough, memory-tormented man from humble origins, represses the fact that when young, he made love to his own sister, an act that propels her into madness and eventually leads to his suicide in a gas oven.

Dy, Roe's sister-in-law who cares for his young son, Christopher, while his fire duties call him away from home. Sharp-tempered and snobbish, she detests the Fire Service personnel and their mean surroundings.

Christopher, Roe's son, who is under the care and tutelage of Dy. A five-year-old at novel's outset, Christopher gradually loses interest in his father as a result of his prolonged separation from him and increasingly adopts the upper-class attitudes of Dy at the same time his father is shedding his preconceived notions about people of "lower station in life."

Hilly, Fire Service driver for Pye who becomes romantically involved with Roe.

Hilly's love helps Roe move away from the pain of his wife's death, and he admires her frank, commonsensical approach to life.

Prudence, upper-class lover of Pye who eventually tires of him and dismisses him from her thoughts. She is Hilly's opposite in many ways, for she is rich and cultivated, though narrow and bigoted. Her interest in the British working class only extends to brief romantic adventures with firemen.

Arthur Piper, oldest fireman with London's Fire Service, who saw duty in World War I. He constantly plays up to his superior officers in an absurd, wheedling fashion.

Shiner Wright, heroic, rugged Fire Service veteran who is killed fighting a huge conflagration in the area around London's docks, which was set ablaze by Nazi bombs.

Trant, Roe's and Pye's commanding officer, a stern, rule-bound man having little interest in the men and women in his command.

Mary Howells, menial worker at the Fire Service station known for her interest in passing along information about others.

John D. Raymer

THE CENCI

Author: Antonin Artaud (1896-1948)
Type of work: Play
Time of action: The sixteenth century
First produced: Les Cenci, 1935 (English translation, 1964, in *Complete Works*)

Count Cenci, the malevolently evil patriarch of a wealthy Renaissance family. In his late sixties, he is arrogant, blasphemous, and sadistically cruel to all the members of his family. His primary motivation in practicing evil is that he identifies himself with nature and, therefore, must abandon himself to his desires. After bribing the Pope to pardon him for murdering some old enemies, he organizes a luxurious orgy, during which he

triumphantly announces the deaths of his two sons and threatens both his wife, Lucretia, and his daughter, Beatrice. After repeatedly raping Beatrice, he is murdered by assassins hired by Beatrice and Lucretia but not before arranging for their deaths with the Pope, to whom he has willed his entire estate.

Beatrice Cenci, a young, beautiful, and

highly sensitive virgin. The only daughter of the wicked Count, she is terrified of what he has blatantly threatened to do to her and spends half the play trying to avoid him. After her father rapes her, she is forced to either submit to his repeated assaults or to murder him. Her major revelation in the play is that her only choice is to be a victim or a victimizer and that either choice will send her to eternal damnation. Just before she is executed by order of the Pope, she realizes that her major crime was in being born.

Lucretia Cenci, the second wife of the Count and the stepmother of Beatrice, Bernardo, and Giacomo. A middle-aged beauty, she is alternately terrified and mystified by her husband's unmotivated sadistic behavior. She, Beatrice, Giacomo, and Orsino conspire to have the Count murdered by hired assassins; she slips a sleeping potion into her husband's wine to ready him for the murder. She is executed with Beatrice at the play's conclusion.

Bernardo, the younger brother of Beatrice and unaware of the murder conspiracy. Because of his sensitive artistic nature, he has difficulty in believing the degradation taking place in the court. The Count, however, spares his life because he wants him to be the surviving sufferer. He is forced by the Pope to witness the torture and death of his beloved sister and stepmother and collapses at the end in a paroxysm of agony.

Camillo, a Cardinal and Papal Legate. Although he is completely aware of the Count's evil projects, he nevertheless arranges a pardon from the Pope for some of his earlier atrocities. He successfully maintains his middle position in case the Count is successfully overthrown. Once he arranges for the Papacy to become sole heir to the Count's property and possessions, however, he permits the family drama to play itself out to its inevitably tragic conclusion.

Orsino, a prelate, priest, and coconspirator in the plot to murder the Count. Middle aged and desperately in love with Beatrice, he initially plans to support Beatrice in punishing her father for his sexual assaults on her. Once she rejects him, though, he helps to arrange the Count's assassination knowing full well that it will destroy the family and he will have his revenge upon Beatrice.

Giacomo Cenci, one of the Count's elder sons. Once he discovers that his father is raping his sister and that the Pope is to inherit the Count's considerable holdings, he becomes one of the planners of the Count's murder, as he has nothing to lose. He escapes punishment by fleeing the country.

Patrick Meanor

THE CENTAUR

Author: John Updike (1932-   )
Type of work: Novel
Time of action: Monday morning to Thursday morning of the second week of January, 1947
First published: 1963

George Caldwell (Chiron), a general science teacher at Olinger High School and, at the mythic level, the centaur who is the teacher of the gods. At fifty years old and in physical pain, Caldwell is fearful about death and uncertain about the value of his own teaching. Despite his doubt and self-deprecation, however, Caldwell shows a deep sensitivity to the needs and fears of others. During the three days depicted in the novel, he and his son, Peter, are forced by car trouble and a snowstorm to spend two nights together away from home. They encounter a world that is realistic in detail and yet explicitly mythic in its emotional and spiritual resonance.

Peter Caldwell (Prometheus), George's son, a fifteen-year-old high school student who is, at the mythic level, the Titan who brought fire to humans and was chained to a rock on Mount Olympus as punishment. Chiron accepted death in exchange for Prometheus' freedom. In the period of the novel, Peter is troubled by psoriasis, a skin condition inherited from his mother, and fearful about his father's illness. Furthermore, Peter is struggling to understand his emerging sexuality and his relationship to the community of his childhood. A promising art student, he contrasts the grimy, uncultured bleakness of Olinger with images of glamor and wealth in New York City. Ironically, in telling the story fourteen years later, Peter has become an Abstract Expressionist painter in New York City, but his life with his Afro-American lover seems to lack the "firm stage resonant with metaphor" that he recalls in depicting his adolescence.

Catherine (Cassie) Caldwell (Ceres), George's wife and Peter's mother, she is the goddess Ceres at the mythic level. No longer a beautiful woman, she is intermittently sharp and tender in her responses to George, Peter, and her father, who lives with them. Her greatest fulfillment is in her love of nature. As a result of her desire to live in the rural farmhouse in Firetown, George and Peter must drive eleven miles to Olinger High School, and it is this journey that precipitates their three days of adventure in the novel.

Pop Kramer (Kronos), Cassie's father, who is, at the mythic level, the dethroned Titan, Kronos. He is an aphorism-spouting old man whose certainties contrast with George Caldwell's pained and thoughtful skepticism.

Al Hummel (Hephaestus), a skilled mechanic and the owner of a local garage, he is related to George as Cassie's cousin. At the mythic level, he is the god of fire and craftsmanship. Hummel's hunched and limping body reflects a childhood accident as well as expressing his dismay at the postwar economy and his grief in his childless marriage to Vera, who is notoriously unfaithful. An understanding friend to George, Hummel helped him to get the teaching job in Olinger. On the second night that George and Peter are stranded in Olinger, they trudge through the snow to Hummel's house, where they sleep together in Peter's great-aunt's bed. The next day, Hummel helps them to shovel out their snowbound car for their return to the farmhouse in Firetown.

Vera Hummel (Venus), Al's wife and the girls' basketball coach at the high school. At the mythic level, she is the goddess of love (Venus/Aphrodite), and she is beautiful: amber-haired and slender, with golden skin and clear, delicate features. Her laughter is not, however, simply an expression of spontaneous joy; it is also a release and a consolation for her grief in her marriage to Hummel and, in her role as goddess, for her woe at men's ribald mockery of sexual desire. Her scenes with George and Peter affirm that sexual sensitivity and responsiveness are central issues in Peter's understanding of his father and his own emerging maturity. On the morning after the snowstorm, for example, Vera gives Peter breakfast and talks with him, providing glowing moments of release from the fears and anxieties he has carried throughout the previous three days.

Louis M. Zimmerman (Zeus), the Olinger High School principal and, at the mythic level, the ruler of the heavens. Both resented and respected in the small town, he is self-assertive, lecherous, and impetuous. In his insensitive evaluation of George's teaching, his misappropriation of 140 tickets for a basketball game, and his affair with a woman on the school board, Zimmerman is a major source of George's anxieties about money and his fear of losing his teaching job.

Dr. Harry Appleton (Apollo), a local medical doctor. A plump, pink balding man, he is, at the mythic level, the god of healing. Like Peter, Doc Appleton has psoriasis, and his matter-of-fact concern for Peter's skin condition parallels his humane directness in discussing George's symptoms and fears. His telephone call to Cassie reporting the results of George's X rays lifts the dread that has characterized the three days of adventure.

Hester Appleton (Artemis), Doc Appleton's twin sister and the Olinger High School teacher of French and Latin. At fifty years old, she is plump and virginal, and, at the level of myth, she is the goddess Artemis. With her precise, sensitive use of language and her expressions of concern for George,

Hester affirms his significance as a teacher and as a person.

Ray Deifendorf, a student at Olinger High School and a successful competitor on the losing swimming team that George coaches. Deifendorf is somewhat lewd and insensitive, but he feels deep affection for George, and, years later, Peter learns that Deifendorf has become a high school teacher.

Donald Vanouse

THE CEREMONY OF INNOCENCE

Author: Ronald Ribman (1932-   )
Type of work: Play
Time of action: Winter, 1012, to Christmas, 1013
First produced: 1967

King Ethelred, the poignantly idealistic, moralistic King of England. Against the wishes of many of his advisers and all of his family, he has signed a truce with the Danes, and the plot turns around his dogged but hopeless attempts to stave off the unraveling of the fragile peace. He is a visionary who uses the peace to try to educate the peasants and equip a ship for a voyage of discovery. His ethical sense is rooted in guilt in that the one man he idolized in his youth, his pious stepbrother who was ruling the country, was done away with by his mother so Ethelred could gain the throne. Perhaps for this reason, he is almost truculent in his refusal to compromise on ethical questions. As the play proceeds, he becomes more and more isolated from his pragmatic advisers until he is ready to forfeit his kingdom to maintain his purity.

Edmund, Ethelred's son. Like Hotspur in Shakespeare's *Henry IV, Part I*, Edmund is intemperately concerned with his own and his country's honor. Going further than the king's other advisers, who only offer verbal objections to the truce, the headstrong Edmund physically disrupts the new status quo by destroying the possessions of the Danish king's daughter, Thulja, and later by murder-

ing four Danish farmers resident in England. His hot temper and facility with insults cause his downfall when his taunting of the Danish ambassador is met with a dagger.

Alfreda, Ethelred's aged mother. Sharp-tongued, treacherous, and actively evil, she upbraids her son for fearing violence, telling him that keeping a war stirring distracts the populace. She constantly reminds him that his own position was achieved through murder, and it is her move that finally sunders the peace when she slays Thulja.

Emma, Ethelred's wife, daughter of the Duke of Normandy. She is almost simple-minded in her virulent hatred of the Danes. Her detestation is based on fear and suspicion, and she has little with which to counter the arguments of her husband except a blind loyalty to the brutal practices of her father. She becomes increasingly estranged from her neglectful spouse as he devotes all of his time to his political preoccupations.

Thulja, fifteen-year-old daughter of Danish King Sweyn who has been left as a hostage at the English court to ensure that the Danes abide by the peace treaty. She is a babe in the woods, uncomprehending of the intrigues and depressed by the rebuffs she suffers from the "war" party, who consider her an irritating symbol of a dishonorable peace. Her purity and ability to extend uncalculating sympathy make her the only person with whom Ethelred can share his dreams. Her murder in the English court precipitates the sundering of the truce.

Earl of Kent, the adviser closest to the king, who is able to see the value of Ethelred's dreams and argue for them pragmatically. Because he has a fourteen-year-old, crippled daughter, he feels sympathy for the misplaced Thulja. He is too practical to follow the king in his pacificism when he feels it endangers the country.

Earl of Sussex, the main verbal antagonist of Kent. A blunt, angry leader who proclaims the only worthy morality stems from the point of a sword. Though as honor smitten as Edmund, he is able to curb his feelings when he finds the majority against him.

Bishop of London, a temporizer who holds a middle place between Sussex and Kent. At first, he is committed to peace and economic reconstruction, but he begins to balk when the king tampers with church prerogatives.

King Sweyn, leader of the Danes. Possessor of the superior army, he is willing to abide by the truce to better conditions for his many countrymen who have settled in England. Though worried about leaving a daughter among the English, he is cunning enough to order her to spy out their forces during her residence.

Thorkill, Danish emissary sent to England to learn the facts about the murder of four Danish farmers. Though willing to be mollified by a sufficiently searching inquiry, he is bewildered by the unmannerly behavior of Edmund. He is slow to anger but violent when provoked.

Abbot Oswald, head of a monastery on the Isle of Wight where Ethelred has sought sanctuary from the mounting pressure to declare war. Isolated from the events of the world, he views the power conflicts surrounding the throne with detachment, coupled with an irritating lack of passion.

James Feast

THE CHAIN OF CHANCE

Author: Stanisław Lem (1921-   )
Type of work: Novel
Time of action: The late 1970's
First published: Katar, 1976 (English translation, 1978)

John, the narrator, a laconic fifty-year-old American private detective of French Canadian origin who has been hired to investigate the death of an American named Adams. An unreflective man of action, almost a machine, he seldom becomes nervous or frightened. As an astronaut, he learned how to wait patiently for those moments when quick and decisive action is required. Yet he can make quite impulsive decisions, as when he enlisted in the commandos at the age of eighteen and participated in the invasion of Normandy as a glider infantryman. Dismissed from the Mars program because of allergies to grass and dust, he has been hired to investigate the death of a fellow American who was one of twelve victims of exactly the same unknown causes of death in Naples.

Annabella, a young French girl whom John heroically saves from death from a Japanese terrorist's bomb in the Rome airport. Though newspaper accounts of this event describe her as a teenager, she is in fact younger than that. At first she is apprehensive about John, fearing that he may be part of the terrorist's

253

plot, but she becomes friendly with her protector when he takes her back to her parents.

Dr. Philippe Barth, a distinguished French computer scientist who serves as a consultant to the Sûreté. Because he has been programming a computer to solve problems in which the amount of data exceeds the storage capacity of human memory, John consults him as a last resort to help him unravel the case. He introduces John to a number of specialists whose conflicting advice when taken together enables him to understand the cause of Adams' death.

Lapidus (lä′pē•dōō), a French pharmacologist. His full-length beard and rather rough appearance make him appear like someone who has just returned from being marooned on an uninhabited island. He explains to John the scientific reasons for his belief that Adams and the others were the victims of gradual poisoning.

Saussure (sō•sür′), a French specialist in pure mathematics. Lean and dark, his gold pince-nez gives him an old-fashioned appearance. Intellectually, he is rather a drifter, and he has recently resigned from a project which was attempting to calculate the possibility of extraterrestrial civilizations. He gives John insight into the "chain of chance" which caused the victims' deaths by showing that they were the result of a random causality.

Mayer, a German statistician. A burly man with curly blond hair, he resembles the cartoon Germans of World War I French propaganda. Because he is an applied mathematician, he serves as a foil to the pure, theoretical mathematics of Saussure.

Inspector Pingaud (păṅ•gō′), an elderly officer in the Sûreté. He tells John and Barth of a previous case of poisoning by accidental combinations of random elements which leads them to a successful solution of the Adams case.

Robert L. Berner

A CHAIN OF VOICES

Author: André Brink (1935-   )
Type of work: Novel
Time of action: The 1780's to 1826
First published: 1982

Piet van der Merwe, an Afrikaner farmer and patriarch. Once a strong and forceful man, the aged Piet has become helpless from a stroke. Because the novel is composed solely of monologues by the characters, Piet himself records his part in the events that surround the slave uprising, traces the course of his life to the uprising and his stroke, and reveals his relationships with the other characters. Throughout, he emerges a God-fearing, British-hating, racialist, self-righteous, often cruel man, who unintentionally destroys his family as he seeks to carry out what he believes to be the will of God. In some ways, he is a stereotypical Afrikaner of the era.

Alida, Piet's wife. Aging and worn from her hard life as a farmer's wife on the South African veld, Alida recounts the past years with bitterness: her youth as a beautiful young woman in Cape Town, her stormy marriage, the years of childbirth and hard work, the disappointments and disillusionment. Yet she has attained a sort of peace, having become reconciled to the destructive force unleashed by her husband, reconciled even to her own death, for which she longs.

Ma Rose, an elderly native woman. She is closely connected to the van der Merwe family as servant, mistress to Piet, and nurse to his children. Through her monologues, Ma Rose emerges as the noblest of the characters—endowed with patience, resolve, fairness, and understanding. As she speaks, she enlarges her own character to embrace the long-suffering black race by drawing parallels between the present struggle for freedom with the trials recorded in ancient tribal myths. Of Ma Rose, one of the characters says that her book "was the whole world."

Barend, Piet's eldest son and a farmer. Like his father, whom he longs to please, Barend develops into a cruel, harsh man who mistreats his wife and slaves. During the slave uprising, he proves himself a coward.

Nicolaas, Piet's youngest son and a farmer. Weaker and more sensitive than his father and older brother, Nicolaas destroys himself through his longing to gain their approval. He is his mother's favorite child, but Piet disrupts their relationship.

Galant, a slave. Galant is a handsome and powerfully built black man who was reared with Piet's sons and becomes Nicolaas' slave. Their relationship as slave and master is a subtle, complex one, and finally leads to Nicolaas' murder by Galant.

Hester, Barend's wife. An attractive young woman, she finds her marriage to Barend dismal, especially the sexual violence that she is forced to endure. While pretending to be submissive, she nourishes an inner strength that leads her to freedom, in part through her sexual encounter with Galant, then through the courage she shows during the slave rebellion. Along with Ma Rose, Hester evolves into one of the novel's rare sympathetic characters.

Cecilia, Nicolaas' wife. Plain and drab in appearance, she has developed a harsh and cold air to endure not only the oppression that is the lot of Afrikaaner women but also the indifference of a husband who despises her.

Pamela, a slave woman and Galant's chosen wife. She is forced to become Nicolaas' mistress and bears him a son.

Lydia, a simple, childlike slave woman, and another of Nicolaas' mistresses.

Robert L. Ross

THE CHAIRS

Author: Eugène Ionesco (1912-   )
Type of work: Play
Time of action: The indeterminate future: "four hundred thousand years after Paris has been extinguished"
First produced: Les Chaises, 1952 (English translation, 1958, in *Four Plays by Ionesco*)

Old Man, a "general factotum" aged ninety-five, an employee, or assistant, who serves in a wide range of capacities and does everything. He, like all the characters in this play, both visible and invisible, is made up of contrasts and contradictions. He is both man and child. His speech is composed of words and logical sentences as well as of some nonsense words and syllables and illogical sentences. Although he is a character of flesh and blood, he sometimes appears to be more illusionary than the invisible characters in this play. While awaiting the arrival of guests, he and his wife reminisce about earlier times and play games of make believe (for example, he sits on his wife's lap like a little child and calls for his mother). Although he says he is bored with it all, he continues to play the same games and tell the same story night after night. He invites a large crowd of both great and ordinary people to hear his great message that will benefit humanity. Believing himself to be inadequate to communicate this message to others, he has hired a professional orator to deliver it. He greets invisible guests as they arrive, and talks with these guests while awaiting the orator. When the orator finally arrives, the old man gives him a wordy ineffectual introduction, then saying his life is now fulfilled, he jumps out the tower window to his death.

Old Woman, the old man's ninety-four-year-old wife and "helpmeet." Like the old man, she is made up of contrast and contradiction. She is both mother and wife to the old man. At times she seems stronger and more mature than her husband, telling him that he could have been so much more than what he is if he had had more power in life. At other times, she seems only her husband's shadow as she literally echos the words that he says. She has heard the same bedtime story for seventy-five years but still asks the old man to tell it again. It fascinates her because it is his life, and she purposely makes her mind new, "a clean slate," for him every evening. She helps the old man greet their invisible guests and brings on chairs for them. She also serves as usher and seller of Eskimo pies and programs. She reveals a hidden personality when she reacts like an old prostitute to one of their guests. She claims that she and the old man have a son, but the old man says they have no children. Like the old man, she is extremely

honored that the emperor has come to their house to hear the orator present her husband's message. She echos her husband's words and actions about their dying but states that at least they will name a street after them. She jumps to her death from another window to die at the same moment and be united in time and eternity with the old man.

The Orator, a deaf-mute between forty-five and fifty years old, dressed in the typical garb of a bohemian artist of the nineteenth century. He is built up by the old man to be the greatest professional orator of all time, having documents to prove it. He is also called a friend of the old man. Although he is the third flesh-and-blood character, he is made to seem more like an invisible character than those who are invisible because he does not speak or react to the old man and old woman. He signs autographs in an automatic fashion and is impassive and generally immobile until after the double suicide when he tries in vain to communicate with the invisible audience.

Many other guests, a cross section of humanity, including the Emperor, who have come to hear the Old Man's message. All of them are invisible to the audience and are indicated by empty chairs placed on stage for them to occupy and by the speech and gestures of the Old Man and the Old Woman.

Bettye Choate Kash

THE CHANEYSVILLE INCIDENT

Author: David Bradley (1950-   )
Type of work: Novel
Time of action: The late 1970's, 1930-1965, and precolonial days to the twentieth century
First published: 1981

Dr. John Washington, a history professor and scholar. A cynical, young black man, John returns to his hometown to comfort a dying friend, Jack Crawley, and ends up re-evaluating his own life when he finally understands the circumstances surrounding the

deaths of his father, Moses Washington, and his great-grandfather, C. K. Washington. The beginning of this insight occurs when, after Crawley's funeral, John is presented with the folio bequeathed to him earlier in his father's will. The contents of the folio, along with other clues left by Moses, guide John through a historical puzzle and eventually help him find peace and meaning in his own life.

Moses Washington, John's father, a bootlegger with enough information to blackmail all the rich, white townspeople, who spurn the impoverished black community banished to the Hill. A powerful man within the district, he is feared by both blacks and whites, even though he keeps to himself, spending most of his time tramping through the Pennsylvania hills and checking on the status of his numerous stills. His suicide, mistaken as a murder, is disguised as a hunting accident to prevent an investigation from accidentally uncovering the folio, believed to contain dangerous evidence incriminating the town officials. Like his son, John, Moses is preoccupied with history and struggles to learn the truth about his ancestors. He possesses his grandfather's diary, but the book ends abruptly, and he becomes obsessed with learning what happened to C. K. Eventually, he learns the truth, and the reality brings about his suicide.

Brobdingnag C. K. Washington, John's great-grandfather, a runaway slave. A self-educated man, he is literally branded C. K. by his master as punishment. Nevertheless, he uses his knowledge to forge himself a pass and manages to escape. In Pennsylvania, he falls in love with a free black woman, Harriette Brewer, who shares his dream of helping other slaves become free.

On her first attempt, though, she is caught and sold into slavery. C. K. makes numerous trips to the South trying to find her and becomes infamous for the number of slaves he helps, but he is unable to locate her. Eventually, he marries someone else, who gives birth to Lamen, Moses' father. C. K. is finally caught when helping twelve runaways, but, rather than return to slavery, the thirteen people kill themselves, believing they will reach eternal freedom through death. It is at C. K.'s grave that Moses, too, kills himself.

Peter John Crawley (Old Jack), "the old man with the stories." One of Moses Washington's only close friends, Jack becomes a surrogate father to John after Moses' death. He teaches John how to coexist with nature, gives him a predilection for hot toddies, and keeps alive memories of Moses for the boy. Because of personal experiences with the Ku Klux Klan, he also cultivates within John a deep suspicion of white men, and that distrust causes the young academic to lead a lonely and cold life.

Dr. Judith Powell, a psychiatrist. Lovely and graceful like a ballerina, she is emotional, persistent, and stubborn. Although she is John's girlfriend, because of her white complexion he has a difficult time trusting her. She follows him to his hometown and badgers him until he confides in her his struggle to understand C. K., Moses, and himself.

Coleen Maddy

A CHANGE OF HEART

Author: Michel Butor (1926-   )
Type of work: Novel
Time of action: 1955 or 1956
First published: La Modification, 1957 (English translation, 1959)

Léon Delmont (dĕl•mŏń′), director of the Paris office of the Scabelli typewriter company. He is successful and well off, but at forty-five years old his hair is getting thin and gray. He is a smoker and wears tan shoes and a luminous watch with a purple leather watchband. He is an intellectual and anticlerical (he reads *Letters of Julian the Apostate* on the train) and has strong views about what is good and bad art. He is concerned about his family's material welfare, but his relationship with his wife has gone sour, and he yearns for a new life on a new footing—in Paris, but with his Italian mistress, Cécile. He is now on a train to Rome to tell Cécile that he has found her a job in Paris and is leaving his wife for her. During the train journey, however, he has dreams, nightmares, and reminiscences. Shortly after noticing a sign saying "It is dangerous to lean out," he has a dream in which, for the first time, he has a negative image of Cécile, who wears a look of mistrust similar to that so often worn by his wife Henriette. This thought creates his first doubts and sets in motion his eventual change of heart. He realizes that Cécile, once in Paris, would be different, more like Henriette—the similarity had become apparent during a brief trip to Paris, when she had seemed to share Henriette's contempt for him. If she comes to Paris, he will lose her. So he eventually decides against this plan.

Henriette Delmont, his wife and the mother of their four children. Her hair, like his, is no longer black. She despises him for letting his professional contacts degrade him, and he perceives her as contemptuous, critical, and petty. Almost three years ago she insisted on going with him to Rome, but it was winter and the trip was a failure, possibly making him more open to the affair with Cécile that developed subsequently. She has now become suspicious and resentful.

Madeleine, their eldest child, age seventeen.

Henri and
Thomas, their sons, about twelve years old. They are rascals, distrustful of him, aware that their parents' relationship has deteriorated.

Jacqueline, their youngest child.

Cécile Darcella (där•sĕ•lä′), Léon's mistress, secretary to an attaché at the French Embassy in Rome. She has jet-black hair and wonderful skin with a smooth, silken glow. She shares Léon's anticlericalism and his love for art. To him she seems like youth preserved; she finds him too bourgeois, anxious, unfree. She went with him to Paris once, but the trip was a failure: She complained continually of how little she saw him.

Alexandre Marnal (mär•näl′), an employee of Léon.

Jean Durieu (dü•rēœ′), director of the Durieu Travel Agency, who has promised a job for Cécile in Paris.

The Intellectual, possibly a law professor. He is tallish, pale, not over forty, with gray hair, nails bitten and tobacco-stained, and wearing thick-lensed glasses and a wedding ring. His forehead is prematurely baldish, with three deep furrows. He looks timid; he may be going to give a lecture at Dijon. He carries a dark red, ink-stained briefcase.

The Young Marrieds, probably honeymooners. They are perhaps in their twenties. He is fair, she is darker, gracious, considerate, even apologetic. They go and eat at the first sitting, as Léon does. They carry large, twin suitcases made of fine pale leather. On their way to Syracuse, they embody the theme of marriage preoccupying him.

The Priest, a man of about thirty or thirty-five, already plumpish, with nicotine-stained fingers, though he is otherwise meticulously clean. He is calm but vigorous, even impulsive, however, he looks bored, discontented, tense, dissatisfied—is he contemplating abandoning his present life, as Léon is? He is associated with the sign "It is dangerous to lean out."

The Englishman, short, with a rosy, even florid complexion, very clean, with small, greedy fishlike eyes. He may be slightly older than Léon, since his head is much balder. He wears a black raincoat and a derby hat. He is possibly the agent for a London wine merchant.

The Travelling Salesman, a man with a

coarse profile, huge hands, very strong. He wears a wedding ring. His suitcase is made of cheap, reddish-brown, imitation leather.

The Italian, a man of about forty-five who wears a wedding ring, a cobalt-blue scarf, and pointed, black-and-white shoes splashed with mud. He carries a traveling bag, and is perhaps a salesman representing French products in Italy—the reverse of Léon, for whom he represents an alter ego.

The Worried Little Woman, with the lined face, who is wearing a hat trimmed with a net and big hatpins. She is accompanied by a ten-year-old boy who reminds Léon of his son Thomas when younger.

Patrick Brady

A CHANGE OF SKIN

Author: Carlos Fuentes (1928-   )
Type of work: Novel
Time of action: April 11, 1965, Palm Sunday
First published: Cambio de piel, 1967 (English translation, 1968)

Javier (hä•vyĕr'), a middle-aged Mexican harboring aspirations of being a writer who takes a drive with his American-born wife, Elizabeth; a friend, Franz; and Franz's lover, Isabel, a young Mexican woman. Javier, who met Elizabeth when he was a student in New York City, is at once in love with and bored by her. Because of his ambivalence, he is taken in by the charms of Isabel, though in his imagination he sees her as a vacuous version of his wife. In this surrealistic novel, Javier may or may not have led Elizabeth and Franz to a terrible death inside an Aztec pyramid and may or may not have attempted to strangle Elizabeth and put Franz's body in his car trunk.

Elizabeth, the American-born wife of Javier. Elizabeth, growing restless, finds life with Javier increasingly unfulfilling, sensing as she does that Javier finds her too old for him. She wishes not only that Javier was more attuned to her needs but also that he would be a successful writer rather than an aimless, unproven one.

Franz, a young Czechoslovakian-born friend of Javier who becomes emotionally and sexually involved with Elizabeth while at the same time carrying on his affair with lovely Isabel. He incurs Javier's envy because of his youthful energy, wit, and good looks, and, because of this envy, he may have been murdered by Javier. In any event, Franz, at the very least, creates problems for Javier, and these problems create hostility.

Isabel, the youngest and most naïve of the four principal characters. She lacks Elizabeth's worldliness, mental powers, and acerbic wit, yet her sexual intensity draws Javier's attentions away from Elizabeth. Whether in fact or only in his imagination, Javier wins Isabel's affections only to become disgusted by her lack of depth and maturity. For the most part, Isabel is a pawn caught up in the unhappiness of Javier, Elizabeth, and Franz.

Freddy Lambert, the all-knowing, all-seeing, yet thoroughly mysterious narrator of the story. Lambert not only can overhear dialogue but also can peer deep into characters' minds, capturing their thoughts, dreams, and fantasies.

John D. Raymer

CHANGING PLACES

Author: David Lodge (1935-   )
Type of work: Novel
Time of action: 1969
First published: 1975

Philip Swallow, a forty-year-old lecturer in English at the University of Rummidge (Lodge's fictional Birmingham), a Redbrick college in the English Midlands. At the start of the novel, he lacks confidence, is eager to please, and is very suggestible. Professionally, he lacks ambition and is relatively unknown in scholarly circles, with few publications; however, he is a superlative examiner of undergraduates. A faculty exchange brings him to the campus of the University of Euphoria in the United States and Euphoria's Morris Zapp to Rummidge. Swallow finds his sexual drives rekindled as he has an affair with Melanie Byrd (unknown to him, Morris Zapp's daughter by his first marriage) and with Zapp's estranged wife Désirée. He also becomes caught up in student protests on the American campus. He is revitalized and gains in self-confidence. Swallow also appears in Lodge's *Small World* (1984) and *Nice Work* (1989).

Morris Zapp, a tenured full professor at the University of Euphoria (Lodge's fictional California) in the United States. He is also forty years old. He has been very ambitious and has published five books (four on Jane Austen) before the age of thirty. His enthusiasm for research was largely a means to an end, and when he became tenured his enthusiasm for scholarship waned. He is immensely self-confident and assertive, legendary for his sarcasm and intimidating to both students and colleagues. The faculty exchange brings him to a setting where his academic reputation does not count, his colleagues initially ignore him, and students are not impressed by him. His loneliness leads him to attach himself to and then have an affair with Hilary Swallow, Philip's wife. He comes to the fore when his familiarity with student unrest and the politics of academe enable him to solve Rummidge's first experi-

ence of student protest. In the end, he is reconciled to Désirée and friends with the Swallows. He appears again in the subsequent Lodge novels *Small World* and *Nice Work*.

Désirée Zapp, the wife of Morris Zapp. At the start of the novel, she feels overwhelmed by Morris' strong personality and wants a divorce but agrees to defer action if he moves out of the house. Freed of his presence when he accepts the faculty exchange, she becomes involved in the early women's liberation movement. She eventually invites Philip Swallow to live with her when the home he is renting is damaged by a hill slide; they have an affair. Désirée gains confidence and self-esteem by the conclusion of the novel.

Hilary, née **Broome, Swallow,** the wife of Philip Swallow. The two met when Hilary was an English student and Philip was doing postdoctoral work. They married and went to Euphoria on his fellowship. Returning to England, Hilary became a devoted wife and mother to their three children (Amanda, Robert, and Matthew). Their relationship had become very predictable and dull, though Hilary had not realized this. Shocked by Philip's infidelities in Euphoria, she becomes more assertive in her own household and enters into an affair with Zapp. She fully expects Philip to return to her and the children, and at the end of the novel there is hope that their relationship will be better.

Charles Boon, a graduate of Rummidge who is ostensibly pursuing a graduate degree at Euphoria. He is a popular student leader and talk show host in the American college community. He likes Swallow and assists his former tutor in Swallow's acceptance by some of the dissident elements at Euphoria.

Melanie Byrd, Morris Zapp's daughter from his first marriage. She is young, attractive, and part of the youth culture surrounding the American campus community. Swallow rents an apartment in her building and has his first affair with her (not knowing her relationship to Zapp). His infatuation helps to open him to new views and feelings.

Francis J. Bremer

THE CHANGING ROOM

Author: David Storey (1933-   )
Type of work: Play
Time of action: The 1960's
First produced: 1971

Harry Riley, a janitor working in the dressing room (changing room) of a professional rugby team in northern England. Of all twenty-two characters in the play, Harry is the only one who seems to share no joy or comradeship in the actual work performed by the team. He works, he says, only for the team owner, Sir Frederick Thornton, and in twenty years has never witnessed a rugby game at the stadium. Nevertheless, Harry is the focal point of the play. He asserts that modern living has softened team players, and he maintains that people living with the innovations of "progress" are diminished because they have distanced themselves from hard physical work, which is necessary for a sustaining, substantive life. Harry is a split character, on the one hand often superstitious and ill-informed, but on the other accurately diagnosing a change in team players. Harry is also the first character on stage and the last to exit. His regular sweeping motion as he cleans the floor throughout the play is symbolic of the physical work that Harry feels is important.

Ken Walsh, a team forward who earns a measure of respect from other team players and supporters because of his levity. A laborer by profession, Walsh enjoys the comradeship of playing the game and is a main figure in the interaction between characters that makes up the "plot," or advancement, of the play.

Clifford Owens, team captain who has a managerial and motivational function on the team. Owens is well liked by his teammates and by the club owner, but his professional approach to the team effort illustrates how more and more team players are responding to the sport as a job rather than an avocation. Owens' success demonstrates that his accomplishments as an athlete are not in question but rather that the significance of teamwork is changing among the players over time.

Sir Frederick Thornton, club owner whose presence reminds the players of the class difference between themselves and the wealthy. Thornton respects his players and enjoys a brief camaraderie with the team. Philosophically, he places himself between the conservative backward-looking impulse represented by Harry Riley and the satisfied "progressive" response offered by his assistant, MacKendrick. Thornton's association with the team is more than financial, however, as demonstrated by his distress over a dream in which rugby is played only by robots. Thornton's decision to keep Kendal, even after his injury, indicates that the team owner cares for the well-being of his players.

MacKendrick, the team secretary and accountant. MacKendrick counters Harry's argument that progress diminishes humans by pointing out its substantial benefits: better housing, modern conveniences, higher employment. He feels that life is better and offers more than ever before. MacKendrick, like Thornton, is attracted to the team's spirit even though he administers rather than plays with the team.

261

Kendal (Kenny), an older player whose injury during the game dramatizes the players' very real physical risks. Kendal's injury, like the hard-won game, occurs offstage, emphasizing the interaction among team players and supporters rather than the game itself.

Trevor, a high school teacher who plays on the team. Trevor's presence demonstrates the team's changing composition over time. Players are no longer simply physical men who enjoy the companionship of playing the game as they were twenty or fifty years ago; more often they are white-collar professionals who play to supplement their lives emotionally as well as financially.

Karen Dwyer

THE CHANT OF JIMMIE BLACKSMITH

Author: Thomas Keneally (1935-   )
Type of work: Novel
Time of action: c. 1900
First published: 1972

Jimmie Blacksmith, a half-white, half-aborigine man bent on achieving social status and material success through land ownership, who murders the families of two of his previous employers. Educated by a missionary, the twenty-two-year-old is perceptive and intelligent, but he is snobbish toward his aborigine kinfolk and frustrated by expectations of failure from his white employers. After being cheated out of wages on several jobs as a fence-builder and after witnessing and participating in the brutal treatment of an aborigine murder suspect while working as a police tracker, Jimmie explodes in a berserk rage of vengeance, killing the Newby women and children and, eventually, the Healy family. While eluding an extensive manhunt for several months, he discovers that he cannot claim the cultural identity of the Mungindi tribe. Captured, he converts to Christianity before he is hanged as Australia, so obsessed with bringing him to justice, celebrates its independence.

Mort Blacksmith, Jimmie's half brother, a full-blooded aborigine. Flippant and prone to fits of laughter, the seventeen-year-old Mort embodies innocence and tribal loyalty. Having left his job as a horse-breaker for white farmers, he accompanies his uncle and cousin in a futile effort to convince Jimmie not to marry a white woman, if he is to be considered a Mungindi man. Drawn into Jimmie's violence, he kills a woman and, later during pursuit of the brothers, a man, both acts of apparent self-defense. Attempting to maintain tribal values of love and loyalty, Mort refuses to abandon Jimmie. He is shot to death while trying to save the life of their hostage McCreadie.

Tabidgi (tä·bĭd′·jē), or **Jackie Smolders,** Jimmie and Mort's maternal uncle, a traditional man of the Tullam section of the Mungindi tribe. With his gray beard falling out in tufts, Tabidgi appears ancient relative to his forty-two years. An alcoholic but nevertheless deeply reverent toward his tribe's mystical beliefs, he carries an initiation tooth to Jimmie in order to remind him of his obligation to marry within the aborigine kinship system. When Jimmie begins his murderous rampage, Tabidgi half-consciously participates out of terror; captured soon afterward, he is hanged along with Jimmie.

Peter Blacksmith, Jimmie's fourteen-year-old cousin who travels with Tabidgi to deliver Jimmie's initiation tooth. Kind and compassionate, he cares for Jimmie's wife, Gilda, after he has beaten her and babysits her child. Left behind after the murder of the Newbys, he is acquitted.

Gilda Howie Blacksmith, Jimmie's wife, a poor white eighteen-year-old girl from

262

Sydney. Frail, sickly, and thin-hipped, she marries Jimmie when she discovers that she is pregnant, but her child has been fathered by Mrs. Hayes's cook, a white communist. Jimmie, hoping to gain status through the marriage, rejects her and the child. Though present at the Newby massacre, she is acquitted with Peter.

Wallace Hyberry, a butcher from Balmain, a Sydney suburb, and the public hangman. Incorruptible and aloof from his duties as hangman, he prides himself on his technological expertise but is blind to the larger contexts of Jimmie's crimes. As Grand Master of his fraternal lodge, he is most concerned that the notoriety of Jimmie's violence and elusive flight will deprive him of royal honors when Australia becomes independent.

The Reverend Mr. A. J. Neville, Jimmie's Methodist teacher. Nurturing Jimmie's aspirations for material success and encouraging him to marry a white woman, the condescending and narrow-minded minister dismisses any validity in aboriginal culture and conveys consistent expectations of Jimmie's inferiority, beating him for truancy when Jimmie leaves the missionary briefly to undergo his tribal initiation ritual.

Senior Constable Farrell, a policeman who employs Jimmie as a tracker. With a love for boar hunting and brutal abuse of aborigines in his district, Farrell uses virility as a mask for his homosexuality. His vicious sodomy of an aboriginal inmate feeds Jimmie's guilt and self-hatred, annihilating any respect for the law that Jimmie might have had.

Mr. Healy and **Mrs. Healy,** Irish Catholic farmers who employ Jimmie as a fence-builder. Having cheated Jimmie out of wages, refusing him food or a ride to another town, and denying him a letter of reference, because he himself is illiterate, Mr. Healy precipitates Jimmie's explosion of his long-simmering rage. Mrs. Healy becomes a principal target of Jimmie's rage in that she is, for him, the symbol of success, a landowner's wife, the archetype of submission to her husband's power and status.

Miss Petra Graf, boarder at the Newbys and schoolmistress at nearby Wallah. The stout, aloof, and patronizing young woman is the model of rural propriety. Condescending to Gilda, she fosters the illusions of social status in the rural homestead.

Dowie Stead, Miss Graf's unwilling fiancé, a farmer from Gulargambone. Secretly romantic and a patron of aboriginal prostitutes but outwardly practical, his brown hair, blue eyes, and passive face are a portrait of Nordic coldness. His relentless pursuit of Jimmie is not so much to avenge the murder of Miss Graf as it is to vent his frustration upon discovering that his father has been sharing his black mistress Tessie.

The Newby Family, a fifty-two-year-old farmer near Wallah, his robust and racist wife, and their six children. Given to mocking Jimmie's efforts to succeed and cheating him of wages, Mrs. Newby becomes Jimmie's first victim when she accuses him of lying about a sack of flour. Her two adolescent daughters are also killed with Miss Graf and herself.

Mr. McCreadie, a schoolteacher who becomes Jimmie and Mort's hostage. Asthmatic and sick much of the time he is held captive, he is sensitive and empathetic to the frustration of the aborigines. Treated derisively by Jimmie, he leads them to the sacred site of a "rock womb" of the Manning River tribes, where they discover that the site has been desecrated by a vacationing rugby team. Succeeding in convincing Jimmie that he must abandon Mort and himself in order to gain self-respect, McCreadie is saved from dying of pneumonia by Mort's attempted surrender.

Michael Loudon

CHÉRI and THE LAST OF CHÉRI

Author: Colette (Sidonie-Gabrielle Colette, 1873-1954)
Type of work: Novels
Time of action: 1913 and 1919
First published: Chéri, 1920 (English translation, 1929); *La Fin de Chéri,* 1926 (English translation, 1932)

Frédéric Peloux (pə·lōō'), nicknamed **Chéri** (shär·ē'), in *Chéri* an idle young man of twenty-five with an inherited fortune whose life is related in a series of flashbacks, which concentrate on the years he spends as a lover to Léa, a middle-aged demimondaine. He is an extremely handsome man of medium height with blue-black hair; dark eyes framed by thick, lustrous lashes; a disdainful but pretty mouth; unblemished white skin; and a hard, darkish chest shaped like a shield, During their six-year liaison, Léa teaches Chéri how to live in her world—how to choose friends, wines, food, jewelry, and clothing, as well as how to be the perfect lover. This idyllic life ends when his mother arranges a marriage for him to Edmée, a wealthy young woman of eighteen. Chéri accepts but has no enthusiasm for the marriage and, after a brief period of domesticity, longs for the old days with Léa, which, to his dismay, he discovers cannot be recaptured. In *The Last of Chéri* he is thirty years old, has faintly shadowed eyelids and a leaner physique, and is a veteran of the Great War, in which he has been mistakenly decorated for bravery, even though he finagled military service behind the lines. Chéri refuses to accept the reality of the post-war world; the independent, self-assured woman Edmée has become; impending middle age; or the fact that Léa has grown gracefully into a comfortable old age without him. Unable to work, to recapture the past, to adapt to the present, to relate to his wife and friends, or to accept the loss of Léa and his youth, Chéri spends his time reminiscing about the past with The Pal. Seeing no place for himself in the modern world, he commits suicide with a pistol in her apartment.

Léa de Lonval, née **Léonie Vallon** and nicknamed **Nounoune** (nōō·nōōn'), a beautiful demimondaine who, after a long career as a mistress to a succession of wealthy men, has successfully parlayed the gifts from her admirers into a comfortable fortune. In *Chéri* she is forty-nine, tall and blonde with ruddy cheeks, a beautiful face, a good body, thin-wristed arms, large pure-blue eyes, a proud nose, an opulent bust, an even row of teeth, a good smile, long legs, and a straight back. When the combination of Chéri's marriage and the Great War alters her world forever, she yearns for Chéri and the past but successfully adapts to the changes. In *The Last of Chéri*, she has settled into a happy, chaste old age and adopted a masculine style of dress which gives her an aura of sexless dignity. She stops dyeing her gray hair, cuts it short, and allows herself to become very stout with a fat neck, sagging cheeks, and a double chin. Her ability to live well and happily without him in the modern world puzzles and saddens Chéri.

Edmée (ĕd·mā'), the attractive daughter of a beautiful former courtesan, Marie-Laure. She is married to Chéri in an arranged union. In *Chéri* she is eighteen, has frightened, secretive eyes; thin arms; small breasts; a flat behind; rosy lips; small, squarish teeth; white skin; and fluffy, ash-brown hair with a slight crimp in it. Although Edmée has a fortune of her own, she is a docile wife to Chéri. In *The Last of Chéri* this changes. Hospital administrative work and separation from Chéri during the war bring her to the realization that she enjoys both her career and her independence. She no longer defines herself exclusively in relation to her husband. In the post-war world her career flourishes and, as Chéri withdraws from her, it becomes the most important thing in her life. Moreover, Edmée proves to be a better financial manager than Chéri and takes control of their joint fortune. Perfectly at home in the modern world, Edmée, like Léa, is able to adjust to life with or without Chéri and to thrive.

Charlotte Peloux, a wealthy former ballet dancer and courtesan who boldly rears her son, Chéri, as a child of the demimonde. Mme Peloux is a small, round barrel of a woman with short legs, tiny feet, large eyes, fair hair, a shrill off-key voice, and a coquettish way of standing with her feet in the fifth position. She chooses Edmée for her son and arranges the marriage terms. Although in *Chéri* her chief occupation is afternoon tea with her friends, in *The Last of Chéri* she, too, had become productively involved both with Edmée's hospital and with the modern world.

Desmond, in *Chéri* a penniless hanger-on who has been Chéri's friend since boyhood. His ugliness contrasts with Chéri's good looks. Like Chéri, he avoids military combat, but, unlike Chéri, he thrives in the postwar era. In *The Last of Chéri* he opens a jazz nightclub, which becomes a commercial success by pandering to what Chéri considers to be the worst elements of modern taste. He is now far too busy and too happy to be at Chéri's beck and call.

The Pal, a contemporary of Léa and Charlotte who has a name so ordinary that nobody ever remembers it. She smokes opium and gives it to others. In *The Last of Chéri* it is only in her company that Chéri finds peace by reminiscing about the past. He commits suicide in her apartment, thinking of Léa and the war.

Marie-Laure, Edmée's mother. In her heyday, she was a spectacular beauty. Although in *Chéri* she is in her forties, she dresses as if she were eighteen.

Nancy E. Rupprecht

CHEROKEE

Author: Jean Echenoz (1949-　)
Type of work: Novel
Time of action: The 1980's
First published: 1983 (English translation, 1987)

George Chave (shäv), the protagonist. A tall, thin man in his thirties, he is looking for work in order to please his girlfriend Veronique, but soon he shifts his devotion to Jenny Weltman. Hired as a detective, he arouses the jealousy of other employees by finding a lost wife and a lost parrot. As unexplainable events take place around him, he is pursued by the police, hidden by friends, kidnapped, taken by a cult, and finally united with Jenny.

Fred Shapiro, a mysterious businessman. An expensively dressed man of thirty-eight, he is balding and has a hooked nose. A distant cousin and childhood playmate of George, he had long ago incurred George's dislike when he did not return a rare, borrowed record of "Cherokee." When George encounters him again, however, Fred is able to suggest a job opening. Later Fred kills his uncle, becomes the leader of the Rayonites, seizes George for use in their rituals, and kills a policeman who is storming their stronghold. At the end of the novel, however, Fred is driving the car containing George and Jenny.

Croconyan (krä·kän′yən), a thief. A large, short-haired man, he is strong and resourceful. After George aids him in a bar fight, he becomes a loyal friend, first hiding him in Paris and later joining him in the Alpine retreat.

Ferguson Gibbs, a rich Englishman. A redhaired man, he is involved in business with Fred Shapiro. He abducts George and later becomes a substitute priest of the Rayonites until they turn against him.

Jenny Weltman, the girl for whom George is searching throughout most of the novel. A pretty young woman with blue-gray eyes and blonde hair, she first meets George in the National Library. She acts as a priestess for the Rayonites but finally is reunited with George.

Fernand, a bookseller. A man of sixty-five, dressed in layer upon layer of clothing, he mourns for the writers whom he knew in his youth. After George tries to sell books to him, he suggests that Fred might be able to help him find a job. Fernand is later killed by his nephew, Fred.

Christian Ripert (rə·pĕr'), a detective. A tall, thin man, he is motivated by jealousy of George, who solves cases that he and his partner cannot handle. His pursuit of George does not bring him luck; first Ripert is injured when George pushes him off of a balcony, and then later he is shot and killed by Fred at the Rayonite headquarters.

Martial Bock, another private detective and Ripert's partner. A short, fat man, like Ripert he dresses as gaudily as a pimp. After kidnapping Veronique from the mountain hideout, he and his partner end up joining the police in the siege of the Rayonite headquarters.

Veronique, George's first girlfriend, an office worker. Although she leaves George for a photographer, she later joins both of them, along with Croconyan, at the photographer's home in the Alps, where George tries to hide. It is Veronique who leads the detectives and the police to rescue George from the Rayonites.

Rosemary M. Canfield Reisman

CHEVENGUR

Author: Andrei Platonov (Andrei Platonovich Klimentov, 1899-1951)
Type of work: Novel
Time of action: Shortly before and during the Russian Revolution and Civil War
First published: 1972 (English translation, 1978)

Alexander (Sasha) Dvanov, an orphan and Red Army soldier. Having been orphaned early and thrown out of his foster parents' home, Sasha becomes a mendicant and later joins the Bolsheviks. As a beggar, he is a failure, because he is not brave enough to beg. He embraces Communism instinctively, at first because everyone else is joining and it is frightening to be left alone again; later, he learns more about Communism, but his understanding of it remains on a rudimentary level, as he seeks it among the simplest and best of people. The nebulousness of his political views is best exemplified by his participation in building, together with a number of similar souls, a mythical city of Chevengur that corresponds to their idealistic notion of brotherly love and comradeship. In the end, he fades away into the foggy future of the city, without any assurance that it would ever work, let alone fulfill his dream of a better life for everyone.

Zakhar Pavlovich, Sasha's guardian and a railroad mechanic. A progenitor of Sasha's dreamlike attitude toward life, Zakhar is also a dreamer but of a different kind. He is inordinately gifted as a practical man and a mechanic, as he virtually lives out of nature and is able to make and fix almost anything. He makes things for others, never for himself, and he does it out of curiosity about what makes things what they are and how they work. He lives alone, never needs people, considering machines to be people, and is attracted to unusual projects such as building a wooden clock powered by the rotation of the earth. At the same time, he is able to converse wth anyone in a neighborly way. This combination of friendliness and aloofness draws him to the revolution; without subscribing to its political aims, he believes, again instinctively, that it may do some good.

Stepan Kopenkin, a dedicated revolutionary with some of the strangest notions about Communism. He wants to build a family army to fight the enemies of the poor and the little man. He has an obsession with a German revolutionary, Rosa Luxemburg, carrying her picture sewn into his cap and always using her as a yardstick for measuring a good revolutionary. With his horse, named Proletarian Strength, he resembles Don Quixote more than a fiery Bolshevik. He believes that people would set things right by themselves if they were left in peace and that Rosa, as a symbol of revolution, had thought up everything in advance. Vague like Sasha and, to some degree, Zakhar about the real goals of the revolution, he trusts his instincts, for he believes that within himself he has the gift of revolution. That, however, is only a mask for his desire to live totally free.

Prokofy (Proshka) Dvanov, Sasha's foster brother. A revolutionary of a different kind, Proshka is using the revolution for his own ends. Practical, at times cruelly selfish, he operates almost exclusively on the basis of "what's in it for me." Even though he has worked for many people, he is loved by no one. He has acquired a good knowledge of Marx, but his use of him depends, for exam-

ple, on his girl's mood and the objective circumstances. By and large, he is a predator who needs no people and collects property in place of people, and who loves no one beyond his own door. The only reason he has survived so far is because he is able to manipulate his comrades and because of the uncertainties of the revolution.

Chepurny, the Jap, a revolutionary, the president of Chevengur. Another blind believer in revolution, the Jap calls himself "a naked communist," who has not read a line of Marx but has picked up an idea or two at meetings and now spends his life fighting for it. Since most of Platonov's characters are not persons but embodiments of ideas, the Jap and others should be seen as spokesmen of the times, despite their individual idiosyncrasies.

Sonya Mandrova, Sasha's childhood friend. Abandoned by her mother at birth, Sonya is caught in the maelstrom of the revolution and becomes one of the millions of simple human beings who were forced by circumstances to participate in it. Her juvenile love for Sasha disappears in the vagaries of revolution. She later becomes a cleaner at a factory. She has difficulties in sustaining her attachment to men and refuses to have children, in the belief that if she could have a flower instead of a child she would be a mother, thus revealing a poetic nature that the revolution's harshness has arrested forever.

Vasa D. Mihailovich

CHEYENNE AUTUMN

Author: Mari Sandoz (1896-1966)
Type of work: Novel
Time of action: 1878-1879
First published: 1953

Little Wolf, also called **Brave Man,** bearer of the Sacred Chief's bundle and one of the Old Man Chiefs. In his prime at fifty-seven, Little Wolf is one of two leaders attempting to bring their Northern Cheyenne back to

their Montana homeland from the hated Indian Territory. Distrustful of whites, he believes that their promises are no more than "wind on the grass." When the group divides at the Platte River, Dull Knife hoping to reach safety at Red Cloud's agency nearby, Little Wolf brings his followers to their original destination in the north. His one weakness is his jealousy of Thin Elk.

Dull Knife, also an Old Man Chief. Once a famed warrior, now, in his sixties, he wants only to return north. He naïvely believes that the army will honor its promise to let the Cheyenne return home from the intolerable southern agency. After their capture and their failed attempt to escape from Fort Robinson, Nebraska, he is embittered, a failure in his own eyes.

Little Finger Nail, a young warrior, sweet singer, and artist. In the absence of older leaders, he leads the tribal remnant in their thirteen-day escape from Robinson. He is killed in their last encounter at Warbonnet Creek, his book of pictographs recording their trek strapped to his back, two bullet holes in it.

Wild Hog, a headman. Big and broad at 6 feet, 5 inches tall, he is married to a Sioux. When Dull Knife fails to take charge during their capture, he assumes leadership. Later he attempts suicide, hoping that his family can then be sent to Red Cloud's nearby Sioux agency.

Black Coyote, a prominent subchief, inimical to the whites and a troublemaker for the leaders. After killing Black Crane, he is exiled as a renegade. Later captured and convicted of killing a soldier, he is hanged by whites.

Thin Elk, a joker, ladies' man, and Little Wolf's nemesis. Once ordered to stay away from the chief's wives, he now flirts with a daughter. After the trek, Little Wolf, forgetting a chief's obligation to ignore personal problems, kills him and forfeits his leadership.

Black Crane, an elder, the experienced camp finder, a strong conservative influence. He is killed during an argument with the violent Black Coyote.

Bridge, the frail old medicine man, who sacrifices his health through fasting and prayer so that the Powers will aid the Cheyenne in their flight. Sometimes they help, but he is killed in the outbreak at Robinson.

Comes-in-Sight, a Cheyenne maiden forced to kill her demented father to prevent his raping her. Cheyenne law requires that she and her family be exiled, but they closely follow the sympathetic group.

Yellow Swallow, the sickly nine-year-old son of a Cheyenne and General George Custer. Brought on the flight by relatives, he returns south before reaching the Platte River.

Red Cloud, Oglala Sioux, about fifty-five. Although made a chief by the whites, he is held a virtual prisoner at his own agency. The Oglalas and Cheyenne are intermarried, but he cannot help his friends.

Brave One and
Enemy, heroic women who have survived two massacres before walking the entire distance to Robinson, often carrying small children. They are killed at Warbonnet Creek, northwest of Robinson.

Woman's Dress, a Sioux army scout. Already considered a traitor to the Sioux Chief Crazy Horse, he leads the army to the last stronghold of the Cheyenne attempting to escape from Robinson.

Captain Little Flying Dutchman (Henry W.) Wessells, a short, light-haired, "busy-busy" man, Commandant at Robinson. A rigid rules-follower, he locks the Cheyenne into their barracks without food, heat, or water for days, attempting to force them to return to Indian Territory. When they break out, he kills, wounds, or captures more than two-thirds of them.

Lieutenant William Chase, a young officer in charge of the Cheyenne at Robinson. Sympathetic, he spends his pay on food and treats, but at Warbonnet Creek he aids Wessels in annihilating the remaining Indians.

Lieutenant White Hat (Philo) Clark, an ambitious, experienced Indian fighter. Little Wolf trusts him more than most whites and surrenders to him near Ft. Keogh after Clark allows the band to keep their weapons and horses.

Colonel Caleb Carlton, who hunts the Cheyenne through Nebraska's sandhills and captures Dull Knife's people near Robinson.

General Braided Beard (George) Crook, Commander, Department of the Platte. A su-perb Indian fighter, he nevertheless protests their treatment to Washington, to no avail.

General Bear Coat (Nelson A.) Miles, headquartered at Ft. Keogh on the Yellowstone. An active campaigner against Indians, yet he allows Little Wolf's band to settle on their own reservation in Montana.

Edgar Beecher Bronson, a rancher near Robinson. Sympathetic to the Cheyenne, he later writes a book giving the details of the outbreak.

Helen Winter Stauffer

CHICKEN SOUP WITH BARLEY

Author: Arnold Wesker (1932-   )
Type of work: Play
Time of action: 1936-1956
First produced: 1958

Sarah Kahn, "a small fiery woman, aged thirty-seven, Jewish and of European origin." She lives in the East End of London, where she is mother to Ada and Ronnie, and wife to Harry, whom she constantly nags. Two features immediately characterize her: her warmhearted but unsentimental dynamism and her total commitment to communism. This commitment is less ideological than intuitive, being based on a sense of community and the need to care, an extension of her strong sense of wider family. It is because of this feeling that she remains the one figure who does not become disillusioned as the play progresses. Although personal tragedy overtakes her during the twenty-year span of the play (particularly her husband's physical and mental collapse, and the breakup of her own family and the Jewish East End community), she never loses her warmth or her convictions. In this loosely structured chronicle play, she is the one character who holds the play together. It is not only that Wesker portrays her as the matriarch in a matriarchal society, but also that she embodies for Wesker what is the true essence of socialism: a caring heart that can withstand political oppression, crass materialism, and disillusion. She alone remains unbroken.

Harry Kahn, thirty-five years old at the beginning, working-class and Jewish, and something of a thinker. Although he apparently shares his wife's beliefs, he is totally opposite to her: physically timid, weak, and a compulsive liar. Their incompatibility leads to frequent quarrels that finish with Harry defeated and guilty. In act 2, he suffers a partial stroke, which makes employment difficult; he more or less gives up. By act 3, he has had a second stroke and is a physical wreck, helpless and incontinent. The play suggests his physical weakness is an outward sign of his emotional and spiritual weakness.

Ada Kahn, Sarah and Harry's daughter. As the play opens, Ada is fourteen years old and, like her mother, totally and actively committed to communism, especially in the immediate confrontation with the Fascist "Blackshirts." As the play progresses, she loses her youthful zeal because of a long engagement and even longer separation from

269

her husband, Dave, caused by the Spanish Civil War and World War II and the failure of their utopian scheme to live simply in the country (which forms the basis of *I'm Talking About Jerusalem*, the third play of this trilogy).

Ronnie, Sarah and Harry's son. In act 1, Ronnie is a child; in act 2, a politically committed high school student; but, in act 3, he returns from a job in Paris as a chef. In many ways, Ronnie is Wesker himself, just as the play is the story of Wesker's own family. Ronnie is shown to be particularly sensitive to his parents' failures. He is terrified of becoming as weak as his own father, and he argues fiercely with his mother that communism has failed. The argument leads Sarah to define her socialism of the heart, but Ronnie cannot accept this, at least "not yet."

Cissie Kahn, Harry's sister, and a Trades-Union organizer. She is as strong in character as Sarah, and as committed in her beliefs, but she lacks her sister-in-law's humanity and warmth. She prefers confrontational roles, but, as the play proceeds, she finds less and less support among her union members, until she is finally "retired" from her post.

Dave Simmonds, Ada's husband. Among the Jewish teenage boys in his group, Dave is the most attractive and idealistic. He volunteers to fight in the Spanish Civil War against the Fascists. For most of the play, he is only heard of through Ada, who reveals his disillusionment with the working class and the failure of his rural socialist scheme.

Monty Blatt, another of the keen Jewish teenagers in act 1. He reappears in act 3 with his wife, Bessie, at a reunion with Sarah and Harry. He is now a successful entrepreneur in Manchester and wants to forget his earlier communist leanings, even while continuing to admire Sarah for her continued commitment.

Prince Silver, the third of the teenagers who participate in the demonstration. He also reappears in act 3, now running a second-hand shop and clearly no longer politically active. He makes up one of the players at an unsuccessful game of cards that is in stark contrast to the idealistic dialogue of act 1.

Hymie Kossof, Sarah's brother. He makes a dramatic entry in act 1, having been hurt in the demonstration. Like Prince, he settles down in life. He is also in the game of cards and, like Prince also, refuses to wait up with Sarah for Ronnie to return from Paris—a final symbolic act of desertion.

David Barratt

THE CHICKENCOOP CHINAMAN

Author: Frank Chin (1940-   )
Type of work: Play
Time of action; The late 1960's
First produced: 1972

Tam Lum, a Chinese American writer and filmmaker. Tam Lum is the young writer cast loose from his Chinese heritage, displaced from mainstream American culture, obsessed with creating a unified artistic identity and discovering an appropriate voice and language in which to tell his stories. He is puzzled, cross, mocking, frustrated, isolated, essentially passive, with a touch of the poet and a

gift for telling a story. In the play's major action, Tam Lum journeys to Pittsburgh to interview Charley Popcorn for a documentary film on the life and career of Ovaltine Jack Dancer, a black fighter who had been the childhood hero of Tam Lum and Kenji.

Kenji (Blackjap Kenji), a Japanese American research dentist who has been Tam

270

Lum's friend since childhood. In his youth, Kenji rejected his cultural and racial heritage, just as did Tam Lum. Together, they found heroes and role models in black men, such as Ovaltine Jack Dancer, and in media heroes, such as the Lone Ranger. Tam Lum stays at Kenji's house in Pittsburgh and renews their friendship while in the city to interview Charley Popcorn. In contrast to Tam Lum, Kenji moves toward assimilation during the play. At the end, Lee will stay with Kenji, as his wife or lover, and Robbie, Lee's son, will have the father he seeks.

Lee, an attractive Eurasian or Chinese American woman, whom Kenji has invited to stay in his apartment. Lee is hostile toward men, especially Chinese men. She represents the white, black, and Oriental worlds, which lack sympathy for a person who attempts to create a new self by amalgamating elements of all three cultures. Lee's hostility toward Tam Lum provides the major conflict of act 1. During the play, Lee begins to understand Tam Lum and to appreciate the form his rebellion takes.

Tom, Lee's former husband, a Chinese American writer. Tom is a neat, tidy, completely assimilated Chinese American, a man who has denied his Chinese heritage and past in order to be acceptable to the majority white culture. Tom, as his name indicates, is the opposite of Tam in many ways. Tom has attempted to blend with the white culture, while Tam has resisted assimilation. He represents a white culture that demands too high a price for success: the repudiation of the writer's Chinese heritage. A major scene in act 2 consists of an argument between Tam Lum and Tom over what it means to be Chinese.

Robbie, Lee's twelve-year-old son. Like Tam Lum and Kenji, Robbie is looking for a strong father figure. He represents impressionable youth, which repeats the prejudices of the adult world but neither fully understands nor believes them.

Charley Popcorn, an old black man. Charley is a former boxing trainer who runs a pornographic cinema in Pittsburgh. Tam Lum believes that he is the father of Ovaltine Jack Dancer, but Charley denies it. Tam Lum's major disappointment in the play is his failure to find the father of his childhood hero, who represents to him the ideal father. Charley Popcorn is the object of Tam Lum's quest to Pittsburgh to meet the ideal father.

The Lone Ranger,
Tonto, and
Hong Kong Dream Girl, all fantasy/dream characters who represent Tam Lum's rejection of his Chinese as well as his American heritage.

James W. Robinson, Jr.

CHILDE BYRON

Author: Romulus Linney (1930-   )
Type of work: Play
Time of action: November 27, 1852
First produced: 1977

George Gordon, Lord Byron, famous English Romantic poet, flamboyant society figure, sexual rebel. Fiery and cynical, passionate and candid, Byron confronts his daughter, Ada, on the day of her death and attempts to justify his life to her. As a boy, he is a moody, fat, clubfooted poseur introduced to sex at age nine by his nurse; however, as a young man, he has become an internationally acclaimed poet, a superb athlete, and a notorious sexual veteran who has bedded practically everything presented to him but whose most passionate love affair has been with his half-sister Augusta Leigh.

Exiled for his scandalous behavior once it no longer suits the public fancy, he lives with the Countess Guiccioli, then with the poet Shelley, and finally flees to Greece, where he dies in the fight for Greek independence. Throughout his recital of his life and loves, Byron remains contemptuous of public opinion, insisting that society is basely hypocritical. He emerges as a heroic figure, genuinely hurt but proud and clearsighted about the demands made on an artist by his public. His defiance raises questions about the emotional and artistic costs of fame, about the boundaries between the artist's work and his life.

Augusta Ada, the Countess of Lovelace, a mathematician and designer of a calculating machine, the Analytical Engine, and Byron's daughter by Annabella Millbanke. Thirty-six and dying of cancer, Ada cannot finish her will without confronting the father she never knew but whose infamous life nevertheless seems linked to hers. She conjures up Byron's ghost and demands that he justify his life and paternal neglect. Coolly logical, scientifically skeptical, something of a reasoning machine herself, Ada discovers in the course of her accusations and Byron's explanations that she is in fact very much her father's daughter: The same rebellious spirit animates them both. Each has achieved much, suffered much, been misunderstood and disgraced, and lived with self-exile and self-loathing. Both will be dead at age thirty-six.

Annabella Millbanke, Ada's mother and later a formidable bluestocking. A logical and direct provincial girl with mathematical interests, she first charms Byron by her candor, but once married she is unable to endure what she claims are Byron's perversities, and she demands a separation and custody of their child. She fuels the gossip of Byron's gambling, incest, sodomy, and homosexuality that leads to his eventual exile from England.

Lady Byron, Byron's mother, a coarse, boozy, unstable woman who both indulges and attacks her son.

Chorus of Men and Women, the voices of society that at first overwhelm Byron with rhapsodic adulation, celebrating his scandalous behavior with offers of wine, dinners, and themselves, but that later turn vengeful, insisting on his expulsion from their midst as a pervert and criminal.

Thomas J. Campbell

CHILDHOOD'S END

Author: Arthur C. Clarke (1917-   )
Type of work: Novel
Time of action: The imagined 1950's and the twenty-first century
First published: 1953

Rikki Stormgren, Secretary-General of the United Nations. At sixty, a native of Finland, widowed with grown children, he has devoted his keen mind and diplomatic talents to thirty-five years of public service before being selected by the Overlords as their only liaison with the human race. With a patience born of long experience (and adeptness at poker), he shares a mutual trust of and faith in Karellen, even while kidnapped and held a short time by extremists. His cleverly arranged glimpse of Karellen does not satisfy his curiosity about the Overlords, and for the ensuing thirty years of his retirement he wonders about their purpose.

Karellen, Supervisor of Earth for the alien race called the Overlords. Immortal by human standards, he and his colleagues act as guardians of the colony Earth for the Overmind of the universe. His, and their, charge is to act as midwives in the birth and transformation of a new generation of cosmic minds for ultimate union with the Overmind. Mental geniuses but physically barren, they insist only on global justice and order, ending wars, South African apartheid, and cruelty to animals. The Overlords all seem to be identical, with the physical form of the legendary Devil and requiring sun glasses because of the brighter light than that of their own sun. His mission accomplished, Karellen leaves the dying Earth to visit the next nursery, always probing the mystery of the Overmind.

Jan Rodricks, a University of Cape Town graduate student in engineering physics. Of mixed Negroid and Scottish blood, he is a twenty-seven-year-old romantic and accomplished pianist whose hopes to explore space are dashed by the arrival of the Overlords. Undaunted, he stows away aboard one of their starships, enabling him to visit their home planet and return with them to Earth. He has aged only six months, but the time dilation caused by relativity means that eighty years have passed on his own world. He remains there, transmitting his impressions of the death throes of Earth to the Overlords as they speed away in their starships.

George Greggson, a television studio designer. Devoted to his profession as an art form, he emigrates to the artist colony of New Athens in the South Pacific with his wife of ten years, Jean Morrel, and their two children. Sporting fashionable sidewhiskers, he strives to maintain the spark of human creativity in spite of the cultural leveling influence of the Overlords. Instead, he succumbs to their mission when his children become the first embryos of the new cosmic generation. His hopes dashed, he and his wife elect collective suicide with many of , their fellow colonists in a nuclear blast.

Jean Morrel, a student and the mate of George Greggson. Individualistic like her husband, twenty-six, and platinum blonde, she enjoys dancing and the amenities of modern technological living. She is first Greggson's

mate, then his "contracted" wife. Natural psychic powers lead her to fear vaguely the Overlords, who are alerted to them during an early paranormal séance. At New Athens, she endures antiquated housekeeping chores and avoids discussing paranormal matters until the truth becomes known that her own mind was a channel for the unknown timeless knowledge of the universe that emerges in her children. Their loss to the Overmind drives her and her husband closer together than ever as they share their mutual fate.

Jennifer Anne Greggson, the baby daughter of George and Jean. Referred to by them endearingly as "the Poppet" (a little doll), she never grows beyond infancy before her mind awakens to the call of the Overmind. Confined thereafter to her cradle, at physical rest with her eyes closed, she has to be left alone while she develops her psychic powers, with which she satisfies her own personal needs. Like an earthly contagion, her powers link with the mind of her brother and then with those of all young children of the Earth. Isolated from their elders by the Overlords, they collectively evolve until their ultimate mental and spiritual power enable them to join the Overmind in the universe and to destroy the Earth physically.

Jeffrey Angus Greggson, the brother of Jennifer. A precocious but typical boy of seven, he is intelligent, artistic, and curious about science and the sea. Through dreams, he is the first earthling to be contacted by the Overmind but is bypassed in his evolution by his sister, since he had more acquired mortal habits to unlearn.

Rupert Boyce, a jungle veterinarian in Africa. A brilliant doctor of animals, he is also gregarious, tactless, and oft-married. A connoisseur of "paraphysics," he lends his immense library on the subject to the Overlords, who therefore assist his veterinary work.

Alexander Wainwright, head of the Freedom League. Originally a clergyman, he is tall, handsome, and in his late forties. With complete integrity, he admires the peace and prosperity made possible by the Overlords but labors to restore the freedom of choice and creativity they have taken from the human race. He fails.

Rashaverak, an Overlord and anthropologist. He tirelessly pores over Boyce's books on psychic matters to find explanations for mental breakthroughs.

Thanthalteresco, the **"Inspector,"** an Overlord. Typically inscrutable, he has an insatia-

ble appetite for statistics in probing human behavior to help fathom cosmic knowledge.

Joe, an extremist opponent of the Overlords. Polish, about fifty, and weighing some 250 pounds, he belongs to the outlaw group that kidnaps Stormgren. A complex but honest man in the latter's view, he is also conservative in his politics, frustrated by the seeming conquest by the Overlords. Once exposed by the Overlords, the activities of him and his colleagues are effectively compromised.

Clark G. Reynolds

CHILDREN OF A LESSER GOD

Author: Mark Medoff (1940-   )
Type of work: Play
Time of action: The 1970's
First produced: 1979

James Leeds, in his thirties, a speech teacher at a state school for the deaf. A sensitive, caring, and charismatic teacher, Leeds finds himself challenged by Sarah Norman, a sarcastic and rebellious maid at the school, whom the headmaster has asked him to help in his spare time. Matching her sarcasm with his own wit and with unorthodox methods of instruction, Leeds attracts her to him and is in turn attracted by her beauty and intelligence. Engaging in a battle of wits via sign language, they fall in love and get married, against the warnings of the headmaster. Despite his attempts to understand Sarah and her point of view, Leeds insists on trying to make her over, pressuring her to learn to lip read and to speak rather than remain entirely dependent upon sign language. When a fellow student, Orin Dennis, engages in a combat with Leeds and tries to recruit Sarah into his militant program of reform, she rejects them both, stating that she is her own person. If Leeds is to win her back, he must accept her on her own terms. He learns the damage his attempts to remake her have caused, acknowledges his love and need for her, and attempts a reconciliation. He was played on stage by John Rubinstein, who won

a Tony Award, and in the motion picture by William Hurt.

Sarah Norman, twenty-six years old, a maid at a state school for the deaf. Deaf since birth, Sarah is estranged from her mother and rebellious against the world. She is highly intelligent but uses her wits only for sarcastic retorts against anyone who tries to intrude into her privacy. Physically beautiful, she has used her sexuality as a way to communicate with the opposite sex but has found such brief relationships meaningless. When James Leeds engages her on her own terms in a battle of wits, she reluctantly falls in love with him and marries him, only to find that he is unable to respect her refusal to learn to lip read and speak and so give up what he calls her "angry deaf person's license." When she becomes a battleground between her husband and Orin Dennis over the latter's war against the school regulations and organization, she leaves her husband, insisting that she will not be manipulated and will not be "the creation of other people." Only if her husband can let her be the individual that she is, come into her silence and know her, will she return to him. She

274

was played on stage by Phyllis Frelich, who won a Tony Award and in the motion picture by Marlee Matlin, who won an Academy Award for Best Actress.

Orin Dennis, in his twenties, a student at the state school for the deaf who has some residual hearing and can lip read. Temperamentally militant, Orin is wary of James Leeds, hostile to the headmaster, and tries to manipulate Sarah and Lydia into joining his attack on the school organization and authority and his attempt to restructure them.

Mrs. Norman, Sarah's mother. Abandoned by her husband when Sarah was a little girl, she has been unable to cope with her daughter's handicap and complex personality, with the result that Sarah ran away when she was eighteen. James Leeds helps bring about a tentative reconciliation between them.

Mr. Franklin, in his thirties or forties, the supervising teacher at the state school for the deaf. Alternately pompous and one of the boys, he is skeptical about Leeds's approach to Sarah and even more skeptical of the success of their marriage, of which he disapproves. A bureaucrat, he bristles when his authority is challenged.

Lydia, in her late teens, a student at the state school for the deaf. A lip reader with some residual hearing, Lydia is infatuated with James Leeds and is manipulated by Orin Dennis.

Edna Klein, in her thirties, a lawyer recruited by Orin Dennis to assist in his attempts to restructure the power structure at the state school for the deaf.

Robert E. Morsberger

CHILDREN OF VIOLENCE

Author: Doris Lessing (1919-   )
Type of work: Novel
Time of action: The late 1930's to 1968, with an appendix dated as late as 1997
First published: Martha Quest, 1952; *A Proper Marriage*, 1954; *A Ripple from the Storm*, 1958; *Landlocked*, 1965; *The Four-Gated City*, 1969

Martha Quest, the protagonist. Martha is a rebellious, boorish, and self-absorbed fifteen-year-old who later becomes a robotic Zambesian socialite and wife; an overworked, overly zealous "Party" member; and, ultimately, a more self-assured, independent, telepathic woman. With a broad face, pointed chin, severe hazel eyes, a full mouth, straight dark brows, and loose blonde hair, the adolescent Martha scorns provincialism and hypocrisy, especially the color bar. Stubborn, brooding, touchy and thin-skinned, resentful and confused throughout her teens and early twenties, she moves to the city, only to learn that home study has not prepared her for work. Her first contacts plunge her into a superficial, gay, but dissatisfying life of parties, rowdiness, excessive drinking, and sexual games; at age eighteen, Martha betrays whatever values she thought she had, yielding to her peers, submerging her interests, feelings, and sense of self to their wishes. Witnessing the flimsy charges made against African natives, she aches to commit herself politically but does not. After a series of unsatisfactory affairs with men who merely use her to exorcise their own private demons, she marries a stranger, only to find herself even more trapped by a child she at first struggles to abort. Depressed and alienated, she experiences the biological and emotional bonds of womanhood and the stupor of motherhood. With her social circle pregnant wives, Martha (by now twenty-two) becomes the suburban housewife, with servants, tea parties, and "sundowners." Dreams suggest truths, but Martha remains passive, complacent, and uncommitted, trapped, and limited. Martha reflects her century: the conflicts between old and new, the convulsions, the

275

hopes. Her life is a house of disparate rooms, finally united in a functional whole.

Mrs. May Quest, Martha's much-resented mother. Once a tall, pretty, athletic-looking English girl with light-brown hair and candid blue eyes, she has become a tired matron, unhappy and driven, rejected by her mother, disappointed in her husband and her children, and fearful for her grandchild. She is everything Martha fears she herself will become: narrow, conventional, intolerant, insensitive, fearful, menaced, bigoted and overly dramatic, self-convinced, self-righteous, and basically Victorian. Her attempts to keep Martha "respectable" by meddling in her life alienate Martha. Mrs. Quest officially disowns her daughter after her first divorce but continues to visit her to bring her news of her child and to criticize her new "Red" friends. Mr. Quest's death leaves her lost and directionless: an old woman, unloved, except by a black child her views on race should make her despise. Her failed attempts to befriend her daughter and make sense of her associates demonstrate the communication gap between generations; her trip to England brings on her mental collapse and early death.

Mr. Alfred Quest, Martha's absentminded, "dream-locked" father, a hypochondriac who uses diabetes as an excuse to fail. Mr. Quest is tall, lean, dark, and handsome, slow of speech and movement, with fine dark rakish eyes. He spends his days staring at the Veld, reliving the nightmares of World War I and irritatedly calling for peace in the family. Buried in his memories and "vague philosophical speculations," he occasionally emerges, to be "warm, shrewd, paternal," giving confused advice and winning sympathy. He loves Martha and understands that marriage has not brought her love, but he sinks deeper into his dreamworld, "a small faded, shrunken invalid," until his death.

Joss Cohen, Martha's childhood friend, a Jewish Socialist, who helps Martha see her pretenses. Joss directs Martha's reading and keeps a distant eye on her maturation. He is short, compact, and robust, with "humorous direct eyes and a sarcastic practicality," a stiff, solemn face transformed by a shy smile. A would-be lawyer, he helped his parents with their store first. His uncle gives Martha the job that allows her to leave home, and his cousin Jasmine introduces her to active politics. Martha always measures her lovers against "the sober, the responsible, the intelligent and manly Joss" and finds them wanting, particularly because he shares her feelings and accepts her behavior—no matter what. He enlists her in the socialist cause and competes with his brother to mold her politics and to win her love. Much later, after helping organize a mass movement in the North, he is expelled from Rhodesia and lives in Phoebe's flat in England, where he solicits money to aid Africans. His keen intellect, his atheism and socialism strongly influence Martha's self-image.

Solly Cohen, Martha's other childhood friend, Joss's brother, a Zionist and a Trotskyite. Solly, like his brother, is blandly sarcastic about Martha's behavior, values, and pretensions. He is tall and lanky, with a big head, long, thin neck, long arms, and big, bony hands that make him seem "knobbly" and unintegrated; however, his "enormous, sombre black eyes," brooding abstractedly on his world, attract and impress Martha. He is sharp-featured, lively and critical, sarcastic and hostile. He studies medicine in Cape Town, sets up an Israeli-like communal settlement ("Utopia") in the middle of a "Coloured" section, and later gets involved with Martha's Communist group. His statement that Martha is a "born marrier" who will end up in a "big house in the suburbs" makes Martha doubt the path she has chosen, while his sarcasm and "facts" make her rethink Stalinist views.

Douglas Knowell, nicknamed **"Know-all,"** Martha's first husband, a stereotypical "commercial traveller." A clumsy, fleshy, freckled young man, he has light-blue eyes, a flattened nose, and pale hair. Martha alternates between liking and despising him. Douglas traps Martha in a hasty engagement and wedding, offering her a social and sexual identity, despite her "creeping disgust" for him after the first time they have sex. A stereotypical male chauvinist, he revels in external proofs of manhood and in his wife as a possession. His politically radical ideas are theory, not practice, and he is basically shallow and limited. His ulcers keep him out of the war but not out of the bed of an old acquaintance. When Martha abandons him and their child. Douglas reacts like "a sulky little boy," with melodrama and self-controlled hysteria: using social pressure, violence, and intimidation to manipulate her. The pose of wronged, self-righteous husband helps him find comfort in the arms of an old friend.

Mr. Maynard, a suave, cultivated Zambesian magistrate whose detached, slighly satiric manner reminds Martha vaguely of an older Joss and who therefore wields influence over her. Mr. Maynard is tall, heavy, and commanding, his raised eyebrows and compressed mouth intimidating, his English face a solemn reminder of his heritage. He is an old-fashioned liberal, a cynic, resignedly bored, but also a just man, brave enough to do and say the unconventional, a rebel of sorts. He supports a strong African middle-class for practical reasons and is capable of a calm, brutal objectivity that hides the flickers of concern he has for his son, for Martha, and later for his godchild and grandchild. He concludes that "the more things change, the more they remain the same" and predicts war and racial unrest and Martha's marital failure. He furthers Martha's education by making her take a new look at the intricacies and hypocrisies of politics and by accompanying her to the liberal meetings he knows intrigue her. He presides over Martha's second marriage, keeps an eye on her development, and later enlists her aid to win access to and to educate his grandchild. He represents that element of the older order that flirts with change.

Jasmine Cohen, a liberal-leftist intellectual with years of competent service, a cousin of Joss and Solly, the daughter of a prosperous

Jewish family, later Martha's friend and politically active associate. She is a small dark girl, with black curly hair, a "generous" nose, a "wide emotional mouth," and a dignified walk: neat, slow, precise. Her first love, Abraham Cohen, died in the Spanish Civil War, and her next romance, the hotheaded Jackie Bolton, is shipped off to war. Martha admires her as efficient, organized, self-effacing, devoted, and somehow glamorous. The voice of the collective, committed to "causes," she provides a positive model for Martha and stays behind in Africa, hoping to find a restored vision of Communism but ending up imprisoned for treason in South Africa.

Anton Hesse, a Communist Party member since 1930; a refugee who had worked in the underground against Hitler, endured torture in a concentration camp, and escaped; Martha's nurse in her time of illness and then her second husband. The tall, stiff, thirty-year-old Anton, with his ice-blue eyes and Nordic fairness, scorns political amateurs; his cold logic convinces, but his basic inhumanity, revolutionary snobbery, and doctrinaire jargon alienate. His first wife dead, his affair with an Austrian uninspired, he marries Martha to avoid deportation but proves to be all talk and no action, reason without passion, disappointing in bed and on the podium. When his naturalization papers arrive, he divorces Martha to marry the daughter of an industrialist. His tòtal dependence on women makes Martha rethink relationships and values.

Thomas Stern, a Polish Jew, Martha's lover near the close of her marriage to Anton. A Zionist, a Marxist, a medical corps corporal, and a gardener, Thomas prides himself on being a peasant from Sochaczen. His relatives dead in the Warsaw Ghetto, his friends in the camps or the battlefield, he deplores the stupidity and injustice of war. A large man with blue eyes and a broad face, he is tanned, strong, and sensual. Despite a wife and child whom he loves, he has numerous affairs, but the one with Martha is special. Their daily meeting is Martha's "center" for many months and helps her realize her latent sexual self, naturally and instinctively. His visit to Israel so transforms him, however—he slips into partial madness—that he and Martha cannot recapture their previous intimacy; he devotes himself to African villagers, contracts blackwater fever, and dies. Yet, he lives on for Martha in his manuscript: confused self-revelations that prepare her to face and resolve her own divided impulses and psychological conflicts.

Jack, a thirty-five-year-old painter, Martha's first lover in England. Tall, thin, tanned, and tubercular, with long straight brown hair, brown eyes, a strong face, and a long white wartime scar, Jack is an outsider with painful memories of a sadistic father. He channels his hate, however, into sexual liaisons in order to master his seething inner energies. For Martha, he is a means to an end, opening up new, erotic worlds of ritualistic, therapeutic sex. Years later, he turns cruel and hard, breaking in young girls for a brothel through a slow game of fantasy, power, and degradation that destroys their will.

Mark Coldridge, a well-known "Communist" writer for whom Martha works as secretary and with whom, over a twenty-year period, she acts as colleague, friend, housekeeper, and lover. Of average height, Mark is dark, well featured, and strong but often anxious, tense, and watchful. He takes the place of Thomas in Martha's life and incorporates her vision of a "four-squared city" into his own utopian dreams, dreams expressed in his book *A City in the Desert*. Like Martha ten years earlier, he is angered by life and seeks answers in external means. Disillusioned with communism and ideology, he moves to Africa to establish a utopian desert city that later offers refuge to the few survivors of nuclear decimation. He remarries but never recovers from his first love, Lynda.

Lynda Coldridge, Mark's schizophrenic wife. Lynda is tall and thin and untidy, with gray staring hollow eyes, lovely but nail-bitten hands, gleaming gold hair, and a heartbreakingly beautiful smile. After years spent in and out of mental hospitals, thanks to a traumatic and psychologically crippling childhood and incompetent psychiatrists, she resides in the Coldridge basement, alternating between sanity and insanity. Totally turned toward the telepathic and the psychic, she is Martha's guide to her inner, irrational self, though she herself cannot control her own inward journeys.

Phoebe Coldridge, a well-informed political organizer for the Labour left (much like Jasmine), and Martha's friend. As the mother of spoiled adolescent daughters for whom she makes unappreciated sacrifices, Phoebe reenacts the role of Mrs. Quest, only sympathetically. International in vision, she is an accomplished, multifaceted woman who believes in self-control, duty, and responsibility. She remains committed to economic and racial equality.

Jimmy Woods, Mark's partner, a technologist, inventor, and highly successful science-fiction writer. Jimmy is a short fair man with wispy hair, an overlarge head, small strained-looking eyes, strong spectacles, and a scared smile. A scientific genius, Jimmy seems more machinelike than human: emotionless, personally reticent except for computerlike streams of facts, obsessed with machines that probe and manipulate the brain (a central theme of his fiction and the abhorrent reality of his human experiments).

Francis Coldridge, Mark's son. Short, stocky Francis is obsessed with social acceptance. His wide brown eyes always on the alert, his smile pathetic, his responses withdrawn and watchful, then forcedly jolly (like Martha's youthful "Mattie" role), he is terrified of home, where his role as clown disintegrates and his alienation from his mother pains him. As a young man, he works very hard backstage in a theater and finds a comfortable social group to shield him from his family. Later, he updates the reader on the nuclear incident that so transforms the world and heads a Reconstruction and Rehabilitation team to record memories of recent history before they are lost forever.

278

Paul Coldridge, Mark's handsome nephew. Initially lively, dark, charming, and warm, but basically confused, desperate, and totally at odds with his cousin Francis, Paul is deeply affected by his aunt's madness and his father's defection to Russia. Doted on by his aunt only to be rejected later, Paul turns antisocial and is expelled from school for bad grades and blatant theft. Forlorn, resentful, he makes others uncomfortable and defensive but finally turns his power fantasies into reality, buying up real estate and starting a hairdressing business. As a young man, he has aquiline features, dark liquid eyes, and an animal grace. After being rejected by a girl he loves, he marries his old sweetheart and dies in the nuclear accident.

Gina Macdonald

THE CHILDREN'S HOUR

Author: Lillian Hellman (1905-1984)
Type of work: Play
Time of action: The 1930's
First produced: 1934

Mary Tilford, a malicious schoolgirl. She attends a private girls' school, where she bullies her fellow classmates, disobeys her teachers, and whines when she is not given her way. She has been brought up by an indulgent grandmother who has spoiled her. When her two teachers, Karen Wright and Martha Dobie, try to discipline her, she retaliates by spreading the rumor that they are lesbians. Although the rumor is untrue, Mary sticks to her charge, and her shocked grandmother then removes her from school and convinces the parents of the other children to do likewise, thus destroying the school and ruining the teachers' lives.

Mrs. Tilford, quite advanced in age, an influential and wealthy figure. She dotes on her grandchild Mary. She knows that Mary is petulant, and she initially scoffs at Mary's attack on the teachers, but she is horrified when Mary whispers her charge that Martha and Karen are lesbians. Blinded by her outrage and unwilling to see through Mary's manipulation of the facts, she succeeds not only in closing the school but also in ostracizing the two teachers. When Mrs. Tilford finally learns of Mary's deception, she abjectly asks for Karen's forgiveness and searches for a way to rectify the great harm she has caused the teachers.

Martha Dobie, a young, intense woman devoted to her friendship with Karen and rather jealous of Joe Cardin, Karen's fiancé. When Martha learns of Mary's charge against her, she goes with Karen to confront Mrs. Tilford, who thinks the two women have come merely to brazen things out. Martha and Karen take Mrs. Tilford to court but lose their case when Martha's Aunt Lily refuses to testify on her behalf. Feeling guilty about the breakup of Karen and Joe, and suspecting that she has harbored sexual feelings for Karen, Martha kills herself at the end of the play.

Karen Wright, a teacher who has joined Martha in working hard to establish a school. While she is very close to Martha, she senses a strain between them when she becomes engaged to Joe Cardin, and it may be this strain that Mary is able to manufacture into a lie. Karen is more even-tempered than Martha, and while she is grieved by the failure of their school, she will clearly survive, even though it appears that her fiancé has begun to doubt her and to wonder whether she indeed has a lesbian relationship with Martha.

Dr. Joe Cardin, Karen's fiancé. He tries to expose Mary as a liar; he intercedes on behalf of Martha and Karen with Mrs. Tilford but proves unable to shake Mary's story or to change Mrs. Tilford's mind. Although he tries to stick loyally by the two women, visiting them when everyone else has shunned them, he eventually succumbs to doubts about the relationship between Martha and Karen and reluctantly accepts Karen's suggestion that they should not marry.

Lily Mortar, Martha's aunt and a teacher at the school. She is proud of her career in the theater and loves to harangue students about her experiences on the stage. She is highly critical of Martha and points out that her niece is jealous of Karen and Joe. Her loose talk inadvertently helps Mary in concocting her charges against the teachers. During the trial, when Karen and Martha are trying to establish their innocence, Lily Mortar remains out of town and does not answer their pleas for help. She returns when it is too late, thinking only of herself and apparently oblivious of the grave injury she has done to Karen's and Martha's life.

Carl Rollyson

THE CHINESE WALL

Author: Max Frisch (1911-   )
Type of work: Play
Time of action: 210 B.C. and the mid-twentieth century
First produced: Die chinesische Mauer: Eine Farce, 1946 (English translation, 1961)

The Contemporary, a modern intellectual, who is both the epic narrator of the play and a central character. He moves back and forth in the play's anachronistic time structure, introducing the many historical and literary personages, debating with them, and commenting on their role in history and relation to the modern world. The figures represent recurring archetypal characters that populate the modern imagination, and the narrator hopes to convince them (and the audience) of the need to break the cycle of their behavior. The return of such tyrants as the Chinese emperor Hwang Ti and France's Napoleon Bonaparte could mean the end of humanity in the atomic age. For his eloquent warnings of a nuclear holocaust, the Contemporary receives an award from Hwang Ti, but he proves to be ineffectual. Neither the tyrants nor the people are deterred by his intellectual arguments, and the cycle of destruction begins anew.

Hwang Ti (hwäng tē), Emperor of China from 247 to 210 B.C., the gentle-looking but ruthless founder of China's first central government. To secure his regime from threats outside China, he orders the building of the Great Wall. To maintain totalitarian rule domestically, Hwang Ti demands the absolute praise and allegiance of his people. While seeking to silence the dissent ascribed to an unseen citizen called Min Ko, "The Voice of the People," the fanatical emperor accuses a mute of being "The Voice of the People" and tortures him, trying to extract a confession. Hwang Ti is deposed by a tyrannical prince, who perpetuates the oppression.

Olan, a Chinese farmer's wife. She and her son have made a pilgrimage to Nanking to see the emperor, and she wonders if the complaints about the emperor are true. When her son is tortured as Min Ko, she refuses to admit the truth, namely that he is mute and unable to register dissent. Rather, her motherly pride prompts her to hail him as "The Voice of the People."

The Mute, Olan's son Wang. Because he is the only silent member of a throng cheering the emperor, he is arrested as the traitorous Min Ko, the final enemy in the land.

Mee Lan, daughter of the emperor. She is dissatisfied with the powerful young princes who court her and seeks instead a defender of truth and intelligence such as the Contemporary. Mee Lan's humanistic inquiry of him ("What do you know about man?") is answered brutally by the revolutionary forces who ravish her.

Wu Tsiang, a Chinese prince, betrothed to Mee Lan. He is bitter that she, who despises his love of power, refuses to marry him. The prince promises revenge and leads the revolt that topples the emperor.

The Maskers, historical and literary figures promenading in a polonaise, "like figures on a musical clock," symbolizing the recurrent forms of human thought and behavior.

Allen E. Hye

THE CHOSEN and THE PROMISE

Author: Chaim Potok (1929-   )
Type of work: Novel
Time of action: 1944 to the mid-1950's
First published: The Chosen, 1967; *The Promise,* 1969

Reuven Malter, the narrator of both novels. The son of David Malter, Reuven describes himself as dark-haired, dark-eyed, and very ordinary. He and his father are Orthodox Jews, but "enlightened" ones, a category whose existence is doubted by pious Jews and secularists alike. Reuven is especially talented in mathematics and enjoys symbolic logic. In the course of the novels, Reuven develops from a fifteen-year-old yeshiva (Jewish parochial school) student and baseball enthusiast to a rabbi with a master's degree in philosophy and a teaching position in the graduate department of rabbinics at Hirsch University. Though his intellectual abilities are obvious—his mathematical talent is exceptional and he is an accomplished textual critic of Talmud while still attending college—it is his talent for friendship that particularly distinguishes Reuven. In *The Chosen,* Reuven becomes the brilliant Danny Saunders' friend, the one with whom Danny talks when he most needs (and nowhere else finds) someone to listen and respond to him. Danny's father, Reb Saunders, talks with Danny through Reuven as well: For Reuven, as his father says, "It is never pleasant to be a buffer." Though their friendship bears the brunt of Reb Saunders' violent opposition to David Malter's Zionism, it survives as a dominant, positive force in both their lives. In *The Promise,* Reuven's friendship with

Danny becomes the background for other friendships, especially those with Michael Gordon, whom Danny, as a psychotherapist, treats; Michael's father, Abraham Gordon; and, in a strange way, Reuven's own teacher, Rav Kalman. When Danny despairs of Michael's treatment, it is Reuven whose friendship touches Michael deeply enough to help him talk. The conflict between the imperatives of friendship and the reactionary demands of Rav Kalman challenge Reuven's honesty and force him to learn independent integrity of mind and heart.

Daniel Saunders (Danny), the brilliant son of Reb Saunders, expected as a matter of course to take his father's place as tzaddik (Hasidic spiritual leader). Danny is tall, with deep blue eyes and facial features that look as if they are chiseled from stone. Until he leaves home for graduate school, he wears the earlocks and beard and the somber clothes—dark suit, white shirt, ritual fringes—of the Hasid; in odd contrast to his garb, Danny speaks perfect, unaccented English in his slightly nasal voice. Danny's brilliance and his photographic memory have two central consequences in his life: They lead his father to rear Danny in silence, Reb Saunders' painful way of forcing Danny to be heart as well as head; to learn compassion; and to feel the world's pain within himself. They also drive him (at first under the anonymous guidance of Reuven's father) to read widely, especially in psychology, and, as a result, to break with his father's plans for him and to work for a Ph.D. in clinical psychology at Columbia. In *The Promise*, Danny uses a variation of his father's silence to break through the defensive walls Michael Gordon has raised around his anger and pain. In spite of his emancipation from and reinterpretation of his past (and his marriage to Rachel Gordon), Danny remains firmly rooted in the tradition of Hasidic spirituality and becomes, as his father says he will, "a tzaddik for the world."

David Malter, Reuven's father, a scholar, writer, and teacher. David Malter is a gentle man, small with thinning hair, who catches colds easily and has a weak heart. His Zionist political activities and his critical writings on the Talmud reflect David Malter's uncompromising strength of conviction and independence of intellect. Nevertheless, he is a moderating influence in the lives of Reuven and Danny, insisting that they develop a well-balanced historical perspective of themselves and their people, that they strive to understand those with whom they disagree, that they think clearly and carefully about their judgments and actions, and that they exercise complete honesty.

Reb Saunders, Danny's father, tzaddik of a community of Russian Hasidim who came to America after the Bolshevik Revolution in 1917. Reb Saunders is tall and heavily bearded, with a face that, like Danny's, looks as if it is chiseled from stone. He never writes because he believes that words distort inner reality, yet he is a great Talmudist and a great leader of his people, who regard him with awe as their link to God. Though in nearly every significant area of life he holds views opposed to those of David Malter, Reb Saunders ultimately credits Reuven's father with preventing Danny from abandoning his Jewishness and helping him to remain a keeper of the Commandments.

Michael Gordon, an adolescent boy, long-limbed and skinny, with dreamy blue eyes and wild hair, whose great interest is astronomy. Michael is the son of Abraham Gordon and is psychologically ill, to a large extent because of his unacknowledged anger at his father for his courageous intellectual work, which has made the Gordons anathema to Orthodox Judaism: Michael feels the hate yet cannot deal with his own response to it. Michael, who has a history of resisting therapy—three therapists have tried unsuccessfully to treat him—becomes a client of Danny Saunders, whom Reuven has introduced to the Gordons at their request. Danny is able to be of help to Michael, breaking through his highly developed defenses; his unusual intervention in Michael's illness later becomes the subject of Danny's doctoral dissertation.

Abraham Gordon, father of Michael Gordon, a Jewish philosopher who no longer believes in the received content of Judaism yet believes the tradition worth renewal. A large man, tall and heavy-set, Abraham Gordon teaches at the non-Orthodox Zechariah Frankel Seminary and has been excommunicated by the Orthodox Jewish community. Reuven likes the questions Abraham Gordon asks in his books. Indeed, he asks the same ones, but he cannot accept Gordon's answers. Reuven and Abraham Gordon become close friends, in spite of Rav Kalman's objections.

Rav Jacob Kalman, in *The Promise*, Reuven's Talmud teacher. A survivor of a German concentration camp, Rav Kalman is short and stocky, with dark eyes and thick black hair and beard; he always dresses in a long, old-fashioned black coat, sharply creased pants, and white shirt. An angry and impatient teacher, he brings an aura of darkness to the classroom. In the wake of the Holocaust, in which all of his European students were killed, and inspired by the zeal of the Hasidim, Rav Kalman becomes the self-appointed guardian of a rigidly traditional *Yiddishkeit* (Judaism), denouncing the writings of Abraham Gordon and David Malter in the Yiddish Orthodox press. He threatens to withhold ordination from Reuven because of Reuven's association with Abraham Gordon and is greatly troubled by Reuven's facility with and enjoyment of his father's method of textual criticism. Nevertheless, whether (as he says) because of the love of Torah he hears in Reuven's voice or (as Abraham Gordon says) because of the Holocaust, Rav Kalman signs Reuven's *smicha* (ordination) and agrees to his appointment to the graduate faculty at Hirsch University.

Rav Gershenson, in *The Chosen*, Reuven's college Talmud teacher. Loved by all who have studied under him, Rav Gershenson is a tall man with thick shoulders, a pointed gray beard, and long-fingered hands that are always in motion as he talks. He warns Reuven not to use critical method in his class, though he is not personally opposed to it. In *The Promise*, Rav Gershenson angrily opposes Rav Kalman's rigid religiosity, claiming that Rav Kalman is driving their best students away from *Yiddishkeit* and thus destroying it, not protecting it. Though Rav Gershenson himself has not been courageous enough to write about the Talmud, he urges Reuven never to be afraid to write.

Rachel Gordon, a Brooklyn College student of English literature, particularly interested in James Joyce. Reuven hears of Rachel from a friend and arranges to meet her because of his interest in the books of Abraham Gordon, her uncle. The auburn-haired, thoroughly modern young woman, poised and self-assured, meets Danny through Reuven. Odd, even impossible, as a Saunders-Gordon alliance seems to all concerned, Danny and Rachel fall in love and marry. Rachel brings Danny the twentieth century; Danny brings Rachel God.

Ruth Gordon, Abraham Gordon's wife. A beautiful woman with a degree in French literature, Ruth Gordon has become a partner with her husband in the writing of his books, editing them and managing their revision. She finds Orthodoxy "medieval" and distasteful.

Joseph Gordon, Rachel's father, a pipe-smoking professor of English literature, tall and broad-shouldered, Abraham Gordon's brother.

Sarah Gordon, Rachel's mother, an artist and art historian, slender, gray eyed, and beautiful.

Jonathan A. Glenn

CHRIST STOPPED AT EBOLI

Author: Carlo Levi (1902-1975)
Type of work: Novel
Time of action: 1935-1936
First published: Cristo si è fermato a Eboli, 1945 (English translation, 1947)

Carlo Levi, a physician and political prisoner. Kind and contemplative, artistic and observant, he has a deep compassion for those who are poor, ill, and disadvantaged. A painter by vocation, he would prefer merely to observe without becoming directly involved, but he cannot. The narrator and the protagonist of the story, his political imprisonment consists in being sent to live in a small and remote southern Italian village, where he is closely watched at all times. He records the experiences and the impressions of his sojourn.

Luigi Magalone (mä·jä·lõ′nĕ), the mayor. Smug and self-satisfied, the Fascist mayor wholly enjoys the power and the prestige of his position. He gives orders to the prisoners for the sheer pleasure of seeing his requests enacted and is particularly zealous in the literal and unwavering application of Fascist laws and regulations in his village.

Giulia Venere (vä•nä'rä), Carlo Levi's housekeeper. She is a middle-aged woman, hardworking, unemotional, strong. She is ignorant but is naturally intelligent and practical. Her life is linked to superstitions and traditions. Despite her natural wisdom and knowledge of life, she very firmly believes in the magical power of curses, potions, and incantations. The world has no secrets for her, no illusions, but the realm of the spiritual and of the intangible she holds in great reverence and fear. It is from her that Carlo learns much about the traditions and folklore of the village, and about the villagers themselves.

Don Giuseppe Trajella (trē•hä'lä), the parish priest. Old and ailing, his most visible characteristics are those of rancor and bitterness toward the entire village. Although bright and cultured, he has no interest other than venting and feeding his anger and his unhappiness. He has been in the parish for many years, having been assigned there as punishment for misconduct. The entire village ridicules, persecutes, and torments him.

Doctor Milillo, an elderly physician and uncle of the mayor. He is a man whose seventy years of age have made his movements slow and his voice shaky. A gentle and well-intentioned man, he remembers very little about medicine and is ill-equipped to tend to the sick. He feels threatened by Dr. Levi's arrival and is much reassured by the latter that his place will not be usurped.

Doctor Gibilisco (jē•bē•lē'skō), a physician. Like Doctor Milillo, he too is an elderly practitioner. A meticulous dresser and man of imposing presence, he projects an image of confidence which conceals a profound ignorance of the medical profession. An exacting and mistrusting man, he demands payment from even the poorest of patients. His profession, in his view, gives him superiority over the rest of the villagers and assigns him the right over their life and death.

Donna Caterina Magalone Cuscianna (kōō•shyä'nä), head of the local Fascist Party and sister of the mayor. She is open, cordial, hospitable, and maternal. In addition, she is clever, calculating, and powerful. From her very privileged position as sister of the mayor and head of the Fascist Party in the village, she has as much to say about what happens in town as Magalone himself. Her driving force is hatred toward certain women in the village and in particular toward the pharmacist's daughter, whom she believes to be her husband's lover.

Susan Briziarelli

CHRONICLE OF A DEATH FORETOLD

Author: Gabriel García Márquez (1928-   )
Type of work: Novel
Time of action: The twentieth century
First published: Crónica de una muerte anunciada, 1981 (English translation, 1982)

Santiago Nasar (sän•tyä'gō nä•sär'), a member of the Arab community, slim and pale, with dark curly hair. He is killed in front of his own house at the age of twenty-one. A handsome bachelor, he is described as having had a love for horses, falconry, and church pomp; his other characteristics included flirtatiousness, valor, merriness, peaceableness, and prudence. Normally dressed in khaki with riding boots, he donned unstarched white linen pants and shirts on special occasions. Inheritor of The Divine Face cattle ranch and a firearms enthusiast, he carried a .357 Magnum with armored bullets as he traveled in the country. Although he is killed as the deflowerer of Angela Vicario, his innocent behavior up to the moment of his death suggests that he was wrongly accused of the act.

Angela Vicario (äng'hē•lä vē•kä'ryō), the

284

youngest and prettiest daughter of a poor family. She resists the prospect of marriage to Bayardo San Román and unsuccessfully attempts to pass as a virgin on their wedding night. After Bayardo brings her back home, she is beaten by her mother, Purísima (Pura) del Carmen Vicario. Questioned by her brothers, she names Santiago as the man responsible for deflowering her. In the aftermath of the murder, she grows from a hapless spirit to a mature and witty woman. Previously disinterested in Bayardo, she becomes obsessed with him and remains unmarried, writing hundreds of letters to him in the years after their separation.

Bayardo San Román, who captures the imagination of the villagers when he arrives in town wearing clothing ornamented with silver. About thirty years old, he has a slim waist, golden eyes, and tanned skin. A drinker, he seems to lack a steady occupation but exhibits familiarity with railway engineering, telegraphy, frontier illnesses, card games, and swimming. Soon after seeing Angela, he courts her and proposes to her. When he discovers on their wedding night that she is not a virgin, he carries her to her mother. Afterwards, he is found in a state of severe intoxication and carried out of the town by members of his family. Although he never opens any of Angela's letters, he saves them and eventually returns to her.

Pedro Vicario and
Pablo Vicario, brothers of Angela, identical twins who support their family by slaughtering pigs. Both presented themselves for military service at the age of twenty, but Pablo, six minutes older than Pedro, stayed home to support the family. Pedro entered service, where he contracted a case of blennorrhea. Told that Santiago has dishonored their sister, the brothers undertake to stab him to death. Although they are unrepentant after the deed is done, the narrator notes that they seemed reluctant to carry it off: By informing more than a dozen villagers of their intent, they seem to have been hoping to be stopped. In jail, they are haunted by an odor of Santiago that lingers after his death. Pablo, who suffers a severe case of diarrhea in confinement, becomes a goldsmith upon his release. Pedro, whose chronic pain prevents him from sleeping for eleven months, is cured of his disease while behind bars. After he is freed, he rejoins the military and disappears on a mission.

The narrator, a friend of Santiago. Returning to his home town, he investigates Santiago's murder twenty-seven years after its occurrence. The narrative summarizes the results of his efforts.

Clotilde Armenta, a milk vendor, who appeals to the Vicario twins to refrain from killing Santiago. In an effort to prevent the crime from taking place, she asks all the people she sees to warn Santiago of the danger he is in, attempts to intoxicate the brothers, unsuccessfully tries to restrain Pedro, and shouts a warning to Santiago.

Don Rogelio de la Flor (r̄ō•hĕ′lyō), Clotilde Armenta's husband, and **Colonel Lázaro Aponte** (lä′sä•rō), the mayor, disappoint Clotilde because they do not take strong measures to prevent the murder from occurring. Don Rogelio dies from shock after seeing Santiago's bloody corpse.

Purísima (Pura) del Carmen (pōō•rē′sĕ•mä), Angela's mother, beats her daughter harshly after Bayardo returns her.

Luis Enrique (ĕn•rē′kĕ), the narrator's brother, and **Cristóbal (Cristo) Bedoya,** friends of Santiago. Luis, Cristo, Santiago, and the narrator had been drinking companions of Bayardo's.

Luisa Santiaga (sän•tyä′gä), the narrator's mother, was Santiago's godmother and a blood relative of Pura. She is initially impressed with Bayardo, but her regard for him gradually ebbs. On the day of the murder, she tries to warn Santiago of the threat to his life but is told that she is too late.

David Marc Fischer

THE CIRCLE

Author: W. Somerset Maugham (1874-1965)
Type of work: Play
Time of action: 1919
First produced: 1921

Arnold Champion-Cheney, a Member of Parliament and owner of a country estate, Aston-Adey. At about age thirty-five, he is tall and good-looking, fair complexioned with a clean-cut and sensitive face. Impeccably dressed, he is an example of the prim and proper upper-class Englishman. Though politics is his career, his primary interest appears to be collecting antique furniture. While he loves his wife of three years, he lacks passion and has little interest in sex; he has no inkling that he stands on the verge of losing her. As a gentleman, he shows himself capable of generosity but is averse to self-sacrifice.

Elizabeth Champion-Cheney, Arnold's wife, a charming, pretty woman in her early twenties. Taken for granted by her husband, she is a romantic at heart, idealizing human love relationships. She is truthful, frank, tolerant, and witty, a good hostess, but her husband's career and enthusiasm for antiques leave her cold.

Clive Champion-Cheney, Arnold's father, formerly a member of Parliament, now an affluent upper-class Englishman living in retirement. A single man in his early sixties, he is tall with gray hair, dresses carefully, and bears himself with dignity. Highly intelligent, he is a man of the world, yet his ample wit turns toward the caustic and at times sarcastic. His unexpected arrival at the Champion-Cheney estate creates an awkward situation because the invited guests include his divorced wife. Highly analytical, he is essentially a man of reason rather than emotion.

Lady Catherine Champion-Cheney (Kitty), Arnold's mother and Clive's former wife. She has been for thirty years the mistress of Lord Porteous. She is a gay, small woman with dyed red hair and painted cheeks. She is vain, preoccupied with retaining a youthful appearance. Her mistakes in the play make her appear an object of humor and sympathy, yet she remains a romantic at heart. She is both talkative and sentimental and obviously dependent on her long-standing relationship with Lord Porteous, whom she seeks to possess.

Lord Porteous (Hughie), a former Member of Parliament and former associate of Clive, normally living in exile with Lady Kitty. A bald, elderly gentleman, he is gruff and somewhat snappish, but underneath a crusty exterior he reveals a sentimental streak. He gave up his chance to be prime minister for the love of Kitty and harbors some bitterness that it has not turned out well, though he would never express it.

Edward Luton (Teddie), a youthful manager of a rubber plantation in the Federated Malay States. He has recently been discharged from the English army following World War I. He is pleasant, athletic, well-mannered, and ambitious. Desiring a wife to accompany him back to the Far East, he boldly declares his love for his hostess, Elizabeth. His masculine directness and competitive nature contrast with Arnold's passive and prim character.

Mrs. Anna Shenstone, a guest at the Champion-Cheney home, a pleasant and elegant woman of forty. She has a small role in the play, serving to focus the dialogue and in partnership with Teddie Luton winning at bridge against Kitty and Lord Porteous.

Stanley Archer

286

THE CITADEL

Author: A. J. Cronin (1896-1981)
Type of work: Novel
Time of action: The first third of the twentieth century
First published: 1937

Andrew Manson, the central character in the novel. Coming from a background of poverty, he graduates with the help of an academic prize as a medical doctor from the University of Dundee. He accepts a position as an assistant to Dr. Edward Page in the coal-mining community of Blaenelly in Wales, where Manson is the latest in a series of assistants who are actually expected to run the practice for Page for small remuneration. Manson is idealistic and works hard despite his growing sense of being exploited. He forms a close friendship with Philip Denny, a talented physician in the community, whose tendency to drink excessively makes him less than respectable. After Christine's death, it is with the support of Philip Denny that Manson is able to pull himself together, and they open a clinic for the treatment of lung disease.

Christine, née Barlow, Manson, a schoolteacher in Blaenelly. She meets Manson when he enters her schoolroom to protest her allowing an ill child to return to school. They are attracted to each other and marry. She tutors Andrew in languages to help him prepare for his advanced degrees. Throughout their marriage, she works to keep him committed to the ideals of his youth. Estranged when he is tempted by wealth and status, they are reconciled, but then she dies in a street accident.

Dr. Edward Page, an elderly physician in Blaenelly. He has suffered a stroke and knows that he will never practice again, but he is dominated by his wife, who maintains the fiction that he will recover. He likes Andrew Manson but is incapable of protecting the young doctor from his wife's exploitation.

Mrs. Blodwen Page, Dr. Page's wife. A short, plump woman about forty years old, she has a domineering personality. She will not admit to the miners in her husband's practice that he will never work again and so recruits assistants such as Andrew Manson to do all the work. She pays these assistants meagerly and feeds them as cheaply as she can.

Dr. Philip Denny, a bright, idealistic physician who is assistant to Dr. Lewis in Blaenelly. He welcomes Manson and finds in him a kindred spirit. Though prone to overindulgence in drink, Denny is a more than capable physician with an unconventional approach to life. He helps Manson in Blaenelly and in finding a new post. Later, he persuades Manson to set up a lung clinic and helps his friend overcome the death of Christine.

Dr. Freddy Hampton, a former classmate of Manson, who makes good in London. He has an elaborate practice dedicated to soaking rich patients and develops a circle of acquaintances who call each other in for consultations as a further way to wealth. Hampton seems the epitome of a successful physician to Manson, and Manson is persuaded to join with him. Eventually Manson breaks with Hampton when he realizes that the latter has no true concern for patients.

Francis J. Bremer

CITIES OF SALT

Author: Abdelrahman Munif (1933-   )
Type of work: Novel

Time of action: Between the two world wars
First published: Mudun al-milh: al-Tīh, 1984 (English translation, 1987)

Miteb al-Hathal, a Bedouin tribesman with a special passion for the Wadi al-Uyoun desert oasis, where he and his family live. The appearance of Americans, invited by the Arabian government to explore and drill for oil, changes Miteb's previously stoic and optimistic attitude toward life. With characteristic boldness and candor, he warns people about impending disaster to their lives and even stands up to the regional emir, but no one heeds him. When the Americans level the orchards and gardens to force people to leave what will henceforth be an oil-drilling site, Miteb mounts his Omani camel and disappears for good. Yet, reports of his visitations come from various parts of the region.

Ibn Rashed, a man from Wadi al-Uyoun who acquiesces to the American presence and decides to join the forces of change. He encourages the local population to relocate and becomes a personnel recruiter for the Americans, bringing Bedouins from all over to Harran with promises of good salaries and homes—but the workers find only dehumanizing tents and later barracks. He loses his struggle against Dabbasi for local influence and power and comes to fear paranoically the specter of Miteb al-Hathal. He dies a broken man, a symbol of an Arab who has broken his ties and traditional fidelity to word and tribal values.

The Americans, oil workers at Wadi al-Uyoun, Harran, and the pipeline camps in between. These one-dimensional personalities, almost caricatures of American workers and managers abroad, seem superficially interested in local culture and customs but are quick to defend and implement company policy in the face of local traditions and concerns.

Bedouin workers at Harran, people lured by the promise of good wages, houses, and a future for their families. These people come from all over to work for the Americans. Hard workers and good Muslims, yet unaware of the facts of life in the modern world beyond their personal experience, they seem simple and uncouth animals to the Americans and Westernized Arab company men.

Harrani townspeople, generous, uncomplicated people unaware of much that is transpiring in the modern world beyond their region. Some accede to Ibn Rashed's entreaties that they sell their land to the Americans; however, Dabbasi convinces some of them to hold onto their land at least, in the face of the foreign takeover of their community.

Naim Sh'eira, the Americans' Arab translator, who, like other Arab company men, learns American disdain for his fellow Arab Bedouins.

Emir Khaled al-Mishari, a middle-aged, heavy-set, and dark-skinned man who replaces an earlier emir who had refused to stay in Harran once he saw changes and the Americans there. Ignorant, indecisive, timorous, and self-indulgent, Khaled is fascinated by a succession of such modern gadget gifts as a telescope, a radio, and a telephone. The climactic workers' strike and the community uprising lead to his mental breakdown. People see him yelling into his unconnected telephone in his car speeding from Harran with his entourage.

Fawaz, Miteb al-Hathal's eldest son, somewhat responsible for the family after his father's disappearance. Feeling the youthful Bedouin urge to travel, however, he leaves home on a brief trip, during which he has a vision of Miteb in a storm. On a second trip, he accepts Ibn Rashed's offer of a job in Harran. At the novel's end, he leads a charge of striking workers and Harranis toward the American compound.

Dabbasi, a round-faced man with a small beard in his mid-fifties who comes to Harran and there wins the hearts of the emir and the populace. He marries a Harrani and marries his son Saleh to one as well. His own wedding party is the social event of the day. He eventually defeats Ibn Rashed in their competition for local power and influence.

Abdu Muhammad, Harran's first baker, who falls pathetically in love from a distance with one of the American women brought by boat to the Americans in Harran.

Hajem, a boy assigned with his elder brother, Mizban, to sea-rock cutting in the Harran port expansion project because they are the only Bedouin workers who can swim. After Mizban drowns by catching his foot on an underwater rock, Hajem becomes simple-minded and unable to communicate. The crowd at Mizban's funeral displays community desperation, sadness at their own plight, and their sense that the Americans are responsible for all untoward events. Terminated from his employment, Hajem is sent back inland by Ibn Rashed to his uncle, who later comes to Harran to demand justice and compensation. The uncle is astounded by the disrespectful and untraditional treatment he receives. Their detainment by the deputy emir upsets the workers, which leads ultimately to Ibn Rashed's downfall. The uncle takes his nephew back inland without fanfare and without compensation.

Akoub, a short, middle-aged Armenian truck driver from Aleppo who dies in his truck in Harran some time after newer vehicles and more commercial operations have driven him out of business. All Harran comes to Akoub's funeral, his death marking the end of an older and more personal way of transporting people and things.

Raji, Akoub's fellow truck driver, a tall, skinny, bald, contentious man, quick to anger but goodhearted. He and Akoub eventually become best friends. Akoub's death devastates him. At the novel's end, Raji carries the wounded in his old truck from Harran to Ujra.

Mufaddi al-Jeddan, a traditional practitioner of medicine, a dervish who treats people for free and seeks only such goods as sandals, other clothing, and food as he needs them.

Dr. Suhbi al-Mahmilji, a physician who has lived in Tripoli and Aleppo and has also served as a hajj pilgrimage physician before coming to Harran. Suhbi becomes a favorite of the emir, who chooses him to give the welcoming speech for Crown Prince Khazael, the sultan's deputy, on the occasion of the opening of the Wadi al-Uyoun-Harran pipeline.

Johar, one of the Emir's bodyguards. Later, as the chief security officer for the emir, he establishes a paramilitary organization and terrorizes Bedouin workers and townspeople. He is assumed to have ordered or committed the murder of Mufaddi al-Jeddan.

Khazna al-Hassan, a Bedouin midwife and healer who treats women and children and thinks of Mufaddi al-Jeddan as her brother. She worries about him when he is arrested, cares for him after he has been beaten, and is disconsolate at his death.

Michael Craig Hillmann

THE CITY AND THE HOUSE

Author: Natalia Ginzburg (1916-　　)
Type of work: Novel
Time of action: The 1970's or 1980's
First published: La città e la casa, 1984 (English translation, 1987)

Giuseppe Guaraldi, a writer and scholar, approaching age fifty, who has just ended a long love affair with Lucrezia, a married woman. He sells his apartment against the advice of his friends, leaves his job, and moves to Princeton, New Jersey, to live with his older brother. He imagines an idyllic life with his brother that will provide him with the security he needs after the end of his affair. Instead, he finds that, shortly before his arrival in Princeton, his brother has married Anne Marie, a colleague from the scientific institute where he works. Giuseppe views the marriage as an intrusion and begins a novel to keep himself from being lonely. At first, he dislikes Anne Marie immensely, but, upon the sudden death of his brother, he begins to feel an affinity for her that eventually leads to marriage. Although he and Lucrezia have had a child together, Giuseppe has never acknowledged his son and concentrates on the child of his previous marriage, Alberico, on Anne Marie's daughter, Chantal, and her husband, Danny. When Alberico is murdered by drug dealers, Giuseppe returns to Italy for the funeral and realizes how little he has been connected to his life there.

Lucrezia, Giuseppe's former lover. Although she has been married to Piero for many years, and they have five children together, Lucrezia has had a number of affairs. At the end of her relationship with Giuseppe, she begins an affair with Ignazio Fegiz, an annoying know-it-all with whom she becomes obsessed. She feels restless after her long-term relationship with Giuseppe and uses Ignazio as the means to extricate herself from the country house her friends have used as a symbol of stability in their relatively rootless lives. She is an unsatisfied woman for whom the role of wife and mother has paled, although, in the eyes of her friends, she has performed it beautifully. After she leaves Piero, she finds a dark and unattractive apartment in Rome where she lives with her five children. She discovers that Ignazio is totally committed to another woman and that he is far from being the love of her life. Lucrezia finds herself living alone in Rome, an observer of the disintegration of her friends' lives as well as her own.

Alberico Guaraldi, Giuseppe's homosexual son. Alberico has spent most of his adult life away from his father, who thinks of him as a dilettante. He lives in various countries and pursues his career as a filmmaker. When he succeeds in making a critically acclaimed film, he is as surprised as anyone. He and his father have not been close, less for the fact of his homosexuality than because Alberico is financially independent through an inheritance from his mother's family. He owns an apartment at a time when his father and his father's friends are practically homeless while frequently moving from one apartment to another. While the so-called adults of his family are wandering and searching for meaning in their lives, he has found a creative calling and establishes a family for himself. Alberico, his lover, and their friend Nadia, who comes to live with Alberico when she discovers she is pregnant by another man, form a domestic partnership of relative stability. After she has her child, Alberico and his lover take on the parenting role that she refuses. Their lives revolve around filmmaking, the baby, and drugs. The drugs eventually result in the violent deaths of all three.

Anne Marie Guaraldi, the widow of Giuseppe's brother and Giuseppe's wife after his brother's death. Anne Marie is a humorless and rather cold woman who pursues scientific interests. She was married before she met Giuseppe's brother and has a daughter, Chantal, from that marriage. She is not a motherly woman and rarely sees her daughter. Chantal comes to live with her mother when her husband, Danny, and she separate, but it is Giuseppe who consoles her. Anne Marie does not want to be bothered with the mess of relationships. After her marriage to Giuseppe, they settle into a convenient silence. He writes his Italian novel in his study, and she continues her employment at the scientific institute and socializes with her coworkers. Because Anne Marie refuses to give of herself in a relationship, Giuseppe and Chantal take comfort from each other and have a short love affair. Anne Marie has had three marriages, all of which she considers successful in comparison to her daughter's. Yet, her first marriage ended in divorce, her second husband died early in the relationship, and she sees her marriage to Giuseppe as a convenient way to continue living in the same house. She needs little from her familial relationships, which makes her somewhat of a puzzle to Giuseppe, who feels his unconnectedness so acutely. It is this puzzling aspect and her lack of warmth, in comparison to the motherly and nurturing Lucrezia, that attracted Giuseppe to her after his brother's death. She seems serene to him at first; he later recognizes that this serenity is really disinterest.

Stephanie Korney

THE CITY AND THE PILLAR

Author: Gore Vidal (1925-   )
Type of work: Novel
Time of action: The late 1930's and 1940's
First published: 1948

Jim Willard, a homosexual youth of high school age, roughly seventeen, a junior at the beginning of the novel. He is tall, handsome, an athlete who has played both baseball and tennis, with short blond hair. In high school, Jim already has formed a sexual attraction to a male friend, Bob Ford, with whom he has his first sexual encounter while the two are on a summer camping trip. Jim Willard is a romantic about love, regularly looking back in time to recapture the magic of his first idealized love, even in later affairs with a novelist, a Hollywood film star, a female involvement, and other casual sexual encounters. In his early adulthood—first at sea, later in California, Mexico, the Army, and New York—he pursues the illusion that he has created of high school friend Bob Ford.

Bob Ford, a tall, lean, but muscular high school athlete, with red curly hair and blue eyes, who is Jim Willard's first love. Bob, however, flees high school upon graduation by joining the Merchant Marine. Later, he returns to his Virginia hometown to marry a high school girlfriend, Sally Mergendahl, with whom he fathers a child. Unlike Jim Willard, Bob is a heterosexual who merely engaged in one homosexual experience, and his eventual reunion with Jim Willard is a hostile confrontation.

Collins, a short, squarely built seaman, twenty years old, with dark curly hair, whom Jim Willard encounters when he ships out to try and find Bob Ford. Collins is egotistical, particularly about his success with women sexually, and he takes Jim Willard to a brothel in Seattle where Jim is repulsed by the situation.

Otto Schilling, a half-Austrian, half-Polish tennis instructor at a Beverly Hills hotel where Jim Willard gets an assistant's job teaching tennis. It is through this job connection that Jim Willard meets Hollywood actors who are homosexual, in spite of the censorious advice of Schilling not to become involved in such liaisons.

Ronald Shaw, a "disturbingly handsome" Hollywood actor of Jewish origins (his real name was George Cohen), with whom Jim Willard begins having a homosexual affair shortly after their meeting at a party at Shaw's estate. Shaw is thirty-five years old, with dark curly hair, a classic profile, and light-blue eyes. He is a highly successful film star often featured in period costume epics and whose homosexuality is rumored but not publicly known.

Paul Sullivan, a novelist who is disillusioned with screenwriting. At twenty-eight, he has written critically approved but financially unremunerative novels. Sullivan, reared as a Catholic, has left the church after discovering his homosexuality and after an attempt at marriage. The sandy-haired Sullivan also is something of a masochist about his life, one of those who prefers to be unhappy much of the time and who masks that unhappiness by a cynical, bitter attitude toward the world in general. Sullivan and Jim Willard begin an affair that separates Willard from film actor Ronald Shaw and takes the pair on travels first to New Orleans and later to Mexico and Guatemala, where the pair meet Maria Verlaine.

Maria Verlaine, a dark, exotic, smartly dressed woman given to affairs with artists and frequently attracted to homosexual men as companions (or as would-be lovers). She is worldly-wise, divorced from a French gigolo, and, in middle age, has become increasingly interested in younger men, especially blonds. Although she attempts a physical relationship with Jim Willard, he is unable to respond to her, and their intense encounter is essentially an unconsummated love affair while Jim, Paul Sullivan, and she are at her plantation in the Yucatán.

Sergeant Kervinski, a homosexual noncommissioned officer in Special Services in the Army Air Corps whom Jim Willard encounters when he enlists during World War II. Kervinski is attracted to him, but Willard is unresponsive to the sergeant. Kervinski is slim, dark, fast-talking, and given to making leading suggestive remarks about the sexiness of women to test soldiers' potential as homosexual conquests. Ultimately, Kervinski becomes involved with a young Army corporal whom Jim Willard had tried to seduce in the barracks.

Ken Woodrow, an Army corporal from the Midwest (Cleveland, Ohio), aged twentyone and the gradute of a secretarial college. Ken is a dark-haired young man with gray eyes and a small, slim body. Although initially friendly to barracks buddy Jim Willard, Ken resists Jim's attempt to seduce him one evening but later responds to similar overtures from Sergeant Kervinski.

Jere Real

THE CITY BUILDER

Author: George Konrád (1933-   )
Type of work: Novel
Time of action: The 1970's
First published: A városalapító, 1977 (English translation, 1977)

The narrator, an aged city planner and former professor in a central Hungarian town. He has been awarded many degrees and diplomas and honored for his role in the technical progress of his city in the early days of socialism. Keenly aware of his own physical and moral degeneration, he at times seems obsessed with death and guilt as he lives alone with his memories in an apartment stuffed with an accumulation of useless objects. In the city all around him he sees reminders in concrete of the errors of his life, errors that can be erased only by dynamite. As a city planner, he mapped out for society a future that has become an almost unbearable present in a state ruled by power-hungry bureaucrats, chosen for their cynicism and idle chatter and protected by the organizational system. Born into a wealthy bourgeois family, he became a member of another privileged class, the intelligentsia, after private property was abolished. Although, as an idealistic builder of the city following the devastation of war, he attempted to abolish social stratification, in reality he created merely a modified system of inequalities to replace the former political structure. Once he repeated mindless slogans and believed the hierarchical military to be the most efficient of all organizations. He perfunctorily eulogizes his superior, a former Gestapo spy with thirty-two years in the movement, who has committed suicide. Reflecting on the dead director, the city builder admits his own lust for power. Later, he inspects an earthquake-torn city, where, he believes, his own son lies buried in the rubble. Finally, he joins a noisy crowd in the town square on New Year's. All greet one another in a friendly manner, and all expect to live until the year's end. Yet the narrator has lingering doubts about the survival of either himself or his society.

The narrator's wife, an attractive, socially active woman who at the age of forty was killed when her car crashed into a tree. The city builder is haunted by memories of her life and death. He sees her lying on a pathologist's marble slab after the fatal accident. He relives her cremation. He recalls divorce proceedings in which both he and she stated that they could not live without each other. He remembers her indefatigable sensuality, her fragrance, her shrieks, her endless activity. She often arrived home late in the evening, laden down with intriguing parcels and exuding fascinating stories. Yet she could be vindictive and stealthy. Nevertheless, the city builder is plagued with guilt for his infidelity while she was alive.

The narrator's son, an apprentice city builder, student of philosophy, and radical intellectual who often violently disagreed with his father's political position. The city builder recalls that from the day his son en-tered his life, he was a touchy tyrant who usurped the attention of the city builder's wife and, indeed, the whole household. An amateur man of the theater, the son was arrested at the age of twenty-two for insulting a state inspector who suspected him of subversion. While serving six months in prison, he fought the guards who abused him, and he sustained permanent injuries to the face and eyes. He was gifted in argumentation but emotionally unstable, alternating between states of frenzy and stupor. His father ultimately believes him to be an earthquake casualty but is unable to find his body.

The narrator's father, a private builder and architect and City Hall alderman who enjoyed wealth and power as the head of the third generation to occupy the fashionable family estate. His greatest professional accomplishment was the designing of the city's neo-Romanesque power plant, a kind of castle for machines rather than people. An authoritarian father given to violence, he paid lip service to religion but reveled in slander and sexual debauchery. His sudden death profoundly affects the city builder, who longs to know what lies on the other side of life.

Janie Caves McCauley

THE CIVIL WARS
A tree is best measured when it is down

Author: Robert Wilson (1941-   )
Type of work: Play
Time of action: Unspecified
First produced: The Dutch Section, 1983; the Cologne Section, 1984; the Rome Section, 1984; the French Section, 1984; the Knee Plays, 1984

Historical and fictional personages, characters that resemble animated wax figures on display. They are derived from a series of "free associational" thoughts, sparked by reflections on the American Civil War, that proved the genesis of the work. Thus, Abraham Lincoln, Mrs. Lincoln, Robert E. Lee, Mrs. Lee, John Wilkes Booth, Mathew Brady, and American Civil War soldiers are among the figures who populate the work's arresting scenarios. Because Wilson also considered his central concept of "civil war" to be applicable to a wide variety of confrontations, including family conflicts, the family of Frederick the Great and an American *fin de siècle* family appear as well. The international scope of Wilson's project (originally scheduled to premiere at the 1984

Summer Olympic Games) is reflected in his use of figures (for example, a Japanese sun goddess, William the Silent, and Giuseppe Garibaldi) who may be identified with the countries that participated in the venture.

The appearance of Hercules in the final act is perhaps in recognition of the ancient origin of the games.

David Marc Fischer

CLEAR LIGHT OF DAY

Author: Anita Desai (1937-   )
Type of work: Novel
Time of action: Summer, 1947, and fifteen years before and after
First published: 1980

Bim Das, a history teacher. The unmarried, eldest Das daughter, Bim, now over forty, still lives in the decaying family home situated on the outskirts of Old Delhi. Slightly heavy and turning gray, Bim is not particularly attractive and makes little effort to be so. Yet her energy and capability, along with her keen understanding, compensate for whatever she lacks physically. Shown through flashbacks in her younger years, Bim has always been at peace with herself and managed to convey that quality to others. She represents the old India: spiritual, peaceful, unselfish, unhurried, sure of life. In some ways, though, she has not come to grips with the present in order to meld it with the past, and therein lies her flaw.

Tara, Bim's sister and an Indian diplomat's wife. Altogether the opposite of her older sister, Tara is attractive, sophisticated, and worldly, having accompanied her husband to various overseas posts. To an extent, her poise is merely an exterior quality, in spite of her seemingly successful marriage, her two teenage daughters, and her role as hostess and wife in diplomatic circles. Representing the new India that was created after independence in 1947, Tara finds herself torn between the past and the present, especially when she visits Bim at the family home and dredges up memories of another time, when life seemed surer and more settled.

Baba Das, Bim and Tara's retarded brother. Although in his thirties, Baba is like a child, innocent and unaffected by events around

him. He is fat and lethargic, dependent on Bim, who caters to his every wish. For most of the day, he plays English-language records from the late 1940's. Like his sisters, he is caught in the web of the past, even in his mindless state.

Bakul, Tara's husband and a diplomat in the Indian foreign service. Handsome, successful, and aggressive, Bakul considers the family's obsession with the past foolish and tedious. He has left the old India behind and entered the larger world, even though he gives lip service to the idea of Mother India as home.

Raja Das, the eldest son of the Das family. During the flashbacks to the gaining of independence in 1947 and the Partition riots, Raja appears as a kind of romantic hero. He reads and writes poetry, dreams of heroics, and possesses the total devotion of his sister Bim, who nurses him to health during a long illness. Coming from a traditional Hindu family, he breaks tradition by marrying a Muslim woman, then leaves Delhi for Hyderabad, where he becomes a rich businessman. Although he does not appear in the latter section of the novel, he is described by Bim as having turned into an excessively fat, arrogant, and pretentious sort of man.

Mira-masi, aunt of the Das children. A traditional Indian woman, she served as their nurse during childhood.

Robert L. Ross

A CLOCKWORK ORANGE

Author: Anthony Burgess (John Anthony Burgess Wilson, 1917-   )
Type of work: Novel
Time of action: An undetermined future
First published: 1962

Alex, the narrator, who speaks in "nadsat" (a teenagers' slang incorporating elements of Elizabethan English and modern Russian). At fifteen, he is the leader of a gang made up of himself and three "droogs" ("droog" is Russian for "friend"), each a year or two older than he. Three years later, he will lead three droogs, each younger than he. His pleasures consist of violence—theft, mugging, vandalism, and rape—and classical music, especially Mozart and Beethoven. His droogs—Georgie, Pete, and Dim—become disaffected under his leadership and betray him by leaving him to be captured by the police. He spends two years in prison, where he undergoes psychological conditioning (the "Ludovico Technique") that leaves him physically incapable of violence and enjoyment of music. Unable to make a moral choice, that is, to choose either good or evil, and capable only of acting in accordance with what society considers good, he is released from prison. He is victimized and abused by society until, restored to his true self at the age of eighteen, he undergoes a transition to responsible maturity.

F. Alexander, the middle-aged author of a sociological work entitled *A Clockwork Orange*, referring to the modern world's tendency to translate humans into vegetable-like automata. His wife dies after being beaten and raped by Alex and his gang. He takes in and cares for ex-prisoner Alex, who has been severely beaten by police thugs, unaware at first that Alex is the person who had brutalized his wife. When he learns the truth, he seeks to kill Alex.

Prison Chaplain, called "charlie" or "charles" in nadsat. He tries to dissuade Alex from accepting the Ludovico treatment as the price of early release from prison. He and F. Alexander, in their turn, uphold the necessity of moral choice.

Dim, a member of Alex's first gang. He is slow-witted, huge, and strong. He wields a chain and flails Alex across the eyes with it when the gang deserts their leader at the scene of the crime for which Alex is imprisoned. The crime is the fatal beating by Alex of a middle-aged woman, who cares for a menagerie of cats, in the course of robbing her house. Dim later becomes a policeman and is one of the police thugs who trounce Alex.

Dr. Brodsky, a fat, curly-haired practitioner of behaviorist psychology. He subjects Alex to the "Ludovico Technique," which ensures that Alex will become intolerably nauseated and ill at thoughts or acts of violence or at the sound of classical music.

Georgie, a member of Alex's first gang, who seeks to supplant Alex as its leader. His death occurs while Alex is in prison.

Pete, a member of Alex's first gang. He is the least averse to Alex, although he participates in the gang's betrayal of their leader. He later marries and leads the life of a good citizen.

Alex's father, a caring but weak-willed parent who is dominated by his son. As a workingman, he conforms to the soulless society of which he is a part.

Alex's mother, a weepy, weary, well-meaning woman, who is quite as ineffectual as her husband.

Billyboy, leader of a gang in rivalry with Alex's gang. Beaten by Alex in a brawl, he reappears in two years as a policeman and, along with Dim, brutally beats his former enemy.

P. R. Deltoid, Alex's Post-Corrective Adviser. He tries unsuccessfully to deal with Alex's truancy and, after Alex is arrested, spits in his face.

Jack, an elderly professorial man, who is beaten up by Alex and his gang but, two years later, leads a group of elderly library patrons in administering a beating to the behavioristically conditioned and consequently unresisting Alex.

Dr. Branom, the zealous and sycophantic assistant of Dr. Brodsky.

Joe, a workingman in his thirties. As a lodger, he preempts the room and usurps the filial position of the imprisoned and then released Alex. Eventually, he surrenders his lodgings after a run-in with the police for loitering.

Bully, a member of Alex's second gang. Like Georgie, he aspires to the leadership held by Alex. Like Dim, he is big and strong.

Rick, a member of Alex's second gang. He has a face "like a frog's."

Len, a member of Alex's second gang.

Z. Dolin, a political activist seeking to make a case against the incumbent party by exposing the inhumanity of Alex's conditioning. He is aided in his efforts by F. Alexander.

Something Something Rubinstein, a colleague of Z. Dolin.

D.B. da Silva, a colleague of Z. Dolin.

Rex, a policeman and the driver of the car in which Dim and Billyboy take Alex out into the country to be beaten.

Georgina, Pete's wife, well groomed and attractive. She is amused by Alex's garbled (nadsat) language.

Roy Arthur Swanson

CLOSELY WATCHED TRAINS

Author: Bohumil Hrabal (1914-   )
Type of work: Novel
Time of action: Winter, 1945, during World War II
First published: Ostře sledované vlaky, 1965 (English translation, 1968)

Miloš Hrma (mē′lōsh hûr′mä), the narrator, an apprentice train dispatcher. Inexperienced and innocent at twenty-two, Miloš views the bizarre and brutal events around him with morally noncommittal curiosity. Following his first sexual encounter, which is a failure, he attempts suicide. Although rescued, he remains preoccupied by doubts regarding his manhood until drawn into a plot to blow up a Nazi ammunition train. In acting deliberately, he finds the answer to his persistent question, "Am I a man?"

Ladislav Hubička (hōō′bĭch′kə), the senior dispatcher. Hubička, whose name means "nice lips," draws Miloš' envy and admiration by his success with women. He is under investigation for imprinting all the station's

rubber stamps on the bare buttocks of the female telegraphist late one night. A fearless nonconformist, he is a key figure in the plot to blow up the munitions train.

Lánský, the stationmaster. Lánský takes great pride in his Venetian armchair, Persian carpet, and marble clock. Hot-tempered and exacting as a boss and as a husband, he dissipates his rages by bellowing into a heating vent. Although careful to conform outwardly to Nazi rule, he symbolically protests the brutal takeover of neighboring Poland by killing all his Nuremberg pigeons (a German breed) and replacing them with Polish silverpoints.

Virginia Svatá, the station telegraphist. An

attractive, fun-loving young woman, Virginia willingly participates in Hubička's lascivious escapade and refuses to incriminate him during the investigation.

Masha, a conductor, Miloš' girlfriend. Young and exuberant, Masha easily forms a mutual attachment to Miloš while they are painting a fence together. Blaming her own inexperience for their sexual fiasco, she sticks by Milŏs after his suicide attempt, making a date with him shortly before the sabotage is to be carried out.

Viktoria Freie, a member of the Czech resistance. The name of this well-endowed beauty means "victorious freedom" and is probably a code name. Viktoria not only delivers the bomb that is to be used in the sabotage, but she also provides Miloš with an unforgettable sexual initiation that dispels his self-doubt and inspires him to act courageously.

Councillor Zednicek, head of a commission to determine whether a criminal charge should be lodged against Hubička for his indiscretion. Zednicek has a son in the German army and is himself an opportunistic collaborator with the Nazis.

Slušny (slōōsh'nē), the traffic chief who arrives at the station with Councillor Zednicek. He enjoys exercising his authority and intimidating the subordinate employees of the railroad.

Mrs. Lánská, the stationmaster's wife. Although her tender care of her geese and other animals seems contradicted by the ease with which she slaughters them, she is still respected by Miloš, who seeks her tutelage in lovemaking.

Countess Kinská, an equestrienne whose family castle stands as a reminder of Czech aristocracy. She stops at the station on her rides and converses with Lánský while Hubička weaves erotic fantasies about her.

Miloš' father, a train engineer who retired early. He collects and salvages all kinds of scrap.

Miloš' grandfather, a circus hypnotist, killed in an attempt to turn back German tanks by means of hypnosis.

Miloš' great-grandfather, a veteran who was wounded at age eighteen during a student uprising. He flaunted his disability pension by drinking rum in front of people hard at work and finally died from one of the many beatings he provoked.

Miloš' mother, a nurturing maternal figure who polishes the buttons on Miloš' uniform and watches for him from behind a window curtain.

Great-Aunt Beatrice, a nurse who takes care of dying burn victims and is well acquainted with death.

Marian Price

CLOUD NINE

Author: Caryl Churchill (1938-   )
Type of work: Play
Time of action: The late nineteenth century and 1979
First produced: 1979

Clive, a British administrator stationed in Africa. A stereotypical Victorian, Clive constantly cites his duty to God, the British Empire, the queen, and his family as motivation

for his behavior. Like the other characters, Clive is a caricature who is both humorous and a painful reminder of social problems. As a Victorian colonialist, he is narrow-minded, hypocritical, and blind to the injustice done to the native Africans upon whom his comforts depend. He continues to dominate his family and the natives only with difficulty, however, and act 1 ends with Clive's son watching silently as the faithful native servant raises a rifle to shoot Clive. Apparently Clive is not killed, however, since he reappears very briefly at the end of act 2 to lament the fall of the British Empire. Clive's Victorian system of colonial repression parallels the system of sexual repression in the 1970's of act 2.

Betty, Clive's wife. In act 1, Betty "is played by a man because she wants to be what men want her to be." She identifies her duty as waiting patiently for Clive and the other men to order and control the world. In act 2, Betty, who has left Clive, is played by a woman, because she is coming to know herself better. At the play's close, Betty from act 1 reappears and the two Bettys embrace, indicating how far Betty has come in achieving wholeness and promising a world of reconciliation.

Joshua, Clive's black servant, "played by a white man because he wants to be what whites want him to be." Joshua separates himself from other natives and serves as Clive's spy. An unspoken pact with Clive permits Joshua the minor rebellion of impertinence to Betty, so long as he remains absolutely subservient to Clive. His raising of the rifle against Clive at the end of act 1 suggests a native effort to break free of British imperialism.

Edward, Clive's nine-year-old son, played in act 1 by a woman in order to highlight Clive's effort "to impose traditional male behavior on him." Edward is a lying, sneaking, sniveling child who blames others for his failures and escapes punishment for misbehavior by mouthing all the manly platitudes in which Clive believes. Edward is the product of Victorian colonialism, but his incipient homosexuality indicates that he, too, is about to break out of control. In act 2, Edward, now thirty-four, works as a gardener

in England. His bisexuality indicates his general uneasiness in the world, but he has grown into a mature appreciation of home, children, and settled relationships.

Victoria, Clive's two-year-old daughter, played in act 1 by a dummy, which is what her good Victorian parents expect her to be. In act 2, Victoria, now twenty-seven, is played by a woman because she is beginning to realize her own identity. She confronts all the women's issues of the 1970's, seeking to balance career, marriage, parenting, and new sexual relationships. She even begins to deal with her mother, moving from calling her "Mummy" to calling her "Betty."

Maud, Clive's mother-in-law, who lives with him and provides a constant reminder of the good old days when Victorian ideals were more firmly in control.

Ellen, Edward's governess, who has difficulty making him behave as Clive wishes. She is in love with Betty, but at the end of act 1 she marries Harry Bagley.

Harry Bagley, an explorer and a friend of Clive's. Betty is attracted to him, and they carry on a flirtation, but Harry is really a homosexual. His socially acceptable marriage to Ellen denies both individuals' sexual preferences and represents repressive Victorian control over sexual behavior. Harry reappears briefly and silently in act 2 when Gerry picks him up for a homosexual encounter.

Mrs. Saunders, a widow who is having an affair with Clive, played by the same actress who plays Ellen, to indicate the parallels between their characters. Clive finds her as dark and mysterious as the continent, and her freedom of thought and behavior hints at the eventual emancipation of Victorian women.

Martin, Victoria's husband in act 2. He works to be helpful and supportive of his emancipated wife but has as much difficulty creating new patterns of behavior as do the women and occasionally continues to dominate Victoria.

Lin, Victoria's lesbian friend in act 2, whose professed hatred for men highlights Victoria's more moderate position.

Cathy, Lin's daughter, whose desire to carry a rifle and wear pink dresses indicates the uneasiness of sexual roles in the 1970's. Cathy is played by a man "partly as a reversal of Edward being played by a woman"

and partly to indicate the "emotional force of young children."

Gerry, Edward's homosexual lover, who is as inconsiderate, manipulative, and insensitive to Edward as Clive was to Betty in act 1.

Soldier, the ghost of Lin's brother, who has been killed while serving with the British army in Northern Ireland, where the colonialism of act 1 is playing out its bitter end.

Helen Lojek

THE CLOVEN VISCOUNT

Author: Italo Calvino (1923-1985)
Type of work: Novel
Time of action: The late eighteenth century
First published: Il visconte dimezzato, 1952 (English translation, 1962)

Viscount Medardo of Terralba, a young Italian nobleman from a small principality on the coast of Italy. Fighting against the Turks, he is split in two by a cannonball; one surviving half is saved by doctors, and he returns home. Once there, he displays a perverted and evil nature, shown especially in his penchant for splitting things — fruits, frogs, mushrooms — in two parts. His courtship of the peasant girl Pamela further reveals his sadistic inclinations. The other part of Medardo, which has also survived and was healed by hermits, returns to Terralba; this portion of the viscount is all virtue and makes his presence known by a series of good deeds, many of which inevitably require redressing the harm done by his evil half. Just as the people of Terralba are oppressed and terrified by the bad portion of the viscount, however, they soon find themselves harassed and limited by the good portion. These opposing parts become known to the people of Terralba as "The Bad 'Un" and "The Good 'Un." Inevitably, the two sides come into a conflict which can be resolved only by their reunion.

The narrator, Medardo's nephew, a young boy seven or eight years old. A shrewd and

observant child, with much common sense, he serves as a generally accurate and unbiased witness of events. Left mostly to himself by his family, he is free to roam the hills and coasts of Terralba and so follow the other characters throughout the novel.

Dr. Trelawney, a shipwrecked English physician living in Terralba. In his sixties, Dr. Trelawney is a short man with a face lined like an old chestnut, and long, thin legs. He wears an old coat with fading trimmings, a tricorn hat, and a wig. He has traveled over the world, including voyages with the famous Captain Cook, but knows nothing of the globe, since he remained in his cabin playing cards the whole time. He is immensely fond of *cancarone*, the harsh and heavy local wine, and he practices very little medicine, seeming to be afraid of the body and disease; there is some doubt as to whether he is actually a medical doctor at all. Instead of healing, he conducts implausible scientific research, such as his attempts to capture will-o'-the-wisps and preserve their essence in bottles.

Ezekiel, a large, bearded, dour man, leader of the exiled Huguenots who live on a hilltop in Terralba. Although banished because of their religion, the Huguenots have lost all outward traces of its form or content and live a bleak existence best expressed in Ezekiel's frequent oath: "Famine and plague."

Esau, the youngest son of Ezekiel. He smokes, drinks, steals, and cheats at dice and cards. He is ignorant of religion and indifferent to the threats of his father.

Galateo, one of the lepers who lives in the village of Pratofungo on the coast of Terralba. Exiled because of their physical condition, the lepers have given themselves up to a life of revelry, merriment, and debauchery, hiding their deformities under garlands of flowers.

Pamela, a young peasant girl, plump and barefoot. She tends goats and ducks and lives in a small cottage with her animals and family. Although naïve and unschooled, she is clever enough to recognize the dangers in the courtship of "The Bad 'Un" and hides in a cave in the mountains until discovered by "The Good 'Un." Sensibly, she refrains from marriage to either half of the viscount, instinctively preferring a complete husband.

Sebastiana, the old nurse of the Medardo family. She has seen generations of them come and go, and perhaps because of this knowledge she is exiled by "The Bad 'Un" to live with the lepers in Pratofungo.

Michael Witkoski

THE CLOWN

Author: Heinrich Böll (1917-1985)
Type of work: Novel
Time of action: c. 1962
First published: Ansichten eines Clowns, 1963 (English translation, 1965)

Hans Schnier (shnēr), a professional clown. All events in this first-person novel are seen through the eyes of Hans, the twenty-seven-year-old son of a wealthy industrialist. He is not, however, the typical son of a rich businessman. As a youth, he showed little aptitude for school, and he has never had any interest in business. Instead, Hans has the character traits and temperament of an artist: He is spontaneous, impulsive, creative, naïve, innocent, and he cannot feign feelings that he does not possess. Nor can he, as someone once urged him, "be a man." To "be a man," he would have to become like everyone else, which he cannot and will not do. Similarly, he cannot act on his father's criticism that he lacks the very quality that makes a man a man: the ability to accept a situation. Hans, unlike most of his friends and acquaintances, does not want to accept the past and gloss it over, nor does he want to be merely swept along by the new tide of democracy. These qualities make him a misfit and an outsider. The loss of Marie de-

stroys his primary link to the real world. Without her, he turns more and more to drink and ends up alone, playing his guitar and singing for a few coins from passersby at the train station.

Marie Derkum (dĕr'kūm), the young woman whom Hans considers to be his wife, although they are not legally married. Sweet, trusting, religious, Marie is in many ways the antithesis of Hans: She is from a very poor background, was good in school, and is a devout Catholic. In time, her desire to return to the good graces of the church and to have a conventional, church-sanctioned marriage overcomes her love of Hans and she leaves him to marry Prelate Züpfner.

Alfons Schnier, the director of a coal-mining company and father of Hans. When Hans was growing up, his mother was the dominant personality in the family, but he also has vivid memories of his father, such as how he courageously defended Hans when, as a boy of about ten, he called Herbert Kalick a "Nazi swine." Schnier is now a handsome, distinguished-looking man in his sixties, who has recently discovered that he has a talent as an entertaining television talk-show guest. He offers his son financial assistance, but only on the condition that Hans take formal training from the best teacher. Hans does not accept his father's offer.

Mrs. Schnier, Hans's mother, a housewife and socialite. Hans considers her to be stupid, stingy, and hypocritical. During the war, she was a staunch racist and a fanatical German nationalist. She even sent her only daughter, sixteen-year-old Henrietta, to fight (and die) on the home front. Now Mrs. Schnier is president of the Executive Committee of the Societies for the Reconciliation of Racial Differences. Hans has never forgiven his mother for the death of his beloved sister, and he has not seen her since he left home to live with Marie and become a professional clown, over five years earlier.

Heribert Züpfner (tsüpf'nər), a Catholic prelate, about the same age as Hans. Züpfner, who as a youth was kind to Hans and occasionally went out with Marie, is one of several prominent young Catholics among Hans and Marie's friends, including Sommerwild and Kinkel. By convincing Marie to leave Hans for him, he shatters Hans's world.

Herbert Kalick (kä'lĭck), a recent recipient of the Federal Cross of Merit for his work in spreading democratic ideas among young people. When he was a youth of fourteen, Kalick, while serving as the leader of Hans's Hitler Youth group, was responsible for the death of one small boy and for the persecution of another lad who could not prove his Aryan background. Now a shining light in the new democratic movement, Kalick has recently invited Hans to his house to ask forgiveness for his past mistakes. Hans, however, cannot forgive and strikes him before leaving without accepting the offer of reconciliation.

Leo Schnier, Hans's younger brother, who became a Catholic and is now a seminary student. He is generous, undemanding, and generally supportive of his brother.

Martin Derkum, a not very successful shopkeeper and Marie's father. He is an intellectual and thought by many to be a Communist. Kind, generous, and not the chameleon, changing with each new situation, typical of the times, he is one of the few men Hans respects.

H. J. Weatherford

COCK-A-DOODLE DANDY

Author: Sean O'Casey (John Casey, 1880-1964)
Type of work: Play
Time of plot: Shortly after World War II
First produced: 1949

Michael Marthraun (măr'thrôn), a grasping and stingy man in late middle age who has the good fortune to own some peat bogs that will increase his modest fortune. Eager to squeeze every ounce of profit from his peat, Marthraun bitterly resists Sailor Mahan's efforts to raise the price of hauling the peat to town, an act that would allow Mahan to pay his drivers a more respectable wage. Marthraun has recently remarried, but he re-sents his young wife, Lorna, especially when she dares to disagree with him and support the drivers' pleas for higher wages. He is even more suspicious of the modern ways of his lovely daughter, Loreleen, whose short dresses, nylons, and cosmetics make her a disturbing presence in the whole parish. Marthraun is particularly bedeviled by the mysterious enchantments of the mythic rooster, or cock, a symbol of sexuality.

Sailor Mahan (māy'ăn), at one time a sailor but now the owner of a fleet of lorries, or trucks. He is a middle-aged man whose experience in various seaports has made him less puritanical than Marthraun. Though more tolerant of Loreleen than Marthraun or the priest, he is also a hypocrite and a lecher. When Loreleen desperately needs a loan to leave the parish, he arranges a meeting with her but uses the occasion to attempt to seduce her (before she is given a reprieve by the intervention of an angry mob). Mahan is another person bedeviled by the appearances of the mysterious demonic rooster.

The Mysterious Cock, a magical black rooster that appears and disappears somewhat capriciously. Representing the power of sexuality, he bothers and torments the puritanical men of the parish of Nyadnanave, causing them to hear strange sounds and see frightening sights, such as whiskey boiling and dishes being thrown about. His most important moment comes when he causes a tremendous wind in scene 3.

Lorna Marthraun, the pretty young wife of Marthraun. She is a woman of spirit who supports her stepdaughter, Loreleen, and finally rebels against Marthraun's mean-spirited stinginess. Lorna apparently married Marthraun only because her paralytic sister, Julia, needed money for a trip to Lourdes, in desperate hope of a miraculous cure there. At the end of the play, Lorna decides to leave the parish when she sees that Loreleen has been driven away.

Loreleen Marthraun, Michael's daughter by his first marriage. Loreleen is a lovely young woman of about twenty who has adopted more modern manners and clothes as the result of living in London. Her makeup, short skirts, and nylons make her a bewitching presence in the dour parish of Nyadnanave; however, many of the people, including her father and the priest, consider her to be so disturbing that they begin to believe that she is a witch. After a mob led by Father Domineer tries to stone her for alleged sexual immorality, and after Sailor Mahan tries to seduce her, she packs her belongings and leaves on foot, without shoes.

Marion, the maid in the Marthraun household, a saucy and pretty young woman of twenty-five or so. She is a familiar character type who comments satirically on the action, and her charms contribute to the sexual confusion of the puritanical males. She is loved by the Messenger and loves him in return; however, this romance is not sufficient to keep her in the parish, for she follows Loreleen and Lorna into exile at the end of the play.

The Messenger, Robin Adair, bringer of news and telegrams who serenades Marion on his accordion. A jaunty young man, he is sometimes more like an incarnation of the Greek god Hermes than a real person; however, he can merely observe the foolish behavior of the men of the parish, not change it. Robin comforts Loreleen when she is persecuted by the villagers and shows the ability to control the demonic cock with ease. At the end of the play, he pronounces judgment on Michael Marthraun and prepares to follow Marion to a more tolerant environment, while leaving the parish to its folly.

Father Domineer, the parish priest of Nyadnanave. The priest is a harsh and brutal man who views Loreleen and her modern manners and clothes as the veritable incarnation of Satan. A middle-aged bigot and reactionary, he strikes one of Mahan's truck drivers and kills him, merely because the man is living out of wedlock with a local woman. After leading an angry mob that abuses Loreleen, he confronts her and demands that she repent and abandon her liberated ways. Father Domineer sees the demonic cock as his mortal enemy and tries to exorcise the unruly rooster from the parish.

Shanaar (shä·năr'), an elderly itinerant sage who travels about the parish spreading suspicion and dark peasant superstitions. Full of pagan fears of mysterious forces, Shanaar advises Marthraun to ignore whatever he cannot understand or finds frightening.

One-Eyed Larry, an ignorant peasant youth who follows Father Domineer around and tries to assist him at the exorcism.

The Sergeant, a beefy middle-aged man who represents the civil authority of the parish. He pursues the demonic rooster across the country but is embarrassed by losing his trousers in the mighty wind conjured up by the cock's supernatural power.

Julia, Lorna's younger sister, a paralytic girl without much time to live. In desperation, she sets out on a trip to Lourdes, hoping for a miraculous cure by the Virgin. Despite Father Domineer's blessing, she returns home in despair with her condition unchanged. As she faces a bleak future, the Messenger counsels her to have courage.

Edgar L. Chapman

A COFFIN FOR DIMITRIOS

Author: Eric Ambler (1909-   )
Type of work: Novel
Time of action: 1938
First published: 1939, in Great Britain as *The Mask of Dimitrios* (U.S. edition, 1939)

Charles Latimer, an English writer of detective stories in his early forties. Formerly, Latimer was a professor of political economy at a minor English university until the success of his stories freed him from academe. On a visit to Istanbul in 1938, Latimer meets Colonel Haki, an admirer of detective novels, who in passing gives Latimer the opportunity of viewing a body that the Turkish police have identified as that of Dimitrios Makropoulos, known to them since 1922. Latimer, on a whim and as an exercise in detection, decides to trace Dimitrios' career. In Paris he surprisingly discovers the real Dimitrios and only narrowly avoids being murdered by him.

Dimitrios Makropoulos, also known as **Talas, Taladis, Rougemont,** and **Monsieur C. K.,** a murderer, thief, spy, pimp, drug dealer, and businessman. Dimitrios, of Greek extraction, was born in 1889. Coming to the attention of the Turkish police in 1922, in subsequent years he engaged in various illegal activities in several European countries. By 1938, he is a director of the Eurasian Credit Trust. It is not Dimitrios' body that is discovered floating in the Bosporus but that of Manus Visser, who had been blackmailing the Greek. Dimitrios killed Visser and disguised the corpse, making it appear to be the body of the long-sought

Dimitrios. Blackmailed again, Dimitrios and his new blackmailer kill each other in a Parisian shootout.

Mr. Peters (Frederik Petersen), drug dealer and former convict. A fat and unhealthy-looking Dane of fifty-five, Peters first knew Dimitrios in the late 1920's in Paris, where Peters owned a nightclub. Dimitrios convinced Peters, along with several others, to work for him in what became a widespread and profitable drug operation. Eventually, Dimitrios absconded with the profits, but he first turned Peters and the rest over to the police. Later learning of Dimitrios' new identity, Peters decides to blackmail Dimitrios. He joins forces with Latimer because the latter had seen the "fake" Dimitrios. The two confront Dimitrios, who pays the blackmail, but the next day Dimitrios traces his blackmailers to the house in Paris owned by Peters and formerly used by Dimitrios. There, Dimitrios and Peters kill each other.

Colonel Haki, head of the Turkish secret police. Meeting Latimer at a party in Istanbul, Haki, a fan of detective fiction, offers Latimer the plot for a future story; however, when Haki is summoned to the morgue to examine a recently retrieved body identified as that of Dimitrios Makropoulos, Latimer accompanies him. Haki, ruthless and assured, has no doubt that the body was that of Dimitrios.

Dhris Mohammed, a black Moslem figpicker in Smyrna. In 1922, Dimitrios and Dhris robbed and killed a moneylender. Dhris was later arrested, but before he was hanged he blamed the murder on Dimitrios, who had already escaped. It was on this occasion that Dimitrios first came to the attention of the police.

N. Marukakis, a middle-aged Greek journalist in Sofia, Bulgaria. Still following the career of the supposedly dead Dimitrios, Latimer turns to Marukakis for information regarding an attempted political assassination that occurred in 1923 and that involved Dimitrios. Latimer learns that the incident had been financed by the Eurasian Credit Trust, a shadowy bank registered in Monaco. Marukakis also introduced Latimer to Irana Preveza.

Irana Preveza, the madam of a Sofia nightclub and brothel. A former prostitute, Preveza knew Dimitrios in 1923. She had lent him funds which he never repaid, and fifteen years later Preveza is still bitter and angry. She was the first person interviewed by Latimer who had actually known Dimitrios.

Wladyslaw Grodek, a master spy. Living in Switzerland and now retired at the age of about sixty, Grodek tells Latimer about the time when he employed Dimitrios in Belgrade in 1926. Dimitrios, using a combination of blackmail and force, was successful in obtaining secret naval plans for Grodek but then turned on Grodek, who was working for the Italians, and sold the plans to the French government instead.

Bulić, a low-level Yugoslav bureaucrat in the Ministry of Marine. A dissatisfied man in his forties with a younger wife, Bulić allows himself to become compromised by Grodek and Dimitrios in a crooked gambling affair and provides the naval plans. He is later arrested and sentenced to prison.

Manus Visser, a drug dealer. A Dutchman, Visser was part of Dimitrios' drug operation in Paris and served time in prison in 1931 after Dimitrios had informed the police of the names of his former associates. Years later, Visser discovered Dimitrios' new identity, Monsieur C. K., and successfully blackmailed him. Visser, however, was eventually murdered by Dimitrios, who disguised Visser's body as his own. It was thus Visser's body that Colonel Haki identifies as that of Dimitrios.

Eugene S. Larson

A COIN IN NINE HANDS

Author: Marguerite Yourcenar (Marguerite de Crayencour, 1903-1987)
Type of work: Novel
Time of action: 1933
First published: Denier du rêve, 1934; revised, 1959 (English translation, 1982)

Marcella Ardeati Sarte (sâr′tā), Dr. Alessandro Sarte's wife. She declares herself as realizing her vocation in her revolt against authority, law, and justice, as established by rulers such as Julius Caesar and Benito Mussolini. Marcella's true vocation is to feel allied to all of those who are humiliated, oppressed, and committed to rebellion. She is demonically bound to her vocation: to assassinate Mussolini. Her harshness is in re-

sponse to that dictator's authoritarian willfulness. Destruction fascinates Marcella, and Dr. Alessandro Sarte repeatedly sees her as a medusa or a vampire. Marcella's death, after the failed assassination attempt, illustrates that in this ongoing drama of life, the fateful role to play is that of a corpse.

Dr. Alessandro Sarte, a medical celebrity and the husband of Marcella. He has failed in both of his functions, however, as he cannot heal Lina Chiari's breast cancer and he cannot understand his wife. The doctor hides behind the mask of social success and uses his patients for the opportunity to exploit their bank accounts or to assimilate medical gestures to those of a lover. He seems to be cold, hard, bitter, and distressed. He likes hunting for deer with royalty and driving beautiful sports cars to attract women. For him, all women are interchangeable. Dr. Sarte, who sees the film *Sir Julius* while sitting next to Angiola, makes love to her but despises Angiola and all women in her.

Ruggiero di Credo (rōo·zhyĕr'ō dē krä'dō), former Italian consul to Biscra. He married a vulgar Jewish Algerian woman, and they have two children, Rosalia and Angiola. His baroque domain of Gemera, in Sicily, which he inherited, is decaying. Faithful to the Bourbons, he disdained the dynasty of the Savoys, and, living in Sicily, he had no interest in the fall of Papal Rome to the north. His hats resemble either halos or helmets. When he joins the army for four years, his wife betrays him. The splendor of Gemera remains but a dream for him and his family, and after it is destroyed they leave for Rome, in the hope of exploiting his aristocratic ancestors and relatives. Life has stolen his dreams, but it is Ruggiero's constant misinterpretation of reality that leads to his isolation in an asylum and death.

Rosalia di Credo, uneducated daughter of Ruggiero di Credo who becomes a votive candle vendor in Rome. Here, Rosalia remains devoted to the dream of her past, Gemera, and to both her father and her sister, Angiola. While Rosalia is selling votive candles, her own wishes are seldom granted, and her solitary destiny without love and happiness is her immediate reality. Rosalia and Angiola propose two opposed ways of understanding life. While Rosalia takes care of her father until she has to put him into an asylum, she continues to weep for all the sorrows of love, and she suffers for both her father and her sister. Rosalia still hopes that generosity will win. Her life is only sustained by the hope that her sister will return to her, when, in fact, Angiola will destroy herself in many love affairs.

Angiola (ăn·zhyō'lä), Rosalia's sister. Though educated in a fashionable school run by aristocratic nuns in Florence, Angiola contracts lovers and marriages from all classes, from tailor to maharaja, but remains unfaithful to all of them, even to her husband Paolo Farina, who pays the mortgage for Gemera, until she leaves him.

Paolo Farina, a young lawyer. He is married to Angiola, but she leaves him for another lover. Paolo then immediately hopes to possess Lina Chiari.

Lina Chiari, a prostitute. She soon realizes that true love cannot be bought. When Lina discovers that she has breast cancer, her future seems to be stripped of all hope. Her lipstick and artificial smile cover up her despair.

Old Giulio Lovisi, the owner of a cosmetics store and a villa in Ostia. He is married to Giuseppa, and their daughter, Giovanna, is married to the writer Carlo Stevo, a socialist whom Giulio would like to "own." Carlo disappears while in jail for crimes against the state. Giulio often lights votive candles and says his prayers in an incoherent and automatic way. He remains enslaved to money worries and family problems, and he realizes the irreversible decline of his feelings for his wife, whose corpulence, sour disposition, and many shortcomings can only worsen. When a wish is granted to Giulio, his agony of hoping is perpetuated.

Carlo Stevo, husband of Giovanna Lovisi. Carlo dies in jail.

Giovanna Lovisi-Stevo, Carlo's wife and Giulio's daughter. She takes care of their crippled child in the hope of seeing her husband again. The angelic and golden world of the Church is the antithesis of Giovanna's life. Giovanna is embittered, solitary, and prone to temptations while waiting in vain for the return of her husband.

Miss Jones, Giulio's salesgirl. When fired from her job because of Giuseppa's jealousy, she says her prayers in the hope of returning to England and regrets her madness in having come to Italy, where none of her dreams has come true. Small miseries make up the lives of Giulio and Miss Jones. Their prayers sustain their hopes, which are the only things that give meaning to their lives.

Old Mother Dida of Ponte Porzio, the wife of Fruttuoso. She has faced a ruthless fate in her husband, a good-for-nothing who had given her many children and poverty, and she is now encrusting her life in routine and habit. Selling flowers near the film theater and the Conti Palace, she has outlived her husband, a king, and three popes. Indifferent to politics and religion, she loves Father Cicca and his organist without any religious faith. Despite her stinginess, she offers the ten-lira coin received from Dr. Sarte to the exhausted Clément Roux.

Clément Roux (rōo), a French artist about seventy years old. He has no interest in the modern architectural and political world of Rome. He meets with Massimo Iacofleff, but their ensuing conversation is completely at cross purposes, as neither listens to the other.

Massimo Iacofleff (yă′kō•flĕf), a double agent. He tells Clément about his complicity with Marcella, when they traded in false passports in Vienna, and how he is now worried that Marcella might have despised him when she died alone during her failed assassination attempt.

Marlies Kronegger

COLD STORAGE

Author: Ronald Ribman (1932-   )
Type of work: Play
Time of action: The 1970's
First produced: 1977

Joseph Parmigian, a man in his mid-sixties, a dying cancer patient in a hospital in New York City. He is the married owner of a fruit and vegetable store in Greenwich Village, of Armenian background, and is still hungry for experience and knowledge. An opinionated wiseacre who, with brass, sarcasm, and broad humor, smashes through the reserved shell of his fellow patient Landau, Parmigian, prodding and provoking, demands that Landau reveal his dreams. Parmigian has never felt settled or satisfied with life, and his wacky exuberance is balanced by a bleak vision of the ultimate meaninglessness of things and contradictory subcurrents typified by his revelation of "the best time to commit suicide, when you're in a good mood." In the end, though, it is not so much this out-of-place, deathbed Rabelaisianism that inspires Landau to break his reticence, but Parmigian's confession that he is at the end of his tether in trying to face up to approaching death.

Richard Landau, a man in his mid-forties who is in the hospital for "exploratory" surgery. He is a Jewish investment adviser who recommends art and antiques to wealthy clients; he is married, with two daughters. He is vaguely discontented with the whirl of modern life and seeks solace in the eternal verities as they are offered by fine china and antique furniture. He is quietly self-possessed, alternately tantalized and scandalized by Parmigian's verbal antics. Though he is drawn into the conversation by the older man's ability to reconstruct, without knowing him, the general contours of his life, Landau still skillfully parries efforts to get him to reveal himself. When he does reveal himself, he discloses an obsession that proves sobering to Parmigian. Landau is searching through psychiatry and introspection for a clearer memory of his parents, who gave him over to another family in Nazi Germany to save him from the concentration camps in which they perished. This inward, backward quest has stopped Landau from living in the present, though his self-confrontation in the hospital brings about his spiritual rebirth, ironically midwifed by a man on the brink of death.

Miss Madurga, the young, attractive Hispanic private-duty nurse of Landau and for-merly Parmigian's nurse. She appears briefly at the opening of act 1 to serve as a bridge to begin the conversation between the two patients and at the the close of act 1 to wheel Landau off. She is imperturbable and straight-faced; there is no nonsense about her.

James Feast

THE COLLECTOR

Author: John Fowles (1926-   )
Type of work: Novel
Time of action: The early 1960's
First published: 1963

Fredrick Clegg, a clerk in the Town Hall Annexe in Southhampton, England, until he wins seventy-three thousand pounds in a lottery and quits his job. Painfully diffident and ashamed of being a member of the uneducated, working class of British society, when Clegg wins the lottery at age thirty-seven he has both the determination and the financial power to realize his greatest ambition: He wants to possess Miranda Grey, the daughter of a doctor and a member of England's cultured, educated upper class. Believing that once Miranda spends time with him she will see that he is worthy of her interest and affection, Clegg purchases a secluded house several miles outside Lewes, England, decorates it the way he mistakenly thinks Miranda would like it, and remodels the cellar and equips it with plumbing and electricity so it will be habitable; he next purchases clothes, records, and books, and he places these in the cellar apartment—not for himself but for Miranda. In fact, after he kidnaps her, the cellar of his house becomes her prison for two months until she dies of pneumonia, at which time Clegg buries her body in his backyard. Throughout his retrospective account of his time with Miranda, he frequently assures the reader that he never meant to harm her, that his interest in her was nonsexual, and that he would have got a doctor for her if she had not proved herself to be unworthy of his trust and admiration. What he never says directly but shows by his actions and attitudes is that he hates women; if they arouse his otherwise repressed sexual desire, he perceives them as disgusting and worthless whores. He ultimately views Miranda as such a woman, consequently allows her to die, and then, after burying her, begins to stalk his next victim, a young woman who physically resembles Miranda.

Miranda Grey, a second-year art student at the Slade Art School in London. Twenty years old when Clegg kidnaps her, Miranda begins writing a diary that makes up approximately half of the novel's narrative. In her diary entries, she attempts to analyze Clegg and her predicament as his prisoner and attempts to come to great self-understanding with regard to her religious faith, her sexuality, her talents as an artist, and her relationships with her family and various men in her life (most specifically with George Pastan, an artist twice her age whom she had begun to view as her mentor but whom she had refused as a lover; her ongoing analysis of this relationship serves as a significant means by which Miranda is able to unveil and embrace the person she is—instead of the person, according to her society, she should be). When Clegg captures her, Miranda is a pacifist who believes in nonviolence at any cost; although she strays from her belief in pacifism when she physically attacks Clegg several weeks after her abduction, she is filled with self-disgust for stoop-

307

ing to his level and letting herself down. She realizes with certainty that she is a moral person unashamed of being moral. She also discovers that her morality should not pre-clude a sexual relationship with her mentor-friend George Pastan.

David A. Carpenter

THE COLOR PURPLE

Author: Alice Walker (1944-   )
Type of work: Novel
Time of action: The 1920's through the 1940's
First published: 1982

Celie, a survivor of sexual and physical abuse, who writes intimate letters to God and to her sister Nettie, and the owner of Celie Folkpants, Unlimited. Described as black, poor, and ugly, she is fourteen at the beginning of the story. Celie is a terrorized and passive girl with little belief in herself who undergoes a major transformation in attitude and becomes an outrageous, audacious, courageous, and willful woman who enjoys her lesbian sexuality. She gives birth to two children, conceived while she is being repeatedly raped by Alphonso, whom she believes to be her father; both children are quickly taken from her by him. Celie is married off to Mr. Albert—— but falls in love with Shug Avery, a former lover of her husband. Celie nurses Shug through an illness, they become lovers, and, later, they move to Memphis, where Celie starts a pants company. Celie returns to Georgia when she inherits her parents' house.

Nettie, Celie's younger sister, a missionary in Africa. Considered to be very pretty and very clever, Nettie loves Celie and remains devoted to her throughout her life. During a separation of some twenty years, she writes to Celie regularly, telling her of her experiences in Africa. Nettie helps take care of and watches over Celie's two children, who have been adopted by the missionary couple whom Nettie accompanies to Africa, and eventually reunites the family.

Mr. Albert——, a poor farmer. Abusive and dissatisfied with himself and his life, Mr. —— is in love with Shug, but, because he is incapable of disobeying his father, he married another woman. He beats Celie, his second wife, because she is not Shug. He also conceals all the letters that Nettie sends to Celie. Mr. —— thinks little of treating Celie as less than human until she stands up to him and then leaves, at which point he becomes physically and spiritually ill, recovers, begins to lead a moral life, and becomes friends with Celie.

Shug Avery, whose real name is **Lillie,** also called **The Queen Honeybee,** a blues singer. Confident, flamboyant, and independent, Shug is considered to be immoral by some church folk but is nevertheless popular and admired as a performer. She is wise in the cultural values of the black community, and her presence has a transforming effect, especially on Celie but also on others. Shug moves in with Celie and Mr. —— and is first Mr. ——'s and then Celie's lover. She marries Grady, becomes lovers with a young blues flutist named Germaine, and eventually returns as Celie's lover.

Harpo, the owner of a juke joint and Mr. ——'s oldest son. As a young man, very tall, skinny, and dark-skinned, he is insecure in his manhood and frustrated by his inability to make his wife do as he commands. When his wife leaves him because she is exasperated by his attempts to beat her, he turns their house into a juke joint that provides Shug Avery and others with a place to sing the blues.

Sofia Butler, the defiant wife of Harpo. Big,

strong, and ruddy-looking, her personality is that of a fighter, and she refuses to be pushed around by anyone. When the mayor's wife sees her on the street and asks her to be her maid, Sofia curses, responds to the mayor's slap by knocking him down, and is then beaten severely by the police. She is sentenced to jail for twelve years but spends most of that time as maid to the mayor's wife.

Alphonso, called **Pa** by Celie, mistaken by Celie and Nettie as their father but really their stepfather. He is a mean man who has sexual relations with a number of young girls, some of whom he marries. When he rapes Celie, he tells her to say nothing to anyone but God; thus, her subsequent letters are addressed to Him.

Mary Agnes, called **Squeak,** Harpo's lover and a late-blooming blues singer. Described as yellow-skinned, Mary Agnes facilitates Sofia's release from prison into the service of the mayor's wife by calling upon her white uncle, the prison warden, who rapes her during this visit. She leaves Harpo to go with Celie and Shug to Memphis to start a sing-

ing career, becomes lovers with Shug's husband and moves to Panama with him, then returns to Memphis and her singing career.

Grady, Shug's husband, who moves to Panama with Mary Agnes in order to run a marijuana plantation.

Olivia, Celie's daughter and oldest child, an independent thinker who is reared in Africa by the Reverend Samuel —— and his wife, Corrine.

Adam Omatangu, Celie's son, a thoughtful and sensitive young man who writes verses and loves to sing. Adam obtains the second name of Omatangu when he marries an African woman.

Tashi Omatangu, wife of Adam, one of the Olinka people who joins the *mbeles* in order to fight against white colonialists in Africa but is persuaded by Adam to become married to him and return with him to the United States.

Leslie W. Lewis

COLOURS IN THE DARK

Author: James Reaney (1926-   )
Type of work: Play
Time of action: The twentieth century
First produced: 1967

Pa, the father, who can read palms and tell the color of things even while blindfolded. He also plays the man initiated into an understanding of his own life during the Sundog ritual. He is the cruel schoolmaster who whips the children for their faults in spelling, the wealthy and powerful executive who is the first to die in the Dance of Death, and the grocer who pulls his customer backward and forward through time by the string attached to her parcel. He recites the poem on the Royal Visit. He plays the teacher of the writing class and the student who baby-sits for the limbless young man.

Ma, the mother, who blindfolds the child

suffering from the measles, the lawyer at the trial of the cruel schoolmaster, and the announcer of the significance of the colors at the beginning of the "color" acts. She is the waspish antisuffragette mistress of the Winnipeg boardinghouse and also a girl boarder at the same boardinghouse. She is the Wind Lady, who dances with her rain doll, and the rich young lady whose swimming pool and vacations in Antigua cannot save her from the Dance of Death.

Gramp, the grandfather, the bear who threatens to eat the small berry-picking girl, and James McIntyre the Ingeroll cheese poet. He is Mr. Winemeyer, the wise sculptor hermit.

He is the aggressively pedantic Professor Button, who decries religious faith but whose knowledge of languages is no match for Bible Sal's ability to speak in tongues. He plays Tecumseh in the schoolmaster's trial, the Minister at the Christening, and the Death King in the Dance of Death scene.

Gram, the grandmother, a Sundog and the lady who initiates the father into a knowledge of himself at the Sundog ritual. She is Granny Crack and the old beggar woman who wanders the countryside and hangs out all the clothing of her life on a line. She is the music teacher, the old farmwife who ladles out horse soup, and the girl at the Winnipeg boardinghouse. She is also the Death Lady in the Dance of Death.

Son, the son, one of the boys on a bicycle trip who meets the reclusive Mr. Winemeyer

and the judge at the trial of the cruel schoolmaster. He is the grocery boy, the accuser at the Sundog ritual, and the university student who is a friend of Bible Sal. He is also a boarder at the Winnipeg boardinghouse. He plays the young man with no arms and no legs who yearns for someone to accept and love him.

Niece, the daughter, the girl, and the Bride. She is Bible Sal, whose religious devotion drives her to attempt to copy out the entire Bible. Bible Sal visits the lecture of Professor Button, a teacher of Old Testament studies at University College, University of Toronto, and she counters his cynical faithlessness with a display of her ability to speak in tongues, a gift she did not previously know she had. She is also the maid at the Winnipeg boardinghouse.

Catherine Swanson

COME BACK, LITTLE SHEBA

Author: William Inge (1913-1973)
Type of work: Play
Time of action: The late 1940's
First produced: 1950

Doc Delaney, a chiropractor in a Midwestern city. This outwardly gentle, courteous, patient man in his early forties is inwardly seething because of his frustrating life. He had felt compelled to drop out of medical school about twenty years before and marry Lola because he had made her pregnant. Married to a woman who is his social and intellectual inferior, disappointed in his ambitions and by the fact that Lola was rendered sterile by the botched delivery of their stillborn first child, Doc became an alcoholic who was nearly homicidal when intoxicated. He squandered all the money he had inherited and allowed his practice to go to ruin. For the past eleven months he has belonged to Alcoholics Anonymous and is trying to rebuild his shattered life.

Lola Delaney, a housewife. Married to Doc

at eighteen, Lola has remained mentally an adolescent for the past twenty years. In contrast to her shy, introverted husband, she has no internal resources and is totally dependent on other people. She has let herself become fat, and she neglects her housekeeping along with her personal appearance. At eighteen, she had been strikingly attractive and much sought after by young men. Since this was the only area in which she ever experienced success and satisfaction, she has never gotten over her youthful illusions about romantic love. Her small lost dog, Little Sheba, symbolizes for her on an unconscious level her own lost youth and beauty, which she hopes somehow will come back to her.

Marie, a college student who boards with the Delaneys. At the age of eighteen or nineteen, she is pretty, cheerful, sprightly, and friendly—a ray of sunshine in this unhappy household. Both Doc and Lola project their own fantasies onto this fairly ordinary girl. Doc sees her as pure and almost saintly. Lola sees her quite simply as herself at that same age. Marie's passionate relationship with Turk, in which Lola takes a strong vicarious interest, triggers Doc's repressed rage and leads directly to the violent climax of the play. Through their emotional involvement with Marie, both Doc and Lola eventually come to realize their mistaken illusions about the glamour of youth.

Turk, a college athlete, good-looking, aggressive, muscular, and narcissistic. Although only nineteen or twenty, he has been in military service and has acquired a superficial sophistication. His attitude toward young women is predatory. He is only interested in sex, and though Marie is strongly attracted to him on this level, she knows he is not marriage material. Doc hates him because he is sensual and uninhibited, everything Doc is not. When Doc realizes the two young students are sleeping together right under his roof, he gets roaring drunk and threatens to kill Turk as well as Lola, whom he blames for acting as a pander in the illicit affair.

Bruce, Marie's fiancé, who lives in a different city. This intelligent, ambitious, well-mannered young man comes from an upper-middle-class family and is already making strong headway in the business world. Marie regards him as a good catch, but he does not fire her blood the way Turk does. When she and Bruce go off to get married at the end of the play, it is clear that they will have a conventional middle-class marriage without any physical excitement.

Mrs. Coffman, a housewife, the Delaneys' next-door neighbor. This middle-aged mother of seven children serves as a contrast to the slovenly, irresponsible Lola. Mrs. Coffman speaks with a German accent and has the hardworking, no-nonsense attitude often associated with members of that ethnic group. She is kindhearted, however, and proves helpful to Lola in her hour of need.

Bill Delaney

THE COMEDIANS

Author: Graham Greene (1904-   )
Type of work: Novel
Time of action: The early 1960's
First published: 1966

Brown, the narrator, a part-Englishman from Monaco who has inherited a hotel in Haiti. Jaded, cynical, and detached, Brown has returned to Haiti in his late fifties because he has no real home and the hotel is all he owns. After run-ins with François "Papa Doc" Duvalier's secret police and after he has betrayed his friend Jones and his mistress Martha through his misplaced suspicion of them, he escapes from the fear-ridden country to the Dominican Republic, where he becomes a partner in a mortician's concern.

"Major" Jones, a former theater manager in his late forties who pretends to have been a war hero. A man sought by the police in several countries, he is nevertheless very likable, because he has a kindness about him and he always "makes people laugh." Tricked by Brown into joining the cause of the resistance against Papa Doc, he dies heroically in an effort to allow his fellow rebels to escape.

William Abel Smith, an elderly, idealistic vegetarian who has come to Haiti because he believes that avoidance of meat would neutralize destructive passions and because he wishes to start a Haitian vegetarian institute. Having run on the vegetarian ticket in the

1948 election, he is accepted as a former presidential candidate by the naïve authorities and even granted some credibility. His attempts to help people usually backfire disastrously, as when he gives beggars money that is immediately snatched by the secret police, but he is instrumental several times in helping Brown.

Mrs. Smith, Smith's wife, as idealistic as her husband. She is devoted to Smith and is even more likely than he to take immediate, direct action when perceiving injustice.

Martha Pineda, Brown's mistress. Married to a South American diplomat who knows about the affair and tolerates it, she is torn between her love for Brown and her attachment to her son Angel. As emotional and committed as Brown is restrained and detached, Martha is pulled back and forth between commitments until the end of the novel, at which time it is clear that she will follow her husband, who has been transferred, and will no longer see Brown.

Dr. Magiot, the elderly Communist doctor, is committed to people rather than causes. He reappears throughout the action to do what he can to alleviate suffering, but at the end he too is betrayed and killed by the supporters of Papa Doc. His last letter, received by Smith after Magiot's death, urges Smith to join the committed—not to "abandon all faith."

Captain Concasseur, an officer in the Tonton Macoute, Papa Doc's secret police, who, like his colleagues, wears black sunglasses in daylight to maximize his effect of terror. Concasseur enjoys torturing and destroying, but his fun terrorizing Brown is broken up by the Smiths. Concasseur is eventually killed by the rebels, before they are killed by other members of the Tonton Macoute.

Henri Philipot, the young nephew of a slain Haitian minister, gives up his writing of obscure verse to join the rebels. He survives to tell of the death of Jones and the others.

Janet McCann

THE COMFORTERS

Author: Muriel Spark (1918-   )
Type of work: Novel
Time of action: The 1950's
First published: 1957

Caroline Rose, a woman of about thirty, Cambridge-educated, "thin, angular, sharp, enquiring . . . well-dressed and good-looking." After converting to Catholicism, she renounces sex, stops living with her lover, Laurence Manders, and goes on a religious retreat. When she hears ghostly voices and a typewriter, she thinks that she is mad but soon guesses that the typewriter is typing the novel of her life and the lives of others. She wonders if this mysterious "author" is a figure from some other dimension—perhaps a soul from purgatory, perhaps Satan himself. She breaks her leg when she and Laurence have a serious automobile accident. More and more, her thoughts influence the novel;

she senses its approaching end. At a climactic picnic, she falls into the river with Georgina Hogg, struggles free, and saves herself. She seems to envision a happy ending— though whether in fiction or reality is unclear.

Laurence Manders, a man of about thirty, a lapsed Catholic who works as a sports commentator for the British Broadcasting Corporation. Despite the fact that Caroline leaves him, he still loves her, and he worries about her sanity. At the end, he discovers Caroline's notes for her novel and protests that she misrepresents him. Perhaps he is rewarded by a happy ending.

Georgina Hogg, a woman of about fifty, the cousin and first wife of Mervyn Hogg and the mother of Albert. She is sanctimonious, bullying, self-centered, and universally hated. Her hair is white; her pale-blue eyes have no lashes; her bosom is tremendous. She was Laurence's nursery governess and now works at a religious retreat center. There are hints that she is not a real person; on the way to a picnic which plays a crucial part in the plot, she falls asleep in the car and disappears like a witch. Later, she struggles with Caroline in the river and is apparently drowned. No body is recovered.

Louisa Jepp, seventy-eight years old, the daughter of a gypsy, mother of Lady Manders and grandmother of Laurence. Short and fat, she is a determined woman; her thin black hair frames a lined face with deep-set spectacled black eyes. Her home, "Smuggler's Retreat," is aptly named, for she runs a diamond-smuggling gang. She ends up marrying one of her partners in crime, J. G. L. Webster.

Mervyn Hogg, or **Hogarth,** the father of Albert. He is a bigamist, having married both Georgina Hogg and Eleanor Hogarth. Mervyn is about fifty, a thin, colorless, cynical little man. As part of Mrs. Jepp's smuggling operation, he takes his son to Continental shrines and returns with diamonds encased in plaster statuettes and rosary beads.

Willi Stock (The Baron), fifty years old, born in the Congo, a naturalized British citizen. He may have African blood; he may be a real baron. Amused and aloof, he runs an intellectual bookshop, befriends Caroline, and spreads stories about her. He is Mrs. Jepp's London contact, receiving jewels from Mr. Webster and selling them. He becomes obsessed with the idea that Mervyn is "the foremost diabolist in these islands." He is present when Georgina disappears and is

at the picnic. Finally, he is committed to a mental hospital.

Eleanor Hogarth, a woman of about thirty, a dancer, wife of Mervyn, mistress of Willi, and business partner of Ernest Manders. She was at Cambridge with Caroline, married soon thereafter, and left when she discovered Mervyn's bigamy. She calls Georgina a witch.

Lady Helena Manders, the daughter of Louisa, wife of Sir Edwin, mother of Laurence. A Catholic convert, she builds religious retreat centers. Though she, too, hates Georgina, she charitably finds work for her. She is in the car when Georgina disappears.

Sir Edwin Manders, a lifelong Catholic, Lady Helena's husband, Laurence's father. He manufactures Manders Figs in Syrup. He is often at a retreat but wonders if his disengagement is proper.

Ernest Manders, Sir Edwin's brother, a dancer, Eleanor's business partner, a good Catholic. He is homosexual and effeminate. When he inadvertently blackmails Mervyn, Georgina thinks that the Manders suspect something. His revelations to Helena help precipitate the ending.

Andrew Hogg, or **Hogarth,** about twenty-five years old, the son of Mervyn and Georgina, confined to a wheelchair. He helps his father smuggle diamonds. When the smuggling stops, he is cured (some say miraculously) and goes to Canada to lecture.

J. G. L. Webster, a man of seventy-seven, with white hair and a mustache. He bakes the loaves in which the diamonds are conveyed from the Hogarths to Mrs. Jepp and is her messenger to Willi. Ultimately, he marries Mrs. Jepp.

George Soule

313

COMING UP FOR AIR

Author: George Orwell (Eric Arthur Blair, 1903-1950)
Type of work: Novel
Time of action: The early 1900's and 1938
First published: 1939

George Bowling, an insurance representative, aged forty-five. Fat and sentimental, with a mouth full of false teeth, George is in every way the lower-middle-class Englishman, even to his love of reading and his nostalgia for an Edwardian, pre-World War I past that can no longer be found, except perhaps in memory. In order to escape the increasingly bland and plastic routine in his London suburban home, as well as his complaining wife and children, George fantasizes about taking a trip to his childhood home of Lower Binfield, a small town in rural Oxfordshire. He discovers, however, that one cannot go home again, for Lower Binfield, as many towns have, has become devoid of individuality as a result of "progress." (The childhood carp pool that George has dreamed about fishing in again, for example, has become a rubbish dump in the middle of a housing tract of fake Tudor homes.) George's family home and business of "Samuel Bowling, Corn & Seed Merchant" has been reduced to "Wendy's Tea-Shop." On the one hand, George is a sentimentalist who gets teary over primroses, a middle-aged man who fantasizes about women without being able to do anything about them. On the other hand, he is also someone who only wants peace and an authentic England, and he is right in his predictions about the start of World War II (the novel was published three months before the outbreak of the war) and about what will happen to England after the war, when it will become even more standardized. George Bowling is a fleshy, three-dimensional character who is both a sentimentalist about the past and a prophet of the future. The other characters in the novel pale in comparison to him.

Hilda Bowling, George's wife of fifteen years. Hilda has been worn down by marriage and by trying to rear two children on George's limited income. She no longer shares any of George's dreams and walks through her days with a "perpetual brooding, worried look in her eyes." It is largely because of Hilda—if only in reaction to what their married life has become in fifteen years—that George's adventures take place.

Elsie Waters, George's first lover. George romanticizes his relationship with Elsie, which occurred years before in Lower Binfield. When he finally sees her in the present, however, she has become a shapeless old woman.

Joe Bowling, George's brother, with whom George shared many childhood adventures, particularly fishing, an activity which in his present fantasies has taken on almost epic proportions. Joe is dead now, as is the past that George hoped to find in Lower Binfield.

Porteous, a retired English public-school master and an old friend of George. George respects "old Porteous" but is shocked to realize how out of touch the elder man is. The retired schoolteacher recognizes neither the real threat of Adolf Hitler nor the impending doom of England after the war.

David Peck

COMPANY

Author: Samuel Beckett (1906-1989)
Type of work: Novel

Time of action: The late 1970's
First published: Compagnie, 1980 (English translation, 1980)

A Voice, seemingly speaking in a dark room, unidentified, addressing the Hearer about his past life and present situation; the Voice seems to move about in the unlit space, sometimes far off, sometimes very close to the Hearer; the Voice is tonally flat on all occasions. Sometimes there are long periods in which the Voice is silent. When it is heard, it is always very soft.

The Hearer, as he is called, unidentified by name (although he is given a name, only to have it immediately taken away), clearly a male, lying on his back in the dark. He is a very old man, immobile save for the opening and closing of his eyes. He seems to be Irish; certainly the anecdotes of his childhood indicate that he was born and brought up in Ireland. He does not speak, and it is made clear that he has never been very active intellectually. At first, he is not sure if the Voice is really speaking to him. It seems he has been in the darkened space for a very long time before the Voice begins. The Voice is some company for him, and the third-person narrator allows the reader to know how he reacts to the Voice.

The Narrator, called the **cankerous other,** sometimes the **Deviser,** able to record the words spoken by the Voice and to enter the mind of the Hearer to reveal how the Hearer responds to what is being said about him. Thus the technical device of third-party narration is given character of a kind, and he is described as the Deviser devising the Voice and the Hearer to keep himself company, thus one of the reasons for the title. There is a vague suggestion made that he is really telling a tale of his own life, and he does possess a talent for witty and sometimes feelingful anecdote.

The Commentator, the voice behind it all, who claims to have invented the narratorial voice, the Voice, and the Hearer. He makes a running critical commentary on the story, breaching the credibility of the tale and continually considering other ways of telling it and of changing the nature of the characters, physically and in terms of character and action. The box-within-a-box of normal third-party narration is opened up in this way to critical comment and to the possibility that there may be another writer, perhaps the real writer, behind this voice.

The Hearer's father, unnamed, appearing in some of the anecdotes told about the Hearer's life as a child. A ruddy, round-faced man, wearing a thick mustache, he is a reader of *Punch*, he likes egg sandwiches and long walks, and he is off walking in the rugged countryside at the time of his son's birth. After his death, he occasionally reappears to his son, but as the son gets older these appearances cease.

An old beggar woman, another character out of the Hearer's childhood. Half blind, stone deaf, and not quite sane, she thinks she can fly, and, on one occasion, she throws herself out a second-story window. The Hearer was kind to her.

Mrs. Coote, a friend of his mother. A small, thin, pessimistic woman, who was having tea one day with his mother while he was busy climbing a huge fir tree in the garden and throwing himself down through the branches.

The Hedgehog, an animal found wandering one day by the young Hearer. He puts it in a hat box with a supply of worms but makes sure that the animal is free to come and go. Some time later, he finds the rotting corpse of the Hedgehog in the box. This anecdote, as well as many of the others which the Voice relates, may have been based on incidents in Beckett's childhood.

Charles Pullen

THE COMPANY OF WOMEN

Author: Mary Gordon (1949-   )
Type of work: Novel
Time of action: August, 1963; winter, 1969-1970; and 1977
First published: 1980

Felicitas Maria Taylor, a bright, articulate but sheltered Catholic girl. In the beginning of the novel, she is an early adolescent coming to recognize her special relationship to Father Cyprian among the women who make up his "company"; he has special regard for her intellectual and spiritual potential. Felicitas' talent at Latin and Greek lead her to a classics major at Columbia University, where at the height of the Vietnam War protests she meets and eventually moves in with a radical political science professor, Robert Cavendish, the man who may be the father of her child. Shocked by her unplanned pregnancy, Felicitas nevertheless rejects abortion. Instead, she returns to her mother and they, along with the other members of the company, move to the country to rear the child near Father Cyprian, whose guidance has marked all of their lives.

Charlotte Taylor, Felicitas' widowed mother. Her husband died when Felicitas was six months old. Being the oldest of thirteen children has taught her realism, toughness, and self-reliance in a demanding world, but those qualities do not diminish her devotion to her daughter or to the other women of the company. She is powerless to help in her daughter's painful romance, but she is quick to plan the move to the country to accommodate Felicitas and Linda, and at the novel's end, at the age of sixty-seven, she is planning a new insurance business with a neighbor.

Father Cyprian Leonard, a brilliant acerbic, conservative Roman Catholic priest. He organized the retreats which evolved into the company of Charlotte, Elizabeth, Mary Rose, Clare, and Muriel, the company that continues to surround him each summer. Having struggled up from an impoverished rural background, he uses his sharp mind and tongue to try to direct Felicitas into orthodoxy and away from the sentimentality of popular Catholicism. He was driving in the accident that gave Felicitas a stay in the hospital for a concussion when she was fourteen, and it is his conservative politics that cause her to clash with him over the Vietnam War. At the end of the novel, however, his love for her daughter Linda makes him pray (to his surprise) for the church to reverse its stand on the ordination of women when Linda tells him she intends to become a priest.

Elizabeth, a schoolteacher and lover of literature. In the 1930's, her husband abandoned her with a small child who died young. Quiet and sensitive, she introduces Felicitas to the novels of Jane Austen and is unsure whether her own religion is of the spirit or of literature.

Mary Rose, the simplest of the "company." Father Cyprian helped her during her naïve marriage to a dangerously unbalanced man by having the man committed to a mental hospital; that aid left her Father Cyprian's disciple. Now she works in a film theater, where she worries about the X-rated films and indulges her uncomplicated and generous nature first in befriending Felicitas and then Linda.

Clare, a businesswoman who has high regard for excellence. She has always recognized good quality in the leather goods she deals in, and that is what she appreciates in Father Cyprian, too. Her life outside his "company," however, is marked by detachment and uninvolvement. At the novel's end, she of all the women most misses the city.

Muriel, Father Cyprian's housekeeper. Unloving and unlovable, little in her meager life has prepared her to be otherwise. She recognizes her limitations and the animosity the others often feel toward her pettiness (which often springs from her jealous guarding of Father Cyprian). When Felicitas was in the hospital, Muriel's gift was a packet of religious tracts.

Robert Cavendish, a radical professor of political science at Columbia. He uses the rebellion of the 1960's to indulge his selfishness. Felicitas fails to notice his clichés and superficiality because she is caught up in the romance of his attentions, his unconventionality, and his good looks. He lives with two of his cast-off lovers and a variety of other drifters, who move through his apartment in a haze of drugs and political rhetoric. His interest in Felicitas is almost entirely sexual.

Linda, Felicitas' child, aged seven at the novel's end. She tells Father Cyprian that she intends to become a priest, having satisfied herself that the fact of Jesus' twelve disciples being male is irrelevant to the priesthood.

Leo, a quiet outdoorsman. Felicitas plans to marry him at the novel's end.

Ann D. Garbett

THE COMPROMISE

Author: Sergei Dovlatov (1941-   )
Type of work: Novel
Time of action: November, 1973, to October, 1976
First published: Kompromiss, 1981 (English translation, 1983)

Sergei Dovlatov, a journalist in his midthirties. Educated as a philologist, he is talented, very tall, a former camp guard, and an alcoholic. Something of a dissident (he is part Jewish), he works for an Estonian newspaper; he is separated from his wife and behind in his alimony payments. In telling the reader the truth behind several apparently innocuous "compromising" human interest stories he had written for his newspaper, the narrator presents himself as the center of a kind of novel that ends with the reporter's return to his family in Leningrad. It is Dovlatov as author who in fact recalls the events behind the stories, but the narrator appears to be fictional, if for no other reason than that his surname is almost never mentioned or, if it is, then usually mistakenly by one of the characters: "Dolmatov," "Dokladov," "Zaplatov . . . ."

Mikhail "Misha" Borisovich Shablinsky, a reporter for the "industry desk" at the newspaper, an excellent writer but cynical and ruthlessly successful with women. He finally decides to get married, however, and therefore breaks up with Marina—who is inherited by Dovlatov. Shablinsky is an established journalist and a member of the Communist Party, which the narrator, though a superior writer, is not.

Marina, one of the secretarial workers at the newspaper. She is around thirty, single, smokes, knows a lot, and is somewhat bitter about men. She sees Dovlatov as pensive, polite, and honest—in keeping with his pattern of being liked by cast-off women. The narrator is inclined to view their relationship as one of intellectual intimacy, with shades of animosity and sex. To Marina this is love, and she weeps over Dovlatov in frustration.

Henry Franzovich Turonok, the editor-in-chief of Dovlatov's newspaper and an important member of the Communist Party. He continually accuses Dovlatov of political myopia—for not understanding, for example, that in a list of socialist countries Hungary should follow East Germany, because in Hungary they had an uprising. When he assigns Dovlatov to do a story on the birth of the four hundred-thousandth inhabitant of the city of Tallinn, he rejects first a newborn

Ethiopian baby, next a Jewish child, and only at last allows Dovlatov, by then very drunk after waiting around the hospital all night, to write about a 100 percent Russian infant and the infant's parents.

Mikhail Vladimirovich Zhbankov, an alcoholic photographer for the newspaper. He makes a number of disconcerting anti-Semitic remarks, but later turns out to be Jewish himself. He is occasionally assigned to work with

Dovlatov on stories. A typical such story is the achievement of an Estonian milkmaid, Linda Peips, in extracting a record-breaking amount of milk out of one cow. Dovlatov and Zhbankov drive to the collective farm and interview the girl, who does not even speak Russian. They stay on for two days, however, drinking excessively and having sexual intercourse with their young Party hostesses.

Donald M. Fiene

CONCLUDING

Author: Henry Green (Henry Vincent Yorke, 1905-1973)
Type of work: Novel
Time of action: Sometime in the future
First published: 1948

Mr. Rock, the central character, a seventy-six-year-old, white-haired, hard of hearing, and bespectacled man. As a young man, he made a great scientific discovery, and now he is being considered for election to the Academy of Sciences. Rock would rather be left alone in his cottage on the grounds of a state school for girls with his granddaughter, whom he loves. He is gruffly kind to the schoolgirls who are fond of his pets: a cat, a goose, and a pig. Moira often comes to visit him. Rock is concerned when two of the girls are missing; he searches for Mary, an act of virtue, when others cover up her absence, to prepare for the dance.

Miss Mabel Edge, one of the two principals of the Institute, a state school for girls. Short, thin, and white-haired, with white hands, Miss Edge schemes to get rid of Rock in order to have his cottage for a still-to-be-hired handyman. Miss Edge is a spinster who angers Miss Marchbanks with her high-handed ways. At a break from the annual Tamasha, or dance, Miss Edge, high on cigarettes, indirectly asks Mr. Rock to marry her. She is furious when, on the way out, he laughs. Feared by all the staff, Miss Edge has only one friend, Miss Baker.

Miss Hermione Baker, short and fat, the other principal of the school. Like Edge and other bureaucrats, she fears that some complaint will be made against them, and perhaps they will be forced to leave the beautiful estate on which the school is situated. Baker and Edge are colleagues and confederates in the scheme against Rock, but Baker is more restrained and less frantic. She talks often about the black and white farm she knew as a child.

Elizabeth Rock, Rock's thirty-five-year-old granddaughter. She is recovering from a nervous breakdown. Having an affair with Sebastian Birt, she wants to marry him and live with him in her grandfather's cottage. She does not accept the fact that because of state regulations, Birt will be reassigned if they marry. Elizabeth will not allow Sebastian to criticize her grandfather, and she will not allow Rock to criticize Sebastian. At the dance, she plasters herself against Sebastian, not realizing how shocking it is to the spinster principals, who call it a display of animalism.

Sebastian Birt, a first-year economics tutor at the school. Fat and very short, he loves

Elizabeth Rock. Like all the other adult characters, he is worried about keeping his job, keeping his living quarters, and avoiding the censure of the principals. Birt is also loved by Miss Winstanley, another teacher, whom he ignores. He worries that Rock will make trouble, for example by reporting Mary's disappearnce to a state bureaucrat, Swaythling.

Moira, one of the senior students. She has strong blue eyes, an apricot neck and face, golden legs, and short, curly hair. She likes to talk to Rock. When Miss Marchbanks thinks she has Merode isolated in a bathroom, Moira talks to her through a ventilator shaft. Moira takes Mr. Rock to the girls' secret clubhouse, and she kisses him on the lips, but Rock only wants to get away.

Merode, an orphan at the school. She is missing but is then found with a scratched knee outside in the woods in her pajamas and coat. She cries and will not explain how she got there. (Moira tells Rock that the junior girls meet George Adams at night.) Merode and her aunt say that she was sleepwalking. When she is found by Sebastian and Elizabeth, she has a white face and painted toenails. She also has red hair and skin like vanilla ice cream.

Mary, usually a steady girl, but missing the same day as Merode is. Rock and some of the girls fear that she has drowned in the lake. The principals have preferred her as an orderly to wait on them. Mary's divorced parents are in Brazil, and she is substantially alone. The other girls finally conclude that Mary ran away because she was overworked as a waitress and pressured to make good grades in her final exams. At the end of the novel, Mary still has not been found.

George Adams, a woodman whose wife died the previous winter. He thinks that people, including Rock, are scheming to get him out of his cottage. To confound his supposed enemy, he writes an anonymous letter to Miss Edge about the Rock household and "furnicating." The night of the dance, he gets into a rage when Rock walks by but Adams refuses to come out from by the withy and face Rock.

Miss Maggie Blain, the cook at the school, a woman with green eyes and an enormous bosom. She is kind enough to give Rock breakfast each day and to give him swill for his pig. She is touchy, however, and cannot be pushed. She is concerned for her girls and angry that no one told her that Mary was missing.

Miss Marchbanks, who is left in charge when the principals go up to London to a meeting for the day. She is kind to Merode when she is found but is unable to get a coherent story from the girl, who faints when she is pressed. Miss Marchbanks tries to put Alice, Rock's Persian cat, on Merode's lap to soothe her with a pet, but it does not work. Marchbanks has brown eyes and spectacles. She tries to suggest fir trees as decorations for the dance, but her idea is squashed by the principals, who want everything to remain the same from year to year.

Mrs. Manley, Merode's aunt, a middle-aged woman with a fruity voice. When she arrives at the school, she insists on seeing Merode against "the Rules." She also suggests that the principals might be at fault in the girl's disappearance. Mrs. Manley insists that Merode was sleepwalking, and, to save themselves trouble, Edge and Baker seem ready to accept that excuse.

Kate M. Begnal

CONCRETE

Author: Thomas Bernhard (1931-1989)
Type of work: Novel

Time of action: The early 1980's
First published: Beton, 1982 (English translation, 1984)

Rudolph, the narrator of the story, a scholar and musicologist who is obsessed with writing a monograph on the composer Felix Mendelssohn. A neurotic and sickly man who is dependent on medication, he lives alone on his country estate in Peiskam. Rudolph is an extreme perfectionist and highly vulnerable to the slightest distraction. Although he thinks constantly about his monograph, he never seems to get to the point of writing it. He is occasionally interrupted by visits from his vivacious socialite sister. Her domineering personality causes him great difficulties and destroys his concentration. He travels to Palma, Mallorca, at the beginning of the novel when, after one of her visits, he cannot concentrate on his work. There he remembers the tragic story of a young woman whom he had met two years earlier on a previous journey to the island. Her fate plunges him into a depressed state, and he contemplates death and the meaninglessness of his life.

Rudolph's sister, an outgoing and vital woman who leads an active social life in the capital city of Vienna. A successful businesswoman who is involved in all the mundane activities of life, she is clearly the opposite of her sickly and isolated brother. She torments the narrator about his lack of success and his inability to write his treatise. Her visit at the beginning of the novel prompts him to travel to Mallorca.

Anna Härdtl, the young German woman whom the narrator meets on one of his trips to Palma, Mallorca. She is married and operates a small business with her husband in Munich. The business is not going well, and they decide to take their savings and take a vacation in Palma. One morning, she finds that her husband has fallen (or thrown himself) from the balcony of their hotel room and is dead. The narrator befriends her, but he learns, after a brief trip away from Palma, that she has committed suicide. She is buried under a simple concrete slab.

Thomas F. Barry

A CONFEDERACY OF DUNCES

Author: John Kennedy Toole (1937-1969)
Type of work: Novel
Time of action: The early 1960's
First published: 1980

Ignatius J. Reilly, a blowsy, flatulent, thirty-year-old, obese self-styled "philosopher." Always dressed in a green hunting cap, hobbled by phobias, especially a dyspeptic pyloric valve that closes at any provocation, obsessed with his bodily functions (though asexual), and disdainful of the "corrupt twentieth century," Reilly languishes at home, criticizing his widowed mother and her friends, refusing to find work, watching television (especially the shows he considers "offenses against taste and decency"), and, on his Big Red tablets, writing a journal of his "travels" and his medieval world vision. When forced to work (first in the office at Levy Pants, which he almost ruins by discarding the company files and organizing the black workers in what he calls a "Crusade for Moorish Dignity," and then at Paradise Vendors selling "weenies" from a pushcart, all the while eating more hotdogs than he sells), he becomes the catalyst for all the chaotic action in the novel and the intersection point for the characters in the several subplots. His picaresque tour of New Orleans reveals Reilly's complete self-indulgence, his philosophical inconsistencies as he sates himself on the very things he abhors in food and entertainment, and his negative, unfeeling attitude toward all around him. Only at the end of the novel, when his mother has finally recognized that Reilly is coldhearted, selfish, and beyond emotional redemption and so has attempted to commit him to the mental ward, does Reilly show a hint of warmth, as Myrna Minkoff spirits him away.

Irene Reilly, the widowed mother of the protagonist. Lonely and unwilling to see her son as a failure (for he has a master's degree), she suffers from a drinking problem, low self-esteem, a bad elbow, and Reilly's incessant demands and verbal abuse. As her circle of friends enlarges and as she gains a suitor in Claude Robichaux, however, she becomes increasingly disenchanted with her son and finally moves to free herself from his lethargy and criticism.

Myrna Minkoff, a New York "radical" and Reilly's nemesis and erstwhile girlfriend. Through her preaching a politics of sexual liberation and Reilly's own need to prove himself to Minkoff by acting, Minkoff becomes Reilly's foil and fantasy, but in the end his savior.

Claude Robichaux, Mrs. Reilly's elderly suitor. He believes nearly everyone and everything is "communiss."

Angelo Mancuso, a bungling policeman and Reilly's nemesis. An aspiring detective relegated to "undercover" work in restrooms and in disguises on the street, Mancuso befriends Mrs. Reilly and later becomes a hero by chancing to uncover a pornographic distribution operation at the Night of Joy bar.

Lana Lee, owner of the Night of Joy bar. Of chiseled body and stony heart, Lee distributes pornographic cards to school children

when she is not overtaxing her employees, Burma Jones and Darlene, at her lowlife bar.

Burma Jones, the self-styled "colored dude" and low-paid black floor sweeper at the Night of Joy bar. Fearful of Lee's threats to turn him in to the police for vagrancy, he effects his own emancipation and a reward by leading Mancuso to Lee's hidden pornoraphy.

Darlene, a B-girl at the Night of Joy bar. Her intellectual fare is *Life* magazine, and her life's ambition is to stage a striptease act with her pet cockatoo.

Gus Levy, owner of Levy Pants. Disdainful of running a company he inherited from an unloving father, Levy thinks little of management (thus the opening for Reilly) and much of baseball.

Mrs. Levy, Levy's wife. She nags Levy to keep Miss Trixie employed and the Levy daughters in high style.

Mr. Gonzales, the manager of Levy Pants. He struggles to keep alive the business that Levy cannot abide, and he becomes the victim of Reilly's dreams to "save" Levy Pants by prettying up the office while discarding office files.

Miss Trixie, senile bookkeeper at Levy Pants. She only wants to retire and receive the Easter ham long due her from Levy, but she is forced to stay on because of Mrs. Levy's misguided notion that work is good for her.

Mr. Clyde, owner of Paradise Vendors. In his desperation to find vendors for hotdogs and in his pity for Reilly, he outfits Reilly and sends him out into the Dantesque world of the French Quarter.

Randall M. Miller

A CONFEDERATE GENERAL FROM BIG SUR

Author: Richard Brautigan (1935-1984)
Type of work: Novel

Time of action: The 1960's
First published: 1964

Lee Mellon, an unemployed, twenty-three-year-old iconoclast who claims to be a descendant of a Confederate general. Assertive, apolitical, unreflective, and hedonistic, Lee is an existential rebel, a "rebel without a cause," who pursues independence and pleasure with the energetic determination of a military campaign. Amoral and self-centered, Lee manages to survive by panhandling, stealing, extorting, and generally taking advantage of the people he meets. As none of these techniques is very successful, Lee must often rely on his considerable ability to endure material deprivations. After spending a depressing year in an abandoned house in Oakland, a period in which his only triumph is tapping into the local utility's gas line, Lee travels to Big Sur, where he camps out in some ill-built shacks on borrowed land. There he lives from day to day, battling the frogs that keep him awake at night, courting Elizabeth, and contending with Johnston Wade's neurotic antics.

Jesse, the novel's narrator and the chronicler of Lee Mellon's exploits. After a disappointing love affair with a girl named Cynthia, Jesse leaves San Francisco and joins Lee at Big Sur. A sensitive and passive opposite to Lee Mellon, Jesse describes himself as an unemployed minister. In the absence of a spiritual calling or a firm basis for belief, he retreats into an absurdist minimalism—represented by his careful enumeration of the punctuation marks in Ecclesiastes—and a fatalistic acceptance of the world as he finds it. Jesse meets Elaine in a Monterey saloon, and she returns with him to Big Sur. Their affair eases Jesse's lingering sorrow over Cynthia, but it does nothing to fill his spiritual emptiness. His growing passivity and alienation threaten to develop into emotional paralysis as his sexual impotence suggests.

Elizabeth, a part-time prostitute and Lee Mellon's sometime companion at Big Sur. She is an idealized combination of whore and mother who works as a highly skilled and highly paid Los Angeles prostitute for three months out of the year, then returns to her modest house at Big Sur where she rears her childen as vegetarians and refuses to kill even the rattlesnakes.

Elaine, an intelligent and attractive young woman who meets Jesse in a Monterey saloon and becomes his lover. A product of a middle-class background, Elaine is an example of bourgeois alienation. Attracted to the unconventionality of Jesse and Lee, Elaine buys them supplies and drives them back to their Big Sur encampment. There she enjoys the rebellious pleasures of marijuana and sex.

Johnston Wade, a rich, unstable insurance executive whom Lee Mellon dubs "Roy Earle" after the Humphrey Bogart character in the film *High Sierra.* Wade arrives at the Big Sur encampment driving a new Bentley in hysterical flight from his upper-middle-class family. He carries a briefcase containing $100,000. An exaggerated vision of the destructive power of money, Wade spends a night chained to a log by Lee Mellon. By the next day he has regained his composure, if not his sanity, and he leaves to return to his business and family.

Carl Brucker

CONFEDERATES

Author: Thomas Keneally (1935-   )
Type of work: Novel
Time of action: 1862
First published: 1979

322

Usaph Bumpass, a Confederate soldier serving in the regiment of the Shenandoah Volunteers. Malnourished, bedraggled Usaph is a veteran of the war at age twenty-three. A poorly educated farmer, he is secretly envious of his two educated friends, Danny Blalock, a schoolmaster, and Gus Ramseur, a music teacher. Usaph constantly worries about the danger of his lovely wife feeling lonely on their farm and being unfaithful to him. When he receives a letter from her delivered by Decatur Cate, he is sure that Ephie and Cate are lovers.

Ephephtha Bumpass (Ephie), the beautiful wife of Usaph, raised in the swamps of the Carolinas. She is raped when young. She then becomes accustomed but not charmed by men's demands upon her. When Usaph brings her from the swamps to Virginia, she thinks that she has been saved. Then Usaph goes to war, and she is convinced that she is being punished for loving him too much. The worldly Decatur Cate represents refinement to Ephie. She is torn between running off to California with him and remaining faithful to Usaph.

Decatur Cate, a Union sympathizer conscripted into Bumpass' regiment. Gangling, hollow-cheeked, twenty-five years old, Cate is an introspective former portrait painter forced to join the army when Usaph's Aunt Sarrie has him arrested. While painting Ephie's portrait, Cate convinces her to become his lover and go to California. Aunt Sarrie intervenes, and Cate is sent to Usaph's regiment, where he delivers a letter from Ephie. Usaph immediately suspects the worst, and Cate becomes his nemesis.

Thomas "Stonewall" Jackson, a Confederate general and actual historical figure called "Stonewall" for not letting the Union get around his troops. A tall, lean, handsome West Point graduate, Jackson acts as if time were limited. All the other characters' fates are in the hands of the military maneuvers of "Stonewall" Jackson.

Lafcadio Wheat, the commanding colonel of the Shenandoah Volunteers. Tall, black-whiskered, thirty-three years old, Wheat is a former lawyer fond of inspiring his men with jokes and personal stories. Usaph becomes his runner and is with him when he dies.

Gus Ramseur, a Confederate soldier and Bumpass' best friend. A gentleman and a music scholar, golden-bearded Gus is the only man Usaph considers worth saving. Ramseur wants to write an overture of military music after the war.

Horace Searcy, an English war correspondent and Union spy. The daring Searcy is an abolitionist who detests the South. He has a secret commission from U.S. Secretary of War Edwin Stanton to gather intelligence. Because of his reputation as a world-renowned war journalist, Searcy has letters of introduction and safe passage from both the Union and the Confederacy. Searcy's identity is discovered after he relays some vital information to the North about the South's military strategy. He is given passage out of the country on a ship but, before leaving, tries to persuade Dora Whipple to marry him.

Dora Whipple, a Confederate widow who becomes Searcy's lover and accomplice. Mrs. Whipple was already a Union spy working in a military hospital in Richmond when she met Searcy. After becoming the matron at the military hospital in Orange, she sneaks to Searcy's room at night. An accomplice of hers is caught, and her name appears on a list of spies. She is tried but refuses to deny being a spy. Accepting her fate and wishing to join her late husband in death, she refuses Searcy's offer to become his wife and save herself by leaving with him for England.

Aunt Sarrie Muswell, Usaph's aunt who takes care of Ephie during the war. Aunt Sarrie hires Cate to paint Ephie's portrait, then realizes that Ephie is impressed by Cate's worldliness. She arranges for Cate to be conscripted into the military in spite of his limp. She then arranges for Ephie to visit an herbalist when Ephie becomes pregnant.

Danny Blalock, a schoolmaster and fellow Confederate soldier in Bumpass' regiment. Danny and Ash Judd are fond of leaving the regiment to find women. Danny dies a major at Gettysburg.

Ash Judd, a farmer and fellow Confederate

of Bumpass. Twenty years old, he looks up to Danny Blalock. Ash is superstitious and believes that a witch has put a spell on him that will protect him throughout the war. He drowns in his own blood at Washington County.

Sandra Willbanks

THE CONFESSION OF A FOOL

Author: August Strindberg (1849-1912)
Type of work: Novel
Time of action: The 1870's and the 1880's
First published: Die Beichte eines Toren, 1893; *Le Plaidoyer d'un fou*, 1895 (English translation, 1912; also as *A Madman's Defense*, 1967, and *A Madman's Manifesto*, 1971)

Axel, the narrator of the novel and its protagonist. At the book's outset, he is in his late twenties, and his narrative, an autobiographical account of his first marriage, follows him through his early forties. Axel is a librarian at the Royal Stockholm Library, as well as an aspiring, and eventually successful, playwright. A small but intense man, he is interested primarily in scientific and aesthetic pursuits. He also may suffer from acute paranoia, and thus his chronicle forces the reader to question whether the novel is an accurate presentation of the facts or the lunatic ravings of a man who is, or is going, insane. In any event, Axel's problems begin when he is introduced to the Baroness Marie, with whom he immediately becomes obsessed. At first he idealizes her, imagining her a chaste, Madonna-like figure, and he shuns the thought of any romantic inclinations toward her. As it becomes clear, however, that the Baroness is unhappy in her marriage to Baron Gustav—even so far as to condone the Baron's illicit affair with her young cousin, Matilda—Axel finds himself sexually attracted to her. Indeed, he becomes so infatuated with her that the thought of living without her drives him to attempt suicide. Fortunately, or perhaps unfortunately, the attempt fails, the Baroness's marriage collapses, and she and Axel become lovers and marry. Axel idealizes the beginning of

their marriage just as he initially idealized the Baroness herself. His romantic bliss is soon shattered, however, when he begins to suspect that Marie had ulterior motives for marrying him. She has ambitions of becoming an actress, and since Axel has already had some success as a playwright, he wonders if she has married him simply to further her career. Furthermore, he imagines that she may have married him for what little money he has, since the Baron, despite his noble title, is in fact broke. These suspicions lead Axel to believe that Marie does not love him and that, therefore, she must be unfaithful. He becomes jealous of anyone or anything to which she devotes her time, even her dog. Axel is able, for very brief intervals, to cast aside his suspicions and to picture Marie as a loving and devoted wife; when they reassert themselves, however, the Madonna once again becomes a whore. His doubts finally become so intense that he suspects Marie, conscious of his passionate love for her as well as his pathological jealousy, of trying to drive him mad by her constant flirtations. By the novel's conclusion, Axel's paranoia reaches such a crescendo that his marriage dissolves, and he resolves upon completion of his memoir to commit suicide.

Marie, a baroness, who leaves her husband to marry Axel. She is a petite, beautiful

324

woman in her early thirties, and, if Axel's early narrative is to be trusted, she has an angelic quality. She is unhappy with her marriage to Baron Gustav because he is both poor and unfaithful but especially because she wishes to pursue her consuming passion to be an actress. Her marriage to Axel allows her to pursue this career, which yet falters either because she cannot act or because Axel, afraid of losing her and resentful of her success, does not offer sufficient help. If Axel's narrative is to be trusted, and this is doubtful, she is an adultress, fickle to the extreme, a spendthrift, an unfit mother, and a bisexual. Moreover, he claims that she is intent on driving him insane with her flirtations. It appears that she really does care very little about motherhood and that she may have had one affair (among the hundreds of which she is accused), but given

Axel's state of mind, it is impossible to be certain.

Gustav, a baron, Marie's first husband. At thirty, he is disappointed with his life and seems intent on dissipating in drinking, gambling, and womanizing. A baron in title only, he has lost his fortune, his marriage to Marie maintained merely for the sake of appearance. He is having an affair with Matilda, Marie's eighteen-year-old cousin. Marie eventually divorces him and marries Axel.

Matilda, Marie's pretty but empty-headed young cousin. When Axel is first invited to the home of the Baron and Baroness, he supposes that Matilda is Marie's companion. He eventually learns, however, that Matilda is invited there to continue her affair with the Baron, who has lost interest in his wife.

Matthew K. Davis

CONFESSIONS OF A MASK

Author: Yukio Mishima (Kimitake Hiraoka, 1925-1970)
Type of work: Novel
Time of action: The 1920's to the late 1940's
First published: Kamen no kokuhaku, 1949 (English translation, 1958)

Kochan, a student. Born in 1925, Kochan is a sickly child who is subject to periodic bouts of illness. As a result, he is excluded from close personal relationships with boys of his age and grows up with little understanding of what normal boys are like. He is latently homosexual and aware of his attraction for other males at a very early age. Nevertheless, he makes attempts to be like those around him, even going so far as to convince himself that he is in love with Sonoko. It is only when her brother asks if he intends to marry her and after he fails to have any physical response to a prostiute that he finally accepts that he can never be like other men even though he must put on a public act that he is the same as everyone else.

Omi, a student. A young man in his early teens, he is several years older than the stu-

dents in his class and as a result is more physically developed than they are. The combination of his physical attractiveness and the fact that he is considered wicked and therefore a loner attracts Kochan and he falls in love with Omi. Omi is arrogantly superior to the students around him but not unkind to Kochan although he is aware of the passion Kochan feels for him. Omi is expelled from school during the summer break, however, and Kochan never sees him again.

Sonoko, a student. Younger than Kochan, she is the sister of one of his few friends, Kusano. She is a proper Japanese girl, unschooled in love and secluded from life, who slowly develops a deep feeling for Kochan, and he quickly convinces himself that he feels the same way about her. After she and her family leave Tokyo to avoid the air raids, he comes to visit and in his attempt to appear normal he goes so far as to kiss her. It is obviously the first time she has been kissed. When Kochan politely rejects the idea of marrying her, she marries another man. She and Kochan meet after her mar-riage, and they spend a year secretly meeting each other, though they do nothing more than talk. She is aware of the danger in their meeting, and her thoughts remain fixed on her husband.

C. D. Akerley

THE CONFESSIONS OF NAT TURNER

Author: William Styron (1925-   )
Type of work: Novel
Time of action: The early 1800's to November, 1831
First published: 1967

Nat Turner, the narrator and protagonist, a black slave and preacher who is just past thirty years old at the time of narration. Born a slave to the somewhat socially enlightened Turner family, the precocious Nat is educated by the Turners after they discover his attempt to read a book that he has stolen from the family's library. This and other benevolences during his youth raise Nat's expectations without altering the slave's prospects, thus creating a double bind from which Nat never escapes. After his dreams of the freedom promised him by the Turners do not materialize, Nat endures a series of degrading hardships at the hands of the various white people to whom he is sold. These experiences bond Nat with his own race, although he consistently expresses contempt for their subservient actions and mannerisms. The educated slave becomes a pariah—a lonely man who belongs neither to the blacks nor to the whites. Bolstered by the early assurances of his mother and by a later mystic vision that he has been preordained to accomplish great things, Nat becomes a preacher, a comforter of those—black and white—who suffer the oppression of the closed Southern society. His observations of and personal experiences with the slave system lead him to understand the depth of the blacks' hatred of the whites. Nat also intuits that despite the white man's power over the blacks, fear of the slaves pervades even the strongest bastions of the white community. This understanding of the dynamics of the society in which he lives coupled with his mystic vision of his role in life leads Nat to form an elaborate plan of "annihilation and escape" designed to free blacks from white domination. This plot results in a reign of terror—a slave rebellion that ends in the deaths of fifty-five whites and approximately two hundred blacks. The insurrection fails because Nat's "soldiers" are more intent on avenging themselves against the whites than on escaping their subservience. Nat evades the Virginia authorities for nearly two months, but eventually is captured, tried, and hanged for his crimes. Nat's confession reveals a highly complex character who attempts to live in both the black and white worlds and who undergoes a radical transformation from educated preacher to slave champion to murderer as a result of the irresolvable tension between those worlds.

T. R. Gray, the court-appointed lawyer who records Nat's confession, the preface of which is given at the beginning of the book. In attempting to understand Nat's motives, Gray asks the central question of the novel: How could the slave have been so cruel to those who were as kind to him as the system allowed? The attorney treats Nat in a condescending manner, especially when explaining the court system and expressing his opinion that Nat's fellow insurrectionists have made him the scapegoat for their own crimes. Nevertheless, Gray does demonstrate concern for Nat, bringing him a Bible, having his chains loosened, and requesting warm clothing for the prisoner. In admitting to Nat that his trial is a sham, Gray interprets society's final insult for Nat, that is, that other rebel slaves have been tried and released solely to protect the white man's rights of property. Gray thus becomes the chief spokesman for the society that confounds Nat Turner.

Mr. Trezevant, the Commonwealth's attorney who prosecutes Nat.

Judge Jeremiah Cobb, the man who passes the death sentence on Nat yet who demonstrates an understanding of the cruelty of slavery. Nat had come to respect the judge during their conversation before Nat's rebellion.

Lou Ann, Nat's mother, a slave in the Turner household who was reared in the Turner home and who in turn rears her son there. In her position as family cook, she enjoys a favored status accorded by both whites and blacks. She is convinced that her son is intended for greatness and encourages him in this notion. She dies when Nat is fifteen.

McBride, Turner's cruel overseer who rapes Lou Ann while young Nat watches.

Samuel Turner, the slave owner who rears Nat. A truly benevolent man, Turner plans to have Nat educated and freed once he is assured that the precocious slave could make his own way in the world. Turner is deeply troubled by the effects of slavery, such as the separation of families and the cruelty inflicted on adults and children alike. Financial troubles, however, prohibit Turner from carrying out his grand scheme of liberation for Nat. He entrusts his plans for Nat to others who fail to adhere to them. In this respect, he proves to be a very poor judge of character.

Nell Turner, the wife of Samuel. Mrs. Turner is impressed with Nat's intellect and teaches him to read, treating him almost as a pet in her home.

Louisa Turner, daughter of Samuel and Nell. Louisa befriends Nat and assists with his education.

Reverend Eppes, a Baptist preacher, second owner of Nat, who promised Samuel Turner to arrange for Nat's continued education and eventual emancipation. In reality, Eppes uses Nat as his sexual pawn and contributes much to Nat's growing hatred of whites.

Tom Moore, Nat's third master who has bought the young slave from Eppes.

Sara Moore, the wife of Tom and, after his death, the wife of Joseph Travis. Sara is kind to Nat, and although he is fond of her, she is the first victim of the rebellion.

Joseph Travis, Nat's last owner. The Travis family is destroyed in Nat's insurrection.

Willis, a slave of the Turner family and an early friend of Nat. The two boys experience together many of adolescence's rites of passage. Turner's selling of Willis and Nat's unwitting complicity in the business deal precipitate Nat's steadily increasing disillusionment with white people.

Hark, born **Hercules,** a later friend of Nat who participates in the rebellion. Hark's harsh treatment by the Travis family and their overseer poignantly establishes in the novel the cruelty of slavery.

Nelson,
Henry, and
Sam, slaves who with Hark form the inner circle of Nat's strike force in planning and executing the rebellion.

Isan, a rebellious slave whose anger and rage, along with the effects these emotions have on Tom Moore, plant the idea of an uprising in Nat's mind.

Ethelred T. Brantley, a fifty-year-old white former plantation overseer in trouble with the law. Brantley hears Nat preach and, since he has been rejected by the white Christian community, turns to the black preacher for salvation. Nat baptizes himself and Brantley in front of his own followers plus a crowd of forty to fifty whites who pelt the two with rocks. This episode further solidifies plans for rebellion against white oppression.

Margaret Whitehead, the young white girl who befriends Nat. Margaret, with her fine education and profound unawareness of the true plight of Nat and his people, epitomizes the gap between blacks and whites. She is the one person who could have kept Nat from fulfilling his "mission." Yet he kills her when the rebellion breaks out in order to maintain his leadership of the rebel slaves. Margaret regards Nat as asexual, but his feelings for her are clearly human and physical. She, more than any other character, represents promised but unfulfilled dreams.

Lagretta T. Lenker

CONFESSIONS OF ZENO

Author: Italo Svevo (Ettore Schmitz, 1861-1928)
Type of work: Novel
Time of action: The 1880's to 1916
First published: La coscienza di Zeno, 1923 (English translation, 1930)

Zeno Cosini, an Italian businessman in Trieste (then part of Austria). The book is supposed to be a narrative Zeno prepared for his psychoanalyst (Dr. S.). Zeno first discusses his attempts to stop smoking, in which he displays his usual pattern of taking a "health-giving bath of good resolutions" that are never carried out. The same irresolution appears in the two most important aspects of Zeno's life: sex and business. He wins his plain but affectionate wife after proposing in vain to two of her sisters (a third has pronounced him quite mad). Though he comes to love his wife, all of his baths of good intentions cannot keep him from taking a mistress, Carla, a music student. He is generally content to leave his family business in the hands of the manager, Olivi. Even when he joins his brother-in-law, Guido Speier, in a separate venture, he mostly watches passively, until Guido dies, leaving his affairs in a disastrous state; then Zeno steps in and by some lucky speculations recovers part of the losses. When war between Italy and Austria separates him from his family and Olivi, he again asserts himself and proves adept at profiting from wartime shortages. The references to psychoanalysis in the novel invite a Freudian interpretation of Zeno, which is supported by Zeno's extreme hypochondria and his troubled memories of his father. Zeno himself likes to analyze life in terms of health and disease, especially Basedow's disease. The name "Zeno" recalls two Greek philosophers, the one a paradoxical skeptic, the other a stoic.

Giovanni Malfenti, a successful businessman with four daughters. Zeno takes him as a role model and resolves to marry one of the daughters, whom he has never seen.

Ada Malfenti Speier, the eldest and most beautiful daughter, who wisely rejects Zeno and unwisely accepts Guido Speier. She loses her beauty through Basedow's (Graves'?) disease, a form of goiter. After Guido's death, she goes to live with his relatives in Argentina.

Augusta Malfenti Cosini, Zeno's wife. Though not beautiful, she is patient and understanding.

Alberta Malfenti, an intellectual whom Zeno courts briefly.

Anna Malfenti, the youngest sister, who believes Zeno completely mad.

Guido Speier, a young man set up in busi-

328

ness by his father in Trieste. Initially, he makes a good impression, especially in contrast with Zeno; he is handsome and plausible and plays the violin very well, while Zeno plays it very badly. He wins Ada where Zeno failed. It is after they go into business together that he reveals depths of incompetence that are far beyond anything Zeno would undertake; it is Zeno who tries to protect Guido's father's interests and who manages to save some of Guido's estate for Ada. It is Guido's final folly to feign suicide twice to get money from Ada; the second time, he

miscalculates and succeeds in killing himself.

Olivi, the manager who conducts the Cosini business with the prudence and industry that Zeno lacks but without Zeno's "inspirations."

Carla, a music student. Zeno is first her patron and somewhat incompetent adviser, afterward her lover. Carla deserts him to marry her teacher.

John C. Sherwood

THE CONFORMIST

Author: Alberto Moravia (1907-   )
Type of work: Novel
Time of action: 1920-1945
First published: Il conformista, 1951 (English translation, 1952)

Marcello Clerici (klĕr·ē′·chē), the protagonist, a man dominated by psychological tendencies that are reflected in the title of the novel. Since childhood, Clerici has desired to be recognized as being normal. As a young boy, he had several haunting experiences of guilt (the presumed consequence of social abnormality), which follow him into adulthood. One involved pleasure in killing small animals, and then trying to convince himself, through others, that his actions were not abnormal. A second event was his traumatic violent experience with a homosexual stranger. When Marcello receives a special assignment to aid in the assassination of his former professor, a Paris-exiled critic of the Fascist regime, he initially assumes he can maintain a separation between his "normal" life and the brutal world of Fascist politics. This attempt at psychological compartmentalization fails when Clerici decides to combine his honeymoon with the espionage assignment to Paris. Clerici's thwarted search to achieve normalcy carries through after his return to middle-class existence in Italy during the war. While he seems to have overcome the trauma of Lina's death, his discovery that Lino did not die from the gun

wounds he inflicted on him as a youth rekindles the nightmare of the futility of his actions: He had carried feelings of guilt and suffered psychologically for years for something that did not happen.

Lino, a homosexual chauffeur who attempted to lure the young Clerici by promising to give him a real revolver—something Marcello sought to establish his credibility among friends and enemies alike. Lino's treachery leads Marcello to seize the gun and shoot his amorous and confused assailant. Lino's pitiful state is reflected in his invitation to the youth to kill him if he cannot possess Marcello.

Lina, the young and voluptuous French wife of the aging Professor Quadri whose body is described as strong but lithe, like that of a gymnast or dancer. When the newly wed Clericis arrive unannounced at Quadri's Paris residence, Lina remains aloof, if not openly hostile. Like her husband, Lina knows that Clerici's supposedly friendly visit to his former professor is a cover for a Fascist espionage mission. While the professor appears sincere in his desire to win over

Clerici from Fascism, Lina's interest in their Italian visitors is dominated by a lesbian attraction for Giulia.

Orlando, the least-developed character in Moravia's novel. A Fascist secret police agent who has served in many countries, he is assigned with Clerici to carry out the assassination of Professor Quadri. Marcello's view of Orlando is somewhat condescending: Marcello characterizes his face as that of a petty bureaucrat, tenant farmer, or, at most, a small landowner. Orlando's carnal baseness is demonstrated as, once Orlando is assured that the "official" contacts and formal instructions for the espionage mission have been taken care of, he indulges his lust immediately with one of the prostitutes.

Professor Quadri (kwä'drē), a man who is considered a traitor because of his abandonment of the Fascist cause. The formerly eccentric and bookish professor is portrayed as having adjusted quite well to his orderly and visibly comfortable life in exile. Although Quadri is engaged in an international network for anti-Fascist propaganda, his character emerges mainly in personal interaction with his young but sexually imbalanced wife, Lina, and with Marcello, who is the only person with whom he carries on a sustained dialogue. Quadri seems not to condemn Clerici for the political choice he has made. He focuses his efforts on trying to dissuade him from his Fascist beliefs. He apparently does not even suspect that Marcello is torn between his duty to carry out Rome's assassination orders and the temptation to abandon his mission to pursue what he perceives (erroneously) to be Lina's amorous attachment to him.

Giula, the twenty-year-old daughter of a deceased government official who is heir to the "twin divinities of respectability and normality." Although these characteristics are things sought by her fiancé, Marcello, her strong devotion to Catholicism is difficult for him to accept. She is largely unimaginative but possesses a sensual vivacity that clearly attracts masculine attentions. Before meeting Marcello, she suffered the humiliation of having love forced upon her by an older married man. Once married, and despite the circumstances of their honeymoon, Giulia tries to impress Marcello with the enthusiasm of her love. Yet, it is her predictable normalcy that attracts Marcello most. When Giulia finds herself to be the object of Lina's lesbian desires, she is very uncomfortable. It is her (normal) unwillingness to respond to Lina's overtures—despite Marcello's attempts to use this very situation as a way to get Lina away from the assassination target and, supposedly, into a liaison with him—that makes Lina decide to travel from Paris with Quadri, with whom she meets her senseless death.

Byron D. Cannon

THE CONNECTION

Author: Jack Gelber (1932-   )
Type of work: Play
Time of action: The late 1950's
First produced: 1959

Cowboy, a sensible, practical, calm, honest heroin dealer. In the second act of the play, he arrives in Leach's New York apartment, where the other characters have been waiting for him impatiently. He gives them heroin injections in Leach's bathroom while the unsuspecting Sister Salvation is looking around the apartment. Cowboy is weary of the dangers of dealing heroin. When Leach takes an overdose, Cowboy saves his life, but he refuses to be considered the play's hero.

Leach, a clearly discontented heroin addict and the occupant of the apartment in which the play takes place. Trying to dominate the other characters, he gets into an argument with Ernie, who refuses to abide by Leach's rules and who accidentally breaks the boil on Leach's neck. He pays for heroin to be given to the play's author and to the two photographers hired to film the play so that they can lose their conventionality. Feeling cheated by Cowboy when he does not get high on the heroin, he overdoses on stage but will probably survive.

Solly, an educated, conciliatory heroin addict. He is the mouthpiece for the play's philosophy and comments on the antisocial attitude of the twentieth century, on the fascination with warfare in the twentieth century, and on waiting, the heroin addicts' main occupation, which often leads to suicide. He and Leach involve the play's author and its producer as well as the two photographers in the action. Solly is a good storyteller and argues that addiction to heroin is no worse than more conventional addictions to money or clothes.

Ernie, a dissatisfied heroin addict and musician. He is not trusted by any of the other characters because of rumors that he may have killed another addict. Although he announces that he has been hired to play his trumpet, he will not be able to take the job because he had to trade in his instrument at a pawnshop. All he has left is the useless mouthpiece he blows time and again while insulting other characters and the audience. When Leach overdoses, Ernie leaves out of fear.

Sam, an uneducated, good-natured, lethargic heroin addict. Sam dozes on stage during much of the performance and complains that Leach does not let him sleep. He tells long stories and takes Solly as his mentor, whom he asks many questions, for example, why heroin is illegal.

Sister Salvation, an unsuspecting, lonely Salvation Army sister, whom Cowboy brings along to Leach's apartment in order to evade the police. She seems not to notice that Cowboy is giving the other characters heroin, suspecting only that the men have been drinking alcohol in the bathroom. When Solly asks her to leave as long as they are getting along well, she is reluctant to go because she fears loneliness and her approaching death.

Jim Dunn, the seemingly superior producer of the play within the play for which he hired the other characters and musicians. Dressed in a suit, he introduces the players and the play's theme of narcotics, announces the intermission, and expresses his discontent with the performance. He is unable to keep out of the play within the play and interacts with the players he has hired. He tries to control the performances and to execute his sensationalist views of what drama should do.

Jaybird, the author of the play within the play whose staging he, Jim Dunn, two photographers, and the audience watch. He has lived with heroin addicts for several months in order to write an outline for an experimental play on narcotics. This experience and the performance of his play transform him from a "square" into a more open-minded person who also tries heroin. He cannot be an experimental playwright wholeheartedly, however, since he wants to remain in control of his play. He also considers heroism the basis of Western drama, although the play as a whole denies the possibility of heroism.

Josef Raab

THE CONSERVATIONIST

Author: Nadine Gordimer (1923-   )
Type of work: Novel

Time of action: The 1960's
First published: 1974

Mehring, the protagonist, a wealthy South African industrialist and amateur farmer. A large, middle-aged man with graying sideburns, Mehring is attractive to women and a popular addition to dinner parties. He is a frequent international traveler and knows much about base metals but nothing about art, music, or poetry. He has no close relationships in his life: His wife left him eight years ago; his son and he have nothing to say to each other; his mistress has left South Africa; the black laborers on the farm largely ignore him; he has many acquaintances but no real friends. What he does have is a 400-acre farm, which he bought intending to use it for rendezvous with his mistress, who visited the farm only once. Mehring attempts to control his land, to keep it organized and perfect, in the face of unconquerable natural and political forces.

Antonia Mancebo, Mehring's mistress. In her thirties, she has an olive complexion and straight dark hair with only one or two strands of gray, which she does not bother to pluck. She does not, Mehring says, have a beautiful body. Antonia is married to a professor who is often away, but she has close ties to her friends, who include blacks and revolutionaries. She frequently marches in antiapartheid demonstrations and has close brushes with the law. Antonia taunts Mehring for his conservative beliefs, his power, and his money. She cannot understand why he does not leave the farm as it is rather than trying to shape it in his image. Finally, she leaves South Africa rather than condone its policies.

Terry, Mehring's son. Sixteen years old, tall and thin with long blond hair, Terry attends a boarding school, where he experiments with leftist politics and homosexuality. He wears tattered jeans and no shoes and gives his spare clothes away to the blacks on the farm. Mehring has had custody of Terry since the divorce, but as Terry gets older he shows less and less interest in his father, the farm, or the wealth he stands to inherit. During his last school vacation, Terry hitchhikes to Namibia instead of coming home to be with his father. Rather than face conscription into an army whose politics he cannot support, Terry wants to live with his mother in New York.

Jacobus, the black chief herdsman on Mehring's farm. Jacobus is middle-aged or perhaps older, with long and callused hands and blackened teeth. He has been on the farm since before Mehring bought it, and he will be there after Mehring has gone. He has learned how to deal with the white owners who come and go. When Mehring is around, Jacobus calls him "Master," and speaks briefly and haltingly. When Mehring is not on the farm, however, Jacobus speaks expansively and articulately, comes and goes as he pleases on Mehring's tractor, and has the run of the farmhouse. By playing Mehring carefully, Jacobus is always able to get what he wants.

Bismillah, an Indian shopkeeper living on a compound near the farm. The middle-aged Bismillah talks very little, except to his family and Jacobus. He is constantly aware of the threats posed by white bureaucrats, whom he bribes to be allowed to keep his business, and blacks, whom he keeps out with a high, barbed-wire fence and guard dogs. He runs his shop under the supervision of his father and has been successful enough to send his son to be educated. Three generations live in his home, and several blacks live and work in the compound. Bismillah's existence depends on his ability to remain inoffensive to the various groups struggling in South Africa, and he is able to speak Hindi, English, Afrikaans, mine pidgin, and farm pidgin.

Cynthia A. Bily

THE CONTRACTOR

Author: David Storey (1933-   )
Type of work: Play
Time of action: The 1960's
First produced: 1969

Ewbank, the "contractor," a self-made owner of a tent-erecting business who featured as a minor character in Storey's 1963 novel *Radcliffe*. A hardworking, bustling Northerner, very much the boss, with a sharp tongue and a fondness for his tipple, affectionate with his wife and daughter (who is marrying "above" the family), and rather lost with his son, Ewbank (and the play) is really more at home with sleeves rolled up among his all-male "family" of workmen, whose language he speaks. The high point of the celebrations (the wedding takes place offstage) comes when he shares cake and a toast with the men. Glendenning, certainly, he treats like a son, buying him chocolate when he cries. He is himself providing the marquee (the erection and the dismantling of which constitutes the action of the play) for his daughter's wedding reception, at his house. His separate worlds of home and work thus come into collision, bringing him to reflect briefly on the ephemeral, or "nomadic," quality of his life as an erector of tents.

Paul, Ewbank's university-educated son. Well-intentioned and kindly but restless and overly thoughtful, with little sense of self-worth and less of direction (which gives him the appearance of an ineffectual lounger), Paul is Storey's surrogate in the play: a young man out of tune with his family because he has been educated out of his class. In this play, in which work is the focus of dramatic attention and the index of value, it is inevitable that he should find a brief sense of belonging by joining in the erecting of the tent. He refuses his father's offer of handing on the business to him, and decides to leave, destination unknown, at the end of the play.

Kay, Ewbank's foreman, a taciturn, efficient former convict. Kay can be needled for a long time before he finally loses his temper, which he does with Fitzpatrick. The play as a whole focuses not on individual characters (though they are sharply individualized) but on the work and on the dynamics of the group relationships it brings about: Kay quietly orchestrates this work.

Fitzpatrick, an Irish workman. An inveterate scrounger, work-shy, and the most loud-mouthed of Ewbank's five-man gang of misfits, Fitzpatrick forms a "double act" with another Irish workman, Marshall, playing games with words in the working-class music hall tradition of nonstop patter and the "turn." His humor is aggressive, provoking one confrontation with Bennett (rapidly defused) and another with Kay, who sacks him (Ewbank reinstates him).

Bennett, a rather colorless workman. Bennett harbors a grudge against Kay, who he thinks picks on him, and so reveals to the others the fact that Kay has done a "stretch" in prison. In act 3, when the tent is dismantled, it is revealed that his wife has left him.

Glendenning, a mentally retarded workman. Shy and affectionate, with a stammer, quick to tears, Glendenning works honestly and hard while enduring needling from his crude fellow workers.

Old Ewbank, Ewbank's long-retired and senile father, once a ropemaker. Old Ewbank wanders on and off clutching a short (and useless) piece of rope, with old Mrs. Ewbank in tow, like his keeper. As decrepit spokesman for the Northern work ethic and the value of craftsmanship, he unintentionally parodies what he preaches.

Joss Lutz Marsh

CONVERSATION IN THE CATHEDRAL

Author: Mario Vargas Llosa (1936-   )
Type of work: Novel
Time of action: The late 1940's and early 1950's
First published: Conversación en la catedral, 1969 (English translation, 1975)

Santiago Zavala (sän•tya'gō sä•vä'lä), also known as **"Skinny"** and **"Superbrain,"** progressively transformed from the favorite son to an aspiring Communist and finally to a columnist in a dead-end newspaper job. He is the novel's protagonist, and much of the narrative is rendered in his voice and from his perspective. He is a disillusioned intellectual and self-disinherited son of the bourgeoisie, who is determined to forge an authentic existence. When he is unable to break with his past, however, he slowly sinks into despair and cyncisim. His preoccupation throughout the novel is with how both the nation and the individual have been betrayed by the same degrading and corrupt political forces.

Ambrosio Pardo (äm•brō'syō pär'dō), a *zambo* (part black and part Indian), first a chauffeur for Santiago's father, then a worker at a dog pound. His particular mixture of blood carries an implicit tension that is externalized in the novel. He is both an innocent victim of Peru's social order and a victimizer who adapts to a corrupt system in order to survive. Ambrosio's inability to break the social, political, and economic bonds that shackle him illustrate one of the novel's major themes: how society, especially a politically corrupt society, can succeed in shaping and determining its members in perverse and inhuman ways.

Trinidad Lopez, a textile worker and political fanatic. While he appears to be an activist who is aware of the political reality of his time, the narrative raises serious doubts concerning the validity of his assertions. Constantly in and out of jail, Trinidad's activities with his comrade Pedro Flores lead to his final arrest and death. Never really understanding the deeper implications of the *aprista* movement for which he fights, he is nev-

ertheless beaten, tortured, and finally killed for his revolutionary activities. His death, therefore, becomes completely meaningless.

Amalia Cerda (sĕr'dä), a servant, later the wife of Trinidad Lopez, then of Ambrosio. Although politically naïve, she is curious about the activities of Trinidad. Both she and Trinidad are portrayed as victims of the political process; they are both individuals who do not understand the functions of their institutions, yet nevertheless, whose lives are determined by those very institutions.

Don Fermín Zavala, Santiago's father, a wealthy Peruvian industrialist. He has strong ties with the Odría regime and is deeply involved in deals with the government strongman, Cayo Bermúdez. His are the middle-class values against which his son revolts. He is involved in a homosexual relationship with Ambrosio.

Don Cayo Bermúdez (kä'yō bĕr•mōō'dĕs), Minister of Security and right-hand man of Peru's dictator, General Manuel Odría. He represents evil in its most sordid aspects, since he takes charge of the regime's dirty work and permits those who are allied with the dictatorship to acquire a certain respectability. His character is without guilt or conscience. He functions both as the chief instrument of corruption and as one of its victims.

Hortensia (ōr̄•tĕn'sē•ä), a wealthy prostitute and the mistress of Cayo Bermúdez. She and Queta, another prostitute, engage in homosexual relations for the voyeuristic purposes of Cayo Bermúdez. She is murdered by Ambrosio in order to protect Don Fermín from the possibility of blackmail. She intended to blackmail Don Fermín because of his homosexual relationship with Ambrosio.

This act of murder becomes a turning point in the novel because it forever dooms Ambrosio to his marginal social status and forces a confrontation between Santiago and his father.

Genevieve Slomski

COONARDOO
The Well in the Shadow

Author: Katharine Susannah Prichard (1884-1969)
Type of work: Novel
Time of action: The late nineteenth century to the 1920's
First published: 1929

Coonardoo, an aboriginal housemaid at Wytaliba station (homestead) in the north of Western Australia. She has dull golden hair, a thin, reedy voice, pretty hands and feet, and firm, pointed breasts. She is long-legged and wiry and is "as spirited as an unbroken filly": a minx. A year older than Hugh Watt, she is devoted to him and exhibits a devouring love for him. Intelligent and authoritative in the uloo (aboriginal camp), she is patient and gracefully submissive in the homestead. She generously gives herself to Hugh when directed to do so by her husband but has the air of a faithful, deserted animal when he later shuns her and abuses her. She is "of more than usual intelligence" and is the nexus between the white and black characters.

Bessie Watt, a former schoolteacher who (for unfathomed reasons) married Ted Watt, a good-looking, good-natured, feckless, and illiterate drunk who owned the million-acre station Wytaliba and died just after Hugh's birth. The aborigines call her Mumae (father); she understands their culture and is insightful, shrewd, and unsentimental, yet kind and practical. She is a manly, small woman with eyes "hard and blue as winter skies"; she is frugal and manages to pay off a large mortgage: "She had her head screwed on the right way." Though frumpy and indefatigable, she sees the value of education and sends Hugh to Perth for an education. She sees the unsuitability of Jessica as a station wife and forbids Coonardoo's marriage as a child. She is truly "a great little woman," an admirable, hardworking outback person.

Hugh Watt, Bessie's son, who succeeds her as owner of Wytaliba. As a child, he is "a boy with a swag of ideals"; he has a sharp and scratchy voice, is blue-eyed and very assured and bossy, and plays with Coonardoo, learning her tribal lore. He has his mother's work ethic and fortitude, but he lacks her insight and flexibility. Restrained and reserved, he reads the *Iliad* and values honor and courtesy. Though he has habits of independence and solitude and has occasional fits of anger and dejection, he is generally high-minded, kindly, courteous, and gentle. He marries in a purely practical manner and does not understand the roots of loneliness in his family and himself. He is tormented by his having had sex with Coonardoo, yet he truly loves their son, Winni. He is jealous of Sam Geary's lifestyle and success and is tormented by his abuse of Coonardoo. In most ways, he is "a good, ordinary little man."

Jessica Haywood, Hugh's fiancée, who visits Wytaliba when he returns from Perth at age twenty. She is a very pretty, delicate, and blossomy creature who plays the piano. She is upset by unshaven men, aborigines, and the isolation of the bush; she returns, disillusioned, to the city.

Mollie Watt, Hugh's wife and formerly a maid-of-all-work in her aunt's boardinghouse in Geraldton. She enters marriage not for romance but in expectation of social advancement; she has five daughters in five years. She is a small woman with straight dark hair; her face is round, plump, and good-natured. She is a good cook and household manager but has a rasping nature and cannot get along with aborigines—especially when she concludes that Hugh and Coonardoo are the parents of Winni. Though she is accurately described as "sonsy" on her arrival at Wytaliba and gives evidence of being a commonsense person, she has "all the obstinacy of a small mind." To her credit, she lasts ten years in the bush, but her extravagant social life in Perth (and the consequent financial drain on Hugh) results in the bank's foreclosure and the loss of Wytaliba to Sam Geary. Hugh's early praise for her ("You're a brick") is a premature evaluation that he later regrets.

Warieda, the principal stockman and horse-breaker on Wytaliba, where he is the imperious leader of the aborigines. A proud upholder of traditional ways, he "lends" his wife Coonardoo to Hugh when Hugh is grieving over Bessie's death. Warieda is tall and handsome, arresting and magnetic; his wild, bright eyes are challenging; his dark, sinewy arms are like tree branches. Though reared under the aegis of the Watts, he succumbs to the traditional "pointing the bone" by a tribal magician and wanders off and dies.

Sam Geary, the unprincipled, opportunistic, and sensual whiskey-loving owner of a neighboring cattle-and-sheep station. He is brash and brutish and has a jaunty bearing that goes with his feeling that he is always master of the situation and the business superior of Hugh. He is bowlegged, sun-scorched, bullock-shouldered, and slouched; his eyes are bulbous and pale blue; he has straight, fair eyelashes, and tufts of hair protrude from his nostrils. He has a number of aboriginal gins (women) as consorts, though Sheba is his primary one; he teases Hugh for not taking black women for his pleasure and for working so hard. Eventually, he becomes owner of Wytaliba.

Phyllis, the oldest daughter of Hugh and Mollie Watt, who leaves for the coast at age nine and returns a decade later, tired of city social life and determined to carry on the tradition of her grandmother, Bessie, as wife of an optimistic stockman, Bill Gale.

Marian B. McLeod

THE CORN IS GREEN

Author: Emlyn Williams (1905-1987)
Type of work: Play
Time of action: The late 1800's
First produced: 1938

Miss Lily Christabel Moffat, founder of a school for miners' children in Wales. A middle-aged English spinster, Miss Moffat is characterized by her direct, honest, and friendly manner. She is well-educated, well-read, intelligent, and tireless. Her unsentimental businesslike approach to life makes her an anathema to the local squire, who, along with the other locals, opposes her idea of educating the illiterate children of the village. Miss Moffat wins over the community through her sincere concern and energetic devotion to the students, even manipulating the Squire into supporting her efforts to win a scholarship to Oxford for Morgan Evans.

Morgan Evans, a young coal miner. Fifteen at the beginning of the play, Evans is the quick, impudent ringleader of the young miners who come to Miss Moffat's school. He proves himself an extraordinarily gifted student and becomes the focus of Miss Moffat's obsession with bettering the lot of the village children. His strong spirit rebels against Miss Moffat's strict control and his career is almost ruined by a brief liaison with Bessie Watty.

Miss Ronberry, a Welsh gentlewoman of no particular occupation. Entrapped by her own ideas of the proper role of a woman, at thirty, Miss Ronberry is fast becoming a sharp-looking old maid, still seeking a husband from among the suitable male gentry. Her genteel observance of class distinctions as signaled by speaking English instead of Welsh, her sentimental view of life, and her traditional attitudes about women make her of the Squire's camp, yet she is so overwhelmed by the strong will of Miss Moffat that she cannot refuse to become involved in teaching the children.

John Goronwy Jones, a churchgoing village handyman. Even though he claims to be saved by his religion, Mr. Jones remains gloomy, intense, and discontent. Born the son of a grocer, Mr. Jones has been educated at the local grammar school but still cannot surmount class distinctions, so that he belongs neither to the gentry nor to the working class. Even though he resents English domination of Wales and retains his native language, he responds eagerly to Miss Moffat's idea of a school and teaches the younger children.

The Squire, an Englishman and the most prominent citizen of the village. A handsome gentleman of forty, the Squire enjoys his social superiority and power over the lower classes (miners and women). He is deeply offended by Miss Moffat's ideas and manner and uses his influence to thwart Miss Moffat's school. In spite of his vanity and stubbornness, however, he is kind and generous. Miss Moffat cleverly appeals to his pride and wins his support.

Mrs. Watty, Miss Moffat's housekeeper. A middle-aged Cockney woman with an illegitimate daughter and a questionable past. Mrs. Watty bustles about taking care of Miss Moffat with efficiency and kindness. She is an enthusiastic convert to The Militant Righteous Corps.

Bessie Watty, the fourteen-year-old illegitimate daughter of Mrs. Watty. Plump and pretty, Bessie aspires to be ladylike, without success. She loathes the country school life she is forced to lead and longs for her former tawdry London life. She seduces Morgan Evans, becomes pregnant, and is bought off by Miss Moffat.

Jean McConnell

CORONATION

Author: José Donoso (1924-   )
Type of work: Novel
Time of action: The 1950's
First published: Coronación, 1957 (English translation, 1965)

Andrés Abalos, the middle-aged neurotic heir of a proud Chilean family now in decline. Rich, and free of any strong familial ties or occupational obligations, he devotes himself to the reading of French history, his collection of walking sticks, and the avoidance of any type of emotional entanglement or commitment. His complacency changes to panic, however, when he realizes that, after his grandmother's death, he will be left entirely alone without any links to the past and no promise for the future. This psychological crisis is further triggered by his growing obsession with the servant girl Estela, whom he sees as a symbol of youth and hope. His final humiliation at her hands leads him to accept madness as the only escape from a sordid, meaningless world.

Misiá Elisa Grey de Abalos (mē·sē·ä′), Andrés' regal nonagenarian grandmother. Once known for her beauty and modesty, she now poisons the atmosphere of her household with the obscene delusions of her madness. Her sexual taunts and accusations insidiously compel Andrés to admit his attraction for Estela.

Estela, a young peasant girl who is taken from her family to be the companion and nursemaid to Misiá Elisa. At first, submissive and uncomplaining, Estela seems overwhelmed by the big city of Santiago, until she meets and falls in love with Mario. She lies and steals for him to prove her love and, finally, must choose between blind devotion and self-respect. She is desired by Andrés and Mario; their passion for her forces both men to reevaluate the direction of their lives.

Mario, Estela's lover. Young, handsome, and carefree, Mario is known for his dalliance with many women, but the innocence and adoration of Estela quickly break down his defenses. The promise of his life is only darkened by the haunting fear that he will be unable to overcome the cycle of poverty and will be drawn into the criminality and despair of his brother René's world. This fear becomes reality when, trapped by circumstances seemingly beyond his control, he accepts the inevitable and throws in his hat with René. He agrees to the plot to rob the Abalos mansion even though it means Estela's betrayal and humiliation.

René, Mario's manipulative half brother. Always looking for the main chance and blaming everyone else for his failures, his life is a series of scams and petty frauds. He yearns to escape from a wife and family he despises in order to enjoy himself, free from all responsibility. Jealous of his brother, he deliberately tries to ruin Mario's future prospects and sets out to turn him against Estela.

Dora, René's pitiful wife, beaten down by the harshness of her life and the ridicule of René. The pathetic love she still retains for her husband is her only hope.

Carlos, Andrés' friend and confidant. A doctor, he has sacrificed his ideals for money and reputation. His self-satisfied comparison between his full life and the vacuum of his friend's precipitates Andrés' psychological trauma.

Adriana, Carlos' wife. Disillusioned by her husband's constant infidelity, she has converted herself into the perfect wife and mother. This façade is her protection against any emotional participation.

Lourdes, Estela's aunt and longtime servant to the Abalos family. Aging, without any life outside the mansion, she, along with Rosario, lives in the past and devotes herself to the care of her mistress, whom she considers a saint.

Rosario, longtime cook to the Abalos family. Her life also revolves around the gratification of any whim of Misiá Elisa and Misiá Elisa's grandson, Andrés, whom the servants still treat as a child.

Charlene E. Suscavage

CORRECTION

Author: Thomas Bernhard (1931-1989)
Type of work: Novel
Time of action: The early 1970's
First published: Korrektur, 1975 (English translation, 1979)

The narrator, a sickly individual who is obsessed with reconstructing his friend Roithammer's unfinished treatise. He is a middle-aged, highly intellectual, and introspective individual plagued by chronic lung infections. The narrator becomes so involved with his late friend's life that he moves into his former apartment and seems to reach a similar point of suicidal despair.

Roithammer, the narrator's friend who has committed suicide. Roithammer was a brilliant intellectual and scholar whose wide-ranging interests included philosophy, mathematics, architecture, and modern music. For a time he had been a promising student and tutor at the University of Cambridge. He returned, however, to his family estate of Altensam but was stifled by the petty and provincial atmosphere of the surrounding community. This sensitive and highly introspective man was considered an eccentric by the local people. When Roithammer received the inheritance of his father, he planned to design and construct a special round-shaped building for his beloved sister. She, however, died soon after its completion. Roithammer then spent a short time in England and then returned to Altensam in order to write a treatise on his childhood and life in Altensam. He moved into a small attic apartment and worked on ever more succinct versions of his work. Unable to finish his treatise, he becomes increasingly depressed and commits suicide.

Höller, a taxidermist from whom Roithammer rents an attic apartment. He later rents it to the narrator and tells him about his friend's last weeks of life.

Thomas F. Barry

CORREGIDORA

Author: Gayl Jones (1949-   )
Type of work: Novel
Time of action: 1947-1969
First published: 1975

Ursa Corregidora, the narrator, a twenty-five-year-old blues singer at Happy's Cafe in a small town in central Kentucky. She is a beautiful, light-skinned black. Ursa must undergo a hysterectomy as a result of injury when her drunken husband pushes her down some steps; she is pregnant at the time. Her consequent inability to bear children ineffably traumatizes her: It makes her feel less of a woman and also contributes to her sense of guilt that she is somehow failing the generations of women who were her ancestors, because the women in her family have always been told to "make generations" to bear witness to their former slavery under Corregidora, a Brazilian plantation master. Her despair at being the last of the line prolongs her recovery, and she apathetically allows herself to be taken care of by Tadpole, her boss at Happy's, whom she soon marries. Her indifference to him is exemplified in her inability to show love for him; later, she admits a resentment toward all men. Her deep-seated pain finds expression in her singing voice, now richer with the exquisite anguish she has experienced. When Tadpole reacts with the same jealousy as her first husband, Ursa leaves him to sing in another club, the Spider, where she is protected from the advances of men not only by a bodyguard but also by her now instinctive aversion to them. Twenty-two years later, still nursing a reserve of hatred toward him mixed with resignation, she reunites with her first husband.

Mutt Thomas, Ursa's first husband, for whom she feels a strong sexual attraction. He becomes increasingly hostile toward her as a result of jealousy: He wants her to sing only for him. In private, he uses sex as a weapon to punish her; in public, he threatens and embarrasses her. He feels guilty about the consequences of his violence and wants to make amends, waiting abjectly night after night outside the café because he has been forbidden entrance, but Ursa refuses to see him. He disappears for more than twenty years, showing up again at the Spider to take Ursa home.

Tadpole McCormick, the owner of Happy's Cafe, who becomes Ursa's second husband. He is initially patient and loving to Ursa, solicitous of her physical and mental health, and at first her reticence in expressing affection does not bother him. He eventually runs out of patience at the lack of real intimacy in their relationship and turns for solace to a new teenage singer he has hired for the bar. Finally, he and Ursa are divorced.

Mama, Ursa's mother. An independent, closemouthed woman, she has tried to discourage the young Ursa from singing the blues, calling it the devil's music. She relates much of the Corregidora background of lust, brutality, sadism, and incest, and she finally

confides to the adult Ursa the sad story of her own tragic marriage.

Catherine (Cat) Lawson, a fortyish, attractive, wordly-wise hairdresser and former maid who lives across the street from Happy's. She mothers Ursa and gives her perceptive advice. When Ursa discovers Cat's lesbianism, she retreats from their friendship, despite the older woman's attempts to explain herself. As a result, Cat moves back to her hometown, where she loses her hair in a factory accident.

Jeffrene, or **Jeffy,** a fourteen-year-old lesbian who has an affair with Cat Lawson. When Jeffy tries to seduce Ursa in bed one night, Ursa knocks her to the floor in revulsion.

Jim, Mutt's cousin. He acts as Mutt's advocate to the wounded Ursa, who repels his pleas for a reconciliation. His reappearance at the end of the novel foreshadows Mutt's.

Caren S. Silvester

COSMOS

Author: Witold Gombrowicz (1904-1969)
Type of work: Novel
Time of action: The 1960's
First published: Kosmos, 1965 (English translation, 1966)

Witold, the narrator of the novel, a student from Warsaw who does not get along with his parents. He is obsessed with interpreting the random events and objects in his environment. He and a fellow student rent a room in the mountain resort of Zakopane in Poland so that they may study for their examinations. On their first day at the resort, they come across a dead sparrow that has been left hanging by a wire, and Witold ponders whether it is meant to be some kind of message or sign. They begin to discover what appear to be other signs or clues, including more objects left hanging. Witold is also fixated on the physical features of those around

him (such as their hands) and grows obsessed with the mouths of two women who live in the rooming house. He becomes increasingly compelled to look for connections and links between events as if there were some kind of plot or mystery to be unraveled. He is never sure whether the objects they find really do have significance or he has merely interpreted them so. Witold begins to lose his control of reality and creates his own mystery by killing a cat and hanging it himself. He finally finds the body of a man hanging in a tree.

Fuchs, a fellow student and friend of the

narrator, Witold. He often seems bored and vacant. He assists Witold in his efforts to resolve the mystery of the puzzling objects.

Kulka Wojtys (voi'tĭsh), the somewhat plump housewife who rents a room to the two friends.

Leo Wojtys, Kulka's husband. He is a short, bald man who is a retired banker.

Lena, Kulka's daughter. She is an attractive and virginal-looking woman. Witold is obsessed with her freshness and the innocent

eroticism of her mouth. It is her cat that Witold throttles.

Louis, Lena's husband. He is tall, well-built, and intelligent-looking and has well-shaped hands. Witold finds him hanging in a group of trees, an apparent suicide.

Katasia, Kulka's poor relative, who helps in the kitchen. She has a lip disfigurement that gives her somewhat of a sensual and reptilian look. Witold becomes transfixed by the erotic suggestivity of her mouth and lips as well.

Thomas F. Barry

THE COUNTRY GIRLS TRILOGY

Author: Edna O'Brien (1930-   )
Type of work: Novel
Time of action: The 1930's to the 1960's
First published: 1986: *The Country Girls*, 1960; *The Lonely Girl*, 1962; *Girls in Their Married Bliss*, 1964; *Epilogue*, 1986

Caithleen (Kate) Brady, a reserved fourteen-year-old, hypersensitive, bookish, and romantic schoolgirl, when the first part of the trilogy opens in the West of Ireland. With her mother dead, though a continuing, strong negative influence on her daughter, and her brutal, drunken father a constant threat, Kate is vulnerable to the attentions of older men. She is also very vulnerable to the machinations of her extroverted best friend, Baba. Kate is in many ways a quick learner in everything, except self-knowledge (especially as this trait manifests itself in her clinging to older, authoritarian men). Yet her marriage fails because Gaillard does not measure up to her sentimental ideal. Always searching for happiness in a relationship with a man, Kate involves herself in yet another unsatisfactory affair. Desperate and depressed, she has herself sterilized. Throughout her years in London, Kate is supported by her lifelong friend, the irrepressible Baba. In the epilogue, twenty years on, it is she who learns that Kate, who was always afraid of water, has, like her mother before her, been drowned.

Bridget (Baba) Brennan, a nasty, spoiled, fourteen-year-old brat when she first appears in the trilogy. She is also effervescent, iconoclastic, attractive to and attracted by men. She is Kate Brady's lifelong (if dangerous) friend, supporter, and confidante. Baba, a weak student, goes to business school in Dublin, after cleverly engineering their expulsion from the convent, where she detested the rules. She is trained to do nothing in life except spend money and enjoy her pursuit of men. Her sacrilegious, scatological humor is irrepressible and irresistible. Her father is the local hardworking country veterinarian; scarcity of money was never a problem for her. Her mother is the alcoholic in Baba's family. A bout with tuberculosis keeps her out of the picture for much of the girls' Dublin experience. When Baba, at age twenty-five, as ever resilient, marries Frank Durack, a crude but rich Irish building contractor, she is given the time and the money to devote herself fairly exclusively to the pursuit of happiness, largely sexual, and also to provide a safe haven in her home for her friend Kate. Baba has a child by the drummer in a band and coerces the impotent Frank into accepting the baby as his. Displaying a heart of gold beneath her aggressive, abrasive exterior, Baba is always there for her very different friend, Kate. It is Baba who takes care of the funeral arrangements when Kate dies. Of the pair of girls, Baba is the brash one, the "old soldier" who endures.

James (Jimmy) Brady, a drunken, ignorant farmer, Kate's father. He is a "bhoy amongst the bhoys" but brutal to his wife and only child. Three times he goes to Dublin to rescue Kate from the godless, divorced Eugene Gaillard; the first trip, he does succeed in bringing her home.

Lily (Neary) Brady, Kate's long-suffering martyr-mother. She drowns early in the trilogy, but her memory continues to exercise a powerful, permanent influence on her daughter.

Mr. Brennan, D.V.M., Baba's hardworking, kindly father. He spoils his daughter, Baba, and helps Kate by giving her a home when her mother dies and her father is on the rampage.

Martha Brennan, Baba's flighty, alcoholic mother. She is too self-centered to exercise any restraint on her willful daughter.

Jack Holland, a middle-aged village grocer dominated by his old mother. He befriends, protects, and would like to marry young Kate.

Jacques de Maurier (Mr. Gentleman), a spineless, middle-aged lawyer who lives in the village community with his ailing wife but works in Dublin. The object of Kate's fantasies, he lets her down in Dublin. He fails to show up to take her on a Continental trip and disappears out of her life when threatened by her father and his wife's nerves.

Eugene Gaillard, another "foreign" man, a handsome, stylish, rather cold, snobbish, middle-aged maker of documentary films. He initiates Kate into the sophisticated world of "the big house" and adultery. Eventually, he marries Kate, which calms her Catholic anxiety; for his own part, he has no religious affiliation. They have a child, Cash, whom he removes, along with himself and the live-in maid, from Kate. He freezes her with his professed superiority into an extramarital affair, the first of many hopeless liaisons with older, married men in which Kate will engage.

Tom (the Ferret) Duggan, of indeterminate age and one of the many Irish "village characters" who inhabit the world of the girls' country years. His erratic services as driver of his old car (he has only one hand) are procured and paid for by Jack Holland to effect Kate's escape. While driving her to the train station, he proposes himself as a very suitable husband for her, in local terms anyhow: He has a water pump in the yard, a bull, and a brother who is a priest.

Frank Durack, Baba's London-Irish, rich building-contractor husband. He is no match for his quick-witted wife, neither in bed, where he is inept, nor out of it, where he is scarcely more adept, though he would dearly love to move in the best society. His function, for Baba, is to provide the money for her escapades, though even this limited contribution is threatened when he makes bad investments and suffers a paralytic stroke.

Archibald E. Irwin

THE COUP

Author: John Updike (1932-   )
Type of work: Novel

Time of action: 1973, with flashbacks to the 1950's
First published: 1978

Colonel Hakim Félix Ellelloû, the forty-year-old, self-effacing president of the sub-Saharan African state Kush. After the 1968 coup against French colonial authorities, he became minister of defense, then president upon the assassination of his predecessor. Previously, as a student at conservative McCarthy College in Wisconsin, he had his strict Muslim Marxist beliefs confirmed by what he considered capitalist greed and consumerism. He has brought back Candace from the United States but keeps her muffled in purdah. Having visited his people in disguise, he blames their poverty on corrupt King Edumu. A purist, he has the king tried and executed, hoping that rains will then come to the arid desert and end a five-year famine. He is hostile to imperialists of both the United States and Russia who, he feels, would subvert Kush's peanut and cattle culture as surely as Arabs, centuries before, sold West Africans into slavery. Yet he is equally hard on himself and considers his humiliation in the tasteless, bourgeois Bad Quarters well-deserved, especially since the rains soon follow. He agrees to be exiled in southern France and to leave Kush to its fate.

King Edumu IV, a blind, old rebel against French colonialism. He supports Ellelloû's political rise, because he respects the colonel's love for Kush. He is imprisoned and finally decapitated for failing to end his people's poverty and considering trade with the West.

Donald Gibbs, a U.S. official, trying to insinuate American influence into Kush affairs by offering crates of processed, famous-brand cereals. When these are set afire, he dies like a martyr at their pinnacle.

Angelica Gibbs, Donald's wife. She hardly remembers his name but comes to claim his ashes. Refusing to return to a wintry climate, she offers herself to Ezana, who has replaced Ellelloû.

Klipspringer, a State Department representative who has no real knowledge of nor interest in Kush.

Colonel Sirin, strict head of a Soviet intercontinental ballistic missile site in the desert. His underground bunker is decorated with czarist supercomfort.

Michaelis Ezana, a one-time minister of the interior in Kush. Infatuated with Western materialism, he is anxious to make financial deals with the World Bank or any wealthy foreign country. He betrays the nomadic desert economy by helping to build an industrial city and an oil refinery along the Libyan border. He weds the widowed Angelica Gibbs.

Dorfû, a young opportunist who, in conspiracy with Ezana, organizes the coup against Ellelloû. Originally he was an underling, a police guard whose sole function was to read the Koran to the blind king. He evacuates the inhabitants of the small villages, now zoned for agribusiness.

Kutunda, an impoverished companion to a company of traveling well-diggers. After briefly serving as Ellelloû's mistress, she joins the coup against him. Her greed makes her into a bloodthirsty minister of the interior. She becomes sister-mistress of Dorfû.

Sheba, the childlike, petite fourth wife of Ellelloû. She joins him in the caravan heading toward Libya. In a constant dreamlike state, she plays music to overcome the desert delirium but disappears at the end of their quest.

Kadongolimi, the earthy first wife of Ellelloû and fat as a queen termite. Her age allows her to mother Ellelloû and temper his rigorous views with common sense. She dies after he is overthrown.

Candace (Candy) Cunningham, Ellelloû's second wife, she rebelled against her Wisconsin father's racism. In her desire to prove herself a liberated woman, she spends several years in Ellelloû's harem completely shrouded. There she develops a robust coarseness but is not insensitive to his feelings of a mission failed when she finally leaves him to return to the United States.

Sittina, sophisticated third wife of Ellelloû. Educated in Alabama, she is a dress designer and semiprofessional painter. The wife most compatible with the larger world of art that transcends power struggles, she accompanies Ellelloû when he goes into exile in France.

Mr. Cunningham, Candace's father, who would like to see all undesirables placed in concentration camps.

Leonard Casper

COUP DE GRÂCE

Author: Marguerite Yourcenar (Marguerite de Crayencour, 1903-1987)
Type of work: Novel
Time of action: The years following World War I and the Russian Revolution
First published: Le Coup de grâce, 1939 (English translation, 1957)

Erick von Lhomond (lō•môň'), a Prussian soldier who fought with the White Russians against the Bolsheviks during the Russian Civil War. He later became a soldier of fortune, engaged in civil conflicts in Central Europe, the Chaco, Manchuria, and Spain. Tall, lean, blue-eyed, and tanned, he retains his youthful elegance at forty, his age when he narrates the story of his relationship with Conrad and Sophie de Reval twenty years earlier. His narrative begins when he returns to Kratovitsy, his boyhood home, after his training as a White Russian soldier. When he returns, he lives on an old overrrun estate that belongs to the de Reval family: Conrad de Reval, his retarded spinster aunt, a gardener, and Conrad's sister, Sophie. He had lived with the family before, when he was sixteen years old. During that idyllic time on the estate, which was like paradise, Erick and Conrad became best friends. Since that time, Erick's overriding passion has been his love for Conrad. He is indifferent to other people and to political causes and believes that this detachment is the primary reason for his effectiveness as a soldier. He is cold and detached, "morally impotent." When Sophie, Conrad's sister, falls in love with him, his unspoken love for Conrad dooms this relationship to a tragic denouement. After Conrad's death, Erick's rightist political affiliation forces a mortal confrontation with Sophie, who joined the Reds when she realized Erick's feelings for her brother. Erick's emotional and moral detachment determine the outcome of their final meeting.

Conrad de Reval (rĕ•văl'), a young Prussian aristocrat engaged in the cause of the White Russians during the Russian Revolution. He is physically very much like Erick, but his hair is fairer. He combines poetic sensitivity and boyish shyness with daredevil courage. It is his ardent desire to be a writer like Rainer Maria Rilke, but his main occupation in the novel is that of a soldier fighting on the side of the Whites against the Reds. Conrad's primary importance in the novel is that he is a passive catalyst in Erick and Sophie's story. It is Erick's and Sophie's separate and individual love for Conrad that is at the center of their own ambiguous and tragic relationship.

Sophie de Reval, a young Prussian aristocrat who, dressed as a boy, fights with the Reds during the Russian Revolution. She is a romantic figure who possesses strange, wild grace. She is possessed by an obsessive love for Erick and is unaware that his feelings for her brother go beyond friendship. She is confused by his behavior toward her and mistakes his friendship for romantic love. When he rebuffs her, she enters into a series of sexual liaisons, and when she finally realizes that it is Conrad whom Erick loves she is driven to flee her home and family and join the Reds. When Erick sees her for the last time, she has been taken prisoner by the Whites. She has been fighting for the Reds disguised as a boy and in masculine garb looks remarkably like Conrad. When Erick is ordered to execute Sophie, he is forced to confront his own feelings for both the brother and the sister.

Volkmar, a soldier fighting for the White Russian cause. His role in the novel is Erick's rival. He is in love with Sophie, and

Erick has never liked him. After Erick rejects Sophie's romantic advances, she becomes involved with Volkmar. Erick reacts violently to her public displays of affection for Volkmar, and these reactions mislead Sophie to believe that Erick is in love with her.

Gregory Loew, a Jewish bookstore clerk who was also in love with Sophie. He enables her to flee her home in Kratovitsy and join the Reds by lending her his clothes in which to disguise herself as a man.

Anne Callahan

COUPLES

Author: John Updike (1932-   )
Type of work: Novel
Time of action: 1963-1964
First published: 1968

Piet Hanema (pēt), a builder and partner in the firm of Gallagher and Hanema, Real Estate and Contracting. A muscular, restless, red-headed, thirty-four-year-old Korean veteran whose Dutch parents died in an auto accident, he worries about damnation and the aimlessness of his life. An insomniac and a womanizer, he has dreams that are often morbid, and his lusty heterosexuality is a subversive influence on the other Tarbox couples. Hired by Ken and Foxy Whitman to repair their house on Blackberry Lane, he becomes the pregnant woman's lover and later impregnates her himself. After others find out about Foxy's subsequent abortion, Piet separates from his wife, marries Foxy, and moves to San Diego.

Angela Hanema, Piet's wife and a kindergarten teacher. A sweet, serene, stately, thirty-four-year-old, with tiny feet and a dolphinlike body, the angelic Angela has a bland, languid opacity, which causes her to be somewhat boring and frigid. Disappointed that Piet did not fix up the Whitman house for her, she is shaken out of her comfortable domesticity by the consequences of her husband's infidelities. She agrees to sleep with

Freddy Thorne as payment for his arranging Foxy's abortion. In return, Piet agrees to let her start psychotherapy. After divorcing Piet, she becomes a full-time teacher and invites her father to move in with her and her two daughters.

Ruth Hanema, the eldest daughter of Piet and Angela. A placid, stoic, nine-year-old, whose bedroom decorations include pictures of Jacqueline Kennedy, Queen Elizabeth, the Beatles, and a naked Nigerian bride, she thinks most people are retardates and is the object of subtle parental neglect of her emotional needs. Piet sees her as a burgeoning replica of his wife.

Nancy Hanema, the youngest daughter of Piet and Angela. A thumb-sucking worrier, she is obsessed by her own negative self-image and the demise of her hamster, the First Family's infant, and various wild animals, whose carcasses she comes upon. Her insecurities mirror Piet's fears about mortality and God's mysterious ways.

Elizabeth "Foxy" Whitman, the wife of Ken and lover of Piet. A vain, amber-eyed, five-foot, nine-inch Radcliffe graduate from Maryland, she is in her late twenties and trapped in a cold marriage. Somewhat of a tart, she is seen as bitchy and manipulative by those envious of her. Her habits could be slovenly, as evidenced, after the birth of her son Tobias, by the accumulation of unwashed dishes and her use of a piece of dry bacon as a bookmark. After her abortion and estrangement from Ken, she goes to the Virgin Islands, awaiting Piet's decision whether to marry her.

Ken Whitman, a thirty-two-year-old research biologist interested in starfish and photosynthesis. He is a sullen, self-righteous WASP with icy eyes, a grimacing mouth, and hair beginning to gray at the temples. His suppressed personality resembles a computer—or a zombie. Unhappy in mid-career, he fears that Jewish and Oriental colleagues are more brilliant and original. Incapable of deep feelings toward his wife or son, he demands a divorce after finding out about Foxy's affair and abortion. Though he hates Piet, he expresses the hope that Piet will marry Foxy. At the end of the book, he takes up with Janet Appleby.

Constance Fox Roth, Foxy's mother. A jolly, divorced busybody, aging at the throat but otherwise well preserved, she is partial to her poodle, cocktail dresses, and red-tipped filter cigarettes. She likes being called Connie and bears little resemblance to the mother Foxy remembers from childhood. Visiting her daughter and grandson, she is not shocked by Foxy's marital problems but urges her to hold on to Ken.

Freddy Thorne, a dentist and spiritual guru of the Tarbox couples. A plump, bald, glint-eyed, flat-footed, unathletic cynic with soft, clammy skin, a sickly mouth, and a green toenail, he has a tooth doctor's preoccupation with decay, a hyena's appetite for dirty truths, and a conspiratorial distrust of others' intentions. Androgynous, he collects Japanese erotica, is working on a pornographic play, and organizes word games at parties. His nicknames for Piet include Enema, Han-

dlebar, and Handball. His revenge for Piet's sleeping with his wife is a night with Angela, whom he has long found alluring in a rather nonsexual way. At the book's end, Freddy's mind games are replaced by bridge when the remaining couples infrequently get together.

Georgene Thorne, Freddy's wife and Piet's first lover. A short, healthy-looking banker's daughter with a narrow nose, green eyes, a freckled chin, and graying hair, she is a practical, sporting woman (good at tennis), who makes the best of a dreary marriage. Angry at finding Piet with Foxy after the abortion, she jealously informs Ken of his cuckoldom. When her loss of Piet's companionship proves irrevocable, she becomes closer to her children, Whitney and Martha.

Matt Gallagher, Piet's partner. Matt is a straight-laced, judgmental Irish-Catholic, whose opaque morality makes him more critical of Piet's affairs than the quality of his own construction. Prim, proper, priestlike, pinch-mouthed, and clean-shaven, he is unadventurous and unethical, preferring dull rectitude to joyous spirituality. Disdainful of those who attend the Thornes' party on the night of John F. Kennedy's assassination, he advises Piet not to leave Angela for Foxy.

Terry Gallagher, the wife of Matt. A tall, willowy, long-haired woman with a Celtic appearance, she dabbles with pottery and the lute. Amiable and amoral, she has an affair with her sculptor and tells Ken Whitman that he should try to save his marriage now that he has a son.

Roger Guerin, a wealthy businessman and frequent golf partner of Piet. Swarthy and dark-browed, with an incongruously small mouth, he has an inheritance that allows him to inhabit his office primarily as a place from which to arrange luncheon and squash dates. Uncomfortable with women and having suppressed homosexual tendencies, he draws closer to his wife Bea after suffering a sudden financial setback.

Bea Guerin, the wife of Roger. A small,

remote, barren woman, she is competitive on the tennis court, flirtatious when drunk at parties, and malicious toward imagined rivals. She gives other women little affectionate pats and allows men to get rough with her in bed. After Piet slaps her, she admits that her husband has done the same thing and that Eddie Constantine has twisted her wrists. She finally finds joy by adopting a black child, thereby integrating Tarbox.

Frank Appleby, a trust officer in a bank. A florid, ironical Harvard University graduate and Shakespeare buff with large teeth, a bilious smile and an ulcer, he sees life as a series of investments. He takes up with Marcia Smith and, realizing his wife is similarly engaged with Marcia's husband, suggests the two men switch bedrooms during a ski trip. The two couples become so close that others call them the Applesmiths.

Janet Appleby, Frank's wife. A pouty, petulant, plump-faced, big-breasted, valentine-mouthed daughter of a Buffalo businessman, with childish handwriting and an addiction to sleeping pills, she fears that others find her common and uncultured and gravitates between self-conscious modesty and voluptuous displays. Initiating an affair with Harold Smith, after convincing him of their spouses' affair, she finds a measure of self-confidence from twice-weekly therapy sessions. Attracted to Ken Whitman, she offers her body to him after Foxy leaves Tarbox.

Harold Smith, a thirty-eight-year-old broker. A political reactionary with slicked-backed hair, he is a Princeton University graduate and subscriber to *Barron's,* who dances adroitly, enjoys classical music, and uses French expressions to emphasize points, almost as a linguistic tic. Orderly, private, and sexually experienced from frequent liaisons with call girls during business trips, he finds his trysts with Janet Appleby a lively addition to his weekly routine.

Marcia Smith, Harold's thirty-six-year-old wife. The black-haired daughter of a psychiatrist whose brittle personality alternates between a nervous corruptibility and a fragile cheerfulness, she and her husband are sometimes called the Little-Smiths, an appellation originally used to distinguish them from another Tarbox couple that has since moved away.

Eddie Constantine, an airline pilot. A crude, perverse, beer-drinking, fast-driving teller of dirty jokes, he has an adolescent, macho personality, which perhaps disguises homoerotic feelings toward Ben Saltz. After he and Ben purchase a boat, the two couples become so close that they are called the Saltines.

Carol Constantine, the wife of Eddie. A lithe, hip, thin-waisted painter of Greek ancestry, she dyes her hair orange and occasionally displays a cruel streak. Piet's final lover before settling down with Foxy, she proves an ardent sexual partner.

Ben Saltz, an aerospace engineer on the Mariner Venus probe. A doleful, bearded Jew with a rabbinical demeanor, he has an eclectic mind and a ponderous manner. His experiment in hedonism with the Constantines ends with his losing his job. Somewhat ostracized as a result, he takes a new position in Cleveland, Ohio.

Irene Saltz, Ben's wife and head of the Tarbox Fair Housing Committee. An earnest, efficient do-gooder whose causes range from conservation to civil rights, she likes bird-watching and arguing with right-wingers and rails against vestiges of anti-Semitism in Tarbox. Having battled with school authorities over the staging of a Christmas pageant, she almost wins election to the school board.

John Ong, a Korean-born nuclear scientist employed at the Massachusetts Institute of Technology. A small, sober, bony, smiling man whose dainty tennis strokes contrast with his acumen at chess, he speaks with an accent barely comprehensible to the other Tarbox couples.

Bernadette Ong, the wife of John Ong. A

gregarious and somewhat exotic woman of Japanese and Portuguese ancesty, she enjoys the company of the other Tarbox couples but is somewhat of an outsider. While Piet is preoccupied with finding Foxy during a party, she beseeches him for a duty dance.

Dan Mills, the proprietor of the Tarbox boatyard. A dissolute, alcoholic World War II veteran, he once presided over the boatyard crowd until they fell out of fashion and scattered. With his business going bankrupt, he separates from his wife and moves to Florida. His tranquil daughter Merissa becomes the Hanemas' babysitter.

Reverend Horace Pedrick, the pastor of Tarbox Congregational Church. A hairy-eared, skeletal sixty-year-old whose sentiments never stray far from dollars and cents,

he is less a holy man than a pitiful ignoramus. Atop his church is a weathervane shaped like a rooster with a copper penny for an eye. When lightning strikes it and incinerates the church, Pedrick's first reaction is to inquire how much the repairs will cost.

Leon Jazinski, a construction foreman for Gallagher and Hanema. A smug, weedy Pole from New Hampshire without subtlety or respect for tradition (labeled Jack be Nimble by two old carpenters, Adams and Comeau), Leon is an ambitious social climber. His pontifications are as unprofound as his professional work is unaesthetic. Ultimately replacing Piet as Gallagher's junior partner, he and his wife move to a more stylish abode and become Unitarians.

James B. Lane

COUSIN BAZILIO

Author: José Maria Eça de Queiróz (1845-1900)
Type of work: Novel
Time of action: The 1870's
First published: O Primo Basílio, 1878 *(Dragon's Teeth,* 1889; better known as *Cousin Bazilio)*

Luiza, blonde, beautiful wife of Jorge. During Jorge's prolonged absence, she has an affair with her cousin Bazilio. When she discovers that her maid has stolen some of their love notes and letters, she wants to escape to Paris with him. She refuses to accept money from Bazilio to pay off Juliana. In order to keep Juliana from revealing her secret, Luiza grants Juliana her every wish, even to the point of doing her work for her. Luiza's love for Bazilio turns to hate, and she longs for Jorge's return. The strains of hiding her affair and dealing with Juliana's constant demands break her health. In desperation, she writes to Bazilio to send her money so she can extricate herself from the intolerable situation. Before she receives a reply from him, however, Jorge returns. After Luiza recovers from a long illness precipitated by Juliana's death, Jorge confronts her with Bazilio's reply to her letter, causing her sudden relapse and death from brain fever.

Jorge (zhōr'zhā), Luiza's devoted and rather conventional husband, a government mining engineer. He has accepted an extended assignment in the Alentejo, a mining region in southern Portugal. After his return, Juliana's behavior infuriates him, and he wants Luiza to fire her. He is consumed with jealousy when he intercepts Bazilio's letter to Luisa and realizes that she might have been unfaithful to him. He nurses her back to health from one fever, only to cause her final collapse by demanding an explanation for the contents of Bazilio's letter.

Bazilio de Brito, Luiza's wealthy, handsome, and worldly cousin. He carefully orchestrates Luiza's seduction and rents a seedy room for their rendezvous. When Luiza threatens to end their affair because he has become inconsiderate and indifferent, he cynically teaches her new sexual sensations to change her mind. He contrives to leave the

348

country immediately after Luiza runs to him with the news of Juliana's knowledge of their romance. His answer to her written request for hush money is intercepted by Jorge. Upon his return to Lisbon, he hopes to resume his liaison with Luiza. The news of her death, however, does not grieve him. He only regrets that his current mistress has not accompanied him to Lisbon.

Juliana Conceiro Tavira, Luiza's ugly, ailing, bitter, and manipulative maid. She steals incriminating notes and letters from Luiza in the hope of extorting enough money from her for a comfortable retirement. The prospect of extracting a large sum is dashed by Bazilio's departure, and so she elects to demand favors of Luiza. After Luiza has given her everything she wants, Juliana refuses to work. When Jorge demands that she be fired, she forces Luiza to fire Joanna instead. Enraged by Sebastian forcing her to surrender Luiza's letters, she dies of a heart attack.

Sebastian, Jorge's best friend from childhood. He has suspected Luiza's romance with Bazilio. When Luiza requests that he deal with Juliana for her, he retrieves the stolen letters and never betrays Luiza's trust in him.

Leopoldina, Luiza's unhappily married school friend. Jorge has forbidden Luiza to see her because of her bad reputation. She fascinates Luiza with tales about her many lovers.

Ernestinho Ledesma, playwright and cousin of Jorge. In the original version of his successful play about adultery, the wife is killed by the offended husband. When Ernestinho complains about being forced to change the ending so that the unfaithful wife was forgiven, Jorge insists vehemently that an unfaithful wife should be killed.

Juliao Zuzarte (zhōō·lē·ouṅ'), dour physician friend of Jorge. He attends Luiza in her final illness.

Joanna, Luiza's loyal cook. She returns to serve Luiza after Juliana's death.

Felicidade de Noronha, a buxom, heavyset lady, friend of Jorge and Luiza. She has never married, although her infatuation with Councilor Accacio has never diminished.

Councilor Accacio, an old-fashioned, dignified bachelor and a friend of Jorge's father.

Evelyn Toft

THE COWARDS

Author: Josef Škvorecký (1924-   )
Type of work: Novel
Time of action: 1945
First published: Zbabĕlci, 1958 (English translation, 1970)

Danny Smiricky (smǐ'rzhǐts·kē), an eighteen-year-old jazz saxophone player in a provincial town in Czechoslovakia. As the narrator of the novel, young Danny reveals that he is less concerned with the major political upheavals occurring around him during the final days of the Nazi occupation in his town in May, 1945, than with his own personal future. Infatuated with a girl named Irena, Danny fantasizes about the kinds of heroic deeds he could perform to win her heart.

Arrested for a cavalier act of defiance in the face of the Nazi force, Danny is saved from serious reprisal by Dr. Sabata, a friend of his father who serves as an important figure in the town. Danny joins a group of young partisans, in part out of a simple desire to gain possession of a gun, but the partisan unit is pressed into service as part of a newly founded local militia. Danny becomes caught up in a fleeting battle with the retreating Nazis. He then spends the day consoling Irena, who is distracted by a lack of news concerning her lover Zdenek. Frustrated once again, Danny joins his jazz band to take part in a celebration in honor of the Soviet Army, which has entered the town to replace the Germans. As the novel closes, Danny pours into his music his mingled feelings of regret over the passing of his youth and his hope for new joy with an unknown girl waiting for him in the future.

Irena, Danny's would-be girlfriend. Although flattered by Danny's attention, Irena has her heart set on the mountain-climber Zdenek. Her appearance in the novel serves mainly as the foil for Danny's adolescent longings and desires.

Prema (prshĕ'má), the leader of the band of partisan rebels that Danny joins. A fearless and indomitable soul, he and Danny set up a machine gun and stop a file of German soldiers maneuvering with a tank on the outskirts of town.

Benno, a member of Danny's band who has spent some time in a concentration camp because he is of Jewish ancestry. During a brief battle with the retreating Germans, he flees in an ignominious yet comical fashion into the woods.

Bertie Moutelik, a young photographer who industriously takes pictures of the local political and military authorities. He takes a picture of Danny proudly displaying a submachine gun.

Dr. Sabata, a local official who managed to get along smoothly with the occupying Germans yet is ready to greet the newly arrived Soviet forces with equal zeal.

Dr. Bohadlo, the ineffectual leader of Danny's military patrol.

Mrs. Heiserova, the wife of the general director of a textile mill. When Danny asks her to provide temporary housing for some newly released prisoners of war, she initially balks, until she learns that the men are English, not Russian.

Mitzi, the Heisers' maid, who serves as the object of one of Danny's unsuccessful flirtations.

Haryk, one of the members of Danny's band.

Lucie, Haryk's girlfriend, with whom Danny flirts in his ceaseless quest to secure romantic attention.

Julian W. Connolly

CRIMES OF THE HEART

Author: Beth Henley (1952-   )
Type of work: Play
Time of action: Fall, 1974 (five years after Hurricane Camille)
First produced: 1979

Lenny MaGrath, at thirty, the eldest of the MaGrath sisters. The play is set on and around her thirtieth birthday. Lenny is a thoughtful, self-conscious woman who remains concerned about her critically ill grandfather and her own impending spinsterhood. She is protective of her sisters and eventually puts Chick in her place after Chick's vitriolic attack on the MaGrath family. By the play's end, she is encouraged to resume a relationship with one Charlie Hill, a man who replied to Lenny's advertisement in the personal section of a periodical. Her fear that he would reject her because of her missing ovary proves to be unfounded.

Meg MaGrath, at twenty-seven, the middle of the MaGrath sisters. Meg has been living in Hollywood in order to pursue her singing career. She returns in order to be close to her sisters after Babe's shooting of her husband. While she is the most outgoing of the three sisters, she relates to Doc that her life in Hollywood had once led to a nervous breakdown. One of the consequences of her return to Hazelhurst is a rekindling of her romance with Doc.

Babe Botrelle, at twenty-four, the youngest of the MaGrath sisters. Babe is the reason for most of the play's dynamics. She shot her husband, Zackery Botrelle, after he discovered that she had been having an affair with Willie Jay, a fifteen-year-old black boy who came to Babe's house to see the dog she tended for him. Babe is also the most fragile of the sisters and, thus, most like their mother, who scandalously had hanged herself and her cat some years before. Indeed, after Babe's shooting of her husband is resolved in her favor, which occurs after Zackery has circulated incriminating pictures and after Willie Jay is forced to leave town, Babe attempts suicide with a rope and with gas. She discovers, as her mother did, that suicide is a lonely act and is relieved by her failure to succeed.

Chick Boyle, the twenty-nine-year-old first cousin of the MaGrath sisters. She has yellow hair, shiny red lips, and a brassy disposition. She is ashamed of Babe's alleged crime and voices it frequently and indiscriminately. Chick finally goes too far when she berates Babe as a murderer and refers to all the MaGrath sisters as "trash." Lenny drives her out of the house with a broom and forces her to climb the mimosa tree.

Doc Porter, the thirty-year-old ex-boyfriend of Meg. Doc comes over to inform Lenny that her twenty-year-old horse, Billy Boy, had died by being struck by lightning. Doc remains highly infatuated with Meg, even after his marriage to another woman and the birth of his two children. They spend their first date after Meg's return nostalgically reminiscing about the past.

Barnette Lloyd, Babe's twenty-six-year-old lawyer. Barnette is a graduate of the Old Miss law school who returns to Hazelhurst in order to open his own firm. Meg remains dubious of Barnette's competence when she first meets him, but Barnette has a personal vendetta against Babe's husband, who has been state senator from Copiah County. Barnette hopes to uncover all Botrelle's criminal dealings. Barnette also remains fond of Babe and hopes to save her from her abusive husband and from any criminal charges.

Hardin Aasand

THE CRUCIBLE

Author: Arthur Miller (1915-   )
Type of work: Play
Time of action: 1692
First published: 1953

Abigail Williams, a strikingly beautiful seventeen-year-old. She is willful and a flirt. Her rebellion against society is expressed in her wayward behavior, which she transforms into a witch scare by going into fits and stimulating and coercing her girlfriends to do likewise. Abigail senses that the community of Salem, Massachusetts, is uneasy, that it suffers from societal tensions, and that it is prepared to believe that its internal divisions are the result of witchcraft. Before she is through, Abigail and her minions will charge many of the most prominent people in Salem with witchcraft.

Tituba, a black servant from Barbados who

351

introduces the girls to certain superstitious practices. It is her confession that leads to the witchcraft scare.

Reverend Samuel Parris, a stiff, intolerant man who is at first nonplussed by the eccentric behavior of the girls. Soon, however, he turns their antics into an indictment of the community. Interpreting their hysterical fits as sure signs of witchcraft, he exploits them to whip his congregation in line. Finding the witches becomes a way of asserting this pious and credulous man's authority.

John Proctor, a man who has had a brief affair with Abigail. He does not believe her fits are caused by the devil. Although he is estranged from his wife, who knows of his liaison with Abigail, Proctor resists Abigail's advances, knowing that the consequence will be that he and his wife will stand accused of witchcraft.

Elizabeth Proctor, John's estranged and unforgiving wife. Although her husband has admitted his lapse into sin and is thereafter faithful to his wife, his relationship with Abigail always stands between them. As husband and wife, however, they maintain their integrity and refuse to confess to the false accusation of witchcraft, even though their protestations of innocence result in a death sentence.

Giles Corey, one of Salem's prominent citizens who opposes the charges of witchcraft and then is accused himself. Rather than admitting to a false accusation, he endures the torture of being crushed to death.

Reverend John Hale, an expert in matters of witchcraft, he comes to Salem to set up the trials.

Thomas Putnam, a prominent Salem citizen and an argumentative man who turns his quarrels with his neighbors into a hunt for witches.

Mary Warren, one of Abigail's girlfriends. She tries to tell the truth (that the girls were only feigning possession by witches), but she loses courage when Abigail intimidates her.

Rebecca Nurse, one of the most devout members of Salem. Despite her piousness, she is also accused of witchcraft. Her conviction illustrates how widespread the hysteria and paranoia of the community have become.

Judge Hathorne, the hanging judge of the Salem witchcraft trials. Hathorne has little sympathy for the accused and looks upon his responsibility quite sternly.

Carl Rollyson

CRUSOE'S DAUGHTER

Author: Jane Gardam (1928-   )
Type of work: Novel
Time of action: 1898-1985
First published: 1985

Polly Flint, the bright, inquisitive, solitary heroine of the novel. Brought to live in a remote seaside village with two maiden aunts at the age of eight. Polly identifies early on with Robinson Crusoe, feeling herself to be similarly marooned. As a teenager, she visits the home of Arthur and Celia

Thwaite, where she meets a number of "artistic" houseguests, including the young poet Paul Treece. Initially attracted to him, she soon grows impatient with his callowness and boundless enthusiasm. She has a brief affair with his friend Theo Zeit, but her impassioned letters to him while he is fighting in

World War I apparently frighten him off. She is heartbroken for a long period and becomes an alcoholic in middle age. She sets herself the task of translating *Robinson Crusoe* into German, then begins to write critical material on the novel. She also becomes a teacher for the local boarding school. The novel ends with Polly in her eighties, about to be interviewed by a local reporter.

Aunt Frances Younghusband, one of Polly's aunts on her mother's side. Small, gentle, and sweet, she has an "understanding" with the local vicar, Father Pocock. They marry and embark on a mission to India. He dies en route, and later Polly receives a photo from Frances, apparently taken after Pocock's death, showing her with a group of people on shipboard, all dressed as Pierrots. It seems that all of her life Frances had a taste for adventure, which she is now indulging. She dies abroad of dysentery soon thereafter.

Aunt Mary Younghusband, Polly's other aunt. Polly thinks of her at first as the "ice maiden," because she seems so remote and austere. On the day of Frances' wedding, though, she amazes Polly by appearing looking radiantly beautiful. It develops that she was at one time going to marry Arthur Thwaite, but apparently his sister prevented it somehow. In later life, she has become very religious and frequently goes on retreat at the local convent. She dies soon after Frances.

Theodore (Theo) Zeit, an upper-class young man of Polly's age. His family are from Germany originally and are Jewish. His father owns the factory that overshadows the seaside village. He is good-natured, confident, and gives Polly the impression of being completely happy and at ease in the world. They have an affair of sorts, but after he leaves the village to fight in World War I, he marries Delphi Vipont, the pale blonde beauty who lived near the village. He returns to the village briefly after the war but decides to live in Germany. Later, during World War II, he sends his two daughters to

Polly in England to escape the Holocaust. Ultimately, he returns to the village a frail and wasted man.

Charlotte, the maid at the Younghusbands. Frumpy and somewhat dirty in her personal appearance, she is a quiet and rather bad-natured woman. She has great affection for her nephew Stanley, who comes for tea every Wednesday. After he dies of influenza, it is revealed that he is actually her son. Wounded by the Younghusband sisters' lack of sympathy for her grief, she flees the house abruptly, never to return.

Mrs. Agnes Woods, a pale-complexioned, bitter-natured woman who always wears black and carries black knitting with her. She has a secret, unspecified, and admiring relationship with Aunt Frances. After Frances leaves, she suffers a stroke and is virtually incapacitated. When Mary dies, Polly and Alice have an unpleasant time caring for her, until she too dies.

Captain Flint, Polly's father, a jolly, irresponsible, roving man. Polly remembers little of him except that he shared a meat pie with her in the first-class train compartment on their journey up to the aunts' and that he sang and danced for the aunts at their home. He used to leave Polly in the care of various people while he went off traveling by sea. He died when his ship sank, going down with the ship while sipping from a large stone bottle of gin.

Arthur Thwaite, a quiet elderly friend of the Younghusband sisters, who visits annually. He has a drooping mustache and wears a monocle. He hardly speaks at all except to comment on the weather, but Polly is nevertheless very drawn to him. He turns out to be Polly's grandfather; he had once been romantically involved with Aunt Mary, but he also had an affair with Polly's grandmother, the aunts' mother, and from that union Polly's mother was born.

Paul Treece, an energetic, amiable, very talkative young poet. A student at Cambridge, Paul meets Polly while they are both guests at the Thwaite home. Paul is one of the "artistic" people Celia has invited to stay. Restless and excitable, Paul is callow but nevertheless a very talented poet. He is infatuated with Polly and sends her long letters from the front after he eagerly enlists to fight in World War I. He is killed in France.

Alice, a serving girl of about the same age as Polly. Formerly the vicar's maid, she comes over to the Younghusbands when Charlotte leaves. Initially mousy, quiet, and tired-looking, she gradually develops a strong personality and becomes a good friend to Polly. She takes over the running of the boarding-house when Polly succumbs to alcoholism. She ends up marrying Mr. Benson, the schoolteacher who boards with them.

Celia Thwaite, Arthur's sister. An old, garishly painted woman, Celia is a poet who takes enormous pride in the fact that her family at one time knew and entertained people such as Alfred, Lord Tennyson and Virginia Woolf. She likes to surround herself with artistic people and generously opens her house to them. Polly thinks her vain and full of machinations. She may have been responsible for breaking up the relationship between Arthur and Mary years ago.

Catherine Swanson

THE CRYING OF LOT 49

Author: Thomas Pynchon (1937-   )
Type of work: Novel
Time of action: The early 1960's
First published: 1966

Mrs. Oedipa Maas, a surburban California housewife, Young Republican, and executrix of the huge estate of Pierce Inverarity, her former lover. An attractive woman of twenty-eight with long hair, she is intelligent and dissatisfied. Feeling imprisoned even before she got married, she looked for liberation through Pierce, but he died, leaving her the job of sorting out his legacy and character. This challenge becomes a mock religious quest. She is a whiz at interpreting texts, but in this case the more information she accumulates, the more difficult it all is to evaluate and the more paranoid she becomes. The focus of her quest for information is The Tristero, or Trystero, which may or may not exist: a secret countercultural postal system called WASTE, whose symbol is a muted post horn. As every access she discovers to the Trystero can be traced to the Inverarity estate, it appears that the dead capitalist owned even the counterculture and controlled WASTE. In the course of her quest, Oedipa insulates and desensitizes herself against a predatory environment. Consequently, she is not sensitive enough to communicate with Maxwell's Demon, a spirit in a box, and is overcome by the entropy she discovers in herself and in America. She sees life as a void, becomes suicidal, loses her bearings, and takes a man's name, Arnold Snarb, imposed upon her by a stranger. At the end, in paranoia she is hoping for a saving revelation at an auction of Inverarity's stamp collection, a crying.

Pierce Inverarity, a dead real estate mogul with headquarters in San Narciso, Southern California. A "founding father," he gradually seems to possess all of America. He does many impersonations, including The Shadow, and becomes a haunting, ambiguous, demonic god figure to Oedipa. His manipulations are represented by his defense plant, Yoyodyne, and his values by his tacky new housing development, Fangoso Lagoons, which features an artificial lake called "Inverarity," with real human skeletons at the bottom. Oedipa fell in love with Pierce, though she may have meant no more to him than another stamp in his collection.

Wendell "Mucho" Maas, a disc jockey for teenagers at radio station KCUF, and the pathetic husband of Oedipa. Mucho is not macho, calls his wife "Oed" and is "too sensitive." He had to quit his former job as a used-car salesman because he felt too sorry for the customers. As he and Oedipa are increasingly unable to communicate, he seduces teenage girls and takes drugs. Gradually he loses his integrity, his ego dissipates, and he merges with the masses and becomes generic.

Metzger, coexecutor of Inverarity's will, a lawyer and former child motion picture star who performed under the name of Baby Igor. Now thirty-five, he is so good-looking that Oedipa promptly sleeps with him after a game of Strip Botticelli. He lives in his looks, is too artificial to be sure of his sexual orientation, and blames his lack of character on a domineering mother and a cowardly father. Oedipa strikes him as one of "these lib, overeducated broads with the soft heads and bleeding hearts." He leaves her to run off with the very young girlfriend of a member of a rock band called the Paranoids.

Michael Hollister

THE CRYSTAL WORLD

Author: J. G. Ballard (1930-   )
Type of work: Novel
Time of action: The early 1960's
First published: 1966

Dr. Edward Sanders, the assistant director of a leper hospital. A gray-haired, unkempt man of forty, he has spent fifteen years of his life in Africa, ten at the leper hospital. Uneasy because of a mysterious letter form his former mistress, Suzanne Clair, Sanders goes to Mont Royal to check on her. There, he risks death from violent men, as well as from the rapidly spreading plague that crystallizes all living things. Although he escapes with the help of a jeweled cross, he eventually returns to the crystal forest, where he had for the first time felt whole.

Suzanne Clair, the wife of Max Clair and formerly the mistress of Sanders. A tall, dark woman in her thirties, she has been beautiful, but, when Sanders finds her, she bears the unmistakable signs of leprosy. Yet, she is ecstatically happy in the crystal forest, where she leads a train of followers.

Dr. Max Clair, Suzanne's husband and the former colleague of Sanders. A small, plump man in early middle age, he now acts erratically, turning away lepers from his hospi-

tal at Mont Royal so that they will become crystallized and die.

Louise Peret, a French journalist. A broad-hipped, beautiful girl in her twenties, with dark hair and gray eyes, she looks much like a younger Suzanne. Although she becomes Sanders' mistress and cares for him in his illness, she does not share his enthusiasm for the crystal forest and finally breaks off their affair.

Ventress, a former architect, the cabinmate of Sanders on the trip to Port Materre. A slight, dark man of forty, he is restless and violent. Desperately searching for his wife, he escapes death time and time again and even incidentally rescues Sanders. After killing Thorensen, he disappears, probably to die in the forest.

Thorensen, a mine owner. A tall, blond man, he is selfish and possessive. After freeing Ventress' wife, he imprisoned her in his own luxurious, isolated home. After a number of skirmishes, he is shot by Ventress.

355

Serena Thorensen, the former wife of Ventress and the object of his search. A girl in her twenties, with long blonde hair, she is emaciated from tuberculosis. When Sanders last sees her, she is only half-conscious, lying beside the dead Thorensen.

Captain Radek, a doctor in the army medical corps. A tall, slim man, it is he who first explains to Sanders about the crystallization phenomenon. Later, when he is looking for Sanders, he becomes partially crystallized.

When Sanders rescues him and tries to tear off the crystals, Radek rebukes him and begs to go back into the forest.

Fr. Balthus, an apostate and priest from Mont Royal. A pale, nervous man, he first meets Sanders on the boat to Port Materre. Later, he nurses Sanders while he recovers from crystallization and gives him a cross which will enable him to return to safety.

Rosemary M. Canfield Reisman

CURSE OF THE STARVING CLASS

Author: Sam Shepard (Samuel Shepard Rogers, 1943-   )
Type of work: Play
Time of action: The 1970's
First published: 1976, in *Angel City and Other Plays*

Wesley Tate, the young son of a lower-middle-class, rural California family. Feeling strong ties to his family and to the land, Wesley maintains the farm after the others have given up. He sees the sale of the land to real estate developers as having significance far greater than the loss of a mere house. At times, Wesley loses patience with his family members, as evidenced by his lack of sympathy for his sister's ruined 4-H project, to which he responds by urinating on her charts and suggesting that his sister do something truly useful. He is also contemptuous of his mother's attorney friend, to whom he is very rude and accusatory. Although Wesley does not get along with his father, he does feel certain responsibilities toward his family. He cleans up the mess left by one of his father's frequent drunken binges and begins to replace the door the old man has beaten down. Wesley also is aware of some inherited traits, especially his father's passionate temper. Failing to experience the rebirth of spirit his father prescribes, Wesley dons his father's discarded old clothes. Wesley and his mother are the only family members left at the end of the play.

Ella Tate, Wesley's mother. Coming from a higher class background, Ella feels an outsider among the members of her own family. She feels abandoned by her husband and fears that he might try to kill her in one of his drunken rages. Ella insensitively cooks the chicken that her daughter plans to use in an important 4-H project. She also fills her young daughter's mind with an obsession about germs and with false information about the girl's physical maturity. Longing for the more prestigious life-style of the rich, Ella has become involved with an attorney and plans to sell the property and run away to Europe. After returning from jail to visit her daughter, Ella sleeps on the kitchen table. When she awakes, both her husband and her daughter have left, but, confused by Wesley's attire, she repeatedly calls her son by her husband's name.

Emma Tate, Wesley's sister. Outspoken and rebellious, Emma reaches physical maturity on the day the play takes place. She is outraged that her mother has used the chicken she has raised and prepared for her 4-H project, and so she begins to make plans to run away to Mexico. Somewhat loyal to her father, Emma does not like her mother's attorney friend and tells him so. Emma is arrested for riding her horse through the bar her father frequents and shooting the place full of holes. She is released, however, when she makes sexual overtures to the police sergeant. Resolved to embark on a life of crime, Emma takes money and car keys from her mother's purse and leaves just before the car explodes.

Weston Tate, Wesley's father. An alcoholic with a violent temper, Weston is unable to hold a steady job, continues to drive even though his license has been revoked, and is in serious debt to some rough characters. He secretly sells the property to the owner of the Alibi Club for fifteen hundred dollars. When the family refrigerator is empty, Weston simply buys a bag of artichokes. After passing out on the kitchen table, Weston awakes with a sense of being reborn. He uncharacteristically bathes and shaves, discards his dirty old clothes, and does the laundry and cooks breakfast for the family. Although Weston has decided to stay and work the farm, Wesley reminds him that he is still in trouble and encourages him to flee to Mexico.

Taylor, an attorney who speculates in real estate. Taylor has already cheated Weston out of five hundred dollars by selling him a worthless piece of desert real estate; now he is taking advantage of his intimate relationship with Ella to purchase the Tate property without the permission of Weston, whom Taylor has had declared mentally incompetent.

Ellis, the owner of the Alibi Club bar. Wearing a shiny yellow shirt, tight pants, shiny shoes, many rings, and a gold necklace, Ellis is a burly man whose arms are covered with tattoos. Ellis has taken advantage of Weston's drunkenness and indebtedness to purchase the Tate property for a mere fifteen hundred dollars.

Emerson, a small man who, by blowing up the Tates' car, warns Weston to pay his debts.

Slater, the man who accompanies Ellis on his threatening visit.

Sergeant Malcolm, a highway patrol officer who notifies Ella that Emma has been arrested. He will take no action against the other criminals, however, because that is not within his jurisdiction.

Lou Thompson

THE CUSTOM HOUSE

Author: Francis King (1923-   )
Type of work: Novel
Time of action: The 1950's
First published: 1961

Professor William Knox, a British university professor teaching in Kyoto, Japan. Equally impatient with the reticence and formality of the Japanese and the intrusiveness of foreigners, the forty-four-year-old phonetics expert acts as a somewhat weary and ironic commentator on the rapidly changing culture of post-World War II Japan. A widower, he falls in love with his neighbor Setsuko, who, for various reasons, cannot return his love. Knox's stay in Japan ends when he flies out of the country with the disgraced missionary Welling. At the novel's end, he is in Greece, his favorite country, where he learns that Setsuko has left Japan.

The Reverend Michael C. Welling, an Australian missionary. He is physically attractive yet emotionally weak, as is revealed early in the novel when he tries to drive away without aiding a woman whom he sideswipes with his green MG. Welling's cowardice is also revealed through his own remembrances of how he failed to aid his brother during a shark attack and how he conducted himself during the war. His general unhappiness with his work is temporarily ameliorated when he falls in love with Sanae. The married missionary's frequent interaction with his beautiful student, however, soon leads to gossip and controversy. When Sanae is found murdered, the innocent and naïve Welling becomes the primary suspect. Characteristically, he chooses to flee the country rather than to face a prolonged trial and likely conviction.

Setsuko, an American-educated chemist who works in a nuclear weapons lab. The daughter of a Japanese father and Russian mother, she considers herself to be an outsider in all cultures. Her uncharacteristic physical features, American education, and unfortunate relationship with her rich and powerful Japanese uncle all combine to alienate her from Japan and the Japanese. Although she enjoys Knox's company, she cannot return his love. Eventually, she flees Japan under the suspicion of having stolen atomic secrets for the Communists.

Sanae, a young, beautiful Japanese stripper. An orphan, reared by missionaries in Hiroshima, she is both perceptive and determined. Her affair with Furomoto ends when, characteristically, he tires of her, but she uses her pregnancy by Furomoto to threaten blackmail. Suspecting Setsuko of having gone through her things on several occasions, Sanae ransacks Setsuko's room, taking some incriminating papers with her when she leaves. Later, Sanae is found murdered. Whether Sanae is killed because of these secret papers or because of her threat to blackmail Furomoto is left unclear.

Furomoto, a rich and powerful Japanese businessman and artist. Proving insensitive and, at time, ruthless in both his business and private affairs, he elicits antipathy in almost everyone with whom he interacts in the novel. His affairs with Sanae and Setsuko, his niece, have tragic consequences for both

women. His desire to have Sanae disposed of is made clear; whether his wishes are acted upon remains ambiguous.

Aileen Colethorpe, an American artist who rooms with Sanae. Colethorpe is under Furomoto's patronage until she angers him by resisting his artistic dicta. She and Sanae move in with Setsuko and her aunt after Furomoto stops providing the American and her friend with free housing. After Knox has left Japan, she writes him in Greece to tell him about Setsuko's flight from Japan.

Ed Schneider, an American journalist. Cynical, boorish, yet brilliant, he has seen his reputation irreparably damaged by his alcoholism. He speaks Japanese fluently and understands the Japanese people better than any other foreigner.

Asai, a poor student. Although driven by his hatred both of Western intrusions into his country and of the Japanese lack of resolve, he chooses to strike out at the representatives of the Western ideology. In Welling's Bible class, he ridicules Christian beliefs and goads Welling by telling him that he and the others are taking the class only to practice their English. His anarchism leads him to attempt to kill Furomoto, but the bungled bombing results only in his own death and the death of Furomoto's servant. Setsuko's respect for Asai is an early indication of her political sympathies.

The Reverend Harry Ambleside, the English director at the mission. He is admired by Welling, who notes the mix of altruism and ambition that drives Ambleside. Although Welling's lack of courage bothers him, he nevertheless tries to help out his fellow missionary once the scandal breaks. Ambleside's generally unruffled attitude toward religion as well as the Japanese contrasts sharply with Welling's troubled outlook on both.

Tom Rash

THE CUTTLEFISH
Or, The Hyrcanian Worldview

Author: Stanisław Ignacy Witkiewicz (1885-1939)
Type of work: Play
Time of action: The 1920's
First published: Mątwe: Czyli, Hyrkaniczny światopogląd, 1922 (English translation, 1970)

Paul Rockoffer, a disillusioned artist. In a time of increasing dehumanization and mechanization of society, Rockoffer finds the pursuit of art meaningless. Forty-six years old, the fair-haired artist, dressed in black, mourns the waste of his life and the isolation and futility of his existence as an artist. In the face of eternal gray boredom, Rockoffer succumbs to the enticements of bourgeois contentment in his engagement to Ella. He is, however, torn by past yearnings as represented by the sensual statue. At the same time, Pope Julius II offers him a life of total devotion to art, and Hyrcan IV attempts to convince him of the possibilities of absolute power. Despite his waverings between a life of art and a life of power, Rockoffer (having killed off Hyrcan IV), as Hyrcan V, intends to create a reality in which art, philosophy, love, and science will become "one huge mishmash," thereby fulfilling the Nietzschean notion of the artist as superman.

Julius II, sixteenth century pope and patron of the arts. A projection of Rockoffer's mind, he is a visitor from the past and represents Renaissance values of strength, intelligence, commitment, and belief in individualism. As a patron of the arts in his support of such artists as Raphael and Michelangelo, Julius II believes that art transcends all ideological absolutes. Dressed in the Renaissance robes from his portrait by Titian, he serves as a reminder of the waning of Humanism and individualism. At times his viewpoint is caricatured, however, when, in the face of contemporary choices, he too chooses a more pragmatic point of view.

Hyrcan IV, king of Hyrcania. Hyrcan IV is ruler and creator of the imaginary kingdom of Hyrcania, constructed to justify his synthetic philosophy of power. An ultimate pragmatist and believer in the absolutes of power, Hyrcan IV represents the coming age of numbing dictatorship over individual creativity. His costume projects the trappings of power as he appears carrying a sword and wearing a purple cloak and a helmet with a red plume, while underneath the cloak, a golden garment glimmers. As he throws off these garments in the last scene and appears in a well-tailored cutaway, the sham of his Hyrcanian worldview is revealed as yet another ideology that pragmatically suits selfish desires.

Alice d'Or, the statue. Dressed in a tight-fitting dress, the fabric of which resembles alligator skin, the blonde, twenty-six-year-old statue reclines on a pedestal on her stomach. As Rockoffer's former mistress, she attempts to entice him by recalling their former sensuality; however, at this point she exists only as a symbol of his atrophied desire.

Ella, Rockoffer's eighteen-year-old fiancée. Ella represents bourgeois domesticity, as she comes in carrying parcels to furnish their small apartment, with its small gold sofa where their matrimonial bliss will be lived out in the daily rituals of meals and pleasantries. She is the play's cuttlefish, an insidious predator who clouds perspective by diffusing an inky substance. In the *coup de théâtre* of the last scene, however, she sheds her bourgeois limitations showing the courage to join Rockoffer in his attempt to build a new Hyrcania.

Two Matrons, one of them Ella's mother, the other Hyrcan's. Both mothers project the sentimental belief in the right of mothers to be taken care of by their children. Both are taken along to Hyrcania by Rockoffer:

359

Hyrcan IV's mother, as Rockoffer's adopted mother, and Ella's, as mother-in-law.

Two Old Gentlemen, Ella's uncles. They are minor characters representing bourgeois complacency in the face of social change.

Grumpus, the footman. He is old, wearing a gray livery coat with large silver buttons and gray top hat. In his acceptance of the transition of power lies a suggestion that there is no essential change as far as he is concerned.

Christine Kiebuzinska

DA

Author: Hugh Leonard (John Keyes Byrne, 1926-   )
Type of work: Play
Time of action: May, 1968
First produced: 1973

Charlie Tynan, a London playwright. Charlie is Da's foster-child, who, at forty-two, has returned to Ireland to bury his deceased father. He is a troubled man who is unable to exorcise Da's presence from his memory. Charlie's earlier abjuration of Da's rustic sensibility is a source of shame for him, as is his perception of his father as boorish and obstinate. His father's posthumous visitations to Charlie's mind are reflections of his fixation on Da and the remarkable impressions he left on Charlie throughout their embattled relationship.

Nick Tynan (Da), a longtime gardener for the Prynne family. Da is eighty-three at his death but appears in the play at various ages from his fifties to the time of his death. Da is a cantankerous man, even when younger, yet he is proud of his fifty-eight years of diligent service as a gardener for the Prynne family. Though he is contrary to people like Drumm, his insistence on haunting Charlie is a reflection of his forceful personality and dominant role in shaping Charlie's life.

Margaret Tynan (Mother), housewife and mother to Da and Charlie respectively. She is in her late seventies at her reported death, but the play presents her during her late fifties. "Mag," as she is called, is devoted to both Da and Charlie and exhibits a pride in her rearing of Charlie after his natural mother abandoned him. Her one act of defiance is to accept an invitation of tea from an old friend and thus to alienate Da.

Mr. Drumm, a clerk. He is a priggish, arrogant man in his mid-fifties in one flashback as Charlie remembers his first job when he was seventeen. He is a bookish man who appreciates Charlie's literary interests but strongly dislikes Da's antagonistic, perverse treatment of him when he first arrives to hire Charlie. He admonishes Charlie about embracing any of life's opportunities. As a result, by play's end, he returns to Charlie's house after Da's funeral and admits his own shortcomings.

Young Charlie, the seventeen-year-old Charlie appears to be a slightly naïve young man, seeking to break away from his parents' influence, especially that of Da. He is excited about his employment at Drumm's clerical office and somewhat cynical about the elder Charlie when the two exchange words. The elder Charlie must often put his younger incarnation in his place.

Oliver, Charlie's childhood friend. Oliver is in his early forties and appears at the house after Da's funeral. His childish perspective on life belies his strictly mercenary interest in the now-empty house and his hopes to acquire it. He also appears later in the play during a flashback of Charlie's departure for London.

Mary Tate, a twenty-five-year-old woman from Charlie's past. Mary appears once in the play and is notable for her effects on Charlie's libido. Described as the "Yellow Peril" by Charlie, Mary is an aloof, lonely young woman, who teases Charlie when he flirts with her. Her mysterious reputation as a bad girl is quickly stripped from her by Da when he meets her and Charlie on a park bench. Da reveals that she is really a young girl from Glasthule, whose father abandoned her and her family. Her identity restored, she no longer becomes the conquest Charlie had hoped for.

Mrs. Prynne, the daughter of Mr. Jacob Prynne, owner of the garden that Da has tended for more than fifty-eight years. She is fifty years old and apparently prim. While she is kind in her words to Da, her pension contribution to Da of twenty-six pounds per annum is viewed as miserly by young Charlie. Unaware of the slight she has given Da, she exacerbates it further by giving Da a mounted set of fused spectacles from the great fire of the San Francisco earthquake— one of her father's keepsakes.

Hardin Aasand

A DANCE IN THE SUN

Author: Dan Jacobson (1929-   )
Type of work: Novel
Time of action: The early 1950's
First published: 1956

The Narrator, unnamed, a university student who hitchhikes with his friend Frank from Lyndhurst (probably modeled on Kimberley) to Cape Town and, marooned in a small, isolated Karroo village, finds lodging for the night at Fletcher's home. A student of literature, he is humane in his attitude toward Africans, in part because of his fond memories of his family's African servants; he cannot, however, entirely escape the attitudes that are inevitable in a member of a socially superior caste. Essentially innocent when they arrive at the Fletcher residence, he and Frank feel as if they have grown up during the night they stay there.

Frank, the Narrator's friend, a medical student. A tall and rather awkward boy who dresses carelessly, he is shy and even timid, but he is a careful observer of people, with a lively and almost clinical interest in human behavior. Described by the narrator as a clever boy in school, he is quite witty, and, because he is no racist, he makes fun of Fletcher's racism and his grandiose ideas of "world order" with sardonic remarks that are too subtle for Fletcher to understand. In the novel's plot he is a more important character than the narrator because he is present in the confrontation of Fletcher and Ignatius Louw.

Fletcher, a British South African. Rather animal-like in bearing and movement, with a large head and bright, staring eyes, he seems younger than he is. He is verbose and jovial, but he tends to shout at everyone and is the sort of person who insists that everyone agree with him. He is arrogant in his assumptions about his own cleverness, and he is above all a raging racist, who rants to the narrator and Frank his apocalyptic predictions that civilization is being destroyed by the "inferior" races and their liberal supporters. In fact, he is the victim of paranoia, exaggerated in his case by his fear that he will lose the estate that he acquired by marriage.

Mrs. Fletcher, his wife, an Afrikaner. Thin and faded, she is the proud daughter of a Boer pioneer whose accomplishments were formidable; she therefore believes that she has lowered herself by marrying Fletcher. More quietly racist than her husband, she committed a crime against Joseph's sister and her child because of pride and a desperate concern for the reputation of her family.

361

Ignatius "Nasie" Louw (nä′sē), Mrs. Fletcher's young brother. Essentially weak-willed and morally bankrupt, he is nevertheless likable. During the night when the Narrator and Frank are staying with the Fletchers, he returns. He seems to have committed miscegenation with Joseph's sister as an act of defiance against his society, his family, and his Boer father. Now he is consumed with guilt for abandoning her and their child and is enraged at Fletcher for encouraging him to do so. In the end, he runs away.

Joseph, an old African laborer, the brother of Louw's mistress. A tall, well-muscled man, physically scarred by his hard life, he was not willing to remain a servant of the Fletchers and left to see the world. Now, because his sister has disappeared and her "yellow" baby is missing, he asks help from the Narrator and Frank. His sense of family loyalty is as great as Mrs. Fletcher's, and he wants desperately to find the child that is his family's only link to the future. On the other hand, he is quite capable of using his painful situation to his own advantage, and at the end of the novel he has blackmailed Fletcher into giving him a job.

Robert L. Berner

A DANCE OF THE FORESTS

Author: Wole Soyinka (1934-   )
Type of work: Play
Time of action: 1960
First produced: 1960

Forest Father or **Head (Osanyin),** the chief god who controls the universe of this play. In the pantheon of Yoruba gods, he is called Osanyin. He is the supreme arbiter, who rules both men and lesser gods. Because he represents the divine qualities of justice and mercy, he despairs of the continuous evil of humanity's history but believes that humankind may be improved if mortals can be made to admit the consequences of their acts as part of history. He designs the dance to expose past and present wickedness. He is concerned and sympathetic but all-powerful, reserving his supreme power to restrain and ultimately decide the outcome of the dance and therefore the outcome of the world. In his mortal guise, he masquerades as Obaneji, who leads the party into the forest.

Aroni, "the Lame One" who opens the play. He is the messenger of the great Forest Head, and it is he who selects the dead man and woman who reflect the violent past that lives on in the grim practices of the present-day characters.

Eshuro, one of the aspects of Oro, god of the dead, who includes qualities of the Yoruba god of mischief, Eshu. He is spiteful and antagonistic to humankind and demands from Forest Head vengeance against Demoke. He becomes the "figure in red" who controls the "bloody triplets" who, at the point of potential reconciliation, snatch the half-child representing the human future. It is his final chance to destroy the human race, as he so bitterly desires.

Agboreko, an Elder of the Sealed Lips who exists as a soothsayer between the two existences. He is an intermediary between the living people on Earth and the spirits in the Forest.

Rola, the eternal whore, but queen in the ancient court of Mata Kharibu, also called **Madame Tortoise** because of the image that once on her back she will not turn herself over. She is woman as tormentor and sexual sadist. She demands the attentions and subjugation of all men. In one evidence of her cruel nature, she orders the passivist army captain (the Dead Man) to be gelded for rejecting her sexual overtures. Now reduced to an actual prostitute, she continues her sexual scandals in modern times when two of her lovers die, one by murder and one by suicide. She is the female black widow spider in human form.

Adenebi, a corrupt official, indifferent to decency and principle, only concerned with being paid for his patronage. He now has the position of Council Orator and uses pompous rhetoric. In early times he was the Court Historian and cruelly sent innocent men to their deaths. He repeats similar iniquities in the present when he corruptly licenses the overloading of a truck, which crashes, burning sixty-five people to death. He exemplifies political immorality.

Demoke, a figure who represents the artist as a potent force within society. He was a poet in the ancient court and is now a carver. His apprentice, Oremole, was killed by falling down from the tree that they were both carving in honor of the celebration for which the play was written. His act provokes an intense soul-searching. He is not sure that others who accuse him of killing Oremole out of jealousy may not be right. As the articulate and self-aware artist, Demoke represents the nature of man at a profound level. In a painful moment of self-interrogation, he is forced to admit that he did in fact destroy Oremole. In spite of this crime, for him redemption is possible. He catches the half-child and, by allowing its birth, ensures the future for man. Demoke is the redeemer within society because he is an artist.

The Dead Man, a character who is revived from his earlier existence as a captain in the army of the dead emperor Mata Kharibu. He has refused to serve in the emperor's unjust wars. As a punishment, he is sold into slavery and gelded on the instructions of the jealous empress.

The Dead Woman, his wife. She is equally dirty, ragged, and squalid, a far cry from the visions of lovely opulence from the other world that were anticipated to arrive. She was killed while pregnant. If her child can now be brought to birth it will establish the future of the human race. In her crude way, she supplies the continuity of life that derives from motherhood and offers life even under degraded conditions.

John F. Povey

DANGLING MAN

Author: Saul Bellow (1915-   )
Type of work: Novel
Time of action: December 15, 1942, to April 9, 1943
First published: 1944

Joseph, an unemployed man dangling between civilian life and his final draft call to the U.S. army, his induction delayed by bureaucratic red tape. A tall, handsome, flabby, well-educated man of introspective and philosophical habits of mind, he keeps a journal of his feelings and musings, growing more bitter, dispirited, and demoralized as he assesses the damage to his sense of self-identity the seven-month delay has inflicted upon him. The major anxiety he feels is existential, such as how to keep his sense of being intact and unencumbered and how to keep his balance between his personal desires and the coercions of society. The problem of freedom is crucial for Joseph, as he clearly recognizes the environmental pressures toward conformity that threaten his personal freedom: the sorrowful, ugly cityscape of Chicago; the stigma of poverty; the demands of his mistress; and the relationships with his wife, family, and friends, all of whom urge him to make something of himself and behave respectably. In a secular age with no deep structure of belief or a priori models of conduct, he is haunted by the question of how to live as a good man.

Becoming more peevish, irritable, and quarrelsome as the weeks go by, his life an unrelieved tedium of idleness in the single room he and his wife are renting until his departure, Joseph broods about the avidity of his friends and about his own limitations and sense of mortality. He becomes increasingly disappointed in others, separate, distrustful, and alienated. Feeling constantly badgered by the public conscience (which he thinks of as the world internalized), he clings desperately to the one true virtue of preserving oneself: deciding what one can decide and recognizing what is beyond one's control. After quarreling with his wife over his refusal to cash her paycheck and with Captain Briggs, the landlady's son-in-law, about the annoying, alcoholic behavior and petty thievery of a fellow roomer named Mr. Vanaker, Joseph decides to give up his struggle and requests the draft board to expedite his induction. Summoned to report to the army, Joseph has now placed his destiny in the hands of others, feeling no longer accountable for himself. His journal ends on an ambiguous note; having volitionally canceled his freedom and self-determination, he seems to embrace the life of regimentation that lies ahead.

Iva, Joseph's wife. A quiet, dutiful, circumspect woman, she tries to enable Joseph to enjoy his liberty before he leaves for the army. Since he quit his job at the travel agency, she has fully supported him. Joseph has dominated her for the six years of their marriage, trying to form her taste and intellect, but she resists his efforts, succumbing instead to the conventional appeals of fashion magazines, clothes, furniture, and radio entertainment. Concerned about appearances and desiring the good opinion of others, she is easily embarrassed by Joseph's behavior. Growing somewhat rebellious, she becomes quick to defy or quarrel with him. She discourages talk (they do not confide in each other), yet she complains that Joseph neglects her. When she nurses him through a minor illness, she becomes less critical and more endearing to Joseph. Hurt by his failure to consult her in his decision to ask the draft board for an early summons, she wishes Joseph would show more grief at the prospect of their long separation. Against Joseph's wishes, she decides to stay with her parents while he is in the army.

Kitty Daumler, Joseph's mistress. A simple, uncomplicated, down-to-earth woman whom Joseph had first met when he arranged a tour for her, she confidently sets out to seduce him. Although she is careless, messy, unkempt, and somewhat gross, she is sensually attractive, a lively, plump, solid, worldly presence. Irritated by Iva's nagging and pettiness, Joseph visits Kitty's apartment regularly, drawn by her affectionate and generous nature, yet determined to keep the relationship on the level of amiable talk. Inevitably, he succumbs to desire and the relationship becomes sexual. The affair lasts for two months, until Kitty hints that Joseph should leave Iva. Sobered by the consequences of his own unlimited desire, he attempts to return the relationship to its earlier friendly but nonsexual basis. One night, after quarreling with Iva, Joseph visits Kitty to retrieve a book and feels vaguely resentful and insulted to find her with a man. Several weeks later, Kitty sends Joseph a note asking him to drop by, but he is surprised to find he no longer thinks about her.

Clifford Edwards

DANIEL MARTIN

Author: John Fowles (1926-   )
Type of work: Novel
Time of action: The mid-1970's, with flashbacks through the 1940's
First published: 1977

Daniel Martin (Dan), a British playwright turned Hollywood screenwriter. Dan is a forty-five-year-old man in emotional and artistic exile. Reared a vicar's son in Devon and educated at the University of Oxford, Dan is a comfortable atheist, a tentative socialist, and a skilled dialogue technician. He sees life through the distorting and limiting eyes of a filmmaker, objectifying or reinventing reality to fit his needs. Accordingly, he can be quick and clever (and often evasive and patronizing) in real emotional situations; after a failed marriage, he has had numerous satisfying but double-edged romances. He is very self-aware and senses his alienation and the echoes of his past. In returning to his estranged friend Anthony's deathbed, Dan faces that past (what Anthony, Jane, Nell, and he meant to one another) and rediscovers lost honesty and passion, his love of nature, and his belief in meaningful art. In subsequent travels in England and the Middle East, he falls back in love with Jane, the one he suspects he should have spent his life with all along.

Jane Mallory, Dan's former sister-in-law. A forty-five-year-old widow, Jane emerges from years of unfulfilled marriage to Anthony a withdrawn, confused, and defensive woman. She is intelligent, well-spoken, and newly interested in Marxism and sociopolitical reform, but these sentiments cloak the internal battle to accept responsibility for the subterfuges of the past and to find a new direction in life. Jane is a deeply intuitive woman, responsive less to logic than to "right feeling" and as expressive in silence as in words. By accepting Dan's concern and, ultimately, his love, she becomes strong, open, and trusting once again.

Jenny McNeil, Dan's girlfriend. Jenny is a twenty-five-year-old British actress learning the ways of Hollywood. She is a shrewd and challenging woman who loves both Dan and the games and repartee their relationship entails. Modern and independent, with a sense of perspective and humor, Jenny turns bitter and sardonic when Dan ends their relationship.

Caroline Martin (Caro), Dan and Nell's twenty-two-year-old daughter. Caro is a sensible, straightforward young woman who, though less sophisticated than she seems, is ready for the challenges of mature womanhood. She feels awkward with Dan but treasures the chance to grow closer; she has mixed feelings toward Nell and needs to establish her independence. She knows that her affair with her boss, Barney, could hurt her deeply, but she is willing to accept all risks and lessons.

Anthony Mallory, Dan's former best friend. Anthony is a brilliant philosopher and academic who faces death from cancer at the age of forty-five. A dogmatic Catholic, he broke with Dan years before over a play Dan wrote but has since come to a more sober, generous, and responsible view of life. After settling his conscience in a final interview with Dan about their shared history and his widow Jane's future, Anthony abruptly and mystifyingly takes his own life.

Nell Randall, Jane's sister and Dan's former wife. Nell, forty-four years old and happily remarried, is a woman of leisure and society. At base insecure, she thrives on propriety and decorum and needs to feel involved and in control of those around her.

Barney Dillon, an acquaintance of Dan from Oxford, now Caro's boss and lover. Barney is a British television personality who has grown bored with his marriage, cynical about his Fleet Street milieu, and disillusioned with his own transparent achievements.

Andrew Randall, another of Dan's Oxford acquaintances, now Nell's husband. Andrew is a supercilious aristocrat whose naturally hearty manner is often a welcome relief in tense family situations.

Rosamund Mallory (Roz), Anthony and Jane's older daughter. Roz, a twenty-three-year-old research assistant with the British Broadcasting Corporation, is an altogether self-possessed, level-headed, compassionate, and mature young woman.

Paul Mallory, Anthony and Jane's son, a withdrawn and taciturn schoolboy whose only apparent passion is for English field systems.

Nancy Reed, Dan's first love. Nancy is a chubby blue-eyed Devon farm girl who loves adventure and delights in secret pleasures with Dan. Later, she reappears as a stout matron.

Abe and
Mildred Nathan, an older Jewish couple who lend Dan and Jenny their guest cottage in Los Angeles. Abe is an apparently lugubrious and obscene but essentially wise and bighearted veteran of the film industry; Mildred is his quietly supportive wife.

Ben and
Phoebe, the simple, provincial old couple who inhabit and maintain Thorncombe, Dan's Devon farmhouse retreat.

Parson Martin, Dan's father, a rigid and humorless country vicar who loved gardening and opposed the display of emotion.

Millie Martin, Dan's simple, old-fashioned spinster aunt and surrogate mother.

Professor Kirnberger, a brilliant, sensitive German Egyptologist whom Dan and Jane befriend on their Nile cruise.

Jimmy Assad, Dan's urbane Egyptian film contact and guide.

B. P. Mann

THE DARK CHILD

Author: Camara Laye (1928-1980)
Type of work: Novel
Time of action: c. 1933-c. 1947
First published: L'Enfant noir, 1953 (English translation, 1954)

The narrator, Camara Laye (kä•mä•rä lä′ yə), a young Guinean boy from a highly respected family of the Malinké people. Although somewhat timid, he is curious, intelligent, affectionate, and sensitive. As he moves from early childhood through adolescence, Laye's advancement through the colonial French school system takes him away from his home in Kouroussa to Conakry (the capital of Guinea) and, finally, sends him to Paris to continue his studies. The childhood memories he recounts seek to preserve, defend, understand, and, perhaps, mourn the passing of the traditional way of life of his youth. These vignettes include observing his father's mysterious familiarity with a small, black snake ("the guiding spirit of our race"); watching his father and mother at work; experiencing the seasonal rhythms of his grandmother's farming village; participating in various traditional ceremonies of initiation, including that of circumcision.

Laye's departure for Paris at the end of the novel again contrasts the anguish of leaving traditional Africa with the attraction of the unfamiliar Western culture.

His Father, a blacksmith, goldsmith, and sculptor. Steeped in the traditional ways of his people, he has powers that can only be described as supernatural. These powers are most clearly seen in his relationship with a small, black snake and in the spirituality, craftsmanship, and theatricality he exhibits while working with gold. Although he clearly regrets that much of his traditional wisdom and knowledge will not be passed on to his son, he recognizes that the boy's destiny is different from his own: The Africa of the future will need citizens with technical skills and Western education. When the boy is harrassed by older students at the local school, the father is willing to come to blows with the school's principal in order to defend his son's rights. At other moments, when Laye is tempted to abandon his educational project, his father urges him to persevere.

His Mother, a member of another respected Malinké family, she also possesses magical powers. Because the crocodile is her totem, she is able to draw water from the river without fear of these animals. On one occasion, she alone is able to revive a horse who ap-

pears to be under a spell. Provider of food, discipline, and, above all, unqualified love, she is not always able to accept the fact that her son is growing up. She suffers greatly each time an event in his life (whether it be a move to a new school or a traditional African rite of passage) threatens to distance him from her.

Janet L. Solberg

DARKNESS VISIBLE

Author: William Golding (1911-   )
Type of work: Novel
Time of action: After World War II
First published: 1979

Matty "Septimus" Windrave, also called **Windrove** or **Windgrave,** the protagonist, a branded victim of the London firebombing. His past a blank slate, his body horribly burned, his mind psychologically scarred, Matty Windrave remains an outcast throughout his life because of his monstrous condition (a limp, two-toned face, a half-bald skull, a ghastly ear). At the Foundlings School at Greenfield, despite his high-minded craving for knowledge, he is rejected by schoolmasters and classmates alike, a rejection that leads to his quest for spiritual meaning to explain his fate and to point the way toward his destiny. Introspective and enduring, he works as a laborer in Australia (always with superior testimonials) until a mystic experience leads him to write a journal of his mission and directs him back to Greenfield and the beautiful, clever Stanhope twins. There he redeems himself by once again being consumed by fire, in this case, a firebomb that burns down his old school, but that, thanks to Matty, fails to harm the kidnapped Arab child whom he frees. Whether mystic-seer or deluded fanatic, Matty sacrifices himself for an innocent.

Mr. Sebastian Pedigree, a pitiable pederast who taught in the boys' school Matty attended. His deviant inclinations lead to a

child's suicide, his own dismissal, a series of imprisonments, and moral and economic decline. He meets Matty's unspoken pleas for friendship with horror and rejection, blaming him for the tragic pattern of his life. The slightly built and graying Pedigree cannot control the tide of passion that overtakes him in waves, and relies on a multicolored ball to attract young boys to his center of existence, the public toilets. Yet for all sins, he understands suffering and guilt, and is the final witness to Matty's return from the dead. Whether that return is a hallucination or a beatific vision, it is the last thing in life Mr. Pedigree ever sees as he prays for an end to his surging tide of impulses.

Sophy Stanhope, a wholesomely beautiful child and then young lady whose affected innocence hides her evil twist. Having tortured animals as a child, she continues to delight in breaking conventional taboos— lying, stealing, and prostituting herself. She becomes a thrill-seeking, sexual sadist, joining forces with a perverse and amoral thief (Gerry), repeatedly stabbing her sexual conquest (the narcissistic, athletic Fido), and exploiting the knowledge and position of others to further her plot to kidnap and slowly torture and kill a wealthy young Arab Prince from Wandicoot School. Her failure to achieve that end leads to perjury and unsuccessful attempts to blame those around her. Her belief that she and her twin are "everything to each other" is continually disproved.

Toni (Antoinette) Stanhope, Sophy's pale, ethereal twin sister, a political terrorist. Aloof, remote, impenetrable, Toni shares her sister's unearthly beauty and perversion but pursues her evil with more controlled direction and theoretically in the name of some anarchistic political cause. Despite her drifting manner, she takes advantage of Sophy's muddled plot and, with her political associates, helps firebomb the school and take hostages to Africa, from where she broadcasts about freedom and justice. Sim calls her "mad and bad," but Edwin recognizes the truth: "She's not human."

Mr. Stanhope, the ineffectual, sexually driven father of the twins. He coldly dismisses them from his life, mocks their sexuality, and buries himself in his studies.

Sim Goodchild, the very decent, kindly owner of a bookstore near the center of Greenfield. Sim takes people at face value and is tolerant and forgiving. He is at first beguiled by both the Stanhope girls (for whom he had an innocent crush) and Mr. Pedigree, but eventually even his simple innocence learns to see them for what they are. Windrave finds his palm indicative of his soul: "exquisitely beautiful . . . made of light . . . precious."

Ruth Goodchild, his calm, matter-of-fact wife. Mrs. Goodchild has self-convinced worldviews, and it is she who first sees through the Stanhope girls' façade. Seeing Sophy stab one of her boyfriends makes her ill.

Edwin Bell, one of Matty's fellow students, now a tutor at the old school. Embarrassed by the reappearance of Pedigree but convinced of the holiness and vision of Matty, occultist Bell longs for a mystic religious experience and persaudes Sim Goodchild to share in the search. Together they accidentally discover the hiding place Sophy had planned for her kidnap victim.

Gina Macdonald

DAUGHTER OF EARTH

Author: Agnes Smedley (1892-1950)
Type of work: Novel
Time of action: The 1890's to the 1920's
First published: 1929

Marie Rogers, narrator and protagonist, daughter of poor laborers who move through Missouri, Oklahoma, and Colorado in search of work. Although she is a survivor, childhood experiences warp her understanding of love, tenderness, and compassion. She escapes her economically oppressive world to become a secretary, magazine saleswoman, and teacher in the West, and, later, a socialist journalist and dedicated activist in the Indian nationalist movement in New York. She is driven by two unyielding beliefs: that work will give her money to use for education, which will insure her economic independence, and that she can maintain her freedom by resisting the demands of family, sex, and marriage, the complexities of which she does not fully understand. She is passionately committed to struggle against all forms of injustice.

Elly Rogers, mother of Marie and her four siblings. A beautiful young woman, subject to frequent brutality and erratic support from her husband, she works diligently but hopelessly at various menial jobs to maintain her children. She cares deeply for them and desires especially that they be educated, but both dreams and affections are crushed by the struggle for life's essentials. She dies in her late thirties of malnutrition and related causes.

John Rogers, husband of Elly and father of their children. Less practical and more imaginative and fun-loving than his wife, he rarely earns sufficient income working on farms and in mining camps to provide an adequate living for his family. To escape responsibilities, he periodically deserts them, resorts to alcohol, defends himself with physical cruelty, and dreams of a better future.

Annie Rogers, Marie's older sister. She gains limited independence by earning her own money in a laundry, marries Sam Walker at age sixteen, and dies in childbirth within two years.

Beatrice Rogers, Marie's younger sister. Unlike Marie, she initially places higher value on physical strength than on education in the struggle for survival. Although she temporarily joins Marie in work and school and shares meager resources with her, the two sisters never establish a close relationship.

George Rogers, Marie's younger brother, for whom she feels a special bond. When he is jailed for stealing a horse, Marie sends what money she has, accompanied by an unsympathetic letter that haunts her after George is accidentally killed as a young man.

Dan Rogers, Marie's youngest sibling. Unable to secure work elsewhere, he joins the army at age eighteen and fights in Europe during World War I. After the war, he is given land in New Mexico where he works with his father and brother-in-law Sam.

Helen, sister of Elly Rogers. She earns money as a hired girl on the farm, as a laundry worker, and, eventually, as a prostitute. A beautiful woman who appreciates beautiful things, she resists the economic dependence and powerlessness of marriage, supports herself, and generously shares her earnings with Elly and her children.

Knut Larsen, a handsome, cultivated, and educated young Scandinavian and Marie's first husband, whom she marries at eighteen. Though their marriage is based on mutual respect and agreement, Knut is unable to pierce Marie's fear of men, sex, and children. After two abortions and consistent though sincere misunderstanding, the couple is divorced.

Karin Larsen, young, lovely, educated sister of Knut, originally from the East but teaching in Phoenix when Marie meets her. She provides friendship and support for Marie when they move to San Francisco and then in New York.

Anand Manvekar (ä′nänd măn•vē′kär), an intelligent, attractive, energetic, radical leader of the Indian nationalist movement in his thirties and Marie's second husband. They love and admire each other, but ultimately his suspicions about her previous relationship with Juan Diaz, whom he dislikes and distrusts, as well as Anand's and Marie's mutual inability to understand each other's convictions on various personal and political issues, destroy their marriage.

Sardar Ranjit Singh (sär′där răn′jĭt sĭng), a lecturer, writer, and active member of the Indian nationalist movement. He becomes Marie's private tutor, introducing her to the serious discipline of study, particularly of all facets of Indian history and culture.

Juan Diaz (wän dē′äz), a half-Hindu, half-Portuguese activist in the Indian nationalist movement. After sexually attacking Marie, he secures her promise not to reveal the incident. Later, he betrays their mutual confidence, misrepresents her behavior in their relationship, and destroys her credibility and Anand's among their Indian associates.

Talvar Singh (täl′vär sĭng), a young Indian nationalist, who entrusts crucially important information to Marie, which she protects to the point of imprisonment.

Sara McAlpin

369

A DAY IN THE DEATH OF JOE EGG

Author: Peter Nichols (1927-   )
Type of work: Play
Time of action: The mid-1960's
First produced: 1967

Brian (Bri), a thirty-three-year-old school-teacher in Bristol, England. Bri is an adept comedian, jokester, and mimic who has found that humor is the only escape from or cure for the reality of living with a spastic child. He loves his wife Sheila and daughter Joe but feels that circumstances (an unexpected pregnancy and ensuing medical malpractice) have thrown him into an untenable situation. He is moody, emotionally spontaneous, and deeply jealous of Joe for usurping Sheila's attention. An aspiring painter who has lost the creative drive and taken solace in drinking, he dislikes and is ineffective in his job as a schoolteacher. To him, God is a manic-depressive rugby player: Bri is very cynical and will not tolerate false hopes about Joe's condition. Though he propels the elaborate farce that he and Sheila enact to fulfill their life with Joe, he cannot understand why Joe must live and finally acts on his impulse to commit euthanasia.

Sheila, Bri's thirty-five-year-old wife. Sheila is an industrious and warm-hearted woman who loves living things: Besides looking after Bri and Joe, she cares for a menagerie of pets and houseplants. A decade of hard work and frustrated motherhood have left her weary and somewhat humorless. She thinks carefully about human behavior and believes in psychology and the power of the subconscious. She harbors deep guilt about Joe's condition; she feels that her earlier promiscuity and the fear of motherhood it gave her caused her to inhibit Joe's birth and thus damage the child. While Sheila has no patience for Bri's self-pity, she plays along with his humor and farcical approach to their shared tragedy. In her heart, however, she resents his cynicism and clings to her faith, dreaming that she will someday see her daughter miraculously become a full human being.

Josephine (Joe), a ten-year-old spastic girl. Joe is a pretty child who looks physically normal but is spastic, epileptic, multiplegic, and almost totally incapable of willful human expression or activity. Her limbs are stiff; she must be propped up; she is susceptible to illness and seizures; and her feeding, medication, and bodily functions require constant care and attention. At best, she looks about vacantly and moans feebly. She spends her days at a school for spastics.

Freddie Underwood, Bri's college friend, now an affluent industrialist, a socialist, and a director of amateur theater. Freddie is hearty and hale and seems older than his thirty-three years. Likable and good-spirited, he is eager to help Sheila and Bri. Freddie is a cautious rationalist who clings to law and order, however, and he considers Bri's and Sheila's playacting with Joe to be an unhealthy and destructive response to the child's condition. He argues theoretically with Bri against euthanasia.

Pamela Underwood, Freddie's wife. Pamela is a postured and fashionable woman who is obsessed with propriety and appearances. She detests anything "N. P. A." (not physically attractive) and therefore feels no compassion, merely disgust, for Joe, to whom she refers as the "weirdie." Pamela is irritable and impatient and cannot fathom Freddie's desire to help Bri and Sheila. A basically self-centered woman, she devotes all of her attention, with great pride, to her husband and their three beautiful children.

Grace, Bri's mother, a sixty-five-year-old widow. Grace is a fastidious suburbanite who appreciates her routine and the small diversions that fill her life. She chatters freely and cheerfully but, like her son, is subject to moods of gloom and self-pity. She

370

is proud of the sacrifices she made for her husband and son and considers Sheila to be inadequate as a wife for Bri and mother for Joe.

B. P. Mann

DAYS OF THE TURBINS

Author: Mikhail Bulgakov (1891-1940)
Type of work: Play
Time of action: November, 1918, to January, 1919
First produced: Dni Turbinykh, 1926 (English translation, 1934, in *Six Soviet Plays*)

Alexei Vasilyevich Turbin, an artillery colonel in the Russian army. He is serving a Ukrainian Hetman in Kiev who collaborates with the Germans against other Ukrainian nationalists and the Bolsheviks. Alexei understands the precariousness of his position, as he is neither a flaming nationalist nor a friend of the Germans; he only wants to do what he is trained for: to serve as an officer with honor and dignity. When his honor and dignity are threatened, he refuses to continue fighting for a cause that has lost its rationale, preferring to pay for his mistake with his life—not before, however, he absolves everyone serving under him of any obligation to fight to the last along with him. Alexei embodies a gentleman officer and an idealist, contrary to the official Soviet view of any opponents of the Bolsheviks as morally bankrupt hirelings.

Nikolai Turbin, his brother, a cadet. Nikolai worships his older brother and, like him, has a high sense of duty. These two sentiments compel him to refuse his brother's command to leave before the final attack, during which he is badly crippled. In this sense, he is an extension of Alexei, with one difference: Alexei is adamantly anti-Bolshevik, whereas Nikolai's reaction to the coming of the Bolsheviks is not as clear.

Yelena Vasilyevna Talberg, their sister. Yelena is an intelligent woman of excellent upbringing married to a high officer in the Hetman's army. A red-haired beauty, with whom everyone seems to fall in love, she shows the dignity inbred in her brothers,

never losing moral decorum. She also handles the advances of her many suitors with benign firmness and never allows any relationship to sink below the proper level. Consequently, she firmly dissolves her marriage when her husband fails to uphold the standards of moral decency.

Vladimir Robertovich Talberg, a General Staff colonel and Yelena's husband. Talberg, also an active officer, is the direct opposite of Alexei: selfish, unscrupulous, insincere in his marriage, vain, jealous, ready to go to any length in furthering his own cause. He has no qualms in leaving Yelena behind to total uncertainty when he flees to Berlin. For this striking conglomeration of negative traits, he "looks like a rat" in the eyes of at least two of his companions.

Viktor Viktorovich Myshlaevsky (mĭ•shlyī•yěv′skĭy), a captain second grade in the artillery. A good-hearted, loud, and, at times, rowdy officer, as well as a heavy drinker but faithful friend, Myshlaevsky serves his country loyally but to a point. Once he realizes that the cause he has been serving is falling apart, he changes without much soul-searching and without really knowing to what he is changing, as he says, "I'm for the Bolsheviks, only against the Communists."

Leonid Yuryevich Shervinsky, a lieutenant, the Hetman's personal aide-de-camp. Shervinsky's driving force in life is his love for Yelena, for whom he is ready to sacrifice everything. His loyalty to the side for which he is fighting is weak, and the reason he

371

does not betray it is his preoccupation with Yelena and his lack of strong beliefs. He has little difficulty adapting to the Bolsheviks, thanks to his beautiful singing voice and to an uncanny ability to stay afloat in every situation.

Alexander Bronislavovich Studzinsky, a captain in the Hetman's army. Of all the officers except Alexei, Studzinsky is the most loyal to the struggle against the Bolsheviks, even when it seems totally hopeless. In this aspect, he shows a remarkable strength of character.

Lariosik, a cousin of the Turbins' from Zhitomir. A young man who comes to the Turbins to study in Kiev at the time of street fighting, Lariosik adapts quickly to the new situation, perhaps a result of his falling in love with Yelena. Painfully polite, bashful, awkward (he always breaks something), often managing to say the wrong thing, he is still liked by all and seems to fit into the chaotic scene onto which he has stumbled. His naïveté is a refreshing change of pace during the period of somber mood and mortal danger for the Turbins.

Vasa D. Mihailovich

THE DEAD

Author: James Joyce (1882-1941)
Type of work: Short story
Time of action: 1904
First published: 1914

Gabriel Conroy, an unfulfilled teacher and favorite nephew of the Morkan sisters, who live in Dublin, Ireland. A stout, nervous, sensitive man wearing his black hair parted in the middle and glasses with gilt rims, he writes a literary newspaper column and considers himself superior in culture to everyone at the annual Christmastime dance given by his aunts, but he feels like a failure. His after-dinner speech is a sentimental affirmation of traditional Irish character and customs, yet he feels sick of his country. Dutiful but restless, he has insulated himself from life, wears galoshes, and has never been passionately in love. His marriage is dull. After the dance, in their hotel room, he feels a strong desire for his wife Gretta, but she weeps, confesses that she is thinking of Michael Furey, a young lover who died for her, then she falls asleep. Gabriel accepts his failure, feels a generous compassion for his wife and, gazing out the window at the falling snow that is general all over Ireland, identifies himself in humility with all the dead.

Gretta Conroy, a country girl from western Ireland, wife of Gabriel. She has rich bronze hair, frail shoulders, and a grace and mystery. At the dance she is moved by a sweet Irish song that reminds her of Michael Furey, leading to the confession to her husband that she once had romance in her life.

Lily, the caretaker's daughter and housemaid of the Morkan sisters. A pale, slim, growing girl, she makes Gabriel feel a failure when he cheerfully inquires whether she will be getting married soon to her young man and she replies with great bitterness that men nowadays are merely out for what they can get.

Kate Morkan, an elderly piano teacher, Gabriel's aunt and the chief hostess. She is a feeble yet vivacious lady, with old-fashioned braided hair that has not lost its ripe nut color and a face like a shriveled red apple. She fiercely defends the rights of her sister Julia Morkan against the pope and is said by Gabriel in his laudatory speech to have too good a heart, though he actually feels trapped by the culture she represents.

Julia Morkan, Kate's sister and a leading soprano. Grayhaired, dim of mind, and near death, she sings a bridal song with innocence of irony and is excessively praised by Freddy Malins, who is drunk. At the end of the story, she inspires Gabriel's pity in his meditation on the dead.

Mary Jane, a young organist and piano teacher, the only niece of the Morkan sisters, and the main prop of the household. With her aunts, according to Gabriel, she is one of the Three Graces of the Dublin musical world.

Molly Ivors, a friend and a teacher colleague of Gabriel, dedicated to Irish nationalism. A frank, challenging woman with a freckled face, prominent brown eyes, and a brooch on her collar bearing an Irish symbol and motto, she irritates Gabriel by accusing him of being unpatriotic, a West Briton. He sees her as a rude propagandist who represents a new generation that lacks the virtures of the Morkan sisters and Mary Jane. She asserts her independence and leaves the dance early.

Freddy Malins, a houseguest given to drink and indecorum. A man of about forty, with coarse features, protruded lips, disorderly scanty hair, and a sleepy look, he comes late, is drunk, and laughs excessively, but proves himself a decent fellow, nonetheless, by defending a black singer and by paying Gabriel back a loan.

Mrs. Malins, Freddy's mother, visiting from Glasgow. An ineffectual old woman with white hair and a stutter, she has made her son take a pledge not to drink.

Mr. Browne, a non-Catholic guest who knows opera. A swarthy man with a stiff, grizzled mustache, he is forward and offensively common.

Bartell D'Arcy, a conceited and second-rate tenor. He sings the Irish song that moves Gretta to recall Michael Furey, who used to sing the same song, but breaks it off because he has a dreadful cold.

Michael Furey, the romantic passion of Gretta, A Galway boy who died at seventeen. Very delicate and gentle, with big dark eyes, he was poor and employed in the gasworks, yet Gretta felt great with him. When she was about to move away from Galway, he was ill, yet he came and stood in her garden in the rain, and caught his death.

Michael Hollister

THE DEAD CLASS
A Dramatic Séance

Author: Tadeusz Kantor (1915-   )
Type of work: Play
Time of action: Evocation of 1914
First produced: Umarła Klasa, 1975

Old Students, eight elderly people, fellow students of the Old Man Repeater, the Old Man with a Bike, the Old Man in the Loo, and the Old Man Exhibitionist. They are dressed in black with black bowlers, grayish faces, and dead staring eyes. Each student carries a child puppet on his back dressed in school uniform as an effigy of lost childhood and imprisonment in the past.

The Old Man in the Loo, a student. He sits in the school lavatory with his pants about his legs, engrossed in endless accounts and quarrels with God. This repetitive action suggests an eternal regression into the anal stage.

The Old Man with a Bike, a student. He never parts with the beat-up remnant of

373

childhood and ceaselessly rides the bike around the desks, adding yet another symbolic action to the eternal imprisonment in repetition of the members of the dead class.

The Old Man Exhibitionist, a student. His fellow students drag him to the privy, pull his pants down, and he exposes his backside, remaining in that pose for the duration of the lesson on Solomon.

The Old Man Repeater, a miserable looking student who is taunted and bullied by the others. He stubbornly recites his grammar lesson while the rest talk and squirm in total indifference. As the Obituary Distributor, he displays his bent for repetitive action by distributing and reading in a droning monotone the endless list of the dead class.

Charwoman, cleans up the classroom. Her function extends from sweeping up notebooks, paper, and the debris of the dead class to the ritual washing of the cadavers of the dead class, thereby extending her symbolic function to Charwoman-Death. In the final scene, she is transformed into a nightmarish brothel-keeper, who bumps and grinds while the activities in the classroom continue in automatic and repetitive patterns.

The Woman with a Mechanical Cradle, she is wheeled in strapped to what looks like a combination gynecologist's table with stir-rups and an instrument of torture. Each one of the movements of opening and closing of her knees is synchronized to the rocking of the coffinlike Mechanical Cradle, with its rattling wooden balls, in a travesty of the birth-death cycle.

The Woman Behind the Window, she carries the frame of a window, always looking in from the outside in a symbolic action of her separation from life.

Somnambulist Prostitute, the town harlot. She struts shamelessly around the leering oldster students baring her breasts in an automaton-like action.

The Beadle, the preserver of order. He sits passively in his chair, coming to life only to sing the Austrian Empire's national anthem.

Tadeusz Kantor, the creator and director of *The Dead Class*. Since the performance is Kantor's creation, he remains on stage during the duration of the performance, directing the action by indicating climaxes, musical passages, entrances, exits, and the speeding up or slowing down of action. As a result of his presence, the performance is not always played in a particular order and actions may change from performance to performance.

Christine Kiebuzinska

DEAD MAN LEADING

Author: V. S. Pritchett (1900-   )
Type of work: Novel
Time of action: c. 1930
First published: 1937

Harry Johnson, a timber merchant and adventurer who relishes solitude. He is about thirty, strong, muscular, and awkward with big brown eyes, a crinkled forehead, immensely broad shoulders, and a gentle aloof manner. He is the son of a missionary who had disappeared in the same Brazilian forest that Johnson is about to explore along with his two friends, Gilbert Phillips and Charles Wright. Before leaving England, he has had a brief love affair with Wright's stepdaughter, Lucy Mommbrekke. Obsessed by the fear that she may be having a child and that he will be chained to her, he falls ill on the launch that is taking him and Phillips upriver to rendezvous with Wright. He longs to talk to his friends but cannot bring himself to risk their saying that he has lost his nerve. When he recovers from his illness, he and Silva leave in a canvas canoe without telling Phillips and Wright, who overtake them. Johnson is punishing himself and Wright because he feels guilty and wants to be alone. Eventually he forgets the other men and thinks only of his father, the dead man of the title. He is extremely brave: He makes a tremendous but unsuccessful effort to save Wright's life, and, after weeks of cutting through the jungle, he staggers off to find water for Phillips and disappears.

Gilbert Phillips, an English journalist about thirty, tall and fair as a Dane, a friend since boyhood of Johnson, and a former lover of Lucy. He is highly impressionable, a worrier who feels that his safety is tied to Johnson. He wallows in self-pity. After Wright's death, he follows Johnson for many miles through almost impenetrable jungle, because he is afraid to turn back alone. After Johnson's departure in search of water, Phillips is saved by rain, but, terrified of being alone, he stumbles on until rescued by some Germans.

Charles Wright, a former army doctor who is now an explorer. He is trim, erect, and capable, with a wiry strength. He is indignant when he, the leader, feels obliged to follow Johnson, particularly after it becomes evident that the young man is taking a dangerous course differing from the one agreed on. Pity urges him to go hunting with Johnson and try to reason with him. When he is accidentally shot by his own gun, he is carried by Johnson back to the boat, where he dies.

Lucy Mommbrekke, a rather short, soft-bodied, lazy and sensual girl. She has black, closely curling hair above a very white forehead and dark lively eyes. After initiating the love affair with Johnson, she appears to become his adoring slave. Like him, she is unsure in social relationships, and she knows that a marriage between them could not be successful. She begs Phillips to look after Johnson on the expedition. Soon after the men's departure, she marries in order to free herself from her wild intolerable love of Harry.

Calcott, a lank, wasted, bald, dirty Cockney of fifty who owns the house from which the expedition is to start. He has spent thirty years in the country and has a Brazilian wife, whom he beats, and seven children. His acute sense of inferiority makes him suspect every visiting Englishman of snubbing him. His conversation is filled with dire prophesies of the horrid fates that befall travelers in the jungle. He was the last person to see Harry's father.

Silva, a fat man in miniature, he is Portuguese, intelligent, discreet, and greedy for gold. He and Calcott conduct spiritualist séances, although he does not believe in spirits. He arranges for the table-tapping to indicate that Harry's father is not dead and has found gold. Greed is his motive for accompanying Harry.

Dorothy B. Aspinwall

THE DEAN'S DECEMBER

Author: Saul Bellow (1915-   )
Type of work: Novel
Time of action: The 1970's
First published: 1982

Albert Corde, a journalism professor and dean at a university in Chicago. Caught between his intellectual, idealistic belief in morality and the pragmatic, relativistic demands of the modern world, Corde seeks for balance in his life. In the past, he abandoned journalism for the relative seclusion of the academy, but two events draw him back into direct consideration of the world beyond the university: Rick Lester's murder and the death of Corde's mother-in-law in Romania. Rick Lester's death leads Corde into an examination of the morally corrupt and destructive environment of Chicago, the doomed lives of its lower class, and the moral obtuseness of its leaders. In Romania, Corde struggles with a political system that is determined to limit human possibilities. In the end, Corde resigns his academic post and decides to return to a kind of intellectual journalism, striving for a balance between the sterile isolation of the academic life and the cynical pragmatism of the capitalists and communists he encounters.

Minna Corde, Albert's Romanian wife, an astronomy professor at the same university. Minna is Albert Corde's complement. As an accomplished pure scientist and an emotional innocent, Minna contrasts Corde's speculative humanism and worldly experience. Brilliant but uncomplicated, Minna provides her husband with an emotional touchstone that helps him survive.

Valeria Raresh, Minna's mother, who is dying in Bucharest, a former Communist Party member, a former Minister of Health, and a founder of the Communist Party Hospital. Her quiet support for political reform and Minna's defection cost Valeria her position and her privileges, but she is a strong and selfless woman who spends her life doing for others: protecting her daughter by engineering Minna's escape to the West, caring for her younger sister Gigi, upholding the medical ideals of her late husband, and providing quiet leadership for other oppressed medical people in Romania.

Elfrida Zaehner, later **Sorokin,** Albert's sister. Elfrida is wealthy and somewhat ostentatious in her expenditures. Loving her as deeply as he does keeps Corde in sympathetic contact with the genteel world of privilege and prevents him from too readily dismissing the humanity of the upper classes.

Alec Witt, the provost and Corde's superior at his university. Witt is the ultimate pragmatic bureaucrat, superficially polite and considerate but devoid of human compassion or understanding. He loses respect for Corde when he realizes that the dean does not understand or is unwilling to play the "game." Angered by Corde's advocacy in the Lester case, Witt gladly accepts Corde's resignation.

Dewey Spangler, a famous journalist and Albert's boyhood friend. Aging and ill, Spangler persists in pursuing his boyhood rivalry with Corde, embarrassing Corde by reprinting his private remarks in a syndicated column.

Mason Zaehner, Elfrida's deceased husband. Intelligent but determinedly anti-intellectual, he derides Corde's academic life as useless escapism.

Mason Zaehner, Jr., Elfrida's son and Albert's nephew. Mason reacts against the privilege of his upbringing by espousing radical political ideas. His support of Leroy Ebry, who is accused and eventually convicted of murdering Rick Lester, a university student, brings him into angry confrontation with Corde.

Max Detillion, a disreputable lawyer and Corde's cousin. Max cheats the gullible Corde out of thousands of dollars and conducts a shrill, self-serving legal attack against Corde as Leroy Ebry's defense attorney.

Rick Lester, a graduate student at Corde's university, who is murdered by Leroy Ebry. Corde becomes deeply involved in the pursuit of Lester's murderers, feeling particularly protective toward Lester's widow, Lydia.

Tanti Gigi, Valeria Raresh's sister, who has always depended upon the protection of her older sister. Valeria's death leaves Gigi to face the barrenness of Romanian life alone.

Rufus Ridpath, a black prison warden who is dismissed from his position because of charges of misconduct. Corde defends Ridpath, seeing him as a victim of a corrupt political system and an unusual example of a man of courage and principle.

Traian, a Romanian driver who helps the Cordes through the complex process of bribes necessary to navigate the Romanian bureaucracy.

Ioanna, the concierge in Valeria's building and a police informant. Treated as one of the family although everyone knows that she is an informant, Ioanna exemplifies the odd divided loyalties that exist under the Romanian system.

Carl Brucker

DEATH AND THE KING'S HORSEMAN

Author: Wole Soyinka (1934-   )
Type of work: Play
Time of action: The 1940's
First published: 1975

Elesin Oba, the chief horseman of the recently deceased king from a Nigerian village. Full of vitality, Elesin enjoys women, singing, and dancing. Despite his great thirst for life, he is a man of honor and wisdom. He must, therefore, adhere to a native law and custom that mandates that he kill himself prior to the king's burial so as to accompany his master to heaven. Although having an abundance of wives already and being in his final hours on earth, his eyes wander to a young woman who has already been promised to another man; as a result of his stature, the girl is given to him in marriage. Regardless of having yet another reason to live, he is prompted by honor to pursue his death ceremony. When the critical rite is interrupted by the British colonial forces and his suicide prevented, Elesin is disgraced and humiliated. His son whom he had previously disowned for abandoning the tribe to attend school in Europe now disowns him upon his return home for disgracing his people. Elesin is repudiated by friends and tribesmen and is held in prison by the British as a means of protecting his life. After witnessing his son's suicide to right his wrong, he strangles himself with his own shackles.

Praise-Singer, a man who follows Elesin around only to sing praises of him. Although his love for Elesin is great, he knows the world demands the death of his master. During the death ritual, he takes on the role of the deceased king to speak with Elesin. He,

too, is disgraced by Elesin failing to complete the ceremony and, thus, disrupting the order of the universe.

Iyaloja (ē•yä•lō′jĕ), the "mother" of the marketplace. Despite her lofty position above the other women, she is subservient to men and is terrified of offending Elesin, a man of such prominence. Her respect of his mission is so great that she willingly gives her son's fiancée to him in marriage. When Elesin's death is stalled, she scorns him, even calling his seed an abomination.

Simon Pilkings, an English colonialist and district officer of the territory. He is insensitive and impatient of beliefs foreign to him, especially tribal superstition. He does not respect religion (even his own) and often offends people. By seeing things from only his vantage point, he disrupts the order of the tribe's universe, which not only leads to the death of Elesin (whom he was attempting to save) but also to the destruction of Elesin's honor and of his eldest son.

Jane Pilkings, Simon's wife. Although shallow and ignorant, she has educated herself as to the tribal customs and tries not to denigrate them. She is more compassionate than her husband and is the buffer between Simon and the people he tends to offend.

Sergeant Amusa, a black man absorbed into the white man's order, including Her Maj-

377

esty's government service. He is despised by his people for denying his heritage and is considered less than an equal by the British. Although having converted to the Moslem religion, he remains superstitious regarding his own primitive beliefs. Amusa is the man sent to arrest Elesin to prevent his suicide. There, he is humiliated and chided by the native girls as a white man's eunuch.

Joseph, Pilking's native houseboy. He takes his conversion to Christianity seriously and is disturbed by Simon Pilking's sacrilegious speech.

Bride, the young virgin desired by Elesin. Although promised to Iyaloja's son, Iyaloja proudly gives her to the honored Elesin before his valiant death. The bride is impregnated by Elesin, but her unborn child is later cursed by Iyaloja after Elesin fails in his mission of death. The bride remains outside Elesin's jail cell after his incarceration, and it is she who closes his eyes after his suicide.

H.R.H. The Prince, the visiting English prince to the native colony.

The Resident, Simon Pilking's superior. He is an arrogant, silly, and ignorant man who is not at all in touch with the natives. He lacks substance, which is displayed in his fascination with surfaces such as uniforms, tassels, and the like.

Aide-De-Camp, assistant to the resident. He is rude and bigoted and much like his superior.

Olunde, eldest son of Elesin. Despite his father's renunciation of him for leaving the village, Olunde travels to London to become a doctor. In his four years among the English, he has learned that they have no respect for what they do not understand. He returns to the village to warn Pilkings not to interfere with his father's suicide. Olunde rejects his father when he learns of Elesin's failed mission. To redeem his people, though, he takes on his father's task and kills himself.

Steven C. Kowall

THE DEATH OF A BEEKEEPER

Author: Lars Gustafsson (1936-   )
Type of work: Novel
Time of action: The 1970's
First published: En biodlares död, 1978 (English translation, 1981)

Lars Lennart Westin, a retired elementary school teacher, living in virtual isolation in the Swedish province of Västmanland. A lean, spent man, thirty-nine years old, he looks much older. Intensely self-absorbed, he keeps a series of notebooks that record the mundane facts of his life, his imaginative explorations of past and present, and the course of his fatal disease, cancer of the spleen. As the novel begins, he has received a letter from a local hospital, probably containing test results and the diagnosis of his ailment. He burns the letter, unopened. As his story unfolds, he reveals his obsession with pain, the deception and lack of com-

munication that have marked most of his relationships, his desire to understand himself, his resolution never to give up in his various struggles, and his terrible conclusion that his life was real only during his last few months of terminal suffering.

Margaret, Westin's wife for ten years, until their divorce, around 1970. The pale and thin daughter of an intensely bourgeois family dominated by a tyrannical father, Margaret initially shared with Westin an aversion to a hypocritical and uncaring society and a desire for independence. As he reviews their uneventful, unsuccessful marriage, Westin discovers that deception, guilt, and Margaret's need to control him were the foundations of their relationship. He refuses to notify her of his disease.

Ann, a large blonde doctor in her late thirties or early forties. She radiates motherliness, a quality that Westin craves and that forms the basis of their love affair in the last year of his marriage. When Margaret learns of the affair, the two women become allies and give Westin a strange, yet real, sense of peace.

Uffe and
Jonny, two young boys who first meet Westin during the course of his illness. He treats them with affectionate warmth and writes for them the first episode of a science-fiction adventure story, in which the hero must locate and destroy a source of great pain created by the evil Emperor Ming.

Sune Jannson, Westin's uncle, a clever storekeeper and operator in the black market during World War II. Westin admires him as a cunning and persistent individualist and re-counts a wartime incident in which Uncle Sune outwits a contingent of local bureaucrats.

God, imagined by Westin—during a temporary cessation of his pain—as a mother who awakes after twenty million years and begins to answer the prayers of human beings. At first, the answered prayers seem wonderful, but since the motherly God grants all wishes, indiscriminately, the process soon leads to the dissolution of all human relationships and institutions, and language itself.

Nicke, a boyhood friend of Westin's who died in 1952, after a short life of reckless yet successful adventures. Nicke is the last significant character to appear in the novel, in a flashback that reminds Westin to begin again and never to give up. In Westin's flashback, the fearless young Nicke dives deep into the whirlpool of a dangerous canal lock. He dives to retrieve a golden fishing lure but emerges from the water with a different treasure from the bottom: a unique gold coin.

Terry Lass

DEATH OF THE FOX

Author: George Garrett (1929-   )
Type of work: Novel
Time of action: The English Renaissance, from the last days of the reign of Henry VIII to the end of the reign of James I
First published: 1971

Sir Walter Ralegh, Captain of the Guard under Queen Elizabeth and a leading Elizabethan courtier. Ralegh has been a soldier, seafarer, explorer, and counselor to the queen as well as an amateur scientist and engineer, antiquarian, historian, and poet. Known to enemies and friends as "The Fox" for his shrewd pursuit of public and personal ambitions, Ralegh is now an old man under suspended sentence of death for a pro-Spanish plot against King James I fifteen years earlier (1603), yet he is innocent of that charge. Although Ralegh had been proud, headstrong, and lusty as a young man, his years in prison have deepened his meditative and philosophical nature; he reflects upon his own past life as he awaits sentencing and then execution on Lord Mayor's Day, October 29, 1618. Raised to eminence and great wealth under Elizabeth, Ralegh was banished from court in 1592 after his affair with Elizabeth Throckmorton, later his beloved wife Bess. He discovered Guiana for England in 1595, however, and was the old queen's most loyal courtier in her declining years. He was brought to trial by King James shortly after the latter's succession in 1603, and his self-defense at Winchester confounded the king's own lawyers. Imprisoned thereafter in the Tower of London, he was released only in 1617, but his subsequent disastrous expedition to Guiana, which resulted in an unsuccessful attack upon a Spanish stronghold and the death of his son, led to his reimprisonment by the king. Unjustly sentenced to execution at Westminster by Henry Yelverton, James's attorney general, visited by his wife Bess and a scholar friend, Thomas Hariot, on the last night of his life, examined spiritually in the morning and justified by Robert Tounson, Dean of Westminster, Ralegh defends himself publicly before the crowd gathered for his public beheading, affirming his loyalty to King James as well as to the deceased Elizabeth, going to his death freely, nobly, and courageously on Lord Mayor's Day, October 29, 1618.

James Stuart, King of England (1603-1625) and Scotland (1567-1625). Physically unattractive but possessed of a powerful if pedantic intellect, the king is a complex blend of virtues and vices: humorous and festive yet somewhat degraded in his personal behavior; tenacious and shrewd in pursuing his policies yet self-righteous and arbitrary; fatherly toward his subjects, friends, and family, yet vengeful and petulant toward those who oppose him. Uncomfortable among the masses in London and almost pathologically fearful of assassination, the king has begun to find the burdens of the crown wearying and frustrating and prefers the companionship of his favorite, George Villiers ("Steenie"), and the pleasures of hunting and extravagant court entertainments. When his chief policy goals (keeping England at peace and arranging a dynastic marriage with England's old enemy, Spain) are frustrated by

Ralegh's Guiana expedition, he has the old Elizabethan courtier executed against the advice of his dying queen; he leaves the affair to his Lord Chancellor, Francis Bacon, and the London civic authorities while he takes holiday at his estate at Theobalds and the royal lodge at Royston. By disposing of the troublesome Ralegh, James hopes to regain his influence with Spain's ambassador, Count Gondomar, but he also destroys the last living embodiment of the Elizabethan regime.

Elizabeth Tudor, Queen of England (1558-1603), James's predecessor, the greatest of the Tudor monarchs and Ralegh's much-beloved and admired sovereign. Moderately attractive, gifted intellectually and artistically, supremely skillful in choosing and using ambitious and talented subordinates to carry out her policies, she sacrificed personal happiness for the welfare of the nation that she loved beyond any individual. The success of her reign, which began in crisis and instability, rested upon her ability to gain and maintain the trust and admiration of all of her people; this success was furthered by the use of open public spectacle financed by her wealthier subjects. She made herself the embodiment of her nation both before and after the climactic defeat of the Spanish Armada in 1588, and as Ralegh relives that earlier age in his imagination, it seems a splendid dream. While her final years were marked by economic and social difficulties in England and a hardening of her personality and her policies, they were eased by Ralegh's loyal and assiduous service during the rebellion by the Earl of Essex in 1601, the final crisis of the regime.

Mark Allen Heberle

DEATH ON THE INSTALLMENT PLAN

Author: Louis-Ferdinand Céline (Louis-Ferdinand Destouches, 1894-1961)
Type of work: Novel
Time of action: 1900 to World War I
First published: Mort à crédit, 1936 (English translation 1938)

Ferdinand, a doctor, aspiring writer, and narrator of the novel. Personally as well as

professionally disillusioned, he cares for his patients although he believes most human beings are not worth saving and are, in fact, better off dead. The reasons for Ferdinand's deep-seated pessimism are evident in his account of his childhood and adolescence. Beaten and abused by his petit bourgeois father, exploited by his employers, and disenchanted with women and love, he finds little to admire in his fellow man and becomes increasingly cynical and cruel as the novel progresses.

Auguste, Ferdinand's father, an insurance clerk and amateur painter. Handsome, vain, pompous, and cruel, he is well educated but emotionally insecure. A failure both personally and professionally, he frequently criticizes his wife and son for their shortcomings while failing to recognize his own. Given to violent outbursts, he constantly abuses his wife and son verbally as well as physically when things do not go his way professionally. He reveals his reactionary politics by blaming his woes on the Freemasons and Jews.

Clémence, Ferdinand's mother, a shopkeeper. Well intentioned but physically and emotionally fragile, she spends most of her time unsuccessfully attempting to keep the peace between her husband and son. Ambitious for Ferdinand, she helps him find jobs (which he never holds) and convinces Auguste to let him go to study at Meanwell College in England. As the novel progresses, Clémence's health is eventually destroyed through overwork and the beatings administered by Auguste.

Caroline, Ferdinand's maternal grandmother and, like her daughter, a shopkeeper by profession and a tireless worker. One of the novel's few admirable characters, she is devoted to her daughter and grandson, whom she teaches to read. She protects both of them from Auguste, whom she detests. In her efforts to provide for her family's needs, Caroline maintains two workers' cottages. After repairing the plumbing at one of these cottages, she catches pneumonia and dies.

Uncle Édouard, Clémence's brother who

owns a hardware store and is an amateur inventor. Intelligent, successful, modest as well as kind, Édouard is Ferdinand's benefactor. He intervenes quietly in family crises to protect his nephew, pays for his schooling in England, and gets him his job with Courtial des Pereires. At the end of the novel when Ferdinand is completely down on his luck, he takes him in, cares for him, and encourages him to start again.

Roger-Martin Courtial des Pereires (pĕr-är'), an inventor, editor of *Genitron* (a journal for inventors), hot air balloon pilot, and, later, experimental farmer and schoolmaster. An eccentric genius with a weakness for horse racing and prostitutes, Courtial is at once generous and egotistical, sophisticated and naïve. He is a shrewd businessman as well as a hopeless financial manager. He employs Ferdinand as his secretary at *Genitron* and, after the journal's failure, the two, along with Courtial's wife, go to the country to start a school for lower-class children and an experimental potato farm. When Courtial's methods for growing new and better potatoes fail, he commits suicide.

Nora Merrywin, wife of the headmaster of Meanwell College. Nora is beautiful, kind, and modest, and she quickly inspires Ferdinand's passion. As Meanwell College gradually loses most of its students to a new school nearby, Nora grows increasingly despondent. In despair, she seduces Ferdinand and then, riddled with guilt and shame, she drowns herself. Although he is nearby and could save her, Ferdinand chooses to watch her die.

Irène, Courtial's wife and a former midwife by profession. Although attractive as a young woman, she has become physically repugnant as a result of bodily changes brought on by a hysterectomy. A devoted supporter of her husband, she nevertheless chastises him regularly for his infidelities and gambling. She accompanies him in all of his misadventures and is devastated by his suicide.

Richard J. Golsan

DEATHWATCH

Author: Jean Genet (1910-1986)
Type of work: Play
Time of action: Unspecified
First produced: Haute Surveillance, 1949 (English translation, 1954)

Green Eyes, a handsome, twenty-two-year-old, condemned murderer. He is the leader of the cell and revered in the prison for his insidious crime of seducing a girl and then strangling her during sex. His chief rival is a black murderer named Snowball, whom he has secretly befriended and actually admires. Whereas the prisoner Lefranc lauds Snowball as the god of the prison, Maurice, another cellmate, worships Green Eyes. This creates endless contention between Maurice and Lefranc; twice Green Eyes is forced to pull Lefranc from Maurice's throat. Being illiterate, Green Eyes needs Lefranc's help in corresponding with his girlfriend on the outside, even though Green Eyes accuses Lefranc of trying to steal her. Green Eyes is at first obsessed with his girlfriend, as evidenced by her face being tattooed on his chest. Then, realizing that he will probably be executed in two months, he instructs his companions to kill her when they are released from prison. When the guard comes to inform Green Eyes that his girlfriend has arrived for a visit, he refuses to see her. Instead, he gives the guard permission to make a play for her. The third time Lefranc lunges at Maurice, Green Eyes passively stands by to watch the slaughter. Although he does nothing to stop it, he is repulsed by Lefranc's willful murder of Maurice and calls for the guard.

Georgie Lefranc, a twenty-three-year-old insolent convict who is about to be released. He does not share the esteem of a hard-core killer since his crime is only burglary. Lefranc is envious of Green Eyes' popularity and position but finds a condemned black murderer more worthy of his praise. He bickers incessantly with Maurice, whom he has tried to pulverize a number of times until stopped by Green Eyes. Lefranc is Green

Eyes' link to his girlfriend since the latter is illiterate and must rely on Lefranc to write all of his letters. He is coerced by Maurice into an admission of trying to steal Green Eyes' girl. In retaliation, Lefranc taunts Maurice about his homosexual infatuation with Green Eyes. Although Lefranc's jail term is due to expire in three days, he foils his release by strangling Maurice in a fit of rage. He does not acquire the respect for this murder that he assumed he would. Green Eyes is repulsed that Lefranc chose his crime instead of allowing the crime to choose him as Green Eyes claims was true of his murder.

Maurice, an effeminate, seventeen-year-old crook. He worships Green Eyes and despises Lefranc since the latter will not recognize Green Eyes as the head of the prison. His constant needling of Lefranc prompts Lefranc to go for Maurice's throat on two different occasions; twice he is saved by Green Eyes' intervention. Maurice feels the distrust that Green Eyes has of Lefranc, especially in regard to his girlfriend. When Maurice learns of Green Eyes' secret friendship with Snowball, he is heartbroken. He still loves Green Eyes but in a different way. He even speaks of pitying his hero. His relentless taunting of Lefranc brings on a third attack, and this time Green Eyes allows him to be strangled to death.

The Guard, a stern but conscientious and fair prison guard. He dislikes Lefranc for his impertinence and threatens to throw him back into the guardhouse. He is friendly with Green Eyes, even delivering a warm message and cigarettes from Snowball. He is grateful when Green Eyes gives him permission to have a chance at his girl.

Steven C. Kowall

THE DEBUT

Author: Anita Brookner (1938-   )
Type of work: Novel
Time of action: The 1970's
First published: 1981, in Great Britain as *A Start in Life* (U.S. edition, 1981)

Ruth Weiss, a scholar who is writing a multivolume study on the women in Honoré de Balzac's novels and teaching a literature seminar. Caught in appearance and character halfway between the nineteeth and twentieth centuries, forty-year-old Ruth has beautiful long red hair (often worn in a classical chignon) and a slight hesitation in her walk. Scrupulous, passionate, thoughtful, and introspective, she is extreme in everything and feels that her life has been ruined by literature. As the novel opens, Ruth is living alone and seeing her publisher once every six months for dinner. The novel recounts her past: her irregular home life with her parents and grandmother, her growing scholarly interests, and her romantic encounters in London and Paris, especially with Richard Hirst and Professor Duplessis. Her ultimate conviction is that moral fortitude is not enough to succeed in life; it is better, and easier, to be engaging and attractive.

George Weiss, a dealer in rare books. Gregarious, affable, and inaccessible to his daughter Ruth, George is glossy and cheery, and a bit of a dandy; he wears smart tweed suits, uses a cigarette holder, and sports a ready smile. In truth, he is somewhat unhappy, with vaguely unrealized dreams. He adores his wife yet is unfaithful to her with his assistant Miss Moss and then with the widowed Mrs. Sally Jacobs. After his wife learns of the affair with Mrs. Jacobs, George has a stroke and is nursed back to health by Ruth.

Helen Weiss, an actress. Beautiful and successful, thin even into middle age, Helen is girlish and outrageous, not interested in being a mother to Ruth. When she is not working, Helen spends most of her time in bed, smoking and talking with Maggie Cutler, becoming increasingly listless. After the discovery of George's latest affair, Helen refuses to stay under the same roof with him; she dies in a taxi with Ruth on the return from an abortive trip to Molly Edwards' house.

Mrs. Weiss, aging grandmother to Ruth and mother to George. Aware of the irresponsibility of her son and his wife, Mrs. Weiss tries to maintain a normal household for Ruth. She dies after a stroke and three months of being bedridden.

Mrs. Maggie Cutler, the spry, chain-smoking, sloppy housekeeper for the Weisses who becomes Helen's confidante. Maggie finds a husband through a matchmaking agency and leaves Oakwood Court for his company in Folkestone. The Weisses, especially Helen, are outraged at her behavior.

Miss Parker, a teacher. She is one of the first people to take an interest in Ruth. She encourages her to go to university and be a scholar.

Anthea, a college friend of Ruth. Beautiful and popular, Anthea needs Ruth for an acolyte. Anthea's concerns are boys and her appearance, but she also schools Ruth in these subjects, appalled at her ignorance, and encourages her to move away from her parents. Later, Anthea makes a conventional marriage to Brian and becomes a housewife and mother.

Richard Hirst, a psychologist. With unblemished blond good looks and many charms, Richard attracts women of all kinds. Eager for crises, Richard is blissfully unaware of obligations. He treats a dinner invitation from Ruth with casual nonchalance, arriving hours late, oblivious of her hunger and her feelings.

Mrs. Sally Jacobs, a woman who buys George's rare bookshop when he retires. A widow who loves to cook for men, Sally tolerates George's disruption of her orderly flat and thinks she wants him to marry her. When Helen dies, however, Mrs. Jacobs retreats to her sister's house in Manchester and leaves her flat to her nephew Roddy.

Professor Alain Duplessis (dü•plĕ•sī), a famous professor at the Sorbonne. Middle-aged, married, comfortable-looking, and rather heavy, Professor Duplessis makes friends with Ruth in Paris. The friendship promises to turn more romantic when Ruth rents the Dixons' flat and invites him to dinner, but it ends when Ruth is called back to London to care for her ailing parents.

Hugh Dixon, an art dealer in Paris who befriends Ruth and gives her advice about cutting her hair and buying more fashionable clothes.

Jill Dixon, a travel agent and Hugh's wife. Jill tolerates his friendship with Ruth because she does not consider Ruth a threat and because she takes a lover herself.

Molly Edwards, a Christian Scientist and a particular friend of Helen Weiss's. The Weisses spend their last vacation together with Molly at her place at Hove.

Humphrey Wilcox, a writer and friend of George Weiss's. Ruth's landlord at her first place in Paris, Humphrey spies on her when she takes her daily bath.

Rhoda Wilcox, Humphrey's wife. She is dedicated to keeping things quiet so that her husband can write.

Roddy Jacobs, a rare book dealer who succeeds his aunt at George Weiss's previous shop. Plump and conventional, he gets along so well with George after Sally Jacobs' departure to Manchester that Ruth agrees to marry him. Only six months later, Roddy is killed in a car accident.

Patricia Clark

THE DEFENSE

Author: Vladimir Nabokov (1899-1977)
Type of work: Novel
Time of action: The 1910's and 1920's
First published: Zashchita Luzhina, 1929, serial; 1930, book (English translation, 1964)

Aleksandr Ivanovich Luzhin, a world-class chess player. Growing up in an aristocratic Russian household, the solitary Luzhin develops into a brilliant chess prodigy. Estranged from his parents, who do not understand his unique talent, he travels extensively to compete in chess tournaments in Europe. After several years he becomes so immersed in a cerebral world of chess strategies that he loses contact with everyday reality and suffers a mental breakdown during the final match of a major tournament in Berlin. Although he recovers from this breakdown with the assistance of his bride-to-be, who tries to keep him away from any reminders of chess, he gradually falls prey to a new obsession: He believes that the events of his life are manipulated by an invisible chess opponent. Trying desperately to foil the relentless control of this unknown opponent, Luzhin increasingly acts in irrational and unpredictable ways. Frustrated by his inability to escape the snares of his opponent, Luzhin commits suicide by jumping from his bathroom window. His last vision, however, is of a vast chessboard, which he takes to be a sign of his future existence.

Mrs. Luzhin, a young woman with an independent mind and a compassionate spirit. She meets Luzhin at a German resort and finds him so unusual that she decides to accept an abrupt and unmannered marriage proposal. She nurses him carefully after his breakdown, but because he never shares his inner fears with her, she remains unable to help him resist his suicidal anxiety.

Ivan Luzhin, Aleksandr Luzhin's father, a writer of children's books. Although concerned for his son's well-being, Ivan Luzhin does not know how to communicate with him. He had hoped that his son would turn out to be a musical prodigy, and he finds his son's chess genius unsettling. The senior Luzhin also has a difficult relationship with his wife, and he causes her pain when he enters into an adulterous affair. After the 1917 Bolshevik Revolution, Luzhin, Sr., lives alone as an émigré in Berlin. He plans to write a novel based on his son's life, but he dies with his plans unfulfilled.

Valentinov, Luzhin's manager during the youth's rise to international fame. A shameless promoter, Valentinov exploits Luzhin's talent when he is still young, and then returns at the end of the novel, causing Luzhin to take his paranoid suicide leap.

Luzhin's aunt, a coquettish young woman who enters into an adulterous relationship with Luzhin, Sr., and introduces Luzhin, Jr., into the mysteries of chess.

Turati, Luzhin's opponent in the climactic championship match that triggers Luzhin's mental breakdown.

Mrs. Luzhin's parents, Russian émigrés living in Berlin. Mrs. Luzhin's mother disapproves of her daughter's marriage to the eccentric chess player, but her husband provides financial resources to support the couple after their marriage.

A lady from the Soviet Union, a garrulous visitor who visits the Luzhin household in Berlin during the period of Luzhin's recuperation from his mental breakdown. Her comments about Luzhin's aunt crystallizes his anxiety about being attacked by an invisible opponent, and her presence prevents Mrs. Luzhin from paying full attention to her distraught husband.

Julian W. Connolly

A DELICATE BALANCE

Author: Edward Albee (1928-   )
Type of work: Play
Time of action: The 1960's
First produced: 1966

Agnes, a handsome wife and mother, in her late fifties. Haunted by the possibility of losing her mind, which she defines as a kind of "drifting," whereby she would become a stranger in the world, she attempts to maintain order, a "delicate balance," in her world. She deals with the emotional withdrawal of her husband and the "embarrassment" of her sister by taking the verbal initiative to judge and thereby control them. Yet she comes to realize that her hold on reality does depend more on them than she has been willing to admit, and that frightens her.

Tobias, her husband, a few years older. An

emotionally repressed and withdrawn man, he covers his deepest fears with some alcohol and an outward mask of self-control and quiet. Forced by Agnes to make a decision about whether Harry and Edna will stay, he breaks down under the weight of trying to be honest about how he really feels not only about them but also about his own family. He has a hysterical fear of death and of being alone, and this allows him to tolerate demands of his family.

Claire, Agnes' alcoholic younger sister. Called an ingrate and one of the walking wounded by Agnes, she is nevertheless the

385

most honest person in the family. She does not hide her feelings or her dark side; she uses her drinking to annoy and embarrass Agnes, to amuse Tobias, with whom she might have had an affair, to prick Julia's pretentions, and to thumb her nose at society. She is a weary, but tough, survivor.

Julia, Agnes' and Tobias' thirty-six-year-old daughter, recently separated from her fourth husband. Returning home with a sense of failure and with raw emotions, she is like a younger version of Claire, for whom she has much esteem and affection. She needs her childhood room, which symbolizes a measure of order in her chaotic emotional life, and the fact that it is occupied by her godparents causes her to become hysterical. She realizes that her arrival will necessitate changes in the alliances that have held Agnes, Tobias, and Claire in their uncomfortable triangle.

Harry and
Edna, Agnes' and Tobias' best friends and godparents to Julia. Frightened by a "terror," which remains unnameable, they are "intruders" in the household. Like the plague, their fear is contagious, as each character reads his or her own personal agony into it. The women of the house want them to go; Tobias begs them to stay. In leaving by their own choice, they force the family to confront and acknowledge their personal fears. The terror seems to be existential in nature, a glimpse into the passage of time, death, and alienation.

Lori Hall Burghardt

DEMIAN
The Story of Emil Sinclair's Youth

Author: Hermann Hesse (1877-1962)
Type of work: Novel
Time of action: 1905-1915
First published: Demian: Die Geschichte von Emil Sinclairs Jugend, 1919 (English translation, 1923)

Emil Sinclair, the protagonist and author-narrator, who looks back on his youth. At the beginning of the story, he is a ten-year-old schoolboy; he is eighteen at its close. He is the son of well-to-do parents. From a sheltered and bright childhood world, Emil Sinclair is first plunged into a world that he had hitherto regarded as separate from his, the world of the lower classes, surrounded by darkness and mystery. Because he had bragged about having stolen apples once in order to impress an older fellow student, Franz Kromer, Emil is being blackmailed and otherwise harassed by Franz. When he meets Max Demian, another older student, his life changes once again, as Max protects him and forces Kromer to leave Emil alone. Emil's growing pains, his trials and tribulations, are accompanied by Demian's role as a mentor and friend. They recognize each other by the "mark of Cain" on their foreheads, which, though invisible and contrary to the conventional view, is the sign of a nonconformist, of one who believes in the human race as one that is yet to come. Demian gradually leads Emil to this visionary insight that draws a line between himself and the "masses" who are driven by a herdlike instinct. Emil's path toward acceptance of what fate has in store for him is one of self-exploration, including the freedom to become what he is. He later meets Demian again and, for the first time, meets Eva, Demian's mother. When Emil encounters Demian for the last time, Demian has been mortally wounded in battle. After Demian's death, Emil's introspection reveals that his and Demian's images have merged into one.

Max Demian, an older student and Sinclair's friend and mentor. He is a born leader and intellectual. His friendship with the younger Sinclair is based on a kinship of spirit and mind. He introduces Sinclair to a world of inner freedom and natural courage. Sinclair sends him a drawing of the bird (a sparrow hawk) as it breaks out of its shell, represented by a globe, in the escutcheon above the doorway of his house. Demian displays the picture prominently in his mother's house. Demian is a lieutenant in the army and one of the first to go to the front. There, having been mortally wounded, he comes to be in the same field hospital as Emil Sinclair. He declares him independent of his leadership, as Sinclair will find that he has by now internalized Demian's own image and potential.

Pistorius, an organist and former theology student; Sinclair's other mentor. He is stocky and short, with a face that is both "stern around the forehead and eyes and soft around the mouth." Pistorius becomes Sinclair's mentor in the town where Sinclair is attending boarding school. Pistorius, given to myths and cults and their celebration, introduces Sinclair to the Abraxas myth.

Frau Eva, Demian's mother. She is tall, beautiful, and dignified. She tells Sinclair to call her "Frau Eva," a distinction only granted to her closest friends. Her head and face suggest both male and female qualities. She is the object of Sinclair's wordly and spiritual dreams and fantasies. Her world is one of love, fairy tales, and dreams. She is the driving force behind the group around Demian that seeks the spiritual rebirth of humankind.

Franz Kromer, a thirteen-year-old boy in Sinclair's hometown. He is robust and strong, the son of a tailor. He attends public elementary school and is, on occasion, associated with the children of the Latin School. He is given to cruelty, exploiting the inexperience of some of the sheltered younger boys of the upper-middle class of the town. Thus, he comes into contact with Sinclair and blackmails him by threatening to expose him for something about which Sinclair has merely boasted but from which he cannot easily extricate himself: extorting small sums of money every week. After Demian's intervention, Kromer has come to fear Sinclair and avoids any further contact with him.

Knauer (knou′ər), a slight, slender eighteen-year-old youth. He is Sinclair's classmate in the boarding school and seeks his advice and friendship. He is sexually abstinent and seeks the counsel of Sinclair, who is himself sexually inexperienced. He finally attempts to commit suicide but is stopped by Sinclair.

Arthur Tilo Alt

DEMOCRACY

Author: Joan Didion (1934-   )
Type of work: Novel
Time of action: 1952-1975
First published: 1984

Inez Christian Victor, an attractive member of an entrenched, wealthy Hawaiian family that lacks warmth and closeness. At age twenty, in 1955, she weds Harry Victor, who in 1969 becomes a U.S. senator and is later considered to be presidential material. Politics, she decides, costs her her memory and privacy. Consequently, she looks for intimacy in an intermittent affair with Jack Lovett, who, however, as an international adventurer, is rarely available. After his death, she decides to assist refugees in Kuala Lumpur, with whom she can identify emotionally.

387

Paul Christian, a ruthless aristocrat whose business interests often take him away from Hawaii. Obsessed with protecting his wealth and power, he not only drives away his wife and daughter Inez but, in 1975, kills his other daughter, Janet, for making land deals with Japanese American entrepreneur Wendell Omura. He is placed in a state asylum.

Carol Christian, a California model who, in 1934, marries Paul Christian. Naïvely expecting to be embraced by the people of privilege in Hawaii, instead she remains an outsider and, out of loneliness, often keeps her young children at home with her. Still uncomfortable in a society that ignores her, she finally abandons the Islands and starts a career, booking celebrities for radio interviews in San Francisco. After Janet's wedding, word comes of Carol's death in a plane crash near Reno, Nevada.

Janet "Nezzie" Christian Ziegler, Carol's younger daughter. Disturbed by her mother's absence, she looks for stability in real estate. Though she marries Dick Ziegler, who once made a modest fortune in Hong Kong, she undercuts his windward Oahu landholdings and container business, with the complicity of Omura and her uncle Dwight. As a result, she is shot to death by her father for frustrating his dynastic plans.

Harry Victor, succeeds so well as a liberal in the Justice Department that he becomes senator and in 1972 is spoken of as a possible presidential candidate. In the process of becoming a public figure, his sense of personal identity and his role as husband and father suffer. He loses his family but becomes special envoy to the Common Market.

Adlai Victor, Inez's directionless son. He is responsible for an accident that costs a fifteen-year-old girl one eye and a kidney. Sometimes he claims to be attending an "alternative" Boston college as if he were a liberal, but finally he joins the establishment as a clerk for a federal judge.

Jessica Victor, Adlai's twin sister and a heroin addict. At age eighteen she goes to Vietnam even as the war there is worsening and has to be rescued as an "escorted orphan," just before the general evacuation.

Billy Dillion, a public relations front man and arranger of photo opportunities for Harry Victor. He considers Inez's interest in refugees to be too controversial and makes her a consultant on embassy paintings. He tries to prevent Paul Christian from having to stand trial, endeavoring to cover up the business connections and racism behind the murders.

Jack Lovett, a handsome adventurer twice divorced. His mysterious occupation as an international consultant constantly in motion seems connected with CIA control of weapons and fuel. He sees war as a commercial enterprise and claims to be devoid of ethics and emotion, except for his love for Inez ever since they first met in Honolulu in 1952. At Inez's request, he brings Jessica safely out of Vietnam. In Jakarta, finally together with Inez, he drowns accidentally in the shallow end of a hotel pool.

Joan Didion, as a character in her own novel, who knew Inez when they both worked at *Vogue* magazine in 1960. While teaching at Berkeley in 1975, she reads of Janet's murder, then is summoned by Inez to hear out her chronicle of family tragedies in the hope of extracting some meaning from all that has happened. Mainly she serves as listener and sympathetic but limited witness, who allows Inez to reveal whatever she wants to and can about her life among powerful landholders and politicians. She considers Inez's story to be strong evidence that Americans are not immune to history.

Leonard Casper

THE DEMONS

Author: Heimito von Doderer (1896-1966)
Type of work: Novel
Time of action: 1926-1927 and 1955
First published: Die Dämonen: Nach der Chronik des Sektionsrates Geyrenhoff, 1956
   (English translation, 1961)

Councillor Georg von Geyrenhoff (fôn gī'rĕn•hōf), a retired civil servant who assumes the task of narrator, editor, and chronicler of the story of "Our Crowd" and other people during 1926-1927 in Vienna. He revises and edits the story again in 1955, when he feels he can be more objective. He requests others to aid him in writing about events that he can not personally witness, accepts unsolicited manuscripts for inclusion in edited form, and directs a team of assistants who are unaware that they are spies, reporters, and collaborators for him. His major concern in 1955 is to examine the events of twenty-eight years before, including the burning of the Palace of Justice in 1927 by an angry mob of demonstrating workers. For Geyrenhoff, this event led to the "Cannae of Austrian freedom": the takeover of Austria by the Nazis and its destruction in World War II.

Kajetan von Schlaggenberg (kā'yĕt•ən fôn schlä'gĕn•bĕrg), a professional writer, major collaborator on the chronicle, and modern idealogue. Kajetan is enraged by the popular notion that the ideal of feminine beauty is seen in the extremely thin woman. He develops "Kajetan's Theory of the Necessity of Fat Females to the Sex Life of the Superior Man Today." Finally, Geyrenhoff extensively censors this "Chronique Scandaleuse" of fat females because he considers it one of the foolish and dangerous ideologies that imperil society. Kajetan is the greatest provider of information on the second life of the people from all segments of society in Vienna. In 1927, he ends his flirtations with ideologies and becomes a serious novelist.

Anna Kapsreiter (käps'rīt•ər), an elderly widow and author of "Kap's Night Book." This book is a diary of thirteen dreams that Anna has during the early months of 1927. Geyrenhoff includes them in the chronicle without editing because they disclose a most unusual perspicacity of the times. She actually predicts the future, although no one knows that until 1955.

Ruodlieb von der Vläntsch (rōōd'lĕb fôn dâr flĕnsh), author of the manuscript entitled "Specyfyeth of how the sorceresses delt wyth atte Neudegck whan that they were taken Anno MCCCCLXIIIJ." (The German version is rendered in an Early New High German dialect, and the English translation uses a late fifteenth century English dialect.) Like Kajetan's "Chronique Scandaleuse," Geyrenhoff includes this story to offer another example of an absurd and ominous ideology.

René von Stangeler (fôn shtän'gĕl•ər), a brilliant young historian. He secures his professional future when Jan Herzka, the owner of the Ruodlieb von der Vläntsch manuscript and a medieval castle, engages René to read and interpret the manuscript and to direct the modernization of the castle. Professor Bullogg, a medievalist at Harvard, visits René in Vienna in June, 1927, and guides him in the preparation of a critical edition of the manuscript. With all this good fortune in his professional life, he is now in the fortuitous position to be able to marry Grete Siebenschein, his fiancée of long standing.

Financial Counselor Levielle (lə•vēl'), the villain. As longtime adviser to the Ruthmayr family, Levielle tries to embezzle the substantial inheritance that the late Captain Ruthmayr had designated for his illegitimate daughter, Charlotte von Schlaggenberg. Geyrenhoff enlists the help of a group of boys to recover the will. This act leads to Levielle's discovery, and the charlatan is forced to flee to Paris.

Charlotte von Schlaggenberg, often called **Quapp,** Kajetan's sister. Charlotte wants to become a virtuoso violinist but realizes that even with hard work she will not be successful because she lacks the necessary musical gift. She is frequently seen in "Our Crowd" in the company of Imre von Gyurkicz, and, though there are moments of great passion, the tempestuous relationship soon breaks up. When she inherits a significant sum of money, she settles down and marries Géza von Orkay.

Leonhard Kakabsa (kä′käp•sə), a self-educated young factory worker. One day, quite by accident, Leonhard finds a Latin grammar book and starts to learn Latin. Although he has no thought of changing his life-style, he notices that he has attained a considerable degree of linguistic freedom that his fellow workers do not possess. Good fortune is on his side again, because it leads to meeting Mary K. only a short while after he has started his self-help educational program. Through Mary K., Leonhard is introduced to Prince Alfons Croix, who not only offers to pay for his further education but also hires him as a librarian for his distinguished and vast private library. At the same time, Leonhard falls in love with Mary K., and they plan to marry as soon as he is established professionally.

Mary K., a widow who has lost a leg in a streetcar accident. Everyone is astonished at the way Mary K. has recovered from the trauma of her accident. She is now a beautiful and poised woman. Although there is a considerable age difference between Mary K.

and Leonhard, their rare and exquisite love for each other will lead to a perfect marriage.

Friederike Ruthmayr (rōt′mī•ər), a very wealthy widow. The most elegant social events take place at the Palais Ruthmayr during the 1926-1927 social season. Yet there is one unexplainable flaw in this otherwise perfectly respectable person: The story is told by reliable sources that "Our Crowd," while on one of their wild nighttime carousels, stopped at the Palais Ruthmayr, and Friederike joined them by drinking cognac right out of the bottle. She and Geyrenhoff marry, but Friederike dies during the war.

Grete Siebenschein (zē′bən•shīn), René von Strangeler's fiancée and Mary K.'s upstairs neighbor. As the daughter of a typical middle-class family, Grete experiences the usual problems in persuading her parents to approve of René as a suitable husband.

Imre von Gyurkicz (ēm′rä fôn gōōr′kĭsh), a painter and newspaper cartoonist. A Hungarian and member of "Our Crowd," Imre has created a questionable genealogy for himself that he uses to enhance his social position. Politically very active, he is killed during the riots of 1927.

Géza von Orkay (gā′zə fôn ôr′kā), Geyrenhoff's cousin. Géza is an important diplomat at the Hungarian embassy in Vienna. Through Geyrenhoff, he meets Charlotte von Schlaggenberg, whom he marries prior to his transfer to a more important post in Basel. The last meeting of "Our Crowd" takes place at the railway station when they gather to say farewell to the newlyweds.

Thomas H. Falk

THE DEPTFORD TRILOGY

Author: Robertson Davies (1913-   )
Type of work: Novel
Time of action: 1908-1975
First published: 1983: *Fifth Business*, 1970; *The Manticore*, 1972; *World of Wonders*, 1975

Dunstable Ramsay, also called **Dunstan, Dunny, Corky, The Cork,** and **Old Buggerlugs,** a retired history master at Colborne College, a fashionable private boys' school in Toronto. He writes a long memoir in the form of a report to his headmaster to correct the impression left by an article in the alumni magazine, summarizing his career on his retirement. Ramsay's need to set the record straight continually comes from his Scots Presbyterian upbringing in a small Ontario town, which has left him feeling guilty and responsible, as well as judgmental and given to frequent examinations of his conduct and motives. The loss of his leg and the severe burns he suffers in the Battle of Ypres in 1917 set him apart in his adult life and contribute to his identification of himself as "fifth business," a theatrical term describing a character with a small role who is essential to the resolution of the plot. Ramsay's wartime nurse, Diana Marfleet, teaches him about the world outside Deptford and introduces him to physical love. Returning to Canada, Ramsay studies history at the university and becomes interested in myth and hagiology, earning a reputation for both scholarly and popular writings about saints. His study of history and his involvement with the Bollandists reinforce his tendency to examine and report both the dark and the light side of everything.

Percy Boyd Staunton, also called **Boy, Pidgy Boy-Boy,** the pampered son of a Deptford doctor, who abandons medicine to make a fortune in land. Boy successfully expands his father's fortune and becomes an important business and government leader. Boy is handsome and fashionable, the epitome of carefree, beautiful youth in the period between the two world wars; he is described by Ramsay as a "Scott Fitzgerald character." He models himself on the Prince of Wales, whom he serves as aide-de-camp during the prince's Canadian visit. The abdication of the Prince in December, 1936, causes a crisis in the Staunton household. Boy takes out his unhappiness at the downfall of his idol on his wife, who attempts suicide, and on his children, who grow to hate Christmastime. A perfectionist, Boy insists that those around him live up to his image of them. He bullies his first wife, Leola, humiliates his son, and spoils his daughter. After Leola's death, he marries Denyse, a "liberated," manipulating woman who manages his career to satisfy her ambitions for power and position. In his later years, he admits to Ramsay, to whom he has always spoken openly about his feelings, that he feels disappointed by life and would like to "get into a car and drive away from the whole damned thing." His death on the eve of his appointment as Lieutenant Governor of Ontario is assumed to be suicide; his car is pulled out of Toronto harbor and his body found in the driver's seat with his hands on the steering wheel and a stone in his mouth. His death sends his son into analysis in Zurich and indirectly causes Ramsay's heart attack.

Paul Dempster, also called **Cass Fletcher, Julius LeGrande, Faustus LeGrande, Mungo Fetch, Magnus Eisengrim,** a small child with a large head, who suffers physically from his premature birth and emotionally from the isolation forced on him by his mother's bizarre behavior and his father's rigid, unforgiving religion. His account of his life, reported by Ramsay, forms the third volume of the trilogy (*World of Wonders*). Paul is aware that his father blames him for the deterioration of his mother's mind. He is often left in the care of Ramsay, who teaches him magic tricks at which Paul quickly becomes adept and surpasses his teacher. At the age of ten, he sneaks out to the Deptford fair where he is raped and abducted by Willard, a carnival magician and morphine addict, with whom he remains for twelve years, finally taking over the act. Paul continually creates new versions of himself as he travels. He goes to England and is befriended by Sir John and Lady Tresize, who exploit his resemblance to Sir John by using Paul, renamed Mungo Fetch, as a double for the elderly actor. Paul learns about the legitimate stage, improves his appearance and his speaking voice, and leaves behind the crude manners of the carnival and the circus. Paul remains loyal to the Tresizes, who take the place of kind and loving parents in his life. With a later name, Magnus Eisengrim, Paul assumes a new forceful and commanding personality. Onstage he never smiles, and offstage he and his troupe work hard to give an impression of quality and mystery. A performance at Colborne College where Ramsay works leads to the meeting with Boy that results in Boy's death, after which Paul returns to a comfortable retirement with Liesl in Switzerland.

David Staunton (Davey), Boy's unhappy son, a very successful criminal laywer in his fifties. He drinks excessively and has never married. Both his choice of criminal law and his unmarried state are rebellions against Boy, whom he resents for his treatment of Leola and interference in his own life. After Boy's death, David enters analysis with a Jungian, Dr. Johanna Van Haller; his diary of this period forms the second volume of the trilogy (*The Manticore*). David's analysis reveals more about the character of Boy Staunton, including the traumatic effect he had on David when he broke up David's teenage romance with a young Jewish girl, Judy Wolff, and arranged for one of his former mistresses to provide David's sexual initiation. During a break in his analysis, David encounters Ramsay and Liesl and goes with them to spend Christmas at Sorgenfrei. There he has a terrifying experience in a cave with Liesl that leaves him feeling "reborn"; he is able to celebrate Christmas, which he had always hated, and allows Ramsay to throw away the stone that had been in his father's mouth and which he in turn had kept.

Liselotte Naegeli (nāg′ə·lē), also known as **Liesl Vitzliputzli** (lēs′əl vitz·lē·pŭtz′lē), a grotesquely ugly woman (Ramsay calls her a gargoyle) of great intelligence and charm, with a beautiful speaking voice. Her face is simian and her head oversized, as are her hands and feet, as the result of a childhood illness. Having come to terms with her own physical and emotional nature (her looks, her anger, her bisexuality), Liesl serves as the means for Ramsay, Paul, and David to come to a better understanding of themselves. She also takes part in Paul's magic show as the voice of an illusion called The Brazen Head. In that role, her enigmatic answer to the question "Who Killed Boy Staunton?" during a Toronto performance triggers Ramsay's heart attack and David's flight to Zurich.

Father Ignacio Blazon (Padre Blazon), an aged Bollandist Jesuit priest who serves as Ramsay's guide in the study of saints. He is coarse, irreverent, ugly, and dirty but wise. He serves as a father figure for Ramsay.

Mary Dempster, the silly child bride of the Baptist minister Amasa Dempster. After the birth of Paul, she becomes unstable and, after she is found copulating with a tramp in the quarry, she is kept tied up by her husband. She is Dunny's spiritual guide; he loves her and is intent on proving that she is a saint after he sees a vision of her on the battlefield when he is wounded.

Roland Ingestree and
Jurgen Lind, the producer and director of a film about the illusionist Jean-Eugène Robert-Houdin in which Paul stars. They ask for the story of Paul's life and form the framing device for *World of Wonders*. While telling his story, Paul embarrasses Roland for his past unkindness to Paul's mentors, the Tresizes.

Leola Cruikshank, a pretty, vacuous, protected Deptford girl whom both Ramsay and Boy love. She marries Boy but cannot live up to his fast-paced, sophisticated life. She attempts suicide, fails, but never fully recovers her spirit and just "fades." There is some mystery surrounding her death.

Katherine Keller

THE DEPUTY

Author: Rolf Hochhuth (1931-   )
Type of work: Play
Time of action: August, 1942, to November, 1944
First produced: Der Stellvertreter, 1963 (English translation, 1964)

Father Riccardo Fontana, an idealistic young Jesuit priest who opposes the Catholic Church's Concordat with Adolf Hitler, and who tries unsuccessfully to persuade the Pope to speak out against the Nazi atrocities against the Jews. Joining a group destined for Auschwitz, he becomes, in effect, the Pope's representative, or "deputy," accepting for himself the morally correct role he believes the Pope has abdicated.

Kurt Gerstein, an officer (*Oberstürmfuhrer*) in the SS and member of the Protestant Confessing church. Gerstein is a devout Christian who attempts to destroy the Nazi system from within. As an SS officer, he has evidence that the Jews are being gassed in the concentration camps and, knowing the Nazis' fear of the moral authority of the Church, believes that intervention by the Pope could stop the persecution.

Pope Pius XII, Eugenio Pacelli, portrayed with grand gestures and aristocratic coolness, he is a symbol of the Church as an institution. He does not protest the arrest of the Jews except in empty, diplomatic language and wishes the Church to be an impartial go-between for Adolf Hitler and Franklin Delano Roosevelt. The symbolic washing of hands reinforces his refusal to speak out against the mass killings.

The Doctor, an inhuman figure with a charming, likable manner, he sorts the Auschwitz prisoners into the ones who will work and the ones who will die immediately. His role is that of Absolute Evil, confronting Riccardo with doubts about the existence of God.

Count Fontana, a high-ranking lay adviser to the Pope. As Riccardo's father, he makes the personal confrontation between his son

and the Pope possible. He is valuable to the Vatican as a financier and business manager and shows himself to be a man of kindness and feeling who well understands the dynamics and politics of the Vatican.

Cesare Orsenigo, the Apostolic Nuncio in Berlin and Riccardo's superior. The Nuncio is sixty-nine years old and a man of great self-discipline with a candid and tolerant expression. His role is to articulate the position of the Church—that Western civilization must be protected from Russian communism, even if that means dealing with Hitler.

Baron von Rutta, a distinguished aristocrat and member of the Reichs Armaments Cartel. This character, along with Müller-Saale of the Krupp works, articulates the position of the German industrialists, whose main concern is using the Jews as forced labor in order to make profits.

The Abbot, Father General of a religious order. He wants the Pope to speak out for the Jews but is committed to his vow of obedience if he does not. A man of conscience, the Abbot has saved hundreds of lives by protecting individuals who are attempting to escape.

The Cardinal, a suave, somewhat ruthless diplomat in the service of the Pope. A man with remarkable intelligence who rose out of poverty, he considers himself a realist in supporting the Church position that Hitler can be used to block communism.

Professor August Hirt, a Strassburg University anatomist who attempts to prove Nazi racial theories by examining the skulls of concentration camp victims.

Helga, a waitress and later secretary, a

young, attractive blonde who enjoys flirting but is totally oblivious to politics and the evil around her. She falls under the spell of the Doctor and accompanies him to Auschwitz, where she becomes his mistress.

Air Force Lieutenant von Rutta, the Baron's son, a young man of about twenty years who has just won the Knight's Cross. An innocent and likable person, he is a brave soldier and shy with women.

Jacobson, a Jew whom Gerstein hides and then attempts to smuggle out of Germany.

Adolf Eichmann, Obersturmbannführer, a colorless bureaucrat who efficiently plans the transport of the Jews to the camps.

Lieutenant Colonel Dr. Fritsche, a doctor of jurisprudence who allocates inmates to the industrial plants near Auschwitz.

Carlotta, a converted Catholic whose Italian fiancé has died in battle. She is considered a full-blooded Jewess and is sent to Auschwitz.

Dr. Lothar Luccani,
Julia,
Luccani, Sr.,
a boy of nine,
a girl of five,
and Pippa (the baby), a part-Jewish family living within view of the Papal Palace. Luccani, Sr., is a Catholic, and the family has made arrangements to hide in a monastery when the SS comes to arrest them.

Signora Simonetta, a neighbor of the Luccanis who takes care of the baby when the family is taken prisoner.

Susan L. Piepke

DESIGN FOR LIVING

Author: Noël Coward (1899-1973)
Type of work: Play
Time of action: The 1930's
First produced: 1933

Gilda, about thirty, the mistress of Otto and Leo, and wife of Ernest. Gilda is initially attracted to Otto, an unsuccessful painter, and lives with him in his Paris studio, hoping to further his career. Although Gilda does not wish to marry, claiming marriage provides nothing she wants, she is humiliated by the way in which feminine impulses sway her life. When Leo returns from New York a successful playwright, Gilda deserts Otto and goes to live with Leo in London. After eighteen months with Leo, however, Gilda is still unhappy. She distrusts (perhaps envies) Leo's continuing success and dislikes the social life it entails. She also thinks that success has affected the quality of Leo's work, a criticism he resents. While he is away, Otto reappears, and Gilda sleeps with him. After leaving Otto and marrying Ernest, Gilda has not only tired of fulfilling her desire for artistic success via men, but she has also come to believe that she deluded herself into thinking she contributed anything to her lovers' creative lives.

Leo, a playwright, lover of Gilda, friend of Otto and Ernest. Leo is offended that Gilda first chose Otto, and his taking Gilda away has an element of revenge in it. He enjoys his success and refuses to believe that starving in a garret is a prerequisite for effective art. When Gilda leaves, however, he is shattered and turns to Otto. They depend on each other for consolation and then travel together and reclaim Gilda together.

Otto, a painter, lover of Gilda, friend of Leo and Ernest. Otto is furious that Leo and Gilda have betrayed him but, after being apart from them, he realizes he misses his friends too much to bear a grudge. He, like Leo, suffers from Gilda's departure and consoles himself with Leo by going on a cruise with him. He forms part of the *ménage à trois* when all three return to Paris at the end of the play.

Ernest, an art dealer, friend of Otto and Leo, husband of Gilda, apparently an American. Early in the play, he brings news of Leo's success and scolds Gilda for the untidiness of her emotional life. Later, he listens to her complaints about feeling superfluous and informs her that he has bought a penthouse in New York and is intending to settle down. Gilda leaves with him and they are subsequently married. Ernest is resentful when Gilda later leaves him to return to her lovers either because she needs them to need her or because none of them can resist his own impulses. Ernest is made to look foolish when he tries to retain his wife, and all three artists are laughing at him as the curtain goes down.

Jocelyn Creigh Cass

THE DEVILS

Author: John Whiting (1917-1963)
Type of work: Play
Time of action: The seventeenth century
First produced: 1961

Urbain Grandier (ûr·bäṅ' grän·dyä'), the vicar of St. Peter's Church in Loudun, France. Grandier is a brilliant, proud, sensuous man who is obviously superior intellectually and emotionally to most of his parishioners, yet he is a persistently religious person as well. He struggles with his libertine impulses and passionate appreciation of physical beauty, which threaten to deify flesh over spirit. He makes powerful enemies in a deliberate attempt to bring about his own destruction, to test his capacity for suffering and doing penance to God for his rebellious spirit. Women are drawn to him, a fact he often takes advantage of but which ultimately destroys him. When he is accused of witchcraft, he gains the excruciating trial he sought, enduring torture and painful death with a fortitude and grace equal to his former arrogance and sensuality.

Sewerman, a workman with whom Grandier often converses in the street. He is a foil for Grandier's philosophic meditations on the nature of man, casting doubt on Grandier's aspirations, comparing human beings to walking sewer systems. His is a materialistic, skeptical, but honest voice that Grandier respects.

Sister Jeanne of the Angels, the prioress of St. Ursula's Convent, the ultimate weapon for Grandier's destruction, though one he never chose. Indeed, he never met the pathetic, hunchbacked mother superior, except to decline an invitation to be her father confessor. She has observed him longingly, however, from the grating of her barren room. His crime against her is the culmination of a more pervasive one to which she is particularly vulnerable—part of the cultural crime of keeping beauty and tender passion forever beyond her reach. Therefore, she joins her special agony to the ugliness and ferocity of the rest of the world to blot out his careless affront to mediocrity and inferiority. Her claim that he possessed her sexually as a devil has elements of both hysteria and deliberate role-playing.

Mannoury (mä·nōō·rē'), a surgeon, and **Adam,** a chemist, demonstrate the malice, envy, and small-mindedness of some middle-class persons who resent Grandier, as well as the gross sadism that permeates the examination of the nuns at Loudun for evidence of demonic possession. Grandier is contemptuous of their pretensions to knowledge and importance.

Phillipe Trincant (trăn•kō'), a young girl, daughter of the Public Prosecutor. Grandier marries her in a secret ceremony, an action that he explains to the Sewerman as an attempt to find a way to salvation through commitment to another person. When Phillipe gets pregnant, however, Grandier recommends to her father that he marry her off to an old man.

Louis Trincant, the Public Prosecutor, an enemy of Grandier for his treatment of Phillipe.

Cardinal Richelieu (rēsh•lēœ'), a far more formidable enemy whom Grandier has opposed in Richelieu's project to tear down the fortifications of Loudun, part of a campaign to reduce local sovereignty and unify France with a strong central government. This political motivation for the government's part in Grandier's conviction is further enhanced by an old insult Richelieu suffered at the hands of the insolent Grandier before Richelieu became virtually the ruler of France.

De la Rochepozay (rōsh•pō•zā'), the Bishop of Poitiers, an ascetic who despises the senses and condemns all self-assertion.

Jean D'Armagnac (àr•mē•nyăk'), the Governor of Loudun, who, like Grandier, would like to preserve the independence of the city.

Prince Henri de Condé (kŏn•dā'), a decadent nobleman, described as an "exquisite and handsome sodomite." He comes, leaning on painted boys, to observe the nuns pretending to demonic possession. He is nobody's fool and devises a clever test that reveals their fraud. He tells the Commissioner to destroy Grandier for his opposition and his strength, not on such flimsy grounds as demonic possession, of which he is innocent.

Sisters Claire,
Gabrielle, and
Louise, who join Jeanne in an obscene display of possession for the delectation of a prurient audience of townspeople.

The Demons, imaginary, they obtain an almost existential reality as the projection of pain, malice, and lust in an atmosphere of hysteria. They speak through the women, and their laughter is heard in other volatile situations. Their "reality" is balanced by Grandier's transcendent religious experience after which he says he has "created God."

Katherine Snipes

DEVOTION

Author: Botho Strauss (1944-   )
Type of work: Novel
Time of action: Summer, 1976
First published: Die Widmung, 1977 (English translation, 1979)

Richard Schroubek (shrrū'běk), a thirty-one-year-old bookseller by trade, recently abandoned by his girlfriend, Hannah Beyl. For Richard, who calls separation the most terrifying and shattering of all types of personal catastrophe, Hannah's departure means the destruction of all prior connection to and identification with society. Without actually quitting or calling in sick, he simply stops working and sells a Beckmann etching so as financially to support his state of misery. He establishes a postal checking account, forgoing interest for the sake of solitude (he can withdraw money through the mail), and retreats to his apartment. Richard's isolation is interrupted initially only by Frau N., the cleaning woman, and then by Fritz, another man rejected by Hannah. Gradually, the protagonist develops bad habits such as not bathing, not changing clothes regularly, and not cleaning. The general dirtiness and disorderliness of the apartment are greatly intensified by the mishaps to which the protagonist becomes prone.

Hannah Beyl (bīl), the twenty-five-year-old girlfriend who suddenly and without explanation abandons Richard. Later, she spends three days with a man by the name of Fritz, only to leave him just as suddenly. Twice, Hannah seemingly attempts to reestablish contact with Richard, but both times she is satisfied with help from other quarters. It is obvious from her appearance at an eventual meeting with Richard that she has suffered since leaving him. Her eyes are red and her face ashen, she has lost weight, she is drunk, dirty, and unkempt, and she seems to be involved in some questionable financial dealings. Hannah remains indifferent and unresponsive toward Richard, unwilling to engage herself in the dialogue he so desperately desires.

Fritz, a school porter. Fat, in his mid-twenties, and very nervous, Fritz enjoyed a brief affair with Hannah. Apparently deeply disturbed by her sudden disappearance, Fritz pushes his way into Richard's apartment and attempts to enter her study; however, Richard, who regards Fritz's misery and suffering as superficial in comparison to his own, blockades himself in Hannah's former room. It is, therefore, Fritz who receives Hannah's call a few minutes later. He arranges to meet her and is still in her company just prior to Richard and Hannah's rendezvous.

Frau N., the house cleaner. The same age as and originally hired by Hannah, Frau N. stops coming to clean the apartment when Richard can no longer pay her. Richard misses her normality, her loquaciousness, and her constant references to Hannah.

Linda C. DeMeritt

THE DHARMA BUMS

Author: Jack Kerouac (1922-1969)
Type of work: Novel
Time of action: 1955-1956
First published: 1958

Raymond Smith, the first-person narrator, an author and wanderer, based on Kerouac himself. Ray is an intellectual who has turned from the Catholicism of his youth to Buddhism in his search for the ultimate truth of existence. He is disgusted with the shallowness and hypocrisy of American civilization in the 1950's. In fact, his major problem is that he cannot live or get along in the world as it is and must retreat periodically from it. He is able to practice meditation successfully on mountaintops, in forests, and in deserts, but when he comes back to civilization, he feels that he is back in "hell" again. Gradually, through his meditation and conversations with friends, especially Japhy Ryder, his spiritual mentor, he comes to realize the Buddhist wisdom of the emptiness and consequent unity of all things and determines to try and live successfully within the dust and commotion of the city.

Japhy Ryder, an outdoorsman, Buddhist, scholar, and poet who becomes Smith's friend and mentor, based on Gary Snyder. Like Raymond Smith, Japhy recognizes the crass materialism and hypocrisy of American life in the 1950's, but he is able to cope successfully with it and live in the real world. Unlike Ray, who must meditate with his eyes closed, he can meditate with his eyes open and can meditate in a crowded bar as well as on a mountaintop. Japhy participates fully in life and tries to introduce Ray to various aspects of living in the world. He introduces Ray to his many friends and takes him along on two mountain-climbing trips where he teaches Ray about his own philosophy. Japhy leaves for Japan on a study scholarship but first arranges for Ray to spend the summer alone on a mountaintop as a fire lookout, where he hopes Ray will attain enlightenment.

Alvah Goldbook, poet and friend of Raymond Smith, with whom he shares a cottage in Berkeley. While agreeing with Raymond's and Japhy's pessimistic views on American society, he is not as much of a believer in Buddhism as they are. He serves as a more prosaic, down-to-earth counter to Raymond's occasional excesses of esoteric Buddhist philosophy about the nonreality of all things. Alvah is far too busy enjoying life and finding beauty where he might to worry about the reality or nonreality of material objects. His idea is not to be concerned with the ultimate meaning of existence and just take life as it comes.

Cody Pomeray, an old friend of Smith, based on Neal Cassady. Cody, the most important character other than the autobiographical narrator in most of Kerouac's other fiction, functions as a combination

lost-brother figure and idolized friend. In *The Dharma Bums*, Cody has a quite peripheral role, appearing briefly as a reminder to Ray that bad things are happening constantly and people need to be enlightened. Cody's girlfriend commits suicide and gives Ray cause to reflect on the unhappiness he sees around him.

Sean Monahan, an old friend of Japhy Ryder. Sean is the primary example in the book of what it would be like to have the enlightenment of Japhy Ryder and live a normal married life. The only married friend of Japhy and Ray, Sean lives with his wife and two children in a rustic cottage in Marin County. He not only practices Buddhist meditation and reads sutras but also goes off during the day to work as a carpenter. His wife stays at home, walking around barefooted, baking bread, cooking simple but delicious meals, and being mother to two children. His house is the gathering place for those interested in Buddhism or alternative lifestyles.

James V. Muhleman

DIARY OF A MAD OLD MAN

Author: Jun'ichirō Tanizaki (1886-1965)
Type of work: Novel
Time of action: The early 1960's
First published: Fūten rōjin nikki, 1961-1962, serial; 1962, book (English translation, 1965)

Mr. Tokusuke Utsugi, elderly patriarch of a well-to-do Tokyo family. Impotent, toothless, plump, and continually pained by neuralgia, backaches, and circulation problems, Utsugi at seventy-seven is attended at home by a full-time nurse. Long fascinated by visions of his own death and funeral, he journeys to Kyoto to select a fitting burial place. He is increasingly preoccupied with masochistic fantasies involving his daughter-in-law, Satsuko. For her small and grudging favors, he pays with ever more expensive gifts. Even after a series of debilitating seizures in the winter, Utsugi looks forward to

spring, the construction of a swimming pool, and walks in the garden with Satsuko.

Satsuko Utsugi, a beautiful former chorus girl. She has been married to Utsugi's son for ten years, and they occupy the second floor of Utsugi's Tokyo house. Although the mother of a six-year-old son, Satsuko devotes her days to shopping, classical flower arranging, films, boxing matches, and an adulterous affair with Utsugi's nephew, Haruhisa. Motivated by greed or by emotional generosity, she offers her father-in-law kisses for gifts such as a car, a designer scarf, a purse, and a cat's-eye ring. She is regarded by her sisters-in-law as spiteful, sarcastic, lying, cold, and manipulative and is disregarded by her husband.

Jokichi Utsugi, the only son of Tokusuke. A successful thirty-six-year-old businessman away from home a considerable amount of the time, he is seemingly little interested in his wife and family.

Itsuko, Utsugi's widowed daughter. She lives in the Nanzenji district with her two grown sons, Kikutaro and Keijiro, and has never gotten along well with her father.

Kugako, Utsugi's daughter. When the eldest of her three children wishes to marry, Kugako asks her father for a short-term loan of twenty thousand yen. He refuses her. Not long after, Satsuko extracts three million yen from him as the price of a necking session. Family resentment of Satsuko escalates.

Nurse Sasaki, Utsugi's live-in attendant. She sleeps in the bed next to him all but one or two nights a month. She tends to his incessant pains and administers his medications.

Virginia Crane

DIARY OF THE WAR OF THE PIG

Author: Adolfo Bioy Casares (1914-   )
Type of work: Novel
Time of action: The near future
First published: Diario de la guerra del cerdo, 1969 (English translation, 1972)

Don Isidro Vidal (ē•sē′drrō vē•däl′), an elderly widower, the novel's protagonist. Small and slightly built, he has a sharp fox's nose and mustache. He is obsessively proud of his new set of false teeth. Don Isidro is the leader of a social group of elderly men, the "pigs" referred to in the novel's title, who are under attack and are being murdered by a group of young men. He is a compassionate individual who has faith in the fundamental brotherhood of man.

Isidorito Vidal (ē•sē•dō•rē′tō), Don Isidro's son. His meager earnings support both his father and himself. When the gang of youths begins to terrorize the town, Isidorito tries to placate both sides. He participates in the group's activities but sometimes warns the old men when they are targeted as victims. He is murdered by the group when he tries to save his father's life; they consider Isidorito a traitor.

Nélida, the young woman who falls in love with Don Isidro. She is engaged to a young man, but breaks the engagement in order to be with Don Isidro, to whom she is increasingly drawn, as he is to her. When he fears for his life and attempts to hide from the youth group, she shelters him in her apartment.

Arturo Farrall, leader of the gang of youths, the "Young Turks," whose death squads terrorize and murder the town's elderly citizens. The reasons he gives for the "war on the pigs" is that the population is growing too large and that the elderly are becoming a useless burden on society.

Néstor Labarthe (lä•bär′tĕ), an elderly friend of Don Isidro. He is the first of Vidal's group who is murdered. He is thrown over the stands and trampled at a soccer match. His brutal murder, in the presence and possibly with the consent of his own son, causes a serious split in the Young Turks between those who attempt to avoid danger by conforming and those who try to rebel against the terrorism of this youth-oriented society.

Leandro Rey (lĕ•än′drō rā), a Spanish-born elderly friend of Don Isidro. He is nicknamed "The Thinker" by the group of aging men. Unlike the others in the group, he is not retired: He works as a baker. He is described as cold, self-centered, close-fisted, and a formidable adversary in business or at the card table. He is also a terrible glutton.

James Newman (Jimmy), a member of the group of elderly men. He is also called the "M.C." because of his quick mind and lively manner. Of Irish descent, he is tall, ruddy-cheeked, and has a plump face. He always speaks in deadly earnest. He is kidnapped by the youth gang for a time and allegedly turns informer in order to obtain his release.

Dante Révora, a member of Don Isidro's group who tries desperately to look young by dyeing his hair. He has a reputation for being an educated man. He is terrified for his life and thinks that he can escape death by attempting to look younger than he is.

Lucio Arévalo, another member of Don Isidro's group, formerly a newspaperman. He is described as being extremely ugly. Usually ill-shaved, he has cigarette-stained hands and flecks of dandruff on his poncho. He is the picture of an asthmatic, ailing old man. Don Isidro considers it strange that no member of their group has ever set foot into Arévalo's house. Because of his longtime affair with a teenage girl, he ends up in the hospital, kicked and beaten by a gang of youths.

Genevieve Slomski

A DIFFERENT DRUMMER

Author: William Melvin Kelley (1937-   )
Type of work: Novel
Time of action: 1931-1961
First published: 1962

Tucker Caliban, the "different drummer" who precipitates the exodus of the black population from the fictitious southern state in which the story is set when he destroys his farm and departs with his family. The land had previously belonged to the Willsons, the white clan that Tucker's family had served even after Emancipation; Tucker buys the land from David Willson, saying, "You tried to free us once, but we didn't go and now we got to free ourselves." Physically small, with a proportionately large head and wearing wire-rimmed glasses, Tucker often appears inscrutable to the other characters. His actions demonstrate an almost instinctive self-reliance. He refuses, for example, to support the National Society for Colored Affairs because he denies that anyone else can achieve his rights.

Bethra, Tucker's wife, tall, slim, and beautiful. Poised and intelligent, she had been working as the Willsons' maid to earn money to finish college. Her college plans are dropped, however, when she falls almost girlishly in love with Tucker, and they marry. More educated than her husband, Bethra is at first embarrassed by his rejection of her friends' civil rights causes, and she leaves him. She returns, however, in a week, having come to see the truth of his commitment to independent action. Dymphna Willson, who made Bethra her confidante, acknowledges that the black woman has taught her much about life.

Mister Harper, the town philosopher. A retired army officer, he went to West Point but, being too young for the Civil War and too old for World War II, never actually put into practice his military training. His son, however, was killed in World War II, and from then on, feeling "knocked down by life," he stayed in a wheelchair. From his porch, he dispenses analyses of the world's chaotic events to townspeople who daily gather around. For example, he offers the "genetic" explanation for the exodus of the blacks, telling the story of the near-mythic, prodigiously powerful and elusive African who was Tucker's ancestor.

Harry Leland, a sharecropper. He admonishes his son for using the word "nigger"; in contrast with others in the town, he recognizes the need for adapting to change and for getting along with all kinds of people. Having been a sergeant in the Korean War, he theorizes that the blacks are conducting a "strategic withdrawal," a prudent action for which he admires them.

Harold Leland, called **Mister Leland,** Harry Leland's son, an active eight-year-old with sandy hair. He has considered Tucker a friend ever since Tucker bought him some peanuts he had been eyeing in the store window; the reason Tucker gave for the gift was the way in which Harry Leland was rearing Mister Leland. The night Bennett T. Bradshaw is lynched on Tucker's property, Mister Leland hears laughing and singing coming from the spot; he thinks that a party is going on to celebrate Tucker's return and plans to go out there the next morning to see his friend again.

David Willson, a descendant of Dewey Willson, the General, a confederate war hero and state governor; David is considered by the townspeople to be a usurper of the family name. While at college, he became active in left-wing issues and struck up a friendship with Bennett T. Bradshaw, a black intellectual and fellow student. The two roomed together and shared a concern for the wasted potential of their respective peoples. Returning to the South after graduation, David finds work as a journalist for a local newspaper. He is fired, however, once he is exposed as the author of articles espousing a radical stance on racial issues, written under a pen name for a communist magazine in New York City. Anxious that he is not finding work, and with a child on the way, he returns to the Willson home to take up the family business, one that he despises: collecting rents from sharecroppers on Willson land. Feeling himself to be a coward for not living up to his ideals, he retreats emotionally from his wife

and children. He experiences a renewal, however, when he agrees to sell Tucker the land by which Tucker means to free himself.

Camille Willson, David's wife. She met him at a party hosted by bohemian friends, and their courtship included going with him on assignments for the newspaper. She continued to have faith in him even as he kept from her his pseudonymous articles and after, when he gets fired. She offers to move with him to New York City, but he misjudges her sincerity. In the Willson home, she feels like a stranger and despairs at the loss of intimacy in her marriage.

Dewey Willson III, David's college-age son. He has a recurring nightmare in which the General entrusts him with the bleeding head he tears from his own body. On his tenth birthday, Dewey got a new bike and begged Tucker, then thirteen, to teach him to ride. Tucker is later punished because they are late for dinner, the older boy having relented to Dewey's plea that they "try once more." Dewey feels guilty about this injustice but never said anything to Tucker about it. He is with Bennett when the lynching mob drags the black man away, and although he tries to save him, he cannot.

Dymphna Willson, David's teenage daughter. Somewhat selfish and a self-professed schemer, her initial consideration in being friends with Bethra was that Bethra, being black, would not compete with her for boyfriends. By the time Bethra leaves the Willson household, she has taught the younger girl that "the most you can do for people you love is leave them alone"—a wisdom that helps Dymphna come to terms with her parents' relationship.

Bennett T. Bradshaw, David's black college roommate, who had to drop out before graduating to support his family. Active in the Civil Rights movement, he places David's articles in leftist magazines in New York City. Later, David reads in a national magazine that Bennett has been fired from the National Society for Colored Affairs because of alleged communist affiliations and has founded the Resurrected Church of the Black Jesus Christ of America, Inc., a black supremacist group. Bennett appears in town in a chauffeur-driven limousine, investigating Tucker's departure and the ensuing exodus of blacks. He is resentful at becoming obsolete as a leader, given the impact of Tucker's independent action. At the novel's climax, he is beaten, humiliated, and taken away to Tucker's farm to be lynched.

Amy Adelstein

THE DINING ROOM

Author: A. R. Gurney, Jr. (1930-   )
Type of work: Play
Time of action: The twentieth century
First produced: 1982

The Dining Room Table, the focal point in the formal dining room that serves not only as the basic prop but as the inanimate main character for the play's eighteen vignettes analyzing twentieth century WASP life in America. The table is large, elegant, and deeply burnished, with armed chairs at either end, two armless chairs along each side, and several matching chairs against the walls of the room. The table sits on an elegant hardwood floor covered with a fine oriental rug. Into this archetypal dining room come almost sixty different characters, their attitudes toward the table and the dining room helping to define the history of WASP America.

Father, the authoritarian head of an affluent 1930's family, self-important, priggish, sexist. He believes that government programs in the 1930's are ruining the country by encouraging people not to work. At breakfast with his young son and daughter, Father reads the newspaper, gently chastises the maid, and instructs his children on fine points of grammar, table manners, and the proper way to address one's mother. For him, the dining room is a central arena for exercising a highly ritualistic approach to life.

Architect, a professional consultant from the 1970's who presents a remodeling plan to his client, a Psychiatrist, who has just bought the house. Efficient, businesslike, and decisive, the Architect does not see elegance in the dining room, only vast space that can be manipulated for more efficient use. Having grown up in a home with a formal dining room, the Architect is familiar with what the room stands for, but as a child he hated its formality.

Aunt Harriet, a woman near the age of sixty being interviewed by her nephew, Tony, an Amherst College student, unaware that Tony is interviewing her for an anthropology project on the eating habits of the vanishing WASP culture of the Northeastern United States. Steeped in the propriety and traditions of upper-middle-class elegance, Aunt Harriet is very proud of the table setting she is displaying for Tony, who takes photographs for documentation. She comments on the delicacy and value of the crystal, silver, linen, and china, relating each item to the genealogy of the family, and then demonstrates the proper use of the finger bowls.

Jim, a father in his late sixties, emotionally distant from his thirty-year-old daughter Meg, who has separated from her husband. Jim ushers Meg into the dining room since it is a good place to talk, but then he tries to avoid Meg's request to live with them.

Ruth, a hostess preparing the table for an elegant dinner party. Refined, sensitive, generous, and precise, Ruth describes her recurrent dream of a perfect dinner party in the formal dining room of the past, before her

402

grandmother's silver was stolen, before the movers broke the china, and before the finger bowls were misplaced.

Peggy, a mother setting the table for a children's birthday party. Strict in her discipline with the raucous children, Peggy is having an extramarital affair with Ted, the father of one of the children.

Grandfather, the family patriarch at age eighty. Businesslike and thorough in his cross-examination, he receives his fourteen-year-

old grandson in the dining room and gives him money for the boy's education.

Paul, a former stockbroker, now a carpenter, in his middle thirties. He carefully examines the dining room table for the owner of the house and recommends repairs.

Sarah, a teenage girl in the 1970's. In the dining room, she and her girlfriend sneak vodka and gin from the liquor cabinet and prepare to meet their boyfriends to smoke marijuana.

Terry Nienhuis

DINNER AT THE HOMESICK RESTAURANT

Author: Anne Tyler (1941-   )
Type of work: Novel
Time of action: 1944-1979, with reference to Pearl's youth in the early 1900's
First published: 1982

Pearl Cody Tull, eighty-six years old, small, fair-haired, gray-eyed, and indomitable. Her insight into herself and her relationships with her long-absent husband and her three children sharpens and becomes focused as her eyesight fades to blindness. Never able to nurture close relationships, Pearl instead allowed her grim determination and high expectations to drive her husband away; as a single mother, her occasional murderous rages almost obscured her powerful love of and concern for her children. Despite an abiding sense of grievance, Pearl always longs to have the children's confidence and trust, but, especially as adults, they remain at arm's length. Their feelings for her range from near-hatred through tolerance to baffled love. Pearl's only oblique acknowledgement of approaching death is her recognition of her own shortcomings. Perception comes as she lies dying, listening for clues from her own youthful diaries read aloud by Ezra, her mind drifting through the events of her life.

Beck Tull, a salesman, Pearl's husband and father of their three children. The young

Beck, black-haired, boldly blue-eyed, and flashily handsome, rescues Pearl from spinsterhood in a whirlwind courtship and marriage. In 1944, though, disappointed in his career and overwhelmed by the burden of Pearl's unspoken but fierce disappointment in him, he abandons the family, afterward maintaining a link with Pearl through the increasingly rare notes and checks he sends. Because Pearl never openly acknowledges his desertion, Beck hovers on the edge of the family's consciousness for thirty-five years until he appears (at Ezra's invitation) at Pearl's funeral. Now elderly, still dapper if slightly sleazy, Beck is ready for reconciliation and recognition as the Tull patriarch, but his commitment lasts only through the day of the funeral, to the end of the one Tull family dinner ever to lurch to completion at the Homesick Restaurant.

Cody Tull, Pearl's eldest child, tall, dark-haired, and handsome. His youthful rebellious behavior and adult success as a time-study expert mask a deep-seated lack of self-confidence. The focus of his resentment is his brother Ezra, who manages to attract female admiration though he is graceless and passive. Cody, curdled by his grievances, exacts revenge first by ensnaring and marrying Ezra's fiancée Ruth and last by castigating the newly returned and conciliatory Beck. In the first flush of his successful career, Cody buys a farm, dreaming of an idyllic domestic life; his hopes soured, he eventually abandons the farm, leaving Pearl and Ezra to try and shore it up against disintegration, just as they try to maintain the crumbling family.

Ezra Tull, Pearl's second son and middle child. With his pale eyes, shock of fair hair, and wide, shapeless body, Ezra appears soft; his mildness in childhood becomes a passivity in adulthood that is his main flaw but also his saving grace. Ezra simply allows life to happen to him, accepting with unthinking loyalty his mother's angry love, his mentor Mrs. Scarlatti's generosity, and even his catastrophic loss to Cody of Ruth, the only woman ever to rouse him to passion. In his revealingly named Homesick Restaurant, however, Ezra comes alive, crafting dishes to tempt his clients, pouring out his oddly maternal humanity into sturdy soups and comforting, lovingly prepared meals. Time and again, marking the milestones in the lives of his fractious family, Ezra attempts to unite and reconcile the Tulls at meals in the Homesick's forgiving atmosphere, but he is doomed to failure. Ezra's constancy stands always in contrast to his family's restless volatility.

Jenny Tull, Pearl's third child and only daughter, dark-haired, dark-eyed, and intense. Jenny's thin, angular body matures into a beauty that she expends carelessly all of her life. Her becoming a pediatrician seems the natural fulfillment of her intellectual self-discipline; however, as the child most vulnerable to Pearl's alternating devotion and volcanic rages, she also displays a curious ambivalence. Sensitive like Cody, she mostly keeps her emotional distance; yet, also warmly accepting like Ezra, in her third marriage she tumbles contentedly into domestic muddle with her new husband, her daughter Becky, and six stepchildren, all of whose problems she treats with laughing offhandedness that masks her compassion and gratitude for people who really need her.

Ruth Spivey Tull, first Ezra's fiancée but finally Cody's wife. An unschooled, rural tomboy, Ruth is a superb country cook who meets the Tulls when she is employed as a chef at the Homesick. Tiny, freckled, and carrot-haired, with pebbly, pale-blue eyes, the young Ruth's brisk, scrappy manner captivates Ezra and fascinates Cody. Once overwhelmed by and married to Cody, however, Ruth subsides awkwardly into middle-class domesticity, her energy smothered by Cody's moody silences, her little body pathetically lost in unsuitable feminine clothing. As Pearl once followed Beck, Ruth follows Cody to a succession of strange towns and houses, never again able to express her scornful, independent spirit. Her sole satisfaction comes from mothering Luke, their serious, lonely son.

Jill Rollins

DIRTY LINEN and NEW-FOUND-LAND

Author: Tom Stoppard (Tomas Straussler, 1937-   )
Type of work: Play
Time of action: The 1970's
First produced: 1976

Dirty Linen

Maddie Gotobed, the new secretary to the Select Committee of Members of Parliament, which meets in an overspill meeting room in Big Ben. Voluptuous and inexperienced, she has evidently been involved in affairs with all the male Members of Parliament (MPs) on the Select Committee, which has been commissioned to investigate sexual misbehavior in the House of Commons. Each member, as he arrives, slips her a pair of lace panties, evidently left at their last rendezvous, so that by the end of the play she has collected a drawer full of "knickers." Maddie is nobody's fool, however, and by the end of the play, it is she who dictates her own text for the committee's resolution: that MPs have as much right to private life as any other citizens and that as long as they break no laws, their privacy should not be broken to indulge public curiosity.

Cocklebury-Smythe, the first of the MPs on this committee. He longs to move into the House of Lords. Like his fellow committee members, he urges Maddie to put out of her mind the various restaurants (Crockford's, Claridges, and the Coq d'Or) at which they have met.

McTeazle, the second of these nearly interchangeable MPs. He pulls Maddie's panties from his briefcase just at the end of a long, huffy speech explaining recent press allegations of bad behavior among MPs. He, too, urges Maddie to forget the locales of their meetings, some of them the same places she has met Cocklebury-Smythe.

Chamberlain, another of the lecherous MPs on the committee. Though he has a wife and family in Dorking, he still writes Mad-

die a note instructing her to forget more restaurants.

Withenshaw, the chairman of the committee. He is from Lancaster, as his speech sometimes betrays. He may be the author of the original draft of the resolution, a cliché-ridden document that says nothing and that is rapidly being revised in several directions by the committee members.

French, the stickler for detail on the committee. He is the member who moves to scrap Withenshaw's resolution in favor of Maddie's.

New-Found-Land

Arthur, a very junior Home Office official. He and Bernard are making a preliminary review of an American's application for British citizenship. His attempt to tell Bernard about the United States becomes a heroic monologue in which he catalogs every cliché about American life as he surveys the American landscape from Long Island to California.

Bernard, a very senior (and very deaf) Home Office official. He tells Arthur a long story about how he once won a five-pound note from Lloyd George, but he sleeps through Arthur's monologue.

Ann D. Garbett

THE DISPOSSESSED

Author: Ursula K. Le Guin (1929-   )
Type of work: Novel
Time of action: The distant future
First published: 1974

Shevek, a physicist who studies time. Tall, lean, and long-haired, Shevek is a citizen of Annares, a world founded seven generations earlier by the followers of Odo, a woman who developed and organized a syndicalist anarchist movement. A genius in a society that has become increasingly conformist to a

collective will, Shevek has difficulty pursuing and publishing his work, a General Temporal Theory that promises to open possibilities for faster-than-light communication and travel. Against the objections of his society, he travels to the sister planet of Urras, from which the Odonians emigrated, hoping to find there the freedom to present his discoveries. On Urras, however, major discoveries become military secrets to be used for gaining and holding national power. He finally evades the restrictions of both planets by broadcasting his discovery to all the known worlds, making possible instantaneous communication between distant planets. He is nearing age forty when he returns to Annares.

Takver, a fish geneticist. Tall, dark, intelligent, and not very pretty, she becomes Shevek's permanent sexual partner, since marriage does not exist on Annares. Though their work and the social needs of Annares often separate them, they have children and support each other in their careers. She encourages him to compromise with the conservative scientific establishment in order to have his works published off-planet. Later, she helps him form a group to support sharing knowledge with other worlds.

Vea, a wealthy and attractive socialite on Urras. In private visits with her, Shevek learns to understand the spiritual inner workings of Urras society, especially with regard to the relations between the sexes and the psychological and social effects of the private accumulation of power and wealth.

Rulag, an engineer. Though Shevek rarely sees her, Rulag is his mother. When he proposes opening communication with and then traveling to Urras, from which Odonians have separated themselves as if from a source of infection, she becomes the leader of his political opposition.

Sabul, a physicist. He dominates the establishment of physics on Annares, even though it is supposed to be controlled by a syndicate of all physicists. Using fear of "infection" by anti-Odonian thought, he achieves power and status by regulating scientific communication between the two worlds. When Shevek produces a major treatise on time, he must publish it off-world under his and Sabul's names.

Dr. Atro, a Urras physicist. The aged Atro, founder of modern physics, recognizes the importance of Shevek's work and invites him to Urras. Shevek finds him a genial old genius, but caught up in nationalist, propertarian, and sexist attitudes that restrict the freedom of his thought.

Efor, Shevek's servant in his Urras quarters. From observing Efor, Shevek learns about attitudes of the working classes. Efor eventually provides the contacts that put Shevek in touch with revolutionary forces on Urras and that bring him to the Earth embassy from which he broadcasts his theory.

Terry Heller

DISTANT RELATIONS

Author: Carlos Fuentes (1928-   )
Type of work: Novel
Time of action: The early 1980's
First published: Una familia lejana, 1980 (English translation, 1982)

The Comte de Branly, a wealthy French aristocrat whose main interest is foreign travel. At the age of eighty-three, this highly intelligent, cultured man is emaciated and nearly bald but still retains a rigid military bearing. Most of this complex novel of parallel lives and reincarnations concerns the Comte's surrealistic adventure in a strange mansion outside Paris where he is confined as the result of an auto accident. Because of his advanced age, however, it is probable that much of what he believes to have occurred may have been hallucinations. Although he is the viewpoint character, he is the passive victim of circumstances throughout the novel.

The narrator, a Latin American author who has taken France as his adopted country. Only at the end is it revealed that this character is Carlos Fuentes himself. Characteristically, Fuentes has chosen a complex manner of telling his tale: The narrator is supposedly writing out an account of incidents described to him by his friend Branly, and parts of what Branly tells him were narrated to the Comte himself by others. By this device, the author is able to maintain a distance from the events described and is therefore not committed to vouching for them. This complex method of developing the story creates a multidimensional, hallucinatory effect. The reader is forced to make his own interpretations and thus become involved as an active participant in the events.

The Mexican Victor Heredia, a twelve-year-old upper-class Mexican student. This handsome and aristocratic youth has been badly spoiled by a doting father. Victor displays outbursts of a violent temper, beating domestic servants when they displease him and, in one crucial instance, deliberately slamming the door of Branly's Citroën on the chauffeur's hand. When Branly tries to drive the car himself, he runs into a tree and is confined to bed as an involuntary guest of the French Victor Heredia. The young Mexican Victor Heredia is the catalyst of most of what happens in the novel.

The French Victor Heredia, a wealthy businessman with social pretensions who proves to be vulgar and sadistic, in striking contrast to the truly aristocratic Branly. The French Victor Heredia is old but has a youngish face, suggesting an immortal nature like that of a vampire. The young Mexican Victor Heredia, who frequently travels with his father, plays a game of looking in foreign telephone directories to see if anyone is listed with the same name as himself or his father. If he finds such persons, he telephones them and tries to strike up an acquaintance. In this manner, he drags his host the Comte de Branly into their strange encounter with the satanic French Victor Heredia, who takes advantage of the fact that the Comte is confined to bed under his roof to play cruel psychological tricks on him. In the meantime, an unwholesome relationship is developing between the Mexican Victor Heredia and André Heredia.

André Heredia, the son of the French Victor Heredia, a boy about the same age as young Victor. Like his father, André is cruel and overbearing, the product of inferior breeding. At one point, Branly catches the French boy sodomizing the Mexican boy in the backseat of the wrecked Citroën. After this unnatural copulation, the two boys somehow merge into a single new supernatural individual, evidently symbolizing a merging of French and Latin American cultures. The Mexican Victor Heredia disappears for the rest of the story. The reader is left to wonder whether this truly occurred or is attributable to Branly's senility, the trauma of the auto accident, and his host's mistreatment.

Hugo Heredia, a Mexican archaeologist, father of the Mexican Victor Heredia. This dignified scholar's decision to visit France with his son leads to all the shocking events that occur. Hugo is absent throughout most of the story, leaving his son in the care of the Comte de Branly. When his son vanishes, however, having merged identities with André Heredia, the father reacts in a strange manner that makes the reader believe he was in enforced collusion with the French Victor Heredia and anticipated what was going to happen.

Bill Delaney

THE DIVINERS

Author: Margaret Laurence (1926-1987)
Type of work: Novel

Time of action: 1930 to the 1970's
First published: 1974

Morag Gunn, the protagonist, a forty-seven-year-old novelist writing the novel containing her story. As she looks back over her life, she believes that her artistic talent was always evident. When her parents died of poliomyelitis, she was reared by Christie Logan in a poor part of town where Métis like her first lover, Jules, also lived. She grew up listening to Christie haranguing about the muck of life.in the past (for example, Lady Sutherland's clearances and World War I) and present (the townspeople). To him, he was creating pride and identity in Morag by telling her stories about her family, the Gunns, coming from Scotland to Manitoba. Morag also wrote her own stories, which she later reworked to create stories of family history for her daughter, Pique. Writing for local, college, and Vancouver newspapers enlarges Morag's sensitivities about the Métis, the Gersons, and others. Her passion leads to an out-of-wedlock pregnancy, however, just as her spirit of independence leads her to leave her husband.

Jules "Skinner" Tonnerre, Morag's first lover. While Morag was still in her teens, Jules seduced her in his father's shack. He told Morag tales of the Métis view of encounters with Scottish emigrants, such as his grandfather who fought with Riel at Batoche and lost.

Pique Gunn Tonnerre, Morag and Jules's daughter. In a London school, she does not experience prejudice like she does as a teenager in the high school in the small Ontario town of McConnell's Landing. She stands up to her boyfriend, Dan, who expects her to work as a cashier while he spends their money to raise horses. With her father's and her own songs, she sets off again for Manawaka and Galloping Mountain, alone this time, to find her own identity from her roots. Some peace comes from her decisions and actions to express the opposite views she embodies.

Brooke Skelton, a professor of English in Winnipeg and Morag's husband. He woos her in her senior year to satisfy his sexual needs and enhance his professional career: After they move to Toronto, he becomes chairman. He has difficulty expressing his feelings; reared in India by an omah who was dismissed when found in his bed, he grew up stoic like his British mother and father. His obsession to control Morag led to her departure.

Dan McRaith, a Scottish painter in his mid-forties who becomes Morag's lover after they meet in a bookshop in London. Each inspires the artistic endeavors of the other. Morag visits Scotland, where his wife and seven children live in Crombruach, near Culloden. Once in Scotland, Morag realizes the physical place is not as real or as important as what Christie had built in her heart with tales of Piper Gunn and his people coming from there. Dan and Morag correspond for years.

Christie Logan, a garbage collector ("scavenger") in Manawaka and Morag's foster father, who inspired her with stories of Piper Gunn leading Highlanders in Scotland and Canada and tales of World War I. Always ranting, he divines the character of townspeople according to their garbage. He advises her to get out of Manawaka to college, by using the money from the sale of her parents' farm, but is pleased when she returns to Prin's deathbed and, later, his.

Prin Logan, Christie's lethargic, fat wife and kind foster mother to Morag. Prin dresses Morag in clothes from the Nuisance Grounds until Morag, working at Ludlow's in her teens, learns to dress smartly.

Royland, a diviner of water at McConnell's Landing. Previously a preacher, he abused his wife, who ran away and drowned herself. His gift of divining water finally leaves him.

Greta McCormick Coger